PENGUIN CLASSICS

THE PORTABLE FREDERICK DOUGLASS

FREDERICK DOUGLASS was born Frederick Augustus Washington Bailey in February 1818 in Tuckahoe, on the Eastern Shore of Maryland. He was the son of Harriet Bailey, a slave owned by Captain Aaron Anthony. Douglass changed his surname to conceal his identity after escaping slavery in 1838. He spent the first seven years of his life working on the plantation owned by Colonel Edward Lloyd. In 1825 he was sold to Hugh Auld and came to live in Baltimore. Life in the city was a turning point in Douglass's life: it was there that he learned to read, which, he later wrote, was his "pathway from slavery to freedom." In 1833, he returned to the Eastern Shore as the slave of Hugh's brother Thomas Auld, who hired him out to work as a field hand. He made his first unsuccessful attempt to escape two years later. In 1838, he successfully escaped to Philadelphia and then to New York by posing as a free sailor. Within two weeks of his arrival in New York, on September 15, 1838, he married Anna Murray, a freedwoman he met in Baltimore who paid for part of his passage north. Immediately after their marriage, the couple moved to New Bedford, Massachusetts.

By 1839 Douglass was an active member of a black abolitionist group in New Bedford, inspired by William Lloyd Garrison's newspaper *The Liberator.* In 1841 he was hired as a full-time lecturer for the American Anti-Slavery Society and toured throughout the North giving speeches on abolition. While living in Massachusetts, he and his wife had four children: Rosetta, Lewis Henry, Frederick Jr., and Charles Remond.

In 1844, Douglass began to write his autobiography, and in the spring of 1845 *Narrative of the Life of Frederick Douglass, an American Slave* was published, becoming a bestseller. Douglass later published additional autobiographies, *My Bondage and My Freedom* (1855), also a bestseller, and *Life and Times of Frederick Douglass* (1881, 1892). The revelation of the details of his life story placed Douglass in danger of being returned to slavery, and so on August 16, 1845, he sailed from Boston to Liverpool and spent nearly two years in Ireland, Scotland, and England. He was legally emancipated on December 12, 1846, after Ellen and Anna Richardson of Newcastle, England, purchased his freedom for $711.66.

Douglass returned to the United States in 1847, moved to Rochester, New York, and began his long career in journalism. From 1847 to 1863 he owned, edited, and published *The North Star*, *Frederick Douglass' Paper*, and *Douglass' Monthly*, and then ran the *New National Era* from 1870 to 1874. In later years Douglass held several high-profile government appointments, including U.S. marshal and recorder of deeds for the District of Columbia and consul-general to Haiti. He died in Washington, D.C., on February 20, 1895, and after lying in state in the nation's capital, he was buried in the Mount Hope Cemetery in Rochester, New York.

JOHN STAUFFER is a professor of English and African and African American Studies at Harvard University and former chair of the school's American Studies program. His books include *State of Jones* (cowritten with Sally Jenkins and nominated for the Pulitzer Prize in History); *The Black Hearts of Men: Radical Abolitionists and the Transformation of Race,* cowinner of the Frederick Douglass Book Prize; *Giants: The Parallel Lives of Frederick Douglass and Abraham Lincoln*; and *Picturing Frederick Douglass: An Illustrated Biography of the Nineteenth Century's Most Photographed American* (cowritten with Zoe Trodd and Celeste-Marie Bernier).

HENRY LOUIS GATES, JR., is the Alphonse Fletcher University Professor and founding director of the Hutchins Center for African and African American Research at Harvard University. He is editor in chief of the Oxford African American Studies Center and TheRoot.com, and creator of the highly praised PBS documentary *The African Americans: Many Rivers to Cross*. He is general editor for a Penguin Classics series of African American works.

FREDERICK DOUGLASS

The Portable Frederick Douglass

Edited with an Introduction and Notes by
JOHN STAUFFER and
HENRY LOUIS GATES, JR.

General Editor:
HENRY LOUIS GATES, JR.

PENGUIN BOOKS

PENGUIN BOOKS

An imprint of Penguin Random House LLC
375 Hudson Street
New York, New York 10014
penguin.com

LIBRARY OF CONGRESS CATALOGING-IN-PUBLICATION DATA
Names: Douglass, Frederick, 1818–1895, author. | Stauffer, John, 1965– author.
Title: The portable Frederick Douglass / Frederick Douglass ; edited by John Stauffer ; introduction by Henry Louis Gates.
Description: New York : Penguin Classics, [2016] | Includes bibliographical references.
Identifiers: LCCN 2016006199 (print) | LCCN 2016006241 (ebook) | ISBN 9780143106814 (paperback) | ISBN 9781101992265 (ebook)
Subjects: LCSH: Douglass, Frederick, 1818–1895. | African American abolitionists—Biography. | Slaves—United States—Biography. | Antislavery movements—United States—History—19th century. | African Americans—History—Sources. | African American orators. | Speeches, addresses, etc., American—African American authors. | BISAC: HISTORY / United States / Civil War Period (1850–1877). | SOCIAL SCIENCE / Ethnic Studies / African American Studies. | BIOGRAPHY & AUTOBIOGRAPHY / Cultural Heritage.
Classification: LCC E449.D75 A25 2016b (print) | LCC E449.D75 (ebook) | DDC 973.8092—dc23

Printed in the United States of America
1 3 5 7 9 10 8 6 4 2

Contents

Speeches

Journalism

What Is an African American Classic?

I have long nurtured a deep and abiding affection for the Penguin Classics, at least since I was an undergraduate at Yale. I used to imagine that my attraction for these books—grouped together, as a set, in some independent bookstores when I was a student, and perhaps even in some today—stemmed from the fact that my first-grade classmates, for some reason that I can't recall, were required to dress as penguins in our annual all-school pageant, and perform a collective side-to-side motion that our misguided teacher thought she could choreograph into something meant to pass for a "dance." Piedmont, West Virginia, in 1956, was a very long way from Penguin Nation, wherever that was supposed to be! But penguins we were determined to be, and we did our level best to avoid wounding each other with our orange-colored cardboard beaks while stomping out of rhythm in our matching orange, veined webbed feet. The whole scene was madness, one never to be repeated at the Davis Free School. But I never stopped loving penguins. And I have never stopped loving the very audacity of the idea of the Penguin Classics, an affordable, accessible library of the most important and compelling texts in the history of civilization, their black-and-white spines and covers and uniform type giving each text a comfortable, familiar feel, as if we have encountered it, or its cousins, before. I think of the Penguin Classics as the very best and most compelling in human thought, an Alexandrian library in paperback, enclosed in black and white.

I still gravitate to the Penguin Classics when killing time in an airport bookstore, deferring the slow torture of the security lines. Sometimes I even purchase two or three, fantasizing that I can speed-read one of the shorter titles, then make a dent in the longer one, vainly attempting to fill the holes in the liberal arts education that our degrees suggest we have, over the course of a plane ride! Mark Twain once quipped that a classic is "something that everybody wants to have read and nobody wants to read," and perhaps that applies to my airport purchasing habits. For my generation, these titles in the Penguin Classics form the canon—the canon of the texts that a truly well-educated person should have read, and read carefully and closely, at least once. For years I rued the absence of texts by black authors in this series, and longed to be able to make even a small contribution to the diversification of this astonishingly universal list. I watched with great pleasure as titles by African American and African authors began to appear, some two dozen over the past several years. So when Elda Rotor approached me about editing a series of African American classics and collections for Penguin's Portable Series, I eagerly accepted.

Thinking about the titles appropriate for inclusion in these series led me, inevitably, to think about what, for me, constitutes a "classic." And thinking about this led me, in turn, to the wealth of reflections on what defines a work of literature or philosophy somehow speaking to the human condition beyond time and place, a work somehow endlessly compelling, generation upon generation, a work whose author we don't have to look like to identify with, to feel at one with, as we find ourselves transported through the magic of a textual time machine; a work that refracts the image of ourselves that we project onto it, regardless of our ethnicity, our gender, our time, our place. This is what centuries of scholars and writers have meant when they use the word *classic*, and—despite all that we know about the complex intersubjectivity of the production of meaning in the wondrous exchange between a reader and a text—it remains true that classic texts, even in the most conventional, conservative sense of the word *classic*, do exist, and these books will continue to be read long after the generation the text reflects and defines, the generation of readers contemporary with the text's author, is dead and gone. Classic texts speak from their authors' graves, in their names, in their voices. As Italo Calvino once remarked, "A classic is a book that has never finished saying what it has to say."

Faulkner put this idea in an interesting way: "The aim of every artist is to arrest motion, which is life, by artificial means, and hold it fixed so that a hundred years later, when a stranger looks at it, it moves again since it is life." That, I am certain, must be the desire of every writer. But what about the reader? What makes a book a classic to a reader? Here, perhaps, Hemingway said it best: "All good books are alike in that they are truer than if they had really happened and after you are finished reading one you will feel that all that happened to you, and afterwards it belongs to you, the good and the bad, the ecstasy, the remorse and sorrow, the people and the places and how the weather was."

I have been reading black literature since I was fifteen, yanked into the dark discursive universe by an Episcopal priest at a church camp near my home in West Virginia in August 1965, during the terrifying days of the Watts Riots in Los Angeles. Eventually, by fits and starts, studying the literature written by black authors became my avocation; ultimately, it has become my vocation. And, in my own way, I have tried to be an evangelist for it, to a readership larger than my own people, people who, as it were, look like these texts. Here, I am reminded of something W. S. Merwin said about the books he most loved: "Perhaps a classic is a work that one imagines should be common knowledge, but more and more often isn't." I would say, of African and African American literature, that perhaps classic works by black writers are works that one imagines should be common knowledge among the broadest possible readership but that less and less are, as the teaching of reading to understand how words can create the worlds into which books can transport us yields to classroom instruction geared toward passing a state-authorized standardized exam. All literary texts suffer from this wrongheaded approach to teaching, mind you; but it especially affects texts by people of color, and texts by women—texts still struggling, despite enormous gains over the last twenty years, to gain a solid foothold in anthologies and syllabi. For every anthology, every syllabus, every publishing series such as the Penguin Classics constitutes a distinct "canon," an implicit definition of all that is essential for a truly educated person to read.

James Baldwin, who has pride of place in my personal canon of African American authors since it was one of his books that that Episcopal priest gave me to read in that dreadful summer of

1965, argued that "the responsibility of a writer is to excavate the experience of the people who produced him." But surely Baldwin would have agreed with E. M. Forster that the books that we remember, the books that have truly influenced us, are those that "have gone a little further down our particular path than we have yet ourselves." Excavating the known is a worthy goal of the writer as cultural archaeologist; yet, at the same time, so is unveiling the unknown, the unarticulated yet shared experience of the colorless things that make us human: "something we have always known (or thought we knew)," as Calvino puts it, "but without knowing that this author said it first." We might think of the difference between Forster and Baldwin, on the one hand, and Calvino, on the other, as the difference between an author representing what has happened (Forster, Baldwin) in the history of a people whose stories, whose very history itself, has long been suppressed, and what could have happened (Calvino) in the atemporal realm of art. This is an important distinction when thinking about the nature of an African American classic—rather, when thinking about the nature of the texts that constitute the African American literary tradition or, for that matter, the texts in any under-read tradition.

One of James Baldwin's most memorable essays, a subtle meditation on sexual preference, race, and gender, is entitled "Here Be Dragons." So much of traditional African American literature, even fiction and poetry—ostensibly at least once removed from direct statement—was meant to deal a fatal blow to the dragon of racism. For black writers since the eighteenth-century beginnings of the tradition, literature has been one more weapon—a very important weapon, mind you, but still one weapon among many—in the arsenal black people have drawn upon to fight against antiblack racism and for their equal rights before the law. Ted Joans, the black surrealist poet, called this sort of literature from the sixties' Black Arts movement "hand grenade poems." Of what possible use are the niceties of figuration when one must slay a dragon? I can hear you say, give me the blunt weapon anytime! Problem is, it is more difficult than some writers seem to think to slay a dragon with a poem or a novel. Social problems persist; literature too tied to addressing those social problems tends to enter the historical archives, leaving the realm of the literary. Let me state bluntly what should be obvious: Writers are read for how they write, not what they write about.

Frederick Douglass—for this generation of readers one of the most widely read writers—reflected on this matter even in the midst of one of his most fiery speeches addressing the ironies of the sons and daughters of slaves celebrating the Fourth of July while slavery continued unabated. In his now-classic essay "What to the Slave Is the Fourth of July?" (1852), Douglass argued that an immediate, almost transparent form of discourse was demanded of black writers by the heated temper of the times, a discourse with an immediate end in mind: "At a time like this, scorching irony, not convincing argument, is needed . . . a fiery stream of biting ridicule, blasting reproach, withering sarcasm, and stern rebuke. For it is not light that is needed, but fire; it is not the gentle shower, but thunder. We need the storm, the whirlwind, and the earthquake." Above all else, Douglass concludes, the rhetoric of the literature created by African Americans must, of necessity, be a purposeful rhetoric, its ends targeted at attacking the evils that afflict black people: "The feeling of the nation must be quickened; the conscience of the nation must be roused; the propriety of the nation must be startled; the hypocrisy of the nation must be exposed; and its crimes against God and man must be proclaimed and denounced." And perhaps this was so; nevertheless, we read Douglass's writings today in literature classes not so much for their content but to understand, and marvel at, his sublime mastery of words, words—to paraphrase Calvino—that never finish saying what it is they have to say, not because of their "message," but because of the language in which that message is inextricably enfolded.

There are as many ways to define a classic in the African American tradition as there are in any other tradition, and these ways are legion. So many essays have been published entitled "What Is a Classic?" that they could fill several large anthologies. And while no one can say explicitly why generations of readers return to read certain texts, just about everyone can agree that making a best-seller list in one's lifetime is most certainly not an index of fame or influence over time; the longevity of one's readership—of books about which one says, "I am rereading," as Calvino puts it—on the other hand, most certainly is. So, the size of one's readership (through library use, Internet access, and sales) cumulatively is an interesting factor to consider; and because of series such as the Penguin Classics, we can gain a sense, for our purposes, of those texts written by authors in previous generations that have sustained sales—mostly for classroom use—long after their authors were dead.

There can be little doubt that *Narrative of the Life of Frederick Douglass* (1845), *The Souls of Black Folk* (1903), by W. E. B. Du Bois, and *Their Eyes Were Watching God* (1937), by Zora Neale Hurston, are the three most classic of the black classics—again, as measured by consumption—while Langston Hughes's poetry, though not purchased as books in these large numbers, is accessed through the Internet as frequently as that of any other American poet, and indeed profoundly more so than most. Within Penguin's Portable Series list, the most popular individual titles, excluding Douglass's first slave narrative and Du Bois's *Souls*, arc:

Up from Slavery (1903), Booker T. Washington
The Autobiography of an Ex-Coloured Man (1912), James Weldon Johnson
God's Trombones (1926), James Weldon Johnson
Passing (1929), Nella Larsen
The Marrow of Tradition (1898), Charles W. Chesnutt
Incidents in the Life of a Slave Girl (1861), Harriet Jacobs
The Interesting Narrative (1789), Olaudah Equiano
The House Behind the Cedars (1900), Charles W. Chesnutt
My Bondage and My Freedom (1855), Frederick Douglass
Quicksand (1928), Nella Larsen

These titles form a canon of classics of African American literature, judged by classroom readership. If we add Jean Toomer's novel *Cane* (1922), arguably the first work of African American modernism, along with Douglass's first narrative, Du Bois's *The Souls*, and Hurston's *Their Eyes*, we would most certainly have included many of the touchstones of black literature published before 1940, when Richard Wright published *Native Son*.

Every teacher's syllabus constitutes a canon of sorts, and I teach these texts and a few others as the classics of the black canon. Why these particular texts? I can think of two reasons: First, these texts signify or riff upon each other, repeating, borrowing, and extending metaphors book to book, generation to generation. To take just a few examples, Equiano's eighteenth-century use of the trope of the talking book (an image found, remarkably, in five slave narratives published between 1770 and 1811) becomes, with Frederick Douglass, the representation of the quest for freedom as, necessarily, the quest for literacy, for a freedom larger than physical manumission; we might think of this as the representation of metaphysical manumission, of freedom and literacy—the literacy of great literature—inextricably intertwined. Douglass transformed the metaphor of the talking book into the trope of chiasmus, a repetition with a stinging reversal: "You have seen how a man becomes a slave, you will see how a slave becomes a man." Du Bois, with Douglass very much on his mind, transmuted chiasmus a half century later into the metaphor of duality or double consciousness, a necessary condition of living one's life, as he memorably put it, behind a "veil."

Du Bois's metaphor has a powerful legacy in twentieth-century black fiction: James Weldon Johnson, in *Ex-Coloured Man*, literalizes the trope of double consciousness by depicting as his protagonist a man who, at will, can occupy two distinct racial spaces, one black, one white, and who moves seamlessly, if ruefully, between them; Toomer's *Cane* takes Du Bois's metaphor of duality for the inevitably split consciousness that every Negro must feel living in a country in which her or his status as a citizen is liminal at best, or has been erased at worst, and makes of this the metaphor for the human condition itself under modernity, a tellingly bold rhetorical gesture—one designed to make the Negro the metaphor of the human condition. And Hurston, in *Their Eyes*, extends Toomer's revision even further, depicting a character who can gain her voice only once she can name this condition of duality or double consciousness and then glide gracefully and lyrically between her two selves, an "inside" self and an "outside" one.

More recently, Alice Walker, in *The Color Purple*, signifies upon two aspects of the narrative strategy of *Their Eyes*: First, she revisits the theme of a young black woman finding her voice, depicting a protagonist who writes herself into being through letters addressed to God and to her sister, Nettie—letters that grow ever more sophisticated in their syntax and grammar and imagery as she comes to consciousness before our very eyes, letter to letter; and second, Walker riffs on Hurston's use of a vernacular-inflected free indirect discourse to show that black English has the capacity to serve as the medium for narrating a novel through the black dialect that forms a most pliable and expansive language in Celie's letters. Ralph Ellison makes Du Bois's metaphor of the veil a trope of blindness and life underground for his protagonist in *Invisible Man*, a protagonist who, as he types the story of his life from a hole underground, writes himself into being in the first person (in contradistinction to Richard Wright's protagonist, Bigger Thomas, whose reactive tale of fear and flight is told in the third person). Walker's novel also riffs on Ellison's claim for the revolutionary possibilities of writing the self into being, whereas Hurston's protagonist, Janie, speaks herself into being. Ellison himself signified multiply upon Richard Wright's *Native Son*, from the title to the use of the first-person bildungsroman to chart the coming to consciousness of a sensitive protagonist moving from blindness and an inability to do little more than react to his environment, to the insight gained by wresting control of his identity from social forces and strong individuals that would circumscribe and confine his life choices. Toni Morrison, master supernaturalist and perhaps the greatest black novelist of all, trumps Ellison's trope of blindness by returning over and over to the possibilities and limits of insight within worlds confined or circumscribed not by supraforces (à la Wright) but by the confines of the imagination and the ironies of individual and family history, signifying upon Faulkner, Woolf, and Márquez in the process. And Ishmael Reed, the father of black postmodernism and what we might think of as the hip-hop novel, the tradition's master parodist, signifies upon everybody and everything in the black literary tradition, from the slave narratives to the Harlem Renaissance to black nationalism and feminism.

This sort of literary signifying is what makes a literary tradition, well, a "tradition," rather than a simple list of books whose authors happen to have been born in the same country, share the same gender, or would be identified by their peers as belonging to this ethnic group or that. What makes these books special—"classic"—however, is something else. Each text has the uncanny capacity to take the seemingly mundane details of the day-to-day African American experience of its time and transmute those details and the characters' actions into something that transcends its ostensible subject's time and place, its specificity. These texts reveal the human universal through the African American particular: All true art, all classics, do this; this is what "art" is, a revelation of that which makes each of us sublimely human, rendered in the minute details of the actions and thoughts and feelings of a compelling character embedded in a time and place. But as soon as we find ourselves turning to a text for its anthropological or sociological data, we have left the realm of art; we have reduced the complexity of fiction or poetry to an essay, and this is not what imaginative literature is for. Richard Wright, at his best, did this, as did his signifying disciple Ralph Ellison; Louis Armstrong and Duke Ellington, Bessie Smith and Billie Holiday achieved this effect in music; Jacob Lawrence and Romare Bearden achieved it in the visual arts. And this is what Wole Soyinka does in his tragedies, what Toni Morrison does in her novels, what Derek Walcott does in his poetry. And while it is risky to name one's contemporaries in a list such as this, I think that Rita Dove and Jamaica Kincaid achieve this effect as well, as do Colson Whitehead and Edwidge Danticat, in a younger generation. (There are other writers whom I would include in this group had I the space.) By delving ever so deeply into the particularity of the African and African American experience, these authors manage, somehow, to come out the other side, making the race or the gender of their characters almost translucent, less important than the fact that they stand as aspects of ourselves beyond race or gender or time or place, precisely in the same magical way that Hamlet never remains for long stuck as a prince in a court in Denmark.

Each classic black text reveals to us, uncannily, subtly, how the Black Experience is inscribed, inextricably and indelibly, in the human experience, and how the human experience takes one of its myriad forms in blackface, as it were. Together, such texts also demonstrate, implicitly, that African American culture is one of the world's truly great and eternal cultures, as noble and as resplendent as any. And it is to publish such texts, written by African and African American authors, that Penguin has created this new series, which I have the pleasure of editing.

HENRY LOUIS GATES, JR.

Introduction

Frederick Douglass was the most famous African American of the nineteenth century and one of the nation's preeminent writers, speakers, and intellectuals. Frederick Augustus Washington Bailey was born on the Eastern Shore of Maryland in February 1818, the son of Harriet Bailey, a slave, and an unknown white father, perhaps his master or an overseer. He escaped from slavery in 1838 and changed his surname from Bailey to Stanley to Johnson and finally to Douglass. From 1845 until his death in 1895 he published three autobiographies, one novella, and thousands of speeches and essays.[1] For sixteen years, from 1847 to 1863, he edited and published the longest-running black newspaper in the nineteenth century. During the Civil War he befriended Abraham Lincoln, and he met with every subsequent president through Grover Cleveland. He became the first black man to receive a federal appointment requiring Senate approval, serving as U.S. marshal of Washington, D.C., then recorder of deeds, and ultimately as minister resident and consul general to Haiti. One other indication of his extraordinary importance to American culture is that he was the most photographed American in the nineteenth century; remarkably, more distinct photographic poses of Douglass survive than of any of his peers.[2]

Douglass became an American icon both through his mastery of the arts of writing and speaking—he was one of the great essayists and orators of his time—and through his clever use of the growing popularity of photography to disseminate his strikingly handsome and noble image. Over the course of a career spanning some fifty-five years, he used these forms of representation to fashion and refashion a public self that championed the rights of freedom and equality, first for the slaves, then the ex-slaves, but also for women, among other causes. Owing to his rise up from slavery to eminent writer, orator, and statesman, he was often called the first black "self-made" or "representative" man, in the Emersonian sense of that term. Lincoln met with him three times at the White House and reportedly called him "one of the most meritorious men, if not the most meritorious man, in the United States." His close friend and confidant, the physician and abolitionist author James McCune Smith (the first black university-trained medical doctor), called him "a Representative American man," because he had "passed through every gradation of rank comprised in our national make-up and bears upon his person and his soul everything that is American." Douglass made possible "what had hitherto been regarded as an impossible reform." He thus became "a burning and a shining light" for all humanity.[3]

Like his peers, Douglass believed that "true art" could break down racial barriers. True art was for him a language, expressed in three registers: as written words on the page, words spoken as oratory, and visual images crafted as daguerreotypes and photographs. He sought to use these three mediums to disseminate "accurate" and "authentic" representations of African Americans to counteract the pernicious caricatures of black people so commonly found in proslavery journalism and literature and in the seemingly endless proliferation of demeaning visual imagery in American popular culture, ranging from cartoons to the minstrelsy stage.

Borrowing from Aristotle's *Poetics*, Douglass argued that humans' proclivity for "pictures"—their desire to represent themselves and their world—is what, ultimately, distinguishes them from animals. "Man is the only picture-making animal in the world," he said. "He alone of all the inhabitants of earth has the capacity and passion for pictures."[4] For Douglass, true art expressed the essential humanity of all people. Blacks were not subhuman, as racist ideologies claimed, but entitled to the same democratic rights as other humans.[5]

During his lifetime, Douglass was perhaps much better known as an orator than an author. His was an era in which public speaking was one of the principal forms of entertainment and often more lucrative and prestigious than writing. He was considered by many to be the art's exemplar, far more sophisticated at the lectern than Lincoln and other statesmen, and thought to rival such highly regarded speakers as Ralph Waldo Emerson and Wendell Phillips. In fact, by the 1850s he was commanding among the highest speaking fees in the country. He had a rich baritone voice, he was a brilliant mimic, and his imitations of his foes (especially of slaveholders) could draw howls of laughter. His performances coupled irony and sarcasm with pathos and sentimentality. In addition to being tall and strikingly handsome, he was also "majestic in his wrath," as one sympathetic admirer noted. Throughout his long career, he said that he felt more comfortable "speaking to the public ear" than "writing for the public eye," though his first two books sold exceptionally well.[6]

Today Douglass is best remembered for his three autobiographies, especially his lyrical 1845 *Narrative of the Life of Frederick Douglass, an American Slave*, which has entered the canon of African American literature and has often been explicated by literary scholars. Although his *Narrative* made him famous, his second autobiography, *My Bondage and My Freedom* (1855), which brilliantly contrasted his life in freedom versus his life in slavery, was during his life his single most popular published work. Incredibly, *My Bondage* sold five thousand copies in its first three days and twelve thousand copies in less than two months. It went through three editions in three years; the reviewer for the literary magazine *Putnam's Monthly* was so taken with the text that he called Douglass a "genius."[7]

He was also something of a genius at marketing, and using one medium to sell another. He would sell his autobiographies and subscriptions to his newspapers at the venues where he lectured.[8] He published his lectures and his novella in his newspaper. He included autobiographical stories in his journalism and lectures. And his lectures were often published as essays in pamphlet form.

Douglass's "picture-making," then, assumed multiple forms, genres, and modes of presentation—from autobiography and fiction to speeches and journalism—in each of which he excelled. *The Portable Frederick Douglass* is intended to introduce a new generation of readers to the fullest range of Douglass's thinking and expression, including two important but previously unpublished writings: a speech, "Pictures and Progress," which he wrote during the Civil War and which highlights the importance of art as a lever for radical social change; and an essay, "Toussaint L'Ouverture," on the great leader of the revolution of the slaves against their French masters on the island of Saint-Domingue, the island that would be reborn as the Republic of Haiti in 1804.[9]

Douglass became fascinated with language during his years as a slave. As a twelve-year-old boy living in Baltimore, he first realized that words could be weapons. His mistress, Sophia Auld, had given him reading lessons until her husband, Hugh Auld, found out and put a stop to it. "If you give a nigger an inch, he will take an ell," Hugh said to his wife. "A nigger should know nothing but to obey his master—to do as he is told to do. Learning would *spoil* the best nigger in the world. Now, if you teach that nigger"—speaking of myself, Douglass explains—"how to read, there would be no keeping him. It would forever unfit him to be a slave. He would at once become unmanageable, and of no value to his master. As to himself, it could do him no good, but a great deal of harm. It would make him discontented and unhappy."

Very well, Frederick thought, he would gain knowledge:

> These words sank deep into my heart, stirred up sentiments within that lay slumbering, and called into existence an entirely new train of thought. It was a new and special revelation, explaining dark and mysterious things, with which my youthful understanding had struggled, but struggled in vain. I now understood what had been to me a most perplexing difficulty—to wit, the white man's power to enslave the black man.

And what was that power? "From that moment," Douglass says with a grand rhetorical flourish,

> I understood the pathway from slavery to freedom . . . Though conscious of the difficulty of learning without a teacher, I set out with high hope, and a fixed purpose, at whatever cost of trouble, to learn how to read . . . What he most dreaded, that I most desired. What he most loved, that I most hated. That which to him

> was a great evil, to be carefully shunned, was to me a great good, to be diligently sought; and the argument which he so warmly urged, against my learning to read, only served to inspire me with a desire and determination to learn.

Having parried his master's attempt to keep him illiterate, Douglass concludes his deeply moving ode to the inextricable relation between literacy and freedom with a final and quite amusing thrust right at the heart of his old master: "In learning to read, I owe almost as much to the bitter opposition of my master, as to the kindly aid of my mistress. I acknowledge the benefit of both."[10]

Douglass quickly embarked on his "pathway" to freedom: On the streets of Baltimore, he tricked little white boys into giving him spelling lessons, offering biscuits in exchange for words. The boys introduced him to *The Columbian Orator*, a popular elocution manual that they were studying. He purchased a copy with fifty cents he had surreptitiously earned polishing boots.

The Columbian Orator was one of the two books that started Douglass on his journey to eloquence and freedom. Edited by the Massachusetts educator Caleb Bingham (1757–1817)—a Dartmouth graduate—and published in 1797, it was designed for young boys like Frederick, who did not have the privilege of a formal education. It was in essence a self-help book for those who wanted to improve their public speaking abilities. In his introduction, Bingham refers to Demosthenes, the Greek statesman who, though born with a weak voice and a speech impediment, had through rigorous practice surmounted these "natural defects" to become one of the great classical orators. While class disadvantages were certainly very much on Bingham's mind, we wonder if he could possibly have imagined the impact that his textbook would have on a slave boy suffering under the burden of what apologists for slavery saw as the "natural defect" of blackness, a slave boy who would become one of the country's most effective speakers and writers by the middle of the nineteenth century.

From Bingham's selections Douglass first became aware of the aesthetic and political power of a rhetorical trope called chiasmus—a form of repetition and reversal that balances words, clauses, or sections of a work against each other. Perhaps the most important example of Douglass's use of chiasmus with maximum effect is his often-cited sentence "You have seen how a man was made a slave; you shall see how a slave was made a man," which is the structural center of his 1845 slave narrative. Repetition with a difference, as he discovered, could produce an aesthetically pleasing and politically powerful effect.[11]

The Columbian Orator's content was surprisingly radical for a self-help book, in the context of the politics of slavery in antebellum America; several of its three dozen or so selections—essays, dialogues, speeches, and poems—denounced slavery and emphasized that all people are created equal. Indeed, by the 1850s some prominent Southern newspapers included it on a blacklist of abolitionist books, seeking to ban it from Southern schools and homes.[12] "Every opportunity I got, I used to read this book," Douglass writes in his *Narrative*. "The more I read, the more I was led to abhor and detest my enslavers." The book made freedom "ever present" to him: "Freedom now appeared, to disappear no more forever. It was heard in every sound, and seen in every thing."[13]

The other book at the heart of Douglass's canon was the King James Bible. In a version of the trope of the talking book so important to the narrative strategies of the eighteenth-century slave narratives, Douglass writes that he heard Sophia Auld read from the Bible, which awakened his curiosity in "this *mystery* of reading, and roused in me the desire to learn." Indeed, it was the Bible that prompted him to ask Mistress Auld to teach him to read in the first placc. Thc Bible would be quite important to Douglass in his quest to master literacy: he writes that he collected ripped-out pages of the Bible from the "street gutters of Baltimore," then "washed and dried them" and read them over and over. Later, on Maryland's Eastern Shore, he led a Sabbath school for other slaves and taught them lessons from scripture.[14] Like *The Columbian Orator*, the King James Bible was designed to be "understood even [by] the very vulgar," as the translators noted in their preface to the first (1611) edition. It became another fount of solace, strength, and eloquence for Douglass.[15] "In the darkest hours of my career in slavery," he writes in his *Narrative*, "this living word of faith and spirit of hope departed not from me, but remained like ministering angels to cheer me through the gloom."[16]

There is an extraordinary moment in all three autobiographies in which a mournful Douglass stands alone on the banks of the

Chesapeake Bay, gazing longingly at the ships, "freedom's swift-winged angels that fly round the world."[17] He places readers with him on the banks of the Chesapeake, so that they will understand what freedom to a slave looks and feels like. It is one of the great scenes of world literature. At once a Job-like lament and a prayer for deliverance, this eloquent apostrophe to the ships speaks movingly to the inspiring and liberating influence of *The Columbian Orator* and the Bible:

> You are loosed from your moorings, and are free; I am fast in my chains, and am a slave! You move merrily before the gentle gale, and I sadly before the bloody whip! You are freedom's swift-winged angels, that fly round the world; I am confined in bands of iron! O that I were free! O, that I were on one of your gallant decks, and under your protecting wing! Alas! betwixt me and you, the turbid waters roll. Go on, go on. O that I could also go! . . . O, why was I born a man, of whom to make a brute!

His growing literacy gained through mastery of these two books, exemplified by this apostrophe to the ships at the Chesapeake, led directly to what Douglass consistently identified as the central turning point in his life: his fight to a "draw" with the "slave breaker" Edward Covey, more or less a wrestling match that led to his spiritual, his psychological, and eventually his physical freedom. It was the first time Frederick had fought a white man, and the effects were thrilling. After forcing Covey to retreat, he defined himself as a free man in fact, even if he remained "a slave in form."[18] Soon after the fight he tried but failed to run away, which prompted his master, Thomas Auld, to send him back to Baltimore, curiously enough, rather than giving him the harsher punishment some runaways received—beatings, maiming, or being sold during the "Second Middle Passage" to work large plantations (such as cotton plantations) in the lower South.

In Baltimore Douglass first became known for his eloquence. He joined a debating club called the Baltimore Mental Improvement Society. Here, free black people, who constituted 85 percent of the total black population of Baltimore, met to hone their public speaking skills and hear lectures. And here, he met his future wife, Anna Murray, a free black woman. Although the only member of the Mental Improvement Society who was a slave, Douglass played a prominent role in the society's debates. One night, after a triumphant debate, he declared that he would never stop rising until he was a United States senator. It was a revolutionary statement that betrayed his boundless faith both in the American ideals of individual progress and elevation and more specifically in the power of language to remake himself and transform society.[19]

The eloquence of the *Narrative* stems partly from Douglass's having first *orated* his life story. In 1841, three years after Douglass fled from slavery and settled in New Bedford, Massachusetts, William Lloyd Garrison, the editor of *The Liberator* and leader of the American Anti-Slavery Society, heard him speak at an antislavery meeting on the island of Nantucket and was so impressed that he hired him more or less on the spot as a full-time lecturer for the society. Immediately, Douglass began traveling around the Northern states, speaking "from experience," as he said, and telling stories about his life as a slave.[20] Although he discussed other subjects, the focal point of these early speeches was his own story of bondage and escape. Much as the Word had prompted him to become free, he now used words, often drawn from the Bible, to convert his audiences to the antislavery cause. In certain respects his 1845 *Narrative* is a written synthesis of the speeches he had been delivering—rehearsing, really—on thc abolitionist circuit during the previous four years.

His latter two autobiographies, published in 1855 and 1881, respectively, are also in part written syntheses of his speeches, coupled with examples of his journalism and pastiches of his earlier autobiographical writings. The first part of *My Bondage*, "Life as a Slave," is closely modeled on his *Narrative*. The second part, "Life as a Freeman," narrates his career as an orator with the American Anti-Slavery Society and culminates with the beginning of his career as the publisher and editor of *The North Star* (which became *Frederick Douglass' Paper* in 1851 and *Douglass' Monthly* in 1859). It ends with a sixty-page appendix in small print that contains excerpts of six speeches plus one letter that he had published in his newspaper. Similarly, the first half of *Life and Times* (1881) is modeled closely on the *Narrative* and *My Bondage* to 1855. The remaining 350 pages of this

700-page book contain long excerpts of his speeches and journalism. Oratory and journalism heavily informed the structure of his later autobiographical writings.

Each autobiography narrates the life from a distinct political vantage point. In the *Narrative*, he writes as a fugitive and an employee of Garrison's American Anti-Slavery Society, which considered the Constitution and federal government corrupt but opposed violent means to end slavery. In *My Bondage*, he is a self-employed publisher and editor, an eminent orator, and a militant, political abolitionist. And in *Life and Times*, he is a postwar Republican elder statesman, respectable, famous, and wealthy.

Throughout these autobiographical writings, Douglass portrays himself as a performance artist who continually evolves while relying on his powerful command of rhetoric to destroy slavery and racism. One remarkable example of his radical self-fashioning is the changes he makes to his genealogy. In each of his three autobiographies he alters the identities of his mother and father and his relationships to them (see the appendix).

In the *Narrative* Douglass draws attention to his white father and thus his white heritage. He says he scarcely knew his slave mother, Harriet Bailey, and notes that she had a "darker complexion than either my grandmother or grandfather," Isaac and Betsey Bailey, both of whom were "quite dark." His father was a white man, he declares without qualification, and "the opinion was also whispered that my master was my father," Douglass tells us in the first chapter of his book. Two years after writing these words, in 1847, after English abolitionists purchased his freedom, Douglass identifies his father, "or the man who was called my father," as Thomas Auld, a central character in all three autobiographies.[21]

Ten years later, in *My Bondage and My Freedom*, Douglass highlights the heritage of his slave mother, Harriet Bailey, and thus his black heritage. Now he says that his knowledge of her is "very distinct." He describes her as very black and very beautiful: "She was tall, and finely proportioned; of deep black, glossy complexion; had regular features, and . . . was remarkably sedate in her manners." Apparently she was also masculine in appearance, for her son likened her to a drawing he had come across, in James Prichard's *Natural History of Man*, of Rameses the Great, the

Egyptian king of the nineteenth dynasty. "The features of [the drawing of Rameses] so resemble those of my mother, that I often recur to it with something of the feeling which I suppose others experience when looking upon the pictures of dear departed ones."

But now, Douglass also implies that his father may have had black ancestry, qualifying his claim ten years earlier that his father was a white man and his master: "My father was a white man, or nearly white." Now he suggests that Aaron Anthony, Thomas Auld's father-in-law, was his probable father. He describes Anthony's rare, fatherly acts of affection toward him: "Could the reader have seen him gently leading me by the hand—as he sometimes did—patting me on the head, speaking to me in soft, caressing tones and calling me his 'little Indian boy,' he would have deemed him a kind old man, and, really, almost fatherly."[22]

In *Life and Times*, though noting, "Of my father I know nothing," Douglass unites his black and white genealogical strands, especially when describing his second marriage, in 1884, to Helen Pitts, a white woman:

> People who had remained silent over the unlawful relations of the white slave masters with their colored slave women loudly condemned me for marrying a wife a few shades lighter than myself. They would have had no objection to my marrying a person much darker in complexion than myself, but to marry one much lighter, and of the complexion of my father rather than of that of my mother, was, in the popular eye, a shocking offense, and one for which I was to be ostracized by white and black alike.

He has become neither white nor black but both. In his 1886 essay "The Future of the Colored Race," he suggests that this new identity is becoming more and more common. The United States has long been understood as having "two distinct and separate streams of human life running through it": "all black on the one side, all white on the other." But since the Civil War, "an intermediate race has arisen, which is neither white nor black, neither Caucasian nor Ethiopian, and this intermediate race is constantly increasing." As the nation's representative

American and African American, Douglass embodied this intermediate race.[23]

Such genealogical self-fashionings articulate a radically evolving persona that explodes the very foundations of slavery and race, both of which depend upon some individuals being "fatally fixed in that condition for life."[24] Slavery creates a low ceiling above which no one can rise, and racism reflects the belief that some humans are *permanently* inferior to other humans. For Douglass (and many other revolutionaries), stasis implied acceptance of existing social structures and hierarchies, including racism and slavery. Douglass recognized, however, that substantive social change in America required a revolutionary conception of both self and society.

The manner in which he restructured his family tree, specifically the identity of or his relation to his mother and father, also reflected the larger political purposes for which Douglass wanted or expected his text to be employed. Claiming descent from a white father did not help to strengthen the argument that white and black people were, by nature, equal, if it could be argued that Douglass's obviously superior intelligence derived from his European rather than his African ancestry, an argument which of course was made. To counter that argument, he enlarged the role of his black mother in his life and in the shaping of his mind, even arguing somewhat wistfully a year before he published *My Bondage and My Freedom* that the intellect "uniformly" derives from the maternal side of one's ancestry.[25]

Douglass's retrospective refashionings of his parents' identities seem to have been motivated by the "self" he was positing at the time he crafted each autobiography. Each "self" unfolding in each text, he suggests, is a logical extension of the self birthed by his mother and shaped by her, his father, and his grandmother, even if his descriptions of his mother and father, and the depth of his relationships with his mother and grandmother, vary from text to text. Douglass seems to be arguing for an *internal* consistency between the persona being posited in each autobiography (mother, father, or grandmother) and his *own* persona as narrator, rather than seeking consistency *among* these three distinct personae. As a result, he needed to conjure up more details as he got older, when the normal course of human memory is to forget details the older one gets. That no scholar seems to have noticed these inconsistencies before Peter Walker explicated them in such fine detail we find as remarkable as we find Douglass's audacity in so boldly reinventing himself in such distinct ways over the course of his three autobiographies.[26]

Douglass's fluid conception of the self united his evolving autobiographical art and his shifting politics. Just as he rejected the idea of a fixed self, so too did he repudiate fixed social stations and rigid hierarchies. Indeed, he defined himself as a "picture-maker," both of the self and of society. As he put it in "Pictures and Progress":

> Poets, prophets, and reformers [Douglass considered himself all three] are all picture-makers—and this ability is the secret of their power and of their achievements. They see what ought to be by the reflection of what is, and endeavor to remove the contradiction.

The 160 separate photographs of Douglass, from his earliest known portrait as a young man, with what might be taken over a century later as something of an "Afro," to his postmortem portrait, convey something of his faith in photography and of his fluid conception of identity and society. His "pictures" document his continual evolution and his desire to reform society, which would, he believed, inspire others to radical reform as well. As he emphasized, "the moral and social influence of pictures" was more important in shaping national culture than "the making of its laws."[27]

Douglass's only work of fiction, *The Heroic Slave* (1853), is also one of the earliest examples of African American fiction. The novella fictionalizes the historical persona of Madison Washington, a Virginia slave who escaped to Canada, returned to free his wife, and was reenslaved in the attempt. After being sold to a trader, Madison Washington was sent south to New Orleans on the slave ship *Creole*, where he led a successful mutiny in 1841. It was one of the most successful slave rebellions in North American history, with 133 slaves becoming free, and only one crewman and two slaves killed. Early reports of the mutiny in the abolitionist press helped push Douglass away from the pacifism of Garrisonian nonresistance toward a more radical position on the uses of violence to achieve black freedom.[28]

The Heroic Slave is a pastiche of genres, combining history, fiction, journalism, oratory, and autobiography to create a black hero who bears a striking resemblance to Douglass himself. Douglass structures his novella around a series of dialogues between Madison Washington, proslavery Southerners, and Mr. Listwell, a radical white abolitionist who "listens well" to what blacks say and is modeled on Douglass's friend the wealthy abolitionist Gerrit Smith. The narrator closely identifies with Washington's heroism, much as Douglass identified with the historical Washington in his speeches and journalism from 1845 until he published the novella.

Initially, Douglass planned to write a history of the *Creole* rebellion that centered on Washington. In early 1852 he planned a trip to Nassau, no doubt hoping to meet Washington and obtain "ample materials" for writing about the rebellion. But the publication of Harriet Beecher Stowe's *Uncle Tom's Cabin* in March 1852 convinced him of the truth-telling power of fiction. As Douglass knew, truth telling, even more than eloquence or artistry, was his most powerful weapon in fighting slavery and racism. Masterfully adorned truth telling was even more powerful. The journalistic accounts of the *Creole* rebellion, including Douglass's, had been comparatively ineffective, because they had to rely on scant and conflicting evidence from depositions taken by whites aboard the *Creole*. The success of Stowe's novel inspired him to couple his rhetorical gifts with historical accuracy and write the story as fiction.[29]

The result is a work that is far more authentic and influential than the existing nonfiction accounts. Douglass likens Madison Washington to the disciplined and eloquent revolutionary heroes "whose names he bore." He also casts Washington as a cosmopolitan black nationalist hero who sees *any* society as a site where slave rebels and abolitionists can live as free and equal citizens. In Canada and Nassau, Madison Washington is "protected" by the British lion's "mighty paw from the talons and the beak of the American eagle," much as Douglass as a fugitive had found protection and legal freedom in the British Isles, after the success of his *Narrative* exposed him to likely reenslavement had he stayed in America. "I have no love for America," he announced after returning to the United States in 1847. "I have no patriotism. I have no country." What he loved was "humanity all over the globe." His endorsement of a radical cosmopolitanism was not inconsistent with his persona as a representative American and African American. As James McCune Smith noted, he represented what we might think of as a universal potential of enlightened humanism, much like America's founding document.[30]

While Douglass's autobiographies, speeches, and novella have been canonized and celebrated, his journalism has been underappreciated.[31] Yet his paper provided, as did Garrison's *Liberator* and Horace Greeley's *New-York Tribune*, some of the most trenchant cultural criticism in the nineteenth century.

Douglass modeled his paper on Garrison's *Liberator*. He had begun reading it in 1838, after fleeing north and settling in New Bedford, Massachusetts. "The paper became my meat and drink. My soul was set all on fire," he wrote.[32] Becoming an editor reflected another aspect of his rise up from slavery, for editors were both public intellectuals and entrepreneurs, leaders of society in ways that orators were not. He borrowed from his former mentor by creating a four-page weekly and employing a punchy, fast-paced, and physical style that conveyed the felt experience of racism and slavery in America. But whereas Garrison was unrelenting in his attacks, Douglass loved irony, humor, and ambiguity, and so his prose sounded more genteel. Like the *Liberator*, Douglass's paper sought universal emancipation and black uplift without ignoring other reform movements such as women's rights, labor, and temperance. But while Garrison downplayed politics, Douglass foregrounded it. In its variety of content and voices, his paper imagined a new community that transcended the nation-state and envisioned "all rights for all," which became the paper's motto.

As an essayist, Douglass understood American politics and culture as well as any peer. He was one of the first journalists to recognize that the Fugitive Slave Act of 1850, which virtually legitimized the kidnapping of free blacks, would inspire millions of formerly law-abiding Northerners to act on "higher law," protect fugitives already living in the North from recapture, and help slaves fleeing slavery in the South to escape to Canada.

Similarly, he accurately predicted that the Dred Scott decision (1857), which declared that even free black people were not citizens and which threatened to extend slavery throughout the territories and even into free states, would convert countless more Northerners to the antislavery cause. He foresaw that John Brown's raid on Harpers Ferry in 1859 would prompt Republicans to choose a more conservative nominee (Lincoln) than the two front-runners, William Seward and Salmon Chase.

Immediately after the 1861 events at Fort Sumter, he recognized that the easiest way to win the war was to emancipate slaves and arm them along with free black volunteers, which took the Lincoln administration almost two years to appreciate and implement. Even before the Civil War ended, he warned that emancipation might not end slavery and that blacks were in danger of becoming slaves "of society at large" rather than free citizens. He warned of a postwar counterrevolution that would preserve slavery in another form, and in 1891 he called for an American Toussaint, "who may convert the Gulf States into another Santo Domingo." In short, his writings prognosticated a major arc of American society, from the growth of the Slave Power that led to civil war and emancipation, to the "redemption" of the South after the collapse of Reconstruction, which reconstituted what we might think of as black unfreedom by another name.[33]

Given his influence and fame, Douglass possibly "abolitionized" more readers and listeners than any other American. He stood apart from his peers in his ability to reveal, in great depth and richness, the psychologies of slavery and freedom, and in employing novelistic structures in his nonfiction. His writings and speeches influenced many other contemporaneous works, from William Wells Brown's *Narrative* (1847) and Herman Melville's *White Jacket* (1850) and *Benito Cereno* (1855) to Harriet Beecher Stowe's *Uncle Tom's Cabin* (1852), Charles Dickens's *Great Expectations* (1861), Harriet Jacobs's *Incidents in the Life of a Slave Girl* (1861), Elizabeth Keckley's *Behind the Scenes* (1868), and Mark Twain's *Adventures of Huckleberry Finn* (1884). After his death, they would inspire later generations of writings, from Booker T. Washington's *Up from Slavery* (1901) and Charles Chesnutt's *Marrow of Tradition* (1901), to W. E. B. Du Bois's *Souls of Black Folk* (1903), James Weldon Johnson's *Autobiography of an Ex-Colored Man* (1912), Zora Neale Hurston's *Their Eyes Were Watching God* (1937), Richard Wright's *Black Boy* (1945), Ralph Ellison's *Invisible Man* (1952), on down to Martin Luther King Jr.'s speeches, James Baldwin's *Fire Next Time* (1963), Malcolm X's *Autobiography* (1965), and Barack Obama's *Dreams from My Father* (1995).[34]

Perhaps the most enduring legacy of Douglass's writings and speeches is that they highlight the degree to which language itself becomes a mode of liberation, "first as a source of hope, later as a strategy of escape and a form of power," as Henry Louis Gates, Jr., and David Blight have noted.[35] He mastered the form of chiasmus (or rhetorical reversal), describing with great beauty and power the transformation from ignorance to knowledge, from darkness to light, from being lost to being found, from slavery to freedom, barbarism to civility, corruption to decency. His writings describe selves and societies that continually evolve, in states of constant flux, encouraging each new generation of readers to discover through his stories their *own* stories, to find through his words their own sources of strength and inspiration, and to seek through his imagery their own swift-winged angels that move merrily before the gentle gale.

JOHN STAUFFER AND HENRY LOUIS GATES, JR.

Suggestions for Further Reading

Andrews, William L., ed. *Critical Essays on Frederick Douglass.* Boston: G. K. Hall, 1991.

———. *To Tell a Free Story: The First Century of Afro-American Autobiography, 1760–1865.* Urbana: University of Illinois Press, 1986.

Blassingame, John W., and John R. McKivigan, eds. *The Frederick Douglass Papers, Series One, Two*, and *Three.* New Haven, CT: Yale University Press, 1979–.

Blight, David W., ed. *The Columbian Orator.* New York: New York University Press, 1998.

———. *Frederick Douglass' Civil War: Keeping Faith in Jubilee.* Baton Rouge: Louisiana State University Press, 1991.

Chesnutt, Charles W. *Frederick Douglass.* Boston: Small, Maynard & Co., 1899.

Davis, David Brion. *Inhuman Bondage: The Rise and Fall of Slavery in the New World.* New York: Oxford University Press, 2006.

Douglass' Monthly, vols. 1–5, 1859–63. New York: Negro Universities Press, 1969.

Foner, Philip S., ed. *The Life and Writings of Frederick Douglass.* 5 vols. New York: International Publishers, 1950–75.

Gates, Henry Louis, Jr. *Figures in Black: Words, Signs, and the "Racial" Self.* New York: Oxford University Press, 1987.

———, ed. *Frederick Douglass: Autobiographies.* New York: Library of America, 1994.

———. "Frederick Douglass's Camera Obscura: Representing the Antislave 'Clothed and in Their Own Form,'" *Critical Inquiry* 42:1 (Fall 2015).

Lee, Maurice S., ed. *The Cambridge Companion to Frederick Douglass.* Cambridge: Cambridge University Press, 2009.

Levine, Robert S. *Martin Delany, Frederick Douglass, and the Politics of Representative Identity.* Durham: University of North Carolina Press, 1997.

Levine, Robert S., John Stauffer, and John R. McKivigan, eds. *The Heroic Slave: A Cultural and Critical Edition.* New Haven, CT: Yale University Press, 2015.

Martin, Waldo E., Jr. *The Mind of Frederick Douglass.* Chapel Hill: University of North Carolina Press, 1986.

McDowell, Deborah E., and Arnold Rampersad, eds. *Slavery and the Literary Imagination.* Baltimore, MD: Johns Hopkins University Press, 1989.

McFeely, William S. *Frederick Douglass.* New York: W. W. Norton, 1995.

Moses, Wilson Jeremiah. *Creative Conflict in African American Thought: Frederick Douglass, Alexander Crummell, Booker T. Washington, W. E. B. Du Bois, and Marcus Garvey.* Cambridge: Cambridge University Press, 2004.

Preston, Dickson J. *Young Frederick Douglass: The Maryland Years.* Baltimore, MD: Johns Hopkins University Press, 1980.

Quarles, Benjamin. *Frederick Douglass.* New York: Da Capo Press, 1997.

Stauffer, John. *The Black Hearts of Men: Radical Abolitionists and the Transformation of Race.* Cambridge, MA: Harvard University Press, 2002.

———. *Giants: The Parallel Lives of Frederick Douglass and Abraham Lincoln.* New York: Twelve, 2008.

Stauffer, John, Zoe Trodd, and Celeste-Marie Bernier. *Picturing Frederick Douglass: An Illustrated Biography of the Nineteenth Century's Most Photographed American.* New York: W. W. Norton, 2015.

Sundquist, Eric J., ed. *Frederick Douglass: New Literary and Historical Essays.* Cambridge: Cambridge University Press, 1990.

———. *To Wake the Nations: Race in the Making of American Literature.* Cambridge, MA: Harvard University Press, 1993.

Walker, Peter F. *Moral Choices: Memory, Desire, and Imagination in Nineteenth-Century American Abolition.* Baton Rouge: Louisiana State University Press, 1978.

Williamson, Scott C. *The Narrative Life: The Moral and Religious Thought of Frederick Douglass.* Macon, GA: Mercer University Press, 2002.

A Note on the Text

The source for each text is listed in the headnote at the beginning of each piece. Spelling and punctuation have been lightly regularized throughout, and minor typographical errors have been corrected. Each chapter from Douglass's autobiographies is excerpted in full, with the exception of chapter 16 of *Life and Times of Frederick Douglass*.

The Portable Frederick Douglass

AUTOBIOGRAPHICAL WRITINGS

NARRATIVE OF THE LIFE OF FREDERICK DOUGLASS, AN AMERICAN SLAVE (1845)

This is the book that made Douglass famous. It also exposed him to recapture, prompting him to move to the British Isles for two years, where sympathizers purchased his legal freedom.

SOURCE: *Narrative of the Life of Frederick Douglass, an American Slave* (Boston: Anti-Slavery Office, 1845)

PREFACE.

In the month of August, 1841, I attended an anti-slavery convention in Nantucket, at which it was my happiness to become acquainted with FREDERICK DOUGLASS, the writer of the following Narrative. He was a stranger to nearly every member of that body; but, having recently made his escape from the southern prison-house of bondage, and feeling his curiosity excited to ascertain the principles and measures of the abolitionists,—of whom he had heard a somewhat vague description while he was a slave,—he was induced to give his attendance, on the occasion alluded to, though at that time a resident in New Bedford.

Fortunate, most fortunate occurrence!—fortunate for the millions of his manacled brethren, yet panting for deliverance from their awful thraldom!—fortunate for the cause of negro emancipation, and of universal liberty!—fortunate for the land of his birth, which he has already done so much to save and bless!—fortunate for a large circle of friends and acquaintances, whose sympathy and affection he has strongly secured by the many sufferings he has endured, by his virtuous traits of character, by his ever-abiding remembrance of those who are in bonds, as being bound with them!—fortunate for the multitudes, in various parts of our republic, whose minds he has enlightened on the subject of slavery, and who have been melted to tears by his pathos, or roused to virtuous indignation by his stirring eloquence against the enslavers of men!—fortunate for himself, as it at once brought him into the field of public usefulness, "gave the world assurance of a MAN,"[1] quickened the slumbering energies of his soul, and consecrated him to the great work of breaking the rod of the oppressor, and letting the oppressed go free!

I shall never forget his first speech at the convention—the extraordinary emotion it excited in my own mind—the powerful impression it created upon a crowded auditory, completely taken by surprise—the applause which followed from the beginning to the end of his felicitous remarks. I think I never hated slavery so intensely as at that moment; certainly, my perception of the enormous outrage which is inflicted by it, on the godlike nature of its victims, was rendered far more clear than ever. There stood one, in physical proportion and stature commanding and exact—in intellect richly endowed—in natural eloquence a prodigy—in soul manifestly "created but a little lower than the angels"[2]—yet a slave, ay, a fugitive slave,—trembling for his safety, hardly daring to believe that on the American soil, a single white person could be found who would befriend him at all hazards, for the love of God and humanity! Capable of high attainments as an intellectual and moral being—needing nothing but a comparatively small amount of cultivation to make him an ornament to society and a blessing to his race—by the law of the land, by the voice of the people, by the terms of the slave code, he was only a piece of property, a beast of burden, a chattel personal, nevertheless!

A beloved friend from New Bedford prevailed on Mr. DOUGLASS to address the convention. He came forward to the platform with a hesitancy and embarrassment, necessarily the attendants of a sensitive mind in such a novel position. After apologizing for his ignorance, and reminding the audience that slavery was a poor school for the human intellect and heart, he proceeded to narrate some of the facts in his own history as a slave, and in the course of his speech gave utterance to many noble thoughts and thrilling reflections. As soon as he had taken his seat, filled with hope and admiration, I rose, and declared that PATRICK HENRY, of revolutionary fame, never made a speech more eloquent in the cause of liberty, than the one we had just listened to from the lips of that hunted fugitive. So I believed at that time—such is my belief now. I reminded the audience of the peril which surrounded this self-emancipated young man at the North,—even in Massachusetts, on the soil of the Pilgrim Fathers, among the descendants of revolutionary sires; and I appealed to them, whether they would ever allow him to be carried back into slavery,—law or no law, constitution or no constitution. The response was unanimous and in thunder-tones—"NO!" "Will you succor and protect him as a brother-man—a resident of the old Bay State?" "YES!" shouted the whole mass, with an energy so startling, that the ruthless tyrants south of Mason and Dixon's line might almost have heard the mighty burst of feeling, and recognized it as the pledge of an invincible determination, on the part of those who gave it, never to betray him that wanders, but to hide the outcast, and firmly to abide the consequences.

It was at once deeply impressed upon my mind, that, if Mr. DOUGLASS could be persuaded to consecrate his time and talents to the promotion of the anti-slavery enterprise, a powerful impetus would be given to it, and a stunning blow at the same time inflicted on northern prejudice against a colored complexion. I therefore endeavored to instil hope and courage into his mind, in order that he might dare to engage in a vocation so anomalous and responsible for a person in his situation; and I was seconded in this effort by warm-hearted friends, especially by the late General Agent of the Massachusetts Anti-Slavery Society, Mr. JOHN A. COLLINS,[3] whose judgment in this instance entirely coincided with my own. At first, he could give no encouragement; with unfeigned diffidence, he expressed his conviction that he was not adequate to the performance of so great a task; the path marked out was wholly an untrodden one; he was sincerely apprehensive that he should do more harm than good. After much deliberation, however, he consented to make a trial; and ever since that period, he has acted as a lecturing agent, under the auspices either of the American or the Massachusetts Anti-Slavery Society. In labors he has been most abundant; and his success in combating prejudice, in gaining proselytes, in agitating the public mind, has far surpassed the most sanguine expectations that were raised at the commencement of his brilliant career. He has borne himself with gentleness and meekness, yet with true manliness of character. As a public speaker, he excels in pathos, wit, comparison, imitation, strength of reasoning, and fluency of language. There is in him that union of head and heart, which is indispensable to an enlightenment of the heads and a winning of the hearts of others. May his strength continue to be equal to his day! May he continue to "grow in grace, and in the knowledge of God,"[4] that he may be increasingly serviceable in the cause of bleeding humanity, whether at home or abroad!

It is certainly a very remarkable fact, that one of the most efficient advocates of the slave population, now before the public, is a fugitive slave, in the person of FREDERICK DOUGLASS; and that the free colored population of the United States are as ably represented by one of their own number, in the person of CHARLES LENOX REMOND,[5] whose eloquent appeals have extorted the highest applause of multitudes on both sides of the Atlantic. Let the calumniators of the colored race despise themselves for their baseness and illiberality of spirit, and henceforth cease to talk of the natural inferiority of those who require nothing but time and opportunity to attain to the highest point of human excellence.

It may, perhaps, be fairly questioned, whether any other portion of the population of the earth could have endured the privations, sufferings and horrors of slavery, without having become more degraded in the scale of humanity than the slaves of African descent. Nothing has been left undone to cripple their intellects, darken their minds, debase their moral nature, obliterate all traces of their relationship to mankind; and yet how wonderfully they have sustained the mighty load of a most frightful bondage, under which they have been groaning for centuries! To illustrate the effect of slavery on the white man,—to show that he has no powers of endurance, in such a condition, superior to those of his black brother,—DANIEL O'CONNELL, the distinguished advocate of universal emancipation, and the mightiest champion of prostrate but not conquered Ireland, relates the following anecdote in a speech delivered by him in the Conciliation

Hall, Dublin, before the Loyal National Repeal Association, March 31, 1845. "No matter," said Mr. O'CONNELL, "under what specious term it may disguise itself, slavery is still hideous. *It has a natural, an inevitable tendency to brutalize every noble faculty of man.* An American sailor, who was cast away on the shore of Africa, where he was kept in slavery for three years, was, at the expiration of that period, found to be imbruted and stultified—he had lost all reasoning power; and having forgotten his native language, could only utter some savage gibberish between Arabic and English, which nobody could understand, and which even he himself found difficulty in pronouncing. So much for the humanizing influence of THE DOMESTIC INSTITUTION!" Admitting this to have been an extraordinary case of mental deterioration, it proves at least that the white slave can sink as low in the scale of humanity as the black one.

Mr. DOUGLASS has very properly chosen to write his own Narrative, in his own style, and according to the best of his ability, rather than to employ some one else. It is, therefore, entirely his own production; and, considering how long and dark was the career he had to run as a slave,—how few have been his opportunities to improve his mind since he broke his iron fetters,—it is, in my judgment, highly creditable to his head and heart. He who can peruse it without a tearful eye, a heaving breast, an afflicted spirit,—without being filled with an unutterable abhorrence of slavery and all its abettors, and animated with a determination to seek the immediate overthrow of that execrable system,—without trembling for the fate of this country in the hands of a righteous God, who is ever on the side of the oppressed, and whose arm is not shortened that it cannot save,—must have a flinty heart, and be qualified to act the part of a trafficker "in slaves and the souls of men." I am confident that it is essentially true in all its statements; that nothing has been set down in malice, nothing exaggerated, nothing drawn from the imagination; that it comes short of the reality, rather than overstates a single fact in regard to SLAVERY AS IT IS. The experience of FREDERICK DOUGLASS, as a slave, was not a peculiar one; his lot was not especially a hard one; his case may be regarded as a very fair specimen of the treatment of slaves in Maryland, in which State it is conceded that they are better fed and less cruelly treated than in Georgia, Alabama, or Louisiana.

Many have suffered incomparably more, while very few on the plantations have suffered less, than himself. Yet how deplorable was his situation! what terrible chastisements were inflicted upon his person! what still more shocking outrages were perpetrated upon his mind! with all his noble powers and sublime aspirations, how like a brute was he treated, even by those professing to have the same mind in them that was in Christ Jesus! to what dreadful liabilities was he continually subjected! how destitute of friendly counsel and aid, even in his greatest extremities! how heavy was the midnight of woe which shrouded in blackness the last ray of hope, and filled the future with terror and gloom! what longings after freedom took possession of his breast, and how his misery augmented, in proportion as he grew reflective and intelligent,—thus demonstrating that a happy slave is an extinct man! how he thought, reasoned, felt, under the lash of the driver, with the chains upon his limbs! what perils he encountered in his endeavors to escape from his horrible doom! and how signal have been his deliverance and preservation in the midst of a nation of pitiless enemies!

This Narrative contains many affecting incidents, many passages of great eloquence and power; but I think the most thrilling one of them all is the description DOUGLASS gives of his feelings, as he stood soliloquizing respecting his fate, and the chances of his one day being a freeman, on the banks of the Chesapeake Bay—viewing the receding vessels as they flew with their white wings before the breeze, and apostrophizing them as animated by the living spirit of freedom. Who can read that passage, and be insensible to its pathos and sublimity? Compressed into it is a whole Alexandrian library of thought, feeling, and sentiment—all that can, all that need be urged, in the form of expostulation, entreaty, rebuke, against that crime of crimes,—making man the property of his fellow-man! O, how accursed is that system, which entombs the godlike mind of man, defaces the divine image, reduces those who by creation were crowned with glory and honor to a level with four-footed beasts, and exalts the dealer in human flesh above all that is called God! Why should its existence be prolonged one hour? Is it not evil, only evil, and that continually? What does its presence imply but the absence of all fear of God, all regard for man, on the part of the people of the United States? Heaven speed its eternal overthrow!

So profoundly ignorant of the nature of slavery are many persons, that they are stubbornly incredulous whenever they read or listen to any recital of the cruelties which are daily inflicted on its victims. They do not deny that the slaves are held as property; but that terrible fact seems to convey to their minds no idea of injustice, exposure to outrage, or savage barbarity. Tell them of cruel scourgings, of mutilations and brandings, of scenes of pollution and blood, of the banishment of all light and knowledge, and they affect to be greatly indignant at such enormous exaggerations, such wholesale misstatements, such abominable libels on the character of the southern planters! As if all these direful outrages were not the natural results of slavery! As if it were less cruel to reduce a human being to the condition of a thing, than to give him a severe flagellation, or to deprive him of necessary food and clothing! As if whips, chains, thumb-screws, paddles, bloodhounds, overseers, drivers, patrols, were not all indispensable to keep the slaves down, and to give protection to their ruthless oppressors! As if, when the marriage institution is abolished, concubinage, adultery, and incest, must not necessarily abound; when all the rights of humanity are annihilated, any barrier remains to protect the victim from the fury of the spoiler; when absolute power is assumed over life and liberty, it will not be wielded with destructive sway! Skeptics of this character abound in society. In some few instances, their incredulity arises from a want of reflection; but, generally, it indicates a hatred of the light, a desire to shield slavery from the assaults of its foes, a contempt of the colored race, whether bond or free. Such will try to discredit the shocking tales of slaveholding cruelty which are recorded in this truthful Narrative; but they will labor in vain. Mr. DOUGLASS has frankly disclosed the place of his birth, the names of those who claimed ownership in his body and soul, and the names also of those who committed the crimes which he has alleged against them. His statements, therefore, may easily be disproved, if they are untrue.

In the course of his Narrative, he relates two instances of murderous cruelty,—in one of which a planter deliberately shot a slave belonging to a neighboring plantation, who had unintentionally gotten within his lordly domain in quest of fish; and in the other, an overseer blew out the brains of a slave who had fled to a stream of water to escape a bloody scourging. Mr. DOUGLASS states that in neither of these instances was any thing done by way of legal arrest or judicial investigation. The Baltimore American, of March 17, 1845, relates a similar case of atrocity, perpetrated with similar impunity—as follows:—"*Shooting a Slave.*—We learn, upon the authority of a letter from Charles county, Maryland, received by a gentleman of this city, that a young man, named Matthews, a nephew of General Matthews, and whose father, it is believed, holds an office at Washington, killed one of the slaves upon his father's farm by shooting him. The letter states that young Matthews had been left in charge of the farm; that he gave an order to the servant, which was disobeyed, when he proceeded to the house, *obtained a gun, and, returning, shot the servant.* He immediately, the letter continues, fled to his father's residence, where he still remains unmolested."—Let it never be forgotten, that no slaveholder or overseer can be convicted of any outrage perpetrated on the person of a slave, however diabolical it may be, on the testimony of colored witnesses, whether bond or free. By the slave code, they are adjudged to be as incompetent to testify against a white man, as though they were indeed a part of the brute creation. Hence, there is no legal protection in fact, whatever there may be in form, for the slave population; and any amount of cruelty may be inflicted on them with impunity. Is it possible for the human mind to conceive of a more horrible state of society?

The effect of a religious profession on the conduct of southern masters is vividly described in the following Narrative, and shown to be any thing but salutary. In the nature of the case, it must be in the highest degree pernicious. The testimony of Mr. DOUGLASS, on this point, is sustained by a cloud of witnesses, whose veracity is unimpeachable. "A slaveholder's profession of Christianity is a palpable imposture. He is a felon of the highest grade. He is a man-stealer. It is of no importance what you put in the other scale."

Reader! are you with the man-stealers in sympathy and purpose, or on the side of their down-trodden victims? If with the former, then are you the foe of God and man. If with the latter, what are you prepared to do and dare in their behalf? Be faithful, be vigilant, be untiring in your efforts to break every yoke, and let the oppressed go free. Come what may—cost what it may—inscribe on the banner which you unfurl to the breeze, as your religious and political motto—"NO COMPROMISE WITH SLAVERY! NO UNION WITH SLAVEHOLDERS!"

WM. LLOYD GARRISON.

BOSTON, *May 1, 1845*.

LETTER FROM WENDELL PHILLIPS, ESQ.

BOSTON, *April 22, 1845.*

My Dear Friend:

You remember the old fable of "The Man and the Lion," where the lion complained that he should not be so misrepresented "when the lions wrote history."

I am glad the time has come when the "lions write history." We have been left long enough to gather the character of slavery from the involuntary evidence of the masters. One might, indeed, rest sufficiently satisfied with what, it is evident, must be, in general, the results of such a relation, without seeking farther to find whether they have followed in every instance. Indeed, those who stare at the half-peck of corn a week, and love to count the lashes on the slave's back, are seldom the "stuff" out of which reformers and abolitionists are to be made. I remember that, in 1838, many were waiting for the results of the West India experiment, before they could come into our ranks. Those "results" have come long ago; but, alas! few of that number have come with them, as converts. A man must be disposed to judge of emancipation by other tests than whether it has increased the produce of sugar,—and to hate slavery for other reasons than because it starves men and whips women,—before he is ready to lay the first stone of his anti-slavery life.

I was glad to learn, in your story, how early the most neglected of God's children waken to a sense of their rights, and of the injustice done them. Experience is a keen teacher; and long before you had mastered your A B C, or knew where the "white sails" of the

Chesapeake were bound, you began, I see, to gauge the wretchedness of the slave, not by his hunger and want, not by his lashes and toil, but by the cruel and blighting death which gathers over his soul.

In connection with this, there is one circumstance which makes your recollections peculiarly valuable, and renders your early insight the more remarkable. You come from that part of the country where we are told slavery appears with its fairest features. Let us hear, then, what it is at its best estate—gaze on its bright side, if it has one; and then imagination may task her powers to add dark lines to the picture, as she travels southward to that (for the colored man) Valley of the Shadow of Death, where the Mississippi sweeps along.

Again, we have known you long, and can put the most entire confidence in your truth, candor, and sincerity. Every one who has heard you speak has felt, and, I am confident, every one who reads your book will feel, persuaded that you give them a fair specimen of the whole truth. No one-sided portrait,—no wholesale complaints,—but strict justice done, whenever individual kindliness has neutralized, for a moment, the deadly system with which it was strangely allied. You have been with us, too, some years, and can fairly compare the twilight of rights, which your race enjoy at the North, with that "noon of night" under which they labor south of Mason and Dixon's line. Tell us whether, after all, the half-free colored man of Massachusetts is worse off than the pampered slave of the rice swamps!

In reading your life, no one can say that we have unfairly picked out some rare specimens of cruelty. We know that the bitter drops, which even you have drained from the cup, are no incidental aggravations, no individual ills, but such as must mingle always and necessarily in the lot of every slave. They are the essential ingredients, not the occasional results, of the system.

After all, I shall read your book with trembling for you. Some years ago, when you were beginning to tell me your real name and birthplace, you may remember I stopped you, and preferred to remain ignorant of all. With the exception of a vague description, so I continued, till the other day, when you read me your memoirs. I hardly knew, at the time, whether to thank you or not for the sight of them, when I reflected that it was still dangerous, in Massachusetts, for honest men to tell their names! They say the fathers, in

1776, signed the Declaration of Independence with the halter about their necks. You, too, publish your declaration of freedom with danger compassing you around. In all the broad lands which the Constitution of the United States overshadows, there is no single spot,—however narrow or desolate,—where a fugitive slave can plant himself and say, "I am safe." The whole armory of Northern Law has no shield for you. I am free to say that, in your place, I should throw the MS. into the fire.

You, perhaps, may tell your story in safety, endeared as you are to so many warm hearts by rare gifts, and a still rarer devotion of them to the service of others. But it will be owing only to your labors, and the fearless efforts of those who, trampling the laws and Constitution of the country under their feet, are determined that they will "hide the outcast," and that their hearths shall be, spite of the law, an asylum for the oppressed, if, some time or other, the humblest may stand in our streets, and bear witness in safety against the cruelties of which he has been the victim.

Yet it is sad to think, that these very throbbing hearts which welcome your story, and form your best safeguard in telling it, are all beating contrary to the "statute in such case made and provided." Go on, my dear friend, till you, and those who, like you, have been saved, so as by fire, from the dark prison-house, shall stereotype these free, illegal pulses into statutes; and New England, cutting loose from a blood-stained Union, shall glory in being the house of refuge for the oppressed;—till we no longer merely "*hide* the outcast," or make a merit of standing idly by while he is hunted in our midst; but, consecrating anew the soil of the Pilgrims as an asylum for the oppressed, proclaim our *welcome* to the slave so loudly, that the tones shall reach every hut in the Carolinas, and make the broken-hearted bondman leap up at the thought of old Massachusetts.

God speed the day!
Till then, and ever,
Yours truly,
WENDELL PHILLIPS.

FREDERICK DOUGLASS.

CHAPTER I.

I was born in Tuckahoe, near Hillsborough, and about twelve miles from Easton, in Talbot county, Maryland. I have no accurate knowledge of my age, never having seen any authentic record containing it. By far the larger part of the slaves know as little of their ages as horses know of theirs, and it is the wish of most masters within my knowledge to keep their slaves thus ignorant. I do not remember to have ever met a slave who could tell of his birthday. They seldom come nearer to it than planting-time, harvest-time, cherry-time, spring-time, or fall-time. A want of information concerning my own was a source of unhappiness to me even during childhood. The white children could tell their ages. I could not tell why I ought to be deprived of the same privilege. I was not allowed to make any inquiries of my master concerning it. He deemed all such inquiries on the part of a slave improper and impertinent, and evidence of a restless spirit. The nearest estimate I can give makes me now between twenty-seven and twenty-eight years of age. I come to this, from hearing my master say, some time during 1835, I was about seventeen years old.

My mother was named Harriet Bailey. She was the daughter of Isaac and Betsey Bailey, both colored, and quite dark. My mother was of a darker complexion than either my grandmother or grandfather.

My father was a white man. He was admitted to be such by all I ever heard speak of my parentage. The opinion was also whispered that my master was my father; but of the correctness of this opinion, I know nothing; the means of knowing was withheld from me. My mother and I were separated when I was but an infant—before I knew her as my mother. It is a common custom, in the part of Maryland from which I ran away, to part children from their mothers at a very early age. Frequently, before the child has reached its twelfth month, its mother is taken from it, and hired out on some farm a considerable distance off, and the child is placed under the care of an old woman, too old for field labor. For what this separation is done, I do not know, unless it be to hinder the development of the child's affection toward its mother, and to blunt and destroy the natural affection of the mother for the child. This is the inevitable result.

I never saw my mother, to know her as such, more than four or five times in my life; and each of these times was very short in duration, and at night. She was hired by a Mr. Stewart, who lived about twelve miles from my home. She made her journeys to see me in the night, travelling the whole distance on foot, after the performance of her day's work. She was a field hand, and a whipping is the penalty of not being in the field at sunrise, unless a slave has special permission from his or her master to the contrary—a permission which they seldom get, and one that gives to him that gives it the proud name of being a kind master. I do not recollect of ever seeing my mother by the light of day. She was with me in the night. She would lie down with me, and get me to sleep, but long before I waked she was gone. Very little communication ever took place between us. Death soon ended what little we could have while she lived, and with it her hardships and suffering. She died when I was about seven years old, on one of my master's farms, near Lee's Mill. I was not allowed to be present during her illness, at her death, or burial. She was gone long before I knew any thing about it. Never having enjoyed, to any considerable extent, her soothing presence, her tender and watchful care, I received the tidings of her death with much the same emotions I should have probably felt at the death of a stranger.

Called thus suddenly away, she left me without the slightest intimation of who my father was. The whisper that my master was my father, may or may not be true; and, true or false, it is of but little consequence to my purpose whilst the fact remains, in all its glaring odiousness, that slaveholders have ordained, and by law established, that the children of slave women shall in all cases follow the condition of their mothers; and this is done too obviously to administer to their own lusts, and make a gratification of their wicked desires profitable as well as pleasurable; for by this cunning arrangement, the slaveholder, in cases not a few, sustains to his slaves the double relation of master and father.

I know of such cases; and it is worthy of remark that such slaves invariably suffer greater hardships, and have more to contend with, than others. They are, in the first place, a constant offence to their mistress. She is ever disposed to find fault with them; they can seldom do any thing to please her; she is never better pleased than when she sees them under the lash, especially when she suspects her husband of showing to his mulatto children favors which he withholds from his black slaves. The master is frequently compelled to sell this class of his slaves, out of deference to the feelings of his white wife; and, cruel as the deed may strike any one to be, for a man to sell his own children to human flesh-mongers, it is often the dictate of humanity for him to do so; for, unless he does this, he must not only whip them himself, but must stand by and see one white son tie up his brother, of but few shades darker complexion than himself, and ply the gory lash to his naked back; and if he lisp one word of disapproval, it is set down to his parental partiality, and only makes a bad matter worse, both for himself and the slave whom he would protect and defend.

Every year brings with it multitudes of this class of slaves. It was doubtless in consequence of a knowledge of this fact, that one great statesman of the south predicted the downfall of slavery by the inevitable laws of population. Whether this prophecy is ever fulfilled or not, it is nevertheless plain that a very different-looking class of people are springing up at the south, and are now held in slavery, from those originally brought to this country from Africa; and if their increase will do no other good, it will do away the force of the argument, that God cursed Ham, and therefore American slavery is right. If the lineal descendants of Ham are alone to be scripturally enslaved, it is certain that slavery at the south must soon become unscriptural; for thousands are ushered into the world, annually, who, like myself, owe their existence to white fathers, and those fathers most frequently their own masters.

I have had two masters. My first master's name was Anthony. I do not remember his first name. He was generally called Captain Anthony—a title which, I presume, he acquired by sailing a craft on the Chesapeake Bay. He was not considered a rich slaveholder. He owned two or three farms, and about thirty slaves. His farms and slaves were under the care of an overseer. The overseer's name was Plummer. Mr. Plummer was a miserable drunkard, a profane swearer, and a savage monster. He always went armed with a cowskin and a heavy cudgel. I have known him to cut and slash the women's heads so horribly, that even master would be enraged at his cruelty, and would threaten to whip him if he did not mind himself. Master, however, was not a humane slaveholder. It required extraordinary barbarity on the part of an overseer to affect him. He was a cruel man, hardened by a long life of slaveholding. He would at times seem to take great pleasure in whipping a slave. I have often been awakened at the dawn of day by the most heart-rending shrieks of an own aunt of mine, whom he used to tie up to a joist, and whip upon her naked back till she was literally covered with blood. No words, no tears, no prayers, from his gory victim, seemed to move his iron heart from its bloody purpose. The louder she screamed, the harder he whipped; and where the blood ran fastest, there he whipped longest. He would whip her to make her scream, and whip her to make her hush; and not until overcome by fatigue, would he cease to swing the blood-clotted cowskin. I remember the first time I ever witnessed this horrible exhibition. I was quite a child, but I well remember it. I never shall forget it whilst I remember any thing. It was the first of a long series of such outrages, of which I was doomed to be a witness and a participant. It struck me with awful force. It was the blood-stained gate, the entrance to the hell of slavery, through which I was about to pass. It was a most terrible spectacle. I wish I could commit to paper the feelings with which I beheld it.

This occurrence took place very soon after I went to live with my old master, and under the following circumstances. Aunt Hester went out one night,—where or for what I do not know,—and happened to be absent when my master desired her presence. He had ordered her not to go out evenings, and warned her that she must never let him catch her in company with a young man, who was paying attention to her, belonging to Colonel Lloyd. The young man's name was Ned Roberts, generally called Lloyd's Ned. Why master was so careful of her, may be safely left to conjecture. She was a woman of noble form, and of graceful proportions, having very few equals, and fewer superiors, in personal appearance, among the colored or white women of our neighborhood.

Aunt Hester had not only disobeyed his orders in going out, but had been found in company with Lloyd's Ned; which circumstance, I found, from what he said while whipping her, was the chief offence. Had he been a man of pure morals himself, he might have been thought interested in protecting the innocence of my aunt; but those who knew him will not suspect him of any such virtue. Before he commenced whipping Aunt Hester, he took her into the kitchen, and stripped her from neck to waist, leaving her neck, shoulders, and back, entirely naked. He then told her to cross her hands, calling her at the same time a d——d b——h. After crossing her hands, he tied them with a strong rope, and led her to a stool under a large hook in the joist, put in for the purpose. He made her get upon the stool, and tied her hands to the hook. She now stood fair for his infernal purpose. Her arms were stretched up at their full length, so that she stood upon the ends of her toes. He then said to her, "Now, you d——d b——h, I'll learn you how to disobey my orders!" and after rolling up his sleeves, he commenced to lay on the heavy cowskin, and soon the warm, red blood (amid heart-rending shrieks from her, and horrid oaths from him) came dripping to the floor. I was so terrified and horror-stricken at the sight, that I hid myself in a closet, and dared not venture out till long after the bloody transaction was over. I expected it would be my turn next. It was all new to me. I had never seen any thing like it before. I had always lived with my grandmother on the outskirts of the plantation, where she was put to raise the children of the younger women. I had therefore been, until now, out of the way of the bloody scenes that often occurred on the plantation.

CHAPTER II.

My master's family consisted of two sons, Andrew and Richard; one daughter, Lucretia, and her husband, Captain Thomas Auld. They lived in one house, upon the home plantation of Colonel

Edward Lloyd. My master was Colonel Lloyd's clerk and superintendent. He was what might be called the overseer of the overseers. I spent two years of childhood on this plantation in my old master's family. It was here that I witnessed the bloody transaction recorded in the first chapter; and as I received my first impressions of slavery on this plantation, I will give some description of it, and of slavery as it there existed. The plantation is about twelve miles north of Easton, in Talbot county, and is situated on the border of Miles River. The principal products raised upon it were tobacco, corn, and wheat. These were raised in great abundance; so that, with the products of this and the other farms belonging to him, he was able to keep in almost constant employment a large sloop, in carrying them to market at Baltimore. This sloop was named Sally Lloyd, in honor of one of the colonel's daughters. My master's son-in-law, Captain Auld, was master of the vessel; she was otherwise manned by the colonel's own slaves. Their names were Peter, Isaac, Rich, and Jake. These were esteemed very highly by the other slaves, and looked upon as the privileged ones of the plantation; for it was no small affair, in the eyes of the slaves, to be allowed to see Baltimore.

Colonel Lloyd kept from three to four hundred slaves on his home plantation, and owned a large number more on the neighboring farms belonging to him. The names of the farms nearest to the home plantation were Wye Town and New Design. "Wye Town" was under the overseership of a man named Noah Willis. New Design was under the overseership of a Mr. Townsend. The overseers of these, and all the rest of the farms, numbering over twenty, received advice and direction from the managers of the home plantation. This was the great business place. It was the seat of government for the whole twenty farms. All disputes among the overseers were settled here. If a slave was convicted of any high misdemeanor, became unmanageable, or evinced a determination to run away, he was brought immediately here, severely whipped, put on board the sloop, carried to Baltimore, and sold to Austin Woolfolk, or some other slave-trader, as a warning to the slaves remaining.

Here, too, the slaves of all the other farms received their monthly allowance of food, and their yearly clothing. The men and women slaves received, as their monthly allowance of food, eight pounds of pork, or its equivalent in fish, and one bushel of corn meal. Their yearly clothing consisted of two coarse linen shirts, one pair of linen trousers, like the shirts, one jacket, one pair of trousers for winter, made of coarse negro cloth, one pair of stockings, and one pair of shoes; the whole of which could not have cost more than seven dollars. The allowance of the slave children was given to their mothers, or the old women having the care of them. The children unable to work in the field had neither shoes, stockings, jackets, nor trousers, given to them; their clothing consisted of two coarse linen shirts per year. When these failed them, they went naked until the next allowance-day. Children from seven to ten years old, of both sexes, almost naked, might be seen at all seasons of the year.

There were no beds given the slaves, unless one coarse blanket be considered such, and none but the men and women had these. This, however, is not considered a very great privation. They find less difficulty from the want of beds, than from the want of time to sleep; for when their day's work in the field is done, the most of them having their washing, mending, and cooking to do, and having few or none of the ordinary facilities for doing either of these, very many of their sleeping hours are consumed in preparing for the field the coming day; and when this is done, old and young, male and female, married and single, drop down side by side, on one common bed,—the cold, damp floor,—each covering himself or herself with their miserable blankets; and here they sleep till they are summoned to the field by the driver's horn. At the sound of this, all must rise, and be off to the field. There must be no halting; every one must be at his or her post; and woe betides them who hear not this morning summons to the field; for if they are not awakened by the sense of hearing, they are by the sense of feeling: no age nor sex finds any favor. Mr. Severe, the overseer, used to stand by the door of the quarter, armed with a large hickory stick and heavy cowskin, ready to whip any one who was so unfortunate as not to hear, or, from any other cause, was prevented from being ready to start for the field at the sound of the horn.

Mr. Severe was rightly named: he was a cruel man. I have seen him whip a woman, causing the blood to run half an hour at the time; and this, too, in the midst of her crying children, pleading for their mother's release. He seemed to take pleasure in manifesting his fiendish barbarity. Added to his cruelty, he was a profane swearer. It was enough to chill the blood and stiffen the hair of an ordinary man to hear him talk. Scarce a sentence escaped him but that was commenced or concluded by some horrid oath. The field was the place to witness his cruelty and profanity. His presence made it both the field of blood and of blasphemy. From the rising till the going down of the sun, he was cursing, raving, cutting, and slashing among the slaves of the field, in the most frightful manner. His career was short. He died very soon after I went to Colonel Lloyd's; and he died as he lived, uttering, with his dying groans, bitter curses and horrid oaths. His death was regarded by the slaves as the result of a merciful providence.

Mr. Severe's place was filled by a Mr. Hopkins. He was a very different man. He was less cruel, less profane, and made less noise, than Mr. Severe. His course was characterized by no extraordinary demonstrations of cruelty. He whipped, but seemed to take no pleasure in it. He was called by the slaves a good overseer.

The home plantation of Colonel Lloyd wore the appearance of a country village. All the mechanical operations for all the farms were performed here. The shoemaking and mending, the blacksmithing, cartwrighting, coopering, weaving, and grain-grinding, were all performed by the slaves on the home plantation. The whole place wore a business-like aspect very unlike the neighboring farms. The number of houses, too, conspired to give it advantage over the neighboring farms. It was called by the slaves the *Great House Farm.* Few privileges were esteemed higher, by the slaves of the out-farms, than that of being selected to do errands at the Great House Farm. It was associated in their minds with greatness. A representative could not be prouder of his election to a seat in the American Congress, than a slave on one of the out-farms would be of his election to do errands at the Great House Farm. They regarded it as evidence of great confidence reposed in them by their overseers; and it was on this account, as well as a constant desire to be out of the field from under the driver's lash, that they esteemed it a high privilege, one worth careful living for. He was called the smartest and most trusty fellow, who had this honor conferred upon him the most frequently. The competitors for this office sought as diligently to please their overseers, as the office-seekers in the political parties seek to please and deceive the people. The same traits of character might be seen in Colonel Lloyd's slaves, as are seen in the slaves of the political parties.

The slaves selected to go to the Great House Farm, for the monthly allowance for themselves and their fellow-slaves, were peculiarly enthusiastic. While on their way, they would make the dense old woods, for miles around, reverberate with their wild songs, revealing at once the highest joy and the deepest sadness. They would compose and sing as they went along, consulting neither time nor tune. The thought that came up, came out—if not in the word, in the sound;—and as frequently in the one as in the other. They would sometimes sing the most pathetic sentiment in the most rapturous tone, and the most rapturous sentiment in the most pathetic tone. Into all of their songs they would manage to weave something of the Great House Farm. Especially would they do this, when leaving home. They would then sing most exultingly the following words:—

> *"I am going away to the Great House Farm!*
> *O, yea! O, yea! O!"*

This they would sing, as a chorus, to words which to many would seem unmeaning jargon, but which, nevertheless, were full of meaning to themselves. I have sometimes thought that the mere hearing of those songs would do more to impress some minds with the horrible character of slavery, than the reading of whole volumes of philosophy on the subject could do.

I did not, when a slave, understand the deep meaning of those rude and apparently incoherent songs. I was myself within the circle; so that I neither saw nor heard as those without might see and hear. They told a tale of woe which was then altogether beyond my feeble comprehension; they were tones loud, long, and deep; they breathed the prayer and complaint of souls boiling over with the bitterest anguish. Every tone was a testimony against slavery, and a prayer to God for deliverance from chains. The hearing of those wild notes always depressed my spirit, and filled me with ineffable sadness. I have frequently found myself in tears while hearing them. The mere recurrence to those songs, even now, afflicts me; and while I am writing these lines, an expression of feeling has already found its way down my cheek. To those songs I trace my first glimmering conception of the dehumanizing character of slavery. I can never get rid of that conception. Those songs still follow me, to deepen my hatred of slavery, and quicken my sympathies for my brethren in bonds. If any one wishes to be impressed with the soul-killing effects of slavery, let him go to Colonel Lloyd's plantation, and, on allowance-day, place himself in the deep pine woods, and there let him, in silence, analyze the sounds that shall pass through the chambers of his soul,—and if he is not thus impressed, it will only be because "there is no flesh in his obdurate heart."

I have often been utterly astonished, since I came to the north, to find persons who could speak of the singing, among slaves, as evidence of their contentment and happiness. It is impossible to conceive of a greater mistake. Slaves sing most when they are most unhappy. The songs of the slave represent the sorrows of his heart; and he is relieved by them, only as an aching heart is relieved by its tears. At least, such is my experience. I have often sung to drown my sorrow, but seldom to express my happiness. Crying for joy, and singing for joy, were alike uncommon to me while in the jaws of slavery. The singing of a man cast away upon a desolate island might be as appropriately considered as evidence of contentment and happiness, as the singing of a slave; the songs of the one and of the other are prompted by the same emotion.

CHAPTER III.

Colonel Lloyd kept a large and finely cultivated garden, which afforded almost constant employment for four men, besides the chief gardener, (Mr. M'Durmond.) This garden was probably the greatest attraction of the place. During the summer months, people came from far and near—from Baltimore, Easton, and Annapolis—to see it. It abounded in fruits of almost every description, from the hardy apple of the north to the delicate orange of the south. This garden was not the least source of trouble on the plantation. Its excellent fruit was quite a temptation to the hungry swarms of boys, as well as the older slaves, belonging to the colonel, few of whom had the virtue or the vice to resist it. Scarcely a day passed, during the summer, but that some slave had to take the lash for stealing fruit. The colonel had to resort to all kinds of stratagems to keep his slaves out of the garden. The last and most successful one was that of tarring his fence all around; after which, if a slave was caught with any tar upon his person, it was deemed sufficient proof that he had either been into the garden, or had tried to get in. In either case, he was severely whipped by the chief gardener. This plan worked well; the slaves became as fearful of tar as of the lash. They seemed to realize the impossibility of touching *tar* without being defiled.

The colonel also kept a splendid riding equipage. His stable and carriage-house presented the appearance of some of our large city livery establishments. His horses were of the finest form and noblest blood. His carriage-house contained three splendid coaches, three or four gigs, besides dearborns and barouches of the most fashionable style.

This establishment was under the care of two slaves—old Barney and young Barney—father and son. To attend to this establishment was their sole work. But it was by no means an easy employment; for in nothing was Colonel Lloyd more particular than in the management of his horses. The slightest inattention to these was unpardonable, and was visited upon those, under whose care they were placed, with the severest punishment; no excuse could shield them, if the colonel only suspected any want of attention to his horses—a supposition which he frequently indulged, and one which, of course, made the office of old and young Barney a very trying one. They never knew when they were safe from punishment. They were frequently whipped when least deserving, and escaped whipping when most deserving it. Every thing depended upon the looks of the horses, and the state of Colonel Lloyd's own mind when his horses were brought to him for use. If a horse did not move fast enough, or hold his head high enough, it was owing to some fault of his keepers. It was painful to stand near the stable-door, and hear the various complaints against the keepers when a horse was taken out for use. "This horse has not had proper attention. He has not been sufficiently rubbed and curried, or he has not been properly fed; his food was too wet or too dry; he got it too soon or too late; he was too hot or too cold; he had too much hay, and not enough of grain; or he had too much grain, and not enough of hay; instead of old Barney's attending to the horse, he had very improperly left it to his son." To all these complaints, no matter how unjust, the slave must answer never a word. Colonel Lloyd could not brook any contradiction from a slave. When he spoke, a slave must stand, listen, and tremble; and such was literally the case. I have seen Colonel Lloyd make old Barney, a man between fifty and sixty years of age, uncover his bald head, kneel down upon the cold, damp ground, and receive upon his naked and toil-worn shoulders more than thirty lashes at the time. Colonel Lloyd had three sons—Edward, Murray, and Daniel,—and three sons-in-law, Mr. Winder, Mr. Nicholson, and Mr. Lowndes. All of these lived at the Great House Farm, and enjoyed the luxury of whipping the servants when they pleased, from old Barney down to William Wilkes, the coach-driver. I have seen Winder make one of the house-servants stand off from him a suitable distance to be touched with the end of his whip, and at every stroke raise great ridges upon his back.

To describe the wealth of Colonel Lloyd would be almost equal to describing the riches of Job. He kept from ten to fifteen house-servants. He was said to own a thousand slaves, and I think this estimate quite within the truth. Colonel Lloyd owned so many that he did not know them when he saw them; nor did all the slaves of the out-farms know him. It is reported of him, that, while riding along the road one day, he met a colored man, and addressed him in the usual manner of speaking to colored people on the public highways of the south: "Well, boy, whom do you belong to?" "To Colonel Lloyd," replied the slave. "Well, does the colonel treat you well?" "No, sir," was the ready reply. "What, does he work you too hard?" "Yes, sir." "Well, don't he give you enough to eat?" "Yes, sir, he gives me enough, such as it is."

The colonel, after ascertaining where the slave belonged, rode on; the man also went on about his business, not dreaming that he had been conversing with his master. He thought, said, and heard nothing more of the matter, until two or three weeks afterwards.

The poor man was then informed by his overseer that, for having found fault with his master, he was now to be sold to a Georgia trader. He was immediately chained and handcuffed; and thus, without a moment's warning, he was snatched away, and forever sundered, from his family and friends, by a hand more unrelenting than death. This is the penalty of telling the truth, of telling the simple truth, in answer to a series of plain questions.

It is partly in consequence of such facts, that slaves, when inquired of as to their condition and the character of their masters, almost universally say they are contented, and that their masters are kind. The slaveholders have been known to send in spies among their slaves, to ascertain their views and feelings in regard to their condition. The frequency of this has had the effect to establish among the slaves the maxim, that a still tongue makes a wise head. They suppress the truth rather than take the consequences of telling it, and in so doing prove themselves a part of the human family. If they have any thing to say of their masters, it is generally in their masters' favor, especially when speaking to an untried man. I have been frequently asked, when a slave, if I had a kind master, and do not remember ever to have given a negative answer; nor did I, in pursuing this course, consider myself as uttering what was absolutely false; for I always measured the kindness of my master by the standard of kindness set up among slaveholders around us. Moreover, slaves are like other people, and imbibe prejudices quite common to others. They think their own better than that of others. Many, under the influence of this prejudice, think their own masters are better than the masters of other slaves; and this, too, in some cases, when the very reverse is true. Indeed, it is not uncommon for slaves even to fall out and quarrel among themselves about the relative goodness of their masters, each contending for the superior goodness of his own over that of the others. At the very same time, they mutually execrate their masters when viewed separately. It was so on our plantation. When Colonel Lloyd's slaves met the slaves of Jacob Jepson, they seldom parted without a quarrel about their masters; Colonel Lloyd's slaves contending that he was the richest, and Mr. Jepson's slaves that he was the smartest, and most of a man. Colonel Lloyd's slaves would boast his ability to buy and sell Jacob Jepson. Mr. Jepson's slaves would boast his ability to whip Colonel Lloyd. These quarrels would almost always end in a fight between the parties, and those that whipped were supposed to have gained the point at issue. They seemed to think that the greatness of their masters was transferable to themselves. It was considered as being bad enough to be a slave; but to be a poor man's slave was deemed a disgrace indeed!

CHAPTER IV.

Mr. Hopkins remained but a short time in the office of overseer. Why his career was so short, I do not know, but suppose he lacked the necessary severity to suit Colonel Lloyd. Mr. Hopkins was succeeded by Mr. Austin Gore, a man possessing, in an eminent degree, all those traits of character indispensable to what is called a first-rate overseer. Mr. Gore had served Colonel Lloyd, in the capacity of overseer, upon one of the out-farms, and had shown himself worthy of the high station of overseer upon the home or Great House Farm.

Mr. Gore was proud, ambitious, and persevering. He was artful, cruel, and obdurate. He was just the man for such a place, and it was just the place for such a man. It afforded scope for the full exercise of all his powers, and he seemed to be perfectly at home in it. He was one of those who could torture the slightest look, word, or gesture, on the part of the slave, into impudence, and would treat it accordingly. There must be no answering back to him; no explanation was allowed a slave, showing himself to have been wrongfully accused. Mr. Gore acted fully up to the maxim laid down by slaveholders,—"It is better that a dozen slaves suffer under the lash, than that the overseer should be convicted, in the presence of the slaves, of having been at fault." No matter how innocent a slave might be—it availed him nothing, when accused by Mr. Gore of any misdemeanor. To be accused was to be convicted, and to be convicted was to be punished; the one always following the other with immutable certainty. To escape punishment was to escape accusation; and few slaves had the fortune to do either, under the overseership of Mr. Gore. He was just proud enough to demand the most debasing homage of the slave, and quite servile enough to crouch, himself, at the feet of the master. He was ambitious enough to be contented with nothing short of the highest rank of overseers, and persevering enough to reach the height of his ambition. He was cruel enough to inflict the severest punishment, artful enough to descend to the lowest trickery, and obdurate enough to be insensible to the voice of a reproving conscience. He was, of all the overseers, the most dreaded by the slaves. His presence was painful; his eye flashed confusion; and seldom was his sharp, shrill voice heard, without producing horror and trembling in their ranks.

Mr. Gore was a grave man, and, though a young man, he indulged in no jokes, said no funny words, seldom smiled. His words were in perfect keeping with his looks, and his looks were in perfect keeping with his words. Overseers will sometimes indulge in a witty word, even with the slaves; not so with Mr. Gore. He spoke but to command, and commanded but to be obeyed; he dealt sparingly with his words, and bountifully with his whip, never using the former where the latter would answer as well. When he whipped, he seemed to do so from a sense of duty, and feared no consequences. He did nothing reluctantly, no matter how disagreeable; always at his post, never inconsistent. He never promised but to fulfil. He was, in a word, a man of the most inflexible firmness and stone-like coolness.

His savage barbarity was equalled only by the consummate coolness with which he committed the grossest and most savage deeds upon the slaves under his charge. Mr. Gore once undertook to whip one of Colonel Lloyd's slaves, by the name of Demby. He had given Demby but few stripes, when, to get rid of the scourging, he ran and plunged himself into a creek, and stood there at the depth of his shoulders, refusing to come out. Mr. Gore told him that he would give him three calls, and that, if he did not come out at the third call, he would shoot him. The first call was given. Demby made no response, but stood his ground. The second and third calls were given with the same result. Mr. Gore then, without consultation or deliberation with any one, not even giving Demby an additional call, raised his musket to his face, taking deadly aim at his standing victim, and in an instant poor

Demby was no more. His mangled body sank out of sight, and blood and brains marked the water where he had stood.

A thrill of horror flashed through every soul upon the plantation, excepting Mr. Gore. He alone seemed cool and collected. He was asked by Colonel Lloyd and my old master, why he resorted to this extraordinary expedient. His reply was, (as well as I can remember,) that Demby had become unmanageable. He was setting a dangerous example to the other slaves,—one which, if suffered to pass without some such demonstration on his part, would finally lead to the total subversion of all rule and order upon the plantation. He argued that if one slave refused to be corrected, and escaped with his life, the other slaves would soon copy the example; the result of which would be, the freedom of the slaves, and the enslavement of the whites. Mr. Gore's defence was satisfactory. He was continued in his station as overseer upon the home plantation. His fame as an overseer went abroad. His horrid crime was not even submitted to judicial investigation. It was committed in the presence of slaves, and they of course could neither institute a suit, nor testify against him; and thus the guilty perpetrator of one of the bloodiest and most foul murders goes unwhipped of justice, and uncensured by the community in which he lives. Mr. Gore lived in St. Michael's, Talbot county, Maryland, when I left there; and if he is still alive, he very probably lives there now; and if so, he is now, as he was then, as highly esteemed and as much respected as though his guilty soul had not been stained with his brother's blood.

I speak advisedly when I say this,—that killing a slave, or any colored person, in Talbot county, Maryland, is not treated as a crime, either by the courts or the community. Mr. Thomas Lanman, of St. Michael's, killed two slaves, one of whom he killed with a hatchet, by knocking his brains out. He used to boast of the commission of the awful and bloody deed. I have heard him do so laughingly, saying, among other things, that he was the only benefactor of his country in the company, and that when others would do as much as he had done, we should be relieved of "the d——d niggers."

The wife of Mr. Giles Hick[s], living but a short distance from where I used to live, murdered my wife's cousin, a young girl between fifteen and sixteen years of age, mangling her person in the most horrible manner, breaking her nose and breastbone with a stick, so that the poor girl expired in a few hours afterward. She was immediately buried, but had not been in her untimely grave but a few hours before she was taken up and examined by the coroner, who decided that she had come to her death by severe beating. The offence for which this girl was thus murdered was this:—She had been set that night to mind Mrs. Hick[s]'s baby, and during the night she fell asleep, and the baby cried. She, having lost her rest for several nights previous, did not hear the crying. They were both in the room with Mrs. Hicks. Mrs. Hicks, finding the girl slow to move, jumped from her bed, seized an oak stick of wood by the fireplace, and with it broke the girl's nose and breastbone, and thus ended her life. I will not say that this most horrid murder produced no sensation in the community. It did produce sensation, but not enough to bring the murderess to punishment. There was a warrant issued for her arrest, but it was never served. Thus she escaped not only punishment, but even the pain of being arraigned before a court for her horrid crime.

Whilst I am detailing bloody deeds which took place during my stay on Colonel Lloyd's plantation, I will briefly narrate another, which occurred about the same time as the murder of Demby by Mr. Gore.

Colonel Lloyd's slaves were in the habit of spending a part of their nights and Sundays in fishing for oysters, and in this way made up the deficiency of their scanty allowance. An old man belonging to Colonel Lloyd, while thus engaged, happened to get beyond the limits of Colonel Lloyd's, and on the premises of Mr. Beal Bondly. At this trespass, Mr. Bondly took offence, and with his musket came down to the shore, and blew its deadly contents into the poor old man.

Mr. Bondly came over to see Colonel Lloyd the next day, whether to pay him for his property, or to justify himself in what he had done, I know not. At any rate, this whole fiendish transaction was soon hushed up. There was very little said about it at all, and nothing done. It was a common saying, even among little white boys, that it was worth a half-cent to kill a "nigger," and a half-cent to bury one.

CHAPTER V.

As to my own treatment while I lived on Colonel Lloyd's plantation, it was very similar to that of the other slave children. I was not old enough to work in the field, and there being little else than field work to do, I had a great deal of leisure time. The most I had to do was to drive up the cows at evening, keep the fowls out of the garden, keep the front yard clean, and run of errands for my old master's daughter, Mrs. Lucretia Auld. The most of my leisure time I spent in helping Master Daniel Lloyd in finding his birds, after he had shot them. My connection with Master Daniel was of some advantage to me. He became quite attached to me, and was a sort of protector of me. He would not allow the older boys to impose upon me, and would divide his cakes with me.

I was seldom whipped by my old master, and suffered little from any thing else than hunger and cold. I suffered much from hunger, but much more from cold. In hottest summer and coldest winter, I was kept almost naked—no shoes, no stockings, no jacket, no trousers, nothing on but a coarse tow linen shirt, reaching only to my knees. I had no bed. I must have perished with cold, but that, the coldest nights, I used to steal a bag which was used for carrying corn to the mill. I would crawl into this bag, and there sleep on the cold, damp, clay floor, with my head in and feet out. My feet have been so cracked with the frost, that the pen with which I am writing might be laid in the gashes.

We were not regularly allowanced. Our food was coarse corn meal boiled. This was called *mush*. It was put into a large wooden tray or trough, and set down upon the ground. The children were then called, like so many pigs, and like so many pigs they would come and devour the mush; some with oyster-shells, others with pieces of shingle, some with naked hands, and none with spoons.

He that ate fastest got most; he that was strongest secured the best place; and few left the trough satisfied.

I was probably between seven and eight years old when I left Colonel Lloyd's plantation. I left it with joy. I shall never forget the ecstasy with which I received the intelligence that my old master (Anthony) had determined to let me go to Baltimore, to live with Mr. Hugh Auld, brother to my old master's son-in-law, Captain Thomas Auld. I received this information about three days before my departure. They were three of the happiest days I ever enjoyed. I spent the most part of all these three days in the creek, washing off the plantation scurf, and preparing myself for my departure.

The pride of appearance which this would indicate was not my own. I spent the time in washing, not so much because I wished to, but because Mrs. Lucretia had told me I must get all the dead skin off my feet and knees before I could go to Baltimore; for the people in Baltimore were very cleanly, and would laugh at me if I looked dirty. Besides, she was going to give me a pair of trousers, which I should not put on unless I got all the dirt off me. The thought of owning a pair of trousers was great indeed! It was almost a sufficient motive, not only to make me take off what would be called by pig-drovers the mange, but the skin itself. I went at it in good earnest, working for the first time with the hope of reward.

The ties that ordinarily bind children to their homes were all suspended in my case. I found no severe trial in my departure. My home was charmless; it was not home to me; on parting from it, I could not feel that I was leaving any thing which I could have enjoyed by staying. My mother was dead, my grandmother lived far off, so that I seldom saw her. I had two sisters and one brother, that lived in the same house with me; but the early separation of us from our mother had well nigh blotted the fact of our relationship from our memories. I looked for home elsewhere, and was confident of finding none which I should relish less than the one which I was leaving. If, however, I found in my new home hardship, hunger, whipping, and nakedness, I had the consolation that I should not have escaped any one of them by staying. Having already had more than a taste of them in the house of my old master, and having endured them there, I very naturally inferred my ability to endure them elsewhere, and especially at Baltimore; for I had something of the feeling about Baltimore that is expressed in the proverb, that "being hanged in England is preferable to dying a natural death in Ireland." I had the strongest desire to see Baltimore. Cousin Tom, though not fluent in speech, had inspired me with that desire by his eloquent description of the place. I could never point out any thing at the Great House, no matter how beautiful or powerful, but that he had seen something at Baltimore far exceeding, both in beauty and strength, the object which I pointed out to him. Even the Great House itself, with all its pictures, was far inferior to many buildings in Baltimore. So strong was my desire, that I thought a gratification of it would fully compensate for whatever loss of comforts I should sustain by the exchange. I left without a regret, and with the highest hopes of future happiness.

We sailed out of Miles River for Baltimore on a Saturday morning. I remember only the day of the week, for at that time I had no knowledge of the days of the month, nor the months of the year. On setting sail, I walked aft, and gave to Colonel Lloyd's plantation what I hoped would be the last look. I then placed myself in the bows of the sloop, and there spent the remainder of the day in looking ahead, interesting myself in what was in the distance rather than in things near by or behind.

In the afternoon of that day, we reached Annapolis, the capital of the State. We stopped but a few moments, so that I had no time to go on shore. It was the first large town that I had ever seen, and though it would look small compared with some of our New England factory villages, I thought it a wonderful place for its size—more imposing even than the Great House Farm!

We arrived at Baltimore early on Sunday morning, landing at Smith's Wharf, not far from Bowley's Wharf. We had on board the sloop a large flock of sheep; and after aiding in driving them to the slaughterhouse of Mr. Curtis on Louden Slater's Hill, I was conducted by Rich, one of the hands belonging on board of the sloop, to my new home in Alliciana Street, near Mr. Gardner's ship-yard, on Fell's Point.

Mr. and Mrs. Auld were both at home, and met me at the door with their little son Thomas, to take care of whom I had been given. And here I saw what I had never seen before; it was a white face beaming with the most kindly emotions; it was the face of my new mistress, Sophia Auld. I wish I could describe the rapture that flashed through my soul as I beheld it. It was a new and strange sight to me, brightening up my pathway with the light of happiness. Little Thomas was told, there was his Freddy,—and I was told to take care of little Thomas; and thus I entered upon the duties of my new home with the most cheering prospect ahead.

I look upon my departure from Colonel Lloyd's plantation as one of the most interesting events of my life. It is possible, and even quite probable, that but for the mere circumstance of being removed from that plantation to Baltimore, I should have to-day, instead of being here seated by my own table, in the enjoyment of freedom and the happiness of home, writing this Narrative, been confined in the galling chains of slavery. Going to live at Baltimore laid the foundation, and opened the gateway, to all my subsequent prosperity. I have ever regarded it as the first plain manifestation of that kind providence which has ever since attended me, and marked my life with so many favors. I regarded the selection of myself as being somewhat remarkable. There were a number of slave children that might have been sent from the plantation to Baltimore. There were those younger, those older, and those of the same age. I was chosen from among them all, and was the first, last, and only choice.

I may be deemed superstitious, and even egotistical, in regarding this event as a special interposition of divine Providence in my favor. But I should be false to the earliest sentiments of my soul, if I suppressed the opinion. I prefer to be true to myself, even at the hazard of incurring the ridicule of others, rather than to be false, and incur my own abhorrence. From my earliest recollection, I date the entertainment of a deep conviction that slavery would not always be able to hold me within its foul embrace; and in the darkest hours of my career in slavery, this living word of faith and spirit of hope departed not from me, but remained like ministering angels to cheer me through the gloom. This good spirit was from God, and to him I offer thanksgiving and praise.

CHAPTER VI.

My new mistress proved to be all she appeared when I first met her at the door,—a woman of the kindest heart and finest feelings. She had never had a slave under her control previously to myself, and prior to her marriage she had been dependent upon her own industry for a living. She was by trade a weaver; and by constant application to her business, she had been in a good degree preserved from the blighting and dehumanizing effects of slavery. I was utterly astonished at her goodness. I scarcely knew how to behave towards her. She was entirely unlike any other white woman I had ever seen. I could not approach her as I was accustomed to approach other white ladies. My early instruction was all out of place. The crouching servility, usually so acceptable a quality in a slave, did not answer when manifested toward her. Her favor was not gained by it; she seemed to be disturbed by it. She did not deem it impudent or unmannerly for a slave to look her in the face. The meanest slave was put fully at ease in her presence, and none left without feeling better for having seen her. Her face was made of heavenly smiles, and her voice of tranquil music.

But, alas! this kind heart had but a short time to remain such. The fatal poison of irresponsible power was already in her hands, and soon commenced its infernal work. That cheerful eye, under the influence of slavery, soon became red with rage; that voice, made all of sweet accord, changed to one of harsh and horrid discord; and that angelic face gave place to that of a demon.

Very soon after I went to live with Mr. and Mrs. Auld, she very kindly commenced to teach me the A, B, C. After I had learned this, she assisted me in learning to spell words of three or four letters. Just at this point of my progress, Mr. Auld found out what was going on, and at once forbade Mrs. Auld to instruct me further, telling her, among other things, that it was unlawful, as well as unsafe, to teach a slave to read. To use his own words, further, he said, "If you give a nigger an inch, he will take an ell. A nigger should know nothing but to obey his master—to do as he is told to do. Learning would *spoil* the best nigger in the world. Now," said he, "if you teach that nigger (speaking of myself) how to read, there would be no keeping him. It would forever unfit him to be a slave. He would at once become unmanageable, and of no value to his master. As to himself, it could do him no good, but a great deal of harm. It would make him discontented and unhappy." These words sank deep into my heart, stirred up sentiments within that lay slumbering, and called into existence an entirely new train of thought. It was a new and special revelation, explaining dark and mysterious things, with which my youthful understanding had struggled, but struggled in vain. I now understood what had been to me a most perplexing difficulty—to wit, the white man's power to enslave the black man. It was a grand achievement, and I prized it highly. From that moment, I understood the pathway from slavery to freedom. It was just what I wanted, and I got it at a time when I the least expected it. Whilst I was saddened by the thought of losing the aid of my kind mistress, I was gladdened by the invaluable instruction which, by the merest accident, I had gained from my master. Though conscious of the difficulty of learning without a teacher, I set out with high hope, and a fixed purpose, at whatever cost of trouble, to learn how to read. The very decided manner with which he spoke, and strove to impress his wife with the evil consequences of giving me instruction, served to convince me that he was deeply sensible of the truths he was uttering. It gave me the best assurance that I might rely with the utmost confidence on the results which, he said, would flow from teaching me to read. What he most dreaded, that I most desired. What he most loved, that I most hated. That which to him was a great evil, to be carefully shunned, was to me a great good, to be diligently sought; and the argument which he so warmly urged, against my learning to read, only served to inspire me with a desire and determination to learn. In learning to read, I owe almost as much to the bitter opposition of my master, as to the kindly aid of my mistress. I acknowledge the benefit of both.

I had resided but a short time in Baltimore before I observed a marked difference, in the treatment of slaves, from that which I had witnessed in the country. A city slave is almost a freeman, compared with a slave on the plantation. He is much better fed and clothed, and enjoys privileges altogether unknown to the slave on the plantation. There is a vestige of decency, a sense of shame, that does much to curb and check those outbreaks of atrocious cruelty so commonly enacted upon the plantation. He is a desperate slaveholder, who will shock the humanity of his non-slaveholding neighbors with the cries of his lacerated slave. Few are willing to incur the odium attaching to the reputation of being a cruel master; and above all things, they would not be known as not giving a slave enough to eat. Every city slaveholder is anxious to have it known of him, that he feeds his slaves well; and it is due to them to say, that most of them do give their slaves enough to eat. There are, however, some painful exceptions to this rule. Directly opposite to us, on Philpot Street, lived Mr. Thomas Hamilton. He owned two slaves. Their names were Henrietta and Mary. Henrietta was about twenty-two years of age, Mary was about fourteen; and of all the mangled and emaciated creatures I ever looked upon, these two were the most so. His heart must be harder than stone, that could look upon these unmoved. The head, neck, and shoulders of Mary were literally cut to pieces. I have frequently felt her head, and found it nearly covered with festering sores, caused by the lash of her cruel mistress. I do not know that her master ever whipped her, but I have been an eye-witness to the cruelty of Mrs. Hamilton. I used to be in Mr. Hamilton's house nearly every day. Mrs. Hamilton used to sit in a large chair in the middle of the room, with a heavy cowskin always by her side, and scarce an hour passed during the day but was marked by the blood of one of these slaves. The girls seldom passed her without her saying, "Move faster, you *black gip!*" at the same time giving them a blow with the cowskin over the head or shoulders, often drawing the blood. She would then say, "Take that, you *black gip!*"—continuing, "If you don't move faster, I'll move you!" Added to the cruel lashings to which these slaves were subjected, they were kept nearly half-starved.

They seldom knew what it was to eat a full meal. I have seen Mary contending with the pigs for the offal thrown into the street. So much was Mary kicked and cut to pieces, that she was oftener called "*pecked*" than by her name.

CHAPTER VII.

I lived in Master Hugh's family about seven years. During this time, I succeeded in learning to read and write. In accomplishing this, I was compelled to resort to various stratagems. I had no regular teacher. My mistress, who had kindly commenced to instruct me, had, in compliance with the advice and direction of her husband, not only ceased to instruct, but had set her face against my being instructed by any one else. It is due, however, to my mistress to say of her, that she did not adopt this course of treatment immediately. She at first lacked the depravity indispensable to shutting me up in mental darkness. It was at least necessary for her to have some training in the exercise of irresponsible power, to make her equal to the task of treating me as though I were a brute.

My mistress was, as I have said, a kind and tender-hearted woman; and in the simplicity of her soul she commenced, when I first went to live with her, to treat me as she supposed one human being ought to treat another. In entering upon the duties of a slaveholder, she did not seem to perceive that I sustained to her the relation of a mere chattel, and that for her to treat me as a human being was not only wrong, but dangerously so. Slavery proved as injurious to her as it did to me. When I went there, she was a pious, warm, and tender-hearted woman. There was no sorrow or suffering for which she had not a tear. She had bread for the hungry, clothes for the naked, and comfort for every mourner that came within her reach. Slavery soon proved its ability to divest her of these heavenly qualities. Under its influence, the tender heart became stone, and the lamblike disposition gave way to one of tiger-like fierceness. The first step in her downward course was in her ceasing to instruct me. She now commenced to practise her husband's precepts. She finally became even more violent in her opposition than her husband himself. She was not satisfied with simply doing as well as he had commanded; she seemed anxious to do better. Nothing seemed to make her more angry than to see me with a newspaper. She seemed to think that here lay the danger. I have had her rush at me with a face made all up of fury, and snatch from me a newspaper, in a manner that fully revealed her apprehension. She was an apt woman; and a little experience soon demonstrated, to her satisfaction, that education and slavery were incompatible with each other.

From this time I was most narrowly watched. If I was in a separate room any considerable length of time, I was sure to be suspected of having a book, and was at once called to give an account of myself. All this, however, was too late. The first step had been taken. Mistress, in teaching me the alphabet, had given me the *inch*, and no precaution could prevent me from taking the *ell*.

The plan which I adopted, and the one by which I was most successful, was that of making friends of all the little white boys whom I met in the street. As many of these as I could, I converted into teachers. With their kindly aid, obtained at different times and in different places, I finally succeeded in learning to read. When I was sent of errands, I always took my book with me, and by going one part of my errand quickly, I found time to get a lesson before my return. I used also to carry bread with me, enough of which was always in the house, and to which I was always welcome; for I was much better off in this regard than many of the poor white children in our neighborhood. This bread I used to bestow upon the hungry little urchins, who, in return, would give me that more valuable bread of knowledge. I am strongly tempted to give the names of two or three of those little boys, as a testimonial of the gratitude and affection I bear them; but prudence forbids;—not that it would injure me, but it might embarrass them; for it is almost an unpardonable offence to teach slaves to read in this Christian country. It is enough to say of the dear little fellows, that they lived on Philpot Street, very near Durgin and Bailey's ship-yard. I used to talk this matter of slavery over with them. I would sometimes say to them, I wished I could be as free as they would be when they got to be men. "You will be free as soon as you are twenty-one, *but I am a slave for life!* Have not I as good a right to be free as you have?" These words used to trouble them; they would express for me the liveliest sympathy, and console me with the hope that something would occur by which I might be free.

I was now about twelve years old, and the thought of being *a slave for life* began to bear heavily upon my heart. Just about this time, I got hold of a book entitled "The Columbian Orator." Every opportunity I got, I used to read this book. Among much of other interesting matter, I found in it a dialogue between a master and his slave. The slave was represented as having run away from his master three times. The dialogue represented the conversation which took place between them, when the slave was retaken the third time. In this dialogue, the whole argument in behalf of slavery was brought forward by the master, all of which was disposed of by the slave. The slave was made to say some very smart as well as impressive things in reply to his master—things which had the desired though unexpected effect; for the conversation resulted in the voluntary emancipation of the slave on the part of the master.

In the same book, I met with one of Sheridan's mighty speeches on and in behalf of Catholic emancipation. These were choice documents to me. I read them over and over again with unabated interest. They gave tongue to interesting thoughts of my own soul, which had frequently flashed through my mind, and died away for want of utterance. The moral which I gained from the dialogue was the power of truth over the conscience of even a slaveholder. What I got from Sheridan was a bold denunciation of slavery, and a powerful vindication of human rights. The reading of these documents enabled me to utter my thoughts, and to meet the arguments brought forward to sustain slavery; but while they relieved me of one difficulty, they brought on another even more painful than the one of which I was relieved. The more I read, the more I was led to abhor and detest my enslavers. I could regard them in no other light than a band of successful robbers, who had left their homes, and gone to Africa, and stolen us from our homes, and in a strange land reduced us to slavery. I loathed them as being the meanest as well as the most wicked of men. As I read and contemplated the subject, behold! that very discontentment which Master Hugh had predicted would follow my learning to read had already come, to torment and sting my soul to unutterable anguish. As I writhed under it, I would at times feel that learning to read had been a curse rather than a blessing. It had given me a view of my wretched condition, without the remedy. It opened my eyes to the horrible pit, but to no ladder upon which to get out. In moments of agony, I envied my fellow-slaves for their stupidity. I have often wished myself a beast. I preferred the condition of the meanest reptile to my own. Any thing, no matter what, to get rid of thinking! It was this everlasting thinking of my condition that tormented me. There was no getting rid of it. It was pressed upon me by every object within sight or hearing, animate or inanimate. The silver trump of freedom had roused my soul to eternal wakefulness. Freedom now appeared, to disappear no more forever. It was heard in every sound, and seen in every thing. It was ever present to torment me with a sense of my wretched condition. I saw nothing without seeing it, I heard nothing without hearing it, and felt nothing without feeling it. It looked from every star, it smiled in every calm, breathed in every wind, and moved in every storm.

I often found myself regretting my own existence, and wishing myself dead; and but for the hope of being free, I have no doubt but that I should have killed myself, or done something for which I should have been killed. While in this state of mind, I was eager to hear any one speak of slavery. I was a ready listener. Every little while, I could hear something about the abolitionists. It was some time before I found what the word meant. It was always used in such connections as to make it an interesting word to me. If a slave ran away and succeeded in getting clear, or if a slave killed his master, set fire to a barn, or did any thing very wrong in the mind of a slaveholder, it was spoken of as the fruit of *abolition*. Hearing the word in this connection very often, I set about learning what it meant. The dictionary afforded me little or no help. I found it was "the act of abolishing;" but then I did not know what was to be abolished. Here I was perplexed. I did not dare to ask any one about its meaning, for I was satisfied that it was something they wanted me to know very little about. After a patient waiting, I got one of our city papers, containing an account of the number of petitions from the north, praying for the abolition of slavery in the District of Columbia, and of the slave trade between the States. From this time I understood the words *abolition* and *abolitionist*, and always drew near when that word was spoken, expecting to hear something of importance to myself and fellow-slaves. The light broke in upon me by degrees. I went one day down on the wharf of Mr. Waters; and seeing two Irishmen unloading a scow of stone, I went, unasked, and helped them. When we had finished, one of them came to me and asked me if I were a slave. I told him I was. He asked, "Are ye a slave for life?" I told him that I was. The good Irishman seemed to be deeply affected by the statement. He said to the other that it was a pity so fine a little fellow as myself should be a slave for life. He said it was a shame to hold me. They both advised me to run away to the north; that I should find friends there, and that I should be free. I pretended not to be interested in what they said, and treated them as if I did not understand them; for I feared they might be treacherous. White men have been known to encourage slaves to escape, and then, to get the reward, catch them and return them to their masters. I was afraid that these seemingly good men might use me so; but I nevertheless remembered their advice, and from that time I resolved to run away. I looked forward to a time at which it would be safe for me to escape. I was too young to think of doing so immediately; besides, I wished to learn how to write, as I might have occasion to write my own pass. I consoled myself with the hope that I should one day find a good chance. Meanwhile, I would learn to write.

The idea as to how I might learn to write was suggested to me by being in Durgin and Bailey's ship-yard, and frequently seeing the ship carpenters, after hewing, and getting a piece of timber ready for use, write on the timber the name of that part of the ship for which it was intended. When a piece of timber was intended for the larboard side, it would be marked thus—"L." When a piece was for the starboard side, it would be marked thus—"S." A piece for the larboard side forward, would be marked thus—"L.F." When a piece was for starboard side forward, it would be marked thus—"S.F." For larboard aft, it would be marked thus—"L.A." For starboard aft, it would be marked thus—"S.A." I soon learned the names of these letters, and for what they were intended when placed upon a piece of timber in the ship-yard. I immediately commenced copying them, and in a short time was able to make the four letters named. After that, when I met with any boy who I knew could write, I would tell him I could write as well as he. The next word would be, "I don't believe you. Let me see you try it." I would then make the letters which I had been so fortunate as to learn, and ask him to beat that. In this way I got a good many lessons in writing, which it is quite possible I should never have gotten in any other way. During this time, my copy-book was the board fence, brick wall, and pavement; my pen and ink was a lump of chalk. With these, I learned mainly how to write. I then commenced and continued copying the Italics in Webster's Spelling Book, until I could make them all without looking on the book. By this time, my little Master Thomas had gone to school, and learned how to write, and had written over a number of copy-books. These had been brought home, and shown to some of our near neighbors, and then laid aside. My mistress used to go to class meeting at the Wilk Street meeting-house every Monday afternoon, and leave me to take care of the house. When left thus, I used to spend the time in writing in the spaces left in Master Thomas's copy-book, copying what he had written. I continued to do this until I could write a hand very similar to that of Master Thomas. Thus, after a long, tedious effort for years, I finally succeeded in learning how to write.

CHAPTER VIII.

In a very short time after I went to live at Baltimore, my old master's youngest son Richard died; and in about three years and six months after his death, my old master, Captain Anthony, died, leaving only his son, Andrew, and daughter, Lucretia, to share his estate. He died while on a visit to see his daughter at Hillsborough. Cut off thus unexpectedly, he left no will as to the disposal of his property. It was therefore necessary to have a valuation of the property, that it might be equally divided between Mrs. Lucretia and Master Andrew. I was immediately sent for, to be valued with the other property. Here again my feelings rose up in detestation of slavery. I had now a new conception of my degraded condition. Prior to this, I had become, if not insensible to my lot, at least partly so. I left Baltimore with a young heart overborne with sadness, and a soul full of apprehension. I took passage with Captain Rowe, in the schooner Wild Cat, and, after a sail of about twenty-four hours, I found myself near the place of my birth. I had now been absent from it almost, if not quite, five years. I, however, remembered the place very well. I was only about five years old when I left it, to go and live with my old master on Colonel Lloyd's plantation; so that I was now between ten and eleven years old.

We were all ranked together at the valuation. Men and women, old and young, married and single, were ranked with horses, sheep, and swine. There were horses and men, cattle and women, pigs and children, all holding the same rank in the scale of being, and were all subjected to the same narrow examination. Silvery-headed age and sprightly youth, maids and matrons, had to undergo the same indelicate inspection. At this moment, I saw more clearly than ever the brutalizing effects of slavery upon both slave and slaveholder.

After the valuation, then came the division. I have no language to express the high excitement and deep anxiety which were felt among us poor slaves during this time. Our fate for life was now to be decided. We had no more voice in that decision than the brutes among whom we were ranked. A single word from the white men was enough—against all our wishes, prayers, and entreaties—to sunder forever the dearest friends, dearest kindred, and strongest ties known to human beings. In addition to the pain of separation, there was the horrid dread of falling into the hands of Master Andrew. He was known to us all as being a most cruel wretch,—a common drunkard, who had, by his reckless mismanagement and profligate dissipation, already wasted a large portion of his father's property. We all felt that we might as well be sold at once to the Georgia traders, as to pass into his hands; for we knew that that would be our inevitable condition,—a condition held by us all in the utmost horror and dread.

I suffered more anxiety than most of my fellow-slaves. I had known what it was to be kindly treated; they had known nothing of the kind. They had seen little or nothing of the world. They were in very deed men and women of sorrow, and acquainted with grief. Their backs had been made familiar with the bloody lash, so that they had become callous; mine was yet tender; for while at Baltimore I got few whippings, and few slaves could boast of a kinder master and mistress than myself; and the thought of passing out of their hands into those of Master Andrew—a man who, but a few days before, to give me a sample of his bloody disposition, took my little brother by the throat, threw him on the ground, and with the heel of his boot stamped upon his head till the blood gushed from his nose and ears—was well calculated to make me anxious as to my fate. After he had committed this savage outrage upon my brother, he turned to me, and said that was the way he meant to serve me one of these days,—meaning, I suppose, when I came into his possession.

Thanks to a kind Providence, I fell to the portion of Mrs. Lucretia, and was sent immediately back to Baltimore, to live again in the family of Master Hugh. Their joy at my return equalled their sorrow at my departure. It was a glad day to me. I had escaped a worse than lion's jaws. I was absent from Baltimore, for the purpose of valuation and division, just about one month, and it seemed to have been six.

Very soon after my return to Baltimore, my mistress, Lucretia, died, leaving her husband and one child, Amanda; and in a very short time after her death, Master Andrew died. Now all the property of my old master, slaves included, was in the hands of strangers,—strangers who had had nothing to do with accumulating it. Not a slave was left free. All remained slaves, from the youngest to the oldest. If any one thing in my experience, more than another, served to deepen my conviction of the infernal character of slavery, and to fill me with unutterable loathing of slaveholders, it was their base ingratitude to my poor old grandmother. She had served my old master faithfully from youth to old age. She had been the source of all his wealth; she had peopled his plantation with slaves; she had become a great grandmother in his service. She had rocked him in infancy, attended him in childhood, served him through life, and at his death wiped from his icy brow the cold death-sweat, and closed his eyes forever. She was nevertheless left a slave—a slave for life—a slave in the hands of strangers; and in their hands she saw her children, her grandchildren, and her great-grandchildren, divided, like so many sheep, without being gratified with the small privilege of a single word, as to their or her own destiny. And, to cap the climax of their base ingratitude and fiendish barbarity, my grandmother, who was now very old, having outlived my old master and all his children, having seen the beginning and end of all of them, and her present owners finding she was of but little value, her frame already racked with the pains of old age, and complete helplessness fast stealing over her once active limbs, they took her to the woods, built her a little hut, put up a little mud-chimney, and then made her welcome to the privilege of supporting herself there in perfect loneliness; thus virtually turning her out to die! If my poor old grandmother now lives, she lives to suffer in utter loneliness; she lives to remember and mourn over the loss of children, the loss of grandchildren, and the loss of great-grandchildren. They are, in the language of the slave's poet, Whittier,—

"Gone, gone, sold and gone
To the rice swamp dank and lone,
Where the slave-whip ceaseless swings,
Where the noisome insect stings,
Where the fever-demon strews
Poison with the falling dews,
Where the sickly sunbeams glare
Through the hot and misty air.—
Gone, gone, sold and gone
To the rice swamp dank and lone,
From Virginia hills and waters—
Woe is me, my stolen daughters!"

The hearth is desolate. The children, the unconscious children, who once sang and danced in her presence, are gone. She gropes her way, in the darkness of age, for a drink of water. Instead of the voices of her children, she hears by day the moans of the dove, and by night the screams of the hideous owl. All is gloom. The grave is at the door. And now, when weighed down by the pains and aches of old age, when the head inclines to the feet, when the beginning and ending of human existence meet, and helpless infancy and painful old age combine together—at this time, this most needful time, the time for the exercise of that tenderness and affection which children only can exercise towards a declining parent—my poor old grandmother, the devoted mother of twelve children, is left all alone, in yonder little hut, before a few dim embers. She stands—she sits—she staggers—she falls—she groans—she dies—and there are none of her children or grandchildren present, to wipe from her wrinkled brow the cold sweat of death, or to place beneath the sod her fallen remains. Will not a righteous God visit for these things?

In about two years after the death of Mrs. Lucretia, Master Thomas married his second wife. Her name was Rowena Hamilton. She was the eldest daughter of Mr. William Hamilton. Master now lived in St. Michael's. Not long after his marriage, a misunderstanding took place between himself and Master Hugh; and as a means of punishing his brother, he took me from him to live with himself at St. Michael's. Here I underwent another most painful separation. It, however, was not so severe as the one I dreaded at the division of property; for, during this interval, a great change had taken place in Master Hugh and his once kind and affectionate wife. The influence of brandy upon him, and of slavery upon her, had effected a disastrous change in the characters of both; so that, as far as they were concerned, I thought I had little to lose by the change. But it was not to them that I was attached. It was to those little Baltimore boys that I felt the strongest attachment. I had received many good lessons from them, and was still receiving them, and the thought of leaving them was painful indeed. I was leaving, too, without the hope of ever being allowed to return. Master Thomas had said he would never let me return again. The barrier betwixt himself and brother he considered impassable.

I then had to regret that I did not at least make the attempt to carry out my resolution to run away; for the chances of success are tenfold greater from the city than from the country.

I sailed from Baltimore for St. Michael's in the sloop Amanda, Captain Edward Dodson. On my passage, I paid particular attention to the direction which the steamboats took to go to Philadelphia. I found, instead of going down, on reaching North Point they went up the bay, in a north-easterly direction. I deemed this knowledge of the utmost importance. My determination to run away was again revived. I resolved to wait only so long as the offering of a favorable opportunity. When that came, I was determined to be off.

CHAPTER IX.

I have now reached a period of my life when I can give dates. I left Baltimore, and went to live with Master Thomas Auld, at St. Michael's, in March, 1832. It was now more than seven years since I lived with him in the family of my old master, on Colonel Lloyd's plantation. We of course were now almost entire strangers to each other. He was to me a new master, and I to him a new slave. I was ignorant of his temper and disposition; he was equally so of mine. A very short time, however, brought us into full acquaintance with each other. I was made acquainted with his wife not less than with himself. They were well matched, being equally mean and cruel. I was now, for the first time during a space of more than seven years, made to feel the painful gnawings of hunger—a something which I had not experienced before since I left Colonel Lloyd's plantation. It went hard enough with me then, when I could look back to no period at which I had enjoyed a sufficiency. It was tenfold harder after living in Master Hugh's family, where I had always had enough to eat, and of that which was good. I have said Master Thomas was a mean man. He was so. Not to give a slave enough to eat, is regarded as the most aggravated development of meanness even among slaveholders. The rule is, no matter how coarse the food, only let there be enough of it. This is the theory; and in the part of Maryland from which I came, it is the general practice,—though there are many exceptions. Master Thomas gave us enough of neither coarse nor fine food. There were four slaves of us in the kitchen—my sister Eliza, my aunt Priscilla, Henny, and myself; and we were allowed less than a half of a bushel of corn-meal per week, and very little else, either in the shape of meat or vegetables. It was not enough for us to subsist upon. We were therefore reduced to the wretched necessity of living at the expense of our neighbors. This we did by begging and stealing, whichever came handy in the time of need, the one being considered as legitimate as the other. A great many times have we poor creatures been nearly perishing with hunger, when food in abundance lay mouldering in the safe and smoke-house, and our pious mistress was aware of the fact; and yet that mistress and her husband would kneel every morning, and pray that God would bless them in basket and store!

Bad as all slaveholders are, we seldom meet one destitute of every element of character commanding respect. My master was one of this rare sort. I do not know of one single noble act ever performed by him. The leading trait in his character was meanness; and if there were any other element in his nature, it was made subject to this. He was mean; and, like most other mean men, he lacked the ability to conceal his meanness. Captain Auld was not born a slaveholder. He had been a poor man, master only of a Bay craft. He came into possession of all his slaves by marriage; and of all men, adopted slaveholders are the worst. He was cruel, but cowardly. He commanded without firmness. In the enforcement of his rules, he was at times rigid, and at times lax. At times, he spoke to his slaves with the firmness of Napoleon and the fury of a demon; at other times, he might well be mistaken for an inquirer who had lost his way. He did nothing of himself. He might have passed for a lion, but for his ears. In all things noble which he attempted, his own meanness shone most conspicuous. His airs, words, and actions, were the airs, words, and actions of born slaveholders, and, being assumed, were awkward enough. He was not even a good imitator. He possessed all the disposition to deceive, but wanted the power. Having no resources within himself, he was compelled to be the copyist of many, and being such, he was forever the victim of inconsistency; and of consequence he was an object of contempt, and was held as such even by his slaves. The luxury of having slaves of his own to wait upon him was something new and unprepared for. He was a slaveholder without the ability to hold slaves. He found himself incapable of managing his slaves either by force, fear, or fraud. We seldom called him "master;" we generally called him "Captain Auld," and were hardly disposed to title him at all. I doubt not that our conduct had much to do with making him appear awkward, and of consequence fretful. Our want of reverence for him must have perplexed him greatly. He wished to have us call him master, but lacked the firmness necessary to command us to do so. His wife used to insist upon our calling him so, but to no purpose. In August, 1832, my master attended a Methodist camp-meeting held in the Bay-side, Talbot county, and there experienced religion. I indulged a faint hope that his conversion would lead him to emancipate his slaves, and that, if he did not do this, it would, at any rate, make him more kind and humane. I was disappointed in both these respects. It neither made him to be humane to his slaves, nor to emancipate them. If it had any effect on his character, it made him more cruel and hateful in all his ways; for I believe him to have been a much worse man after his conversion than before. Prior to his conversion, he relied upon his own depravity to shield and sustain him in his savage barbarity; but after his conversion, he found religious sanction and support for his slaveholding cruelty. He made the greatest pretensions to piety. His house was the house of prayer. He prayed morning, noon, and night. He very soon distinguished himself among his brethren, and was soon made a class-leader and exhorter. His activity in revivals was great, and he proved himself an instrument in the hands of the church in converting many souls. His house was the preachers' home. They used to take great pleasure in coming there to put up; for while he starved us, he stuffed them. We have had three or four preachers there at a time. The names of those who used to come most frequently while I lived there, were Mr. Storks, Mr. Ewery, Mr. Humphry, and Mr. Hickey. I have also seen Mr. George Cookman at our house. We slaves loved Mr. Cookman. We believed him to be a good man. We thought him instrumental in getting Mr. Samuel Harrison, a very rich slaveholder, to emancipate his slaves; and by some means got the impression that he was laboring to effect the emancipation of all the slaves. When he was at our house, we were sure to be called in to prayers. When the others were there, we were sometimes called in and sometimes not. Mr. Cookman took more notice of us than either of the other ministers. He could not come among us without betraying his sympathy for us, and, stupid as we were, we had the sagacity to see it.

While I lived with my master in St. Michael's, there was a white young man, a Mr. Wilson, who proposed to keep a Sabbath school for the instruction of such slaves as might be disposed to learn to read the New Testament. We met but three times, when Mr. West and Mr. Fairbanks, both class-leaders, with many others, came upon us with sticks and other missiles, drove us off, and forbade us to meet again. Thus ended our little Sabbath school in the pious town of St. Michael's.

I have said my master found religious sanction for his cruelty. As an example, I will state one of many facts going to prove the charge. I have seen him tie up a lame young woman, and whip her with a heavy cowskin upon her naked shoulders, causing the warm red blood to drip; and, in justification of the bloody deed, he would quote this passage of Scripture—"He that knoweth his master's will, and doeth it not, shall be beaten with many stripes."[6]

Master would keep this lacerated young woman tied up in this horrid situation four or five hours at a time. I have known him to tie her up early in the morning, and whip her before breakfast; leave her, go to his store, return at dinner, and whip her again, cutting her in the places already made raw with his cruel lash. The secret of master's cruelty toward "Henny" is found in the fact of her being almost helpless. When quite a child, she fell into the fire, and burned herself horribly. Her hands were so burnt that she never got the use of them. She could do very little but bear heavy burdens. She was to master a bill of expense; and as he was a mean man, she was a constant offence to him. He seemed desirous of getting the poor girl out of existence. He gave her away once to his sister; but, being a poor gift, she was not disposed to keep her. Finally, my benevolent master, to use his own words, "set her adrift to take care of herself." Here was a recently-converted man, holding on upon the mother, and at the same time turning out her helpless child, to starve and die! Master Thomas was one of the many pious slaveholders who hold slaves for the very charitable purpose of taking care of them.

My master and myself had quite a number of differences. He found me unsuitable to his purpose. My city life, he said, had had a very pernicious effect upon me. It had almost ruined me for every good purpose, and fitted me for every thing which was bad. One of my greatest faults was that of letting his horse run away, and go down to his father-in-law's farm, which was about five miles from St. Michael's. I would then have to go after it. My reason for this kind of carelessness, or carefulness, was, that I could always get something to eat when I went there. Master William Hamilton, my master's father-in-law, always gave his slaves enough to eat. I never left there hungry, no matter how great the need of my speedy return. Master Thomas at length said he would stand it no longer. I had lived with him nine months, during which time he had given me a number of severe whippings, all to no good purpose. He resolved to put me out, as he said, to be broken; and, for this purpose, he let me for one year to a man named Edward Covey. Mr. Covey was a poor man, a farm-renter. He rented the place upon which he lived, as also the hands with which he tilled it. Mr. Covey had acquired a very high reputation for breaking young slaves, and this reputation was of immense value to him. It enabled him to get his farm tilled with much less expense to himself than he could have had it done without such a reputation. Some slaveholders thought it not much loss to allow Mr. Covey to have their slaves one year, for the sake of the training to which they were subjected, without any other compensation. He could hire young help with great ease, in consequence of this reputation. Added to the natural good qualities of Mr. Covey, he was a professor of religion—a pious soul—a member and a class-leader in the Methodist church. All of this added weight to his reputation as a "nigger-breaker." I was aware of all the facts, having been made acquainted with them by a young man who had lived there. I nevertheless made the change gladly; for I was sure of getting enough to eat, which is not the smallest consideration to a hungry man.

CHAPTER X.

I left Master Thomas's house, and went to live with Mr. Covey, on the 1st of January, 1833. I was now, for the first time in my life, a field hand. In my new employment, I found myself even more awkward than a country boy appeared to be in a large city. I had been at my new home but one week before Mr. Covey gave me a very severe whipping, cutting my back, causing the blood to run, and raising ridges on my flesh as large as my little finger. The details of this affair are as follows: Mr. Covey sent me, very early in the morning of one of our coldest days in the month of January, to the woods, to get a load of wood. He gave me a team of unbroken oxen. He told me which was the in-hand ox, and which the off-hand one. He then tied the end of a large rope around the horns of the in-hand ox, and gave me the other end of it, and told me, if the oxen started to run, that I must hold on upon the rope. I had never driven oxen before, and of course I was very awkward. I, however, succeeded in getting to the edge of the woods with little difficulty; but I had got a very few rods into the woods, when the oxen took fright, and started full tilt, carrying the cart against trees, and over stumps, in the most frightful manner. I expected every moment that my brains would be dashed out against the trees. After running thus for a considerable distance, they finally upset the cart, dashing it with great force against a tree, and threw themselves into a dense thicket. How I escaped death, I do not know. There I was, entirely alone, in a thick wood, in a place new to me. My cart was upset and shattered, my oxen were entangled among the young trees, and there was none to help me. After a long spell of effort, I succeeded in getting my cart righted, my oxen disentangled, and again yoked to the cart. I now proceeded with my team to the place where I had, the day before, been chopping wood, and loaded my cart pretty heavily, thinking in this way to tame my oxen. I then proceeded on my way home. I had now consumed one half of the day. I got out of the woods safely, and now felt out of danger. I stopped my oxen to open the woods gate; and just as I did so, before I could get hold of my ox-rope, the oxen again started, rushed through the gate, catching it between the wheel and the body of the cart, tearing it to pieces, and coming within a few inches of crushing me against the gate-post. Thus twice, in one short day, I escaped death by the merest chance. On my return, I told Mr. Covey what had happened, and how it happened. He ordered me to return to the woods again immediately. I did so, and he followed on after me. Just as I got into the woods, he came up and told me to stop my cart, and that he would teach me how to trifle away my time, and break gates. He then went to a large gum-tree, and with his axe cut three large switches, and, after trimming them up neatly with his pocket-knife, he ordered me to take off my clothes. I made him no answer, but stood with my clothes on. He repeated his order. I still made him no answer, nor did I move to strip myself. Upon this he rushed at me with the fierceness of a tiger, tore off my clothes, and lashed me till he had worn out his switches, cutting me so savagely as to leave the marks visible for a long time after. This whipping was the first of a number just like it, and for similar offences.

I lived with Mr. Covey one year. During the first six months, of that year, scarce a week passed without his whipping me. I was seldom free from a sore back. My awkwardness was almost always his excuse for whipping me. We were worked fully up to the point of endurance. Long before day we were up, our horses fed, and by the first approach of day we were off to the field with our hoes and ploughing teams. Mr. Covey gave us enough to eat, but scarce time to eat it. We were often less than five minutes taking our meals. We were often in the field from the first approach of day till its last lingering ray had left us; and at saving-fodder time, midnight often caught us in the field binding blades.

Covey would be out with us. The way he used to stand it, was this. He would spend the most of his afternoons in bed. He would then come out fresh in the evening, ready to urge us on with his words, example, and frequently with the whip. Mr. Covey was one of the few slaveholders who could and did work with his hands. He was a hard-working man. He knew by himself just what a man or a boy could do. There was no deceiving him. His work went on in his absence almost as well as in his presence; and he had the faculty of making us feel that he was ever present with us. This he did by surprising us. He seldom approached the spot where we were at work openly, if he could do it secretly. He always aimed at taking us by surprise. Such was his cunning, that we used to call him, among ourselves, "the snake." When we were at work in the cornfield, he would sometimes crawl on his hands and knees to avoid detection, and all at once he would rise nearly in our midst, and scream out, "Ha, ha! Come, come! Dash on, dash on!" This being his mode of attack, it was never safe to stop a single minute. His comings were like a thief in the night.

He appeared to us as being ever at hand. He was under every tree, behind every stump, in every bush, and at every window, on the plantation. He would sometimes mount his horse, as if bound to St. Michael's, a distance of seven miles, and in half an hour afterwards you would see him coiled up in the corner of the wood-fence, watching every motion of the slaves. He would, for this purpose, leave his horse tied up in the woods. Again, he would sometimes walk up to us, and give us orders as though he was upon the point of starting on a long journey, turn his back upon us, and make as though he was going to the house to get ready; and, before he would get half way thither, he would turn short and crawl into a fence-corner, or behind some tree, and there watch us till the going down of the sun.

Mr. Covey's *forte* consisted in his power to deceive. His life was devoted to planning and perpetrating the grossest deceptions. Every thing he possessed in the shape of learning or religion, he made conform to his disposition to deceive. He seemed to think himself equal to deceiving the Almighty. He would make a short prayer in the morning, and a long prayer at night; and, strange as it may seem, few men would at times appear more devotional than he. The exercises of his family devotions were always commenced with singing; and, as he was a very poor singer himself, the duty of raising the hymn generally came upon me. He would read his hymn, and nod at me to commence. I would at times do so; at others, I would not. My non-compliance would almost always produce much confusion. To show himself independent of me, he would start and stagger through with his hymn in the most discordant manner. In this state of mind, he prayed with more than ordinary spirit. Poor man! such was his disposition, and success at deceiving, I do verily believe that he sometimes deceived himself into the solemn belief, that he was a sincere worshipper of the most high God; and this, too, at a time when he may be said to have been guilty of compelling his woman slave to commit the sin of adultery. The facts in the case are these: Mr. Covey was a poor man; he was just commencing in life; he was only able to buy one slave; and, shocking as is the fact, he bought her, as he said, for a *breeder.* This woman was named Caroline. Mr. Covey bought her from Mr. Thomas Lowe, about six miles from St. Michael's. She was a large, able-bodied woman, about twenty years old. She had already given birth to one child, which proved her to be just what he wanted. After buying her, he hired a married man of Mr. Samuel Harrison, to live with him one year; and him he used to fasten up with her every night! The result was, that, at the end of the year, the miserable woman gave birth to twins. At this result Mr. Covey seemed to be highly pleased, both with the man and the wretched woman. Such was his joy, and that of his wife, that nothing they could do for Caroline during her confinement was too good, or too hard, to be done. The children were regarded as being quite an addition to his wealth.

If at any one time of my life more than another, I was made to drink the bitterest dregs of slavery, that time was during the first six months of my stay with Mr. Covey. We were worked in all weathers. It was never too hot or too cold; it could never rain, blow, hail, or snow, too hard for us to work in the field. Work, work, work, was scarcely more the order of the day than of the night. The longest days were too short for him, and the shortest nights too long for him. I was somewhat unmanageable when I first went there, but a few months of this discipline tamed me. Mr. Covey succeeded in breaking me. I was broken in body, soul, and spirit. My natural elasticity was crushed, my intellect languished, the disposition to read departed, the cheerful spark that lingered about my eye died; the dark night of slavery closed in upon me; and behold a man transformed into a brute!

Sunday was my only leisure time. I spent this in a sort of beast-like stupor, between sleep and wake, under some large tree. At times I would rise up, a flash of energetic freedom would dart through my soul, accompanied with a faint beam of hope, that flickered for a moment, and then vanished. I sank down again, mourning over my wretched condition. I was sometimes prompted to take my life, and that of Covey, but was prevented by a combination of hope and fear. My sufferings on this plantation seem now like a dream rather than a stern reality.

Our house stood within a few rods of the Chesapeake Bay, whose broad bosom was ever white with sails from every quarter of the habitable globe. Those beautiful vessels, robed in purest white, so delightful to the eye of freemen, were to me so many shrouded ghosts, to terrify and torment me with thoughts of my wretched condition. I have often, in the deep stillness of a summer's Sabbath, stood all alone upon the lofty banks of that noble bay, and traced, with saddened heart and tearful eye, the countless number of sails moving off to the mighty ocean. The sight of these always affected me powerfully. My thoughts would compel utterance; and there, with no audience but the Almighty, I would pour out my soul's complaint, in my rude way, with an apostrophe to the moving multitude of ships:—

"You are loosed from your moorings, and are free; I am fast in my chains, and am a slave! You move merrily before the gentle gale, and I sadly before the bloody whip! You are freedom's swift-winged angels, that fly round the world; I am confined in bands of iron! O that I were free! O, that I were on one of your gallant decks, and under your protecting wing! Alas! betwixt me and you, the turbid waters roll. Go on, go on. O that I could also go! Could I but swim! If I could fly! O, why was I born a man, of whom to make a brute! The glad ship is gone; she hides in the dim distance. I am left in the hottest hell of unending slavery. O God, save me! God, deliver me! Let me be free! Is there any God? Why am I a slave? I will run away. I will not stand it. Get caught, or get clear, I'll try it. I had as well die with ague as the fever. I have only one life to lose. I had as well be killed running as die standing. Only think of it; one hundred miles straight north, and I am free! Try it? Yes! God helping me, I will. It cannot be that I shall live and die a slave. I will take to the water. This very bay shall yet bear me into freedom. The steamboats steered in a north-east course from North Point. I will do the same; and when I get to the head of the bay, I will turn my canoe adrift, and walk straight through Delaware into Pennsylvania. When I get there, I shall not be required to have a pass; I can travel without being disturbed. Let but the first opportunity offer, and, come what will, I am off. Meanwhile, I will try to bear up under the yoke. I am not the only slave in the world. Why should I fret? I can bear as much as any of them. Besides, I am but a boy, and all boys are bound to some one. It may be that my misery in slavery will only increase my happiness when I get free. There is a better day coming."

Thus I used to think, and thus I used to speak to myself; goaded almost to madness at one moment, and at the next reconciling myself to my wretched lot.

I have already intimated that my condition was much worse, during the first six months of my stay at Mr. Covey's, than in the last six. The circumstances leading to the change in Mr. Covey's course toward me form an epoch in my humble history. You have seen how a man was made a slave; you shall see how a slave was made a man. On one of the hottest days of the month of August, 1833, Bill Smith, William Hughes, a slave named Eli, and myself, were engaged in fanning wheat. Hughes was clearing the fanned wheat from before the fan, Eli was turning, Smith was feeding, and I was carrying wheat to the fan. The work was simple, requiring strength rather than intellect; yet, to one entirely unused to such work, it came very hard. About three o'clock of that day, I broke down; my strength failed me; I was seized with a violent aching of the head, attended with extreme dizziness; I trembled in every limb. Finding what was coming, I nerved myself up, feeling it would never do to stop work. I stood as long as I could stagger to the hopper with grain. When I could stand no longer, I fell, and felt as if held down by an immense weight. The fan of course stopped; every one had his own work to do; and no one could do the work of the other, and have his own go on at the same time.

Mr. Covey was at the house, about one hundred yards from the treading-yard where we were fanning. On hearing the fan stop, he left immediately, and came to the spot where we were. He hastily inquired what the matter was. Bill answered that I was sick, and there was no one to bring wheat to the fan. I had by this time crawled away under the side of the post and rail-fence by which the yard was enclosed, hoping to find relief by getting out of the sun. He then asked where I was. He was told by one of the hands. He came to the spot, and, after looking at me awhile, asked me what was the matter. I told him as well as I could, for I scarce had strength to speak. He then gave me a savage kick in the side, and told me to get up. I tried to do so, but fell back in the attempt. He gave me another kick, and again told me to rise. I again tried, and succeeded in gaining my feet; but, stooping to get the tub with which I was feeding the fan, I again staggered and fell. While down in this situation, Mr. Covey took up the hickory slat with which Hughes had been striking off the half-bushel measure, and with it gave me a heavy blow upon the head, making a large wound, and the blood ran freely; and with this again told me to get up. I made no effort to comply, having now made up my mind to let him do his worst. In a short time after receiving this blow, my head grew better. Mr. Covey had now left me to my fate. At this moment I resolved, for the first time, to go to my master, enter a complaint, and ask his protection. In order to [do] this, I must that afternoon walk seven miles; and this, under the circumstances, was truly a severe undertaking. I was exceedingly feeble; made so as much by the kicks and blows which I received, as by the severe fit of sickness to which I had been subjected. I, however, watched my chance, while Covey was looking in an opposite direction, and started for St. Michael's. I succeeded in getting a considerable distance on my way to the woods, when Covey discovered me, and called after me to come back, threatening what he would do if I did not come. I disregarded both his calls and his threats, and made my way to the woods as fast as my feeble state would allow; and thinking I might be overhauled by him if I kept the road, I walked through the woods, keeping far enough from the road to avoid detection, and near enough to prevent losing my way. I had not gone far before my little strength again failed me. I could go no farther. I fell down, and lay for a considerable time. The blood was yet oozing from the wound on my head. For a time I thought I should bleed to death; and think now that I should have done so, but that the blood so matted my hair as to stop the wound. After lying there about three quarters of an hour, I nerved myself up again, and started on my way, through bogs and briers, barefooted and bareheaded, tearing my feet sometimes at nearly every step; and after a journey of about seven miles, occupying some five hours to perform it, I arrived at master's store. I then presented an appearance enough to affect any but a heart of iron. From the crown of my head to my feet, I was covered with blood. My hair was all clotted with dust and blood; my shirt was stiff with blood. My legs and feet were torn in sundry places with briers and thorns, and were also covered with blood. I suppose I looked like a man who had escaped a den of wild beasts, and barely escaped them. In this state I appeared before my master, humbly entreating him to interpose his authority for my protection. I told him all the circumstances as well as I could, and it seemed, as I spoke, at times to affect him. He would then walk the floor, and seek to justify Covey by saying he expected I deserved it. He asked me what I wanted. I told him, to let me get a new home; that as sure as I lived with Mr. Covey again, I should live with but to die with him; that Covey would surely kill me; he was in a fair way for it. Master Thomas ridiculed the idea that there was any danger of Mr. Covey's killing me, and said that he knew Mr. Covey; that he was a good man, and that he could not think of taking me from him; that, should he do so, he would lose the whole year's wages; that I belonged to Mr. Covey for one year, and that I must go back to him, come what might; and that I must not trouble him with any more stories, or that he would himself *get hold of me.* After threatening me thus, he gave me a very large dose of salts, telling me that I might remain in St. Michael's that night, (it being quite late,) but that I must be off back to Mr. Covey's early in the morning; and that if I did not, he would *get hold of me*, which meant that he would whip me. I remained all night, and, according to his orders, I started off to Covey's in the morning, (Saturday morning,) wearied in body and broken in spirit. I got no supper that night, or breakfast that morning. I reached Covey's about nine o'clock; and just as I was getting over the fence that divided Mrs. Kemp's fields from ours, out ran Covey with his cowskin, to give me another whipping. Before he could reach me, I succeeded in getting to the cornfield; and as the corn was very high, it afforded me the means of hiding. He seemed very angry, and searched for me a long time. My behavior was altogether unaccountable. He finally gave up the chase, thinking, I suppose, that I must come home for something to eat; he would give himself no further trouble in looking for me. I spent that day mostly in the woods, having the alternative before me,—to go home and be whipped to death, or stay in the woods and be starved to death. That night, I fell in with Sandy Jenkins, a slave with whom I was somewhat acquainted. Sandy had a free wife who lived about four miles from Mr. Covey's; and it being Saturday, he was on his way to see her. I told him my circumstances, and he very kindly invited me to go home with him. I went home with him, and talked this whole matter over, and got his advice as to what course it was best for me to pursue. I found Sandy an old adviser. He told me, with great solemnity, I must go back to Covey; but that before I went, I must go with him into another part of the woods, where there was a certain *root*, which, if I would take some of it with me, carrying it *always on my right side*, would render it impossible for Mr. Covey, or any other white man, to whip me. He said he had carried it for years; and since he had done so, he had never received a blow, and never expected to while he carried it. I at first rejected the idea, that the simple carrying of a root in my pocket would have any such effect as he had said, and was not disposed to take it; but Sandy impressed the necessity with much earnestness, telling me it could do no harm, if it did no good. To please him, I at length took the root, and, according to his direction, carried it upon my right side. This was Sunday morning. I immediately started for home; and upon entering the yard gate, out came Mr. Covey on his way to meeting. He spoke to me very kindly, bade me drive the pigs from a lot near by, and passed on towards the church. Now, this singular conduct of Mr. Covey really made me begin to think that there was something in the *root* which Sandy had given me; and had it been on any other day than Sunday, I could have attributed the conduct to no other cause than the influence of that root; and as it was, I was half inclined to think the *root* to be something more than I at first had taken it to be. All went well till Monday morning. On this morning, the virtue of the *root* was fully tested. Long before daylight, I was called to go and rub, curry, and feed, the horses. I obeyed, and was glad to obey. But whilst thus engaged, whilst in the act of throwing down some blades from the loft, Mr. Covey entered the stable with a long rope; and just as I was half out of the loft, he caught hold of my legs, and was about tying me. As soon as I found what he was up to, I gave a sudden spring, and as I did so, he holding to my legs, I was brought sprawling on the stable floor. Mr. Covey seemed now to think he had me, and could do what he pleased; but at this moment—from whence came the spirit I don't know—I resolved to fight; and, suiting my action to the resolution, I seized Covey hard by the throat; and as I did so, I rose. He held on to me, and I to him. My resistance was so entirely unexpected, that Covey seemed taken all aback. He trembled like a leaf. This gave me assurance, and I held him uneasy, causing the blood to run where I touched him with the ends of my fingers. Mr. Covey soon called out to Hughes for help. Hughes came, and, while Covey held me, attempted to tie my right hand. While he was in the act of doing so, I watched my chance, and gave him a heavy kick close under the ribs. This kick fairly sickened Hughes, so that he left me in the hands of Mr. Covey. This kick had the effect of not only weakening Hughes, but Covey also. When he saw Hughes bending over with pain, his courage quailed. He asked me if I meant to persist in my resistance. I told him I did, come what might; that he had used me like a brute for six months, and that I was determined to be used so no longer. With that, he strove to drag me to a stick that was lying just out of the stable door. He meant to knock me down. But just as he was leaning over to get the stick, I seized him with both hands by his collar, and brought him by a sudden snatch to the ground. By this time, Bill came. Covey called upon him for assistance. Bill wanted to know what he could do. Covey said, "Take hold of him, take hold of him!" Bill said his master hired him out to work, and not to help to whip me; so he left Covey and myself to fight our own battle out. We were at it for nearly two hours. Covey at length let me go, puffing and blowing at a great rate, saying that if I had not resisted, he would not have whipped me half so much. The truth was, that he had not whipped me at all. I considered him as getting entirely the worst end of the bargain; for he had drawn no blood from me, but I had from him. The whole six months afterwards, that I spent with Mr. Covey, he never laid the weight of his finger upon me in anger. He would occasionally say, he didn't want to get hold of me again. "No," thought I, "you need not; for you will come off worse than you did before."

This battle with Mr. Covey was the turning-point in my career as a slave. It rekindled the few expiring embers of freedom, and revived within me a sense of my own manhood. It recalled the departed self-confidence, and inspired me again with a determination to be free. The gratification afforded by the triumph was a full compensation for whatever else might follow, even death itself. He only can understand the deep satisfaction which I experienced, who has himself repelled by force the bloody arm of slavery. I felt as I never felt before. It was a glorious resurrection, from the tomb of slavery, to the heaven of freedom. My long-crushed spirit rose, cowardice departed, bold defiance took its place; and I now resolved that, however long I might remain a slave in form, the day had passed forever when I could be a slave in fact. I did not hesitate to let it be known of me, that the white man who expected to succeed in whipping, must also succeed in killing me.

From this time I was never again what might be called fairly whipped, though I remained a slave four years afterwards. I had several fights, but was never whipped.

It was for a long time a matter of surprise to me why Mr. Covey did not immediately have me taken by the constable to the whipping-post, and there regularly whipped for the crime of raising my hand against a white man in defence of myself. And the only explanation I can now think of does not entirely satisfy me; but such as it is, I will give it. Mr. Covey enjoyed the most unbounded reputation for being a first-rate overseer and negro-breaker. It was of considerable importance to him. That reputation was at stake; and had he sent me—a boy about sixteen years old—to the public whipping-post, his reputation would have been lost; so, to save his reputation, he suffered me to go unpunished.

My term of actual service to Mr. Edward Covey ended on Christmas day, 1833. The days between Christmas and New Year's day are allowed as holidays; and, accordingly, we were not required to perform any labor, more than to feed and take care of the stock. This time we regarded as our own, by the grace of our masters; and we therefore used or abused it nearly as we pleased. Those of us who had families at a distance, were generally allowed to spend the whole six days in their society. This time, however, was spent in various ways. The staid, sober, thinking and industrious ones of our number would employ themselves in making corn-brooms, mats, horse-collars, and baskets; and another class of us would spend the time in hunting opossums, hares, and coons. But by far the larger part engaged in such sports and merriments as playing ball, wrestling, running foot-races, fiddling, dancing, and drinking whisky; and this latter mode of spending the time was by far the most agreeable to the feelings of our masters. A slave who would work during the holidays was considered by our masters as scarcely deserving them. He was regarded as one who rejected the favor of his master. It was deemed a disgrace not to get drunk at Christmas; and he was regarded as lazy indeed, who had not provided himself with the necessary means, during the year, to get whisky enough to last him through Christmas.

From what I know of the effect of these holidays upon the slave, I believe them to be among the most effective means in the hands of the slaveholder in keeping down the spirit of insurrection. Were the slaveholders at once to abandon this practice, I have not the slightest doubt it would lead to an immediate insurrection among the slaves. These holidays serve as conductors, or safety-valves, to carry off the rebellious spirit of enslaved humanity. But for these, the slave would be forced up to the wildest desperation; and woe betide the slaveholder, the day he ventures to remove or hinder the operation of those conductors! I warn him that, in such an event, a spirit will go forth in their midst, more to be dreaded than the most appalling earthquake.

The holidays are part and parcel of the gross fraud, wrong, and inhumanity of slavery. They are professedly a custom established by the benevolence of the slaveholders; but I undertake to say, it is the result of selfishness, and one of the grossest frauds committed upon the down-trodden slave. They do not give the slaves this time because they would not like to have their work during its continuance, but because they know it would be unsafe to deprive them of it. This will be seen by the fact, that the slaveholders like to have their slaves spend those days just in such a manner as to make them as glad of their ending as of their beginning. Their object seems to be, to disgust their slaves with freedom, by plunging them into the lowest depths of dissipation. For instance, the slaveholders not only like to see the slave drink of his own accord, but will adopt various plans to make him drunk. One plan is, to make bets on their slaves, as to who can drink the most whisky without getting drunk; and in this way they succeed in getting whole multitudes to drink to excess. Thus, when the slave asks for virtuous freedom, the cunning slaveholder, knowing his ignorance, cheats him with a dose of vicious dissipation, artfully labelled with the name of liberty. The most of us used to drink it down, and the result was just what might be supposed: many of us were led to think that there was little to choose between liberty and slavery.

We felt, and very properly too, that we had almost as well be slaves to man as to rum. So, when the holidays ended, we staggered up from the filth of our wallowing, took a long breath, and marched to the field,—feeling, upon the whole, rather glad to go, from what our master had deceived us into a belief was freedom, back to the arms of slavery.

I have said that this mode of treatment is a part of the whole system of fraud and inhumanity of slavery. It is so. The mode here adopted to disgust the slave with freedom, by allowing him to see only the abuse of it, is carried out in other things. For instance, a slave loves molasses; he steals some. His master, in many cases, goes off to town, and buys a large quantity; he returns, takes his whip, and commands the slave to eat the molasses, until the poor fellow is made sick at the very mention of it. The same mode is sometimes adopted to make the slaves refrain from asking for more food than their regular allowance. A slave runs through his allowance, and applies for more. His master is enraged at him; but, not willing to send him off without food, gives him more than is necessary, and compels him to eat it within a given time. Then, if he complains that he cannot eat it, he is said to be satisfied neither full nor fasting, and is whipped for being hard to please! I have an abundance of such illustrations of the same principle, drawn from my own observation, but think the cases I have cited sufficient. The practice is a very common one.

On the first of January, 1834, I left Mr. Covey, and went to live with Mr. William Freeland, who lived about three miles from St. Michael's. I soon found Mr. Freeland a very different man from Mr. Covey. Though not rich, he was what would be called an educated southern gentleman. Mr. Covey, as I have shown, was a well-trained negro-breaker and slave-driver. The former (slaveholder though he was) seemed to possess some regard for honor, some reverence for justice, and some respect for humanity. The latter seemed totally insensible to all such sentiments. Mr. Freeland had many of the faults peculiar to slaveholders, such as being very passionate and fretful; but I must do him the justice to say, that he was exceedingly free from those degrading vices to which Mr. Covey was constantly addicted. The one was open and frank, and we always knew where to find him. The other was a most artful deceiver, and could be understood only by such as were skilful enough to detect his cunningly-devised frauds. Another advantage I gained in my new master was, he made no pretensions to, or profession of, religion; and this, in my opinion, was truly a great advantage. I assert most unhesitatingly, that the religion of the south is a mere covering for the most horrid crimes,—a justifier of the most appalling barbarity,—a sanctifier of the most hateful frauds,—and a dark shelter under, which the darkest, foulest, grossest, and most infernal deeds of slaveholders find the strongest protection. Were I to be again reduced to the chains of slavery, next to that enslavement, I should regard being the slave of a religious master the greatest calamity that could befall me. For of all slaveholders with whom I have ever met, religious slaveholders are the worst. I have ever found them the meanest and basest, the most cruel and cowardly, of all others. It was my unhappy lot not only to belong to a religious slaveholder, but to live in a community of such religionists. Very near Mr. Freeland lived the Rev. Daniel Weeden, and in the same neighborhood lived the Rev. Rigby Hopkins. These were members and ministers in the Reformed Methodist Church. Mr. Weeden owned, among others, a woman slave, whose name I have forgotten. This woman's back, for weeks, was kept literally raw, made so by the lash of this merciless, *religious* wretch. He used to hire hands. His maxim was, Behave well or behave ill, it is the duty of a master occasionally to whip a slave, to remind him of his master's authority. Such was his theory, and such his practice.

Mr. Hopkins was even worse than Mr. Weeden. His chief boast was his ability to manage slaves. The peculiar feature of his government was that of whipping slaves in advance of deserving it. He always managed to have one or more of his slaves to whip every Monday morning. He did this to alarm their fears, and strike terror into those who escaped. His plan was to whip for the smallest offences, to prevent the commission of large ones. Mr. Hopkins could always find some excuse for whipping a slave. It would astonish one, unaccustomed to a slaveholding life, to see with what wonderful ease a slaveholder can find things, of which to make occasion to whip a slave. A mere look, word, or motion,—a mistake, accident, or want of power,—are all matters for which a slave may be whipped at any time. Does a slave look dissatisfied? It is said, he has the devil in him, and it must be whipped out. Does he speak loudly when spoken to by his master? Then he is getting high-minded, and should be taken down a button-hole lower. Does he forget to pull off his hat at the approach of a white person? Then he is wanting in reverence, and should be whipped for it. Does he ever venture to vindicate his conduct, when censured for it? Then he is guilty of impudence,—one of the greatest crimes of which a slave can be guilty. Does he ever venture to suggest a different mode of doing things from that pointed out by his master? He is indeed presumptuous, and getting above himself; and nothing less than a flogging will do for him. Does he, while ploughing, break a plough,—or, while hoeing, break a hoe? It is owing to his carelessness, and for it a slave must always be whipped. Mr. Hopkins could always find something of this sort to justify the use of the lash, and he seldom failed to embrace such opportunities. There was not a man in the whole county, with whom the slaves who had the getting their own home, would not prefer to live, rather than with this Rev. Mr. Hopkins. And yet there was not a man any where round, who made higher professions of religion, or was more active in revivals,—more attentive to the class, love-feast, prayer and preaching meetings, or more devotional in his family,—that prayed earlier, later, louder, and longer,—than this same reverend slave-driver, Rigby Hopkins.

But to return to Mr. Freeland, and to my experience while in his employment. He, like Mr. Covey, gave us enough to eat; but, unlike Mr. Covey, he also gave us sufficient time to take our meals. He worked us hard, but always between sunrise and sunset. He required a good deal of work to be done, but gave us good tools with which to work. His farm was large, but he employed hands enough to work it, and with ease, compared with many of his neighbors. My treatment, while in his employment, was heavenly, compared with what I experienced at the hands of Mr. Edward Covey.

Mr. Freeland was himself the owner of but two slaves. Their names were Henry Harris and John Harris. The rest of his hands he hired. These consisted of myself, Sandy Jenkins,* and Handy Caldwell. Henry and John were quite intelligent, and in a very little while after I went there, I succeeded in creating in them a strong desire to learn how to read. This desire soon sprang up in the others also. They very soon mustered up some old spelling-books, and nothing would do but that I must keep a Sabbath school. I agreed to do so, and accordingly devoted my Sundays to teaching these my loved fellow-slaves how to read. Neither of them knew his letters when I went there. Some of the slaves of the neighboring farms found what was going on, and also availed themselves of this little opportunity to learn to read. It was understood, among all who came, that there must be as little display about it as possible. It was necessary to keep our religious masters at St. Michael's unacquainted with the fact, that, instead of spending the Sabbath in wrestling, boxing, and drinking whisky, we were trying to learn how to read the will of God; for they had much rather see us engaged in those degrading sports, than to see us behaving like intellectual, moral, and accountable beings. My blood boils as I think of the bloody manner in which Messrs. Wright Fairbanks and Garrison West, both class-leaders, in connection with many others, rushed in upon us with sticks and stones, and broke up our virtuous little Sabbath school, at St. Michael's—all calling themselves Christians! humble followers of the Lord Jesus Christ! But I am again digressing.

I held my Sabbath school at the house of a free colored man, whose name I deem it imprudent to mention; for should it be known, it might embarrass him greatly, though the crime of holding the school was committed ten years ago. I had at one time over forty scholars, and those of the right sort, ardently desiring to learn. They were of all ages, though mostly men and women. I look back to those Sundays with an amount of pleasure not to be expressed. They were great days to my soul. The

* This is the same man who gave me the roots to prevent my being whipped by Mr. Covey. He was "a clever soul." We used frequently to talk about the fight with Covey, and as often as we did so, he would claim my success as the result of the roots which he gave me. This superstition is very common among the more ignorant slaves. A slave seldom dies but that his death is attributed to trickery.

work of instructing my dear fellow-slaves was the sweetest engagement with which I was ever blessed. We loved each other, and to leave them at the close of the Sabbath was a severe cross indeed. When I think that these precious souls are to-day shut up in the prison-house of slavery, my feelings overcome me, and I am almost ready to ask, "Does a righteous God govern the universe? and for what does he hold the thunders in his right hand, if not to smite the oppressor, and deliver the spoiled out of the hand of the spoiler?" These dear souls came not to Sabbath school because it was popular to do so, nor did I teach them because it was reputable to be thus engaged. Every moment they spent in that school, they were liable to be taken up, and given thirty-nine lashes. They came because they wished to learn. Their minds had been starved by their cruel masters. They had been shut up in mental darkness. I taught them, because it was the delight of my soul to be doing something that looked like bettering the condition of my race. I kept up my school nearly the whole year I lived with Mr. Freeland; and, beside my Sabbath school, I devoted three evenings in the week, during the winter, to teaching the slaves at home. And I have the happiness to know, that several of those who came to Sabbath school learned how to read; and that one, at least, is now free through my agency.

The year passed off smoothly. It seemed only about half as long as the year which preceded it. I went through it without receiving a single blow. I will give Mr. Freeland the credit of being the best master I ever had, *till I became my own master.* For the ease with which I passed the year, I was, however, somewhat indebted to the society of my fellow-slaves. They were noble souls; they not only possessed loving hearts, but brave ones. We were linked and interlinked with each other. I loved them with a love stronger than any thing I have experienced since. It is sometimes said that we slaves do not love and confide in each other. In answer to this assertion, I can say, I never loved any or confided in any people more than my fellow-slaves, and especially those with whom I lived at Mr. Freeland's. I believe we would have died for each other. We never undertook to do any thing, of any importance, without a mutual consultation. We never moved separately. We were one; and as much so by our tempers and dispositions, as by the mutual hardships to which we were necessarily subjected by our condition as slaves.

At the close of the year 1834, Mr. Freeland again hired me of my master, for the year 1835. But, by this time, I began to want to live *upon free land* as well as *with Freeland;* and I was no longer content, therefore, to live with him or any other slaveholder. I began, with the commencement of the year, to prepare myself for a final struggle, which should decide my fate one way or the other. My tendency was upward. I was fast approaching manhood, and year after year had passed, and I was still a slave. These thoughts roused me—I must do something. I therefore resolved that 1835 should not pass without witnessing an attempt, on my part, to secure my liberty. But I was not willing to cherish this determination alone. My fellow-slaves were dear to me. I was anxious to have them participate with me in this, my life-giving determination. I therefore, though with great prudence, commenced early to ascertain their views and feelings in regard to their condition, and to imbue their minds with thoughts of freedom. I bent myself to devising ways and means for our escape, and meanwhile strove, on all fitting occasions, to impress them with the gross fraud and inhumanity of slavery. I went first to Henry, next to John, then to the others. I found, in them all, warm hearts and noble spirits. They were ready to hear, and ready to act when a feasible plan should be proposed. This was what I wanted. I talked to them of our want of manhood, if we submitted to our enslavement without at least one noble effort to be free. We met often, and consulted frequently, and told our hopes and fears, recounted the difficulties, real and imagined, which we should be called on to meet. At times we were almost disposed to give up, and try to content ourselves with our wretched lot; at others, we were firm and unbending in our determination to go. Whenever we suggested any plan, there was shrinking—the odds were fearful. Our path was beset with the greatest obstacles; and if we succeeded in gaining the end of it, our right to be free was yet questionable—we were yet liable to be returned to bondage. We could see no spot, this side of the ocean, where we could be free. We knew nothing about Canada. Our knowledge of the north did not extend farther than New York; and to go there, and be forever harassed with the frightful liability of being returned to slavery—with the certainty of being treated tenfold worse than before—the thought was truly a horrible one, and one which it was not easy to overcome. The case sometimes stood thus: At every gate through which we were to pass, we saw a watchman—at every ferry a guard—on every bridge a sentinel—and in every wood a patrol. We were hemmed in upon every side. Here were the difficulties, real or imagined—the good to be sought, and the evil to be shunned. On the one hand, there stood slavery, a stern reality, glaring frightfully upon us,—its robes already crimsoned with the blood of millions, and even now feasting itself greedily upon our own flesh. On the other hand, away back in the dim distance, under the flickering light of the north star, behind some craggy hill or snow-covered mountain, stood a doubtful freedom—half frozen—beckoning us to come and share its hospitality. This in itself was sometimes enough to stagger us; but when we permitted ourselves to survey the road, we were frequently appalled. Upon either side we saw grim death, assuming the most horrid shapes. Now it was starvation, causing us to eat our own flesh;—now we were contending with the waves, and were drowned;—now we were overtaken, and torn to pieces by the fangs of the terrible bloodhound. We were stung by scorpions, chased by wild beasts, bitten by snakes, and finally, after having nearly reached the desired spot,—after swimming rivers, encountering wild beasts, sleeping in the woods, suffering hunger and nakedness,—we were overtaken by our pursuers, and, in our resistance, we were shot dead upon the spot! I say, this picture sometimes appalled us, and made us

> "rather bear those ills we had,
> Than fly to others, that we knew not of."[7]

In coming to a fixed determination to run away, we did more than Patrick Henry, when he resolved upon liberty or death. With us it was a doubtful liberty at most, and almost certain death if we failed. For my part, I should prefer death to hopeless bondage.

Sandy, one of our number, gave up the notion, but still encouraged us. Our company then consisted of Henry Harris, John Harris, Henry Bailey, Charles Roberts, and myself. Henry Bailey was my uncle, and belonged to my master. Charles married my aunt: he belonged to my master's father-in-law, Mr. William Hamilton.

The plan we finally concluded upon was, to get a large canoe belonging to Mr. Hamilton, and upon the Saturday night previous to Easter holidays, paddle directly up the Chesapeake Bay. On our arrival at the head of the bay, a distance of seventy or eighty miles from where we lived, it was our purpose to turn our canoe adrift, and follow the guidance of the north star till we got beyond the limits of Maryland. Our reason for taking the water route was, that we were less liable to be suspected as runaways; we hoped to be regarded as fishermen; whereas, if we should take the land route, we should be subjected to interruptions of almost every kind. Any one having a white face, and being so disposed, could stop us, and subject us to examination.

The week before our intended start, I wrote several protections, one for each of us. As well as I can remember, they were in the following words, to wit:—

> "THIS is to certify that I, the undersigned, have given the bearer, my servant, full liberty to go to Baltimore, and spend the Easter holidays. Written with mine own hand, &c., 1835.
>
> "WILLIAM HAMILTON,
>
> "Near St. Michael's, in Talbot county, Maryland."

We were not going to Baltimore; but, in going up the bay, we went toward Baltimore, and these protections were only intended to protect us while on the bay.

As the time drew near for our departure, our anxiety became more and more intense. It was truly a matter of life and death with us. The strength of our determination was about to be fully tested. At this time, I was very active in explaining every difficulty, removing every doubt, dispelling every fear, and inspiring all with the firmness indispensable to success in our undertaking; assuring them that half was gained the instant we made the move; we had talked long enough; we were now ready to move; if not now, we never should be; and if we did not intend to move now, we had as well fold our arms, sit down, and acknowledge ourselves fit only to be slaves. This, none of us were prepared to acknowledge. Every man stood firm; and at our last meeting, we pledged ourselves afresh, in the most solemn manner, that, at the time appointed, we would certainly start in pursuit of freedom. This was in the middle of the week, at the end of which we were to be off. We went, as usual, to our several fields of labor, but with bosoms highly agitated with thoughts of our truly hazardous undertaking. We tried to conceal our feelings as much as possible; and I think we succeeded very well.

After a painful waiting, the Saturday morning, whose night was to witness our departure, came. I hailed it with joy, bring what of sadness it might. Friday night was a sleepless one for me. I probably felt more anxious than the rest, because I was, by common consent, at the head of the whole affair. The responsibility of success or failure lay heavily upon me. The glory of the one, and the confusion of the other, were alike mine. The first two hours of that morning were such as I never experienced before, and hope never to again. Early in the morning, we went, as usual, to the field. We were spreading manure; and all at once, while thus engaged, I was overwhelmed with an indescribable feeling, in the fulness of which I turned to Sandy, who was near by, and said, "We are betrayed!" "Well," said he, "that thought has this moment struck me." We said no more. I was never more certain of any thing.

The horn was blown as usual, and we went up from the field to the house for breakfast. I went for the form, more than for want of any thing to eat that morning. Just as I got to the house, in looking out at the lane gate, I saw four white men, with two colored men. The white men were on horseback, and the colored ones were walking behind, as if tied. I watched them a few moments till they got up to our lane gate. Here they halted, and tied the colored men to the gate-post. I was not yet certain as to what the matter was. In a few moments, in rode Mr. Hamilton, with a speed betokening great excitement. He came to the door, and inquired if Master William was in. He was told he was at the barn. Mr. Hamilton, without dismounting, rode up to the barn with extraordinary speed. In a few moments, he and Mr. Freeland returned to the house. By this time, the three constables rode up, and in great haste dismounted, tied their horses, and met Master William and Mr. Hamilton returning from the barn; and after talking awhile, they all walked up to the kitchen door. There was no one in the kitchen but myself and John. Henry and Sandy were up at the barn. Mr. Freeland put his head in at the door, and called me by name, saying, there were some gentlemen at the door who wished to see me. I stepped to the door, and inquired what they wanted. They at once seized me, and, without giving me any satisfaction, tied me—lashing my hands closely together. I insisted upon knowing what the matter was. They at length said, that they had learned I had been in a "scrape," and that I was to be examined before my master; and if their information proved false, I should not be hurt.

In a few moments, they succeeded in tying John. They then turned to Henry, who had by this time returned, and commanded him to cross his hands. "I won't!" said Henry, in a firm tone, indicating his readiness to meet the consequences of his refusal. "Won't you?" said Tom Graham, the constable. "No, I won't!" said Henry, in a still stronger tone. With this, two of the constables pulled out their shining pistols, and swore, by their Creator, that they would make him cross his hands or kill him. Each cocked his pistol, and, with fingers on the trigger, walked up to Henry, saying, at the same time, if he did not cross his hands, they would blow his damned heart out. "Shoot me, shoot me!" said Henry; "you can't kill me but once. Shoot, shoot,—and be damned! *I won't be tied!*" This he said in a tone of loud defiance; and at the same time, with a motion as quick as lightning, he with one single stroke dashed the pistols from the hand of each constable. As he did this, all hands fell upon him, and, after beating him some time, they finally overpowered him, and got him tied.

During the scuffle, I managed, I know not how, to get my pass out, and, without being discovered, put it into the fire. We were all now tied; and just as we were to leave for Easton jail, Betsy Freeland, mother of William Freeland, came to the door with her hands full of biscuits, and divided them between Henry and John. She then delivered herself of a speech, to the following effect:—addressing herself to me, she said, "*You devil! You yellow devil!* it was you that put it into the heads of Henry and John to run away. But for you, you long-legged mulatto devil! Henry nor John would never have thought of such a thing." I made no reply, and was immediately hurried off towards St. Michael's. Just a moment previous to the scuffle with Henry, Mr. Hamilton suggested the propriety of making a search for the protections which he had understood Frederick had written for himself and the rest. But, just at the moment he was about carrying his proposal into effect, his aid was needed in helping to tie Henry; and the excitement attending the scuffle caused them either to forget, or to deem it unsafe, under the circumstances, to search. So we were not yet convicted of the intention to run away.

When we got about half way to St. Michael's, while the constables having us in charge were looking ahead, Henry inquired of me what he should do with his pass. I told him to eat it with his biscuit, and own nothing; and we passed the word around, "*Own nothing;*" and "*Own nothing!*" said we all. Our confidence in each other was unshaken. We were resolved to succeed or fail together, after the calamity had befallen us as much as before. We were now prepared for any thing. We were to be dragged that morning fifteen miles behind horses, and then to be placed in the Easton jail. When we reached St. Michael's, we underwent a sort of examination. We all denied that we ever intended to run away. We did this more to bring out the evidence against us, than from any hope of getting clear of being sold; for, as I have said, we were ready for that. The fact was, we cared but little where we went, so we went together. Our greatest concern was about separation. We dreaded that more than any thing this side of death. We found the evidence against us to be the testimony of one person; our master would not tell who it was; but we came to a unanimous decision among ourselves as to who their informant was. We were sent off to the jail at Easton. When we got there, we were delivered up to the sheriff, Mr. Joseph Graham, and by him placed in jail. Henry, John, and myself, were placed in one room together—Charles, and Henry Bailey, in another. Their object in separating us was to hinder concert.

We had been in jail scarcely twenty minutes, when a swarm of slave traders, and agents for slave traders, flocked into jail to look at us, and to ascertain if we were for sale. Such a set of beings I never saw before! I felt myself surrounded by so many fiends from perdition. A band of pirates never looked more like their father, the devil. They laughed and grinned over us, saying, "Ah, my boys! we have got you, haven't we?" And after taunting us in various ways, they one by one went into an examination of us, with intent to ascertain our value. They would impudently ask us if we would not like to have them for our masters. We would make them no answer, and leave them to find out as best they could. Then they would curse and swear at us, telling us that they could take the devil out of us in a very little while, if we were only in their hands.

While in jail, we found ourselves in much more comfortable quarters than we expected when we went there. We did not get much to eat, nor that which was very good; but we had a good clean room, from the windows of which we could see what was going on in the street, which was very much better than though we had been placed in one of the dark, damp cells. Upon the whole, we got along very well, so far as the jail and its keeper were concerned. Immediately after the holidays were over, contrary to all our expectations, Mr. Hamilton and Mr. Freeland came up to Easton, and took Charles, the two Henrys, and John, out of jail, and carried them home, leaving me alone. I regarded this separation as a final one. It caused me more pain than any thing else in the whole transaction. I was ready for any thing rather than separation. I supposed that they had consulted together, and had decided that, as I was the whole cause of the intention of the others to run away, it was hard to make the innocent suffer with the guilty; and that they had, therefore, concluded to take the others home, and sell me, as a warning to the others that remained. It is due to the noble Henry to say, he seemed almost as reluctant at leaving the prison as at leaving home to come to the prison. But we knew we should, in all probability, be separated, if we were sold; and since he was in their hands, he concluded to go peaceably home.

I was now left to my fate. I was all alone, and within the walls of a stone prison. But a few days before, and I was full of hope. I expected to have been safe in a land of freedom; but now I was covered with gloom, sunk down to the utmost despair. I thought the possibility of freedom was gone. I was kept in this way about one week, at the end of which, Captain Auld, my master, to my surprise and utter astonishment, came up, and took me out, with the intention of sending me, with a gentleman of his acquaintance, into Alabama. But, from some cause or other, he did not send me to Alabama, but concluded to send me back to Baltimore, to live again with his brother Hugh, and to learn a trade.

Thus, after an absence of three years and one month, I was once more permitted to return to my old home at Baltimore. My master sent me away, because there existed against me a very great prejudice in the community, and he feared I might be killed.

In a few weeks after I went to Baltimore, Master Hugh hired me to Mr. William Gardner, an extensive ship-builder, on Fell's Point. I was put there to learn how to calk. It, however, proved a very unfavorable place for the accomplishment of this object. Mr. Gardner was engaged that spring in building two large man-of-war brigs, professedly for the Mexican government. The vessels were to be launched in the July of that year, and in failure thereof, Mr. Gardner was to lose a considerable sum; so that when I entered, all was hurry. There was no time to learn any thing. Every man had to do that which he knew how to do. In entering the ship-yard, my orders from Mr. Gardner were, to do whatever the carpenters commanded me to do. This was placing me at the beck and call of about seventy-five men. I was to regard all these as masters. Their word was to be my law. My situation was a most trying one. At times I needed a dozen pair of hands. I was called a dozen ways in the space of a single minute. Three or four voices would strike my ear at the same moment. It was—"Fred., come help me to cant this timber here."—"Fred., come carry this timber yonder."—"Fred., bring that roller here."—"Fred., go get a fresh can of water."—"Fred., come help saw off the end of this timber."—"Fred., go quick, and get the crowbar."—"Fred., hold on the end of this fall."—"Fred., go to the blacksmith's shop, and get a new punch."—"Hurra, Fred.! run and bring me a cold chisel."—"I say, Fred., bear a hand, and get up a fire as quick as lightning under that steam-box."—"Halloo, nigger! come, turn this grindstone."—"Come, come! move, move! and *bowse* this timber forward."—"I say, darky, blast your eyes, why don't you heat up some pitch?"—"Halloo! halloo! halloo!" (Three voices at the same time.) "Come here!—Go there!—Hold on where you are! Damn you, if you move, I'll knock your brains out!"

This was my school for eight months; and I might have

remained there longer, but for a most horrid fight I had with four of the white apprentices, in which my left eye was nearly knocked out, and I was horribly mangled in other respects. The facts in the case were these: Until a very little while after I went there, white and black ship-carpenters worked side by side, and no one seemed to see any impropriety in it. All hands seemed to be very well satisfied. Many of the black carpenters were freemen. Things seemed to be going on very well. All at once, the white carpenters knocked off, and said they would not work with free colored workmen. Their reason for this, as alleged, was, that if free colored carpenters were encouraged, they would soon take the trade into their own hands, and poor white men would be thrown out of employment. They therefore felt called upon at once to put a stop to it. And, taking advantage of Mr. Gardner's necessities, they broke off, swearing they would work no longer, unless he would discharge his black carpenters. Now, though this did not extend to me in form, it did reach me in fact. My fellow-apprentices very soon began to feel it degrading to them to work with me. They began to put on airs, and talk about the "niggers" taking the country, saying we all ought to be killed; and, being encouraged by the journeymen, they commenced making my condition as hard as they could, by hectoring me around, and sometimes striking me. I, of course, kept the vow I made after the fight with Mr. Covey, and struck back again, regardless of consequences; and while I kept them from combining, I succeeded very well; for I could whip the whole of them, taking them separately. They, however, at length combined, and came upon me, armed with sticks, stones, and heavy handspikes. One came in front with a half brick. There was one at each side of me, and one behind me. While I was attending to those in front, and on either side, the one behind ran up with the handspike, and struck me a heavy blow upon the head. It stunned me. I fell, and with this they all ran upon me, and fell to beating me with their fists. I let them lay on for a while, gathering strength. In an instant, I gave a sudden surge, and rose to my hands and knees. Just as I did that, one of their number gave me, with his heavy boot, a powerful kick in the left eye. My eyeball seemed to have burst. When they saw my eye closed, and badly swollen, they left me. With this I seized the handspike, and for a time pursued them. But here the carpenters interfered, and I thought I might as well give it up. It was impossible to stand my hand against so many. All this took place in sight of not less than fifty white ship-carpenters, and not one interposed a friendly word; but some cried, "Kill the damned nigger! Kill him! kill him! He struck a white person." I found my only chance for life was in flight. I succeeded in getting away without an additional blow, and barely so; for to strike a white man is death by Lynch law,—and that was the law in Mr. Gardner's ship-yard; nor is there much of any other out of Mr. Gardner's ship-yard.

I went directly home, and told the story of my wrongs to Master Hugh; and I am happy to say of him, irreligious as he was, his conduct was heavenly, compared with that of his brother Thomas under similar circumstances. He listened attentively to my narration of the circumstances leading to the savage outrage, and gave many proofs of his strong indignation at it. The heart of my once overkind mistress was again melted into pity. My puffed-out eye and blood-covered face moved her to tears. She took a chair by me, washed the blood from my face, and, with a mother's tenderness, bound up my head, covering the wounded eye with a lean piece of fresh beef. It was almost compensation for my suffering to witness, once more, a manifestation of kindness from this, my once affectionate old mistress. Master Hugh was very much enraged. He gave expression to his feelings by pouring out curses upon the heads of those who did the deed. As soon as I got a little the better of my bruises, he took me with him to Esquire Watson's, on Bond Street, to see what could be done about the matter. Mr. Watson inquired who saw the assault committed. Master Hugh told him it was done in Mr. Gardner's ship-yard, at midday, where there were a large company of men at work. "As to that," he said, "the deed was done, and there was no question as to who did it." His answer was, he could do nothing in the case, unless some white man would come forward and testify. He could issue no warrant on my word. If I had been killed in the presence of a thousand colored people, their testimony combined would have been insufficient to have arrested one of the murderers. Master Hugh, for once, was compelled to say this state of things was too bad. Of course, it was impossible to get any white man to volunteer his testimony in my behalf, and against the white young men. Even those who may have sympathized with me were not prepared to do this. It required a degree of courage unknown to them to do so; for just at that time, the slightest manifestation of humanity toward a colored person was denounced as abolitionism, and that name subjected its bearer to frightful liabilities. The watchwords of the bloody-minded in that region, and in those days, were, "Damn the abolitionists!" and "Damn the niggers!" There was nothing done, and probably nothing would have been done if I had been killed. Such was, and such remains, the state of things in the Christian city of Baltimore.

Master Hugh, finding he could get no redress, refused to let me go back again to Mr. Gardner. He kept me himself, and his wife dressed my wound till I was again restored to health. He then took me into the ship-yard of which he was foreman, in the employment of Mr. Walter Price. There I was immediately set to calking, and very soon learned the art of using my mallet and irons. In the course of one year from the time I left Mr. Gardner's, I was able to command the highest wages given to the most experienced calkers. I was now of some importance to my master. I was bringing him from six to seven dollars per week. I sometimes brought him nine dollars per week: my wages were a dollar and a half a day. After learning how to calk, I sought my own employment, made my own contracts, and collected the money which I earned. My pathway became much more smooth than before; my condition was now much more comfortable. When I could get no calking to do, I did nothing. During these leisure times, those old notions about freedom would steal over me again. When in Mr. Gardner's employment, I was kept in such a perpetual whirl of excitement, I could think of nothing, scarcely, but my life; and in thinking of my life, I almost forgot my liberty. I have observed this in my experience of slavery,—that whenever my condition was improved, instead of its increasing my contentment, it only increased my desire to be free, and set me to thinking of plans to gain my freedom. I have found that, to make a contented slave, it is necessary to make a thoughtless one. It is necessary to darken his moral and mental vision, and, as far as possible, to annihilate the power of reason. He must be able to detect no inconsistencies in slavery; he must be made to feel that slavery is right; and he can be brought to that only when he ceases to be a man.

I was now getting, as I have said, one dollar and fifty cents per day. I contracted for it; I earned it; it was paid to me; it was rightfully my own; yet, upon each returning Saturday night, I was compelled to deliver every cent of that money to Master Hugh. And why? Not because he earned it,—not because he had any hand in earning it,—not because I owed it to him,—nor because he possessed the slightest shadow of a right to it; but solely because he had the power to compel me to give it up. The right of the grim-visaged pirate upon the high seas is exactly the same.

CHAPTER XI.

I now come to that part of my life during which I planned, and finally succeeded in making, my escape from slavery. But before narrating any of the peculiar circumstances, I deem it proper to make known my intention not to state all the facts connected with the transaction. My reasons for pursuing this course may be understood from the following: First, were I to give a minute statement of all the facts, it is not only possible, but quite probable, that others would thereby be involved in the most embarrassing difficulties. Secondly, such a statement would most undoubtedly induce greater vigilance on the part of slaveholders than has existed heretofore among them; which would, of course, be the means of guarding a door whereby some dear brother bondman might escape his galling chains. I deeply regret the necessity that impels me to suppress any thing of importance connected with my experience in slavery. It would afford me great pleasure indeed, as well as materially add to the interest of my narrative, were I at liberty to gratify a curiosity, which I know exists in the minds of many, by an accurate statement of all the facts pertaining to my most fortunate escape. But I must deprive myself of this pleasure, and the curious of the gratification which such a statement would afford. I would allow myself to suffer under the greatest imputations which evil-minded men might suggest, rather than exculpate myself, and thereby run the hazard of closing the slightest avenue by which a brother slave might clear himself of the chains and fetters of slavery.

I have never approved of the very public manner in which some of our western friends have conducted what they call the *underground railroad*, but which, I think, by their open declarations, has been made most emphatically the *upperground railroad*. I honor those good men and women for their noble daring, and applaud them for willingly subjecting themselves to bloody persecution, by openly avowing their participation in the escape of slaves. I, however, can see very little good resulting from such a course, either to themselves or the slaves escaping; while, upon the other hand, I see and feel assured that those open declarations are a positive evil to the slaves remaining, who are seeking to escape. They do nothing towards enlightening the slave, whilst they do much towards enlightening the master. They stimulate him to greater watchfulness, and enhance his power to capture his slave. We owe something to the slaves south of the line as well as to those north of it; and in aiding the latter on their way to freedom, we should be careful to do nothing which would be likely to hinder the former from escaping from slavery. I would keep the merciless slaveholder profoundly ignorant of the means of flight adopted by the slave. I would leave him to imagine himself surrounded by myriads of invisible tormentors, ever ready to snatch from his infernal grasp his trembling prey. Let him be left to feel his way in the dark; let darkness commensurate with his crime hover over him; and let him feel that at every step he takes, in pursuit of the flying bondman, he is running the frightful risk of having his hot brains dashed out by an invisible agency. Let us render the tyrant no aid; let us not hold the light by which he can trace the footprints of our flying brother. But enough of this. I will now proceed to the statement of those facts, connected with my escape, for which I am alone responsible, and for which no one can be made to suffer but myself.

In the early part of the year 1838, I became quite restless. I could see no reason why I should, at the end of each week, pour the reward of my toil into the purse of my master. When I carried to him my weekly wages, he would, after counting the money, look me in the face with a robber-like fierceness, and ask, "Is this all?" He was satisfied with nothing less than the last cent. He would, however, when I made him six dollars, sometimes give me six cents, to encourage me. It had the opposite effect. I regarded it as a sort of admission of my right to the whole. The fact that he gave me any part of my wages was proof, to my mind, that he believed me entitled to the whole of them. I always felt worse for having received any thing; for I feared that the giving me a few cents would ease his conscience, and make him feel himself to be a pretty honorable sort of robber. My discontent grew upon me. I was ever on the look-out for means of escape; and, finding no direct means, I determined to try to hire my time, with a view of getting money with which to make my escape. In the spring of 1838, when Master Thomas came to Baltimore to purchase his spring goods, I got an opportunity, and applied to him to allow me to hire my time. He unhesitatingly refused my request, and told me this was another stratagem by which to escape. He told me I could go nowhere but that he could get me; and that, in the event of my running away, he should spare no pains in his efforts to catch me. He exhorted me to content myself, and be obedient. He told me, if I would be happy, I must lay out no plans for the future. He said, if I behaved myself properly, he would take care of me. Indeed, he advised me to complete thoughtlessness of the future, and taught me to depend solely upon him for happiness. He seemed to see fully the pressing necessity of setting aside my intellectual nature, in order to contentment in slavery. But in spite of him, and even in spite of myself, I continued to think, and to think about the injustice of my enslavement, and the means of escape.

About two months after this, I applied to Master Hugh for the privilege of hiring my time. He was not acquainted with the fact that I had applied to Master Thomas, and had been refused. He too, at first, seemed disposed to refuse; but, after some reflection, he granted me the privilege, and proposed the following terms: I was to be allowed all my time, make all contracts with those for whom I worked, and find my own employment; and, in return for this liberty, I was to pay him three dollars at the end of each week; find myself in calking tools, and in board and clothing. My board was two dollars and a half per week. This, with the wear and tear of clothing and calking tools, made my regular expenses about six dollars per week. This amount I was compelled to make up, or relinquish the privilege of hiring my time. Rain or shine, work or no work, at the end of each week the money must be forthcoming, or I must give up my privilege. This arrangement, it will be perceived, was decidedly in my master's favor. It relieved him of all need of looking after me. His money was sure. He received all the benefits of slaveholding without its evils; while I endured all the evils of a slave, and suffered all the care and anxiety of a freeman. I found it a hard bargain. But, hard as it was, I thought it better than the old mode of getting along. It was a step towards freedom to be allowed to bear the responsibilities of a freeman, and I was determined to hold on upon it. I bent myself to the work of making money. I was ready to work at night as well as day, and by the most untiring perseverance and industry, I made enough to meet my expenses, and lay up a little money every week. I went on thus from May till August. Master Hugh then refused to allow me to hire my time longer. The ground for his refusal was a failure on my part, one Saturday night, to pay him for my week's time. This failure was occasioned by my attending a camp meeting about ten miles from Baltimore. During the week, I had entered into an engagement with a number of young friends to start from Baltimore to the camp ground early Saturday evening; and being detained by my employer, I was unable to get down to Master Hugh's without disappointing the company. I knew that Master Hugh was in no special need of the money that night. I therefore decided to go to camp meeting, and upon my return pay him the three dollars. I staid at the camp meeting one day longer than I intended when I left. But as soon as I returned, I called upon him to pay him what he considered his due. I found him very angry; he could scarce restrain his wrath. He said he had a great mind to give me a severe whipping. He wished to know how I dared go out of the city without asking his permission. I told him I hired my time, and while I paid him the price which he asked for it, I did not know that I was bound to ask him when and where I should go. This reply troubled him; and, after reflecting a few moments, he turned to me, and said I should hire my time no longer; that the next thing he should know of, I would be running away. Upon the same plea, he told me to bring my tools and clothing home forthwith. I did so; but instead of seeking work, as I had been accustomed to do previously to hiring my time, I spent the whole week without the performance of a single stroke of work. I did this in retaliation. Saturday night, he called upon me as usual for my week's wages. I told him I had no wages; I had done no work that week. Here we were upon the point of coming to blows. He raved, and swore his determination to get hold of me. I did not allow myself a single word; but was resolved, if he laid the weight of his hand upon me, it should be blow for blow. He did not strike me, but told me that he would find me in constant employment in future. I thought the matter over during the next day, Sunday, and finally resolved upon the third day of September, as the day upon which I would make a second attempt to secure my freedom. I now had three weeks during which to prepare for my journey. Early on Monday morning, before Master Hugh had time to make any engagement for me, I went out and got employment of Mr. Butler, at his ship-yard near the drawbridge, upon what is called the City Block, thus making it unnecessary for him to seek employment for me. At the end of the week, I brought him between eight and nine dollars. He seemed very well pleased, and asked me why I did not do the same the week before. He little knew what my plans were. My object in working steadily was to remove any suspicion he might entertain of my intent to run away; and in this I succeeded admirably. I suppose he thought I was never better satisfied with my condition than at the very time during which I was planning my escape. The second week passed, and again I carried him my full wages; and so well pleased was he, that he gave me twenty-five cents, (quite a large sum for a slaveholder to give a slave,) and bade me to make a good use of it. I told him I would.

Things went on without very smoothly indeed, but within there was trouble. It is impossible for me to describe my feelings as the time of my contemplated start drew near. I had a number of warm-hearted friends in Baltimore,—friends that I loved almost as I did my life,—and the thought of being separated from them forever was painful beyond expression. It is my opinion that thousands would escape from slavery, who now remain, but for the strong cords of affection that bind them to their friends. The thought of leaving my friends was decidedly the most painful thought with which I had to contend. The love of them was my tender point, and shook my decision more than all things else. Besides the pain of separation, the dread and apprehension of a failure exceeded what I had experienced at my first attempt. The appalling defeat I then sustained returned to torment me. I felt assured that, if I failed in this attempt, my case would be a hopeless one—it would seal my fate as a slave forever. I could not hope to get off with any thing less than the severest punishment, and being placed beyond the means of escape. It required no very vivid imagination to depict the most frightful scenes through which I should have to pass, in case I failed. The wretchedness of slavery, and the blessedness of freedom, were perpetually before me. It was life and death with me. But I remained firm, and, according to my resolution, on the third day of September, 1838, I left my chains, and succeeded in reaching New York without the slightest interruption of any kind. How I did so,—what means I adopted,—what direction I travelled, and by what mode of conveyance,—I must leave unexplained, for the reasons before mentioned.

I have been frequently asked how I felt when I found myself in a free State. I have never been able to answer the question with any satisfaction to myself. It was a moment of the highest excitement I ever experienced. I suppose I felt as one may imagine the unarmed mariner to feel when he is rescued by a friendly man-of-war from the pursuit of a pirate. In writing to a dear friend, immediately after my arrival at New York, I said I felt like one who had escaped a den of hungry lions. This state of mind, however, very soon subsided; and I was again seized with a feeling of great insecurity and loneliness. I was yet liable to be taken back, and subjected to all the tortures of slavery. This in itself was enough to damp the ardor of my enthusiasm. But the loneliness overcame me. There I was in the midst of thousands, and yet a perfect stranger; without home and without friends, in the midst of thousands of my own brethren—children of a common Father, and yet I dared not to unfold to any one of them my sad condition. I was afraid to speak to any one for fear of speaking to the wrong one, and thereby falling into the hands of money-loving kidnappers, whose business it was to lie in wait for the panting fugitive, as the ferocious beasts of the forest lie in wait for their prey. The motto which I adopted when I started from slavery was this—"Trust no man!" I saw in every white man an enemy, and in almost every colored man cause for distrust. It was a most painful situation; and, to understand it, one must needs experience it, or imagine himself in similar circumstances. Let him be a fugitive slave in a strange land—a land given up to be the hunting-ground for slaveholders—whose inhabitants are legalized kidnappers—where he is every moment subjected to the terrible liability of being seized upon by his fellow-men, as the hideous crocodile seizes upon his prey!—I say, let him place himself in my situation—without home or friends—without money or credit—wanting shelter, and no one to give it—wanting bread, and no money to buy it,—and at the same time let him feel that he is pursued by merciless men-hunters, and in total darkness as to what to do, where to go, or where to stay,—perfectly helpless both as to the means of defence and means of escape,—in the midst of plenty, yet suffering the terrible gnawings of hunger,—in the midst of houses, yet having no home,—among fellow-men, yet feeling as if in the midst of wild beasts, whose greediness to swallow up the trembling and half-famished fugitive is only equalled by that with which the monsters of the deep swallow up the helpless fish upon which they subsist,—I say, let him be placed in this most trying situation,—the situation in which I was placed,—then, and not till then, will he fully appreciate the hardships of, and know how to sympathize with, the toil-worn and whip-scarred fugitive slave.

Thank Heaven, I remained but a short time in this distressed situation. I was relieved from it by the humane hand of Mr. DAVID RUGGLES,[8] whose vigilance, kindness, and perseverance, I shall never forget. I am glad of an opportunity to express, as far as words can, the love and gratitude I bear him. Mr. Ruggles is now afflicted with blindness, and is himself in need of the same kind offices which he was once so forward in the performance of toward others. I had been in New York but a few days, when Mr. Ruggles sought me out, and very kindly took me to his boarding-house at the corner of Church and Lespenard Streets. Mr. Ruggles was then very deeply engaged in the memorable *Darg* case,[9] as well as attending to a number of other fugitive slaves, devising ways and means for their successful escape; and, though watched and hemmed in on almost every side, he seemed to be more than a match for his enemies.

Very soon after I went to Mr. Ruggles, he wished to know of me where I wanted to go; as he deemed it unsafe for me to remain in New York. I told him I was a calker, and should like to go where I could get work. I thought of going to Canada; but he decided against it, and in favor of my going to New Bedford, thinking I should be able to get work there at my trade. At this time, Anna,* my intended wife, came on; for I wrote to her immediately after my arrival at New York, (notwithstanding my homeless, houseless, and helpless condition,) informing her of my successful flight, and wishing her to come on forthwith. In a few days after her arrival, Mr. Ruggles called in the Rev. J. W. C. Pennington,[10] who, in the presence of Mr. Ruggles, Mrs. Michaels, and two or three others, performed the marriage ceremony, and gave us a certificate, of which the following is an exact copy:—

> "THIS may certify, that I joined together in holy matrimony Frederick Johnson† and Anna Murray, as man and wife, in the presence of Mr. David Ruggles and Mrs. Michaels.
>
> "JAMES W. C. PENNINGTON.
>
> "*New York, Sept.* 15, 1838."

Upon receiving this certificate, and a five-dollar bill from Mr. Ruggles, I shouldered one part of our baggage, and Anna took up the other, and we set out forthwith to take passage on board of the steamboat John W. Richmond for Newport, on our way to New Bedford. Mr. Ruggles gave me a letter to a Mr. Shaw in Newport, and told me, in case my money did not serve me to New Bedford, to stop in Newport and obtain further assistance; but upon our arrival at Newport, we were so anxious to get to a place of safety, that, notwithstanding we lacked the necessary money to pay our fare, we decided to take seats in the stage, and promise to pay when we got to New Bedford. We were encouraged to do this by two excellent gentlemen, residents of New

* She was free.

† I had changed my name from Frederick *Bailey* to that of *Johnson*.

Bedford, whose names I afterward ascertained to be Joseph Ricketson and William C. Taber. They seemed at once to understand our circumstances, and gave us such assurance of their friendliness as put us fully at ease in their presence. It was good indeed to meet with such friends, at such a time. Upon reaching New Bedford, we were directed to the house of Mr. Nathan Johnson, by whom we were kindly received, and hospitably provided for. Both Mr. and Mrs. Johnson took a deep and lively interest in our welfare. They proved themselves quite worthy of the name of abolitionists. When the stage-driver found us unable to pay our fare, he held on upon our baggage as security for the debt. I had but to mention the fact to Mr. Johnson, and he forthwith advanced the money.

We now began to feel a degree of safety, and to prepare ourselves for the duties and responsibilities of a life of freedom. On the morning after our arrival at New Bedford, while at the breakfast-table, the question arose as to what name I should be called by. The name given me by my mother was, "Frederick Augustus Washington Bailey." I, however, had dispensed with the two middle names long before I left Maryland, so that I was generally known by the name of "Frederick Bailey." I started from Baltimore bearing the name of "Stanley." When I got to New York, I again changed my name to "Frederick Johnson," and thought that would be the last change. But when I got to New Bedford, I found it necessary again to change my name. The reason of this necessity was, that there were so many Johnsons in New Bedford, it was already quite difficult to distinguish between them. I gave Mr. Johnson the privilege of choosing me a name, but told him he must not take from me the name of "Frederick." I must hold on to that, to preserve a sense of my identity. Mr. Johnson had just been reading the "Lady of the Lake," and at once suggested that my name be "Douglass."[11] From that time until now I have been called "Frederick Douglass;" and as I am more widely known by that name than by either of the others, I shall continue to use it as my own.

I was quite disappointed at the general appearance of things in New Bedford. The impression which I had received respecting the character and condition of the people of the north, I found to be singularly erroneous. I had very strangely supposed, while in slavery, that few of the comforts, and scarcely any of the luxuries, of life were enjoyed at the north, compared with what were enjoyed by the slaveholders of the south. I probably came to this conclusion from the fact that northern people owned no slaves. I supposed that they were about upon a level with the non-slaveholding population of the south. I knew *they* were exceedingly poor, and I had been accustomed to regard their poverty as the necessary consequence of their being non-slaveholders. I had somehow imbibed the opinion that, in the absence of slaves, there could be no wealth, and very little refinement. And upon coming to the north, I expected to meet with a rough, hard-handed, and uncultivated population, living in the most Spartan-like simplicity, knowing nothing of the ease, luxury, pomp, and grandeur of southern slaveholders. Such being my conjectures, any one acquainted with the appearance of New Bedford may very readily infer how palpably I must have seen my mistake.

In the afternoon of the day when I reached New Bedford, I visited the wharves, to take a view of the shipping. Here I found myself surrounded with the strongest proofs of wealth. Lying at the wharves, and riding in the stream, I saw many ships of the finest model, in the best order, and of the largest size. Upon the right and left, I was walled in by granite warehouses of the widest dimensions, stowed to their utmost capacity with the necessaries and comforts of life. Added to this, almost every body seemed to be at work, but noiselessly so, compared with what I had been accustomed to in Baltimore. There were no loud songs heard from those engaged in loading and unloading ships. I heard no deep oaths or horrid curses on the laborer. I saw no whipping of men; but all seemed to go smoothly on. Every man appeared to understand his work, and went at it with a sober, yet cheerful earnestness, which betokened the deep interest which he felt in what he was doing, as well as a sense of his own dignity as a man. To me this looked exceedingly strange. From the wharves I strolled around and over the town, gazing with wonder and admiration at the splendid churches, beautiful dwellings, and finely-cultivated gardens; evincing an amount of wealth, comfort, taste, and refinement, such as I had never seen in any part of slaveholding Maryland.

Every thing looked clean, new, and beautiful. I saw few or no dilapidated houses, with poverty-stricken inmates; no half-naked children and barefooted women, such as I had been accustomed to see in Hillsborough, Easton, St. Michael's, and Baltimore. The people looked more able, stronger, healthier, and happier, than those of Maryland. I was for once made glad by a view of extreme wealth, without being saddened by seeing extreme poverty. But the most astonishing as well as the most interesting thing to me was the condition of the colored people, a great many of whom, like myself, had escaped thither as a refuge from the hunters of men. I found many, who had not been seven years out of their chains, living in finer houses, and evidently enjoying more of the comforts of life, than the average of slaveholders in Maryland. I will venture to assert that my friend Mr. Nathan Johnson (of whom I can say with a grateful heart, "I was hungry, and he gave me meat; I was thirsty, and he gave me drink; I was a stranger, and he took me in"[12]) lived in a neater house; dined at a better table; took, paid for, and read, more newspapers; better understood the moral, religious, and political character of the nation,—than nine tenths of the slaveholders in Talbot county Maryland. Yet Mr. Johnson was a working man. His hands were hardened by toil, and not his alone, but those also of Mrs. Johnson. I found the colored people much more spirited than I had supposed they would be. I found among them a determination to protect each other from the blood-thirsty kidnapper, at all hazards. Soon after my arrival, I was told of a circumstance which illustrated their spirit. A colored man and a fugitive slave were on unfriendly terms. The former was heard to threaten the latter with informing his master of his whereabouts. Straightway a meeting was called among the colored people, under the stereotyped notice, "Business of importance!" The betrayer was invited to attend. The people came at the appointed hour, and organized the meeting by appointing a very religious old gentleman as president, who, I believe, made a prayer, after which he addressed the meeting as follows: "*Friends, we have got him here, and I would recommend that you young men just take him outside the door, and kill him!*" With this, a number of them bolted at him; but they were intercepted by some more timid than themselves, and the betrayer escaped their vengeance, and has not been seen in New Bedford since. I believe there have been no more such threats, and should there be hereafter, I doubt not that death would be the consequence.

I found employment, the third day after my arrival, in stowing a sloop with a load of oil. It was new, dirty, and hard work for me; but I went at it with a glad heart and a willing hand. I was now my own master. It was a happy moment, the rapture of which can be understood only by those who have been slaves. It was the first work, the reward of which was to be entirely my own. There was no Master Hugh standing ready, the moment I earned the money, to rob me of it. I worked that day with a pleasure I had never before experienced. I was at work for myself and newly-married wife. It was to me the starting-point of a new existence. When I got through with that job, I went in pursuit of a job of calking; but such was the strength of prejudice against color, among the white calkers, that they refused to work with me, and of course I could get no employment.* Finding my trade of no immediate benefit, I threw off my calking habiliments, and prepared myself to do any kind of work I could get to do. Mr. Johnson kindly let me have his wood-horse and saw, and I very soon found myself a plenty of work. There was no work too hard—none too dirty. I was ready to saw wood, shovel coal, carry the hod, sweep the chimney, or roll oil casks,—all of which I did for nearly three years in New Bedford, before I became known to the anti-slavery world.

In about four months after I went to New Bedford, there came a young man to me, and inquired if I did not wish to take the "Liberator." I told him I did; but, just having made my escape from slavery, I remarked that I was unable to pay for it then. I, however, finally became a subscriber to it. The paper came, and I read it from week to week with such feelings as it would be quite idle for me to attempt to describe. The paper became my meat and my drink. My soul was set all on fire. Its sympathy for my brethren in bonds—its scathing denunciations of slaveholders—its faithful exposures of slavery—and its powerful attacks upon the upholders of the institution—sent a thrill of joy through my soul, such as I had never felt before!

* I am told that colored persons can now get employment at calking in New Bedford—a result of anti-slavery effort.

I had not long been a reader of the "Liberator," before I got a pretty correct idea of the principles, measures and spirit of the anti-slavery reform. I took right hold of the cause. I could do but little; but what I could, I did with a joyful heart, and never felt happier than when in an anti-slavery meeting. I seldom had much to say at the meetings, because what I wanted to say was said so much better by others. But, while attending an anti-slavery convention at Nantucket, on the 11th of August, 1841, I felt strongly moved to speak, and was at the same time much urged to do so by Mr. William C. Coffin, a gentleman who had heard me speak in the colored people's meeting at New Bedford. It was a severe cross, and I took it up reluctantly. The truth was, I felt myself a slave, and the idea of speaking to white people weighed me down. I spoke but a few moments, when I felt a degree of freedom, and said what I desired with considerable ease. From that time until now, I have been engaged in pleading the cause of my brethren—with what success, and with what devotion, I leave those acquainted with my labors to decide.

APPENDIX.

I find, since reading over the foregoing Narrative that I have, in several instances, spoken in such a tone and manner, respecting religion, as may possibly lead those unacquainted with my religious views to suppose me an opponent of all religion. To remove the liability of such misapprehension, I deem it proper to append the following brief explanation. What I have said respecting and against religion, I mean strictly to apply to the *slaveholding religion* of this land, and with no possible reference to Christianity proper; for, between the Christianity of this land, and the Christianity of Christ, I recognize the widest possible difference—so wide, that to receive the one as good, pure, and holy, is of necessity to reject the other as bad, corrupt, and wicked. To be the friend of the one, is of necessity to be the enemy of the other. I love the pure, peaceable, and impartial Christianity of Christ: I therefore hate the corrupt, slaveholding, women-whipping, cradle-plundering, partial and hypocritical Christianity of this land.

Indeed, I can see no reason, but the most deceitful one, for calling the religion of this land Christianity. I look upon it as the climax of all misnomers, the boldest of all frauds, and the grossest of all libels. Never was there a clearer case of "stealing the livery of the court of heaven to serve the devil in." I am filled with unutterable loathing when I contemplate the religious pomp and show, together with the horrible inconsistencies, which every where surround me. We have men-stealers for ministers, women-whippers for missionaries, and cradle-plunderers for church members. The man who wields the blood-clotted cowskin during the week fills the pulpit on Sunday, and claims to be a minister of the meek and lowly Jesus. The man who robs me of my earnings at the end of each week meets me as a class-leader on Sunday morning, to show me the way of life, and the path of salvation. He who sells my sister, for purposes of prostitution, stands forth as the pious advocate of purity. He who proclaims it a religious duty to read the Bible denies me the right of learning to read the name of the God who made me. He who is the religious advocate of marriage robs whole millions of its sacred influence, and leaves them to the ravages of wholesale pollution. The warm defender of the sacredness of the family relation is the same that scatters whole families,—sundering husbands and wives, parents and children, sisters and brothers,—leaving the hut vacant, and the hearth desolate. We see the thief preaching against theft, and the adulterer against adultery. We have men sold to build churches, women sold to support the gospel, and babes sold to purchase Bibles for the *poor heathen! all for the glory of God and the good of souls!* The slave auctioneer's bell and the church-going bell chime in with each other, and the bitter cries of the heart-broken slave are drowned in the religious shouts of his pious master. Revivals of religion and revivals in the slave-trade go hand in hand together. The slave prison and the church stand near each other. The clanking of fetters and the rattling of chains in the prison, and the pious psalm and solemn prayer in the church, may be heard at the same time. The dealers in the bodies and souls of men erect their stand in the presence of the pulpit, and they mutually help each other. The dealer gives his blood-stained gold to support the pulpit, and the pulpit, in return, covers his infernal business with the garb of Christianity. Here we have religion and robbery the allies of each other—devils dressed in angels' robes, and hell presenting the semblance of paradise.

"Just God! and these are they,
  Who minister at thine altar, God of right!
Men who their hands, with prayer and blessing, lay
  On Israel's ark of light.

"What! preach, and kidnap men?
  Give thanks, and rob thy own afflicted poor?
Talk of thy glorious liberty, and then
  Bolt hard the captive's door?

"What! servants of thy own
  Merciful Son, who came to seek and save
The homeless and the outcast, fettering down
  The tasked and plundered slave!

"Pilate and Herod friends!
  Chief priests and rulers, as of old, combine!
Just God and holy! is that church which lends
  Strength to the spoiler thine?"

The Christianity of America is a Christianity, of whose votaries it may be as truly said, as it was of the ancient scribes and Pharisees, "They bind heavy burdens, and grievous to be borne, and lay them on men's shoulders, but they themselves will not move them with one of their fingers. All their works they do for to be seen of men.——They love the uppermost rooms at feasts, and the chief seats in the synagogues, ... and to be called of men, Rabbi, Rabbi.——But woe unto you, scribes and Pharisees, hypocrites! for ye shut up the kingdom of heaven against men; for ye neither go in yourselves, neither suffer ye them that are entering to go in. Ye devour widows' houses, and for a pretence make long prayers; therefore ye shall receive the greater damnation. Ye compass sea and land to make one proselyte, and when he is made, ye make him twofold more the child of hell than yourselves.——Woe unto you, scribes and Pharisees, hypocrites! for ye pay tithe of mint, and anise, and cumin, and have omitted the weightier matters of the law, judgment, mercy, and faith; these ought ye to have done, and not to leave the other undone. Ye blind guides! which strain at a gnat, and swallow a camel. Woe unto you, scribes and Pharisees, hypocrites! for ye make clean the outside of the cup and of the platter; but within, they are full of extortion and excess.——Woe unto you, scribes and Pharisees, hypocrites! for ye are like unto whited sepulchres, which indeed appear beautiful outward, but are within full of dead men's bones, and of all uncleanness. Even so ye also outwardly appear righteous unto men, but within ye are full of hypocrisy and iniquity."

Dark and terrible as is this picture, I hold it to be strictly true of the overwhelming mass of professed Christians in America. They strain at a gnat, and swallow a camel. Could any thing be more true of our churches? They would be shocked at the proposition of fellowshipping a *sheep*-stealer; and at the same time they hug to their communion a *man*-stealer, and brand me with being an infidel, if I find fault with them for it. They attend with Pharisaical strictness to the outward forms of religion, and at the same time neglect the weightier matters of the law, judgment, mercy, and faith. They are always ready to sacrifice, but seldom to show mercy. They are they who are represented as professing to love God whom they have not seen, whilst they hate their brother whom they have seen. They love the heathen on the other side of the globe. They can pray for him, pay money to have the Bible put into his hand, and missionaries to instruct him; while they despise and totally neglect the heathen at their own doors.

Such is, very briefly, my view of the religion of this land; and to avoid any misunderstanding, growing out of the use of general terms, I mean, by the religion of this land, that which is revealed in the words, deeds, and actions, of those bodies, north and south, calling themselves Christian churches, and yet in union with slaveholders. It is against religion, as presented by these bodies, that I have felt it my duty to testify.

I conclude these remarks by copying the following portrait of the religion of the south, (which is, by communion and fellowship, the religion of the north,) which I soberly affirm is "true to the life," and without caricature or the slightest exaggeration. It is said to have been drawn, several years before the present anti-slavery agitation began, by a northern Methodist preacher, who, while residing at the south, had an opportunity to see slaveholding morals, manners, and piety, with his own eyes. "Shall I not visit for these things? saith the Lord. Shall not my soul be avenged on such a nation as this?"[13]

"A PARODY.[14]

"Come, saints and sinners, hear me tell
How pious priests whip Jack and Nell,
And women buy and children sell,
And preach all sinners down to hell,
  And sing of heavenly union.

"They'll bleat and baa, dona like goats,
Gorge down black sheep, and strain at motes,
Array their backs in fine black coats,
Then seize their negroes by their throats,
  And choke, for heavenly union.

"They'll church you if you sip a dram,
And damn you if you steal a lamb;
Yet rob old Tony, Doll, and Sam,
Of human rights, and bread and ham;
  Kidnapper's heavenly union.

"They'll loudly talk of Christ's reward,
And bind his image with a cord,
And scold, and swing the lash abhorred,
And sell their brother in the Lord
  To handcuffed heavenly union.

"They'll read and sing a sacred song,
And make a prayer both loud and long,
And teach the right and do the wrong,
Hailing the brother, sister throng,
  With words of heavenly union.

"We wonder how such saints can sing,
Or praise the Lord upon the wing,
Who roar, and scold, and whip, and sting,
And to their slaves and mammon cling,
  In guilty conscience union.

"They'll raise tobacco, corn, and rye,
And drive, and thieve, and cheat, and lie,
And lay up treasures in the sky,
By making switch and cowskin fly,
  In hope of heavenly union.

"They'll crack old Tony on the skull,
And preach and roar like Bashan bull,
Or braying ass, of mischief full,
Then seize old Jacob by the wool,
  And pull for heavenly union.

"A roaring, ranting, sleek man-thief,
Who lived on mutton, veal, and beef,
Yet never would afford relief
To needy, sable sons of grief,
  Was big with heavenly union.

"'Love not the world,' the preacher said,
And winked his eye, and shook his head;
He seized on Tom, and Dick, and Ned,
Cut short their meat, and clothes, and bread,
  Yet still loved heavenly union.

"Another preacher whining spoke
Of One whose heart for sinners broke:
He tied old Nanny to an oak,
And drew the blood at every stroke,
  And prayed for heavenly union.

"Two others oped their iron jaws,
And waved their children-stealing paws;

There sat their children in gewgaws;
By stinting negroes' backs and maws,
  They kept up heavenly union.

"All good from Jack another takes,
And entertains their flirts and rakes,
Who dress as sleek as glossy snakes,
And cram their mouths with sweetened cakes;
  And this goes down for union."

Sincerely and earnestly hoping that this little book may do something toward throwing light on the American slave system, and hastening the glad day of deliverance to the millions of my brethren in bonds—faithfully relying upon the power of truth, love, and justice, for success in my humble efforts—and solemnly pledging my self anew to the sacred cause,—I subscribe myself,

FREDERICK DOUGLASS.
LYNN, *Mass., April 28, 1845.*

THE END.

FROM *MY BONDAGE AND MY FREEDOM* (1855)

This is the most intellectual, psychological, and radical of Douglass's three autobiographies. In these three chapters taken from the book's second part, Life as a Freeman, he describes his transition to freedom, his early antislavery work, and the scourge of American racism in contrast with its dearth in the British Isles.

SOURCE: *My Bondage and My Freedom* (New York and Auburn, New York: Miller, Orton & Mulligan, 1855)

CHAPTER XXII.

LIBERTY ATTAINED.

TRANSITION FROM SLAVERY TO FREEDOM—A WANDERER IN NEW YORK—FEELINGS ON REACHING THAT CITY—AN OLD ACQUAINTANCE MET—UNFAVORABLE IMPRESSIONS—LONELINESS AND INSECURITY—APOLOGY FOR SLAVES WHO RETURN TO THEIR MASTERS—COMPELLED TO TELL MY CONDITION—SUCCORED BY A SAILOR—DAVID RUGGLES—THE UNDER-GROUND RAILROAD—MARRIAGE—BAGGAGE TAKEN FROM ME—KINDNESS OF NATHAN JOHNSON—THE AUTHOR'S CHANGE OF NAME—DARK NOTIONS OF NORTHERN CIVILIZATION—THE CONTRAST—COLORED PEOPLE IN NEW BEDFORD—AN INCIDENT ILLUSTRATING THEIR SPIRIT—THE AUTHOR AS A COMMON LABORER—DENIED WORK AT HIS TRADE—THE FIRST WINTER AT THE NORTH—REPULSE AT THE DOORS OF THE CHURCH—SANCTIFIED HATE—THE LIBERATOR AND ITS EDITOR.

There is no necessity for any extended notice of the incidents of this part of my life. There is nothing very striking or peculiar about my career as a freeman, when viewed apart from my life as a slave. The relation subsisting between my early experience and that which I am now about to narrate, is, perhaps, my best apology for adding another chapter to this book.

Disappearing from the kind reader, in a flying cloud or balloon, (pardon the figure,) driven by the wind, and knowing not where I should land—whether in slavery or in freedom—it is proper that I should remove, at once, all anxiety, by frankly making known where I alighted. The flight was a bold and perilous one; but here I am, in the great city of New York, safe and sound, without loss of blood or bone. In less than a week after leaving Baltimore, I was walking amid the hurrying throng, and gazing upon the dazzling wonders of Broadway. The dreams of my childhood and the purposes of my manhood were now fulfilled. A free state around me, and a free earth under my feet! What a moment was this to me! A whole year was pressed into a single day. A new world burst upon my agitated vision. I have often been asked, by kind friends to whom I have told my story, how I felt when first I found myself beyond the limits of slavery; and I must say here, as I have often said to them, there is scarcely anything about which I could not give a more satisfactory answer. It was a moment of joyous excitement, which no words can describe. In a letter to a friend, written soon after reaching New York, I said I felt as one might be supposed to feel, on escaping from a den of hungry lions. But, in a moment like that, sensations are too intense and too rapid for words. Anguish and grief, like darkness and rain, may be described, but joy and gladness, like the rainbow of promise, defy alike the pen and pencil.

For ten or fifteen years I had been dragging a heavy chain, with a huge block attached to it, cumbering my every motion. I had felt myself doomed to drag this chain and this block through life. All efforts, before, to separate myself from the hateful encumbrance, had only seemed to rivet me the more firmly to it. Baffled and discouraged at times, I had asked myself the question, May not this, after all, be God's work? May He not, for wise ends, have doomed me to this lot? A contest had been going on in my mind for years, between the clear consciousness of right and the plausible errors of superstition; between the wisdom of manly courage, and the foolish weakness of timidity. The contest was now ended; the chain was severed; God and right stood vindicated. I WAS A FREEMAN, and the voice of peace and joy thrilled my heart.

Free and joyous, however, as I was, joy was not the only sensation I experienced. It was like the quick blaze, beautiful at the first, but which subsiding, leaves the building charred and desolate. I was soon taught that I was still in an enemy's land. A sense of loneliness and insecurity oppressed me sadly. I had been but a few hours in New York, before I was met in the streets by a fugitive slave, well known to me, and the information I got from him respecting New York, did nothing to lessen my apprehension of danger. The fugitive in question was "Allender's Jake," in Baltimore; but, said he, I am "WILLIAM DIXON," in New York![1] I knew Jake well, and knew when Tolly Allender and Mr. Price (for the latter employed Master Hugh as his foreman, in his shipyard on Fell's Point) made an attempt to recapture Jake, and failed. Jake told me all about his circumstances, and how narrowly he escaped being taken back to slavery; that the city was now full of southerners, returning from the springs; that the black people in New York were not to be trusted; that there were hired men on the lookout for fugitives from slavery, and who, for a few dollars, would betray me into the hands of the slave-catchers; that I must trust no man with my secret; that I must not think of going either on the wharves to work, or to a boarding-house to board; and, worse still, this same Jake told me it was not in his power to help me. He seemed, even while cautioning me, to be fearing lest, after all, I might be a party to a second attempt to recapture him. Under the inspiration of his thought, I must suppose it was, he gave signs of a wish to get rid of me, and soon left me—his whitewash brush in hand—as he said, for his work. He was soon lost to sight among the throng, and I was alone again, an easy prey to the kidnappers, if any should happen to be on my track.

New York, seventeen years ago, was less a place of safety for a runaway slave than now, and all know how unsafe it now is, under the new fugitive slave bill. I was much troubled. I had very little money—enough to buy me a few loaves of bread, but not enough to pay board, outside a lumber yard. I saw the wisdom of keeping away from the ship yards, for if Master Hugh pursued me, he would naturally expect to find me looking for work among the calkers. For a time, every door seemed closed against me. A sense of my loneliness and helplessness crept over me, and covered me with something bordering on despair. In the midst of thousands of my fellowmen, and yet a perfect stranger! In the midst of human brothers, and yet more fearful of them than of hungry wolves! I was without home, without friends, without work, without money, and without any definite knowledge of which way to go, or where to look for succor.

Some apology can easily be made for the few slaves who have, after making good their escape, turned back to slavery, preferring the actual rule of their masters, to the life of loneliness, apprehension, hunger, and anxiety, which meets them on their first arrival in a free state. It is difficult for a freeman to enter into the feelings of such fugitives. He cannot see things in the same light with the slave, because he does not, and cannot, look from the same point from which the slave does. "Why do you tremble," he says to the slave—"you are in a free state;" but the difficulty is, in realizing that he is in a free state, the slave might reply. A freeman cannot understand why the slave-master's shadow is bigger, to the slave, than the might and majesty of a free state; but when he reflects that the slave knows more about the slavery of his master than he does of the might and majesty of the free state, he has the explanation. The slave has been all his life learning the power of his master—being trained to dread his approach—and only a few hours learning the power of the state. The master is to him a stern and flinty reality, but the state is little more than a dream. He has been accustomed to regard every white man as the friend of his master, and every colored man as more or less under the control of his master's friends—the white people. It takes stout nerves to stand up, in such circumstances. A man, homeless, shelterless, breadless, friendless, and moneyless, is not in a condition to assume a very proud or joyous tone; and in just this condition was I, while wandering about the streets of New York city, and lodging, at least one night, among the barrels on one of its wharves. I was not only free from slavery, but I was free from home, as well. The reader will easily see that I had something more than the simple fact of being free to think of, in this extremity.

I kept my secret as long as I could, and at last was forced to go in search of an honest man—a man sufficiently *human* not to betray me into the hands of slave-catchers. I was not a bad reader of the human face, nor long in selecting the right man, when once compelled to disclose the facts of my condition to some one.

I found my man in the person of one who said his name was Stewart. He was a sailor, warm-hearted and generous, and he listened to my story with a brother's interest. I told him I was running for my freedom—knew not where to go—money almost gone—was hungry—thought it unsafe to go to the shipyards for work, and needed a friend. Stewart promptly put me in the way of getting out of my trouble. He took me to his house, and went in search of the late David Ruggles, who was then the secretary of the New York Vigilance Committee, and a very active man in all anti-slavery works. Once in the hands of Mr. Ruggles, I was comparatively safe. I was hidden with Mr. Ruggles several days. In the meantime, my intended wife, Anna, came on from Baltimore—to whom I had written, informing her of my safe arrival at New York—and, in the presence of Mrs. Mitchell and Mr. Ruggles, we were married, by Rev. James W. C. Pennington.

Mr. Ruggles* was the first officer on the under-ground rail-

* He was a whole-souled man, fully imbued with a love of his afflicted and hunted people, and took pleasure in being to me, as was his wont, "Eyes to the blind, and legs to the lame." This brave and devoted man suffered much from the persecutions common to all who have been prominent benefactors. He at last became blind, and needed a friend to guide him, even as he had been a guide to others. Even in his blindness, he exhibited his manly character. In search of health, he became a physician. When hope of gaining his own was gone, he had hope for others. Believing in hydropathy, he established, at Northampton, Massachusetts, a large "*Water Cure,*" and became one of the most successful of all engaged in that mode of treatment.

road with whom I met after reaching the north, and, indeed, the first of whom I ever heard anything. Learning that I was a calker by trade, he promptly decided that New Bedford was the proper place to send me. "Many ships," said he, "are there fitted out for the whaling business, and you may there find work at your trade, and make a good living." Thus, in one fortnight after my flight from Maryland, I was safe in New Bedford, regularly entered upon the exercise of the rights, responsibilities, and duties of a freeman.

I may mention a little circumstance which annoyed me on reaching New Bedford. I had not a cent of money, and lacked two dollars toward paying our fare from Newport, and our baggage—not very costly—was taken by the stage driver, and held until I could raise the money to redeem it. This difficulty was soon surmounted. Mr. Nathan Johnson, to whom we had a line from Mr. Ruggles, not only received us kindly and hospitably, but, on being informed about our baggage, promptly loaned me two dollars with which to redeem my little property. I shall ever be deeply grateful, both to Mr. and Mrs. Nathan Johnson, for the lively interest they were pleased to take in me, in this the hour of my extremest need. They not only gave myself and wife bread and shelter, but taught us how to begin to secure those benefits for ourselves. Long may they live, and may blessings attend them in this life and in that which is to come!

Once initiated into the new life of freedom, and assured by Mr. Johnson that New Bedford was a safe place, the comparatively unimportant matter, as to what should be my name, came up for consideration. It was necessary to have a name in my new relations. The name given me by my beloved mother was no less pretentious than "Frederick Augustus Washington Bailey." I had, however, before leaving Maryland, dispensed with the *Augustus Washington*, and retained the name *Frederick Bailey*. Between Baltimore and New Bedford, however, I had several different names, the better to avoid being over-hauled by the hunters, which I had good reason to believe would be put on my track. Among honest men an honest man may well be content with one name, and to acknowledge it at all times and in all places; but toward fugitives, Americans are not honest. When I arrived at New Bedford, my name was Johnson; and finding that the Johnson family in New Bedford were already quite numerous—sufficiently so to produce some confusion in attempts to distinguish one from another—there was the more reason for making another change in my name. In fact, "Johnson" had been assumed by nearly every slave who had arrived in New Bedford from Maryland, and this, much to the annoyance of the original "Johnsons" (of whom there were many) in that place. Mine host, unwilling to have another of his own name added to the community in this unauthorized way, after I spent a night and a day at his house, gave me my present name. He had been reading the "Lady of the Lake," and was pleased to regard me as a suitable person to wear this, one of Scotland's many famous names. Considering the noble hospitality and manly character of Nathan Johnson, I have felt that he, better than I, illustrated the virtues of the great Scottish chief. Sure I am, that had any slave-catcher entered his domicile, with a view to molest any one of his household, he would have shown himself like him of the "stalwart hand."

The reader will be amused at my ignorance, when I tell the notions I had of the state of northern wealth, enterprise, and civilization. Of wealth and refinement, I supposed the north had none. My Columbian Orator, which was almost my only book, had not done much to enlighten me concerning northern society. The impressions I had received were all wide of the truth. New Bedford, especially, took me by surprise, in the solid wealth and grandeur there exhibited. I had formed my notions respecting the social condition of the free states, by what I had seen and known of free, white, non-slaveholding people in the slave states. Regarding slavery as the basis of wealth, I fancied that no people could become very wealthy without slavery. A free white man, holding no slaves, in the country, I had known to be the most ignorant and poverty-stricken of men, and the laughing stock even of slaves themselves—called generally by them, in derision, "*poor white trash.*" Like the non-slaveholders at the south, in holding no slaves, I supposed the northern people like them, also, in poverty and degradation. Judge, then, of my amazement and joy, when I found—as I did find—the very laboring population of New Bedford living in better houses, more elegantly furnished—surrounded by more comfort and refinement—than a majority of the slaveholders on the Eastern Shore of Maryland. There was my friend, Mr. Johnson, himself a colored man, (who at the south would have been regarded as a proper marketable commodity,) who lived in a better house—dined at a richer board—was the owner of more books—the reader of more newspapers—was more conversant with the political and social condition of this nation and the world—than nine-tenths of all the slaveholders of Talbot county, Maryland. Yet Mr. Johnson was a working man, and his hands were hardened by honest toil. Here, then, was something for observation and study. Whence the difference? The explanation was soon furnished, in the superiority of mind over simple brute force. Many pages might be given to the contrast, and in explanation of its causes. But an incident or two will suffice to show the reader as to how the mystery gradually vanished before me.

My first afternoon, on reaching New Bedford, was spent in visiting the wharves and viewing the shipping. The sight of the broad brim and the plain, Quaker dress, which met me at every turn, greatly increased my sense of freedom and security. "I am among the Quakers," thought I, "and am safe."[2] Lying at the wharves and riding in the stream, were full-rigged ships of finest model, ready to start on whaling voyages. Upon the right and the left, I was walled in by large granite-fronted warehouses, crowded with the good things of this world. On the wharves, I saw industry without bustle, labor without noise, and heavy toil without the whip. There was no loud singing, as in southern ports, where ships are loading or unloading—no loud cursing or swearing—but everything went on as smoothly as the works of a well adjusted machine. How different was all this from the noisily fierce and clumsily absurd manner of labor-life in Baltimore and St. Michael's! One of the first incidents which illustrated the superior mental character of northern labor over that of the south, was the manner of unloading a ship's cargo of oil. In a southern port, twenty or thirty hands would have been employed to do what five or six did here, with the aid of a single ox attached to the end of a fall. Main strength, unassisted by skill, is slavery's method of labor. An old ox, worth eighty dollars, was doing, in New Bedford, what would have required fifteen thousand dollars worth of human bones and muscles to have performed in a southern port. I found that everything was done here with a scrupulous regard to economy, both in regard to men and things, time and strength. The maid servant, instead of spending at least a tenth part of her time in bringing and carrying water, as in Baltimore, had the pump at her elbow. The wood was dry, and snugly piled away for winter. Wood-houses, in-door pumps, sinks, drains, self-shutting gates, washing machines, pounding barrels, were all new things, and told me that I was among a thoughtful and sensible people. To the ship-repairing dock I went, and saw the same wise prudence. The carpenters struck where they aimed, and the calkers wasted no blows in idle flourishes of the mallet. I learned that men went from New Bedford to Baltimore, and bought old ships, and brought them here to repair, and made them better and more valuable than they ever were before. Men talked here of going whaling on a four *years'* voyage with more coolness than sailors where I came from talked of going a four *months'* voyage.

I now find that I could have landed in no part of the United States, where I should have found a more striking and gratifying contrast to the condition of the free people of color in Baltimore, than I found here in New Bedford. No colored man is really free in a slaveholding state. He wears the badge of bondage while nominally free, and is often subjected to hardships to which the slave is a stranger; but here in New Bedford, it was my good fortune to see a pretty near approach to freedom on the part of the colored people. I was taken all aback when Mr. Johnson—who lost no time in making me acquainted with the fact—told me that there was nothing in the constitution of Massachusetts to prevent a colored man from holding any office in the state. There, in New Bedford, the black man's children—although anti-slavery was then far from popular—went to school side by side with the white children, and apparently without objection from any quarter. To make me at home, Mr. Johnson assured me that no slaveholder could take a slave from New Bedford; that there were men there who would lay down their lives, before such an outrage could be perpetrated. The colored people themselves were of the best metal, and would fight for liberty to the death.

Soon after my arrival in New Bedford, I was told the following story, which was said to illustrate the spirit of the colored people in that goodly town: A colored man and a fugitive slave happened to have a little quarrel, and the former was heard to threaten the latter with informing his master of his whereabouts. As soon as this threat became known, a notice was read from the desk of what was then the only colored church in the place, stating that business of importance was to be then and there transacted. Special measures had been taken to secure the attendance of the would-be Judas, and had proved successful. Accordingly, at the hour appointed, the people came, and the betrayer also. All the usual formalities of public meetings were scrupulously gone through, even to the offering prayer for Divine direction in the duties of the occasion. The president himself performed this part of the ceremony, and I was told that he was unusually fervent. Yet, at the close of his prayer, the old man (one of the numerous family of Johnsons) rose from his knees, deliberately surveyed his audience, and then said, in a tone of solemn resolution, "*Well, friends, we have got him here, and I would now recommend that you young men should just take him outside the door and kill him.*" With this, a large body of the congregation, who well understood the business they had come there to transact, made a rush at the villain, and doubtless would have killed him, had he not availed himself of an open sash, and made good his escape. He has never shown his head in New Bedford since that time. This little incident is perfectly characteristic of the spirit of the colored people in New Bedford. A slave could not be taken from that town seventeen years ago, any more than he could be so taken away now. The reason is, that the colored people in that city are educated up to the point of fighting for their freedom, as well as speaking for it.

Once assured of my safety in New Bedford, I put on the habiliments of a common laborer, and went on the wharf in search of work. I had no notion of living on the honest and generous sympathy of my colored brother, Johnson, or that of the abolitionists. My cry was like that of Hood's laborer, "Oh! only give me work."[3] Happily for me, I was not long in searching. I found employment, the third day after my arrival in New Bedford, in stowing a sloop with a load of oil for the New York market. It was new, hard, and dirty work, even for a calker, but I went at it with a glad heart and a willing hand. I was now my own master—a tremendous fact—and the rapturous excitement with which I seized the job, may not easily be understood, except by some one with an experience something like mine. The thoughts—"I can work! I can work for a living; I am not afraid of work; I have no Master Hugh to rob me of my earnings"—placed me in a state of independence, beyond seeking friendship or support of any man. That day's work I considered the real starting point of something like a new existence. Having finished this job and got my pay for the same, I went next in pursuit of a job at calking. It so happened that Mr. Rodney French, late mayor of the city of New Bedford, had a ship fitting out for sea, and to which there was a large job of calking and coppering to be done. I applied to that noble-hearted man for employment, and he promptly told me to go to work; but going on the float-stage for the purpose, I was informed that every white man would leave the ship if I struck a blow upon her. "Well, well," thought I, "this is a hardship, but yet not a very serious one for me." The difference between the wages of a calker and that of a common day laborer, was an hundred per cent. in favor of the former; but then I was free, and free to work, though not at my trade. I now prepared myself to do anything which came to hand in the way of turning an honest penny; sawed wood—dug cellars—shoveled coal—swept chimneys with Uncle Lucas Debuty—rolled oil casks on the wharves—helped to load and unload vessels—worked in Ricketson's candle works—in Richmond's brass foundery, and elsewhere; and thus supported myself and family for three years.

The first winter was unusually severe, in consequence of the high prices of food; but even during that winter we probably suffered less than many who had been free all their lives. During the hardest of the winter, I hired out for nine dollars a month; and out of this rented two rooms for nine dollars per quarter, and supplied my wife—who was unable to work—with food and some necessary articles of furniture. We were closely pinched to bring our wants within our means; but the jail stood over the way, and I had a wholesome dread of the consequences of running in debt. This winter past, and I was up with the times—got plenty of work—got well paid for it—and felt that I had not done a foolish thing to leave Master Hugh and Master Thomas. I was now living in a new world, and was wide awake to its advantages. I early began to attend the meetings of the colored people of New Bedford, and to take part in them. I was somewhat amazed to see colored men drawing up resolutions and offering them for consideration. Several colored young men of New Bedford, at that period, gave promise of great usefulness. They were educated, and possessed what seemed to me, at that time, very superior talents. Some of them have been cut down by death, and others have removed to different parts of the world, and some remain there now, and justify, in their present activities, my early impressions of them.

Among my first concerns on reaching New Bedford, was to become united with the church, for I had never given up, in reality, my religious faith. I had become lukewarm and in a backslidden state, but I was still convinced that it was my duty to join the Methodist church. I was not then aware of the powerful influence of that religious body in favor of the enslavement of my race, nor did I see how the northern churches could be responsible for the conduct of southern churches; neither did I fully understand how it could be my duty to remain separate from the church, because bad men were connected with it. The slaveholding church, with its Coveys, Weedens, Aulds, and Hopkins, I could see through at once, but I could not see how Elm Street church, in New Bedford, could be regarded as sanctioning the christianity of these characters in the church at St. Michael's. I therefore resolved to join the Methodist church in New Bedford, and to enjoy the spiritual advantage of public worship. The minister of the Elm Street Methodist church, was the Rev. Mr. Bonney; and although I was not allowed a seat in the body of the house, and was proscribed on account of my color, regarding this proscription simply as an accommodation of the unconverted congregation who had not yet been won to Christ and his brotherhood, I was willing thus to be proscribed, lest sinners should be driven away from the saving power of the gospel. Once converted, I thought they would be sure to treat me as a man and a brother. "Surely," thought I, "these christian people have none of this feeling against color. They, at least, have renounced this unholy feeling." Judge, then, dear reader, of my astonishment and mortification, when I found, as soon I did find, all my charitable assumptions at fault.

An opportunity was soon afforded me for ascertaining the exact position of Elm Street church on that subject. I had a chance of seeing the religious part of the congregation by themselves; and although they disowned, in effect, their black brothers and sisters, before the world, I did think that where none but the saints were assembled, and no offense could be given to the wicked, and the gospel could not be "blamed," they would certainly recognize us as children of the same Father, and heirs of the same salvation, on equal terms with themselves.

The occasion to which I refer, was the sacrament of the Lord's Supper, that most sacred and most solemn of all the ordinances of the christian church. Mr. Bonney had preached a very solemn and searching discourse, which really proved him to be acquainted with the inmost secrets of the human heart. At the close of his discourse, the congregation was dismissed, and the church remained to partake of the sacrament. I remained to see, as I thought, this holy sacrament celebrated in the spirit of its great Founder.

There were only about a half dozen colored members attached to the Elm Street church, at this time. After the congregation was dismissed, these descended from the gallery, and took a seat against the wall most distant from the altar. Brother Bonney was very animated, and sung very sweetly, "Salvation 'tis a joyful sound," and soon began to administer the sacrament. I was anxious to observe the bearing of the colored members, and the result was most humiliating. During the whole ceremony, they looked like sheep without a shepherd. The white members went forward to the altar by the bench full; and when it was evident that all the whites had been served with the bread and wine, Brother Bonney—pious Brother Bonney—after a long pause, as if inquiring whether all the white members had been served, and fully assuring himself on that important point, then raised his voice to an unnatural pitch, and looking to the corner where his black sheep seemed penned, beckoned with his hand, exclaiming, "Come forward, colored friends!—come forward! You, too, have an interest in the blood of Christ. God is no respecter of persons. Come forward, and take this holy sacrament to your comfort." The colored members—poor, slavish souls—went forward, as invited. I went *out*, and have never been in that church since, although I honestly went there with a view to joining that body. I found it impossible to respect the religious profession of any who were under the dominion of this wicked prejudice, and I could not, therefore, feel that in joining them, I was joining a christian church, at all. I tried other churches in New Bedford, with the same result, and, finally, I attached myself to a small body of colored Methodists, known as the Zion Methodists.[4] Favored with the affection and confidence of the members of this humble communion, I was soon made a class-leader and a local preacher among them. Many seasons of peace and joy I experienced among them, the remembrance of which is still precious, although I could not see it to be my duty to remain with that body, when I found that it consented to the same spirit which held my brethren in chains.

In four or five months after reaching New Bedford, there came a young man to me, with a copy of the "Liberator," the paper edited by WILLIAM LLOYD GARRISON, and published by ISAAC KNAPP,[5] and asked me to subscribe for it. I told him I had but just escaped from slavery, and was of course very poor, and remarked further, that I was unable to pay for it then; the agent, however, very willingly took me as a subscriber, and appeared to be much pleased with securing my name to his list. From this time I was brought in contact with the mind of William Lloyd Garrison. His paper took its place with me next to the bible.

The Liberator was a paper after my own heart. It detested slavery—exposed hypocrisy and wickedness in high places—made no truce with the traffickers in the bodies and souls of men; it preached human brotherhood, denounced oppression, and, with all the solemnity of God's word, demanded the complete emancipation of my race. I not only liked—I *loved* this paper, and its editor. He seemed a match for all the opponents of emancipation, whether they spoke in the name of the law, or the gospel. His words were few, full of holy fire, and straight to the point. Learning to love him, through his paper, I was prepared to be pleased with his presence. Something of a hero worshiper, by nature, here was one, on first sight, to excite my love and reverence.

Seventeen years ago, few men possessed a more heavenly countenance than William Lloyd Garrison, and few men evinced a more genuine or a more exalted piety. The bible was his text book—held sacred, as the word of the Eternal Father—sinless perfection—complete submission to insults and injuries—literal obedience to the injunction, if smitten on one side to turn the other also. Not only was Sunday a Sabbath, but all days were Sabbaths, and to be kept holy. All sectarism false and mischievous—the regenerated, throughout the world, members of one body, and the HEAD Christ Jesus. Prejudice against color was rebellion against God. Of all men beneath the sky, the slaves, because most neglected and despised, were nearest and dearest to his great heart. Those ministers who defended slavery from the bible, were of their "father the devil;"[6] and those churches which fellowshiped slaveholders as christians, were synagogues of Satan, and our nation was a nation of liars. Never loud or noisy—calm and serene as a summer sky, and as pure. "You are the man, the Moses, raised up by God, to deliver his modern Israel from bondage,"[7] was the spontaneous feeling of my heart, as I sat away back in the hall and listened to his mighty words; mighty in truth—mighty in their simple earnestness.

I had not long been a reader of the Liberator, and listener to its editor, before I got a clear apprehension of the principles of the anti-slavery movement. I had already the spirit of the movement, and only needed to understand its principles and measures. These I got from the Liberator, and from those who believed in that paper. My acquaintance with the movement increased my hope for the ultimate freedom of my race, and I united with it from a sense of delight, as well as duty.

Every week the Liberator came, and every week I made myself master of its contents. All the anti-slavery meetings held in New Bedford I promptly attended, my heart burning at every true utterance against the slave system, and every rebuke of its friends and supporters. Thus passed the first three years of my residence in New Bedford. I had not then dreamed of the possibility of my becoming a public advocate of the cause so deeply imbedded in my heart. It was enough for me to listen—to receive and applaud the great words of others, and only whisper in private, among the white laborers on the wharves, and elsewhere, the truths which burned in my breast.

CHAPTER XXIII.

INTRODUCED TO THE ABOLITIONISTS.

FIRST SPEECH AT NANTUCKET—MUCH SENSATION—EXTRAORDINARY SPEECH OF MR. GARRISON—AUTHOR BECOMES A PUBLIC LECTURER—FOURTEEN YEARS' EXPERIENCE—YOUTHFUL ENTHUSIASM—A BRAND NEW FACT—MATTER OF THE AUTHOR'S SPEECH—HE COULD NOT FOLLOW THE PROGRAMME—HIS FUGITIVE SLAVESHIP DOUBTED—TO SETTLE ALL DOUBT HE WRITES HIS EXPERIENCE OF SLAVERY—DANGER OF RECAPTURE INCREASED.

In the summer of 1841, a grand anti-slavery convention was held in Nantucket, under the auspices of Mr. Garrison and his friends. Until now, I had taken no holiday since my escape from slavery. Having worked very hard that spring and summer, in Richmond's brass foundery—sometimes working all night as well as all day—and needing a day or two of rest, I attended this convention, never supposing that I should take part in the proceedings. Indeed, I was not aware that any one connected with the convention even so much as knew my name. I was, however, quite mistaken. Mr. William C. Coffin, a prominent abolitionist in those days of trial, had heard me speaking to my colored friends, in the little school-house on Second street, New Bedford, where we worshiped. He sought me out in the crowd, and invited me to say a few words to the convention. Thus sought out, and thus invited, I was induced to speak out the feelings inspired by the occasion, and the fresh recollection of the scenes through which I had passed as a slave. My speech on this occasion is about the only one I ever made, of which I do not remember a single connected sentence. It was with the utmost difficulty that I could stand erect, or that I could command and articulate two words without hesitation and stammering. I trembled in every limb. I am not sure that my embarrassment was not the most effective part of my speech, if speech it could be called. At any rate, this is about the only part of my performance that I now distinctly remember. But excited and convulsed as I was, the audience, though remarkably quiet before, became as much excited as myself. Mr. Garrison followed me, taking me as his text; and now, whether I had made an eloquent speech in behalf of freedom or not, his was one never to be forgotten by those who heard it. Those who had heard Mr. Garrison oftenest, and had known him longest, were astonished. It was an effort of unequaled power, sweeping down, like a very tornado, every opposing barrier, whether of sentiment or opinion. For a moment, he possessed that almost fabulous inspiration, often referred to but seldom attained, in which a public meeting is transformed, as it were, into a single individuality—the orator wielding a thousand heads and hearts at once, and by the simple majesty of his all controlling thought, converting his hearers into the express image of his own soul. That night there were at least one thousand Garrisonians in Nantucket! At the close of this great meeting, I was duly waited on by Mr. John A. Collins—then the general agent of the Massachusetts anti-slavery society—and urgently solicited by him to become an agent of that society, and to publicly advocate its anti-slavery principles. I was reluctant to take the proffered position. I had not been quite three years from slavery—was honestly distrustful of my ability—wished to be excused; publicity exposed me to discovery and arrest by my master; and other objections came up, but Mr. Collins was not to be put off, and I finally consented to go out for three months, for I supposed that I should have got to the end of my story and my usefulness, in that length of time.

Here opened upon me a new life—a life for which I had had no preparation. I was a "graduate from the peculiar institution," Mr. Collins used to say, when introducing me, *"with my diploma written on my back!"* The three years of my freedom had been spent in the hard school of adversity. My hands had been furnished by nature with something like a solid leather coating, and I had bravely marked out for myself a life of rough labor, suited to the hardness of my hands, as a means of supporting myself and rearing my children.

Now what shall I say of this fourteen years' experience as a public advocate of the cause of my enslaved brothers and sisters? The time is but as a speck, yet large enough to justify a pause for retrospection—and a pause it must only be.

Young, ardent, and hopeful, I entered upon this new life in the full gush of unsuspecting enthusiasm. The cause was good; the men engaged in it were good; the means to attain its triumph, good; Heaven's blessing must attend all, and freedom must soon be given to the pining millions under a ruthless bondage. My whole heart went with the holy cause, and my most fervent prayer to the Almighty Disposer of the hearts of men, were continually offered for its early triumph. "Who or what," thought I, "can withstand a cause so good, so holy, so indescribably glorious. The God of Israel is with us. The might of the Eternal is on our side. Now let but the truth be spoken, and a nation will start forth at the sound!"[8] In this enthusiastic spirit, I dropped into the ranks of freedom's friends, and went forth to the battle. For a time I was made to forget that my skin was dark and my hair crisped. For a time I regretted that I could not have shared the hardships and dangers endured by the earlier workers for the slave's release. I soon, however, found that my enthusiasm had been extravagant; that hardships and dangers were not yet passed; and that the life now before me, had shadows as well as sunbeams.

Among the first duties assigned me, on entering the ranks, was to travel, in company with Mr. George Foster, to secure subscribers to the "Anti-slavery Standard" and the "Liberator." With him I traveled and lectured through the eastern counties of Massachusetts. Much interest was awakened—large meetings assembled. Many came, no doubt, from curiosity to hear what a negro could say in his own cause. I was generally introduced as a *"chattel"*—a *"thing"*—a piece of southern *"property"*—the chairman assuring the audience that *it* could speak. Fugitive slaves, at that time, were not so plentiful as now; and as a fugitive slave lecturer, I had the advantage of being a *"brand new fact"*—the first one out. Up to that time, a colored man was deemed a fool who confessed himself a runaway slave, not only because of the danger to which he exposed himself of being retaken, but because it was a confession of a very *low* origin! Some of my colored friends in New Bedford thought very badly of my wisdom for thus exposing and degrading myself. The only precaution I took, at the beginning, to prevent Master Thomas from knowing where I was, and what I was about, was the withholding my former name, my master's name, and the name of the state and county from which I came. During the first three or four months, my speeches were almost exclusively made up of narrations of my own personal experience as a slave. "Let us have the facts," said the people. So also said Friend George Foster, who always wished to pin me down to my simple narrative. "Give us the facts," said Collins, "we will take care of the philosophy." Just here arose some embarrassment. It was impossible for me to repeat the same old story month after month, and to keep up my interest in it. It was new to the people, it is true, but it was an old story to me; and to go through with it night after night, was a task altogether too mechanical for my nature. "Tell your story, Frederick," would whisper my then revered friend, William Lloyd Garrison, as I stepped upon the platform. I could not always obey, for I was now reading and thinking. New views of the subject were presented to my mind. It did not entirely satisfy me to *narrate* wrongs; I felt like *denouncing* them. I could not always curb my moral indignation for the perpetrators of slaveholding villainy, long enough for a circumstantial statement of the facts which I felt almost everybody must know. Besides, I was growing, and needed room. "People won't believe you ever was a slave, Frederick, if you keep on this way," said Friend Foster. "Be yourself," said Collins, "and tell your story." It was said to me, "Better have a *little* of the plantation manner of speech than not; 'tis not best that you seem too learned." These excellent friends were actuated by the best of motives, and were not altogether wrong in their advice; and still I must speak just the word that seemed to *me* the word to be spoken *by* me.

At last the apprehended trouble came. People doubted if I had ever been a slave. They said I did not talk like a slave, look like a slave, nor act like a slave, and that they believed I had never been south of Mason and Dixon's line. "He don't tell us where he came from—what his master's name was—how he got away—nor the story of his experience. Besides, he is educated, and is, in this, a contradiction of all the facts we have concerning the ignorance of the slaves." Thus, I was in a pretty fair way to be denounced as an impostor. The committee of the Massachusetts anti-slavery society knew all the facts in my case, and agreed with me in the prudence of keeping them private. They, therefore, never doubted my being a genuine fugitive; but going down the aisles of the churches in which I spoke, and hearing the free spoken Yankees saying, repeatedly, *"He's never been a slave, I'll warrant ye,"* I resolved to dispel all doubt, at no distant day, by such a revelation of facts as could not be made by any other than a genuine fugitive.

In a little less than four years, therefore, after becoming a public lecturer, I was induced to write out the leading facts connected with my experience in slavery, giving names of persons, places, and dates—thus putting it in the power of any who doubted, to ascertain the truth or falsehood of my story of being a fugitive slave. This statement soon became known in Maryland, and I had reason to believe that an effort would be made to recapture me.

It is not probable that any open attempt to secure me as a slave could have succeeded, further than the obtainment, by my master, of the money value of my bones and sinews. Fortunately for me, in the four years of my labors in the abolition cause, I had gained many friends, who would have suffered themselves to be taxed to almost any extent to save me from slavery. It was felt that I had committed the double offense of running away, and exposing the secrets and crimes of slavery and slaveholders. There was a double motive for seeking my reënslavement—avarice and vengeance; and while, as I have said, there was little probability of successful recapture, if attempted openly, I was constantly in danger of being spirited away, at a moment when my friends could render me no assistance. In traveling about from place to place—often alone—I was much exposed to this sort of attack. Any one cherishing the design to betray me, could easily do so, by simply tracing my whereabouts through the anti-slavery journals, for my meetings and movements were promptly made known in advance. My true friends, Mr. Garrison and

Mr. Phillips, had no faith in the power of Massachusetts to protect me in my right to liberty. Public sentiment and the law, in their opinion, would hand me over to the tormentors. Mr. Phillips, especially, considered me in danger, and said, when I showed him the manuscript of my story, if in my place, he would throw it into the fire. Thus, the reader will observe, the settling of one difficulty only opened the way for another; and that though I had reached a free state, and had attained a position for public usefulness, I was still tormented with the liability of losing my liberty. How this liability was dispelled, will be related, with other incidents, in the next chapter.

CHAPTER XXIV.

TWENTY-ONE MONTHS IN GREAT BRITAIN.

GOOD ARISING OUT OF UNPROPITIOUS EVENTS—DENIED CABIN PASSAGE—PROSCRIPTION TURNED TO GOOD ACCOUNT—THE HUTCHINSON FAMILY—THE MOB ON BOARD THE CAMBRIA—HAPPY INTRODUCTION TO THE BRITISH PUBLIC—LETTER ADDRESSED TO WILLIAM LLOYD GARRISON—TIME AND LABORS WHILE ABROAD—FREEDOM PURCHASED—MRS. HENRY RICHARDSON—FREE PAPERS—ABOLITIONISTS DISPLEASED WITH THE RANSOM—HOW THE AUTHOR'S ENERGIES WERE DIRECTED—RECEPTION SPEECH IN LONDON—CHARACTER OF THE SPEECH DEFENDED—CIRCUMSTANCES EXPLAINED—CAUSES CONTRIBUTING TO THE SUCCESS OF HIS MISSION—FREE CHURCH OF SCOTLAND—TESTIMONIAL.

The allotments of Providence, when coupled with trouble and anxiety, often conceal from finite vision the wisdom and goodness in which they are sent; and, frequently, what seemed a harsh and invidious dispensation, is converted by after experience into a happy and beneficial arrangement. Thus, the painful liability to be returned again to slavery, which haunted me by day, and troubled my dreams by night, proved to be a necessary step in the path of knowledge and usefulness. The writing of my pamphlet, in the spring of 1845, endangered my liberty, and led me to seek a refuge from republican slavery in monarchical England. A rude, uncultivated fugitive slave was driven, by stern necessity, to that country to which young American gentlemen go to increase their stock of knowledge, to seek pleasure, to have their rough, democratic manners softened by contact with English aristocratic refinement. On applying for a passage to England, on board the Cambria, of the Cunard line, my friend, James N. Buffum,[9] of Lynn, Massachusetts, was informed that I could not be received on board as a cabin passenger. American prejudice against color triumphed over British liberality and civilization, and erected a color test and condition for crossing the sea in the cabin of a British vessel. The insult was keenly felt by my white friends, but to me, it was common, expected, and therefore, a thing of no great consequence, whether I went in the cabin or in the steerage. Moreover, I felt that if I could not go into the first cabin, first-cabin passengers could come into the second cabin, and the result justified my anticipations to the fullest extent. Indeed, I soon found myself an object of more general interest than I wished to be; and so far from being degraded by being placed in the second cabin, that part of the ship became the scene of as much pleasure and refinement, during the voyage, as the cabin itself. The Hutchinson Family,[10] celebrated vocalists—fellow-passengers—often came to my rude forecastle deck, and sung their sweetest songs, enlivening the place with eloquent music, as well as spirited conversation, during the voyage. In two days after leaving Boston, one part of the ship was about as free to me as another. My fellow-passengers not only visited me, but invited me to visit them, on the saloon deck. My visits there, however, were but seldom. I preferred to live within my privileges, and keep upon my own premises. I found this quite as much in accordance with good policy, as with my own feelings. The effect was, that with the majority of the passengers, all color distinctions were flung to the winds, and I found myself treated with every mark of respect, from the beginning to the end of the voyage, except in a single instance; and in that, I came near being mobbed, for complying with an invitation given me by the passengers, and the captain of the "Cambria," to deliver a lecture on slavery. Our New Orleans and Georgia passengers were pleased to regard my lecture as an insult offered to them, and swore I should not speak. They went so far as to threaten to throw me overboard, and but for the firmness of Captain Judkins, probably would have (under the inspiration of *slavery* and *brandy*) attempted to put their threats into execution. I have no space to describe this scene, although its tragic and comic peculiarities are well worth describing. An end was put to the *melee*, by the captain's calling the ship's company to put the salt water mobocrats in irons. At this determined order, the gentlemen of the lash scampered, and for the rest of the voyage conducted themselves very decorously.

This incident of the voyage, in two days after landing at Liverpool, brought me at once before the British public, and that by no act of my own. The gentlemen so promptly snubbed in their meditated violence, flew to the press to justify their conduct, and to denounce me as a worthless and insolent negro. This course was even less wise than the conduct it was intended to sustain; for, besides awakening something like a national interest in me, and securing me an audience, it brought out counter statements, and threw the blame upon themselves, which they had sought to fasten upon me and the gallant captain of the ship.

Some notion may be formed of the difference in my feelings and circumstances, while abroad, from the following extract from one of a series of letters addressed by me to Mr. Garrison, and published in the Liberator. It was written on the first day of January, 1846:

"MY DEAR FRIEND GARRISON: Up to this time, I have given no direct expression of the views, feelings, and opinions which I have formed, respecting the character and condition of the people of this land. I have refrained thus, purposely. I wish to speak advisedly, and in order to do this, I have waited till, I trust, experience has brought my opinions to an intelligent maturity. I have been thus careful, not because I think what I say will have much effect in shaping the opinions of the world, but because whatever of influence I may possess, whether little or much, I wish it to go in the right direction, and according to truth. I hardly need say that, in speaking of Ireland, I shall be influenced by no prejudices in favor of America. I think my circumstances all forbid that. I have no end to serve, no creed to uphold, no government to defend; and as to nation, I belong to none. I have no protection at home, or resting-place abroad. The land of my birth welcomes me to her shores only as a slave, and spurns with contempt the idea of treating me differently; so that I am an outcast from the society of my childhood, and an outlaw in the land of my birth. 'I am a stranger with thee, and a sojourner, as all my fathers were.'[11] That men should be patriotic, is to me perfectly natural; and as a philosophical fact, I am able to give it an *intellectual* recognition. But no further can I go. If ever I had any patriotism, or any capacity for the feeling, it was whipped out of me long since, by the lash of the American soul-drivers.

"In thinking of America, I sometimes find myself admiring her bright blue sky, her grand old woods, her fertile fields, her beautiful rivers, her mighty lakes, and star-crowned mountains. But my rapture is soon checked, my joy is soon turned to mourning. When I remember that all is cursed with the infernal spirit of slaveholding, robbery, and wrong; when I remember that with the waters of her noblest rivers, the tears of my brethren are borne to the ocean, disregarded and forgotten, and that her most fertile fields drink daily of the warm blood of my outraged sisters; I am filled with unutterable loathing, and led to reproach myself that anything could fall from my lips in praise of such a land. America will not allow her children to love her. She seems bent on compelling those who would be her warmest friends, to be her worst enemies. May God give her repentance, before it is too late, is the ardent prayer of my heart. I will continue to pray, labor, and wait, believing that she cannot always be insensible to the dictates of justice, or deaf to the voice of humanity.

"My opportunities for learning the character and condition of the people of this land have been very great. I have traveled almost from the Hill of Howth to the Giant's Causeway, and from the Giant's Causeway to Cape Clear. During these travels, I have met with much in the character and condition of the people to approve, and much to condemn; much that has thrilled me with pleasure, and very much that has filled me with pain. I will not, in this letter, attempt to give any description of those scenes which have given me pain. This I will do hereafter. I have enough, and more than your subscribers will be disposed to read at one time, of the bright side of the picture. I can truly say, I have spent some of the happiest moments of my life since landing in this country. I seem to have undergone a transformation. I live a new life. The warm and generous coöperation extended to me by the friends of my despised race; the prompt and liberal manner with which the press has rendered me its aid; the glorious enthusiasm with which thousands have flocked to hear the cruel wrongs of my down-trodden and long-enslaved fellow-countrymen portrayed; the deep sympathy for the slave, and the strong abhorrence of the slaveholder, everywhere evinced; the cordiality with which members and ministers of various religious bodies, and of various shades of religious opinion, have embraced me, and lent me their aid; the kind hospitality constantly proffered to me by persons of the highest rank in society; the spirit of freedom that seems to animate all with whom I come in contact, and the entire absence of everything that looked like prejudice against me, on account of the color of my skin—contrasted so strongly with my long and bitter experience in the United States, that I look with wonder and amazement on the transition. In the southern part of the United States, I was a slave, thought of and spoken of as property; in the language of the LAW, '*held, taken, reputed, and adjudged to be a chattel in the hands of my owners and possessors, and their executors, administrators, and assigns, to all intents, constructions, and purposes whatsoever.*' (Brev. Digest, 224.) In the northern states, a fugitive slave, liable to be hunted at any moment, like a felon, and to be hurled into the terrible jaws of slavery—doomed by an inveterate prejudice against color to insult and outrage on every hand, (Massachusetts out of the question)—denied the privileges and courtesies common to others in the use of the most humble means of conveyance—shut out from the cabins on steamboats—refused admission to respectable hotels—caricatured, scorned, scoffed, mocked, and maltreated with impunity by any one, (no matter how black his heart,) so he has a white skin. But now behold the change! Eleven days and a half gone, and I have crossed three thousand miles of the perilous deep. Instead of a democratic government, I am under a monarchical government. Instead of the bright, blue sky of America, I am covered with the soft, grey fog of the Emerald Isle. I breathe, and lo! the chattel becomes a man. I gaze around in vain for one who will question my equal humanity, claim me as his slave, or offer me an insult. I employ a cab—I am seated beside white people—I reach the hotel—I enter the same door—I am shown into the same parlor—I dine at the same table—and no one is offended. No delicate nose grows deformed in my presence. I find no difficulty here in obtaining admission into any place of worship, instruction, or amusement, on equal terms with people as white as any I ever saw in the United States. I meet nothing to remind me of my complexion. I find myself regarded and treated at every turn with the kindness and deference paid to white people. When I go to church, I am met by no upturned nose and scornful lip to tell me, '*We don't allow niggers in here!*'

"I remember, about two years ago, there was in Boston, near the south-west corner of Boston Common, a menagerie. I had long desired to see such a collection as I understood was being exhibited there. Never having had an opportunity while a slave, I resolved to seize this, my first, since my escape. I went, and as I approached the entrance to gain admission, I was met and told by the doorkeeper, in a harsh and contemptuous tone, '*We don't allow niggers in here.*' I also remember attending a revival meeting in the Rev. Henry Jackson's meeting-house, at New Bedford, and going up the broad aisle to find a seat, I was met by a good deacon, who told me, in a pious tone, '*We don't allow niggers in here!*' Soon after my arrival in New Bedford, from the south, I had a strong desire to attend the Lyceum, but was told, '*They don't allow niggers in here!*' While passing from New York to Boston, on the steamer Massachusetts, on the night of the 9th of December, 1843, when chilled amost through with the cold, I went into the cabin to get a little warm. I was soon touched upon the shoulder, and told, '*We don't allow niggers in here!*' On arriving in Boston, from an anti-slavery tour, hungry and tired, I went into an eating-house, near my friend, Mr. Campbell's, to get some refreshments. I was met by a lad in a white apron, '*We don't allow niggers in here!*' A week or two before leaving the United States, I had a meeting appointed at

Weymouth, the home of that glorious band of true abolitionists, the Weston family, and others. On attempting to take a seat in the omnibus to that place, I was told by the driver, (and I never shall forget his fiendish hate,) *'I don't allow niggers in here!'* Thank heaven for the respite I now enjoy! I had been in Dublin but a few days, when a gentleman of great respectability kindly offered to conduct me through all the public buildings of that beautiful city; and a little afterward, I found myself dining with the lord mayor of Dublin. What a pity there was not some American democratic christian at the door of his splendid mansion, to bark out at my approach, *'They don't allow niggers in here!'* The truth is, the people here know nothing of the republican negro hate prevalent in our glorious land. They measure and esteem men according to their moral and intellectual worth, and not according to the color of their skin. Whatever may be said of the aristocracies here, there is none based on the color of a man's skin. This species of aristocracy belongs preëminently to 'the land of the free, and the home of the brave.' I have never found it abroad, in any but Americans. It sticks to them wherever they go. They find it almost as hard to get rid of, as to get rid of their skins.

"The second day after my arrival at Liverpool, in company with my friend, Buffum, and several other friends, I went to Eaton Hall, the residence of the Marquis of Westminster, one of the most splendid buildings in England. On approaching the door, I found several of our American passengers, who came out with us in the Cambria, waiting for admission, as but one party was allowed in the house at a time. We all had to wait till the company within came out. And of all the faces, expressive of chagrin, those of the Americans were preëminent. They looked as sour as vinegar, and as bitter as gall, when they found I was to be admitted on equal terms with themselves. When the door was opened, I walked in, on an equal footing with my white fellow-citizens, and from all I could see, I had as much attention paid me by the servants that showed us through the house, as any with a paler skin. As I walked through the building, the statuary did not fall down, the pictures did not leap from their places, the doors did not refuse to open, and the servants did not say, *'We don't allow niggers in here!'*

"A happy new-year to you, and all the friends of freedom."

My time and labors, while abroad, were divided between England, Ireland, Scotland, and Wales. Upon this experience alone, I might write a book twice the size of this, *"My Bondage and my Freedom."* I visited and lectured in nearly all the large towns and cities in the United Kingdom, and enjoyed many favorable opportunities for observation and information. But books on England are abundant, and the public may, therefore, dismiss any fear that I am meditating another infliction in that line; though, in truth, I should like much to write a book on those countries, if for nothing else, to make grateful mention of the many dear friends, whose benevolent actions toward me are ineffaceably stamped upon my memory, and warmly treasured in my heart. To these friends I owe my freedom in the United States. On their own motion, without any solicitation from me, (Mrs. Henry Richardson, a clever lady, remarkable for her devotion to every good work, taking the lead,) they raised a fund sufficient to purchase my freedom, and actually paid it over, and placed the papers* of my manumission in my hands, before

* The following is a copy of these curious papers, both of my transfer from Thomas to Hugh Auld, and from Hugh to myself:

"Know all men by these Presents, That I, Thomas Auld, of Talbot county, and state of Maryland, for and in consideration of the sum of one hundred dollars, current money, to me paid by Hugh Auld, of the city of Baltimore, in the said state, at and before the sealing and delivery of these presents, the receipt whereof, I, the said Thomas Auld, do here by acknowledge, have granted, bargained, and sold, and by these presents do grant, bargain, and sell unto the said Hugh Auld, his executors, administrators, and assigns, ONE NEGRO MAN, by the name of FREDERICK BAILY, or DOUGLASS, as he calls himself—he is now about twenty-eight years of age—to have and to hold the said negro man for life. And I, the said Thomas Auld, for myself, my heirs, executors, and administrators, all and singular, the said FREDERICK BAILY, *alias* DOUGLASS, unto the said Hugh Auld, his executors, administrators, and assigns, ONE NEGRO MAN, by the name of FREDERICK BAILY, or DOUGLASS, against all and every other person or persons whatsoever, shall and will warrant and forever defend by these presents. In witness whereof, I set my hand and seal, this thirteenth day of November, eighteen hundred and forty-six. THOMAS AULD.

"Signed, sealed, and delivered in presence of Wrightson Jones.

"JOHN C. LEAS."

The authenticity of this bill of sale is attested by N. Harrington, a justice of the peace of the state of Maryland, and for the county of Talbot, dated same day as above.

"To all whom it may concern; Be it known, that I, Hugh Auld, of the city of Baltimore, in Baltimore county, in the state of Maryland, for divers good they would tolerate the idea of my returning to this, my native country. To this commercial transaction I owe my exemption from the democratic operation of the fugitive slave bill of 1850. But for this, I might at any time become a victim of this most cruel and scandalous enactment, and be doomed to end my life, as I began it, a slave. The sum paid for my freedom was one hundred and fifty pounds sterling.

Some of my uncompromising anti-slavery friends in this country failed to see the wisdom of this arrangement, and were not pleased that I consented to it, even by my silence. They thought it a violation of anti-slavery principles—conceding a right of property in man—and a wasteful expenditure of money. On the other hand, viewing it simply in the light of a ransom, or as money extorted by a robber, and my liberty of more value than one hundred and fifty pounds sterling, I could not see either a violation of the laws of morality, or those of economy, in the transaction.

It is true, I was not in the possession of my claimants, and could have easily remained in England, for the same friends who had so generously purchased my freedom, would have assisted me in establishing myself in that country. To this, however, I could not consent. I felt that I had a duty to perform—and that was, to labor and suffer with the oppressed in my native land. Considering, therefore, all the circumstances—the fugitive slave bill included—I think the very best thing was done in letting Master Hugh have the hundred and fifty pounds sterling, and leaving me free to return to my appropriate field of labor. Had I been a private person, having no

causes and considerations, me thereunto moving, have released from slavery, liberated, manumitted, and set free, and by these presents do hereby release from slavery, liberate, manumit, and set free, MY NEGRO MAN, named FREDERICK BAILY, otherwise called DOUGLASS, being of the age of twenty-eight years, or thereabouts, and able to work and gain a sufficient livelihood and maintenance; and him the said negro man, named FREDERICK BAILY, otherwise called FREDERICK DOUGLASS, I do declare to be henceforth free, manumitted, and discharged from all manner of servitude to me, my executors, and administrators forever.

"In witness whereof, I, the said Hugh Auld, have hereunto set my hand and seal, the fifth of December, in the year one thousand eight hundred and forty-six.

HUGH AULD.

"Sealed and delivered in the presence of T. Hanson Belt.

"JAMES N. S. T. WRIGHT."

other relations or duties than those of a personal and family nature, I should never have consented to the payment of so large a sum for the privilege of living securely under our glorious republican form of government. I could have remained in England, or have gone to some other country; and perhaps I could even have lived unobserved in this. But to this I could not consent. I had already become somewhat notorious, and withal quite as unpopular as notorious; and I was, therefore, much exposed to arrest and recapture.

The main object to which my labors in Great Britain were directed, was the concentration of the moral and religious sentiment of its people against American slavery. England is often charged with having established slavery in the United States, and if there were no other justification than this, for appealing to her people to lend their moral aid for the abolition of slavery, I should be justified. My speeches in Great Britain were wholly extemporaneous, and I may not always have been so guarded in my expressions, as I otherwise should have been. I was ten years younger then than now, and only seven years from slavery. I cannot give the reader a better idea of the nature of my discourses, than by republishing one of them, delivered in Finsbury chapel, London, to an audience of about two thousand persons, and which was published in the "London Universe," at the time.

Those in the United States who may regard this speech as being harsh in its spirit and unjust in its statements, because delivered before an audience supposed to be anti-republican in their principles and feelings, may view the matter differently, when they learn that the case supposed did not exist. It so happened that the great mass of the people in England who attended and patronized my anti-slavery meetings, were, in truth, about as good republicans as the mass of Americans, and with this decided advantage over the latter—they are lovers of republicanism for all men, for black men as well as for white men. They are the people who sympathize with Louis Kossuth and Mazzini,[12] and with the oppressed and enslaved, of every color and nation, the world over. They constitute the democratic element in British politics, and are as much opposed to the union of church and state as we, in America, are to such an union. At the meeting where this speech was delivered, Joseph Sturge[13]—a world-wide philanthropist, and a member of the society of Friends—presided, and addressed the meeting.

George William Alexander, another Friend, who has spent more than an American fortune in promoting the anti-slavery cause in different sections of the world, was on the platform; and also Dr. Campbell,[14] (now of the "British Banner,") who combines all the humane tenderness of Melancthon, with the directness and boldness of Luther.[15] He is in the very front ranks of non-conformists, and looks with no unfriendly eye upon America. George Thompson,[16] too, was there; and America will yet own that he did a true man's work in relighting the rapidly dying-out fire of true republicanism in the American heart, and be ashamed of the treatment he met at her hands. Coming generations in this country will applaud the spirit of this much abused republican friend of freedom. There were others of note seated on the platform, who would gladly ingraft upon English institutions all that is purely republican in the institutions of America. Nothing, therefore, must be set down against this speech on the score that it was delivered in the presence of those who cannot appreciate the many excellent things belonging to our system of government, and with a view to stir up prejudice against republican institutions.

Again, let it also be remembered—for it is the simple truth—that neither in this speech, nor in any other which I delivered in England, did I ever allow myself to address Englishmen as against Americans. I took my stand on the high ground of human brotherhood, and spoke to Englishmen as men, in behalf of men. Slavery is a crime, not against Englishmen, but against God, and all the members of the human family; and it belongs to the whole human family to seek its suppression. In a letter to Mr. Greeley, of the New York Tribune, written while abroad, I said:

"I am, nevertheless, aware that the wisdom of exposing the sins of one nation in the ear of another, has been seriously questioned by good and clear-sighted people, both on this and on your side of the Atlantic. And the thought is not without weight on my own mind. I am satisfied that there are many evils which can be best removed by confining our efforts to the immediate locality where such evils exist. This, however, is by no means the case with the system of slavery. It is such a giant sin—such a monstrous aggregation of iniquity—so hardening to the human heart—so destructive to the moral sense, and so well calculated to beget a character, in every one around it, favorable to its own continuance,—that I feel not only at liberty, but abundantly justified, in appealing to the whole world to aid in its removal."

But, even if I had—as has been often charged—labored to bring American institutions generally into disrepute, and had not confined my labors strictly within the limits of humanity and morality, I should not have been without illustrious examples to support me. Driven into semi-exile by civil and barbarous laws, and by a system which cannot be thought of without a shudder, I was fully justified in turning, if possible, the tide of the moral universe against the heaven-daring outrage.

Four circumstances greatly assisted me in getting the question of American slavery before the British public. First, the mob on board the Cambria, already referred to, which was a sort of national announcement of my arrival in England. Secondly, the highly reprehensible course pursued by the Free Church of Scotland,[17] in soliciting, receiving, and retaining money in its sustentation fund for supporting the gospel in Scotland, which was evidently the ill-gotten gain of slaveholders and slave-traders. Third, the great Evangelical Alliance[18]—or rather the attempt to form such an alliance, which should include slaveholders of a certain description—added immensely to the interest felt in the slavery question. About the same time, there was the World's Temperance Convention, where I had the misfortune to come in collision with sundry American doctors of divinity—Dr. Cox[19] among the number—with whom I had a small controversy.

It has happened to me—as it has happened to most other men engaged in a good cause—often to be more indebted to my enemies than to my own skill or to the assistance of my friends, for whatever success has attended my labors. Great surprise was expressed by American newspapers, north and south, during my stay in Great Britain, that a person so illiterate and insignificant as myself could awaken an interest so marked in England. These papers were not the only parties surprised. I was myself not far behind them in surprise. But the very contempt and scorn, the systematic and extravagant disparagement of which I was the object, served, perhaps, to magnify my few merits, and to render me of some account, whether deserving or not. A man is sometimes made great, by the greatness of the abuse a portion of mankind may think proper to heap upon him. Whether I was of as much consequence as the English papers made me out to be, or not, it was easily seen, in England, that I could not be the ignorant and worthless creature, some of the American papers would have them believe I was. Men, in their senses, do not take bowie-knives to kill mosquitoes, nor pistols to shoot flies; and the American passengers who thought proper to get up a mob to silence me, on board the Cambria, took the most effective method of telling the British public that I had something to say.

But to the second circumstance, namely, the position of the Free Church of Scotland, with the great Doctors Chalmers, Cunningham, and Candlish[20] at its head. That church, with its leaders, put it out of the power of the Scotch people to ask the old question, which we in the north have often most wickedly asked—"*What have we to do with slavery?*" That church had taken the price of blood into its treasury, with which to build *free* churches, and to pay *free* church ministers for preaching the gospel; and, worse still, when honest John Murray, of Bowlien Bay—now gone to his reward in heaven—with William Smeal, Andrew Paton, Frederick Card, and other sterling anti-slavery men in Glasgow, denounced the transaction as disgraceful and shocking to the religious sentiment of Scotland, this church, through its leading divines, instead of repenting and seeking to mend the mistake into which it had fallen, made it a flagrant sin, by undertaking to defend, in the name of God and the bible, the principle not only of taking the money of slave-dealers to build churches, but of holding fellowship with the holders and traffickers in human flesh. This, the reader will see, brought up the whole question of slavery, and opened the way to its full discussion, without any agency of mine. I have never seen a people more deeply moved than were the people of Scotland, on this very question. Public meeting succeeded public meeting. Speech after speech, pamphlet after pamphlet, editorial after editorial, sermon after sermon, soon lashed the conscientious Scotch people into a perfect *furore*. "SEND BACK THE MONEY!" was indignantly cried out, from Greenock to Edinburgh, and from Edinburgh to Aberdeen. George Thompson, of London, Henry C. Wright,[21] of the United States, James N. Buffum, of Lynn, Massachusetts, and myself were on the anti-slavery side; and Doctors

Chalmers, Cunningham, and Candlish on the other. In a conflict where the latter could have had even the show of right, the truth, in our hands as against them, must have been driven to the wall; and while I believe we were able to carry the conscience of the country against the action of the Free Church, the battle, it must be confessed, was a hard-fought one. Abler defenders of the doctrine of fellowshiping slaveholders as christians, have not been met with. In defending this doctrine, it was necessary to deny that slavery is a sin. If driven from this position, they were compelled to deny that slaveholders were responsible for the sin; and if driven from both these positions, they must deny that it is a sin in such a sense, and that slaveholders are sinners in such a sense, as to make it wrong, in the circumstances in which they were placed, to recognize them as christians. Dr. Cunningham was the most powerful debater on the slavery side of the question; Mr. Thompson was the ablest on the anti-slavery side. A scene occurred between these two men, a parallel to which I think I never witnessed before, and I know I never have since. The scene was caused by a single exclamation on the part of Mr. Thompson.

The general assembly of the Free Church was in progress at Cannon Mills, Edinburgh. The building would hold about twenty-five hundred persons; and on this occasion it was densely packed, notice having been given that Doctors Cunningham and Candlish would speak, that day, in defense of the relations of the Free Church of Scotland to slavery in America. Messrs. Thompson, Buffum, myself, and a few anti-slavery friends, attended, but sat at such a distance, and in such a position, that, perhaps, we were not observed from the platform. The excitement was intense, having been greatly increased by a series of meetings held by Messrs. Thompson, Wright, Buffum, and myself, in the most splendid hall in that most beautiful city, just previous to the meetings of the general assembly. "SEND BACK THE MONEY!" stared at us from every street corner; "SEND BACK THE MONEY!" in large capitals, adorned the broad flags of the pavement; "SEND BACK THE MONEY!" was the heading of leading editorials in the daily newspapers. This day, at Cannon Mills, the great doctors of the church were to give an answer to this loud and stern demand. Men of all parties and all sects were most eager to hear.

Something great was expected. The occasion was great, the men great, and great speeches were expected from them.

In addition to the outside pressure upon Doctors Cunningham and Candlish, there was wavering in their own ranks. The conscience of the church itself was not ease. A dissatisfaction with the position of the church touching slavery, was sensibly manifest among the members, and something must be done to counteract this untoward influence. The great Dr. Chalmers was in feeble health, at the time. His most potent eloquence could not now be summoned to Cannon Mills, as formerly. He whose voice was able to rend asunder and dash down the granite walls of the established church of Scotland, and to lead a host in solemn procession from it, as from a doomed city, was now old and enfeebled. Besides, he had said his word on this very question; and his word had not silenced the clamor without, nor stilled the anxious heavings within. The occasion was momentous, and felt to be so. The church was in a perilous condition. A change of some sort must take place in her condition, or she must go to pieces. To stand where she did, was impossible. The whole weight of the matter fell on Cunningham and Candlish. No shoulders in the church were broader than theirs; and I must say, badly as I detest the principles laid down and defended by them, I was compelled to acknowledge the vast mental endowments of the men. Cunningham rose; and his rising was the signal for almost tumultuous applause. You will say this was scarcely in keeping with the solemnity of the occasion, but to me it served to increase its grandeur and gravity. The applause, though tumultuous, was not joyous. It seemed to me, as it thundered up from the vast audience, like the fall of an immense shaft, flung from shoulders already galled by its crushing weight. It was like saying, "Doctor, we have borne this burden long enough, and willingly fling it upon you. Since it was you who brought it upon us, take it now, and do what you will with it, for we are too weary to bear it."

Doctor Cunningham proceeded with his speech, abounding in logic, learning, and eloquence, and apparently bearing down all opposition; but at the moment—the fatal moment—when he was just bringing all his arguments to a point, and that point being, that neither Jesus Christ nor his holy apostles regarded slaveholding as a sin, George Thompson, in a clear, sonorous, but rebuking voice, broke the deep stillness of the audience, exclaiming, "HEAR! HEAR! HEAR!" The effect of this simple and common exclamation is almost incredible. It was as if a granite wall had been suddenly flung up against the advancing current of a mighty river. For a moment, speaker and audience were brought to a dead silence. Both the doctor and his hearers seemed appalled by the audacity, as well as the fitness of the rebuke. At length a shout went up to the cry of *"Put him out!"* Happily, no one attempted to execute this cowardly order, and the doctor proceeded with his discourse. Not, however, as before, did the learned doctor proceed. The exclamation of Thompson must have reëchoed itself a thousand times in his memory, during the remainder of his speech, for the doctor never recovered from the blow.

The deed was done, however; the pillars of the church—*the proud, Free Church of Scotland*—were committed, and the humility of repentance was absent. The Free Church held on to the blood-stained money, and continued to justify itself in its position—and of course to apologize for slavery—and does so till this day. She lost a glorious opportunity for giving her voice, her vote, and her example to the cause of humanity; and to-day she is staggering under the curse of the enslaved, whose blood is in her skirts. The people of Scotland are, to this day, deeply grieved at the course pursued by the Free Church, and would hail, as a relief from a deep and blighting shame, the "sending back the money" to the slaveholders from whom it was gathered.

One good result followed the conduct of the Free Church; it furnished an occasion for making the people of Scotland thoroughly acquainted with the character of slavery, and for arraying against the system the moral and religious sentiment of that country. Therefore, while we did not succeed in accomplishing the specific object of our mission, namely—procure the sending back of the money—we were amply justified by the good which really did result from our labors.

Next comes the Evangelical Alliance. This was an attempt to form a union of all evangelical christians throughout the world. Sixty or seventy American divines attended, and some of them went there merely to weave a world-wide garment with which to clothe evangelical slaveholders. Foremost among these divines, was the Rev. Samuel Hanson Cox, moderator of the New School Presbyterian General Assembly. He and his friends spared no pains to secure a platform broad enough to hold American slaveholders, and in this they partly succeeded. But the question of slavery is too large a question to be finally disposed of, even by the Evangelical Alliance. We appealed from the judgment of the Alliance, to the judgment of the people of Great Britain, and with the happiest effect. This controversy with the Alliance might be made the subject of extended remark, but I must forbear, except to say, that this effort to shield the christian character of slaveholders greatly served to open a way to the British ear for anti-slavery discussion, and that it was well improved.

The fourth and last circumstance that assisted me in getting before the British public, was an attempt on the part of certain doctors of divinity to silence me on the platform of the World's Temperance Convention. Here I was brought into point blank collision with Rev. Dr. Cox, who made me the subject not only of bitter remark in the convention, but also of a long denunciatory letter published in the New York Evangelist and other American papers. I replied to the doctor as well as I could, and was successful in getting a respectful hearing before the British public, who are by nature and practice ardent lovers of fair play, especially in a conflict between the weak and the strong.

Thus did circumstances favor me, and favor the cause of which I strove to be the advocate. After such distinguished notice, the public in both countries was compelled to attach some importance to my labors. By the very ill usage I received at the hands of Dr. Cox and his party, by the mob on board the Cambria, by the attacks made upon me in the American newspapers, and by the aspersions cast upon me through the organs of the Free Church of Scotland, I became one of that class of men, who, for the moment, at least, "have greatness forced upon them."[22] People became the more anxious to hear for themselves, and to judge for themselves, of the truth which I had to unfold. While, therefore, it is by no means easy for a stranger to get fairly before the British public, it was my lot to accomplish it in the easiest manner possible.

Having continued in Great Britain and Ireland nearly two years, and being about to return to America—not as I left it, a slave, but a freeman—leading friends of the cause of emancipation in that country intimated their intention to make me a testimonial, not only on grounds of personal regard to myself, but also to the cause to which they were so ardently devoted. How far any such thing could have succeeded, I do not know; but many reasons led me to prefer that my friends should simply give me the means of obtaining a printing press and printing materials, to enable me to start a paper, devoted to the interests of my enslaved and oppressed people. I told them that perhaps the greatest hinderance to the adoption of abolition principles by the people of the United States, was the low estimate, everywhere in that country, placed upon the negro, as a man; that because of his assumed natural inferiority, people reconciled themselves to his enslavement and oppression, as things inevitable, if not desirable. The grand thing to be done, therefore, was to change the estimation in which the colored people of the United States were held; to remove the prejudice which depreciated and depressed them; to prove them worthy of a higher consideration; to disprove their alleged inferiority, and demonstrate their capacity for a more exalted civilization than slavery and prejudice had assigned to them. I further stated, that, in my judgment, a tolerably well conducted press, in the hands of persons of the despised race, by calling out the mental energies of the race itself; by making them acquainted with their own latent powers; by enkindling among them the hope that for them there is a future; by developing their moral power; by combining and reflecting their talents—would prove a most powerful means of removing prejudice, and of awakening an interest in them. I further informed them—and at that time the statement was true—that there was not, in the United States, a single newspaper regularly published by the colored people; that many attempts had been made to establish such papers; but that, up to that time, they had all failed. These views I laid before my friends. The result was, nearly two thousand five hundred dollars were speedily raised toward starting my paper. For this prompt and generous assistance, rendered upon my bare suggestion, without any personal efforts on my part, I shall never cease to feel deeply grateful; and the thought of fulfilling the noble expectations of the dear friends who gave me this evidence of their confidence, will never cease to be a motive for persevering exertion.

Proposing to leave England, and turning my face toward America, in the spring of 1847, I was met, on the threshold, with something which painfully reminded me of the kind of life which awaited me in my native land. For the first time in the many months spent abroad, I was met with proscription on account of my color. A few weeks before departing from England, while in London, I was careful to purchase a ticket, and secure a berth for returning home, in the Cambria—the steamer in which I left the United States—paying therefor the round sum of forty pounds and nineteen shillings sterling. This was first cabin fare. But on going aboard the Cambria, I found that the Liverpool agent had ordered my berth to be given to another, and had forbidden my entering the saloon! This contemptible conduct met with stern rebuke from the British press. For, upon the point of leaving England, I took occasion to expose the disgusting tyranny, in the columns of the London Times. That journal, and other leading journals throughout the United Kingdom, held up the outrage to unmitigated condemnation. So good an opportunity for calling out a full expression of British sentiment on the subject, had not before occurred, and it was most fully embraced. The result was, that Mr. Cunard came out in a letter to the public journals, assuring them of his regret at the outrage, and promising that the like should never occur again on board his steamers; and the like, we believe, has never since occurred on board the steamships of the Cunard line.

It is not very pleasant to be made the subject of such insults; but if all such necessarily resulted as this one did, I should be very happy to bear, patiently, many more than I have borne, of the same sort. Albeit, the lash of proscription, to a man accustomed to equal social position, even for a time, as I was, has a sting for the soul hardly less severe than that which bites the flesh and draws the blood from the back of the plantation slave. It was rather hard, after having enjoyed nearly two years of equal social privileges in England, often dining with gentlemen of great literary, social, political, and religious eminence—never, during the whole time, having met with a single word, look, or gesture, which gave me the slightest reason to think my color was an offense to anybody—now to be cooped up in the stern of the Cambria, and denied the right to enter the saloon, lest my dark presence should be deemed an offense to some of my democratic fellow-passengers. The reader will easily imagine what must have been my feelings.

FROM *LIFE AND TIMES OF FREDERICK DOUGLASS* (1881)

In these excerpts from the second part of his third autobiography, Douglass details his escape from slavery, which he omitted from his earlier narratives, and his postwar reunion with his former master, Thomas Auld.

SOURCE: *Life and Times of Frederick Douglass* (Hartford, CT: Park Publishing Co., 1881)

CHAPTER I.

ESCAPE FROM SLAVERY.

REASONS FOR NOT HAVING REVEALED THE MANNER OF ESCAPE—NOTHING OF ROMANCE IN THE METHOD—DANGER—FREE PAPERS—UNJUST TAX—PROTECTION PAPERS—"FREE TRADE AND SAILORS' RIGHTS"—AMERICAN EAGLE—RAILROAD TRAIN—UNOBSERVING CONDUCTOR—CAPT. MCGOWAN—HONEST GERMAN—FEARS—SAFE ARRIVAL IN PHILADELPHIA—DITTO IN NEW YORK.

In the first narrative of my experience in slavery, written nearly forty years ago, and in various writings since, I have given the public what I considered very good reasons for withholding the manner of my escape. In substance these reasons were, first, that such publication at any time during the existence of slavery might be used by the master against the slave, and prevent the future escape of any who might adopt the same means that I did.

The second reason was, if possible, still more binding to silence—for publication of details would certainly have put in peril the persons and property of those who assisted. Murder itself was not more sternly and certainly punished in the State of Maryland than was the aiding and abetting the escape of a slave. Many colored men, for no other crime than that of giving aid to a fugitive slave, have, like Charles T. Torrey, perished in prison. The abolition of slavery in my native State and throughout the country, and the lapse of time, render the caution hitherto observed no longer necessary. But, even since the abolition of slavery, I have sometimes thought it well enough to baffle curiosity by saying that while slavery existed there were good reasons for not telling the manner of my escape, and since slavery had ceased to exist there was no reason for telling it. I shall now, however, cease to avail myself of this formula, and, as far as I can, endeavor to satisfy this very natural curiosity. I should perhaps have yielded to that feeling sooner, had there been anything very heroic or thrilling in the incidents connected with my escape, for I am sorry to say I have nothing of that sort to tell; and yet the courage that could risk betrayal and the bravery which was ready to encounter death if need be, in pursuit of freedom, were essential features in the undertaking. My success was due to address rather than to courage; to good luck rather than to bravery. My means of escape were provided for me by the very men who were making laws to hold and bind me more securely in slavery. It was the custom in the State of Maryland to require of the free colored people to have what were called free papers. This instrument they were required to renew very often, and by charging a fee for this writing, considerable sums from time to time were collected by the State. In these papers the name, age, color, height and form of the free man were described, together with any scars or other marks upon his person which would assist in his identification. This device of slaveholding ingenuity, like other devices of wickedness, in some measure defeated itself—since more than one man could be found to answer the same general description. Hence many slaves could escape by personating the owner of one set of papers; and this was often done as follows: A slave nearly or sufficiently answering the description set forth in the papers, would borrow or hire them till he could by their means escape to a free state, and then, by mail or otherwise, return them to the owner. The operation was a hazardous one for the lender as well as for the borrower. A failure on the part of the fugitive to send back the papers would imperil his benefactor, and the discovery of the papers in possession of the wrong man would imperil both the fugitive and his friend. It was therefore an act of supreme trust on the part of a freeman of color thus to put in jeopardy his own liberty that another might be free. It was, however, not unfrequently bravely done, and was seldom discovered. I was not so fortunate as to sufficiently resemble any of my free acquaintances as to answer the description of their papers. But I had one friend—a sailor—who owned a sailor's protection, which answered somewhat the purpose of free papers—describing his person and certifying to the fact that he was a free American sailor. The instrument had at its head the American eagle, which at once gave it the appearance of an authorized document. This protection did not, when in my hands, describe its bearer very accurately. Indeed, it called for a man much darker than myself, and close examination of it would have caused my arrest at the start. In order to avoid this fatal scrutiny on the part of the railroad official, I had arranged with Isaac Rolls, a hackman, to bring my baggage to the train just on the moment of starting, and jumped upon the car myself when the train was already in motion. Had I gone into the station and offered to purchase a ticket, I should have been instantly and carefully examined, and undoubtedly arrested. In choosing this plan upon which to act, I considered the jostle of the train, and the natural haste of the conductor in a train crowded with passengers, and relied upon my skill and address in playing the sailor as described in my protection, to do the rest. One element in my favor was the kind feeling which prevailed in Baltimore and other seaports at the time, towards "those who go down to the sea in ships." "Free trade and sailors' rights" expressed the sentiment of the country just then. In my clothing I was rigged out in sailor style. I had on a red shirt and a tarpaulin hat and black cravat, tied in sailor fashion, carelessly and loosely about my neck. My knowledge of ships and sailor's talk came much to my assistance, for I knew a ship from stem to stern, and from keelson to cross-trees, and could talk sailor like an "old salt." On sped the train, and I was well on the way to Havre de Grace before the conductor came into the negro car to collect tickets and examine the papers of his black passengers. This was a critical moment in the drama. My whole future depended upon the decision of this conductor. Agitated I was while this ceremony was proceeding, but still, externally at least, I was apparently calm and self-possessed. He went on with his duty—examining several colored passengers before reaching me. He was somewhat harsh in tone and peremptory in manner until he reached me, when, strangely enough, and to my surprise and relief, his whole manner changed. Seeing that I did not readily produce my free papers, as the other colored persons in the car had done, he said to me in a friendly contrast with that observed towards the others: "I suppose you have your free papers?" To which I answered: "No, sir; I never carry my free papers to sea with me." "But you have something to show that you are a free man, have you not?" "Yes, sir," I answered; "I have a paper with the American eagle on it, that will carry me round the world." With this I drew from my deep sailor's pocket my seaman's protection, as before described. The merest glance at the paper satisfied him, and he took my fare and went on about his business. This moment of time was one of the most anxious I ever experienced. Had the conductor looked closely at the paper, he could not have failed to discover that it called for a very different looking person from myself, and in that case it would have been his duty to arrest me on the instant and send me back to Baltimore from the first station. When he left me with the assurance that I was all right, though much relieved, I realized that I was still in great danger: I was still in Maryland, and subject to arrest at any moment. I saw on the train several persons who would have known me in any other clothes, and I feared they might recognize me, even in my sailor "rig," and report me to the conductor, who would then subject me to a closer examination, which I knew well would be fatal to me.

Though I was not a murderer fleeing from justice, I felt, perhaps, quite as miserable as such a criminal. The train was moving at a very high rate of speed for that time of railroad travel, but to my anxious mind, it was moving far too slowly. Minutes were hours, and hours were days during this part of my flight. After Maryland I was to pass through Delaware—another slave State, where slave-catchers generally awaited their prey, for it was not in the interior of the State, but on its borders, that these human hounds were most vigilant and active. The border lines between slavery and freedom were the dangerous ones, for the fugitives. The heart of no fox or deer, with hungry hounds on his trail, in full chase, could have beaten more anxiously or noisily than did mine from the time I left Baltimore till I reached Philadelphia. The passage of the Susquehanna river at Havre de Grace was at that time made by ferry-boat, on board of which I met a young colored man by the name of Nichols, who came very near betraying me. He was a "hand" on the boat, but instead of minding his business, he insisted upon knowing me, and asking me dangerous questions as to where I was going, and when I was coming back, etc. I got away from my old and inconvenient acquaintance as soon as I could decently do so, and went to another part of the boat. Once across the river I encountered a new danger. Only a few days before I had been at work on a revenue cutter, in Mr. Price's ship-yard, under the care of Captain McGowan. On the meeting at this point of the two trains, the one going south stopped on the track just opposite to the one going north, and it so happened that this Captain McGowan sat at a window where he could see me very distinctly, and would certainly have recognized me had he looked at me but for a second. Fortunately, in the hurry of the moment, he did not see me, and the trains soon passed each other on their respective ways. But this was not the only hair-breadth escape. A German blacksmith, whom I knew well, was on the train with me, and looked at me very intently, as if he thought he had seen me somewhere before in his travels. I really believe he knew me, but had no heart to betray me. At any rate he saw me escaping and held his peace.

The last point of imminent danger, and the one I dreaded most, was Wilmington. Here we left the train and took the steamboat for Philadelphia. In making the change I again apprehended arrest, but no one disturbed me, and I was soon on the broad and beautiful Delaware, speeding away to the Quaker City. On reaching Philadelphia in the afternoon I inquired of a colored man how I could get on to New York? He directed me to the Willow street depot, and thither I went, taking the train that night. I reached New York Tuesday morning, having completed the journey in less than twenty-four hours. Such is briefly the manner of my escape from slavery—and the end of my experience as a slave. Other chapters will tell the story of my life as a freeman.

CHAPTER XVI.

"TIME MAKES ALL THINGS EVEN."

RETURN TO THE "OLD MASTER"—A LAST INTERVIEW—CAPTAIN AULD'S ADMISSION, "HAD I BEEN IN YOUR PLACE I SHOULD HAVE DONE AS YOU DID"—SPEECH AT EASTON—THE OLD JAIL THERE—INVITED TO A SAIL ON THE REVENUE CUTTER GUTHRIE—HON. JOHN L. THOMAS—VISIT TO THE OLD PLANTATION—HOME OF COLONEL LLOYD—KIND RECEPTION AND ATTENTIONS—FAMILIAR SCENES—OLD MEMORIES—BURIAL GROUND—HOSPITALITY—GRACIOUS RECEPTION FROM MRS. BUCHANAN—A LITTLE GIRL'S FLORAL GIFT—A PROMISE OF A "GOOD TIME COMING"—SPEECH AT HARPER'S FERRY, DECORATION DAY, 1881—STORER COLLEGE—HON. A. J. HUNTER.

The leading incidents to which it is my purpose to call attention and make prominent in the present chapter will, I think, address the imagination of the reader with peculiar and poetic force, and might well enough be dramatized for the stage. They certainly afford another striking illustration of the trite saying that "truth is stranger than fiction."

The first of these events occurred four years ago, when, after a period of more than forty years, I visited and had an interview with Captain Thomas Auld at St. Michaels, Talbot county, Maryland. It will be remembered by those who have followed the thread of my story that St. Michaels was at one time the place of my home and the scene of some of my saddest experiences of slave life, and that I left there, or rather was compelled to leave there, because it was believed that I had written passes for several slaves to enable them to escape from slavery, and that prominent slaveholders in that neighborhood had, for this alleged offense, threatened to shoot me on sight, and to prevent the execution of this threat my master had sent me to Baltimore.

My return, therefore, in peace, to this place and among the same people, was strange enough in itself; but that I should, when there, be formally invited by Captain Thomas Auld, then over eighty years old, to come to the side of his dying bed, evidently with a view to a friendly talk over our past relations, was a fact still more strange, and one which, until its occurrence, I could never have thought possible. To me Captain Auld had sustained the relation of master—a relation which I had held in extremest abhorrence, and which for forty years I had denounced in all bitterness of spirit and fierceness of speech. He had struck down my personality, had subjected me to his will, made property of my body and soul, reduced me to a chattel, hired me out to a noted slave breaker to be worked like a beast and flogged into submission, taken my hard earnings, sent me to prison, offered me for sale, broken up my Sunday-school, forbidden me to teach my fellow-slaves to read on pain of nine and thirty lashes on my bare back and had, without any apparent disturbance of his conscience, sold my body to his brother Hugh and pocketed the price of my flesh and blood. I, on my part, had traveled through the length and breadth of this country and of England, holding up this conduct of his, in common with that of other slaveholders, to the reprobation of all men who would listen to my words. I had by my writings made his name and his deeds familiar to the world in four different languages, yet here we were, after four decades, once more face to face—he on his bed, aged and tremulous, drawing near the sunset of life, and I, his former slave, United States Marshal of the district of Columbia, holding his hand and in friendly conversation with him in a sort of final settlement of past differences preparatory to his stepping into his grave, where all distinctions are at an end, and where the great and the small, the slave and his master, are reduced to the same level. Had I been asked in the days of slavery to visit this man I should have regarded the invitation as one to put fetters on my ankles and handcuffs on my wrists. It would have been an invitation to the auction-block and the slave-whip. I had no business with this man under the old regime but to keep out of his way. But now that slavery was destroyed, and the slave and the master stood upon equal ground, I was not only willing to meet him, but was very glad to do so. The conditions were favorable for remembrance of all his good deeds, and generous extenuation of all his evil ones. He was to me no longer a slaveholder either in fact or in spirit, and I regarded him as I did myself, a victim of the circumstances of birth, education, law, and custom.

Our courses had been determined for us, not by us. We had both been flung, by powers that did not ask our consent, upon a mighty current of life, which we could neither resist nor control. By this current he was a master, and I a slave; but now our lives were verging towards a point where differences disappear, where even the constancy of hate breaks down and where the clouds of pride, passion and selfishness vanish before the brightness of infinite light. At such a time, and in such a place, when a man is about closing his eyes on this world and ready to step into the eternal unknown, no word of reproach or bitterness should reach him or fall from his lips; and on this occasion there was to this rule no transgression on either side.

As this visit to Capt. Auld has been made the subject of mirth by heartless triflers, and by serious-minded men regretted as a weakening of my life-long testimony against slavery, and as the report of it, published in the papers immediately after it occurred, was in some respects defective and colored, it may be proper to state exactly what was said and done at this interview.

It should in the first place be understood that I did not go to St. Michaels upon Capt. Auld's invitation, but upon that of my colored friend, Charles Caldwell; but when once there, Capt. Auld sent Mr. Green, a man in constant attendance upon him during his sickness, to tell me he would be very glad to see me, and wished me to accompany Green to his house, with which request I complied. On reaching the house I was met by Mr. Wm. H. Bruff, a son-in-law of Capt. Auld, and Mrs. Louisa Bruff, his daughter, and was conducted by them immediately to the bedroom of Capt. Auld. We addressed each other simultaneously, he calling me "Marshal Douglass," and I, as I had always called him, "Captain Auld." Hearing myself called by him "Marshal Douglass," I instantly broke up the formal nature of the meeting by saying, "not *Marshal*, but Frederick to you as formerly." We shook hands cordially, and in the act of doing so, he, having been long stricken with palsy, shed tears as men thus afflicted will do when excited by any deep emotion. The sight of him, the changes which time had wrought in him, his tremulous hands constantly in motion, and all the circumstances of his condition affected me deeply, and for a time choked my voice and made me speechless. We both, however, got the better of our feelings, and conversed freely about the past.

Though broken by age and palsy, the mind of Capt. Auld was remarkably clear and strong. After he had become composed I asked him what he thought of my conduct in running away and going to the north. He hesitated a moment as if to properly formulate his reply, and said: "Frederick, I always knew you were too smart to be a slave, and had I been in your place, I should have done as you did." I said, "Capt. Auld, I am glad to hear you say this. I did not run away from *you*, but from *slavery*; it was not that I loved Caesar less, but Rome more." I told him that I had made a mistake in my narrative, a copy of which I had sent him, in attributing to him ungrateful and cruel treatment of my grandmother; that I had done so on the supposition that in the division of the property of my old master, Mr. Aaron Anthony, my grandmother had fallen to him, and that he had left her in her old age, when she could be no longer of service to him, to pick up her living in solitude with none to help her, or, in other words, had turned her out to die like an old horse. "Ah!" he said, "that was a mistake, I never owned your grandmother; she in the division of the slaves was awarded to my brother-in-law, Andrew Anthony; but," he added quickly, "I brought her down here and took care of her as long as she lived." The fact is, that, after writing my narrative describing the condition of my grandmother, Capt. Auld's attention being thus called to it, he rescued her from her destitution. I told him that this mistake of mine was corrected as soon as I discovered it, and that I had at no time any wish to do him injustice; that I regarded both of us as victims of a system. "Oh, I never liked slavery," he said, "and I meant to emancipate all of my slaves when they reached the age of twenty-five years." I told him I had always been curious to know how old I was and that it had been a serious trouble to me, not to know when was my birthday. He said he could not tell me that, but he thought I was born in February, 1818. This date made me one year younger than I had supposed myself from what was told me by Mistress Lucretia, Captain Auld's former wife, when I left Lloyd's for Baltimore in the Spring of 1825; she having then said that I was eight, going on nine. I know that it was in the year 1825 that I went to Baltimore, because it was in that year that Mr. James Beacham built a large frigate at the foot of Alliceana street, for one of the South American Governments. Judging from this, and from certain events which transpired at Col. Lloyd's such as a boy under eight years old, without any knowledge of books, would hardly take cognizance of, I am led to believe that Mrs. Lucretia was nearer right as to my age than her husband.

Before I left his bedside Captain Auld spoke with a cheerful confidence of the great change that awaited him, and felt himself about to depart in peace. Seeing his extreme weakness I did not protract my visit. The whole interview did not last more than twenty minutes, and we parted to meet no more. His death was soon after announced in the papers, and the fact that he had once owned me as a slave was cited as rendering that event noteworthy.

FICTION

THE HEROIC SLAVE (1853)

In his only work of fiction, Douglass tells the story of the 1841 *Creole* mutiny, the most successful slave revolt in American history in terms of numbers liberated (133) versus killed (3). Drawing from existing reports, he casts the leader, Madison Washington, as a revolutionary hero who combines eloquence with physical force to combat slavery and racism.

SOURCE: "The Heroic Slave," *Autographs for Freedom* (Boston: John P. Jewett & Co., 1853)

PART I.

Oh! child of grief, why weepest thou?
  Why droops thy sad and mournful brow?
Why is thy look so like despair?
  What deep, sad sorrow lingers there?[1]

The State of Virginia is famous in American annals for the multitudinous array of her statesmen and heroes. She has been dignified by some the mother of statesmen. History has not been sparing in recording their names, or in blazoning their deeds. Her high position in this respect, has given her an enviable distinction among her sister States. With Virginia for his birth-place, even a man of ordinary parts, on account of the general partiality for her sons, easily rises to eminent stations. Men, not great enough to attract special attention in their native States, have, like a certain distinguished citizen in the State of New York, sighed and repined that they were not born in Virginia. Yet not all the great ones of the Old Dominion have, by the fact of their birth-place, escaped undeserved obscurity. By some strange neglect, *one* of the truest, manliest, and bravest of her children,—one who, in after years, will, I think, command the pen of genius to set his merits forth, holds now no higher place in the records of that grand old Commonwealth than is held by a horse or an ox. Let those account for it who can, but there stands the fact, that a man who loved liberty as well as did Patrick Henry,—who deserved it as much as Thomas Jefferson,—and who fought for it with a valor as high, an arm as strong, and against odds as great, as he who led all the armies of the American colonies through the great war for freedom and independence, lives now only in the chattel records of his native State.

Glimpses of this great character are all that can now be presented. He is brought to view only by a few transient incidents, and these afford but partial satisfaction. Like a guiding star on a stormy night, he is seen through the parted clouds and the howling tempests; or, like the gray peak of a menacing rock on a perilous coast, he is seen by the quivering flash of angry lightning, and he again disappears covered with mystery.

Curiously, earnestly, anxiously we peer into the dark, and wish even for the blinding flash, or the light of northern skies to reveal him. But alas! he is still enveloped in darkness, and we return from the pursuit like a wearied and disheartened mother, (after a tedious and unsuccessful search for a lost child,) who returns weighed down with disappointment and sorrow. Speaking of marks, traces, possibles, and probabilities, we come before our readers.

In the spring of 1835, on a Sabbath morning, within hearing of the solemn peals of the church bells at a distant village, a Northern traveller through the State of Virginia drew up his horse to drink at a sparkling brook, near the edge of a dark pine forest. While his weary and thirsty steed drew in the grateful water, the rider caught the sound of a human voice, apparently engaged in earnest conversation.

Following the direction of the sound, he descried, among the tall pines, the man whose voice had arrested his attention. "To whom can he be speaking?" thought the traveller. "He seems to be alone." The circumstance interested him much, and he became intensely curious to know what thoughts and feelings, or, it might be, high aspirations, guided those rich and mellow accents. Tieing his horse at a short distance from the brook, he stealthily drew near the solitary speaker; and, concealing himself by the side of a huge fallen tree, he distinctly heard the following soliloquy:—

"What, then, is life to me? it is aimless and worthless, and worse than worthless. Those birds, perched on yon swinging boughs, in friendly conclave, sounding forth their merry notes in seeming worship of the rising sun, though liable to the sportsman's fowling-piece, are still my superiors. They *live free*, though they may die slaves. They fly where they list by day, and retire in freedom at night. But what is freedom to me, or I to it? I am a *slave*,—born a slave, an abject slave,—even before I made part of this breathing world, the scourge was platted for my back; the fetters were forged for my limbs. How mean a thing am I. That accursed and crawling snake, that miserable reptile, that has just glided into its slimy home, is freer and better off than I. He escaped my blow, and is safe. But here am I, a man,—yes, *a man!*—with thoughts and wishes, with powers and faculties as far as angel's flight above that hated reptile,—yet he is my superior, and scorns to own me as his master, or to stop to take my blows. When he saw my uplifted arm, he darted beyond my reach, and turned to give me battle. I dare not do as much as that. I neither run nor fight, but do meanly stand, answering each heavy blow of a cruel master with doleful wails and piteous cries. I am galled with irons; but even these are more tolerable than the consciousness, the *galling* consciousness of cowardice and indecision. Can it be that I *dare* not run away? *Perish the thought*, I *dare* do any thing which may be done by another. When that young man struggled with the waves *for life*, and others stood back appalled in helpless horror, did I not plunge in, forgetful of life, to save his? The raging bull from whom all others fled, pale with fright, did I not keep at bay with a single pitchfork? Could a coward do that? *No*,—*no*,—I wrong myself,—I am no coward. *Liberty* I will have, or die in the attempt to gain it. This working that others may live in idleness! This cringing submission to insolence and curses! This living under the constant dread and apprehension of being sold and transferred, like a mere brute, is *too* much for me. I will stand it no longer. What others have done, I will do. These trusty legs, or these sinewy arms shall place me among the free. Tom escaped; so can I. The North Star will not be less kind to me than to him. I will follow it. I will at least make the trial. I have nothing to lose. If I am caught, I shall only be a slave. If I am shot, I shall only lose a life which is a burden and a curse. If I get clear, (as something tells me I shall,) liberty, the inalienable birth-right of every man, precious and priceless, will be mine. My resolution is fixed. *I shall be free*."

At these words the traveller raised his head cautiously and noiselessly, and caught, from his hiding-place, a full view of the unsuspecting speaker. Madison (for that was the name of our hero) was standing erect, a smile of satisfaction rippled upon his expressive countenance, like that which plays upon the face of one who has but just solved a difficult problem, or vanquished a malignant foe; for at that moment he was free, at least in spirit. The future gleamed brightly before him, and his fetters lay broken at his feet. His air was triumphant.

Madison was of manly form. Tall, symmetrical, round, and strong. In his movements he seemed to combine, with the strength of the lion, a lion's elasticity. His torn sleeves disclosed arms like polished iron. His face was "black, but comely."[2] His eye, lit with emotion, kept guard under a brow as dark and as glossy as the raven's wing. His whole appearance betokened Herculean strength; yet there was nothing savage or forbidding in his aspect. A child might play in his arms, or dance on his shoulders. A giant's strength, but not a giant's heart was in him. His broad mouth and nose spoke only of good nature and kindness. But his voice, that unfailing index of the soul, though full and melodious, had that in it which could terrify as well as charm. He was just the man you would choose when hardships were to be endured, or danger to be encountered,—intelligent and brave. He had the head to conceive, and the hand to execute. In a word, he was one to be sought as a friend, but to be dreaded as an enemy.

As our traveller gazed upon him, he almost trembled at the thought of his dangerous intrusion. Still he could not quit the place. He had long desired to sound the mysterious depths of the thoughts and feelings of a slave. He was not, therefore, disposed to allow so providential an opportunity to pass unimproved. He resolved to hear more; so he listened again for those mellow and mournful accents which, he says, made such an impression upon him as can never be erased. He did not have to wait long. There came another gush from the same full fountain; now bitter, and now sweet. Scathing denunciations of the cruelty and injustice of slavery; heart-touching narrations of his own personal suffering, intermingled with prayers to the God of the oppressed for help and deliverance, were followed by presentations of the dangers and difficulties of escape, and formed the burden of his eloquent utterances; but his high resolution clung to him,—for he ended each speech by an emphatic declaration of his purpose to be free. It seemed that the very repetition of this, imparted a glow to his countenance. The hope of freedom seemed to sweeten, for a season, the bitter cup of slavery, and to make it, for a time, tolerable; for when in the very whirlwind of anguish,—when his heart's cord seemed screwed up to snapping tension, hope sprung up and soothed his troubled spirit. Fitfully he would exclaim, "How can I leave her? Poor thing! what can she do when I am gone? Oh! oh! 'tis impossible that I can leave poor Susan!"

A brief pause intervened. Our traveller raised his head, and saw again the sorrow-smitten slave. His eye was fixed upon the ground. The strong man staggered under a heavy load. Recovering himself, he argued thus aloud: "All is uncertain here. Tomorow's sun may not rise before I am sold, and separated from her I love. What, then, could I do for her? I should be in more hopeless slavery, and she no nearer to liberty,—whereas if I were free,—my arms my own,—I might devise the means to rescue her."

This said, Madison cast around a searching glance, as if the thought of being overheard had flashed across his mind. He said no more, but, with measured steps, walked away, and was lost to the eye of our traveller amidst the wildering woods.

Long after Madison had left the ground, Mr. Listwell (our traveller) remained in motionless silence, meditating on the extraordinary revelations to which he had listened. He seemed fastened to the spot, and stood half hoping, half fearing the return of the sable preacher to his solitary temple. The speech of Madison rung through the chambers of his soul, and vibrated through his entire frame. "Here is indeed a man," thought he, "of rare endowments,—a child of God,—guilty of no crime but the color of his skin,—hiding away from the face of humanity, and pouring out his thoughts and feelings, his hopes and resolutions to the lonely woods;

to him those distant church bells have no grateful music. He shuns the church, the altar, and the great congregation of christian worshippers, and wanders away to the gloomy forest, to utter in the vacant air complaints and griefs, which the religion of his times and his country can neither console nor relieve. Goaded almost to madness by the sense of the injustice done him, he resorts hither to give vent to his pent up feelings, and to debate with himself the feasibility of plans, plans of his own invention, for his own deliverance. From this hour I am an abolitionist. I have seen enough and heard enough, and I shall go to my home in Ohio resolved to atone for my past indifference to this ill-starred race, by making such exertions as I shall be able to do, for the speedy emancipation of every slave in the land."

PART II.

The gaudy, blabbling and remorseful day
Is crept into the bosom of the sea;
And now loud-howling wolves arouse the jades
That drag the tragic melancholy night;
Who with their drowsy, slow, and flagging wings
Clip dead men's graves, and from their misty jaws
Breathe foul contagions, darkness in the air.

Shakspeare.[3]

Five years after the foregoing singular occurrence, in the winter of 1840, Mr. and Mrs. Listwell sat together by the fireside of their own happy home, in the State of Ohio. The children were all gone to bed. A single lamp burnt brightly on the centre-table. All was still and comfortable within; but the night was cold and dark; a heavy wind sighed and moaned sorrowfully around the house and barn, occasionally bringing against the clattering windows a stray leaf from the large oak trees that embowered their dwelling. It was a night for strange noises and for strange fancies. A whole wilderness of thought might pass through one's mind during such an evening. The smouldering embers, partaking of the spirit of the restless night, became fruitful of varied and fantastic pictures, and revived many bygone scenes and old impressions. The happy pair seemed to sit in silent fascination, gazing on the fire. Suddenly this *reverie* was interrupted by a heavy growl. Ordinarily such an occurrence would have scarcely provoked a single word, or excited the least apprehension. But there are certain seasons when the slightest sound sends a jar through all the subtle chambers of the mind; and such a season was this. The happy pair started up, as if some sudden danger had come upon them. The growl was from their trusty watch-dog.

"What can it mean? certainly no one can be out on such a night as this," said Mrs. Listwell.

"The wind has deceived the dog, my dear; he has mistaken the noise of falling branches, brought down by the wind, for that of the footsteps of persons coming to the house. I have several times to-night thought that I heard the sound of footsteps. I am sure, however, that it was but the wind. Friends would not be likely to come out at such an hour, or such a night; and thieves are too lazy and self-indulgent to expose themselves to this biting frost; but should there be any one about, our brave old Monte, who is on the lookout, will not be slow in sounding the alarm."

Saying this they quietly left the window, whither they had gone to learn the cause of the menacing growl, and re-seated themselves by the fire, as if reluctant to leave the slowly expiring embers, although the hour was late. A few minutes only intervened after resuming their seats, when again their sober meditations were disturbed. Their faithful dog now growled and barked furiously, as if assailed by an advancing foe. Simultaneously the good couple arose, and stood in mute expectation. The contest without seemed fierce and violent. It was, however, soon over,—the barking ceased, for, with true canine instinct, Monte quickly discovered that a friend, not an enemy of the family, was coming to the house, and instead of rushing to repel the supposed intruder, he was now at the door, whimpering and dancing for the admission of himself and his newly made friend.

Mr. Listwell knew by this movement that all was well; he advanced and opened the door, and saw by the light that streamed out into the darkness, a tall man advancing slowly towards the house, with a stick in one hand, and a small bundle in the other. "It is a traveller," thought he, "who has missed his way, and is coming to inquire the road. I am glad we did not go to bed earlier,—I have felt all the evening as if somebody would be here to-night."

The man had now halted a short distance from the door, and looked prepared alike for flight or battle. "Come in, sir, don't be alarmed, you have probably lost your way."

Slightly hesitating, the traveller walked in; not, however, without regarding his host with a scrutinizing glance. "No, sir," said he, "I have come to ask you a greater favor."

Instantly Mr. Listwell exclaimed, (as the recollection of the Virginia forest scene flashed upon him,) "Oh, sir, I know not your name, but I have seen your face, and heard your voice before. I am glad to see you. *I know all.* You are flying for your liberty,—be seated,—be seated,—banish all fear. You are safe under my roof."

This recognition, so unexpected, rather disconcerted and disquieted the noble fugitive. The timidity and suspicion of persons escaping from slavery are easily awakened, and often what is intended to dispel the one, and to allay the other, has precisely the opposite effect. It was so in this case. Quickly observing the unhappy impression made by his words and action, Mr. Listwell assumed a more quiet and inquiring aspect, and finally succeeded in removing the apprehensions which his very natural and generous salutation had aroused.

Thus assured, the stranger said, "Sir, you have rightly guessed, I am, indeed, a fugitive from slavery. My name is Madison,—Madison Washington my mother used to call me. I am on my way to Canada, where I learn that persons of my color are protected in all the rights of men; and my object in calling upon you was, to beg the privilege of resting my weary limbs for the night in your barn. It was my purpose to have continued my journey till morning; but the piercing cold, and the frowning darkness compelled me to seek shelter; and, seeing a light through the lattice of your window, I was encouraged to come here to beg the privilege named. You will do me a great favor by affording me shelter for the night."

"A resting-place, indeed, sir, you shall have; not, however, in my barn, but in the best room of my house. Consider yourself, if you please, under the roof of a friend; for such I am to you, and to all your deeply injured race."

While this introductory conversation was going on, the kind

lady had revived the fire, and was diligently preparing supper; for she, not less than her husband, felt for the sorrows of the oppressed and hunted ones of earth, and was always glad of an opportunity to do them a service. A bountiful repast was quickly prepared, and the hungry and toil-worn bondman was cordially invited to partake thereof. Gratefully he acknowledged the favor of his benevolent benefactress; but appeared scarcely to understand what such hospitality could mean. It was the first time in his life that he had met so humane and friendly a greeting at the hands of persons whose color was unlike his own; yet it was impossible for him to doubt the charitableness of his new friends, or the genuineness of the welcome so freely given; and he therefore, with many thanks, took his seat at the table with Mr. and Mrs. Listwell, who, desirous to make him feel at home, took a cup of tea themselves, while urging upon Madison the best that the house could afford.

Supper over, all doubts and apprehensions banished, the three drew around the blazing fire, and a conversation commenced which lasted till long after midnight.

"Now," said Madison to Mr. Listwell, "I was a little surprised and alarmed when I came in, by what you said; do tell me, sir, *why* you thought you had seen my face before, and by what you knew me to be a fugitive from slavery; for I am sure that I never was before in this neighborhood, and I certainly sought to conceal what I supposed to be the manner of a fugitive slave."

Mr. Listwell at once frankly disclosed the secret; describing the place where he first saw him; rehearsing the language which he (Madison) had used; referring to the effect which his manner and speech had made upon him; declaring the resolution he there formed to be an abolitionist; telling how often he had spoken of the circumstance, and the deep concern he had ever since felt to know what had become of him; and whether he had carried out the purpose to make his escape, as in the woods he declared he would do.

"Ever since that morning," said Mr. Listwell, "you have seldom been absent from my mind, and though now I did not dare to hope that I should ever see you again, I have often wished that such might be my fortune; for, from that hour, your face seemed to be daguerreotyped on my memory."

Madison looked quite astonished, and felt amazed at the narration to which he had listened. After recovering himself he said, "I well remember that morning, and the bitter anguish that wrung my heart; I will state the occasion of it. I had, on the previous Saturday, suffered a cruel lashing; had been tied up to the limb of a tree, with my feet chained together, and a heavy iron bar placed between my ankles. Thus suspended, I received on my naked back forty stripes, and was kept in this distressing position three or four hours, and was then let down, only to have my torture increased; for my bleeding back, gashed by the cow-skin, was washed by the overseer with old brine, partly to augment my suffering, and partly, as he said, to prevent inflammation. My crime was that I had stayed longer at the mill, the day previous, than it was thought I ought to have done, which, I assured my master and the overseer, was no fault of mine; but no excuses were allowed. 'Hold your tongue, you impudent rascal,' met my every explanation. Slave-holders are so imperious when their passions are excited, as to construe every word of the slave into insolence. I could do nothing but submit to the agonizing infliction. Smarting still from the wounds, as well as from the consciousness of being whipt for no cause, I took advantage of the absence of my master, who had gone to church, to spend the time in the woods, and brood over my wretched lot. Oh, sir, I remember it well,—and can never forget it."

"But this was five years ago; where have you been since?"

"I will try to tell you," said Madison. "Just four weeks after that Sabbath morning, I gathered up the few rags of clothing I had, and started, as I supposed, for the North and for freedom. I must not stop to describe my feelings on taking this step. It seemed like taking a leap into the dark. The thought of leaving my poor wife and two little children caused me indescribable anguish; but consoling myself with the reflection that once free, I could, possibly, devise ways and means to gain their freedom also, I nerved myself up to make the attempt. I started, but ill-luck attended me; for after being out a whole week, strange to say, I still found myself on my master's grounds; the third night after being out, a season of clouds and rain set in, wholly preventing me from seeing the North Star, which I had trusted as my guide, not dreaming that clouds might intervene between us.

"This circumstance was fatal to my project, for in losing my star,

I lost my way; so when I supposed I was far towards the North, and had almost gained my freedom, I discovered myself at the very point from which I had started. It was a severe trial, for I arrived at home in great destitution; my feet were sore, and in travelling in the dark, I had dashed my foot against a stump, and started a nail, and lamed myself. I was wet and cold; one week had exhausted all my stores; and when I landed on my master's plantation, with all my work to do over again,—hungry, tired, lame, and bewildered,—I almost cursed the day that I was born. In this extremity I approached the quarters. I did so stealthily, although in my desperation I hardly cared whether I was discovered or not. Peeping through the rents of the quarters, I saw my fellow-slaves seated by a warm fire, merrily passing away the time, as though their hearts knew no sorrow. Although I envied their seeming contentment, all wretched as I was, I despised the cowardly acquiescence in their own degradation which it implied, and felt a kind of pride and glory in my own desperate lot. I dared not enter the quarters,—for where there is seeming contentment with slavery, there is certain treachery to freedom. I proceeded towards the great house, in the hope of catching a glimpse of my poor wife, whom I knew might be trusted with my secrets even on the scaffold. Just as I reached the fence which divided the field from the garden, I saw a woman in the yard, who in the darkness I took to be my wife; but a nearer approach told me it was not she. I was about to speak; had I done so, I would not have been here this night; for an alarm would have been sounded, and the hunters been put on my track. Here were hunger, cold, thirst, disappointment, and chagrin, confronted only by the dim hope of liberty. I tremble to think of that dreadful hour. To face the deadly cannon's mouth in warm blood unterrified, is, I think, a small achievement, compared with a conflict like this with gaunt starvation. The gnawings of hunger conquers by degrees, till all that a man has he would give in exchange for a single crust of bread. Thank God, I was not quite reduced to this extremity.

"Happily for me, before the fatal moment of utter despair, my good wife made her appearance in the yard. It was she; I knew her step. All was well now. I was, however, afraid to speak, lest I should frighten her. Yet speak I did; and, to my great joy, my voice was known. Our meeting can be more easily imagined than described. For a time hunger, thirst, weariness, and lameness were forgotten. But it was soon necessary for her to return to the house. She being a house-servant, her absence from the kitchen, if discovered, might have excited suspicion. Our parting was like tearing the flesh from my bones; yet it was the part of wisdom for her to go. She left me with the purpose of meeting me at midnight in the very forest where you last saw me. She knew the place well, as one of my melancholy resorts, and could easily find it, though the night was dark.

"I hastened away, therefore, and concealed myself, to await the arrival of my good angel. As I lay there among the leaves, I was strongly tempted to return again to the house of my master and give myself up; but remembering my solemn pledge on that memorable Sunday morning, I was able to linger out the two long hours between ten and midnight. I may well call them long hours. I have endured much hardship; I have encountered many perils; but the anxiety of those two hours, was the bitterest I ever experienced. True to her word, my wife came laden with provisions, and we sat down on the side of a log, at that dark and lonesome hour of the night. I cannot say we talked; our feelings were too great for that; yet we came to an understanding that I should make the woods my home, for if I gave myself up, I should be whipped and sold away; and if I started for the North, I should leave a wife doubly dear to me. We mutually determined, therefore, that I should remain in the vicinity. In the dismal swamps I lived, sir, five long years,—a cave for my home during the day. I wandered about at night with the wolf and the bear,—sustained by the promise that my good Susan would meet me in the pine woods at least once a week. This promise was redeemed, I assure you, to the letter, greatly to my relief. I had partly become contented with my mode of life, and had made up my mind to spend my days there; but the wilderness that sheltered me thus long took fire, and refused longer to be my hiding-place.

"I will not harrow up your feelings by portraying the terrific scene of this awful conflagration. There is nothing to which I can liken it. It was horribly and indescribably grand. The whole world seemed on fire, and it appeared to me that the day of judgment had come; that the burning bowels of the earth had burst forth, and that the end of all things was at hand. Bears and wolves, scorched from their mysterious hiding-places in the earth, and all the wild inhabitants of the untrodden forest, filled with a common dismay, ran forth, yelling, howling, bewildered amidst the smoke and flame. The very heavens seemed to rain down fire through the towering trees; it was by the merest chance that I escaped the devouring element. Running before it, and stopping occasionally to take breath, I looked back to behold its frightful ravages, and to drink in its savage magnificence. It was awful, thrilling, solemn, beyond compare. When aided by the fitful wind, the merciless tempest of fire swept on, sparkling, creaking, cracking, curling, roaring, out-doing in its dreadful splendor a thousand thunderstorms at once. From tree to tree it leaped, swallowing them up in its lurid, baleful glare; and leaving them leafless, limbless, charred, and lifeless behind. The scene was overwhelming, stunning,—nothing was spared,—cattle, tame and wild, herds of swine and of deer, wild beasts of every name and kind,—huge night-birds, bats, and owls, that had retired to their homes in lofty tree-tops to rest, perished in that fiery storm. The long-winged buzzard and croaking raven mingled their dismal cries with those of the countless myriads of small birds that rose up to the skies, and were lost to the sight in clouds of smoke and flame. Oh, I shudder when I think of it! Many a poor wandering fugitive, who, like myself, had sought among wild beasts the mercy denied by our fellow men, saw, in helpless consternation, his dwelling-place and city of refuge reduced to ashes forever. It was this grand conflagration that drove me hither; I ran alike from fire and from slavery."

After a slight pause, (for both speaker and hearers were deeply moved by the above recital,) Mr. Listwell, addressing Madison, said, "If it does not weary you too much, do tell us something of your journeyings since this disastrous burning,—we are deeply interested in everything which can throw light on the hardships of persons escaping from slavery; we could hear you talk all night; are there no incidents that you could relate of your travels hither? or are they such that you do not like to mention them."

"For the most part, sir, my course has been uninterrupted; and, considering the circumstances, at times even pleasant. I have suffered little for want of food; but I need not tell you how I got it. Your moral code may differ from mine, as your customs and usages are different. The fact is, sir, during my flight, I felt myself robbed by society of all my just rights; that I was in an enemy's land, who sought both my life and my liberty. They had transformed me into a brute; made merchandise of my body, and, for all the purposes of my flight, turned day into night,—and guided by my own necessities, and in contempt of their conventionalities, I did not scruple to take bread where I could get it."

"And just there you were right," said Mr. Listwell; "I once had doubts on this point myself, but a conversation with Gerrit Smith, (a man, by the way, that I wish you could see, for he is a devoted friend of your race, and I know he would receive you gladly,) put an end to all my doubts on this point. But do not let me interrupt you."

"I had but one narrow escape during my whole journey," said Madison.

"Do let us hear of it," said Mr. Listwell.

"Two weeks ago," continued Madison, "after travelling all night, I was overtaken by daybreak, in what seemed to me an almost interminable wood. I deemed it unsafe to go farther, and, as usual, I looked around for a suitable tree in which to spend the day. I liked one with a bushy top, and found one just to my mind. Up I climbed, and hiding myself as well as I could, I, with this strap, (pulling one out of his old coat-pocket,) lashed myself to a bough, and flattered myself that I should get a *good night's* sleep that day; but in this I was soon disappointed. I had scarcely got fastened to my natural hammock, when I heard the voices of a number of persons, apparently approaching the part of the woods where I was. Upon my word, sir, I dreaded more these human voices than I should have done those of wild beasts. I was at a loss to know what to do. If I descended, I should probably be discovered by the men; and if they had dogs I should, doubtless, be *'treed.'* It was an anxious moment, but hardships and dangers have been the accompaniments of my life; and have, perhaps, imparted to me a certain hardness of character, which, to some extent, adapts me to them. In my present predicament, I decided to hold my place in the treetop, and abide the consequences. But here I must disappoint you; for the men, who were all colored, halted at least a hundred yards from me, and began with their axes, in right good earnest, to attack the trees. The sound of their laughing axes was like the report of as many well-charged pistols. By and by there came down at least a dozen trees with a terrible crash. They leaped upon the fallen trees with an air of victory. I could see no dog with them, and felt myself comparatively safe, though I could not forget the possibility that some freak or fancy might bring the axe a little nearer my dwelling than comported with my safety.

"There was no sleep for me that day, and I wished for night. You may imagine that the thought of having the tree attacked under me was far from agreeable, and that it very easily kept me on the look-out. The day was not without diversion. The men at work seemed to be a gay set; and they would often make the woods resound with that uncontrolled laughter for which we, as a race, are remarkable. I held my place in the tree till sunset,—saw the men put on their jackets to be off. I observed that all left the ground except one, whom I saw sitting on the side of a stump, with his head bowed, and his eyes apparently fixed on the ground. I became interested in him. After sitting in the position to which I have alluded ten or fifteen minutes, he left the stump, walked directly towards the tree in which I was secreted, and halted almost under the same. He stood for a moment and looked around, deliberately and reverently took off his hat, by which I saw that he was a man in the evening of life, slightly bald and quite gray. After laying down his hat carefully, he knelt and prayed aloud, and such a prayer, the most fervent, earnest, and solemn, to which I think I ever listened. After reverently addressing the Almighty, as the all-wise, all-good, and the common Father of all mankind, he besought God for grace, for strength, to bear up under, and to endure, as a good soldier, all the hardships and trials which beset the journey of life, and to enable him to live in a manner which accorded with the gospel of Christ. His soul now broke out in humble supplication for deliverance from bondage. 'O thou,' said he, 'that hearest the raven's cry,[4] take pity on poor me! O deliver me! O deliver me! in mercy, O God, deliver me from the chains and manifold hardships of slavery! With thee, O Father, all things are possible.[5] Thou canst stand and measure the earth. Thou hast beheld and drove asunder the nations,—all power is in thy hand,—thou didst say of old, "I have seen the affliction of my people, and am come to deliver them,"[6]—Oh look down upon our afflictions, and have mercy upon us.' But I cannot repeat his prayer, nor can I give you an idea of its deep pathos. I had given but little attention to religion, and had but little faith in it; yet, as the old man prayed, I felt almost like coming down and kneel by his side, and mingle my broken complaint with his.

"He had already gained my confidence; as how could it be otherwise? I knew enough of religion to know that the man who prays in secret is far more likely to be sincere than he who loves to pray standing in the street, or in the great congregation. When he arose from his knees, like another Zacheus,[7] I came down from the tree. He seemed a little alarmed at first, but I told him my story, and the good man embraced me in his arms, and assured me of his sympathy.

"I was now about out of provisions, and thought I might safely ask him to help me replenish my store. He said he had no money; but if he had, he would freely give it me. I told him I had *one dollar*; it was all the money I had in the world. I gave it to him, and asked him to purchase some crackers and cheese, and to kindly bring me the balance; that I would remain in or near that place, and would come to him on his return, if he would whistle. He was gone only about an hour. Meanwhile, from some cause or other, I know not what, (but as you shall see very wisely,) I changed my place. On his return I started to meet him; but it seemed as if the shadow of approaching danger fell upon my spirit, and checked my progress. In a very few minutes, closely on the heels of the old man, I distinctly saw *fourteen men*, with something like guns in their hands."

"Oh! the old wretch!" exclaimed Mrs. Listwell, "he had betrayed you, had he?"

"I think not," said Madison, "I cannot believe that the old man was to blame. He probably went into a store, asked for the articles for which I sent, and presented the bill I gave him; and it is so unusual for slaves in the country to have money, that fact, doubtless, excited suspicion, and gave rise to inquiry. I can easily believe that the truthfulness of the old man's character compelled him to disclose the facts; and thus were these blood-thirsty men put on my track. Of course I did not present myself; but hugged my hiding-place securely. If discovered and attacked, I resolved to sell my life as dearly as possible.

"After searching about the woods silently for a time, the whole company gathered around the old man; one charged him with lying, and called him an old villain; said he was a thief; charged him with stealing money; said if he did not instantly tell where he got it, they would take the shirt from his old back, and give him thirty-nine lashes.

"'I did *not* steal the money,' said the old man, 'it was given me, as I told you at the store; and if the man who gave it me is not here, it is not my fault.'

"'Hush! you lying old rascal; we'll make you smart for it. You shall not leave this spot until you have told where you got that money.'

"They now took hold of him, and began to strip him; while others went to get sticks with which to beat him. I felt, at the moment, like rushing out in the midst of them; but considering that the old man would be whipped the more for having aided a fugitive slave, and that, perhaps, in the *melée* he might be killed outright, I disobeyed this impulse. They tied him to a tree, and began to whip him. My own flesh crept at every blow, and I seem to hear the old man's piteous cries even now. They laid thirty-nine lashes on his bare back, and were going to repeat that number, when one of the company besought his comrades to desist. 'You'll kill the d—d old scoundrel! You've already whipt a dollar's worth out of him, even if he stole it!' 'O yes,' said another, 'let him down. He'll never tell us another lie, I'll warrant ye!' With this, one of the company untied the old man, and bid him go about his business.

"The old man left, but the company remained as much as an hour, scouring the woods. Round and round they went, turning up the underbrush, and peering about like so many bloodhounds. Two or three times they came within six feet of where I lay. I tell you I held my stick with a firmer grasp than I did in coming up to your house tonight. I expected to level one of them at least. Fortunately, however, I eluded their pursuit, and they left me alone in the woods.

"My last dollar was now gone, and you may well suppose I felt the loss of it; but the thought of being once again free to pursue my journey, prevented that depression which a sense of destitution causes; so swinging my little bundle on my back, I caught a glimpse of the *Great Bear* (which ever points the way to my beloved star,) and I started again on my journey. What I lost in money I made up at a hen-roost that same night, upon which I fortunately came."

"But you did'nt eat you food raw? How did you cook it?" said Mrs. Listwell.

"O no, Madam," said Madison, turning to his little bundle;—"I had the means of cooking." Here he took out of his bundle an old-fashioned tinder-box, and taking up a piece of a file, which he brought with him, he struck it with a heavy flint, and brought out at least a dozen sparks at once. "I have had this old box," said he, "more than five years. It is the *only* property saved from the fire in the dismal swamp. It has done me good service. It has given me the means of broiling many a chicken!"

It seemed quite a relief to Mrs. Listwell to know that Madison had, at least, lived upon cooked food. Women have a perfect horror of eating uncooked food.

By this time thoughts of what was best to be done about getting Madison to Canada, began to trouble Mr. Listwell; for the laws of Ohio were very stringent against any one who should aid, or who were found aiding a slave to escape through that State. A citizen, for the simple act of taking a fugitive slave in his carriage, had just been stripped of all his property, and thrown penniless upon the world. Notwithstanding this, Mr. Listwell was determined to see Madison safely on his way to Canada. "Give yourself no uneasiness," said he to Madison, "for if it cost my farm, I shall see you safely out of the States, and on your way to a land of liberty. Thank God that there is *such* a land so near us! You will spend to-morrow with us, and to-morrow night I will take you in my carriage to the Lake. Once upon that, and you are safe."

"Thank you! thank you," said the fugitive; "I will commit myself to your care."

For the *first* time during *five* years, Madison enjoyed the luxury of resting his limbs on a comfortable bed, and inside a human habitation. Looking at the white sheets, he said to Mr. Listwell, "What, sir! you don't mean that I shall sleep in that bed?"

"Oh yes, oh yes."

After Mr. Listwell left the room, Madison said he really hesitated whether or not he should lie on the floor; for that was *far* more comfortable and inviting than any bed to which he had been used.

We pass over the thoughts and feelings, the hopes and fears, the plans and purposes, that revolved in the mind of Madison during the day that he was secreted at the house of Mr. Listwell. The reader will be content to know that nothing occurred to endanger his liberty, or to excite alarm. Many were the little attentions bestowed upon him in his quiet retreat and hiding-place. In the evening, Mr. Listwell, after treating Madison to a new suit of winter clothes, and replenishing his exhausted purse with five dollars, all in silver, brought out his two-horse wagon, well provided with buffaloes, and silently started off with him to Cleveland. They arrived there without interruption, a few minutes before sunrise the next morning. Fortunately the steamer Admiral lay at the wharf, and was to start for Canada at nine o'clock. Here the last anticipated danger was surmounted. It was feared that just at this point the hunters of men might be on the lookout, and, possibly, pounce upon their victim. Mr. Listwell saw the captain of the boat; cautiously sounded him on the matter of carrying liberty-loving passengers, before he introduced his precious charge. This done, Madison was conducted on board. With usual generosity this true subject of the emancipating queen welcomed Madison, and assured him that he should be safely landed in Canada, free of charge. Madison now felt himself no more a piece of merchandise, but a passenger, and, like any other passenger, going about his business, carrying with him what belonged to him, and nothing which rightfully belonged to anybody else.

Wrapped in his new winter suit, snug and comfortable, a pocket full of silver, safe from his pursuers, embarked for a free country, Madison gave every sign of sincere gratitude, and bade his kind benefactor farewell, with such a grip of the hand as bespoke a heart full of honest manliness, and a soul that knew how to appreciate kindness. It need scarcely be said that Mr. Listwell was deeply moved by the gratitude and friendship he had excited in a nature so noble as that of the fugitive. He went to his home that day with a joy and gratification which knew no bounds. He had done something "to deliver the spoiled out of the hands of the spoiler,"[8] he had given bread to the hungry, and clothes to the naked;[9] he had befriended a man to whom the laws of his country forbade all friendship,—and in proportion to the odds against his righteous deed, was the delightful satisfaction that gladdened his heart. On reaching home, he exclaimed, "*He is safe,—he is safe,—he is safe,*"—and the cup of his joy was shared by his excellent lady. The following letter was received from Madison a few days after.

"WINDSOR, CANADA WEST, DEC. 16, 1840.

My dear Friend,—for such you truly are:—

Madison is out of the woods at last; I nestle in the mane of the British lion, protected by his mighty paw from the talons and the beak of the American eagle. I AM FREE, and breathe an atmosphere too pure for *slaves*, slave-hunters, or slave-holders. My heart is full. As many thanks to you, sir, and to your kind lady, as there are pebbles on the shores of Lake Erie; and may the blessing of God rest upon you both. You will never be forgotten by your profoundly grateful friend,

MADISON WASHINGTON."

PART III.

———His head was with his heart,
And that was far away!

Childe Harold.[10]

Just upon the edge of the great road from Petersburg, Virginia, to Richmond, and only about fifteen miles from the latter place, there stands a somewhat ancient and famous public tavern, quite notorious in its better days, as being the grand resort for most of the leading gamblers, horse-racers, cock-fighters, and slave-traders from all the country round about. This old rookery, the nucleus of all sorts of birds, mostly those of ill omen, has, like everything else peculiar to Virginia, lost much of its ancient consequence and splendor; yet it keeps up some appearance of gaiety and high life, and is still frequented, even by respectable travellers, who are unacquainted with its past history and present condition. Its fine old portico looks well at a distance, and gives the building an air of grandeur. A nearer view, however, does little to sustain this pretension. The house is large, and its style imposing, but time and dissipation, unfailing in their results, have made ineffaceable marks upon it, and it must, in the common course of events, soon be numbered with the things that were. The gloomy mantle of ruin is, already, outspread to envelop it, and its remains, even but now remind one of a human skull, after the flesh has mingled with the earth. Old hats and rags fill the places in the upper windows once occupied by large panes of glass, and the moulding boards along the roofing have dropped off from their places, leaving holes and crevices in the rented wall for bats and swallows to build their nests in. The platform of the portico, which fronts the highway is a rickety affair, its planks are loose, and in some places entirely gone, leaving effective mantraps in their stead for nocturnal ramblers. The wooden pillars, which once supported it, but which now hang as encumbrances, are all rotten, and tremble with the touch. A part of the stable, a fine old structure in its day, which has given comfortable shelter to hundreds of the noblest steeds of "the Old Dominion" at once, was blown down many years ago, and never has been, and probably never will be, rebuilt. The doors of the barn are in wretched condition; they will shut with a little human strength to help their worn out hinges, but not otherwise. The side of the great building seen from the road is much discolored in sundry places by slops poured from the upper windows, rendering it unsightly and offensive in other respects. Three or four great dogs, looking as dull and gloomy as the mansion itself, lie stretched out along the door-sills under the portico; and double the number of loafers, some of them completely rum-ripe, and others ripening, dispose themselves like so many sentinels about the front of the house. These latter understand the science of scraping acquaintance to perfection. They know every-body, and almost every-body knows them. Of course, as their title implies, they have no regular employment. They are (to use an expressive phrase) *hangers on*, or still better, they are what sailors would denominate *holders-on to the slack, in every-body's mess, and in nobody's watch.* They are, however, as good as the newspaper for the events of the day, and they sell their knowledge almost as cheap. Money they seldom have; yet they always have capital the most reliable. They make their way with a succeeding traveller by intelligence gained from a preceding one. All the great names of Virginia they know by heart, and have seen their owners often. The history of the house is folded in their lips, and they rattle off stories in connection with it, equal to the guides at Dryburgh Abbey.[11] He must be a shrewd man, and well skilled in the art of evasion, who gets out of the hands of these fellows without being at the expense of a treat.

It was at this old tavern, while on a second visit to the State of Virginia in 1841, that Mr. Listwell, unacquainted with the fame of the place, turned aside, about sunset, to pass the night. Riding up to the house, he had scarcely dismounted, when one of the half dozen bar-room fraternity met and addressed him in a manner exceedingly bland and accommodating.

"Fine evening, sir."

"Very fine," said Mr. Listwell. "This is a tavern, I believe?"

"O yes, sir, yes; although you may think it looks a little the worse for wear, it was once as good a house as any in Virginy. I make no doubt if ye spend the night here, you'll think it a good house yet; for there aint a more accommodating man in the country than you'll find the landlord."

Listwell. "The most I want is a good bed for myself, and a full manger for my horse. If I get these, I shall be quite satisfied."

Loafer. "Well, I alloys like to hear a gentleman talk for his horse; and just becase the horse can't talk for itself. A man that don't care about his beast, and don't look arter it when he's travelling, aint much in my eye anyhow. Now, sir, I likes a horse, and I'll guarantee your horse will be taken good care on here. That old stable, for all you see it looks so shabby now, once sheltered the great *Eclipse*, when he run here agin *Batchelor* and *Jumping Jemmy*. Them was fast horses, but he beat 'em both."

Listwell. "Indeed."

Loafer. "Well, I rather reckon you've travelled a right smart distance to-day, from the look of your horse?"

Listwell. "Forty miles only."

Loafer. "Well! I'll be darned if that aint a pretty good *only*. Mister, that beast of yours is a singed cat, I warrant you. I never see'd a creature like that that was'nt good on the road. You've come about forty miles, then?"

Listwell. "Yes, yes, and a pretty good pace at that."

Loafer. "You're somewhat in a hurry, then, I make no doubt? I reckon I could guess if I would, what you're going to Richmond for? It would'nt be much of a guess either; for it's rumored hereabouts, that there's to be the greatest sale of niggers at Richmond to-morrow that has taken place there in a long time; and I'll be bound you're a going there to have a hand in it."

Listwell. "Why, you must think, then, that there's money to be made at that business?"

Loafer. "Well, 'pon my honor, sir, I never made any that way myself; but it stands to reason that it's a money making business; for almost all other business in Virginia is dropped to engage in this. One thing is sartain, I never see'd a nigger-buyer yet that had'nt a plenty of money, and he was'nt as free with it as water. I has known one on 'em to treat as high as twenty times in a night; and, ginerally speaking, they's men of edication, and knows all about the government. The fact is, sir, I alloys like to hear 'em talk, bekase I alloys can learn something from them."

Listwell. "What may I call your name, sir?"

Loafer. "Well, now, they calls me Wilkes. I'm known all around by the gentlemen that comes here. They all knows old Wilkes."

Listwell. "Well, Wilkes, you seem to be acquainted here, and I see you have a strong liking for a horse. Be so good as to speak a kind word for mine to the hostler to-night, and you'll not lose anything by it."

Loafer. "Well, sir, I see you don't say much, but you've got an insight into things. It's alloys wise to get the good will of them that's acquainted about a tavern; for a man don't know when he goes into a house what may happen, or how much he may need a friend." Here the loafer gave Mr. Listwell a significant grin, which expressed a sort of triumphant pleasure at having, as he supposed, by his tact succeeded in placing so fine appearing a gentleman under obligations to him.

The pleasure, however, was mutual; for there was something so insinuating in the glance of this loquacious customer, that Mr. Listwell was very glad to get quit of him, and to do so more successfully, he ordered his supper to be brought to him in his private room, private to the eye, but not to the ear. This room was directly over the bar, and the plastering being off, nothing but pine boards and naked laths separated him from the disagreeable company below,—he could easily hear what was said in the bar-room, and was rather glad of the advantage it afforded, for, as you shall see, it furnished him important hints as to the manner and deportment he should assume during his stay at that tavern.

Mr. Listwell says he had got into his room but a few moments, when he heard the officious Wilkes below, in a tone of disappointment, exclaim, "Whar's that gentleman?" Wilkes was evidently expecting to meet with his friend at the bar-room, on his return, and had no doubt of his doing the handsome thing. "He has gone to his room," answered the landlord, "and has ordered his supper to be brought to him."

Here some one shouted out, "Who is he, Wilkes? Where's he going?"

"Well, now, I'll be hanged if I know; but I'm willing to make any man a bet of this old hat agin a five dollar bill, that that gent is as full of money as a dog is of fleas. He's going down to Richmond to buy niggers, I make no doubt. He's no fool, I warrant ye."

"Well, he acts d—d strange," said another, "anyhow. I likes to see a man, when he comes up to a tavern, to come straight into the bar-room, and show that he's a man among men. Nobody was going to bite him."

"Now, I don't blame him a bit for not coming in here. That man knows his business, and means to take care on his money," answered Wilkes.

"Wilkes, you're a fool. You only say that, becase you hope to get a few coppers out on him."

"You only measure my corn by your half-bushel, I won't say that you're only mad becase I got the chance of speaking to him first."

"O Wilkes! you're known here. You'll praise up any body that will give you a copper; besides, 'tis my opinion that that fellow who took his long slab-sides up stairs, for all the world just like a half-scared woman, afraid to look honest men in the face, is a *Northerner*, and as mean as dish-water."

"Now what will you bet of that," said Wilkes.

The speaker said, "I make no bets with you, 'kase you can get that fellow up stairs there to say anything."

"Well," said Wilkes, "I am willing to bet any man in the company that *that* gentleman is a *nigger*-buyer. He did'nt tell me so right down, but I reckon I knows enough about men to give a pretty clean guess as to what they are arter."

The dispute as to *who* Mr. Listwell was, what his business, where he was going, etc., was kept up with much animation for some time, and more than once threatened a serious disturbance of the peace. Wilkes had his friends as well as his opponents. After this sharp debate, the company amused themselves by drinking whiskey, and telling stories. The latter consisting of quarrels, fights, *rencontres*, and duels, in which distinguished persons of that neighborhood, and frequenters of that house, had been actors. Some of these stories were frightful enough, and were told, too, with a relish which bespoke the pleasure of the parties with the horrid scenes they portrayed. It would not be proper here to give the reader any idea of the vulgarity and dark profanity which rolled, as "a sweet morsel,"[12] under these corrupt tongues. A more brutal set of creatures, perhaps, never congregated.

Disgusted, and a little alarmed withal, Mr. Listwell, who was not accustomed to such entertainment, at length retired, but not to sleep. He was *too* much wrought upon by what he had heard to rest quietly, and what snatches of sleep he got, were interrupted by dreams which were anything than pleasant. At eleven o'clock, there seemed to be several hundreds of persons crowding into the house. A loud and confused clamour, cursing and cracking of whips, and the noise of chains startled him from his bed; for a moment he would have given the half of his farm in Ohio to have been at home. This uproar was kept up with undulating course, till near morning. There was loud laughing,—loud singing,—loud cursing,—and yet there seemed to be weeping and mourning in the midst of all. Mr. Listwell said he had heard enough during the forepart of the night to convince him that a buyer of men and women stood the best chance of being respected. And he, therefore, thought it best to say nothing which might undo the favorable opinion that had been formed of him in the bar-room by at least one of the fraternity that swarmed about it. While he would not avow himself a purchaser of slaves, he deemed it not prudent to disavow it. He felt that he might, properly, refuse to cast such a pearl before parties which, to him, were worse than swine. To reveal himself, and to impart a knowledge of his real character and sentiments would, to say the least, be imparting intelligence with the certainty of seeing it and himself both abused. Mr. Listwell confesses, that this reasoning did not altogether satisfy his conscience, for, hating slavery as he did, and regarding it to be the immediate duty of every man to cry out against it, "without compromise and without concealment,"[13] it was hard for him to admit to himself the possibility of circumstances wherein a man might, properly, hold his tongue on the subject. Having as little of the spirit of a martyr as Erasmus, he concluded, like the latter, that it was wiser to trust the mercy of God for his soul, than the humanity of slave-traders for his body. Bodily fear, not conscientious scruples, prevailed.

In this spirit he rose early in the morning, manifesting no surprise at what he had heard during the night. His quondam friend was soon at his elbow, boring him with all sorts of questions. All, however, directed to find out his character, business, residence, purposes, and destination. With the most perfect appearance of good nature and carelessness, Mr. Listwell evaded these meddlesome inquiries, and turned conversation to general topics, leaving himself and all that specially pertained to him, out of discussion. Disengaging himself from their troublesome companionship, he made his way towards an old bowling-alley, which was connected with the house, and which, like all the rest, was in very bad repair.

On reaching the alley Mr. Listwell saw, for the first time in his life, a slave-gang on their way to market. A sad sight truly. Here were one hundred and thirty human beings,—children of a common Creator—guilty of no crime—men and women, with hearts, minds, and deathless spirits, chained and fettered, and bound for the market, in a christian country,—in a country boasting of its liberty, independence, and high civilization! Humanity converted into merchandise, and linked in iron bands, with no regard to decency or humanity! All sizes, ages, and sexes, mothers, fathers, daughters, brothers, sisters,—all huddled together, on their way to market to be sold and separated from home, and from each other *forever.*

And all to fill the pockets of men too lazy to work for an honest living, and who gain their fortune by plundering the helpless, and trafficking in the souls and sinews of men. As he gazed upon this revolting and heart-rending scene, our informant said he almost doubted the existence of a God of justice! And he stood wondering that the earth did not open and swallow up such wickedness.

In the midst of these reflections, and while running his eye up and down the fettered ranks, he met the glance of one whose face he thought he had seen before. To be resolved, he moved towards the spot. It was MADISON WASHINGTON! Here was a scene for the pencil! Had Mr. Listwell been confronted by one risen from the dead, he could not have been more appalled. He was completely stunned. A thunderbolt could not have struck him more dumb. He stood, for a few moments, as motionless as one petrified; collecting himself, he at length exclaimed, "*Madison! is that you?*"

The noble fugitive, but little less astonished than himself, answered cheerily, "O yes, sir, they've got me again."

Thoughtless of consequences for the moment, Mr. Listwell ran up to his old friend, placing his hands upon his shoulders, and looked him in the face! Speechless they stood gazing at each other as if to be doubly resolved that there was no mistake about the matter, till Madison motioned his friend away, intimating a fear lest the keepers should find him there, and suspect him of tampering with the slaves.

"They will soon be out to look after us. You can come when they go to breakfast, and I will tell you all."

Pleased with this arrangement, Mr. Listwell passed out of the alley; but only just in time to save himself, for, while near the door, he observed three men making their way to the alley. The thought occurred to him to await their arrival, as the best means of diverting the ever ready suspicions of the guilty.

While the scene between Mr. Listwell and his friend Madison was going on, the other slaves stood as mute spectators,—at a loss to know what all this could mean. As he left, he heard the man chained to Madison ask, "Who is that gentleman?"

"He is a friend of mine. I cannot tell you now. Suffice it to say he is a friend. You shall hear more of him before long, but mark me! whatever shall pass between that gentleman and me, in your hearing, I pray you will say nothing about it. We are all chained here together,—ours is a common lot; and that gentleman is not less *your* friend than *mine*." At these words, all mysterious as they were, the unhappy company gave signs of satisfaction and hope. It seems that Madison, by that mesmeric power which is the invariable accompaniment of genius, had already won the confidence of the gang, and was a sort of general-in-chief among them.

By this time the keepers arrived. A horrid trio, well fitted for their demoniacal work. Their uncombed hair came down over foreheads "*villainously low*,"[14] and with eyes, mouths, and noses to match. "Hallo! hallo!" they growled out as they entered. "Are you all there!"

"All here," said Madison.

"Well, well, that's right! your journey will soon be over. You'll be in Richmond by eleven to-day, and then you'll have an easy time on it."

"I say, gal, what in the devil are you crying about?" said one of them. "I'll give you something to cry about, if you don't mind." This was said to a girl, apparently not more than twelve years old, who had been weeping bitterly. She had, probably, left behind her a loving mother, affectionate sisters, brothers, and friends, and her tears were but the natural expression of her sorrow, and the only solace. But the dealers in human flesh have *no* respect for such sorrow. They look upon it as a protest against their cruel injustice, and they are prompt to punish it.

This is a puzzle not easily solved. *How* came he here? what can I do for him? may I not even now be in some way compromised in this affair? were thoughts that troubled Mr. Listwell, and made him eager for the promised opportunity of speaking to Madison.

The bell now sounded for breakfast, and keepers and drivers, with pistols and bowie-knives gleaming from their belts, hurried in, as if to get the best places. Taking the chance now afforded, Mr. Listwell hastened back to the bowling-alley. Reaching Madison, he said, "Now *do* tell me all about the matter. Do you know me?"

"Oh, yes," said Madison, "I know you well, and shall never forget you nor that cold and dreary night you gave me shelter. I must be short," he continued, "for they'll soon be out again. This, then, is the story in brief. On reaching Canada, and getting over the excitement of making my escape, sir, my thoughts turned to my poor wife, who had well deserved my love by her virtuous fidelity and undying affection for me. I could not bear the thought of leaving her in the cruel jaws of slavery, without making an effort to rescue her. First, I tried to get money to buy her; but oh! the process was *too slow.* I despaired of accomplishing it. She was in all my thoughts by day, and my dreams by night. At times I could almost hear her voice, saying, 'O Madison! Madison! will you then leave me here? can you leave me here to die? No! no! you will come! you will come!' I was wretched. I lost my appetite. I could neither work, eat, nor sleep, till I resolved to hazard my own liberty, to gain that of my wife! But I must be short. Six weeks ago I reached my old master's place. I laid about the neighborhood nearly a week, watching my chance, and, finally, I ventured upon the desperate attempt to reach my poor wife's room by means of a ladder. I reached the window, but the noise in raising it frightened my wife, and she screamed and fainted. I took her in my arms, and was descending the ladder, when the dogs began to bark furiously, and before I could get to the woods the white folks were roused. The cool night air soon restored my wife, and she readily recognized me. We made the best of our way to the woods, but it was now *too* late,—the dogs were after us as though they would have torn us to pieces. It was all over with me now! My old master and his two sons ran out with loaded rifles, and before we were out of gunshot, our ears were assailed with '*Stop! stop! or be shot down.*' Nevertheless we ran on. Seeing that we gave no heed to their calls, they fired, and my poor wife fell by my side dead, while I received but a slight flesh wound. I now became desperate, and stood my ground, and awaited their attack over her dead body. They rushed upon me, with their rifles in hand. I parried their blows, and fought them 'till I was knocked down and overpowered."

"Oh! it was madness to have returned," said Mr. Listwell.

"Sir, I could not be free with the galling thought that my poor wife was still a slave. With her in slavery, my body, not my spirit, was free. I was taken to the house,—chained to a ring-bolt,—my wounds dressed. I was kept there three days. All the slaves, for miles around, were brought to see me. Many slave-holders came with their slaves, using me as proof of the completeness of their power, and of the impossibility of slaves getting away. I was taunted, jeered at, and berated by them, in a manner that pierced me to the soul. Thank God, I was able to smother my rage, and to bear it all with seeming composure. After my wounds were nearly healed, I was taken to a tree and stripped, and I received sixty lashes on my naked back. A few days after, I was sold to a slave-trader, and placed in this gang for the New Orleans market."

"Do you think your master would sell you to me?"

"O no, sir! I was sold on condition of my being taken South. Their motive is revenge."

"Then, then," said Mr. Listwell, "I fear I can do nothing for you. Put your trust in God, and bear your sad lot with the manly fortitude which becomes a man. I shall see you at Richmond, but don't recognize me." Saying this, Mr. Listwell handed Madison ten dollars; said a few words to the other slaves; received their hearty "God bless you," and made his way to the house.

Fearful of exciting suspicion by too long delay, our friend went to the breakfast table, with the air of one who half reproved the greediness of those who rushed in at the sound of the bell. A cup of coffee was all that he could manage. His feelings were too bitter and excited, and his heart was too full with the fate of poor Madison (whom he loved as well as admired) to relish his breakfast; and although he sat long after the company had left the table, he really did little more than change the position of his knife and fork. The strangeness of meeting again one whom he had met on two several occasions before, under extraordinary circumstances, was well calculated to suggest the idea that a supernatural power, a wakeful providence, or an inexorable fate, had linked their destiny together; and that no efforts of his could disentangle him from the mysterious web of circumstances which enfolded him.

On leaving the table, Mr. Listwell nerved himself up and walked firmly into the bar-room. He was at once greeted again by that talkative chatter-box, Mr. Wilkes.

"Them's a likely set of niggers in the alley there," said Wilkes.

"Yes, they're fine looking fellows, one of them I should like to purchase, and for him I would be willing to give a handsome sum."

Turning to one of his comrades, and with a grin of victory,

Wilkes said, "Aha, Bill, did you hear that? I told you I know'd that gentleman wanted to buy niggers, and would bid as high as any purchaser in the market."

"Come, come," said Listwell, "don't be too loud in your praise, you are old enough to know that prices rise when purchasers are plenty."

"That's a fact," said Wilkes, "I see you knows the ropes—and there's not a man in old Virginy whom I'd rather help to make a good bargain than you, sir."

Mr. Listwell here threw a dollar at Wilkes, (which the latter caught with a dexterous hand,) saying, "Take that for your kind good will." Wilkes held up the dollar to his right eye, with a grin of victory, and turned to the morose grumbler in the corner who had questioned the liberality of a man of whom he knew nothing.

Mr. Listwell now stood as well with the company as any other occupant of the bar-room.

We pass over the hurry and bustle, the brutal vociferations of the slave-drivers in getting their unhappy gang in motion for Richmond; and we need not narrate every application of the lash to those who faltered in the journey. Mr. Listwell followed the train at a long distance, with a sad heart; and on reaching Richmond, left his horse at a hotel, and made his way to the wharf in the direction of which he saw the slave-coffle driven. He was just in time to see the whole company embark for New Orleans. The thought struck him that, while mixing with the multitude, he might do his friend Madison one last service, and he stept into a hardware store and purchased three strong *files*. These he took with him, and standing near the small boat, which lay in waiting to bear the company by parcels to the side of the brig that lay in the stream, he managed, as Madison passed him, to slip the files into his pocket, and at once darted back among the crowd.

All the company now on board, the imperious voice of the captain sounded, and instantly a dozen hardy seamen were in the rigging, hurrying aloft to unfurl the broad canvas of our Baltimore built American Slaver. The sailors hung about the ropes, like so many black cats, now in the round-tops, now in the cross-trees, now on the yard-arms; all was bluster and activity. Soon the broad fore topsail, the royal and top gallant sail were spread to the breeze. Round went the heavy windlass, clank, clank went the fall-bit,—the anchors weighed,—jibs, mainsails, and topsails hauled to the wind, and the long, low, black slaver, with her cargo of human flesh, careened and moved forward to the sea.

Mr. Listwell stood on the shore, and watched the slaver till the last speck of her upper sails faded from sight, and announced the limit of human vision. "Farewell! farewell! brave and true man! God grant that brighter skies may smile upon your future than have yet looked down upon your thorny pathway."

Saying this to himself, our friend lost no time in completing his business, and in making his way homewards, gladly shaking off from his feet the dust of Old Virginia.

PART IV.

Oh, where's the slave so lowly
Condemn'd to chains unholy,
Who could he burst
His bonds at first
Would pine beneath them slowly?

Moore.[15]

———Know ye not
Who would be free, *themselves* must strike the blow.

Childe Harold.[16]

What a world of inconsistency, as well as of wickedness, is suggested by the smooth and gliding phrase, AMERICAN SLAVE TRADE; and how strange and perverse is that moral sentiment which loathes, execrates, and brands as piracy and as deserving of death the carrying away into captivity men, women, and children from the *African coast*; but which is neither shocked nor disturbed by a similar traffic, carried on with the same motives and purposes, and characterized by even *more* odious peculiarities on the coast of our MODEL REPUBLIC. We execrate and hang the wretch guilty of this crime on the coast of Guinea, while we respect and applaud the guilty participators in this murderous business on the enlightened shores of the Chesapeake. The inconsistency is so flagrant and glaring, that it would seem to cast a doubt on the doctrine of the innate moral sense of mankind.

Just two months after the sailing of the Virginia slave brig, which the reader has seen move off to sea so proudly with her human cargo for the New Orleans market, there chanced to meet, in the Marine Coffee-house at Richmond, a company of *ocean birds,* when the following conversation, which throws some light on the subsequent history, not only of Madison Washington, but of the hundred and thirty human beings with whom we last saw him chained.

"I say, shipmate, you had rather rough weather on your late passage to Orleans?" said Jack Williams, a regular old salt, tauntingly, to a trim, compact, manly looking person, who proved to be the first mate of the slave brig in question.

"Foul play, as well as foul weather," replied the firmly knit personage, evidently but little inclined to enter upon a subject which terminated so ingloriously to the captain and officers of the American slaver.

"Well, betwixt you and me," said Williams, "that whole affair on board of the Creole was miserably and disgracefully managed. Those black rascals got the upper hand of ye altogether; and, in my opinion, the whole disaster was the result of ignorance of the real character of *darkies* in general. With half a dozen *resolute* white men, (I say it not boastingly,) I could have had the rascals in irons in ten minutes, not because I'm so strong, but I know how to manage 'em. With my back against the *caboose,* I could, myself, have flogged a dozen of them; and had I been on board, by every monster of the deep, every black devil of 'em all would have had his neck stretched from the yard-arm. Ye made a mistake in yer manner of fighting 'em. All that is needed in dealing with a set of rebellious *darkies*, is to show that yer not afraid of 'em. For my own part, I would not honor a dozen niggers by pointing a gun at one on 'em,—a good stout whip, or a stiff rope's end, is better than all the guns at Old Point to quell a *nigger* insurrection. Why, sir, to take a gun to a *nigger* is the best way you can select to tell him you are afraid of him, and the best way of inviting his attack."

This speech made quite a sensation among the company, and a part of them indicated solicitude for the answer which might be made to it. Our first mate replied, "Mr. Williams, all that you've now said sounds very well *here* on shore, where, perhaps, you have studied negro character. I do not profess to understand the subject as well as yourself; but it strikes me, you apply the same rule in dissimilar cases. It is quite easy to talk of flogging niggers here on land, where you have the sympathy of the community, and the whole physical force of the government, State and national, at your command; and where, if a negro shall lift his hand against a white man, the whole community, with one accord, are ready to unite in shooting him down. I say, in such circumstances, it's easy to talk of flogging negroes and of negro cowardice; but, sir, I deny that the negro is, naturally, a coward, or that your theory of managing slaves will stand the test of *salt* water. It may do very well for an overseer, a contemptible hireling, to take advantage of fears already in existence, and which his presence has no power to inspire; to swagger about whip in hand, and discourse on the timidity and cowardice of negroes; for they have a smooth sea and a fair wind. It is one thing to manage a company of slaves on a Virginia plantation, and quite another thing to quell an insurrection on the lonely billows of the Atlantic, where every breeze speaks of courage and liberty. For the negro to act cowardly on shore, may be to act wisely; and I've some doubts whether *you,* Mr. Williams, would find it very convenient were you a slave in Algiers, to raise your hand against the bayonets of a whole government."

"By George, shipmate," said Williams, "you're coming rather *too* near. Either I've fallen very low in your estimation, or your notions of negro courage have got up a button-hole too high. Now I more than ever wish I'd been on board of that luckless craft. I'd have given ye practical evidence of the truth of my theory. I don't doubt there's some difference in being at sea. But a nigger's a nigger, on sea or land; and is a coward, find him where you will; a drop of blood from one on 'em will skeer a hundred. A knock on the nose, or a kick on the shin, will tame the wildest *'darkey'* you can fetch me. I say again, and will stand by it, I could, with half a dozen good men, put the whole nineteen on 'em in irons, and have carried them safe to New Orleans too. Mind, I don't blame you, but I do say, and every gentleman here will bear me out in it, that the fault was somewhere, or them niggers would never have got off as they have done. For my part I feel ashamed to have the idea go abroad, that a ship load of slaves can't be safely taken from Richmond to New Orleans. I should like, merely to redeem the character of Virginia sailors, to take charge of a ship load on 'em to-morrow."

Williams went on in this strain, occasionally casting an imploring glance at the company for applause for his wit, and sympathy for his contempt of negro courage. He had, evidently, however, waked up the wrong passenger; for besides being in the right, his opponent carried that in his eye which marked him a man not to be trifled with.

"Well, sir," said the sturdy mate, "you can select your own method for distinguishing yourself;—the path of ambition in this direction is quite open to you in Virginia, and I've no doubt that you will be highly appreciated and compensated for all your valiant achievements in that line; but for myself, while I do not profess to be a giant, I have resolved never to set my foot on the deck of a slave ship, either as officer, or common sailor again; I have got enough of it."

"Indeed! indeed!" exclaimed Williams, derisively.

"Yes, *indeed,*" echoed the mate; "but don't misunderstand me. It is not the high value that I set upon my life that makes me say what I have said; yet I'm resolved never to endanger my life again in a cause which my conscience does not approve. I dare say *here* what many men *feel*, but *dare not speak*, that this whole slave-trading business is a disgrace and scandal to Old Virginia."

"Hold! hold on! shipmate," said Williams, "I hardly thought you'd have shown your colors so soon,—I'll be hanged if you're not as good an abolitionist as Garrison himself."

The mate now rose from his chair, manifesting some excitement. "What do you mean, sir," said he, in a commanding tone. "*That man does not live who shall offer me an insult with impunity.*"

The effect of these words was marked; and the company clustered around. Williams, in an apologetic tone, said, "Shipmate! keep your temper. I mean't no insult. We all know that Tom Grant is no coward, and what I said about your being an abolitionist was simply this: you *might* have put down them black mutineers and murderers, but your conscience held you back."

"In that, too," said Grant, "you were mistaken. I did all that any man with equal strength and presence of mind could have done. The fact is, Mr. Williams, you underrate the courage as well as the skill of these negroes, and further, you do not seem to have been correctly informed about the case in hand at all."

"All I know about it is," said Williams, "that on the ninth day after you left Richmond, a dozen or two of the niggers ye had on board, came on deck and took the ship from you;—had her steered into a British port, where, by the by, every woolly head of them went ashore and was free. Now I take this to be a discreditable piece of business, and one demanding explanation."

"There are a great many discreditable things in the world," said Grant. "For a ship to go down under a calm sky is, upon the first flush of it, disgraceful either to sailors or caulkers. But when we learn, that by some mysterious disturbance in nature, the waters parted beneath, and swallowed the ship up, we lose our indignation and disgust in lamentation of the disaster, and in awe of the Power which controls the elements."

"Very true, very true," said Williams, "I should be very glad to have an explanation which would relieve the affair of its present discreditable features. I have desired to see you ever since you got home, and to learn from you a full statement of the facts in the case. To me the whole thing seems unaccountable. I cannot see how a dozen or two of ignorant negroes, not one of whom had ever been to sea before, and all of them were closely ironed between decks, should be able to get their fetters off, rush out of the hatchway in open daylight, kill two white men, the one the captain and the other their master, and then carry the ship into a British port, where every '*darkey*' of them was set free. There must have been great carelessness, or cowardice somewhere!"

The company which had listened in silence during most of this discussion, now became much excited. One said, I agree with Williams; and several said the thing looks black enough. After the temporary tumultous exclamations had subsided,—

"I see," said Grant, "how you regard this case, and how difficult it will be for me to render our ship's company blameless in your eyes. Nevertheless, I will state the fact precisely as they came under my own observation. Mr. Williams speaks of 'ignorant negroes,' and, as a general rule, they are ignorant; but had he been on board the *Creole* as I was, he would have seen cause to admit that there are exceptions to this general rule. The leader of the mutiny in question was just as shrewd a fellow as ever I met in my life, and was as well fitted to lead in a dangerous enterprise as any one white man in ten thousand. The name of this man, strange to say, (ominous of greatness,) was MADISON WASHINGTON. In the short time he had been on board, he had secured the confidence of every officer. The negroes fairly worshipped him. His manner and bearing were such, that no one could suspect him of a murderous purpose. The only feeling with which we regarded him was, that he was a powerful, good-disposed negro. He seldom spake to any one, and when he did speak, it was with the utmost propriety. His words were well chosen, and his pronunciation equal to that of any schoolmaster. It was a mystery to us *where* he got his knowledge of language; but as little was said to him, none of us knew the extent of his intelligence and ability till it was too late. It seems he brought three files with him on board, and must have gone to work upon his fetters the first night out; and he must have worked well at that; for on the day of the rising, he got the irons *off eighteen* besides himself.

"The attack began just about twilight in the evening. Apprehending a squall, I had commanded the second mate to order all hands on deck, to take in sail. A few minutes before this I had seen Madison's head above the hatchway, looking out upon the white-capped waves at the leeward. I think I never saw him look more good-natured. I stood just about midship, on the larboard side. The captain was pacing the quarter-deck on the starboard side, in company with Mr. Jameson, the owner of most of the slaves on board. Both were armed. I had just told the men to lay aloft, and was looking to see my orders obeyed, when I heard the discharge of a pistol on the starboard side; and turning suddenly around, the very deck seemed covered with fiends from the pit. The nineteen negroes were all on deck, with their broken fetters in their hands, rushing in all directions. I put my hand quickly in my pocket to draw out my jack-knife; but before I could draw it, I was knocked senseless to the deck. When I came to myself, (which I did in a few minutes, I suppose, for it was yet quite light,) there was not a white man on deck. The sailors were all aloft in the rigging, and dared not come down. Captain Clarke and Mr. Jameson lay stretched on the quarter-deck,—both dying,—while Madison himself stood at the helm unhurt.

"I was completely weakened by the loss of blood, and had not recovered from the stunning blow which felled me to the deck; but it was a little too much for me, even in my prostrate condition, to see our good brig commanded by a *black murderer.* So I called out to the men to come down and take the ship, or die in the attempt. Suiting the action to the word, I started aft. 'You murderous villain,' said I, to the imp at the helm, and rushed upon him to deal him a blow, when he pushed me back with his strong, black arm, as though I had been a boy of twelve. I looked around for the men. They were still in the rigging. Not one had come down. I started towards Madison again. The rascal now told me to stand back. 'Sir,' said he, 'your life is in my hands. I could have killed you a dozen times over during this last half hour, and could kill you now. You call me a *black murderer.* I am not a murderer. God is my witness that LIBERTY, not *malice,* is the motive for this night's work. I have done no more to those dead men yonder, than they would have done to me in like circumstances. We have struck for our freedom, and if a true man's heart be in you, you will honor us for the deed. We have done that which you applaud your fathers for doing, and if we are murderers, *so were they.*'

"I felt little disposition to reply to this impudent speech. By heaven, it disarmed me. The fellow loomed up before me. I forgot his blackness in the dignity of his manner, and the eloquence of his speech. It seemed as if the souls of both the great dead (whose names he bore) had entered him. To the sailors in the rigging he said: 'Men! the battle is over,—your captain is dead. I have complete command of this vessel. All resistance to my authority will be in vain. My men have won their liberty, with no other weapons but their own BROKEN FETTERS. We are nineteen in number. We do not thirst for your blood, we demand only our rightful freedom. Do not flatter yourselves that I am ignorant of chart or compass. I know both. We are now only about sixty miles from Nassau. Come down, and do your duty. Land us in Nassau, and not a hair of your heads shall be hurt.'

"I shouted, *Stay where you are, men,*—when a sturdy black fellow ran at me with a handspike, and would have split my head open, but for the interference of Madison, who darted between me and the blow. 'I know what you are up to,' said the latter to me. 'You want to navigate this brig into a slave port, where you would have us all hanged; but you'll miss it; before this brig shall touch a slave-cursed shore while I am on board, I will myself put a match to the magazine, and blow her, and be blown with her, into a thousand fragments. Now I have saved your life twice within these last twenty minutes,—for, when you lay helpless on deck, my men were about to kill you. I held them in check. And if you now (seeing I am your friend and not your enemy) persist in your resistance to my authority, I give you fair warning, YOU SHALL DIE.'

"Saying this to me, he cast a glance into the rigging where the terror-stricken sailors were clinging, like so many frightened monkeys, and commanded them to come down, in a tone from which there was no appeal; for four men stood by with muskets in hand, ready at the word of command to shoot them down.

"I now became satisfied that resistance was out of the question; that my best policy was to put the brig into Nassau, and secure the assistance of the American consul at that port. I felt sure that the authorities would enable us to secure the murderers, and bring them to trial.

"By this time the apprehended squall had burst upon us. The wind howled furiously,—the ocean was white with foam, which, on account of the darkness, we could see only by the quick flashes of lightning that darted occasionally from the angry sky. All was alarm and confusion. Hideous cries came up from the slave women. Above the roaring billows a succession of heavy thunder rolled along, swelling the terrific din. Owing to the great darkness, and a sudden shift of the wind, we found ourselves in the trough of the sea. When shipping a heavy sea over the starboard bow, the bodies of the captain and Mr. Jameson were washed overboard. For awhile we had dearer interests to look after than slave property. A more savage thunder-gust never swept the ocean. Our brig rolled and creaked as if every bolt would be started, and every thread of oakum would be pressed out of the seams. To the pumps! to the pumps! I cried, but not a sailor would quit his grasp. Fortunately this squall soon passed over, or we must have been food for sharks.

"During all the storm, Madison stood firmly at the helm,—his keen eye fixed upon the binnacle. He was not indifferent to the dreadful hurricane; yet he met it with the equanimity of an old sailor. He was silent but not agitated. The first words he uttered after the storm had slightly subsided, were characteristic of the man. 'Mr. mate, you cannot write the bloody laws of slavery on those restless billows. The ocean, if not the land, is free.' I confess, gentlemen, I felt myself in the presence of a superior man; one who, had he been a white man, I would have followed willingly and gladly in any honorable enterprise. Our difference of color was the only ground for difference of action. It was not that his principles were wrong in the abstract; for they are the principles of 1776. But I could not bring myself to recognize their application to one whom I deemed my inferior.

"But to my story. What happened now is soon told. Two hours after the frightful tempest had spent itself, we were plump at the wharf in Nassau. I sent two of our men immediately to our consul with a statement of facts, requesting his interference in our behalf. What he did, or whither he did anything, I don't know; but, by order of the authorities, a company of *black* soldiers came on board, for the purpose, as they said, of protecting the property. These impudent rascals, when I called on them to assist me in keeping the slaves on board, sheltered themselves adroitly under their instructions only to protect property,—and said they did not recognize *persons* as *property*. I told them that by the laws of Virginia and the laws of the United States, the slaves on board were as much property as the barrels of flour in the hold. At this the stupid block-heads showed their *ivory*, rolled up their white eyes in horror, as if the idea of putting men on a footing with merchandise were revolting to their humanity. When these instructions were understood among the negroes, it was impossible for us to keep them on board. They deliberately gathered up their baggage before our eyes, and, against our remonstrances, poured through the gangway,—formed themselves into a procession on the wharf,—bid farewell to all on board, and, uttering the wildest shouts of exultation, they marched, amidst the deafening cheers of a multitude of sympathizing spectators, under the triumphant leadership of their heroic chief and deliverer, MADISON WASHINGTON."

SPEECHES

"WHAT TO THE SLAVE IS THE FOURTH OF JULY?" (1852)

Douglass was invited to give the prestigious Fourth of July oration by the Ladies' Anti-Slavery Society of Rochester. He spoke to a mostly white audience, eliciting "much applause" for his eloquence. In his intricate three-part structure, he lauds the nation's past accomplishments, condemns present conditions, and ends with hope for the nation's future.

SOURCE: "What to the Slave Is the Fourth of July?" Oration delivered in Corinthian Hall (Rochester: Lee, Mann & Co., 1852)

Mr. President, Friends and Fellow Citizens:

HE who could address this audience without a quailing sensation, has stronger nerves than I have. I do not remember ever to have appeared as a speaker before any assembly more shrinkingly, nor with greater distrust of my ability, than I do this day. A feeling has crept over me, quite unfavorable to the exercise of my limited powers of speech. The task before me is one which requires much previous thought and study for its proper performance. I know that apologies of this sort are generally considered flat and unmeaning. I trust, however, that mine will not be so considered. Should I seem at ease, my appearance would much misrepresent me. The little experience I have had in addressing public meetings, in country school houses, avails me nothing on the present occasion.

The papers and placards say, that I am to deliver a 4th [of] July oration. This certainly, sounds large, and out of the common way, for me. It is true that I have often had the privilege to speak in this beautiful Hall, and to address many who now honor me with their presence. But neither their familiar faces, nor the perfect gage I think I have of Corinthian Hall, seems to free me from embarrassment.

The fact is, ladies and gentlemen, the distance between this platform and the slave plantation, from which I escaped, is considerable—and the difficulties to be overcome in getting from the latter to the former, are by no means slight. That I am here to-day, is, to me, a matter of astonishment as well as of gratitude. You will not, therefore, be surprised, if in what I have to say, I evince no elaborate preparation, nor grace my speech with any high sounding exordium. With little experience and with less learning, I have been able to throw my thoughts hastily and imperfectly together; and trusting to your patient and generous indulgence, I will proceed to lay them before you.

This, for the purpose of this celebration, is the 4th of July. It is the birthday of your National Independence, and of your political freedom. This, to you, is what the Passover was to the emancipated people of God. It carries your minds back to the day, and to the act of your great deliverance; and to the signs, and to the wonders, associated with that act, and that day. This celebration also marks the beginning of another year of your national life; and reminds you that the Republic of America is now 76 years old. I am glad, fellow-citizens, that your nation is so young. Seventy-six years, though a good old age for a man, is but a mere speck in the life of a nation. Three score years and ten is the allotted time for individual men;[1] but nations number their years by thousands. According to this fact, you are, even now only in the beginning of you national career, still lingering in the period of childhood. I repeat, I am glad this is so. There is hope in the thought, and hope is much needed, under the dark clouds which lower above the horizon. The eye of the reformer is met with angry flashes, portending disastrous times; but his heart may well beat lighter at the thought that America is young, and that she is still in the impressible stage of her existence. May he not hope that high lessons of wisdom, of justice and of truth, will yet give direction to her destiny? Were the nation older, the patriot's heart might be sadder, and the reformer's brow heavier. Its future might be shrouded in gloom, and the hope of its prophets go out in sorrow. There is consolation in the thought, that America is young.—Great streams are not easily turned from channels, worn deep in the course of ages. They may sometimes rise in quiet and stately majesty, and inundate the land, refreshing and fertilizing the earth with their mysterious properties. They may also rise in wrath and fury, and bear away, on their angry waves, the accumulated wealth of years of toil and hardship. They, however, gradually flow back to the same old channel, and flow on as serenely as ever. But, while the river may not be turned aside, it may dry up, and leave nothing behind but the withered branch, and the unsightly rock, to howl in the abyss-sweeping wind, the sad tale of departed glory. As with rivers so with nations.

Fellow-citizens, I shall not presume to dwell at length on the associations that cluster about this day. The simple story of it is, that, 76 years ago, the people of this country were British subjects. The style and title of your "sovereign people" (in which you now glory) was not then born. You were under the British Crown. Your fathers esteemed the English Government as the home government; and England as the fatherland. This home government, you know, although a considerable distance from your home, did, in the exercise of its parental prerogatives, impose upon its colonial children, such restraints, burdens and limitations, as, in its mature judgment, it deemed wise, right and proper.

But, your fathers, who had not adopted the fashionable idea of this day, of the infallibility of government, and the absolute character of its acts, presumed to differ from the home government in respect to the wisdom and the justice of some of those burdens and restraints. They went so far in their excitement as to pronounce the measures of government unjust, unreasonable, and oppressive, and altogether such as ought not to be quietly submitted to. I scarcely need say, fellow-citizens, that my opinion of those measures fully accords with that of your fathers. Such a declaration of agreement on my part, would not be worth much to anybody. It would, certainly, prove nothing, as to what part I might have taken, had I lived during the great controversy of 1776. To say *now* that America was right, and England wrong, is exceedingly easy. Everybody can say it; the dastard, not less than the noble brave, can flippantly discant on the tyranny of England towards the American Colonies. It is fashionable to do so; but there was a time when, to pronounce against England, and in favor of the cause of the colonies, tried men's souls. They who did so were accounted in their day, plotters of mischief, agitators and rebels, dangerous men. To side with the right, against the wrong, with the weak against the strong, and with the oppressed against the oppressor! *here* lies the merit, and the one which, of all others, seems unfashionable in our day. The cause of liberty may be stabbed by the men who glory in the deeds of your fathers. But, to proceed.

Feeling themselves harshly and unjustly treated, by the home government, your fathers, like men of honesty, and men of spirit, earnestly sought redress. They petitioned and remonstrated; they did so in a decorous, respectful, and loyal manner. Their conduct was wholly unexceptionable. This, however, did not answer the purpose. They saw themselves treated with sovereign indifference, coldness and scorn. Yet they persevered. They were not the men to look back.

As the sheet anchor takes a firmer hold, when the ship is tossed by the storm, so did the cause of your fathers grow stronger, as it breasted the chilling blasts of kingly displeasure. The greatest and best of British statesmen admitted its justice, and the loftiest eloquence of the British Senate came to its support. But, with that blindness which seems to be the unvarying characteristic of tyrants, since Pharaoh and his hosts were drowned in the Red sea, the British Government persisted in the exactions complained of.

The madness of this course, we believe, is admitted now, even by England; but we fear the lesson is wholly lost on our present rulers.

Oppression makes a wise man mad. Your fathers were wise men, and if they did not go mad, they became restive under this treatment. They felt themselves the victims of grievous wrongs, wholly incurable in their colonial capacity. With brave men there is always a remedy for oppression. Just here, the idea of a total separation of the colonies from the crown was born! It was a startling idea, much more so, than we, at this distance of time, regard it. The timid and the prudent (as has been intimated) of that day, were, of course, shocked and alarmed by it.

Such people lived then, had lived before, and will, probably, ever have a place on this planet; and their course, in respect to any great change, (no matter how great the good to be attained, or the wrong to be redressed by it,) may be calculated with as much precision as can be the course of the stars. They hate all changes, but silver, gold and copper change! Of this sort of change they are always strongly in favor.

These people were called tories in the days of your fathers; and the appellation, probably, conveyed the same idea that is meant by a more modern, though a somewhat less euphonious term, which we often find in our papers, applied to some of our old politicians.

Their opposition to the then dangerous thought was earnest and powerful; but, amid all their terror and affrighted vociferations against it, the alarming and revolutionary idea moved on, and the country with it.

On the 2d of July, 1776, the old Continental Congress, to the dismay of the lovers of ease, and the worshippers of property, clothed that dreadful idea with all the authority of national sanction. They did so in the form of a resolution; and as we seldom hit upon resolutions, drawn up in our day, whose transparency is at all equal to this, it may refresh your minds and help my story if I read it.

> Resolved, That these united colonies *are*, and of right, ought to be free and Independent States; that they are absolved from all allegiance to the British Crown; and that all political connection between them and the State of Great Britain *is*, and ought to be, dissolved.

Citizens, your fathers made good that resolution. They succeeded; and to-day you reap the fruits of their success. The freedom gained is yours; and you, therefore, may properly celebrate this anniversary. The 4th of July is the first great fact in your nation's history—the very ring-bolt in the chain of your yet undeveloped destiny.

Pride and patriotism, not less than gratitude, prompt you to celebrate and to hold it in perpetual remembrance. I have said that the Declaration of Independence is the RINGBOLT to the chain of your nation's destiny; so, indeed, I regard it. The principles contained in that instrument are saving principles. Stand by those principles, be true to them on all occasions, in all places, against all foes, and at whatever cost.

From the round top of your ship of state, dark and threatening clouds may be seen. Heavy billows, like mountains in the distance, disclose to the leeward huge forms of flinty rocks! That *bolt* drawn, that *chain* broken, and all is lost. *Cling to this day—cling to it,* and to its principles, with the grasp of a storm-tossed mariner to a spar at midnight.

The coming into being of a nation, in any circumstances, is an interesting event. But, besides general considerations, there were peculiar circumstances which make the advent of this republic an event of special attractiveness.

The whole scene, as I look back to it, was simple, dignified and sublime.

The population of the country, at the time, stood at the insignificant number of three millions. The country was poor in the munitions of war. The population was weak and scattered, and the country a wilderness unsubdued. There were then no means of concert and combination, such as exist now. Neither steam nor lightning had then been reduced to order and discipline. From the Potomac to the Delaware was a journey of many days. Under these, and innumerable other disadvantages, your fathers declared for liberty and independence and triumphed.

Fellow Citizens, I am not wanting in respect for the fathers of this republic. The signers of the Declaration of Independence were brave men. They were great men too—great enough to give fame to a great age. It does not often happen to a nation to raise, at one time, such a number of truly great men. The point from which I am compelled to view them is not, certainly the most favorable; and yet I cannot contemplate their great deeds with less than admiration. They were statesmen, patriots and heroes, and for the good they did, and the principles they contended for, I will unite with you to honor their memory.

They loved their country better than their own private interests; and, though this is not the highest form of human excellence, all will concede that it is a rare virtue, and that when it is exhibited, it ought to command respect. He who will, intelligently, lay down his life for his country, is a man whom it is not in human nature to despise. Your fathers staked their lives, their fortunes, and their sacred honor, on the cause of their country. In their admiration of liberty, they lost sight of all other interests.

They were peace men; but they preferred revolution to peaceful submission to bondage. They were quiet men; but they did not shrink from agitating against oppression. They showed forbearance; but that they knew its limits. They believed in order; but not in the order of tyranny. With them, nothing was "*settled*" that was not right. With them, justice, liberty and humanity were "*final;*" not slavery and oppression. You may well cherish the memory of such men. They were great in their day and generation. Their solid manhood stands out the more as we contrast it with these degenerate times.

How circumspect, exact and proportionate were all their movements! How unlike the politicians of an hour! Their statesmanship looked beyond the passing moment, and stretched away in strength into the distant future. They seized upon eternal principles, and set a glorious example in their defence. Mark them!

Fully appreciating the hardships to be encountered, firmly believing in the right of their cause, honorably inviting the scrutiny of an on-looking world, reverently appealing to heaven to attest their sincerity, soundly comprehending the solemn responsibility they were about to assume, wisely measuring the terrible odds against them, your fathers, the fathers of this republic, did, most deliberately, under the inspiration of a glorious patriotism, and with a sublime faith in the great principles of justice and freedom, lay deep, the corner-stone of the national superstructure, which has risen and still rises in grandeur around you.

Of this fundamental work, this day is the anniversary. Our eyes are met with demonstrations of joyous enthusiasm. Banners and penants wave exultingly on the breeze. The din of business, too, is hushed. Even mammon seems to have quitted his grasp on this day. The ear-piercing fife and the stirring drum unite their accents with the ascending peal of a thousand church bells. Prayers are made, hymns are sung, and sermons are preached in honor of this day; while the quick martial tramp of a great and multitudinous nation, echoed back by all the hills, valleys and mountains of a vast continent, bespeak the occasion one of thrilling and universal interest—a nation's jubilee.

Friends and citizens, I need not enter further into the causes which led to this anniversary. Many of you understand them better than I do. You could instruct me in regard to them. That is a branch of knowledge in which you feel, perhaps, a much deeper interest than your speaker. The causes which led to the separation of the colonies from the British crown have never lacked for a tongue. They have all been taught in your common schools, narrated at your firesides, unfolded from your pulpits, and thundered from your legislative halls, and are as familiar to you as household words. They form the staple of your national poetry and eloquence.

I remember, also, that, as a people, Americans are remarkably familiar with all facts which make in their own favor. This is esteemed by some as a national trait—perhaps a national weakness. It is a fact, that whatever makes for the wealth or for the reputation of Americans, and can be had *cheap!* will be found by Americans. I shall not be charged with slandering Americans, if I say I think the American side of any question may be safely left in American hands.

I leave, therefore, the great deeds of your fathers to other gentlemen whose claim to have been regularly descended will be less likely to be disputed than mine!

THE PRESENT.

My business, if I have any here to-day, is with the present. The accepted time with God and his cause is the ever-living now.

> "Trust no future, however pleasant,
> Let the dead past bury its dead;
> Act, act in the living present,
> Heart within, and God overhead."[2]

We have to do with the past only as we can make it useful to the present and to the future. To all inspiring motives, to noble deeds which can be gained from the past, we are welcome. But now is the time, the important time. Your fathers have lived, died, and have done their work, and have done much of it well. You live and must die, and you must do your work. You have no right to enjoy a child's share in the labor of your fathers, unless your children are to be blest by your labors. You have no right to wear out and waste the hard-earned fame of your fathers to cover your indolence. Sydney Smith[3] tells us that men seldom eulogize the wisdom and virtues of their fathers, but to excuse some folly or wickedness of their own. This truth is not a doubtful one. There are illustrations of it near and remote, ancient and modern. It was fashionable, hundreds of years ago, for the children of Jacob to boast, we have "Abraham to our father,"[4] when they had long lost Abraham's faith and spirit. That people contented themselves under the shadow of Abraham's great name, while they repudiated the deeds which made his name great. Need I remind you that a similar thing is being done all over this country to-day? Need I tell you that the Jews are not the only people who built the tombs of the prophets, and garnished the sepulchres of the righteous? Washington could not die till he had broken the chains of his slaves. Yet his monument is built up by the price of human blood, and the traders in the bodies and souls of men, shout—"We have Washington to *our father*."—Alas! that it should be so; yet so it is.

> "The evil that men do, lives after them,
> The good is oft' interred with their bones."[5]

Fellow-citizens, pardon me, allow me to ask, why am I called upon to speak here to-day? What have I, or those I represent, to do with your national independence? Are the great principles of political freedom and of natural justice, embodied in that Declaration of Independence, extended to us? and am I, therefore, called upon to bring our humble offering to the national altar, and to confess the benefits and express devout gratitude for the blessings resulting from your independence to us?

Would to God, both for your sakes and ours, that an affirmative answer could be truthfully returned to these questions! Then would my task be light, and my burden easy and delightful. For *who* is there so cold, that a nation's sympathy could not warm him? Who so obdurate and dead to the claims of gratitude, that would not thankfully acknowledge such priceless benefits? Who so stolid and selfish, that would not give his voice to swell the hallelujahs of a nation's jubilee, when the chains of servitude had been torn from his limbs? I am not that man. In a case like that, the dumb might eloquently speak, and the "lame man leap as an hart."[6]

But, such is not the state of the case. I say it with a sad sense of the disparity between us. I am not included within the pale of this glorious anniversary! Your high independence only reveals the immeasurable distance between us. The blessings in which you, this day, rejoice, are not enjoyed in common.—The rich inheritance of justice, liberty, prosperity and independence, bequeathed by your fathers, is shared by you, not by me. The sunlight that brought life and healing to you, has brought stripes and death to me. This Fourth [of] July is *yours,* not *mine. You* may rejoice, *I* must mourn. To drag a man in fetters into the grand illuminated temple of liberty, and call upon him to join you in joyous anthems, were inhuman mockery and sacrilegious irony. Do you mean, citizens, to mock me, by asking me to speak to-day? If so, there is a parallel to your conduct. And let me warn you that it is dangerous to copy the example of a nation whose crimes, towering up to heaven, were thrown down by the breath of the Almighty, burying that nation in irrecoverable ruin! I can to-day take up the plaintive lament of a peeled and woe-smitten people!

"By the rivers of Babylon, there we sat down. Yea! we wept when we remembered Zion. We hanged our harps upon the willows in the midst thereof. For there, they that carried us away captive, required of us a song; and they who wasted us required of us mirth, saying, Sing us one of the songs of Zion. How can we sing the Lord's song in a strange land? If I forget thee, O Jerusalem, let my right hand forget her cunning. If I do not remember thee, let my tongue cleave to the roof of my mouth."[7]

Fellow-citizens; above your national, tumultous joy, I hear the mournful wail of millions! whose chains, heavy and grievous yesterday, are, to-day, rendered more intolerable by the jubilee shouts that reach them. If I do forget, if I do not faithfully remember those bleeding children of sorrow this day, "may my right hand forget her cunning, and may my tongue cleave to the roof of my mouth!" To forget them, to pass lightly over their wrongs, and to chime in with the popular theme, would be treason most scandalous and shocking, and would make me a reproach before God and the world. My subject, then, fellow-citizens, is AMERICAN SLAVERY. I shall see, this day, and its popular characteristics, from the slave's point of view. Standing, there, identified with the American bondman, making his wrongs mine, I do not hesitate to declare, with all my soul, that the character and conduct of this nation never looked blacker to me than on this 4th of July! Whether we turn to the declarations of the past, or to the professions of the present, the conduct of the nation seems equally hideous and revolting. America is false to the past, false to the present, and solemnly binds herself to be false to the future. Standing with God and the crushed and bleeding slave on this occasion, I will, in the name of humanity which is outraged, in the name of liberty which is fettered, in the name of the constitution and the Bible, which are disregarded and trampled upon, dare to call in question and to denounce, with all the emphasis I can command, everything that serves to perpetuate slavery—the great sin and shame of America! "I will not equivocate; I will not excuse;"[8] I will use the severest language I can command; and yet not one word shall escape me that any man, whose judgment is not blinded by prejudice, or who is not at heart a slaveholder, shall not confess to be right and just.

But I fancy I hear some one of my audience say, it is just in this circumstance that you and your brother abolitionists fail to make a favorable impression on the public mind. Would you argue more, and denounce less, would you persuade more, and rebuke less, your cause would be much more likely to succeed. But, I submit, where all is plain there is nothing to be argued. What point in the anti-slavery creed would you have me argue? On what branch of the subject do the people of this country need light? Must I undertake to prove that the slave is a man? That point is conceded already. Nobody doubts it. The slave-holders themselves acknowledge it in the enactment of laws for their government. They acknowledge it when they punish disobedience on the part of the slave. There are seventy-two crimes in the State of Virginia, which, if committed by a black man, (no matter how ignorant he be,) subject him to the punishment of death; while only two of the same crimes will subject a white man to the like punishment.—What is this but the acknowledgement that the slave is a moral, intellectual and responsible being. The manhood of the slave is conceded. It is admitted in the fact that Southern statute books are covered with enactments forbidding, under severe fines and penalties, the teaching of the slave to read or to write.—When you can point to any such laws, in reference to the beasts of the field, then I may consent to argue the manhood of the slave. When the dogs in your streets, when the fowls of the air, when the cattle on your hills, when the fish of the sea, and the reptiles that crawl, shall be unable to distinguish the slave from a brute, *then* will I argue with you that the slave is a man!

For the present, it is enough to affirm the equal manhood of the negro race. Is it not astonishing that, while we are ploughing, planting and reaping, using all kinds of mechanical tools, erecting houses, constructing bridges, building ships, working in metals of brass, iron, copper, silver and gold; that, while we are reading, writing and cyphering, acting as clerks, merchants and secretaries, having among us lawyers, doctors, ministers, poets, authors, editors, orators and teachers; that, while we are engaged in all manner of enterprises common to other men, digging gold in California, capturing the whale in the Pacific, feeding sheep and cattle on the hill-side, living, moving, acting, thinking, planning, living in families as husbands, wives and children, and, above all, confessing and worshipping the Christian's God, and looking hopefully for life and immortality beyond the grave, we are called upon to prove that we are men!

Would you have me argue that man is entitled to liberty? that he is the rightful owner of his own body? You have already declared it. Must I argue the wrongfulness of slavery? Is that a question for Republicans? Is it to be settled by the rules of logic and argumentation, as a matter beset with great difficulty, involving a doubtful application of the principle of justice, hard to be understood? How should I look to-day, in the presence of Americans, dividing, and subdividing a discourse, to show that men have a natural right to freedom? speaking of it relatively, and positively, negatively, and affirmatively. To do so, would be to make myself ridiculous, and to offer an insult to your understanding.—There is not a man beneath the canopy of heaven, that does not know that slavery is wrong *for him*.

What, am I to argue that it is wrong to make men brutes, to rob them of their liberty, to work them without wages, to keep them ignorant of their relations to their fellow men, to beat them with sticks, to flay their flesh with the lash, to load their limbs with irons, to hunt them with dogs, to sell them at auction, to sunder their families, to knock out their teeth, to burn their flesh, to starve them into obedience and submission to their masters? Must I argue that a system thus marked with blood, and stained with pollution, is *wrong?* No I will not! I have better employment for my time and strength, than such arguments would imply.

What, then, remains to be argued? Is it that slavery is not divine; that God did not establish it; that our doctors of divinity are mistaken? There is blasphemy in the thought. That which is inhuman, cannot be divine! *Who* can reason on such a proposition? They that can, may; I cannot. The time for such argument is past.

At a time like this, scorching irony, not convincing argument, is needed. O! had I the ability, and could I reach the nation's ear, I would, to-day, pour out a fiery stream of biting ridicule, blasting reproach, withering sarcasm, and stern rebuke. For it is not light that is needed, but fire; it is not the gentle shower, but thunder. We need the storm, the whirlwind, and the earthquake. The feeling of the nation must be quickened; the conscience of the nation must be roused; the propriety of the nation must be startled; the hypocrisy of the nation must be exposed; and its crimes against God and man must be proclaimed and denounced.

What, to the American slave, is your 4th of July? I answer; a day that reveals to him, more than all other days in the year, the gross injustice and cruelty to which he is the constant victim. To him, your celebration is a sham; your boasted liberty, an unholy license; your national greatness, swelling vanity; your sounds of rejoicing are empty and heartless; your denunciations of tyrants, brass fronted impudence; your shouts of liberty and equality, hollow mockery; your prayers and hymns, your sermons and thanksgivings, with all your religious parade, and solemnity, are, to him, mere bombast, fraud, deception, impiety, and hypocrisy—a thin veil to cover up crimes which would disgrace a nation of savages. There is not a nation on the earth guilty of practices, more shocking and bloody, than are the people of these United States, at this very hour.

Go where you may, search where you will, roam through all the monarchies and despotisms of the old world, travel through South America, search out every abuse, and when you have found the last, lay your facts by the side of the every day practices of this nation, and you will say with me, that, for revolting barbarity and shameless hypocrisy, America reigns without a rival.

THE INTERNAL SLAVE TRADE.

Take the American slave-trade, which we are told by the papers, is especially prosperous just now. Ex-Senator Benton[9] tells us that the price of men was never higher than now. He mentions the fact to show that slavery is in no danger. This trade is one of the peculiarities of American institutions. It is carried on in all the large towns and cities in one half of this confederacy; and millions are pocketed every year, by dealers in this horrid traffic. In several states, this trade is a chief source of wealth. It is called (in contradistinction to the foreign slave-trade) *"the internal slave-trade."* It is, probably, called so, too, in order to divert from it the horror with which the foreign slave-trade is contemplated. That trade has long since been denounced by this government, as piracy. It has been denounced with burning words, from the high places of the nation, as an execrable traffic. To arrest it, to put an end to it, this nation keeps a squadron, at immense cost, on the coast of Africa. Everywhere, in this country, it is safe to speak of this foreign slave-trade, as a most inhuman traffic, opposed alike to the laws of God and of man. The duty to extirpate and destroy it, is admitted even by our DOCTORS OF DIVINITY. In order to put an end to it, some of these last have consented that their colored brethren (nominally free) should leave this country, and establish themselves on the western coast of Africa! It is, however, a notable fact, that, while so much execration is poured out by Americans, upon those engaged in the foreign slave-trade, the men engaged in the slave-trade between the states pass without condemnation, and their business is deemed honorable.

Behold the practical operation of this internal slave-trade, the American slave-trade, sustained by American politics and American religion. Here you will see men and women, reared like swine, for the market. You know what is a swine-drover? I will show you a man-drover. They inhabit all our Southern States. They perambulate the country, and crowd the highways of the nation, with droves of human stock. You will see one of these human flesh jobbers, armed with pistol, whip and bowie-knife, driving a company of a hundred men, women, and children, from the Potomac to the slave market at New Orleans. These wretched people are to be sold singly, or in lots, to suit purchasers. They are food for the cotton-field, and the deadly sugar-mill. Mark the sad procession, as it moves wearily along, and the inhuman wretch who drives them. Hear his savage yells and his blood-chilling oaths, as he hurries on his affrighted captives! There, see the old man, with locks thinned and gray. Cast one glance, if you please, upon that young mother, whose shoulders are bare to the scorching sun, her briny tears falling on the brow of the babe in her arms. See, too, that girl of thirteen, weeping, *yes*! weeping, as she thinks of the mother from whom she has been torn! The drove moves tardily. Heat and sorrow have nearly consumed their strength; suddenly you hear a quick snap, like the discharge of a rifle; the fetters clank, and the chain rattles simultaneously; your ears are saluted with a scream, that seems to have torn its way to the centre of your soul! The crack you heard, was the sound of the slave-whip; the scream you heard, was from the woman you saw with the babe. Her speed had faltered under the weight of her child and her chains! that gash on her shoulder tells her to move on. Follow this drove to New Orleans. Attend the auction; see men examined like horses; see the forms of women rudely and brutally exposed to the shocking gaze of American slave-buyers. See this drove sold and separated for ever; and never forget the deep, sad sobs that arose from that scattered multitude. Tell me citizens, WHERE, under the sun, you can witness a spectacle more fiendish and shocking. Yet this is but a glance at the American slave-trade, as it exists, at this moment, in the ruling part of the United States.

I was born amid such sights and scenes. To me the American slave-trade is a terrible reality. When a child, my soul was often pierced with a sense of its horrors. I lived on Philpot Street, Fell's Point, Baltimore, and have watched from the wharves, the slave ships in the Basin, anchored from the shore, with their cargoes of human flesh, waiting for favorable winds to waft them down the Chesapeake. There was, at that time, a grand slave mart kept at the head of Pratt Street, by Austin Woldfolk[10] [*sic*]. His agents were sent into every town and county in Maryland, announcing their arrival, through the papers, and on flaming *"hand-bills,"* headed CASH FOR NEGROES. These men were generally well dressed men, and very captivating in their manners. Ever ready to drink, to treat, and to gamble. The fate of many a slave has depended upon the turn of a single card; and many a child has been snatched from the arms of its mother, by bargains arranged in a state of brutal drunkenness.

The flesh-mongers gather up their victims by dozens, and drive them, chained, to the general depot at Baltimore. When a sufficient number have been collected here, a ship is chartered, for the purpose of conveying the forlorn crew to Mobile, or to New Orleans. From the slave prison to the ship, they are usually driven in the darkness of night; for since the anti-slavery agitation, a certain caution is observed.

In the deep still darkness of midnight, I have been often aroused by the dead heavy footsteps, and the pitious cries of the chained gangs that passed our door. The anguish of my boyish heart was intense; and I was often consoled, when speaking to my mistress in the morning, to hear her say that the custom was very wicked; that she hated to hear the rattle of the chains, and the heart-rending cries. I was glad to find one who sympathised with me in my horror.

Fellow-citizens, this murderous traffic is, to-day, in active operation in this boasted republic. In the solitude of my spirit, I see clouds of dust raised on the highways of the South; I see the bleeding footsteps; I hear the doleful wail of fettered humanity, on the way to the slave-markets, where the victims are to be sold like *horses, sheep,* and *swine,* knocked off to the highest bidder. There I see the tenderest ties ruthlessly broken, to gratify the lust, caprice and rapacity of the buyers and sellers of men. My soul sickens at the sight.

> "Is this the land your Fathers loved,
> The freedom which they toiled to win?
> Is this the earth whereon they moved?
> Are these the graves they slumber in?"[11]

But a still more inhuman, disgraceful, and scandalous state of things remains to be presented.

By an act of the American Congress, not yet two years old, slavery has been nationalized in its most horrible and revolting form. By that act, Mason & Dixon's line has been obliterated; New York has become as Virginia; and the power to hold, hunt, and sell men, women and children, as slaves, remains no longer a mere state institution, but is now an institution of the whole United States. The power is co-extensive with the star-spangled banner, and American Christianity. Where these go, may also go the merciless slave-hunter. Where these are, man is not sacred. He is a bird for the sportsman's gun. By that most foul and fiendish of all human decrees, the liberty and person of every man are put in peril. Your broad republican domain is hunting ground for *men. Not* for thieves and robbers, enemies of society, merely, but for men guilty of no crime. Your law-makers have commanded all good citizens to engage in this hellish sport. Your President, your Secretary of State, your *lords, nobles,* and ecclesiastics, enforce, as a duty you owe to your free and glorious country, and to your God, that you do this accursed thing. Not fewer than forty Americans, have, within the past two years, been hunted down, and, without a moment's warning, hurried away in chains, and consigned to slavery, and excruciating torture. Some of these have had wives and children, dependent on them for bread; but of this, no account was made. The right of the hunter to his prey, stands superior to the right of marriage, and to *all* rights in this republic, the rights of God included! For black men there are neither law, justice, humanity, nor religion. The Fugitive Slave *Law* makes MERCY TO THEM, A CRIME; and bribes the judge who tries them. An American JUDGE GETS TEN DOLLARS FOR EVERY VICTIM HE CONSIGNS to slavery, and five, when he fails to do so. The oath of any two villains is sufficient, under this hell-black enactment, to send the most pious and exemplary black man into the remorseless jaws of slavery! His own testimony is nothing. He can bring no witnesses for himself. The minister of American justice is bound, by the law to hear but *one* side; and *that* side, is the side of the oppressor. Let this damning fact be perpetually told. Let it be thundered around the world, that, in tyrant-killing, king-hating, people-loving, democratic, Christian America, the seats of justice are filled with judges, who hold their offices under an open and palpable *bribe,* and are bound, in deciding in the case of a man's liberty, *to hear only his accusers!*

In glaring violation of justice, in shameless disregard of the forms of administering law, in cunning arrangement to entrap the defenceless, and in diabolical intent, this Fugitive Slave Law stands alone in the annals of tyrannical legislation. I doubt if there be another nation on the globe, having the brass and the baseness to put such a law on the statute-book. If any man in this assembly thinks differently from me in this matter, and feels able to disprove my statements, I will gladly confront him at any suitable time and place he may select.

RELIGIOUS LIBERTY.

I take this law to be one of the grossest infringements of Christian Liberty, and, if the churches and ministers of our country were not stupidly blind, or most wickedly indifferent, they, too, would so regard it.

At the very moment that they are thanking God for the enjoyment of civil and religious liberty, and for the right to worship God according to the dictates of their own consciences, they are utterly silent in respect to a law which robs religion of its chief significance, and makes it utterly worthless to a world lying in wickedness. Did this law concern the "*mint, anise* and *cummin*"[12]—abridge the right to sing psalms, to partake of the sacrament, or to engage in any of the ceremonies of religion, it would be smitten by the thunder of a thousand pulpits. A general shout would go up from the church, demanding *repeal, repeal, instant repeal!*—And it would go hard with that politician who presumed to solicit the votes of the people without inscribing this motto on his banner. Further, if this demand were not complied with, another Scotland would be added to the history of religious liberty, and the stern old covenanters would be thrown into the shade. A John Knox would be seen at every church door, and heard from every pulpit, and Fillmore[13] would have no more quarter than was shown by Knox, to the beautiful, but threacherous Queen Mary of Scotland.—The fact that the church of our country, (with fractional exceptions,) does not esteem "the Fugitive Slave Law" as a declaration of war against religious liberty, implies that that church regards religion simply as a form of worship, an empty ceremony, and *not* a vital principle, requiring active benevolence, justice, love and good will towards man. It esteems sacrifice above mercy; psalm-singing above right doing; solemn meetings above practical righteousness. A worship that can be conducted by persons who refuse to give shelter to the houseless, to give bread to the hungry, clothing to the naked, and who enjoin obedience to a law forbidding these acts of mercy, is a curse, not a blessing to mankind. The Bible addresses all such persons as "scribes, pharisees, hypocrites, who pay tithe of *mint, anise,* and *cummin,* and have omitted the weightier matters of the law, judgment, mercy and faith."

THE CHURCH RESPONSIBLE.

But the church of this country is not only indifferent to the wrongs of the slave, it actually takes sides with the oppressors. It has made itself the bulwark of American slavery, and the shield of American slave-hunters. Many of its most eloquent Divines, who stand as the very lights of the church, have shamelessly given the sanction of religion, and the bible, to the whole slave system.—They have taught that man may, properly, be a slave; that the relation of master and slave is ordained of God; that to send back an escaped bondman to his master is clearly the duty of all the followers of the Lord Jesus Christ; and this horrible blasphemy is palmed off upon the world for christianity.

For my part, I would say, welcome infidelity! welcome atheism! welcome anything! in preference to the gospel, *as preached by those Divines!* They convert the very name of religion into an engine of tyranny, and barbarous cruelty, and serve to confirm more infidels, in this age, than all the infidel writings of Thomas Paine, Voltaire, and Bolingbroke,[14] put together, have done! These ministers make religion a cold and flinty-hearted thing, having neither principles of right action, nor bowels of compassion. They strip the love of God of its beauty, and leave the throne of religion a huge, horrible, repulsive form. It is a religion for oppressors, tyrants, man-stealers, and *thugs*. It is not that *"pure and undefiled religion"* which is from above, and which is *"first pure, then peaceable, easy to be entreated,* full of mercy and good fruits, *without partiality, and without hypocrisy."*[15] But a religion which favors the rich against the poor; which exalts the proud above the humble; which divides mankind into two classes, tyrants and slaves; which says to the man in chains, *stay there*; and to the oppressor, *oppress on*; it is a religion which may be professed and enjoyed by all the robbers and enslavers of mankind; it makes God a respecter of persons, denies his fatherhood of the race, and tramples in the dust the great truth of the brotherhood of man. All this we affirm to be true of the popular church, and the popular worship of our land and nation—a religion, a church and a worship which, on the authority of inspired wisdom, we pronounce to be an abomination in the sight of God. In the language of Isaiah, the American church might be well addressed, "Bring no more vain oblations; incense is an abomination unto me: the new moons and Sabbaths, the calling of assemblies, I cannot away with; it is iniquity, even the solemn meeting. Your new moons, and your appointed feasts my soul hateth. They are a trouble to me; I am weary to bear them; and when ye spread forth your hands I will hide mine eyes from you. Yea! when ye make many prayers, I will not hear. YOUR HANDS ARE FULL OF BLOOD; cease to do evil, learn to do well; seek judgment; relieve the oppressed; judge for the fatherless; plead for the widow."[16]

The American church is guilty, when viewed in connection with what it is doing to uphold slavery; but it is superlatively guilty when viewed in connection with its ability to abolish slavery.

The sin of which it is guilty is one of omission as well as of commission. Albert Barnes but uttered what the common sense of every man at all observant of the actual state of the case will receive as truth, when he declared that "There is no power out of the church that could sustain slavery an hour, if it were not sustained in it."[17]

Let the religious press, the pulpit, the sunday school, the conference meeting, the great ecclesiastical, missionary, bible and tract associations of the land array their immense powers against slavery, and slaveholding; and the whole system of crime and blood would be scattered to the winds, and that they do not do this involves them in the most awful responsibility of which the mind can conceive.

In prosecuting the anti-slavery enterprise, we have been asked to spare the church, to spare the ministry; but *how,* we ask, could such a thing be done? We are met on the threshold of our efforts for the redemption of the slave, by the church and ministry of the country, in battle arrayed against us; and we are compelled to fight or flee. From *what* quarter, I beg to know, has proceeded a fire so deadly upon our ranks, during the last two years, as from the Northern pulpit? As the champions of oppressors, the chosen men of American theology have appeared—men, honored for their so called piety, and their real learning. The LORDS of Buffalo, the SPRINGS of New York, the LATHROPS of Auburn, the COXES and SPENCERS of Brooklyn, the GANNETTS and SHARPS of Boston, the DEWEYS of Washington, and other great religious lights of the land, have, in utter denial of the authority of *Him,* by whom they professed to be called to the ministry, deliberately taught us, against the example of the Hebrews, and against the remonstrance of the Apostles, they teach *that we ought to obey man's law before the law of God.*

My spirit wearies of such blasphemy; and how such men can be supported, as the "standing types and representatives of Jesus Christ," is a mystery which I leave others to penetrate. In speaking of the American church, however, let it be distinctly understood that I mean the *great mass* of the religious organizations of our land. There are exceptions, and I thank God that there are. Noble men may be found, scattered all over these Northern States, of whom Henry Ward Beecher, of Brooklyn, Samuel J.

May, of Syracuse, and my esteemed friend* on the platform, are shining examples; and let me say further, that, upon these men lies the duty to inspire our ranks with high religious faith and zeal, and to cheer us on in the great mission of the slave's redemption from his chains.

RELIGION IN ENGLAND AND RELIGION IN AMERICA.

One is struck with the difference between the attitude of the American church towards the anti-slavery movement, and that occupied by the churches in England towards a similar movement in that country. There, the church, true to its mission of ameliorating, elevating, and improving the condition of mankind, came forward promptly, bound up the wounds of the West Indian slave, and restored him to his liberty. There, the question of emancipation was a high religious question. It was demanded, in the name of humanity, and according to the law of the living God. The Sharps, the Clarksons, the Wilberforces, the Buxtons, the Burchells and the Knibbs, were alike famous for their piety, and for their philanthropy. The anti-slavery movement *there*, was not an anti-church movement, for the reason that the church took its full share in prosecuting that movement: and the anti-slavery movement in this country will cease to be an anti-church movement, when the church of this country shall assume a favorable, instead of a hostile position towards that movement.

Americans! your republican politics, not less than your republican religion, are flagrantly inconsistent. You boast of your love of liberty, your superior civilization, and your pure christianity, while the whole political power of the nation, as embodied in the two great political parties, is solemnly pledged to support and perpetuate the enslavement of three millions of your countrymen. You hurl your anathemas at the crowned headed tyrants of Russia and Austria, and pride yourselves on your Democratic institutions, while you yourselves consent to be the mere *tools* and *body-guards* of the tyrants of Virginia and Carolina.

* Rev. R. R. Raymond.

You invite to your shores fugitives of oppression from abroad, honor them with banquets, greet them with ovations, cheer them, toast them, salute them, protect them, and pour out your money to them like water; but the fugitives from your own land, you advertise, hunt, arrest, shoot and kill. You glory in your refinement, and your universal education; yet you maintain a system as barbarous and dreadful, as ever stained the character of a nation—a system begun in avarice, supported in pride, and perpetuated in cruelty. You shed tears over fallen Hungary, and make the sad story of her wrongs the theme of your poets, statesmen and orators, till your gallant sons are ready to fly to arms to vindicate her cause against her oppressors; but, in regard to the ten thousand wrongs of the American slave, you would enforce the strictest silence, and would hail him as an enemy of the nation who dares to make those wrongs the subject of public discourse! You are all on fire at the mention of liberty for France or for Ireland; but are as cold as an iceberg at the thought of liberty for the enslaved of America.—You discourse eloquently on the dignity of labor; yet, you sustain a system which, in its very essence, casts a stigma upon labor. You can bare your bosom to the storm of British artillery, to throw off a three-penny tax on tea; and yet wring the last hard earned farthing from the grasp of the black laborers of your country. You profess to believe "that, of one blood, God made all nations of men to dwell on the face of all the earth,"[18] and hath commanded all men, everywhere to love one another; yet you notoriously hate, (and glory in your hatred,) all men whose skins are not colored like your own. You declare, before the world, and are understood by the world to declare, that you *"hold these truths to be self evident, that all men are created equal; and are endowed by their Creator with certain inalienable rights; and that, among these are, life, liberty, and the pursuit of happiness;"* and yet, you hold securely, in a bondage, which according to your own Thomas Jefferson, *"is worse than ages of that which your fathers rose in rebellion to oppose,"*[19] *a seventh part* of the inhabitants of your country.

Fellow-citizens! I will not enlarge further on your national inconsistencies. The existence of slavery in this country brands your republicanism as a sham, your humanity as a base pretence, and your christianity as a lie. It destroys your moral power abroad[;] it corrupts your politicians at home. It saps the foundation of religion; it makes your name a hissing, and a bye-word to a mocking earth. It is the antagonistic force in your government, the only thing that seriously disturbs and endangers your *Union.* It fetters your progress; it is the enemy of improvement, the deadly foe of education; it fosters pride; it breeds insolence; it promotes vice; it shelters crime; it is a curse to the earth that supports it; and yet, you cling to it, as if it were the sheet anchor of all your hopes. Oh! be warned! be warned! a horrible reptile is coiled up in your nation's bosom; the venomous creature is nursing at the tender breast of your youthful republic; *for the love of God, tear away,* and fling from you the hideous monster, and *let the weight of twenty millions, crush and destroy it forever!*

THE CONSTITUTION.

But it is answered in reply to all this, that precisely what I have now denounced is, in fact, guaranteed and sanctioned by the Constitution of the United States; that, the right to hold, and to hunt slaves is a part of that Constitution framed by the illustrious Fathers of this Republic.

Then, I dare to affirm, notwithstanding all I have said before, your fathers stooped, basely stooped.

> "To palter with us in a double sense:
> And keep the word of promise to the ear,
> But break it to the heart."[20]

And instead of being the honest men I have before declared them to be, they were the veriest imposters that ever practised on mankind. *This* is the inevitable conclusion, and from it there is no escape; but I differ from those who charge this baseness on the framers of the Constitution of the United States. *It is a slander upon their memory,* at least, so I believe. There is not time now to argue the constitutional question at length; nor have I the ability to discuss it as it ought to be discussed. The subject has been handled with masterly power by Lysander Spooner, Esq., by William Goodell, by Samuel E. Sewall, Esq., and last, though not least, by Gerrit Smith, Esq. These gentlemen have, as I think, fully and clearly vindicated the Constitution from any design to support slavery for an hour.

Fellow-citizens! there is no matter in respect to which, the people of the North have allowed themselves to be so ruinously imposed upon, as that of the pro-slavery character of the Constitution. In *that* instrument I hold there is neither warrant, license, nor sanction of the hateful thing; but interpreted, as it *ought* to be interpreted, the Constitution is a GLORIOUS LIBERTY DOCUMENT. Read its preamble, consider its purposes. Is slavery among them? Is it at the gateway? or is it in the temple? it is neither. While I do not intend to argue this question on the present occasion, let me ask, if it be not somewhat singular that, if the Constitution were intended to be, by its framers and adopters, a slaveholding instrument, why neither *slavery, slaveholding,* nor *slave* can anywhere be found in it. What would be thought of an instrument, drawn up, *legally* drawn up, for the purpose of entitling the city of Rochester to a track of land, in which no mention of land was made? Now, there are certain rules of interpretation, for the proper understanding of all legal instruments. These rules are well established. They are plain, commonsense rules, such as you and I, and all of us, can understand and apply, without having passed years in the study of law. I scout the idea that the question of the constitutionality, or unconstitutionality of slavery, is not a question for the people. I hold that every American citizen has a right to form an opinion of the constitution, and to propagate that opinion, and to use all honorable means to make his opinion the prevailing one. Without this right, the liberty of an American citizen would be as insecure as that of a Frenchman. Ex-Vice-President Dallas[21] tells us that the constitution is an object to which no American mind can be too attentive, and no American heart too devoted. He further says, the constitution, in its words, is plain and intelligible, and is meant for the home-bred, unsophisticated understandings of our fellow-citizens. Senator Berrien tells us that the Constitution is the fundamental law, that which controls all others. The charter of our liberties, which every citizen has a personal interest in understanding thoroughly. The testimony of Senator Breese, Lewis

Cass, and many others that might be named, who are everywhere esteemed as sound lawyers, so regard the constitution. I take it, therefore, that it is not presumption in a private citizen to form an opinion of that instrument.

Now, take the constitution according to its plain reading, and I defy the presentation of a single pro-slavery clause in it. On the other hand it will be found to contain principles and purposes, entirely hostile to the existence of slavery.

I have detained my audience entirely too long already. At some future period I will gladly avail myself of an opportunity to give this subject a full and fair discussion.

Allow me to say, in conclusion, notwithstanding the dark picture I have this day presented, of the state of the nation, I do not despair of this country. There are forces in operation, which must inevitably, work the downfall of slavery. "*The arm of the Lord is not shortened,*"[22] and the doom of slavery is certain. I, therefore, leave off where I began, with *hope*. While drawing encouragement from "the Declaration of Independence," the great principles it contains, and the genius of American Institutions, my spirit is also cheered by the obvious tendencies of the age. Nations do not now stand in the same relation to each other that they did ages ago. No nation can now shut itself up, from the surrounding world, and trot round in the same old path of its fathers without interference. The time *was* when such could be done. Long established customs of hurtful character could formerly fence themselves in, and do their evil work with social impunity. Knowledge was then confined and enjoyed by the privileged few, and the multitude walked on in mental darkness. But a change has now come over the affairs of mankind. Walled cities and empires have become unfashionable. The arm of commerce has borne away the gates of the strong city. Intelligence is penetrating the darkest corners of the globe. It makes its pathway over and under the sea, as well as on the earth. Wind, steam, and lightning are its chartered agents. Oceans no longer divide, but link nations together. From Boston to London is now a holiday excursion. Space is comparatively annihilated.—Thoughts expressed on one side of the Atlantic, are distinctly heard on the other.

The far off and almost fabulous Pacific rolls in grandeur at our feet. The Celestial Empire, the mystery of ages, is being solved. The fiat of the Almighty, "*Let there be Light,*"[23] has not yet spent its force. No abuse, no outrage whether in taste, sport or avarice, can now hide itself from the all-pervading light. The iron shoe, and crippled foot of China must be seen, in contrast with nature. *Africa must rise and put on her yet unwoven garment. "Ethiopia shall stretch out her hand unto God."*[24] In the fervent aspirations of William Lloyd Garrison, I say, and let every heart join in saying it:

God speed the year of jubilee
  The wide world o'er!
When from their galling chains set free,
Th' oppress'd shall vilely bend the knee,
And wear the yoke of tyranny
  Like brutes no more.
That year will come, and freedom's reign,
To man his plundered rights again
  Restore.

God speed the day when human blood
  Shall cease to flow!
In every clime be understood,
The claims of human brotherhood,
And each return for evil, good,
  Not blow for blow;
That day will come all feuds to end,
And change into a faithful friend
  Each foe.

God speed the hour, the glorious hour,
  When none on earth
Shall exercise a lordly power,
Nor in a tyrant's presence cower;
But all to manhood's stature tower,
  By equal birth!
THAT HOUR WILL COME, to each, to all,
And from his prison-house, the thrall
  Go forth.

Until that year, day, hour, arrive,
With head, and heart, and hand I'll strive,
To break the rod, and rend the gyve,
The spoiler of his prey deprive—
  So witness Heaven!
And never from my chosen post,
Whate'er the peril or the cost,
  Be driven.[25]

"THE CLAIMS OF THE NEGRO ETHNOLOGICALLY CONSIDERED" (1854)

With this address to the literary societies of Western Reserve College in Ohio, Douglass became the first African American to deliver a commencement address at a major American university. In it he undermines the claims of leading white scientists by showing the flaws in their methods.

SOURCE: "The Claims of the Negro Ethnologically Considered" (Rochester: Lee, Mann & Co., 1854)

Gentlemen of the Philozetian Society: I propose to submit to you a few thoughts on the subject of the Claims of the Negro, suggested by ethnological science, or the natural history of man. But before entering upon that subject, I trust you will allow me to make a remark or two, somewhat personal to myself. The relation between me and this occasion may justify what, in others, might seem an offence against good taste.

This occasion is to me one of no ordinary interest, for many reasons; and the honor you have done me, in selecting me as your speaker, is as grateful to my heart, as it is novel in the history of American Collegiate or Literary Institutions. Surprised as I am, the public are no less surprised, at the spirit of independence, and the moral courage displayed by the gentlemen at whose call I am here. There is felt to be a principle in the matter, placing it far above egotism or personal vanity; a principle which gives to this occasion a general, and I had almost said, an universal interest. I engage to-day, for the first time, in the exercises of any College Commencement. It is a new chapter in my humble experience. The usual course, at such times, I believe, is to call to the platform men of age and distinction, eminent for eloquence, mental ability, and scholarly attainments—men whose high culture, severe training, great experience, large observation, and peculiar aptitude for teaching qualify them to instruct even the already well instructed, and to impart a glow, a lustre, to the acquirements of those who are passing from the Halls of learning, to the broad theatre of active life. To no such high endeavor as this is your humble speaker fitted; and it was with much distrust and hesitation that he accepted the invitation, so kindly and perseveringly given, to occupy a portion of your attention here to-day.

I express the hope, then, gentlemen, that this acknowledgment of the novelty of my position, and my unaffected and honest confession of inaptitude, will awaken a sentiment of generous indulgence towards the scattered thoughts I have been able to fling together, with a view to presenting them as my humble contribution to these Commencement Exercises.

Interesting to me, personally, as this occasion is, it is still more interesting to you; especially to such of you as have completed your education, and who (not wholly unlike the gallant ship, newly launched, full rigged, and amply fitted, about to quit the placid waters of the harbor for the boisterous waves of the sea) are entering upon the active duties and measureless responsibilities incident to the great voyage of life. Before such, the ocean of mind lies outspread more solemn than the sea, studded with difficulties and perils. Thoughts, theories, ideas, and systems, so various, and so opposite, and leading to such diverse results, suggest the wisdom of the utmost precaution, and the most careful survey, at the start. A false light, a defective chart, an imperfect compass, may cause one to drift in endless bewilderment, or to be landed at last amid sharp, destructive rocks.

On the other hand, guided by wisdom, manned with truth, fidelity and industry, the haven of peace, devoutly wished for by all, may be reached in safety by all. The compensation of the preacher is full, when assured that his words have saved even one from error and from ruin. My joy shall be full, if, on this occasion, I shall be able to give a right direction to any one mind, touching the question now to be considered.

Gentlemen, in selecting the Claims of the Negro as the subject of my remarks to-day, I am animated by a desire to bring before you a matter of living importance—[a] matter upon which action, as well as thought, is required. The relation subsisting between the white and black people of this country is the vital question of the age. In the solution of this question, the scholars of America will have to take an important and controlling part. This is the moral battle field to which their country and their God now call them. In the eye[s] of both, the neutral scholar is an ignoble man. Here, a man must be hot, or be accounted cold, or, perchance, something worse than hot or cold. The lukewarm and the cowardly, will be rejected by earnest men on either side of the controversy. The cunning man who avoids it, to gain the favor of both parties, will be rewarded with scorn; and the timid man who shrinks from it, for fear of offending either party, will be despised. To the lawyer, the preacher, the politician, and to the man of letters, there is no neutral ground. He that is not for us, is against us. Gentlemen, I assume at the start, that wherever else I may be required to speak with bated breath, here, at least, I may speak with freedom the thought nearest my heart. This liberty is implied, by the call I have received to be here; and yet I hope to present the subject so that no man can reasonably say, that an outrage has been committed, or that I have abused the privilege with which you have honored me. I shall aim to discuss the claims of the negro, general and special, in a manner, though not scientific, still sufficiently clear and definite to enable my hearers to form an intelligent judgment respecting them.

The first general claim which may here be set up, respects the manhood of the negro. This is an elementary claim, simple enough, but not without question. It is fiercely opposed. A respectable public journal, published in Richmond, Va., bases its whole defence of the slave system upon a denial of the negro's manhood.

"The white peasant is free, and if he is a man of will and intellect, can rise in the scale of society; or at least his offspring may. He is not deprived by law of those 'inalienable rights,' 'liberty and the pursuit of happiness,' by the use of it. But here is the essence of slavery—that we do declare the negro destitute of these powers. We bind him by law to the condition of the laboring peasant for ever, without his consent, and we bind his posterity after him. Now, the true question is, have we a right to do this? If we have not, all discussions about his comfortable situation and the actual condition of free laborers elsewhere, are quite beside the point. If the negro has the same right to his liberty and the pursuit of his own happiness that the white man has, then we commit the greatest wrong and robbery to hold him a slave—an act at which the sentiment of justice must revolt in every heart—and negro slavery is an institution which that sentiment must sooner or later blot from the face of the earth." —*Richmond Examiner.*

After stating the question thus, the *Examiner* boldly asserts that the negro has no such right—BECAUSE HE IS NOT A MAN!

There are three ways to answer this denial. One is by ridicule; a second is by denunciation; and a third is by argument. I hardly know under which of these modes my answer to-day will fall. I feel myself somewhat on trial; and that this is just the point where there is hesitation, if not serious doubt. I cannot, however, argue; I must assert. To know whether [a] negro is a man, it must first be known what constitutes a man. Here, as well as elsewhere, I take it, that the "coat must be cut according to the cloth." It is not necessary, in order to establish the manhood of any one making the claim, to prove that such an one equals Clay in eloquence, or Webster and Calhoun in logical force and directness;[1] for, tried by such standards of mental power as these, it is apprehended that very few could claim the high designation of *man.* Yet something like this folly is seen in the arguments directed against the humanity of the negro. His faculties and powers, uneducated and unimproved, have been contrasted with those of the highest cultivation; and the world has then been called upon to behold the immense and amazing difference between the man admitted, and the man disputed. The fact that these intellects, so powerful and so controlling, are almost, if not quite, as exceptional to the general rule of humanity in one direction, as the specimen negroes are in the other, is quite overlooked.

Man is distinguished from all other animals, by the possession of certain definite faculties and powers, as well as by physical organization and proportions. He is the only two-handed animal on the earth—the only one that laughs, and nearly the only one that weeps. Men instinctively distinguish between men and brutes. Common sense itself is scarcely needed to detect the absence of manhood in a monkey, or to recognize its presence in a negro. His speech, his reason, his power to acquire and to retain knowledge, his heaven-erected face, his habitudes, his hopes, his fears, his aspirations, his prophecies, plant between him and the brute creation, a distinction as eternal as it is palpable. Away, therefore, with all the scientific moonshine that would connect men with monkeys; that would have the world believe that humanity, instead of resting on its own characteristic pedestal—gloriously independent—is a sort of sliding scale, making one extreme brother to the ou-rang-ou-tang, and the other to angels, and all the rest intermediates! Tried by all the usual, and all the *un*usual tests, whether mental, moral, physical, or psychological, the negro is a MAN—considering him as possessing knowledge, or needing knowledge, his elevation or his degradation, his virtues, or his vices—whichever road you take, you reach the same conclusion, the negro is a MAN. His good and his bad, his innocence and his guilt, his joys and his sorrows, proclaim his manhood in speech that all mankind practically and readily understand[s].

A very recondite author says that "man is distinguished from all other animals, in that he resists as well as adapts himself to his circumstances."[2] He does not take things as he finds them, but goes to work to improve them. Tried by this test, too, the negro is a man. You may see him yoke the oxen, harness the horse, and hold the plow. He can swim the river; but he prefers to fling over it a bridge. The horse bears him on his back—admits his mastery and dominion. The barn-yard fowl know his step, and flock around to receive their morning meal from his sable hand. The dog dances when he comes home, and whines piteously when he is absent. All these know that the negro is a MAN. Now, presuming that what is evident to beast and to bird, cannot need elaborate argument to be made plain to men, I assume, with this brief statement, that the negro is a man.

The first claim conceded and settled, let us attend to the second, which is beset with some difficulties, giving rise to many opinions, different from my own, and which opinions I propose to combat.

There was a time when, if you established the point that a particular being is a man, it was considered that such a being, of course, had a common ancestry with the rest of mankind. But it is not so now. This is, you know, an age of science, and science is favorable to division. It must explore and analyze, until all doubt is set at rest. There is, therefore, another proposition to be stated and maintained, separately, which, in other days, (the days before the Notts, the Gliddens, the Agassiz[es], and Mortons,[3] made their profound discoveries in ethnological science), might have been included in the first.

It is somewhat remarkable, that, at a time when knowledge is so generally diffused, when the geography of the world is so well understood—when time and space, in the intercourse of nations, are almost annihilated—when oceans have become bridges—the earth a magnificent ball—the hollow sky a dome—under which a common humanity can meet in friendly conclave—when nationalities are being swallowed up—and the ends of the earth brought together—I say it is remarkable—nay, it is strange that there should arise a phalanx of learned men—speaking in the name of *science*—to forbid the magnificent reunion of mankind in one brotherhood. A mortifying proof is here given, that the moral growth of a nation, or an age, does not always keep pace with the increase of knowledge, and suggests the necessity of means to increase human love with human learning.

The proposition to which I allude, and which I mean next to assert, is this: that what are technically called the negro race, are a part of the human family, and are descended from a common ancestry, with the rest of mankind. The discussion of this point opens a comprehensive field of inquiry. It involves the question of the unity of the human race. Much has and can be said on both sides of that question.

Looking out upon the surface of the Globe, with its varieties of climate, soil, and formations, its elevations and depressions, its rivers, lakes, oceans, islands, continents, and the vast and striking differences which mark and diversify its multitudinous inhabitants, the question has been raised, and pressed with increasing ardor and pertinacity, (especially in modern times), can all these various tribes, nations, tongues, kindred, so widely separated, and so strangely dissimilar, have descended from a common ancestry? That is the question, and it has been answered variously by men of learning. Different modes of reasoning have been adopted, but the conclusions reached may be divided into two—the one YES, and the other NO. *Which* of these answers is most in accordance with facts, with reason, with the welfare of the world, and reflects most glory upon the wisdom, power, and goodness of the Author of all existence, is the question for consideration with us. On which side is the weight of the argument, rather than which side is absolutely proved?

It must be admitted at the beginning, that, viewed apart from the authority of the Bible, neither the unity, nor diversity of origin of the human family, can be demonstrated. To use the terse expression of the Rev. Dr. Anderson,[4] who speaking on this point, says: "It is impossible to get far enough back for that." This much, however, can be done. The evidence on both sides, can be accurately weighed, and the truth arrived at with almost absolute certainty.

It would be interesting, did time permit, to give here, some of the most striking features of the various theories, which have, of late, gained attention and respect in many quarters of our country—touching the origin of mankind—but I must pass this by. The argument to-day, is to the unity, as against that theory, which affirms the diversity of human origin.

THE BEARINGS OF THE QUESTION.

A moment's reflection must impress all, that few questions have more important and solemn bearings, than the one now under consideration. It is connected with eternal as well as with terrestrial interests. It covers the earth and reaches heaven. The unity of the human race—the brotherhood of man—the reciprocal duties of all to each, and of each to all, are too plainly taught in the Bible to admit of cavil. The credit of the Bible is at stake—and if it be too much to say that it must stand or fall by the decision of this question, *it is* proper to say, that the value of that sacred Book—as a record of the early history of mankind—must be materially affected, by the decision of the question.

For myself I can say, my reason (not less than my feeling, and my faith) welcomes with joy, the declaration of the Inspired Apostle, "that God has made of one blood all nations of men for to dwell upon all the face of the earth." But this grand affirmation of the unity of the human race, and many others like unto it, together with the whole account of the creation, given in the early scriptures, must all get a new interpretation or be overthrown altogether, if a diversity of human origin can be maintained. Most evidently, this aspect of the question makes it important to those who rely upon the Bible, as the sheet anchor of their hopes—and the framework of all religious truth. The young minister must look into this subject and settle it for himself, before he ascends the pulpit, to preach redemption to a fallen race.

The bearing of the question upon Revelation, is not more marked and decided than its relation to the situation of things in our country, at this moment. *One seventh* part of the population of this country is of negro descent. The land is peopled by what may be called the most dissimilar races on the globe. The black and the white—the negro and the European—these constitute the American people—and, in all the likelihoods of the case, they will ever remain the principal inhabitants of the United States, in some form or other. The European population are greatly in the ascendant in numbers, wealth and power. They are the rulers of the country—the masters—the Africans are the slaves—the proscribed portion of the people—and precisely in proportion as the truth of human brotherhood gets recognition, will be the freedom and elevation, in this country, of persons of African descent. In truth, this question is at the bottom of the whole controversy, now going on between the slaveholders on the *one* hand, and the abolitionists on the other. It is the same old question which has divided the selfish from the philanthropic part of mankind in all ages. It is the question whether the rights, privileges, and immunities enjoyed by some ought not to be shared and enjoyed by all.

It is not quite two hundred years ago, when such was the simplicity (I will not now say the pride and depravity) of the Anglo-Saxon inhabitants of the British West Indies, that the learned and pious Godwin, a missionary to the West Indies, deemed it necessary to write a book, to remove what he conceived to be the injurious belief that it was sinful in the sight of God to baptize negroes and Indians.[5] The West Indies have made progress since that time. God's emancipating angel has broken the fetters of slavery in those islands, and the praises of the Almighty are now sung by the sable lips of eight hundred thousand freemen, before deemed only fit for slaves, and to whom even baptismal and burial rights [rites?] were denied.

The unassuming work of *Godwin* may have had some agency in producing this glorious result. One other remark before entering upon the argument. It may be said that views and opinions favoring the unity of the human family, coming from one of lowly condition, are open to the suspicion that "*the wish is father to the thought,*"[6] and so, indeed, it may be. But let it be also remembered, that this deduction from the weight of the argument on the one side, is more than counterbalanced by the pride of race and position arrayed on the other. Indeed, ninety-nine out of every hundred of the advocates of a diverse origin of the human family in this country, are among those who hold it to be the privilege of the *Anglo-Saxon* to enslave and oppress the African—and slaveholders, not a few, like the Richmond *Examiner* to which I have referred, have admitted, that the whole argument in defence of slavery, becomes utterly worthless the moment the African is proved to be equally a man with the Anglo-Saxon. The temptation, therefore, to read the negro out of the human family is exceedingly strong, and may account somewhat for the repeated attempts on the part of Southern pretenders to science, to cast a doubt over the Scriptural account of the origin of mankind. If the origin and motives of most works opposing the doctrine of the unity of the human race could be ascertained, it may be doubted whether *one* such work could boast an honest parentage. Pride and selfishness, combined with mental power, never want for a theory to justify them—and when men oppress their fellow-men, the oppressor ever finds, in the character of the oppressed, a full justification for his oppression. Ignorance and depravity, and the inability to rise from degradation to civilization and respectability, are the most usual allegations against the oppressed. The evils most fostered by slavery and oppression are precisely those which slaveholders and oppressors would transfer from their system to the inherent character of their victims. Thus the very crimes of slavery become slavery's best defence. By making the enslaved a character fit only for slavery, they excuse themselves for refusing to make the slave a freeman. A wholesale method of accomplishing this result is to overthrow the instinctive consciousness of the common brotherhood of man. For, let it be once granted that the human race are of multitudinous origin, naturally different in their moral, physical, and intellectual capacities, and at once you make plausible a demand for classes, grades and conditions, for different methods of culture, different moral, political, and religious institutions, and a chance is left for slavery, as a necessary institution. The debates in Congress on the Nebraska Bill during the past winter, will show how slaveholders have availed themselves of this doctrine in support of slaveholding. There is no doubt that Messrs. Nott, Glidden, Morton, Smith and Agassiz were duly consulted by our slavery propagating statesmen.

ETHNOLOGICAL UNFAIRNESS TOWARDS THE NEGRO.

The lawyers tell us that the credit of a witness is always in order. Ignorance, malice or prejudice, may disqualify a witness, and why not an author? Now, the disposition everywhere evident, among the class of writers alluded to, to separate the negro race from every intelligent nation and tribe in Africa, may fairly be regarded as one proof, that they have staked out the ground beforehand, and that they have aimed to construct a theory in support of a foregone conclusion. The desirableness of isolating the negro race, and especially of separating them from the various peoples of Northern Africa, is too plain to need a remark. Such isolation would remove stupendous difficulties in the way of getting the negro in a favorable attitude for the blows of scientific Christendom.

Dr. Samuel George Morton may be referred to as a fair sample of American Ethnologists. His very able work *Crania Americana*,[7] published in Philadelphia in 1839, is widely read in this country. In this great work his contempt for negroes is ever conspicuous. I take him as an illustration of what had been alleged as true of his class.

The fact that Egypt was one of the earliest abodes of learning and civilization, is as firmly established as are the everlasting hills, defying, with a calm front the boasted mechanical and architectural skill of the nineteenth century—smiling serenely on the assaults and the mutations of time, there she stands in overshadowing grandeur, riveting the eye and the mind of the modern world—upon her, in silent and dreamy wonder. Greece and Rome—and through them Europe and America—have received their civilization from the ancient Egyptians. This fact is not denied by anybody. But Egypt is in Africa. Pity that it had not been in Europe, or in Asia, or better still, in America! Another unhappy circumstance is, that the ancient Egyptians were not white people; but were, undoubtedly, just about as dark in complexion as many in this country who are considered genuine negroes; and that is not all, their hair was far from being of that graceful lankness which adorns the fair Anglo-Saxon head. But the next best thing, after these defects, is a positive unlikeness to the negro. Accordingly, our learned author enters into an elaborate argument to prove that the ancient Egyptians were totally distinct from the negroes, and to deny all relationship between. Speaking of the "Copts and Fellahs," whom every body knows are descendants of the Egyptians, he says, "*The Copts, though now remarkably distinct from the people that surround them, derive from their remote ancestors some mixture of Greek, Arabian, and perhaps even negro blood.*" Now, mark the description given of the Egyptians in this same work: "*Complexion brown, The nose is straight, excepting the end, where it is rounded and wide; the lips are rather thick, and the hair black and curly.*" This description would certainly seem to make it safe to suppose the presence of "*even* negro blood." A man, in our day, with brown complexion, "nose rounded and wide, lips thick, hair black and curly," would, I think, have no difficulty in getting himself recognized as a negro!!

The same authority tells us that the "Copts are supposed by Neibhur, Denon and others, to be the descendants of the ancient Egyptians;" and Dr. Morton adds, that it has often been observed that a strong resemblance may be traced between the

Coptic visage and that presented in the ancient mummies and statues. Again, he says, the "*Copts can be, at most, but the degenerate remains, both physically and intellectually, of that mighty people who have claimed the admiration of all ages.*" Speaking of the Nubians, Dr. Morton says, (page 26)—

"The hair of the Nubian is thick and black—often curled, either by nature or art, and sometimes *partially frizzled,* but *never woolly.*"

Again:—

"Although the Nubians occasionally present their national characters unmixed, they generally show traces of their social intercourse with the Arabs, and *even* with the negroes."

The repetition of the adverb here "*even,*" is important, as showing the spirit in which our great American Ethnologist pursues his work, and what deductions may be justly made from the value of his researches on that account. In everything touching the negro, Dr. Morton, in his *Crania Americana,* betrays the same spirit. He thinks that the *Sphinx* was not the representative of an Egyptian Deity, but was a shrine, worshiped at by the degraded *negroes* of Egypt; and this fact he alleges as the secret of the mistake made by Volney, in supposing that the Egyptians were real negroes. The absurdity of this assertion will be very apparent, in view of the fact that the great Sphinx in question was the chief of a series, full two miles in length. Our author again repels the supposition that the Egyptians were related to negroes, by saying there is no mention made of *color* by the historian, in relating the marriage of Solomon with Pharaoh's daughter; and, with genuine American feeling, he says, such a circumstance as the marrying of an European monarch with the daughter of a negro would not have been passed over in silence in our day. This is a sample of the reasoning of men who reason from *prejudice* rather than from *facts.* It assumes that a *black skin* in the *East* excites the same prejudice which we see here in the West. Having denied all relationship of the negro to the ancient Egyptians, with characteristic American assumption, he says, "It is easy to prove, that whatever may have been the hue of their skin, they belong to the same race with ourselves."

Of course, I do not find fault with Dr. Morton, or any other American, for claiming affinity with Egyptians. All that goes in that direction belongs to my side of the question, and is really right.

The leaning here indicated is natural enough, and may be explained by the fact that an educated man in Ireland ceases to be an Irishman; and an intelligent black man is always supposed to have derived his intelligence from his connection with the white race. To be intelligent is to have one's negro blood ignored.

There is, however, a very important physiological fact, contradicting this last assumption; and that fact is, that intellect is uniformly derived from the maternal side. Mulattoes, in this country, may almost wholly boast of Anglo-Saxon male ancestry.

It is the province of prejudice to blind; and scientific writers, not less than others, write to please, as well as to instruct, and even unconsciously to themselves, (sometimes), sacrifice what is true to what is popular. Fashion is not confined to dress; but extends to philosophy as well—and it is fashionable now, in our land, to exaggerate the differences between the negro and the European. If, for instance, a phrenologist or naturalist undertakes to represent in portraits, the differences between the two races—the negro and the European—he will invariably present the *highest* type of the European, and the *lowest* type of the negro.

The European face is drawn in harmony with the highest ideas of beauty, dignity and intellect. Features regular and brow after the Websterian mold. The negro, on the other hand, appears with features distorted, lips exaggerated, forehead depressed—and the whole expression of the countenance made to harmonize with the popular idea of negro imbecility and degradation. I have seen many pictures of negroes and Europeans, in phrenological and ethnological works; and all, or nearly all, excepting the work of Dr. Prichard, and that other great work, Combs' *Constitution of Man,*[8] have been more or less open to this objection. I think I have never seen a single picture in an American work, designed to give an idea of the mental endowments of the negro, which did any thing like justice to the subject; nay, that was not infamously distorted. The heads of A. CRUMMEL, HENRY H. GARNET, SAM'L R. WARD, CHAS. LENOX REMOND, W. J. WILSON, J. W.

PENNINGTON, J. I. GAINES, M. R. DELANY, J. W. LOGUIN, J. M. WHITFIELD, J. C. HOLLY, and hundreds of others I could mention,[9] are all better formed, and indicate the presence of intellect more than any pictures I have seen in such works; and while it must be admitted that there are negroes answering the description given by the American ethnologists and others, of the negro race, I contend that there is every description of head among them, ranging from the highest Indoo Caucasian downward. If the very best type of the European is always presented, I insist that *justice,* in all such works, demands that the very best type of the negro should also be taken. The importance of this criticism may not be apparent to all;—to the *black* man it is very apparent. He sees the injustice, and writhes under its sting. But to return to Dr. Morton, or rather to the question of the affinity of the negroes to the Egyptians.

It seems to me that a man might as well deny the affinity of the Americans to the Englishman, as to deny such affinity between the negro and the Egyptian. He might make out as many points of difference, in the case of the one as in that of the other. Especially could this be done, if, like ethnologists, in given cases, only typical specimens were resorted to. The lean, slender American, pale and swarthy, if exposed to the sun, wears a very different appearance to the full, round Englishman, of clear, *blonde* complexion. One may trace the progress of this difference in the common portraits of the American Presidents. Just study those faces, beginning with WASHINGTON; and as you come thro' the JEFFERSONS, the ADAMSES, and the MADISONS, you will find an increasing bony and wiry appearance about those portraits, & a greater remove from that serene amplitude which characterises the countenances of the earlier Presidents. I may be mistaken, but I think this is a correct index of the change going on in the nation at large,—converting Englishmen, Germans, Irishmen, and Frenchmen into Americans, and causing them to lose, in a common American character, all traces of their former distinctive national peculiarities.

AUTHORITIES AS TO THE RESEMBLANCE OF THE EGYPTIANS TO NEGROES.

Now, let us see what the best authorities say, as to the personal appearance of the Egyptians. I think it will be at once admitted, that while they differ very strongly from the negro, debased and enslaved, that difference is not greater than may be observed in other quarters of the globe, among people notoriously belonging to the same variety, the same original stock; in a word, to the same family. If it shall be found that the people of Africa have an African character, as general, as well defined, and as distinct, as have the people of Europe, or the people of Asia, the exceptional differences among them afford no ground for supposing a difference of race; but, on the contrary, it will be inferred that the people of Africa constitute one great branch of the human family, whose origin may be as properly referred to the families of Noah, as can be any other branch of the human family from whom they differ. Denon, in his *Travels in Egypt,* describes the Egyptians, as of full, but "delicate and voluptuous forms, countenances sedate and placid, round and soft features, with eyes long and almond shaped, half shut and languishing, and turned up at the outer angles, as if habitually fatigued by the light and heat of the sun; cheeks round; thick lips, full and prominent; mouths large, but cheerful and smiling; complexion dark, ruddy and coppery, and the whole aspect displaying—as one of the most graphic delineators among modern travelers has observed—the genuine African character, of which the *negro* is the exaggerated and extreme representation."[10] Again, Prichard says, (page 152)—

"Herodotus traveled in Egypt, and was, therefore, well acquainted with the people from personal observation. He does not say anything directly, as to the descriptions of their persons, which were too well known to the Greeks to need such an account, but his indirect testimony is very strongly expressed. After mentioning a tradition, that the people of Colchis were a colony from Egypt, Herodotus says, that 'there was one fact strongly in favor of this opinion—the Colchians were *black* in complexion and *woolly* haired.'"

These are the words by which the complexion and hair of negroes are described. In another passage, he says that

"The pigeon, said to have fled to Dodona, and to have founded the Oracle, was declared to be *black,* and that the meaning of the story was this: The Oracle was, in reality, founded by a female captive from the Thebaid: she was *black,* being an Egyptian." "Other Greek writers," says Prichard, "have expressed themselves in similar terms."

Those who have mentioned the Egyptians as a *swarthy* people, according to Prichard, might as well have applied the term *black* to them, since they were doubtless of a chocolate color. The same author brings together the testimony of Eschylus[11] and others as to the color of the ancient Egyptians, all corresponding, more or less, with the foregoing. Among the most direct testimony educed by Prichard, is, first that of Volney, who, speaking of the modern Copts, says:

"They have a puffed visage, swollen eyes, flat nose, and thick lips, and bear much resemblance to mulattoes."

Baron Larrey says, in regard to the same people:

"They have projecting cheek bones, dilating nostrils, thick lips, and hair and beard black and *crisp.*"

Mr. Ledyard, (whose testimony, says our learned authority, is of the more value, as he had no theory to support), says:

"I suspect the *Copts* to have been the *origin* of the *negro* race; the nose and lips correspond with those of the negro; the hair, wherever I can see it among the people here, is curled, *not* like that of the negroes, but like the mulattoes."[12]

Here I leave our learned authorities, as to the resemblance of the Egyptians to negroes.

It is not in my power, in a discourse of this sort, to adduce more than a very small part of the testimony in support of a near relationship between the present enslaved and degraded negroes, and the ancient highly civilized and wonderfully endowed Egyptians. Sufficient has already been adduced, to show a marked similarity in regard to features, hair, color, and I doubt not that the philologist can find equal similarity in the structures of their languages. In view of the foregoing, while it may not be claimed that the ancient Egyptians were negroes,—viz:—answering, in all respects, to the nations and tribes ranged under the general appellation, negro; still, it may safely be affirmed, that a strong affinity and a direct relationship may be claimed by the negro race, to THAT GRANDEST OF ALL THE NATIONS OF ANTIQUITY, THE BUILDERS OF THE PYRAMIDS.

But there are other evidences of this relationship, more decisive than those alleged in a general similarity of personal appearance. Language is held to be very important, by the best ethnologists, in tracing out the remotest affinities of nations, tribes, classes and families. The color of the skin has sometimes been less enduring than the speech of a people. I speak by authority, and follow in the footsteps of some of the most learned writers on the natural and ethnological history of man, when I affirm that one of the most direct and conclusive proofs of the general affinity of Northern African nations with those of West, East and South Africa, is found in the general similarity of their language[s]. The philologist easily discovers, and is able to point out something like the original source of the multiplied tongues now in use in that yet mysterious quarter of the globe. Dr. R. G. LATHAM, F. R. S., corresponding member of the Ethnological Society, New York—in his admirable work, entitled "Man and his Migrations"—says:

"In the languages of Abyssinia, the Gheez and Tigre, admitted, as long as they have been known at all, to be *Semitic,* graduate through the Amharic, the Talasha, the Harargi, the Gafat and other languages, which may be well studied in Dr. Beke's valuable comparative tables, into the Agow tongue, unequivocally indigenous to Abyssinia, and through this into the true negro classes. But, unequivocal as may be the Semitic elements of the Berber, Coptic and Galla, their affinities with the tongues of Western and Southern Africa are more so. I weigh my words when I say, not *equally,* but *more;* changing the expression, for every foot in advance which can be made towards the Semitic tongues in one direction, the African philologist can go a yard towards the negro ones in the other."

In a note, just below this remarkable statement, Dr. Latham says:

"A short table of the Berber and Coptic, as compared with the other African tongues, may be seen in the Classical Museum of the British Association, for 1846. In the *Transactions* of the Philological Society is a grammatical sketch of the Tumali language, by Dr. S. Tutsbek of Munich. The Tumali is a truly negro language, of Kordufan; whilst, in respect to the extent to which its inflections are formed, by internal changes of vowels and accents, it is fully equal to the Semitic tongues of Palestine and Arabia."[13]

This testimony may not serve prejudice, but to me it seems quite sufficient.

SUPERFICIAL OBJECTIONS.

Let us now glance again at the opposition. A volume, on the *Natural History of the Human Species,* by Charles Hamilton Smith, quite false in many of its facts, and as mischievous as false, has been published recently in this country, and will, doubtless, be widely circulated, especially by those to whom the thought of human brotherhood is abhorrent. This writer says, after mentioning sundry facts touching the dense and spherical structure of the negro head:

"This very structure may influence the erect gait, which occasions the practice common also to the Ethiopian, or mixed nations, of carrying burdens and light weights, even to a tumbler full of water, upon the head."

No doubt this seemed a very sage remark to Mr. Smith, and quite important in fixing a character to the negro skull, although different to that of Europeans. But if the learned Mr. Smith had stood, previous to writing it, at our door, (a few days in succession), he might have seen hundreds of Germans and of Irish people, not bearing burdens of "*light* weight," but of *heavy* weight, upon the same vertical extremity. The carrying of burdens upon the head is as old as Oriental Society; and the man writes himself a blockhead, who attempts to find in the custom a proof of original difference. On page 227, the same writer says:

"The voice of the negroes is feeble and hoarse in the male sex."

The explanation of this mistake in our author is found in the fact that an oppressed people, in addressing their superiors—perhaps I ought to say, their oppressors—usually assume a minor tone, as less likely to provoke the charge of intrusiveness. But it is ridiculous to pronounce the voice of the negro feeble; and the learned ethnologist must be hard pushed, to establish differences, when he refers to this as one. Mr. Smith further declares, that

"The typical woolly haired races have never discovered an alphabet, framed a grammatical language, nor made the least step in science or art."[14]

Now, the man is still living, (or was but a few years since), among the Mandingoes of the Western coast of Africa, who has framed an alphabet; and while Mr. Smith may be pardoned for his ignorance of that fact, as an ethnologist, he is inexcusable for not knowing that the Mpongwe language, spoken on both sides of the Gaboon River, at Cape Lopez, Cape St. Catharine, and in the interior, to the distance of two or three hundred miles, is as truly a grammatically framed language as any extant. I am indebted, for this fact, to Rev. Dr. M. B. ANDERSON, President of the Rochester University; and by his leave, here is the Grammar—(holding up the Grammar). Perhaps, of all the attempts ever made to disprove the unity of the human family, and to brand the negro with natural inferiority, the most compendious and barefaced is the book, entitled *Types of Mankind,* by Nott and Glidden.[15] One would be well employed in a series of Lectures directed to an exposure of the unsoundness, if not the wickedness of this work.

THE AFRICAN RACE BUT ONE PEOPLE.

But I must hasten. Having shown that the people of Africa are, probably, one people; that each tribe bears an intimate relation to other tribes and nations in that quarter of the globe, and that the Egyptians may have flung off the different tribes seen there at different times, as implied by the evident relations of their language, and by other similarities; it can hardly be deemed unreasonable to suppose, that the African branch of the human species—from the once highly civilized Egyptian to the barbarians on the banks of the Niger—may claim brotherhood with the great family of Noah, spreading over the more Northern and Eastern parts of the globe. I will now proceed to consider those physical peculiarities of form, features, hair and color, which are supposed by some men to mark the African, not only as an inferior race, but as a distinct species, naturally and originally different from the rest of mankind, and as really to place him nearer to the brute than to man.

THE EFFECT OF CIRCUMSTANCES UPON THE PHYSICAL MAN.

I may remark, just here, that it is impossible, even were it desirable, in a discourse like this, to attend to the anatomical and physiological argument connected with this part of the subject. I am not equal to that, and if I were, the occasion does not require it. The form of the *negro*—(I use the term *negro,* precisely in the sense that you use the term Anglo-Saxon; and I believe, too, that the former will one day be as illustrious as the latter)—has often been the subject of remark. His flat feet, long arms, high cheek bones and retreating forehead are especially dwelt upon, to his disparagement, and just as if there were no white people with precisely the same peculiarities. I think it will ever be found, that the *well* or *ill* condition of any part of mankind, will leave its mark on the physical as well as on the intellectual part of man. A hundred instances might be cited, of whole families who have degenerated, and others who have improved in personal appearance, by a change of circumstances. A man is worked upon by what *he* works on. He may carve out his circumstances, but his circumstances will carve him out as well. I told a boot maker, in Newcastle-upon-Tyne, that I had been a plantation slave. He said I must pardon him; but he could not believe it; no plantation laborer ever had a high instep. He said he had noticed that the coal heavers and work people in low condition had, for the most part, flat feet, and that he could tell, by the shape of the feet, whether a man's parents were in high or low condition. The thing was worth a thought, and I have thought of it, and have looked around me for facts. There is some truth in it; though there are exceptions in individual cases.

The day I landed in Ireland, nine years ago, I addressed, (in company with Father SPRATT and that good man who has been recently made the subject of bitter attack; I allude to the philanthropic JAMES HAUGHTON, of Dublin), a large meeting of the common people of Ireland, on temperance. Never did human faces tell a sadder tale. More than five thousand were assembled; and I say, with no wish to wound the feelings of any Irishman, that these people lacked only a black skin and wooly hair, to complete their likeness to the plantation negro. The open, uneducated mouth—the long, gaunt arm—the badly formed foot and ankle—the shuffling gait—the retreating forehead and vacant expression—and, their petty quarrels and fights—all reminded me of the plantation, and my own cruelly abused people. Yet, *that* is the land of GRATTAN, of CURRAN, of O'CONNELL, and of SHERIDAN.[16] Now, while what I have said is true of the common people, the fact is, there are no more really handsome people in the world, than the educated Irish people. The Irishman educated, is a model gentleman; the Irishman ignorant and degraded, compares in form and feature with the negro!

I am stating facts. If you go into Southern Indiana, you will see what climate and habit can do, even in one generation. The man may have come from New England, but his hard features, sallow complexion, have left little of New England on his brow. The right arm of the blacksmith is said to be larger and stronger than his left. The ship carpenter is at forty round-shouldered. The shoemaker carries the marks of his trade. One locality becomes famous for one thing, another for another. Manchester and Lowell, in America, Manchester and Sheffield, in England, attest this. But what does it all prove? Why, nothing positively, as to the main point; still, it raises the inquiry—May not the condition of men explain their various appearances? Need we go behind the vicissitudes of barbarism for an explanation of the gaunt, wiry, ape like appearance of some of the genuine negroes? Need we look higher than a vertical sun, or lower than the damp, black soil of the Niger, the Gambia, the Senegal, with their heavy and enervating miasma, rising ever from the rank growing and decaying vegetation, for an explanation of the negro's color? If a cause, full and adequate, can be found here, *why seek further*?

The eminent Dr. LATHAM, already quoted, says that nine-tenths of the white population of the globe are found between 30 and 65 degrees North latitude. Only about one-fifth of all the inhabitants of the globe are white; and they are as far from the Adamic complexion as is the negro. The remainder are—*what?* Ranging all the way from the brunette to jet black. There are the red, the reddish copper color, the yellowish, the dark brown, the chocolate color, and so on, to the jet black. On the mountains on the North of Africa, where water freezes in winter at times, branches of the same people who are *black* in the valley are *white* on the mountains. The Nubian, with his beautiful curly hair, finds it becoming frizzled, crisped, and even woolly, as he approaches the great Sahara. The Portuguese, white in Europe, is brown in Asia. The Jews, who are to be found in all countries, never intermarrying, are white in Europe, brown in Asia, and black in Africa. Again, what does it all prove? Nothing, absolutely; nothing which places the question beyond dispute; but it *does* justify the conjecture before referred to, that outward circumstances *may* have something to do with modifying the various phases of humanity; and that color itself is at the control of the world's climate and its various concomitants. It is the sun that paints the peach—and may it not be, that he paints the *man* as well? My reading, on this point, however, as well as my own observation, have convinced me that from the beginning the Almighty, within certain limits, endowed mankind with organizations capable of countless variations in form, feature and color, without having it necessary to begin a new creation for every new variety.

A powerful argument in favor of the oneness of the human family, is afforded in the fact that nations, however dissimilar, may be united in one social state, not only without detriment to each other, but, most clearly, to the advancement of human welfare, happiness and perfection. While it is clearly proved, on the other hand, that those nations freest from foreign elements present the most evident marks of deterioration. Dr. JAMES MCCUNE SMITH, himself a colored man, a gentleman and scholar, alleges—and not without excellent reason—that this, our own great nation, so distinguished for industry and enterprise, is largely indebted to its composite character.[17] We all know, at any rate, that now, what constitutes the very heart of the civilized world—(I allude to England)—has only risen from barbarism to its present lofty eminence, through successive invasions and alliances with her people. The Medes and Persians constituted one of the mightiest empires that ever rocked the globe. The most terrible nation which now threatens the peace of the world,[18] to make its will the law of Europe, is a grand piece of Mosaic work, in which almost every nation has its characteristic feature, from the wild Tartar to the refined Pole.

But, gentlemen, the time fails me, and I must bring these remarks to a close. My argument has swelled beyond its appointed measure. What I intended to make special, has become, in its progress, somewhat general. I meant to speak here to-day, for the lonely and the despised ones, with whom I was cradled, and with whom I have suffered; and now, gentlemen, in conclusion, what if all this reasoning be unsound? What if the negro may not be able to prove his relationship to Nubians, Abyssinians and Egyptians? What if ingenious men are able to find plausible objections to all arguments maintaining the oneness of the human race? What, after all, if they are able to show very good reasons for believing the negro to have been created precisely as we find him on the Gold Coast—along the Senegal and the Niger—I say, what of all this? "*A man's a man for a' that.*"[19] I sincerely believe, that the weight of the argument is in favor of the unity of origin of the human race, or species—that the arguments on the other side are partial, superficial, utterly subversive of the happiness of man, and insulting to the wisdom of God. Yet, what if we grant they are not so? What, if we grant that the case, on our part, is not made out? Does it follow, that the negro should be held in contempt? Does it follow, that to enslave and imbrute him is either *just* or *wise?* I think not. Human rights stand upon a common basis; and by all the reason that they are supported, maintained and defended, for one variety of the human family, they are supported, maintained and defended for *all* the human family; because all mankind have the same wants, arising out of a common nature. A diverse origin does not disprove a common nature, nor does it disprove a united destiny. The essential characteristics of humanity are everywhere the same. In the language of the eloquent CURRAN,[20] "No matter what complexion, whether an Indian or an African sun has burnt upon him," his title deed to freedom, his claim to life and to liberty, to knowledge and to civilization, to society and to

Christianity, are just and perfect. It is registered in the Courts of Heaven, and is enforced by the eloquence of the God of all the earth.

I have said that the negro and white man are likely ever to remain the principal inhabitants of this country. I repeat the statement now, to submit the reasons that support it. The blacks can disappear from the face of the country by three ways. They may be colonized,—they may be exterminated,—or, they may die out. Colonization is out of the question; for I know not what hardships the laws of the land can impose, which can induce the colored citizen to leave his native soil. He was here in its infancy; he is here in its age. Two hundred years have passed over him, his tears and blood have been mixed with the soil, and his attachment to the place of his birth is stronger than iron. It is not probable that he will be exterminated; two considerations must prevent a crime so stupendous as that—the influence of Christianity on the one hand, and the power of self interest on the other; and, in regard to their dying out, the statistics of the country afford no encouragement for such a conjecture. The history of the negro race proves them to be wonderfully adapted to all countries, all climates, and all conditions. Their tenacity of life, their powers of endurance, their malleable toughness, would almost imply especial interposition on their behalf. The ten thousand horrors of slavery, striking hard upon the sensitive soul, have bruised, and battered, and stung, but have not killed. The poor bondman lifts a smiling face above the surface of a sea of agonies, *hoping on, hoping ever.* His tawny brother, the Indian, dies, under the flashing glance of the Anglo-Saxon. *Not* so the negro; civilization cannot kill him. He accepts it—becomes a part of it. In the Church, he is an Uncle Tom; in the State, he is the most abused and least offensive. All the facts in his history mark out for him a destiny, united to America and Americans. Now, whether this population shall, by FREEDOM, INDUSTRY, VIRTUE and INTELLIGENCE, be made a blessing to the country and the world, or whether their multiplied wrongs shall kindle the vengeance of an offended God, will depend upon the conduct of no class of men so much as upon the Scholars of the country. The future public opinion of the land, whether anti-slavery or pro-slavery, whether just or unjust, whether magnanimous or mean, must redound to the honor of the Scholars of the country or cover them with shame. There is but one safe road for nations or for individuals. The fate of a wicked man and of a wicked nation is the same. The flaming sword of offended justice falls as certainly upon the nation as upon the man. God has no children whose rights may be safely trampled upon. The sparrow may not fall to the ground without the notice of his eye, and men are more than sparrows.

Now, gentlemen, I have done. The subject is before you. I shall not undertake to make the application. I speak as unto wise men. I stand in the presence of Scholars. We have met here to-day from vastly different points in the world's condition. I have reached here—if you will pardon the egotism—by little short of a miracle: at any rate, by dint of some application and perseverance. Born, as I was, in obscurity, a stranger to the halls of learning, environed by ignorance, degradation, and their concomitants, from birth to manhood, I do not feel at liberty to mark out, with any degree of confidence, or dogmatism, what is the precise vocation of the Scholar. Yet, this I *can* say, as a denizen of the world, and as a citizen of a country rolling in the sin and shame of Slavery, the most flagrant and scandalous that ever saw the sun, "Whatsoever things are true, whatsoever things are honest, whatsoever things are just, whatsoever things are pure, whatsoever things are lovely, whatsoever things are of good report, if there be any virtue, and if there be any praise, think on these things."[21]

"THE DRED SCOTT DECISION" (1857)

In March 1857 the Supreme Court, in *Dred Scott v. Sandford*, declared that blacks "had no rights which the white man was bound to respect," that the Republican Party's antislavery platform was unconstitutional, and that slavery could expand anywhere in the nation. In responding to the decision, Douglass accurately predicted that it would bolster the antislavery cause by encouraging Northerners to act on "higher law" and conscience rather than judicial interpretations.

SOURCE: *Two Speeches by Frederick Douglass; One on West India Emancipation . . . and the Other on the Dred Scott Decision, Delivered in New York, on the Occasion of the Anniversary of the American Abolition Society, May, 1857* (Rochester: C. P. Dewey, 1857)

MR. CHAIRMAN, FRIENDS, and FELLOW CITIZENS: While four millions of our fellow countrymen are in chains—while men, women, and children are bought and sold on the auction-block with horses, sheep, and swine—while the remorseless slave-whip draws the warm blood of our common humanity—it is meet that we assemble as we have done to-day, and lift up our hearts and voices in earnest denunciation of the vile and shocking abomination. It is not for us to be governed by our hopes or our fears in this great work; yet it is natural on occasions like this, to survey the position of the great struggle which is going on between slavery and freedom, and to dwell upon such signs of encouragement as may have been lately developed, and the state of feeling these signs or events have occasioned in us and among the people generally. It is a fitting time to take an observation to ascertain where we are, and what our prospects are.

To many, the prospects of the struggle against slavery seem far from cheering. Eminent men, North and South, in Church and State, tell us that the omens are all against us. Emancipation, they tell us, is a wild, delusive idea; the price of human flesh was never higher than now; slavery was never more closely entwined about the hearts and affections of the southern people than now; that whatever of conscientious scruple, religious conviction, or public policy, which opposed the system of slavery forty or fifty years ago, has subsided; and that slavery never reposed upon a firmer basis than now. Completing this picture of the happy and prosperous condition of this system of wickedness, they tell us that this state of things is to be set to our account. Abolition agitation has done it all. How deep is the misfortune of my poor, bleeding people, if this be so! How lost their condition, if even the efforts of their friends but sink them deeper in ruin!

Without assenting to this strong representation of the increasing strength and stability of slavery, without denouncing what of untruth pervades it, I own myself not insensible to the many difficulties and discouragements that beset us on every hand. They fling their broad and gloomy shadows across the pathway of every thoughtful colored man in this country. For one, I see them clearly, and feel them sadly. With an earnest, aching heart I have long looked for the realization of the hope of my people. Standing, as it were, barefoot, and treading upon the sharp and flinty rocks of the present, and looking out upon the boundless sea of the future, I have sought, in my humble way, to penetrate the intervening mists and clouds, and, perchance, to descry, in the dim and shadowy distance, the white flag of freedom, the precise speck of time at which the cruel bondage of my people should end, and the long entombed millions rise from the foul grave of slavery and death. But of that time I can know nothing, and you can know nothing. All is uncertain at that point. One thing, however, is certain; slaveholders are in earnest, and mean to cling to their slaves as long as they can, and to the bitter end. They show no sign of a wish to quit their iron grasp upon the sable throats of their victims. Their motto is, "a firmer hold and a tighter grip" for every new effort that is made to break their cruel power. The case is one of life or death with them, and they will give up only when they must do that or do worse.

In one view slaveholders have a decided advantage over all opposition. It is well to notice this advantage—the advantage of complete organization. They are organized; and yet were not at the pains of creating their organizations. The State governments, where the system of slavery exists, are complete slavery organizations. The church organizations in those States are equally at the service of slavery; while the Federal Government, with its army and navy, from the chief magistracy in Washington, to the Supreme Court, and thence to the chief marshalship at New York, is pledged to support, defend, and propagate the crying curse of human bondage. The pen, the purse, and the sword, are united against the simple truth, preached by humble men in obscure places.

This is one view. It is, thank God, only one view; there is another, and a brighter view. David, you know, looked small and insignificant when going to meet Goliath, but looked larger when he had slain his foe.[1] The Malakoff was, to the eye of the world, impregnable, till the hour it fell before the shot and shell of the allied army. Thus hath it ever been. Oppression, organized as ours is, will appear invincible up to the very hour of its fall. Sir, let us look at the other side, and see if there are not some things to cheer our heart and nerve us up anew in the good work of emancipation.

Take this fact—for it is a fact—the anti-slavery movement has, from first to last, suffered no abatement. It has gone forth in all directions, and is now felt in the remotest extremities of the Republic.

It started small, and was without capital either in men or money. The odds were all against it. It literally had nothing to lose, and every thing to gain. There was ignorance to be enlightened, error to be combatted, conscience to be awakened, prejudice to be overcome, apathy to be aroused, the right of speech to be secured, mob violence to be subdued, and a deep, radical change to be inwrought in the mind and heart of the whole nation. This great work, under God, has gone on, and gone on gloriously.

Amid all changes, fluctuations, assaults, and adverses of every kind, it has remained firm in its purpose, steady in its aim, onward and upward, defying all opposition, and never losing a single battle. Our strength is in the growth of anti-slavery conviction, and this has never halted.

There is a significant vitality about this abolition movement. It has taken a deeper, broader, and more lasting hold upon the national heart than ordinary reform movements. Other subjects of much interest come and go, expand and contract, blaze and vanish, but the huge question of American Slavery, comprehending, as it does, not merely the weal or the woe of four millions, and their countless posterity, but the weal or the woe of this entire nation, must increase in magnitude and in majesty with every hour of its history. From a cloud not bigger than a man's hand, it has overspread the heavens. It has risen from a grain not bigger than a mustard seed. Yet see the fowls of the air, how they crowd its branches.[2]

Politicians who cursed it, now defend it; ministers, once dumb, now speak in its praise; and presses, which once flamed with hot denunciations against it, now surround the sacred cause as by a wall of living fire. Politicians go with it as a pillar of cloud by day, and the press as a pillar of fire by night.[3] With these ancient tokens of success, I, for one, will not despair of our cause.

Those who have undertaken to suppress and crush out this agitation for Liberty and humanity, have been most woefully disappointed. Many who have engaged to put it down, have found themselves put down. The agitation has pursued them in all their meanderings, broken in upon their seclusion, and, at the very moment of fancied security, it has settled down upon them like a mantle of unquenchable fire. Clay, Calhoun, and Webster each tried his hand at suppressing the agitation; and they went to their graves disappointed and defeated.

Loud and exultingly have we been told that the slavery question is settled, and settled forever. You remember it was settled thirty-seven years ago, when Missouri was admitted into the Union with a slaveholding constitution, and slavery prohibited in all territory north of thirty-six degrees of north latitude. Just fifteen years afterwards, it was settled again by voting down the right of petition, and gagging down free discussion in Congress.

Ten years after this it was settled again by the annexation of Texas, and with it the war with Mexico. In 1850 it was again settled. This was called a final settlement. By it slavery was virtually declared to be the equal of Liberty, and should come into the Union on the same terms. By it the right and the power to hunt down men, women, and children, in every part of this country, was conceded to our southern brethren, in order to keep them in the Union. Four years after this settlement, the whole question was once more settled, and settled by a settlement which unsettled all the former settlements.[4]

The fact is, the more the question has been settled, the more it has needed settling. The space between the different settlements has been strikingly on the decrease. The first stood longer than any of its successors.

There is a lesson in these decreasing spaces. The first stood fifteen years—the second, ten years—the third, five years—the fourth stood four years—and the fifth has stood the brief space of two years.

This last settlement must be called the Taney settlement. We are now told, in tones of lofty exultation, that the day is lost—all lost—and that we might as well give up the struggle. The highest authority has spoken. The voice of the Supreme Court has gone out over the troubled waves of the National Conscience, saying peace, be still.

This infamous decision of the Slaveholding wing of the Supreme Court maintains that slaves are, within the contemplation of the Constitution of the United States, property; that slaves are property in the same sense that horses, sheep, and swine are property; that the old doctrine that slavery is a creature of local law is false; that the right of the slaveholder to his slave does not depend upon the local law, but is secured wherever the Constitution of the United States extends; that Congress has no right to prohibit slavery anywhere; that slavery may go in safety anywhere under the star-spangled banner; that colored persons of African descent have no rights that white men are bound to respect; that colored men of African descent are not and cannot be citizens of the United States.

You will readily ask me how I am affected by this devilish decision—this judicial incarnation of wolfishness! My answer is, and no thanks to the slaveholding wing of the Supreme Court, my hopes were never brighter than now.

I have no fear that the National Conscience will be put to sleep by such an open, glaring, and scandalous tissue of lies as that decision is, and has been, over and over, shown to be.

The Supreme Court of the United States is not the only power in this world. It is very great, but the Supreme Court of the Almighty is greater. Judge Taney can do many things, but he cannot perform impossibilities. He cannot bale out the ocean, annihilate this firm old earth, or pluck the silvery star of liberty from our Northern sky. He may decide, and decide again; but he cannot reverse the decision of the Most High. He cannot change the essential nature of things—making evil good, and good, evil.

Happily for the whole human family, their rights have been defined, declared, and decided in a court higher than the Supreme Court. "There is a law," says Brougham, "above all the enactments of human codes, and by that law, unchangeable and eternal, man cannot hold property in man."[5]

Your fathers have said that man's right to liberty is self-evident. There is no need of argument to make it clear. The voices of nature, of conscience, of reason, and of revelation, proclaim it as the right of all rights, the foundation of all trust, and of all responsibility. Man was born with it. It was his before he comprehended it. The *deed* conveying it to him is written in the centre of his soul, and is recorded in Heaven. The sun in the sky is not more palpable to the sight than man's right to liberty is to the moral vision. To decide against this right in the person of Dred Scott, or the humblest and most whip-scarred bondman in the land, is to decide against God. It is an open rebellion against God's government. It is an attempt to undo what God [has] done, to blot out the broad distinction instituted by the *Allwise* between men and things, and to change the image and superscription of the everliving God into a speechless piece of merchandise.

Such a decision cannot stand. God will be true though every man be a liar. We can appeal from this hell-black judgment of the Supreme Court, to the court of common sense and common humanity. We can appeal from man to God. If there is no justice on earth, there is yet justice in heaven. You may close your Supreme Court against the black man's cry for justice, but you cannot, thank God, close against him the ear of a sympathising world, nor shut up the Court of Heaven. All that is merciful and just, on earth and in Heaven, will execrate and despise this edict of Taney.

If it were at all likely that the people of these free States would tamely submit to this demonical judgment, I might feel gloomy and sad over it, and possibly it might be necessary for my people to look for a home in some other country. But as the case stands, we have nothing to fear.

In one point of view, we, the abolitionists and colored people, should meet this decision, unlooked for and monstrous as it appears, in a cheerful spirit. This very attempt to blot out forever the hopes of an enslaved people may be one necessary link in the chain of events preparatory to the downfall and complete overthrow of the whole slave system.

The whole history of the anti-slavery movement is studded with proof that all measures devised and executed with a view to allay and diminish the anti-slavery agitation, have only served to increase, intensify, and embolden that agitation. This wisdom of the crafty has been confounded, and the counsels of the ungodly brought to nought. It was so with the Fugitive Slave Bill. It was so with the Kansas-Nebraska Bill; and it will be so with this last and most shocking of all pro-slavery devices, this Taney decision.

When great transactions are involved, where the fate of millions is concerned, where a long enslaved and suffering people are to be delivered, I am superstitious enough to believe that the finger of the Almighty may be seen bringing good out of evil, and making the wrath of man redound to his honor, hastening the triumph of righteousness.

The American people have been called upon, in a most striking manner, to abolish and put away forever the system of slavery. The subject has been pressed upon their attention in all earnestness and sincerity. The cries of the slave have gone forth to the world, and up to the throne of God. This decision, in my view, is a means of keeping the nation awake on the subject. It is another proof that God does not mean that we shall go to sleep, and forget that we are a slaveholding nation.

Step by step we have seen the slave power advancing; poisoning, corrupting, and perverting the institutions of the country; growing more and more haughty, imperious, and exacting. The white man's liberty has been marked out for the same grave with the black man's.

The ballot box is desecrated, God's law set at nought, armed legislators stalk the halls of Congress, freedom of speech is beaten down in the Senate. The rivers and highways are infested by border ruffians, and white men are made to feel the iron heel of slavery. This ought to arouse us to kill off the hateful thing. They are solemn warnings to which the white people, as well as the black people, should take heed.

If these shall fail, judgment, more fierce or terrible, may come. The lightning, whirlwind, and earthquake may come. Jefferson said that he trembled for his country when he reflected that God is just, and his justice cannot sleep forever.[6] The time may come when even the crushed worm may turn under the tyrant's feet. Goaded by cruelty, stung by a burning sense of wrong, in an awful moment of depression and desperation, the bondman and bondwoman at the south may rush to one wild and deadly struggle for freedom. Already slaveholders go to bed with bowie knives, and apprehend death at their dinners. Those who enslave, rob, and torment their cooks, may well expect to find death in their dinner-pots.

The world is full of violence and fraud, and it would be strange if the slave, the constant victim of both fraud and violence, should escape the contagion. He, too, may learn to fight the devil with fire, and for one, I am in no frame of mind to pray that this may be long deferred.

Two remarkable occurrences have followed the presidential election, one was the unaccountable sickness traced to the National Hotel at Washington, and the other was the discovery of a plan among the slaves, in different localities, to slay their oppressors. Twenty or thirty of the suspected were put to death. Some were shot, some hanged, some burned, and some died under the lash. One brave man owned himself well acquainted with the conspiracy, but said he would rather die than disclose the facts. He received seven hundred and fifty lashes, and his noble spirit went away to the God who gave it. The name of this hero has been by the meanness of tyrants suppressed. Such a man redeems his race. He is worthy to be mentioned with the Hoffers and Tells, the noblest heroes of history.[7] These insurrectionary movements have been put down, but they may break out at any time, under the guidance of higher intelligence, and with a more invincible spirit.

The fire thus kindled, may be revived again;
The flames are extinguished, but the embers remain;
One terrible blast may produce an ignition,
Which shall wrap the whole South in wild conflagration.

The pathway of tyrants lies over volcanoes;
The very air they breathe is heavy with sorrows;
Agonizing heart-throbs convulse them while sleeping,
And the wind whispers Death as over them sweeping.

By all the laws of nature, civilization, and of progress, slavery is a doomed system. Not all the skill of politicians, North and South, not all the sophistries of Judges, not all the fulminations of a corrupt press, not all the hypocritical prayers, or the hypocritical refusals to pray of a hollow-hearted priesthood, not all the devices of sin and Satan, can save the vile thing from extermination.

Already a gleam of hope breaks upon us from the south-west. One Southern city has grieved and astonished the whole South by a preference for freedom. The wedge has entered. Dred Scott, of Missouri, goes into slavery, but St. Louis declares for freedom.[8] The judgment of Taney is not the judgment of St. Louis.

It may be said that this demonstration in St. Louis is not to be taken as an evidence of sympathy with the slave; that it is purely a white man's victory. I admit it. Yet I am glad that white men, bad as they generally are, should gain a victory over slavery. I am willing to accept a judgment against slavery, whether supported by white or black reasons—though I would much rather have it supported by both. He that is not against us, is on our part.

Come what will, I hold it to be morally certain that, sooner or later, by fair means or foul means, in quiet or in tumult, in peace or in blood, in judgment or in mercy, slavery is doomed to cease out of this otherwise goodly land, and liberty is destined to become the settled law of this Republic.

I base my sense of the certain overthrow of slavery, in part, upon the nature of the American Government, the Constitution, the tendencies of the age, and the character of the American people; and this, notwithstanding the important decision of Judge Taney.

I know of no soil better adapted to the growth of reform than American soil. I know of no country where the conditions for affecting great changes in the settled order of things, for the development of right ideas of liberty and humanity, are more favorable than here in these United States.

The very groundwork of this government is a good repository of Christian civilization. The Constitution, as well as the Declaration of Independence, and the sentiments of the founders of the Republic, give us a platform broad enough, and strong enough, to support the most comprehensive plans for the freedom and elevation of all the people of this country, without regard to color, class, or clime.

There is nothing in the present aspect of the anti-slavery question which should drive us into the extravagance and nonsense of advocating a dissolution of the American Union as a means of overthrowing slavery, or freeing the North from the malign influence of slavery upon the morals of the Northern people. While the press is at liberty, and speech is free, and the ballot-box is open to the people of the sixteen free States; while the slaveholders are but four hundred thousand in number, and we are fourteen millions; while the mental and moral power of the nation is with us; while we are really the strong and they are the weak, it would look worse than cowardly to retreat from the Union.

If the people of the North have not the power to cope with these four hundred thousand slaveholders inside the Union, I see not how they could do so outside the Union; indeed, I see not how they could get out of the Union. The strength necessary to move the Union must ever be less than is required to break it up. If we have got to conquer the slave power to get out of the Union, I for one would much rather conquer, and stay in the Union. The latter, it strikes me, is the far more rational mode of action.

I make these remarks in no servile spirit, nor in any superstitious reverence for a mere human arrangement. If I felt the Union to be a curse, I should not be far behind the very chiefest of the disunion Abolitionists in denouncing it. But the evil to be met and abolished is not in the Union. The power arrayed against us is not a parchment.

It is not in changing the dead form of the Union, that slavery is to be abolished in this country. We have to do not with the dead, but the living; not with the past, but the living present.

Those who seek slavery in the Union, and who are everlastingly dealing blows upon the Union, in the belief that they are killing slavery, are most woefully mistaken. They are fighting a dead form instead of a living and powerful reality. It is clearly not because of the peculiar character of our Constitution that we have slavery, but the wicked pride, love of power, and selfish perverseness of the American people. Slavery lives in this country not because of any paper Constitution, but in the moral blindness of the American people, who persuade themselves that they are safe, though the rights of others may be struck down.

Besides, I think it would be difficult to hit upon any plan less likely to abolish slavery than the dissolution of the Union. The most devoted advocates of slavery, those who make the interests of slavery their constant study, seek a dissolution of the Union as their final plan for preserving slavery from Abolition, and their ground is well taken. Slavery lives and flourishes best in the absence of civilization; a dissolution of the Union would shut up the system in its own congenial barbarism.

The dissolution of the Union would not give the North one single additional advantage over slavery to the people of the North, but would manifestly take from them many which they now certainly possess.

Within the Union we have a firm basis of anti-slavery operation. National welfare, national prosperity, national reputation and honor, and national scrutiny; common rights, common duties, and common country, are so many bridges over which we can march to the destruction of slavery. To fling away these advantages because James Buchanan is President, or Judge Taney gives a lying decision in favor of slavery, does not enter into my notion of common sense.

Mr. Garrison and his friends have been telling us that, while in the Union, we are responsible for slavery; and in so telling us, he and they have told us the truth. But in telling us that we shall cease to be responsible for slavery by dissolving the Union, he and they have not told us the truth.

There now, clearly, is no freedom from responsibility for slavery, but in the Abolition of slavery. We have gone too far in this business now to sum up our whole duty in the cant phrase of "no Union with slaveholders."

To desert the family hearth may place the recreant husband out of the sight of his hungry children, but it cannot free him from responsibility. Though he should roll the waters of three oceans, between him and them, he could not roll from his soul the burden of his responsibility to them; and, as with the private family, so in this instance with the national family. To leave the slave in his chains, in the hands of cruel masters, who are too strong for him, is not to free ourselves from responsibility. Again: If I were on board of a pirate ship, with a company of men and women whose lives and liberties I had put in jeopardy, I would not clear my soul of their blood by jumping in the long boat, and singing out no union with pirates. My business would be to remain on board, and while I never would perform a single act of piracy again, I should exhaust every means given me by my position, to save the lives and liberties of those against whom I had committed piracy. In like manner, I hold it is our duty to remain inside this Union, and use all the power to restore [to the] enslaved millions their precious and God-given rights. The more we have done by our voice and our votes, in times past, to rivet their galling fetters, the more clearly and solemnly comes the sense of duty to remain, to undo what we have done. Where, I ask, could the slave look for release from slavery if the Union were dissolved? I have an abiding conviction founded upon long and careful study of the certain effects of slavery upon the moral sense of slaveholding communities, that if the slaves are ever delivered from bondage, the power will emanate from the free States. All hope that the slaveholders will be self-moved to this great act of justice, is groundless and delusive. Now, as of old, the Redeemer must come from above, not from beneath. To dissolve the Union would be to withdraw the emancipating power from the field.

But I am told this is the argument of expediency. I admit it, and am prepared to show that what is expedient in this instance is right. "Do justice, though the heavens fall."[9] Yes, that is a good motto, but I deny that it would be doing justice to the slave to dissolve the Union and leave the slave in his chains to get out by the clemency of his master, or the strength of his arms. Justice to the slave is to break his chains, and going out of the union is to leave him in his chains, and without any probable chance of getting out of them.

But I come now to the great question as to the constitutionality of slavery. The recent slaveholding decision, as well as the teachings of anti-slavery men, make this a fit time to discuss the constitutional pretensions of slavery.

The people of the North are a law abiding people. They love order and respect the means to that end. This sentiment has sometimes led them to the folly and wickedness of trampling upon the very life of law, to uphold its dead form. This was so in the execution of that thrice accursed Fugitive Slave Bill. Burns and Simms,[10] were sent back to the hell of slavery after they had looked upon Bunker Hill, and heard liberty thunder in Faneuil Hall. The people permitted this outrage in obedience to the popular sentiment of reverence for law. While men thus respect law, it becomes a serious matter so to interpret the law as to make it operate against liberty. I have a quarrel with those who fling the Supreme Law of this land between the slave and freedom. It is a serious matter to fling the weight of the Constitution against the cause of human liberty, and those who do it, take upon them a heavy responsibility. Nothing but absolute necessity, shall, or ought to drive me to such a concession to slavery.

When I admit that slavery is constitutional, I must see slavery recognized in the Constitution. I must see that it is there plainly stated that one man of a certain description has a right of property in the body and soul of another man of a certain description. There must be no room for a doubt. In a matter so important as the loss of liberty, everything must be proved beyond all reasonable doubt.

The well known rules of legal interpretation bear me out in this stubborn refusal to see slavery where slavery is not, and only to see slavery where it is.

The Supreme Court has, in its day, done something better than make slaveholding decisions. It has laid down rules of interpretation which are in harmony with the true idea and object of law and liberty.

It has told us that the intention of legal instruments must prevail; and that this must be collected from its words.[11] It has told us that language must be construed strictly in favor of liberty and justice.

It has told us where rights are infringed, where fundamental principles are overthrown, [and] where the general system of the law is departed from, the Legislative intention must be expressed with irresistible clearness, to induce a court of justice to suppose a design to effect such objects.

These rules are as old as law. They rise out of the very elements of law. It is to protect human rights, and promote human welfare. Law is in its nature opposed to wrong, and must everywhere be presumed to be in favor of the right. The pound of flesh, but not one drop of blood, is a sound rule of legal interpretation.

Besides there is another rule of law as well [as] of common sense, which requires us to look to the ends for which a law is made, and to construe its details in harmony with the ends sought.

Now let us approach the Constitution from the stand-point thus indicated, and instead of finding in it a warrant for the stupendous system of robbery, comprehended in the term slavery, we shall find it strongly against that system.

"We, the people of the United States, in order to form a more perfect Union, establish justice, insure domestic tranquility, provide for the common defence, promote the general welfare, and secure the blessings of liberty to ourselves and our posterity, do ordain and establish this constitution for the United States of America."

Such are the objects announced by the instrument itself, and they are in harmony with the Declaration of Independence, and the principles of human well-being.

Six objects are here declared, "Union," "defence," "welfare," "tranquility," and "justice," and "liberty."

Neither in the preamble nor in the body of the Constitution is there a single mention of the term *slave* or *slave holder, slave master* or *slave state,* neither is there any reference to the color, or the physical peculiarities of any part of the people of the United States. Neither is there anything in the Constitution standing alone, which would imply the existence of slavery in this country.

"We, the people"—not we, the white people—not we, the citizens, or the legal voters—not we, the privileged class, and excluding all other classes but we, the people; not we, the horses and cattle, but we the people—the men and women, the human inhabitants of the United States, do ordain and establish this Constitution, &c.

I ask, then, any man to read the Constitution, and tell me where if he can, in what particular that instrument affords the slightest sanction of slavery?

Where will he find a guarantee for slavery? Will he find it in the declaration that no person shall be deprived of life, liberty, or property, without due process of law? Will he find it in the declaration that the Constitution was established to secure the blessings of liberty? Will he find it in the right of the people to be secure in their persons and papers, and houses, and effects? Will he find it in the clause prohibiting the enactment by any State of a bill of attainder?

These all strike at the root of slavery, and any one of them, but faithfully carried out, would put an end to slavery in every State in the American Union.

Take, for example, the prohibition of a bill of attainder. That is a law entailing on the child the misfortunes of the parent. This principle would destroy slavery in every State of the Union.

The law of slavery is a law of attainder. The child is property because its parent was property, and suffers as a slave because its parent suffered as a slave.

Thus the very essence of the whole slave code is in open violation of a fundamental provision of the Constitution, and is in open and flagrant violation of all the objects set forth in the Constitution.

While this and much more can be said, and has been said, and much better said, by Lysander Spooner, William Goodell, Beriah Green, and Gerrit Smith, in favor of the entire unconstitutionality of slavery, what have we on the other side?

How is the constitutionality of slavery made out, or attempted to be made out?

First, by discrediting and casting away as worthless the most beneficent rules of legal interpretation; by disregarding the plain and common sense reading of the instrument itself; by showing that the Constitution does not mean what it says, and says what it does not mean, by assuming that the WRITTEN Constitution is to be interpreted in the light of a SECRET and UNWRITTEN understanding of its framers, which understanding is declared to be in favor of slavery. It is in this mean, contemptible, underhand method that the Constitution is pressed into the service of slavery.

They do not point us to the Constitution itself, for the reason that there is nothing sufficiently explicit for their purpose; but they delight in supposed intentions—intentions no where expressed in the Constitution, and every where contradicted in the Constitution.

Judge Taney lays down this system of interpreting in this wise:

"The general words above quoted would seem to embrace the whole human family, and, if they were used in a similar instrument at this day, would be so understood. But it is too clear for dispute that the enslaved African race were not intended to be included, and formed no part of the people who framed and adopted this declaration; for if the language, as understood in that day, would embrace them, the conduct of the distinguished men who framed the Declaration of Independence would have been utterly and flagrantly inconsistent with the principles they asserted; and instead of the sympathy of mankind, to which they appealed, they would have deserved and received universal rebuke and reprobation.

"It is difficult, at this day, to realize the state of public opinion respecting that unfortunate class with the civilized and enlightened portion of the world at the time of the Declaration of Independence and the adoption of the Constitution;[12] but history shows they had, for more than a century, been regarded as beings of an inferior order, and unfit associates for the white race, either socially or politically, and had no rights which white men are bound to respect; and the black man might be reduced to slavery, bought and sold, and treated as an ordinary article of merchandise. This opinion, at that time, was fixed and universal with the civilized portion of the white race. It was regarded as an axiom of morals, which no one thought of disputing, and every one habitually acted upon it, without doubting, for a moment, the correctness of the opinion. And in no nation was this opinion more fixed, and generally acted upon, than in England; the subjects of which government not only seized them on the coast of Africa, but took them, as ordinary merchandise, to where they could make a profit on them. The opinion, thus entertained, was universally maintained on the colonies this side of the Atlantic; accordingly, negroes of the African race were regarded by them as property, and held and bought and sold as such in every one of the thirteen colonies which united in the Declaration of Independence, and afterwards formed the Constitution."

The argument here is, that the Constitution comes down to us from a slaveholding period and a slaveholding people; and that, therefore, we are bound to suppose that the Constitution recognizes colored persons of African descent, the victims of slavery at that time, as debarred forever from all participation in the benefit of the Constitution and the Declaration of Independence, although the plain reading of both includes them in their beneficent range.

As a man, an American, a citizen, a colored man of both Anglo-Saxon and African descent, I denounce this representation as a most scandalous and devilish perversion of the Constitution, and a brazen misstatement of the facts of history.

But I will not content myself with mere denunciation; I invite attention to the facts.

It is a fact, a great historic fact, that at the time of the adoption of the Constitution, the leading religious denominations in this land were anti-slavery, and were laboring for the emancipation of the colored people of African descent.

The church of a country is often a better index of the state of opinion and feeling than is even the government itself.

The Methodists, Baptists, Presbyterians, and the denomination of Friends, were actively opposing slavery, denouncing the system of bondage, with language as burning and sweeping as we employ at this day.

Take the Methodists. In 1780, that denomination said: "The Conference acknowledges that slavery is contrary to the laws of God, man, and nature, and hurtful to society—contrary to the dictates of conscience and true religion, and doing to others that we would not do unto us." In 1784, the same church declared, "that those who buy, sell, or give slaves away, except for the purpose to free them, shall be expelled immediately." In 1785, it spoke even more stringently on the subject. It then said: "We hold in the deepest abhorrence the practice of slavery, and shall not cease to seek its destruction by all wise and proper means."[13]

So much for the position of the Methodist Church in the early history of the Republic, in those days of darkness to which Judge Taney refers.

Let us now see how slavery was regarded by the Presbyterian Church at that early date.

In 1794, the General Assembly of that body pronounced the following judgment in respect to slavery, slaveholders, and slaveholding.

"1st Timothy, 1st chapter, 10th verse: 'The law was made for man-stealers.' 'This crime among the Jews exposed the perpetrators of it to capital punishment.' Exodus, xxi, 13.—And the apostle here classes them with sinners of the first rank. The word he uses in its original import, comprehends all who are concerned in bringing any of the human race into slavery, or in retaining them in it. Stealers of men are all those who bring off slaves or freemen, and keep, sell, or buy them. 'To steal a freeman,' says Grotius, 'is the highest kind of theft.' In other instances, we only steal human property, but when we steal or retain men in slavery, we seize those who, in common with ourselves, are constituted, by the original grant, lords of the earth."[14]

I might quote, at length, from the sayings of the Baptist Church and the sayings of eminent divines at this early period, showing that Judge Taney has grossly falsified history, but will not detain you with these quotations.

The testimony of the church, and the testimony of the founders of this Republic, from the declaration downward, prove Judge Taney false: as false to history as he is to law.

Washington and Jefferson, and Adams, and Jay, and Franklin, and Rush, and Hamilton, and a host of others, held no such degrading views on the subject as are imputed by Judge Taney to the Fathers of the Republic.[15]

All, at that time, looked for the gradual but certain abolition of slavery, and shaped the constitution with a view to this grand result.

George Washington can never be claimed as a fanatic, or as the representative of fanatics. The slaveholders impudently use his name for the base purpose of giving respectability to slavery. Yet, in a letter to Robert Morris, Washington uses this language—language which, at this day, would make him a terror of the slaveholders, and the natural representative of the Republican party.

"There is not a man living, who wishes more sincerely than I do, to see some plan adopted for the abolition of slavery; but there is only one proper and effectual mode by which it can be accomplished, and that is by Legislative authority; and this, as far as my suffrage will go, shall not be wanting."[16]

Washington only spoke the sentiment of his times. There were, at that time, Abolition societies in the slave States—Abolition societies in Virginia, in North Carolina, in Maryland, in Pennsylvania, and in Georgia—all slaveholding States. Slavery was so weak, and liberty so strong, that free speech could attack the monster to its teeth. Men were not mobbed and driven out of the presence of slavery, merely because they condemned the slave system. The system was then on its knees imploring to be spared, until it could get itself decently out of the world.

In the light of these facts, the Constitution was framed, and framed in conformity to it.

It may, however, be asked, if the Constitution were so framed that the rights of all the people were naturally protected by it, how happens it that a large part of the people have been held in slavery ever since its adoption? Have the people mistaken the requirements of their own Constitution?

The answer is ready. The Constitution is one thing, its administration is another, and, in this instance, a very different and opposite thing. I am here to vindicate the law, not the administration of the law. It is the written Constitution, not the unwritten Constitution, that is now before us. If, in the whole range of the Constitution, you can find no warrant for slavery, then we may properly claim it for liberty.

Good and wholesome laws are often found dead on the statute book. We may condemn the practice under them and against them, but never the law itself. To condemn the good law with the wicked practice, is to weaken, not to strengthen our testimony.

It is no evidence that the Bible is a bad book, because those who profess to believe the Bible are bad. The slaveholders of the South, and many of their wicked allies at the North, claim the Bible for slavery; shall we, therefore, fling the Bible away as a pro-slavery book? It would be as reasonable to do so as it would be to fling away the Constitution.

We are not the only people who have illustrated the truth, that a people may have excellent law, and detestable practices. Our Savior denounces the Jews, because they made void the law by their traditions.[17] We have been guilty of the same sin.

The American people have made void our Constitution by just such traditions as Judge Taney and Mr. Garrison have been giving to the world of late, as the true light in which to view the Constitution of the United States. I shall follow neither. It is not what Moses allowed for the hardness of heart, but what God requires, [which] ought to be the rule.

It may be said that it is quite true that the Constitution was designed to secure the blessings of liberty and justice to the people who made it, and to the posterity of the people who made it, but was never designed to do any such thing for the colored people of African descent.

This is Judge Taney's argument, and it is Mr. Garrison's argument, but it is not the argument of the Constitution. The Constitution imposes no such mean and satanic limitations upon its own beneficent operation. And, if the Constitution makes none, I beg to know what right has any body, outside of the Constitution, for the special accommodation of slaveholding villainy, to impose such a construction upon the Constitution?

The Constitution knows all the human inhabitants of this country as "the people." It makes, as I have said before, no discrimination in favor of, or against, any class of the people, but is fitted to protect and preserve the rights of all, without reference to color, size, or any physical peculiarities. Besides, it has been shown by William Goodell and others, that in eleven out of the old thirteen States, colored men were legal voters at the time of the adoption of the Constitution.

In conclusion, let me say, all I ask of the American people is, that they live up to the Constitution, adopt its principles, imbibe its spirit and enforce its provisions.

When this is done, the wounds of my bleeding people will be healed, the chain will no longer rust on their ankles, their backs will no longer be torn by the bloody lash, and liberty, the glorious birthright of our common humanity, will become the inheritance of all the inhabitants of this highly favored country.

"THE SIGNIFICANCE OF EMANCIPATION IN THE WEST INDIES" (1857)

American abolitionists celebrated August 1, Emancipation Day in the British West Indies, as fervently as July 4. Douglass draws from scripture to argue that the British Emancipation Act of 1834 portended emancipation in the United States, much as the Old Testament had prophesied for Christians the coming Messiah.

SOURCE: *Two Speeches by Frederick Douglass; One on West India Emancipation . . . and the Other on the Dred Scott Decision, Delivered in New York, on the Occasion of the Anniversary of the American Abolition Society, May, 1857* (Rochester: C. P. Dewey, 1857)

MR. CHAIRMAN, FRIENDS, and FELLOW CITIZENS: In coming before you to speak a few words, bearing on the great question of human freedom, and having some relation to the sublime event which has brought us together, I am cheered by your numbers, and deeply gratified by the cordial, generous, and earnest reception with which you have been pleased to greet me. I sincerely thank you for this manifestation of your kindly feelings, and if I had as many voices and hearts as you have, I would give as many evidences of my pleasure in meeting you as you have given me, of your pleasure at my appearance before you to-day. As it is I can only say, I sincerely rejoice to be here, and am exceedingly glad to meet you. No man who loves the cause of human freedom, can be other than happy when beholding a multitude of freedom-loving, human faces like that I now see before me.

Sir, it is just ten years and three days ago, when it was my high privilege to address a vast concourse of the friends of Liberty in this same beautiful town, on an occasion similar to the one which now brings us here. I look back to that meeting—I may say, that great meeting—with most grateful emotions. That meeting was great in its numbers, great in the spirit that pervaded it, and great in the truths enunciated by some of the speakers on that occasion.

Sir, that meeting seems to me a thing of yesterday. The time between then and now seems but a speck, and it is hard to realize that ten long years, crowded with striking events, have rolled away: yet such is the solemn fact. Mighty changes, great transactions, have taken place since the first of August, 1847. Territory has been acquired from Mexico; political parties in the country have assumed a more open and shameless subserviency to slavery; the fugitive slave bill has been passed; ancient landmarks of freedom have been overthrown; the government has entered upon a new and dreadful career in favor of slavery; the slave power has become more aggressive; freedom of speech has been beaten down by ruffian and murderous blows; innocent and freedom-loving men have been murdered by scores on the soil of Kansas, and the end is not yet. Of these things, however, I will not speak now; indeed I may leave them entirely to others who are to follow me.

Mr. President, I am deeply affected by the thought that many who were with us ten years ago, and who bore an honorable part in the joyous exercise of that occasion, are now numbered with the silent dead. Sir, I miss one such from this platform. Soon after that memorable meeting, our well-beloved friend, Chas. Van Loon, was cut down, in the midst of his years and his usefulness, and transfered to that undiscovered country, from whose bourne no traveler returns. Many who now hear me, will remember how nobly he bore himself on the occasion of our celebration. You remember how he despised, disregarded and trampled upon the mean spirit of color caste, which was then so rampant and bitter in the country, and his cordial and practical recognition of the great truths of human brotherhood. Some of you will never forget, as I shall never forget, his glorious, towering, spontaneous, copious, truthful, and fountain-like out-gushing eloquence. I never think of that meeting without thinking of Chas. Van Loon. He was a true man, a genuine friend of liberty, and of liberty for all men, without the least regard for any of the wicked distinctions, arbitrarily set up by the pride and depravity of the wealthy and strong, against the rights of the humble and weak. My friends, we should cherish the memory of Chas. Van Loon as a precious treasure, for it is not often that a people like ours, has such a memory to cherish. The poor have but few friends, and we, the colored people, are emphatically and peculiarly, the poor of this land.[1]

Sir, I believe Chas. Van Loon is the only one of those who addressed us at that time, who has been removed from us by the hand of death. Many of the five thousand of the rank and file, have doubtless gone the way of all the earth. We shall see their faces and hear their voices no more, save as we recall them to the mind's eye and ear, by the aid of memory. Some of the marshalls who ordered our procession on that occasion, are no more, and very few of the glorious choir, which filled your grove with songs of joyous freedom, are with us to-day. What death, the common destroyer of all, has not done towards thinning our ranks, the fugitive slave bill has done, and done with terrible effect. It came upon us like a wolf upon the fold, and left our ranks thinned and trembling. The first six months after this whirlwind and pestilence set in, were six of the gloomiest months I ever experienced. It did seem that the infernal regions were broken up, and that devils, not men, had taken possession of our government and our church. The most shocking feature of those times was, that the infernal business of hunting men and women went on under the sanction of heaven as well as earth. Kidnapping proclamations, and kidnapping sermons, the one backed up by the terrors of the gallows, and the others by the terrors of hell, were promulgated at the same time. Our leading divines, had no higher law for the poor, the needy, the hunted, and helpless; their God was with the slaveholder, and the brutal and savage man hunter, carried his warrant from Millard Fillmore, in one pocket, and a sermon from Doctor Lord in the other.[2] I say, sir, these were gloomy days for me. Our people fled in darkening trains from this country, to Canada. There seemed no place for the free black man, in this Republic. It appeared that we were to be driven out of the country by a system of cruelty and violence as murderous and as hellish as that which snatched us from our homes in our fatherland, and planted us here, as the white man's slaves.

Sir, the many changes, vicissitudes, and deaths, which have occurred within the range of our knowledge, during this decade, afford matter for serious thought. I cannot now dwell upon them. Perhaps the occasion does not require that I should dwell upon them, yet I must say, what we all more or less feel, and that is that the flight of the last ten years, with its experience of trial and death, admonish[es] us that we are all hastening down the tide of time, and that our places in the world's activities are soon to be occupied by other generations. They remind us that the present only is ours, and that what our hands now find to do, we should do quickly, and with all our might.

Sir, I have thought much on this subject of the present, and the future, the seen, and the unseen, and about what things should engage our thoughts, and energies while here, and I have come to the conclusion that from no work would I rather go to meet my Eternal Father, than from the work of breaking the fetters from the limbs of his suffering children.

Mr. President (Austin Steward), I am happy to see here to-day many faces that were here ten years ago. I am especially glad to see you here, and to hear your voice. Sir, you have grown venerable in the service of your enslaved people, and I am glad to find that you are not weary in this department of well doing. Time has dealt gently with you this last ten years, and you seem as vigorous now as when I saw you then. You presided on that occasion, you preside now; and notwithstanding the gloomy aspect of the times, I am not without hope, that you will live to preside over a grander celebration than this; a celebration of the American jubilee, in which four millions of our countrymen shall rejoice in freedom. That jubilee will come. You and I may, or we may not live to see it; but whether we do, or do not, God reigns, and Slavery must yet fall; unless the devil is more potent than the Almighty; unless sin is stronger than righteousness, Slavery must perish, and that not very long hence.

Here, too, I am most happy to meet again my loved, and honored and much respected friend, HENRY HIGHLAND GARNET. He was here with us, and spoke to us ten years ago. He has traveled much and labored much since that time. England, Ireland, Scotland, and Wales, have listened to his eloquent advocacy of our cause since then. While in the old world, it was his privilege to associate with refined and cultivated people; and I venture to say that no man from among us, visiting the old country, has left in his pathway a better impression for himself and [his] people than H. H. GARNET. We need a thousand such representative men at home and abroad, to meet and repel the floods of slander of our race, which two thousand millions of dollars invested in our people, as property, constantly provoke. The American government does not need a minister at the court of St. James to look after American interests, more than we need in England a representative of our people against whom all manner of lies are told.

Happy am I too, to meet here to-day, as ten years ago, J. W. LOGUEN, the intrepid and faithful conductor of the Underground Railroad, who has, during the interval of our former celebrations, conveyed from Republican slavery to Monarchical Liberty, not fewer than a thousand souls.

Mr. President, you miss, and we all miss, our old friend, SAML. R. WARD. He was with us ten years ago, and if he were now in the country, he would doubtless be with us here to-day. I will say for Mr. WARD what he can not say for himself. Though absent in body he is with us in spirit. Mr. WARD is now in Jamaica, and I am told is soon to be joined in his new home by his dear family, of whom we have often heard him lovingly speak. They are now in Canada, and he has sent for them to come out to him. I will say another word of Mr. WARD, and that is, he was, in many respects, a head and shoulders above us all. No colored man who has yet attracted public observation in this country, was ever capable of rendering his people greater service than he. And while we all deeply regret that he has seen fit to leave us for other fields of usefulness, we will here and now tender him our best wishes while he may remain abroad, and pledge him an earnest welcome should he ever return to the Empire State.

My friends, you will also miss, as I do, the eloquent CHAS. L.

REMOND. He was on this platform ten years ago. I should have been glad to have met him here to-day, for though he differs from us in his mode of serving our cause, he doubtless fully sympathises with us in the sentiment which brings us together on this occasion.

Mr. President, you will pardon those homely but grateful references to individuals. The great poet has told us that one touch of nature makes all the world akin,[3] and the cause of freedom, I think, makes friends of all its friends. At any rate, I can say that I can love an enemy, if he loves the slave, for I know that if he loves the slave, he loves him intelligently, and if he hates me, he does it ignorantly. I can easily forgive such. Sir, there are other names I might well refer to, as worthy as those already mentioned, but the time would fail. I hasten, therefore, to the consideration of those topics naturally suggested by this occasion.

Friends and fellow-citizens: We have met here to-day to celebrate with all fitting demonstrations of joy and gladness, this the twenty-third anniversary of the inauguration of freedom as the ruling law of the British West Indies. The day and the deed are both greatly distinguished. They are as a city set upon a hill.[4] All civilized men at least, have looked with wonder and admiration upon the great deed of justice and humanity which has made the first of August illustrious among all the days of the year. But to no people on the globe, leaving out the emancipated men and women of the West Indies themselves, does this day address itself with so much force and significance, as to the people of the United States. It has made the name of England known and loved in every Slave Cabin, from the Potomac to the Rio Grande, and has spread alarm, hatred, and dread in all the accursed slave markets of our boasted Republic from Baltimore to New Orleans.

Slavery in America, and slavery every where, never received a more stunning and killing condemnation.

The event we celebrate is the finding and the restoration to the broken ranks of human brotherhood eight hundred thousand lost members of the human family. It is the resurrection of a mighty multitude, from the grave of moral, mental, social, and spiritual death, where ages of slavery and oppression, and lust and pride, and cruelty had bound them. Here they were instantly clothed with all the rights, responsibilities, powers, and duties, of free men and women.

Up to the morning of the first of August, 1834, these people were slaves, numbered with the beasts of the field, marked, branded, priced, valued, and ranged as articles of property. The gates of human brotherhood were bolted and barred against them. They were outside of both law and gospel. The love taught in the Bible, and the justice recorded in the Statute Book did not embrace them: they were outside. Their fellow men had written their names with horses, sheep, and swine, and with horned cattle. They were not governed by the law, but [by] the lash, they were not paid for their work, but whipped on to toil as the American slave now is. Their degradation was complete. They were slaves; and when I have said that, I have said all. The essence of wickedness, the intensified sum of all iniquity, the realization of the idea of a burning hell upon the earth, in which every passion is an unchained devil, let loose to deal out ten thousand pains, and horrors start up to view at the very mention of slavery! It comprehends all that is foul, shocking, and dreadful. Human nature shudders, and turns pale at its presence, and flies from it as from a den of lions, a nest of scorpions, or an army of rattlesnakes. The very soul sickens, and the mind revolts at the thought of slavery, and the true man welcomes instant death in preference to being reduced to its degradation and ruin.

Yet such was the condition of our brothers and sisters in the British West Indies, up to the morning of the first of August, 1834. The wicked love of dominion by man over man, had made strong their fetters and multiplied their chains. But on the memorable morning which we are met to celebrate, one bolt from the moral sky of Britain left these blood-stained irons all scattered and broken throughout the West Indies, and the limbs they had bruised, out-stretched in praise and thanksgiving to God for deliverance. No man of any sensibility can read the account of that great transaction without emotions too great for utterance. There was something Godlike in this decree of the British nation. It was the spirit of the Son of God commanding the devil of slavery to go out of the British West Indies.

It said [to the] tyrant slave-driver, fling away your blood-stained whip, and bury out of sight your broken fetters and chains. Your accursed occupation is gone. It said to the slave, with wounds, bruises, and scars yet fresh upon him, you are emancipated—set free—enfranchised—no longer slaves, but British subjects, and henceforth equal before the British law!

Such my friends, was the change—the revolution—the wonderous transformation which took place in the condition of the colored people in the British West Indies, twenty-three years ago. With the history of the causes, which led to this great consummation, you are perhaps already sufficiently acquainted. I do not intend in my present remarks to enter into the tedious details of this history, although it might prove quite instructive to some in this assembly. It might prove especially interesting to point out various steps in the progress of the British Anti-Slavery movement, and to dwell upon some of the more striking analogies between that and our movement in this country. The materials at this point are ample, did the limits of the hour permit me to bring them forward.

One remark in this connection I will make. The abolition movement in America, like many other institutions of this country, was largely derived from England. The defenders of American slavery often excuse their villainy on the ground that they inherited the system from England. Abolitionism may be traced to the same source, yet I don't see that it is any more popular on that account. Mr. Garrison applied British abolitionism to American slavery. He did that and nothing more. He found its principles here plainly stated and defined; its truths glowingly enunciated, and the whole subject illustrated, and elaborated in a masterly manner. The sin—the crime—the curse of slavery, were all demonstrated in the light of reason, religion, and morality, and by a startling array of facts. We owe Mr. Garrison our grateful homage in that he was among the first of his countrymen who zealously applied the British argument for abolition against American slavery. Even the doctrine of immediate emancipation as against gradualism, is of English, not American origin. It was expounded and enforced by Elizabeth Herrick, and adopted by all the earnest abolitionists in England.[5] It came upon the British nation like *Uncle Tom's Cabin* upon our land after the passing of the fugitive slave law, and it is remarkable that the highest services rendered the anti-slavery cause in both countries, were rendered by women. Elizabeth Herrick, who wrote only a pamphlet, will be remembered as long as the West India Emancipation is remembered, and the name of Harriet Beecher Stowe can never die while the love of freedom lives in the world.

But my friends, it is not with these analogies and minute references that I mean in my present talk, to deal.

I wish you to look at West India Emancipation as one complete transaction of vast and sublime significance, surpassing all power of exaggeration. We hear and read much of the achievements of this nineteenth century, and much can be said, and truthfully said of them. The world has literally shot forward with the speed of steam and lightning. It has probably made more progress during the last fifty years, than in any five hundred years to which we can refer in the history of the race. Knowledge has been greatly increased, and its blessing, widely diffused. Locomotion has been marvelously improved, so that the very ends of the earth are being rapidly brought together. Time to the traveler has been annihilated.

Deep down beneath the stormy surface of the wide, wide waste of waters, a pathway has been formed for human thought. Machinery of almost every conceivable description, and for almost every conceivable purpose, has been invented and applied; ten thousand discoveries and combinations have been made during these last fifty years, till the world has ceased to ask in astonishment "what next?" for there seems scarcely any margin left for a next. We have made hands of iron and brass, and copper and wood, and though we have not been able to endow them with life and soul, yet we have found the means of endowing them with intelligent motion, and of making them do our work, and to do it more easily, quickly and more abundantly than the hands in their palmiest days were able to perform it. I am not here to disparage or underrate this physical and intellectual progress of the race. I thank my God for every advance which is made in this direction.

I fully appreciate the beautiful statement which you farmers, now before me, so highly regard, "that he who makes two blades of grass grow where only one grew before,"[6] is a benefactor. I recognize and honor, as you do, all such benefactors. There is not the slightest danger that those who contribute directly to the world's wealth and ease will ever be forgotten by the world. The world loves its own. A hungry man will not forget the hand that feeds him, though he may forget that Providence which caused the bread to grow. Arkwright, Watt, Fulton, Franklin, Morse, and Daguerre,[7] are names which will not fade from the memories of men. They are grand civilizers, but civilizers after their kind—and great as are their achievements, they sink to nothingness when compared with that great achievement which has given us the first day of August as a sacred day. "What shall it profit a man if he gain the whole world and lose his own soul?"[8] We are to view this grand event in the light of this sublime enquiry.

"Men do not live by bread alone," said the great Redeemer.[9] What is true of individual men, is also true of societies, and nations of men. Nations are not held in their spheres, and perpetuated in health by cunning machinery. Railroads, steamships, electric wires, tons of gold and silver, and precious stones cannot save them. A nation may perish in the midst of them all, or in the absence of them all. The true life principle is not in them.

Egypt died in the sight of all her imposing wealth and her everlasting Pyramids. The polished stone is there, but Egypt is gone. Greece has vanished, her life disappeared as it were, in a trance of artistic beauty, and architectural splendor. Great Babylon, the mother of harlots and the abominations of the earth, fell in the midst of barbaric wealth and glory. The lesson taught by the history of nations is that the preservation or destruction of communities does not depend upon external prosperity. Men do not live by bread alone, so with nations. They are not saved by art, but by honesty. Not by the gilded splendors of wealth, but by the hidden treasure of manly virtue. Not by the multitudinous gratification of the flesh, but by the celestial guideance of the spirit.

It is in this view that West India Emancipation becomes the most interesting and sublime event of the nineteenth century. It was the triumph of a great moral principle, a decisive victory, after a severe and protracted struggle, of freedom over slavery; of justice and mercy against a grim and bloody system of devilish brutality. It was an acknowledgement by a great nation of the sacredness of humanity, as against the claims of power and cupidity.

As such, it stands out as a large and glorious contribution to the moral and spiritual growth of mankind, and just such a contribution as the world needed, and needs now to have repeated a thousand times over, in our own land especially. Look at New York city; beautiful without to be sure. She has great churches, great hotels, great wealth, great commerce, but you all know that she is the victim of a dreadful disease, and that her best friends regard her as a cage of unclean birds in danger at any moment of being swallowed up by a social earthquake. Look at Philadelphia, Baltimore, Louisville, New Orleans. Look where you will, and you will see that while all without is covered and studded with the evidences of prosperity, there is yet no real sense of that stability which conscious rectitude imparts. All the great acts of the nation of late have looked away from the right path. Our very Temple of Justice has inverted and outraged all the principles of justice which it was professedly established to maintain. The government at Washington is mostly exercised in schemes by which it can cheat one section of the country for the benefit of another, and yet, seem honest to all. Where this will end, Heaven only knows.

But I was calling attention to this great example of British justice not in anger, but in sorrow. Great Britain bowing down, confessing and forsaking her sins—her sins against the weak and despised—is a spectacle which nations present but seldom. No achievement in arts or arms, in letters or laws, can equal this. And the world owes Britain more for this example of humility and honest repentance than for all her other contributions to the world's progress.

I know, and you know, it is easy enough for a nation to assume the outward and hollow seemings of humility and repentance. The world is full of such tongue-wise demonstrations. Our own country can show a long list of them. We have thanksgivings and fasts, and are unrivalled in this department of religious observances. On our fast days and fourth of Julys, we seem unto men to fast, but the sequel shows that our confessions and prayers have only come from men whose hearts are crammed with arrogancy, pride and hate.

We have bowed down our heads as a bulrush, and have spread sackcloth and ashes under us,[10] and like the stiff-necked Jews, whose bad practices we imitate more closely than we do their religion, we have exacted all our labors.

I am not here to make invidious and insulting comparisons; but all must allow, that the example of England, in respect to the great act before us, differs widely from our manifestations of sorrow for great national sin. Here we have, indeed, a chosen fast of the Living God, an acceptable day unto the Lord, a day in which the bands of wickedness were loosed; the heavy burdens undone; the oppressed let go free; every yoke broken; the poor that were cast out of the house brought in; and men no longer hiding themselves from their own flesh.

It has been said that corporations have no souls,[11] that with nations might is the standard of right,[12] and that self-interest governs the world.[13]

The abolition of slavery in the West Indies is a shining evidence of the reverse of all this profanity. Nobler ideas and principles of action are here brought to view. The vital, animating, and all-controlling power of the British Abolition movement was religion. Its philosophy was not educated and enlightened selfishness, (such as some are relying upon now to do away with slavery in this country), but the pure, single-eyed spirit of benevolence. It was not impelled or guided by the fine-spun reasonings of political expediency, but by the unmistakable and imperative demands of principle. It was not commerce, but conscience; not considerations of climate and productions of the earth, but the heavenly teachings of Christianity, which every where teaches that God is our Father, and man, however degraded, is our brother.

The men who were most distinguished in carrying forward the movement, from the great Wilberforce downward, were eminent for genuine piety. They worked for the slave as if they had been working for the Son of God. They believed that righteousness exalteth a nation and that sin is a reproach to any people. Hence they united religion with patriotism, and pressed home the claims of both upon the national heart with the tremendous energy of truth and love, till all England cried out with one accord, through Exeter Hall, through the press, through the pulpit, through parliament, and through the very throne itself, *slavery must and shall be destroyed.*

Herein is the true significance of West India Emancipation. It stands out before all the world as a mighty, moral, and spiritual triumph. It is a product of the soul, not of the body. It is a contribution to common honesty without which nations as well as individuals sink to ruin. It is one of those words of life that proceedeth out of the mouth of God, by which nations are established, and kept alive and in moral health.

Now, my friends, how has this great act of freedom and benevolence been received in the United States? How has our American Christian Church and our American Democratic Government received this glorious new birth of National Righteousness?

From our professions as a nation, it might have been expected that a shout of joy and gladness would have shook the hollow sky, that loud hallelujahs would have rolled up to heaven from all our borders, saying, "Glory to God, in the highest, on earth peace and good will toward man. Let the earth be glad."[14] "The Lord God omnipotent reigneth."[15]

Alas, no such responsive note of rejoicing has reached my ear, except from a part of the colored people and their few white friends. As a nation, we are deaf, dumb, and blind to the moral beauty, and transcendent sublimity of West India Emancipation. We have passed it by with averted eyes, regarding it rather as a reflection to be resented than as an example to be imitated. First, we looked for means of impeaching England's motives for abolishing Slavery, and not being able to find any such, we have made ourselves hoarse in denouncing emancipation as a failure.

We have not viewed the great fact in the light of a liberal philosophy, but have applied to it rules of judgment which were not intended to reveal its true character and make known its actual worth. We have taken a microscope to view the stars, and a fish line to measure the ocean's depths.

We have approached it as though it were a railroad, a canal, a steamship, or a newly invented mowing machine, and out of the fullness of our dollar-loving hearts, we have asked with owl-like wisdom, WILL IT PAY? Will it increase the growth of sugar? Will it cheapen tobacco? Will it increase the imports and exports of the Islands? Will it enrich or ruin the planters? How will it effect Jamaican spirits? Can the West Indies be successfully cultivated by free labor? These and sundry other questions, springing out of the gross materialism of our age and nation, have been characteristically put respecting West India Emancipation. All our tests of the grand measure have been such as we might look for from slave-holders themselves. They all proceed from the slaveholders' side, and never from the side of the emancipated slaves.

The effect of freedom upon the emancipated people of the West Indies passes for nothing. It is nothing that the plundered slave is now a freeman; it is nothing with our sagacious, economical philosophers, that the family now takes the place of concubinage; it is nothing that marriage is now respected where before it was a mockery; it is nothing that moral purity has now a chance to spring up, where before pollution was only possible; it is nothing that education is now spreading among the emancipated men and women, bearing its precious fruits, where only ignorance, darkness, superstition and idolatry prevailed before; it is nothing that the whipping post has given way to the school house; it is nothing that the church stands now where the slave prison stood before; all these are nothing, I say, in the eyes of our slavery-cursed country.

But the first and last question, and the only question which we Americans have to press in the premises, is the great American question (viz.) *will it pay?*

Sir, if such a people as ours had heard the beloved disciple of the Lord, exclaiming in the rapture of the apocalyptic vision, "And I saw another angel fly in the midst of heaven, having the everlasting gospel to preach to them that dwell on the earth, and to every nation, kindred, tongue, and people;"[16] they, instead of answering, Amen Glory to God in the Highest, would have responded,—but brother John, *will it pay?* Can money be made out of it? Will it make the rich richer, and the strong stronger? How will it affect property? In the eyes of such people, there is no God but wealth; no right and wrong but profit and loss.

Sir, our national morality and religion have reached a depth of baseness than which there is no lower deep. They both allow that if men can make money by stealing men and women, and by working them up into sugar, rice, and tobacco, they may innocently continue the practice, and that he who condemns it is an unworthy citizen, and a disturber of the church. Money is the measure of morality, and the success or failure of slavery, as a money-making system, determines with many whether the thing is virtuous, or villainous, and whether it should be maintained or abolished. They are for Slavery where climate and soil are said to be for it, and are really not opposed to it any where, though as a nation we have made a show of opposition to it where the system does not exist. With our geographical ethics, and climatic religion, we have naturally sided with the slave-holders and women-whippers of the West Indies, in denouncing the abolition of slavery in the West Indies a failure.

Sir: As to what has been the effect of West India freedom upon the material condition of the people of those Islands, I am happy that there is one on this platform, who can speak with the authority of positive knowledge. Henry Highland Garnet, has lived and labored among those emancipated people. He has enjoyed ample opportunity for forming an intelligent judgment in respect to all that pertains to the subject. I therefore most willingly leave this branch of the subject to him.

One remark, however, I will venture to make—and that is this: I take it that both the friends and the enemies of the emancipated have been too impatient for results. They seem to forget that although a nation can be born in a day, it can mature only in centuries—that though the fetters on the limbs can be broken in an instant, the fetters on the soul can wear off only in the ages.

Degradation, mental, moral, and physical, ground into the very bones of a people by ages of unremitting bondage, will not depart from that people in the course, even of many generations.

West India freedom, though more than twenty-one years old, is yet but an infant. And to predicate its future on its present weakness, awkwardness, and improvidence now, is about as wise as to apply the same rule to your little toothless children. It has taken at least a thousand years to bring some of the leading nations of the earth from the point where the negroes of the West Indies started twenty-three years ago, to their present position. Let considerations like these be duly weighed, and black man though I am, I do not fear the world's judgment.

Now, sir, I like these annual celebrations. I like them because they call us to the contemplation of great interests, and afford an opportunity of presenting salutary truths before the American people. They bring our people together, and enable us to see and commune with each other to mutual profit. If these occasions are conducted wisely, decorously, and orderly, they increase our respectability in the eyes of the world, and silence the slanders of prejudice. If they are otherwise conducted they cover us with shame and confusion. But, sir, these celebrations have been objected to by our slaveholding democracy; they do not think it in good taste. Slaveholders are models of taste. With them, propriety is every thing; honesty, nothing. For a long time they have taught our Congress, and Senate, and Pulpits, what subjects should be discussed, and what objects should command our attention. Senator SUMNER, fails to observe the proscribed rules and he falls upon the Senate floor, stunned and bleeding[17] beneath the ruffian blows of one of our southern models of propriety. By such as these, and by their timid followers, this is called a *British* celebration.

From the inmost core of my soul I pity the mean spirits, who can see in these celebrations nothing but British feeling. The man who limits his admiration of good actions to the country in which he happens to be born, (if he ever was born,) or to the nation or community of which he forms a small part, is a most pitiable object. With him to be one of a nation is more than to be one of the human family. He don't live in the world, but he lives in the United States. Into his little soul the thought of God as our common Father, and of man our common Brother has never entered. To such a soul as that, this celebration cannot but be exceedingly distasteful.

But sarcasm aside, I hold it to be eminently fit that we keep up those celebrations from year to year, at least until we shall have an American celebration to take its place. That the event we thus commemorate transpired in another country, and was wrought out by the labors and sacrifices of the people of another nation, form[s] no valid objection to its grateful, warm, hearty, and enthusiastic celebration by us. In a very high sense, we may claim that great deed as our own. It belongs not exclusively to England and the English people, but to the lovers of Liberty and of mankind the world over. It is one of those glorious emanations of Christianity, which, like the sun in the Heavens, takes no cognizance of national lines or geographical boundaries, but pours its golden floods of living light upon all. In the great Drama of Emancipation, England was the theatre, but universal and every where applying principles of Righteousness, Liberty, and Justice were the actors. The great Ruler of the Universe, the God and Father of all men, to whom be honor, glory, and praise for evermore, roused the British conscience by his truth, moved the British heart, and West India Emancipation was the result. But if only Englishmen may properly celebrate this great concession to justice and liberty, then, sir, we may claim to be Englishmen, Englishmen in the love of Justice and Liberty, Englishmen in magnanimous efforts to protect the weak against the strong, and the slave against the slaveholder. Surely in this sense, it ought to be no disgrace to be an Englishman, even on the soil of the freest people on the globe.

But, Mr. Chairman, we celebrate this day on the broad platform of Philanthropy—whose country is the world, and whose countrymen are all mankind. On this platform we are neither Jews nor Greeks, strangers nor foreigners, but fellow citizens of the household of faith. We are the brothers and friends of Clarkson, Wilberforce, Granville Sharpe, Richard Baxter, John Wesley, Thomas Day, Bishop Portius, and George Fox, and the glorious company of those who first wrought to turn the moral sense of mankind in active opposition to slavery.[18] They labored for freedom not as Englishmen, but as men, and as brothers to men—the world over—and it is meet and right to commemorate and imitate their noble example. So much for the Anti-British objection.

I will now notice a special objection. It is said that we, the colored people, should do something ourselves worthy of celebration, and not be everlastingly celebrating the deeds of a race by which we are despised.

This objection, strange as it may seem, comes from no enemy of our people, but from a friend. He is himself a colored man, a high spirited and patriotic man, eminent for learning and ability, and to my mind, he has few equals, and no superior among us. I thank Dr. J. M'Cune Smith for this objection, since in the answer I may make to it, I shall be able to give a few of my thoughts on the relation subsisting between the white and colored people of this country, a subject which it well becomes us to consider whenever and wherever we congregate.

In so far as this objection to our celebrating the first of August has a tendency to awaken in us a higher ambition than has hitherto distinguished us, and to raise our aims and activities above the dull level of our present physical wants, and so far as it shall tend to stimulate us to the execution of great deeds of heroism worthy to be held in admiration and perpetual remembrance, for one, sir, I say amen to the whole of it. I am free to say, that nothing is more humiliating than the insignificant part we, the colored people, are taking in the great contest now going on with the powers of oppression in this land. I can stand the insults, assaults, misrepresentations, and slanders of the known haters of my race, and brave them all. I look for such opposition. It is a natural incident of the war, and I trust I am to a certain degree prepared for it; but the stolid contentment, the listless indifference, the moral death which reigns over many of our people, we who should be all on fire, beats down my little flame of enthusiasm and leaves me to labor, half robbed of my natural force. This indifference, in us, is outrageous. It is giving aid and comfort to the men who are warring against our very manhood. The highest satisfaction of our oppressors, is to see the negro degraded, divested of public spirit, insensible to patriotism, and to all concern for the freedom, elevation, and respectability of the race.

Senator Toombs with a show of truth, lyingly said in Boston a year or two ago in defence of the slavery of the black race, they are mentally and morally inferior, and that if the whole colored population were swept from this country, there would be nothing in twenty years to tell that such a people had ever existed.[19] He exulted over our assumed ignorance and over our destitution of valuable achievements. Of course the slaveholder uttered a falsehood, but to many it seemed to be a truth, and vast numbers of the American people receive it as a truth to-day, and shape their action accordingly.

The general sentiment of mankind is, that a man who will not fight for himself, when he has the means of doing so, is not worth being fought for by others, and this sentiment is just. For a man who does not value freedom for himself will never value it for others, nor put himself to any inconvenience to gain it for others. Such a man the world says, may lay down until he has sense enough to stand up. It is useless and cruel to put a man on his legs, if the next moment his head is to be brought against a curb-stone.

A man of that type will never lay the world under any obligation to him, but will be a moral pauper, a drag on the wheels of society, and if he, too, be identified with a peculiar variety of the race he will entail disgrace upon his race as well as upon himself. The world in which we live is very accommodating to all sorts of people. It will co-operate with them in any measure which they propose; it will help those who earnestly help themselves, and will hinder those who hinder themselves. It is very polite, and never offers its services unasked. Its favors to individuals are measured by an unerring principle in this: viz.—respect those who respect themselves, and despise those who despise themselves. It is not within the power of unaided human nature to persevere in pitying a people who are insensible to their own wrongs, and indifferent to the attainment of their own rights. The poet was as true to common sense as to poetry when he said,

> "Who would be free, themselves must strike the blow."

When O'Connell, with all Ireland at his back, was supposed to be contending for the just rights and liberties of Ireland, the sympathies of mankind were with him, and even his enemies were compelled to respect his patriotism. Kossuth, fighting for Hungary with his pen long after she had fallen by the sword, commanded the sympathy and support of the liberal world till his own hopes died out. The Turks while they fought bravely for themselves and scourged and drove back the invading legions of Russia, shared the admiration of mankind. They were standing up for their own rights against an arrogant and powerful enemy; but as soon as they let out their fighting to the Allies, admiration gave way to contempt. These are not the maxims and teachings of a cold-hearted world. Christianity itself teaches that a man shall provide for his own house.[20] This covers the whole ground of nations as well as individuals. Nations no more than individuals can innocently be improvident. They should provide for all wants, mental, moral, and religious, and against all evils to which they are liable as nations. In the great struggle now progressing for the freedom and elevation of our people, we should be found at work with all our might, resolved that no man or set of men shall be more abundant in labors, according to the measure of our ability, than ourselves.

I know, my friends, that in some quarters the efforts of colored people meet with very little encouragement. We may fight, but we must fight like the Seapoys of India, under white officers.[21] This class of Abolitionists don't like colored celebrations, they don't like colored conventions, they don't like colored Anti-Slavery fairs for the support of colored newspapers. They don't like any demonstrations whatever in which colored men take a leading part. They talk of the proud Anglo-Saxon blood, as flippantly as those who profess to believe in the natural inferiority of races. Your humble speaker has been branded as an ingrate, because he has ventured to stand up on his own right, and to plead our common cause as a colored man, rather than as a Garrisonian. I hold it to be no part of gratitude to allow our white friends to do all the work, while we merely hold their coats. Opposition of the sort now referred to, is partizan opposition, and we need not mind it. The white people at large will not largely be influenced by it. They will see and appreciate all honest efforts on our part to improve our condition as a people.

Let me give you a word of the philosophy of reform. The whole history of the progress of human liberty shows that all concessions yet made to her august claims, have been born of earnest struggle. The conflict has been exciting, agitating, all-absorbing, and for the time being, putting all other tumults to silence. It must do this or it does nothing. If there is no struggle there is no progress. Those who profess to favor freedom and yet depreciate agitation, are men who want crops without plowing up the ground, they want rain without thunder and lightning. They want the ocean without the awful roar of its many waters.

This struggle may be a moral one, or it may be a physical one, and it may be both moral and physical, but it must be a struggle. Power concedes nothing without a demand. It never did and it never will. Find out just what any people will quietly submit to and you have found out the exact measure of injustice and wrong which will be imposed upon them, and these will continue till they are resisted with either words or blows, or with both. The limits of tyrants are prescribed by the endurance of those whom they oppress. In the light of these ideas, Negroes will be hunted at the North, and held and flogged at the South so long as they submit to those devilish outrages, and make no resistance, either moral or physical. Men may not get all they pay for in this world, but they must certainly pay for all they get. If we ever get free from the oppressions and wrongs heaped upon us, we must pay for their removal. We must do this by labor, by suffering, by sacrifice, and if needs be, by our lives and the lives of others.

Hence, my friends, every mother who, like Margaret Garner,[22] plunges a knife into the bosom of her infant to save it from the hell of our Christian Slavery, should be held and honored as a benefactress. Every fugitive from slavery who like the noble William Thomas[23] at Wilkesbarre, prefers to perish in a river made red by his own blood, to submission to the hell hounds who were hunting and shooting him, should be esteemed as a glorious martyr, worthy to be held in grateful memory by our people. The fugitive Horace, at Mechanicsburgh, Ohio, the other day, who taught the slave catchers from Kentucky that it was safer to arrest white men than to arrest him, did a most excellent service to our cause.[24] Parker and his noble band of fifteen at Christiana,[25] who defended themselves from the kidnappers with prayers and pistols, are entitled to the honor of making the first successful resistance to the Fugitive Slave Bill. But for that resistance, and the rescue of Jerry, and Shadrack,[26] the man-hunters would have hunted our hills and valleys here with the same freedom with which they now hunt their own dismal swamps.

There was an important lesson in the conduct of that noble Krooman in New York, the other day, who, supposing that the American Christians were about to enslave him, betook himself to the mast head, and with knife in hand, said he would cut his throat before he would be made a slave. Joseph Cinque on the deck of the *Amistad*, did that which should make his name dear to us. He bore nature's burning protest against slavery. Madison Washington who struck down his oppressor on the deck of the *Creole*, is more worthy to be remembered than the colored man who shot Pitcaren at Bunker Hill.

My friends, you will observe that I have taken a wide range, and you think it is about time that I should answer the special objection to this celebration. I think so too. This, then, is the truth concerning the inauguration of freedom in the British West Indies. Abolition was the act of the British Government. The motive which led the Government to act, no doubt was mainly a philanthropic one, entitled to our highest admiration and gratitude. The National Religion, the justice, and humanity, cried out in thunderous indignation against the foul abomination, and the government yielded to the storm. Nevertheless a share of the credit of the result falls justly to the slaves themselves. "Though slaves, they were rebellious slaves." They bore themselves well. They did not hug their chains, but according to their opportunities, swelled the general protest against oppression. What Wilberforce was endeavoring to win from the British Senate by his magic eloquence, the Slaves themselves were endeavoring to gain by outbreaks and violence. The combined action of one and the other wrought out the final result. While one showed that slavery was wrong, the other showed that it was dangerous as well as wrong. Mr. Wilberforce, peace man though he was, and a model of piety, availed himself of this element to strengthen his case before the British Parliament, and warned the British government of the danger of continuing slavery in the West Indies. There is no doubt that the fear of the consequences, acting with a sense of the moral evil of slavery led to its abolition. The spirit of freedom was abroad in the Islands. Insurrection for freedom kept the planters in a constant state of alarm and trepidation. A standing army was necessary to keep the slaves in their chains. This state of facts could not be without weight in deciding the question of freedom in these countries.

I am aware that the rebellious disposition of the slaves was said to arise out of the discussions which the abolitionists were carrying on at home, and it is not necessary to refute this alleged explanation. All that I contend for is this: that the slaves of the West Indies did fight for their freedom, and that the fact of their discontent was known in England, and that it assisted in bringing about that state of public opinion which finally resulted in their emancipation. And if this be true, the objection is answered.

Again, I am aware that the insurrectionary movements of the slaves were held by many to be prejudicial to their cause. This is said now of such movements at the South. The answer is that abolition followed close on the heels of insurrection in the West Indies, and Virginia was never nearer emancipation than when General Turner kindled the fires of insurrection at Southampton.

Sir, I have now more than filled up the measure of my time. I thank you for the patient attention given to what I have had to say. I have aimed, as I said at the beginning, to express a few thoughts having some relation to the great interests of freedom both in this country and in the British West Indies, and I have said all that I meant to say, and the time will not permit me to say any more.

"THE TRIALS AND TRIUMPHS OF SELF-MADE MEN" (1860)

Douglass's self-made men speeches were immensely popular from 1860 until his death in 1895. Over time he altered the speech as he remade himself. Here he defines "self-made men" (and women) as radicals who wage war on injustice as they improve themselves.

SOURCE: *Halifax Courier* (UK), January 7, 1860

The LECTURER on rising was received with immense cheering. He said: I appear before you this evening in an unaccustomed position. I usually speak in public on the subject of American slavery, and it is supposed by some in my country that a coloured man has not thoughts worth listening to on any other subject. Partly with a view to show the fallacy of this notion, and partly to give expression to what I think sound and important views of life, I have prepared this lecture.

The various uses to which men put the brief space of human existence, and the proportion which their success in the world bears to their several opportunities, are subjects worthy of the attention and study of all men, and especially of those who have something of life still in prospect. It may not be of very serious consequence, what views of life are presented and urged upon the attention of those who have grown old and hardened in the violent and long continued abuse of life's best privileges. Under the whole heavens there is not a sadder sight—a more affecting and melancholy spectacle—than such men present to the eye of a thoughtful man. Standing upon the very verge of misspent time, and looking back only upon wasted opportunities, a whole life wantonly flung away, such men stud the field of human existence only as warnings. And sad warnings they are. The chance to redeem the time for themselves has come and gone, never to return. The past is covered with regrets, the present is without the life and inspirations of hope, and the future is mantled in gloom.

But to the young, with all the bright world before them where to choose, the case is widely and cheeringly different. By wisdom, by firmness, and by a manly and heroic self-denial, these may wholly escape the sharp and flinty rocks, the false lights, and the treacherous shores, the tempest, and the whirlwinds of passion and sin which have sent other voyagers to the bottom wrecked and ruined. Life is the world's greatest and most significant fact. It is the grand reality that realizes all other realities. All that man can know of the dim and shadowy past, and of the solemn and mysterious future have their explanation mainly in this one great fact. It is the now that makes the then, and the here that makes the hereafter to us all. Death itself is only predicated of life, and itself can only comprehend death.

Without trenching upon the forbidden domains of theology, I may venture to say, that if this life shall only be regarded as an individual fact, standing alone, having no relations or bearings, full and complete in itself, wholly independent of, and disconnected with, any other state or place, we still find it a most glorious fact, and crowded with arguments the most convincing, and with motives the most powerful, in favour of the construction and cultivation of a true and manly character. Such are the transcendent rewards of virtue, knowledge, wisdom, and power, even in this life, and the certain misery which a life of inaction, vice, and ignorance entails, that man is ever under the pressure of the highest motives in favour of self-culture and self-improvement.

How to make the best of this life, as a thing of and for itself,—viewed apart from those other considerations to which I have alluded,—must ever be an important and useful enquiry. For he who has best fitted himself to live and serve his fellow men on earth has best fitted himself to live and serve his God in Heaven. While in the world, a man's work is with the world and for the world. It is something to be a man among shady trees and stately halls—but much more to be a man among men, full of the cares, labours, and joys of this life. It is good to think that in Heaven, all injustice, all wrong, all wars, all ignorance, and all vice, will be at an end; but how incomparably better is it, to wage a vigorous war upon these blighting evils and drive them from the present, so that the will of God may be done on earth as in heaven—(cheers).

There have been many daguerrotypes taken of life. They are as various as they are numerous. Each picture is coloured according to the lights and shades surrounding the artist. To the sailor, life is a ship, richly freighted, and with all sail spread to the breeze. To the farmer, life is a fertile field waving with its golden harvests. To the architect, it stands out as a gorgeous palace or temple, with its pillars, domes, towers, and turrets. To the great dramatic poet, all the world is a stage, and men but players; but to all mankind, the world is a vast school. From the cradle to the grave, the oldest and the wisest, not less than the youngest and the simplest, are but learners; and those who learn most, seem to have most to learn—(hear, hear).

The lecturer then spoke at some length on the anomalies of society; the rich and the poor, the lofty and the lowly, the happy and the miserable. But, he observed, even taking this aspect of society, humanity was a great worker, and it sometimes worked wonders. It was a master of all situations, and a match for all adversities. Notwithstanding the vast disparity between the hut and the hall, these two extremes, as well as others, did sometimes meet in life's eventful journey, and shake hands upon a common platform of knowledge, wisdom, usefulness, virtue, honour, and fame—(cheers).

Nevertheless, life presented many puzzles. It was a puzzle that men could resemble each other so closely, yet differ so widely. Possessed of the same faculties, vitalized by the same life-blood, sustained by the same elements, yet how endless were the dissimilarities and contradictions. While some were Miltons, Bacons, and Shakespeares, illuminating and filling a wondering world with the resplendent glories of their achievements, others were as dull as lead, and rose no higher in life than a mere physical existence. The natural laws for the preservation and development of human faculties were equal, uniform, harmonious, permanent, wise, and perfect;

but the subjects of them abounded in oddities, confusions, opposites, and discords—(hear, hear).

A thousand arrows might be shot at the same object, but, though united in aim, they might be divided in flight. And such was life—equal in quiver, but unequal in aim; matched when dormant, but unmatched, mismatched, and countermatched in action. The boundless realms of the past were covered with these fallen arrows. They were to be met with in history, biography, and the other walks of life. Nothing was more natural or instructive than to walk among those fallen arrows, and estimate the probable amount of skill and force requisite to bring each to its place. "The proper study of mankind is man"[1] was a saying of which men never tired. It expressed a sublime truth, it came fresh to the ear every time repeated, and vibrated the soul like the lightning the wire; it was felt as well as thought; it was felt before it was thought. A single human being was of more interest than all else on earth. The solitary form of the great navigator, Franklin,[2] wedged in between walls of eternal ice, cast all the gloomy wonders of the Arctic Seas into the shade. He was greater to us than the polar night or the north-west passage—there was a charm about him in the simple quality of manhood—(hear, hear).

The voyage of discovery that evening was over the broad ocean of humanity. They might not find that for which they were searching, but they would find that which would make the search worth undertaking. Men were noble and generous when they found a man who came up to their idea of a hero. The lecturer at this point stated that he once saw a swarm of little boys following the great O'Connell, from square to square in the city of Dublin, forgetful of their poverty and wretchedness, despising cold and rain and mud, swept on by a joyous enthusiasm, making the welkin ring with praises of the great Irish liberator. Why did they follow him? The answer was plain—they could not help it; they obeyed the tide of their nature.

The lecturer having enlarged on this view of human nature, he remarked that the title of his lecture that evening involved something like a solecism. He freely admitted that there could not be self-made men in the world; all had begged, borrowed, or stolen from somebody or somewhere—(cheers). Nevertheless, it was a fit and convenient title to the subject matter of his discourse.

Four points were suggested as the natural divisions of his subject. First, the class designated as self-made men. Second, the true theory of their success. Third, the advantages which they derived from the ideas and institutions of the country in which they lived. And the fourth, the criticism and disadvantages to which they were exposed.

In a certain sense, most if not all the great characters whose names shone in history, and whose deeds commanded homage and admiration might be regarded as self-made men; but he meant that evening just what the name imported: those men who had without the ordinary helps of favouring circumstances, raised themselves against great odds from the most humble and cheerless positions in life to usefulness, greatness, honour, influence, and fame. These were the men who had built the ladder on which they climbed and built as they climbed—(hear, hear). Such men, whether they were found in the factory or the college, whether at the handles of the plough or in the professor's chair, whether at the bar or in the pulpit, whether of Anglo-Saxon or of Anglo-African origin, ought to have awarded to them the honour of being self-made men—(cheers).

There were three special explanations given as to the cause of success in self-made men. The first attributed to such men superior mental endowments, and assigned this as the true explanation of success. The second made the most of circumstances, favouring opportunities, accidents, chances, &c. The third made industry and application the great secret of success. All had truth in them, and all were capable of being pressed into untruth.

Mr. Douglass entered into a discussion of each point, but the substance of his own views on them was, that industry and application, together with a regard to favourable circumstances and opportunities were the means of success. The lecturer continued:—Such is my theory of self-made men, and, indeed, of all made men. The credit belongs and must be ascribed to brave, honest, earnest, ceaseless heart and soul industry. By this simple means—open and free to all men—whatever may be said of chances, circumstances, and natural endowments—the simple man may become wise, and the wise man become wiser. Striking examples of the truth of this position are abundant.

Hugh Miller,[3] whose lamented death a few years ago cast a

dark shadow, not only over this land, but across the broad Atlantic, is, perhaps, among the most striking and brilliant examples of industrious application at self-culture. In a country famous for its colleges and other institutions of learning, this brave son of toil mastered geology while wielding the heavy hammer of the mechanic. As was said of Burns, Miller was himself a college. One is really astonished, on reading this man's works, at what he accomplished by simple, patient application, guided by a steady purpose.

The case of Elihu Burritt[4]—a man whose very goodness overshadows his real mental greatness—may be cited. He had to support his bodily wants by his own hands, while maintaining the struggle for an education. But this did not discourage him. Over the glowing forge, the red-hot steel, the polished anvil, amid the noise and dust of the blacksmith's shop, this brave son of toil mastered, I dare not say how many languages, and is now admitted to be among our best American scholars.

That not many books, or very favourable circumstances are essential to successful education, is amply demonstrated in the life of Louis Kossuth. That eminent man came here from the extreme east of Europe, loaded down with Anglo-Saxon ideas, and clothed with an English eloquence which is absolutely overwhelming. When asked where and when he got his knowledge, he tells us that his school-house was an Austrian prison, that his books were the Bible and Shakespeare, and the English Dictionary, and that his schoolmaster was Louis Kossuth—(cheers and laughter).

The United States has produced no self-made man more worthy of mention than Benjamin Bannecker,[5] the black astronomer of the State of Maryland. With honest pride I turn to this black sage as in part blotting out the charge of natural inferiority so often brought against the negro race. You may know his history. He was black—for slavery had not in his day robbed the negro in America of his colour, as well as of his liberty. Bannecker was distinguished as a mathematician, and was among the surveyors who laid out the present capital of the United States—where freedom has been "laid out" ever since. In the corn field, and by the roadside, this sable son of toil picked up an education which brought him to the favourable notice of eminent men on both sides of the Atlantic. He held a creditable correspondence with a man no less distinguished than Thomas Jefferson, one of the early presidents of the United States. At that time presidents were men, and not as now mere platforms. Bannecker was an astronomer as well as a surveyor, and calculated almanacs. One of his almanacs he sent to Mr. Jefferson, which brought him the following letter in return:—

PHILADELPHIA, AUGUST 30, 1790.

Sir,—I thank you sincerely for your letter and the almanac it contains. Nobody wishes more than I do to see such proofs as you exhibit that nature has given our black brethren talents equal to those of other colours of men, and that the appearance of a want of them is owing merely to the degraded condition of their existence both in Africa and in America. I have taken the liberty of sending your almanac to Monsieur Condorcet, secretary of the Academy of Science at Paris, and member of the Philanthropic Society, because I considered it as a document to which your whole colour had a right for their justification against the doubts which have been entertained of them.

I am, with great esteem, Sir,
Your most obedient,
THOMAS JEFFERSON.

William Dietz,[6] of Albany, another black man, now living, has risen from the humble condition of a servant in a private family, to be the manager of an estate worth three million dollars. This black man (for he too is black) who would be read out of the human family by the Notts, Gliddens, Mortons, and other American ethnological writers, is admitted to be one of the best designers and draftsmen in the state of New York. He is not only a draftsman but an inventor, and a very ingenious one. He has recently invented a bridge for spanning the Hudson at Albany, which is calculated to overcome all the objections scientific men have raised in behalf of navigation against the erection of a draw-bridge at that point. This is not all: he has invented and planned a railroad for Broadway, New York city, equally obviating the presence of dust, smoke, noise, and horses, in that grand thorough-fare, and should any railway be allowed there, it will be on the plan suggested and modelled by William Dietz, of Albany. An engraving of this railway has been published and commended by the *Scientific American*. Men read of the inventions of Mr. Dietz, but do not know what I know, and what the American people ought to know, that the inventor is a black man. His achievement if known, would do more to elevate the popular estimate of the coloured race than any number of learned desertations on the natural equality of races. Nothing in logic is so stubborn, and here is a strong one certainly.

There too, stands the bright example of Toussaint L'Ouverture. He is confessed to have been a brave and generous soldier, a clear-headed, calm and sagacious statesman, and the noble liberator and law giver of his brave and dauntless people. A slave during fifty of the best years of his life. A poor scholar, yet rising up in troublous times. I will not extol his merits. He is already a hero of history, poetry, and eloquence. Wordsworth has encircled his memory with a halo of fadeless glory, while Wendell Phillips has borne his name heavenward in a chariot of matchless eloquence.

I might if time permitted, point to a long list of self-made men, and could I ask these by what means they obtained their high positions among their fellowmen, their answer would come with the startling effect of a blast from a quarry—industry and application.

I now come to the relation which ideas and institutions bear to this class of men, and shall have special reference to America. I seldom find anything either in the ideas or institutions of that country, whereof to glory. The one deep dark veil of human bondage, covering as it does every department of the government, and every class of its people, poisoning the very life blood, the morals, religion, manners, and civilization of that great nation, hides from my dim vision much that might otherwise be seen, noble and beautiful and worthy of admiration and of imitation. But pushing aside this black and clotted covering which mantles all our land, as with the shadow of death, I recognize one feature at least of special and peculiar excellence, and that is the relation of America to self-made men.

America is, most unquestionably and pre-eminently, the home and special patron of self-made men. In no country in the world are the conditions more favourable to the production and sustentation of such men than in America. They are found in all the high places, exercising all the powers, and enjoying all the immunities of office and honour. The press flames with the living and quenchless fires of their genius, and the senate listens with respect and admiration to their eloquence. They are foremost men everywhere. They are found among our authors, editors, lawyers, preachers, inventors, poets, philosophers, and statesmen, and the fact that they are self-made is often dwelt upon by the crowd as their highest honour.

Let me give you one or two of the causes of this ample growth of self-made men. One cause, undoubtedly, is to be found in the general respectability of labour, especially in the northern states of the American Union. Work has not yet come to be looked upon as a degradation or disgrace. A man may labour there with his hands, or with his head, or with both hands and head, and yet move in respectable society—that is if he has a white skin. Every stranger landing upon American shores is struck by the easy, independent, and even haughty bearing of the labouring classes. This general respectability of labour is an important element in the production of self-made men.

But a second, and perhaps the most powerful, cause is this: the principle of measuring men by their own individual merits is better observed and enforced there than anywhere else. In Europe

> A king can mak' a belted knight,
> A marquis, duke, and a' that.[7]

But there, a man who wants to be a nobleman, must prove his nobility to his neighbours and the public. The sons of Henry Clay, Daniel Webster, and John C. Calhoun, are put upon trial, and have to make their way in the world like the rest of us, and they must prove themselves real Clays, Websters, and Calhouns, if they attract to themselves any of the respect and generous admiration commanded by their brilliant fathers. Our departed great men drop down from their various circles of greatness, like bright stars from the blue overhanging sky, bearing away with them their own silvery light, leaving the places they have illumined robed in darkness, until the heavens are re-lighted by the glory of other rising stars—(hear, hear, and cheers). On the strength of a great name, and upon the accident of being just what any other man might be, the nephew of his uncle, Mr. Louis Napoleon, has been able to banish from France many of the wisest, best, and bravest patriots and statesmen. On the ruins of broken faith and outraged liberty, he has firmly seated himself on the throne of a despot. But such an experiment on such a capital of name and nephewship could never succeed in America. Nobody there now cares for George Washington, jun., nor for Andrew Jackson, jun., and they stand no better chance of being made presidents of the United States than William or John, or other common men, whose fathers were never heard of twenty miles from home.

But self-made men are by no means invulnerable men. I do not at all subscribe to the maxim that self-made men are the best made men. With many excellent qualities and acquirements, they are apt to possess some which are not so excellent and desirable. It is hard to shake off all the effects of early surroundings. There is, however, one very common defect to be found among such men, to which even I may allude, who may share it; this it is: such men are generally very egotistical. The very nature of the path they have pursued, and the energies they have employed in reaching their position, have served to render them so. A man who is indebted to himself for himself, is apt to think no small pumpkins of himself—(laughter). He has altogether too much to say about being a self-made man. Whatever else shall be forgotten, this is always remembered. "I am a self-made man" is the thread-bare preface to all his words and actions—(cheers).

I have still another criticism to pass upon self-made men; and that is, they too often display a want of respect for the means by which other men have risen above the level of the race. They are too free in disparagement of schools they never attended, and colleges, of which they are ignorant. In this they assume a place that does not become them; for whatever may be their merits they are generally but relative merits—they are out-siders. They may pass judgment upon the best means of self-education, but they may not lay down the law as to the best means of educating others. There never was yet a man who had educated himself who could not, by the same exertion and application and determined perseverance, have been better educated by the helps of the ordinary institutions of learning—(hear, hear).

Thus I have given you a peep at both sides of the class of men taken as my subject, having nothing set down in malice, whatever I may have set down in partiality. The lessons which such men teach are valuable in many respects, chief among them is the dignity of humanity. They teach us, too, the value of work, self-reliance, and manly independence. Let us appreciate such men and award to them the mead of praise due to their heroism—give them equal elbow room—no matter from what land they come or from what race they descend—(cheers).

After all, my friends, let it be remembered—let it be rivetted upon our understandings and anchored in our hearts for ever—that neither self-culture, nor any other kind of culture, can amount to much in this world, unless joined to some truly unselfish and noble purpose. Patriotism, religion, philanthropy—some grand motive power other than the simple hope of personal reward must be present, or the candle is under the bushel and will certainly remain there. We all need some grand, some soul-enlarging, some soul-sustaining object to draw out the best energies of our natures and to lift us to the plains of true nobleness and manly life—(cheers).

And is it not a consoling thought that, rich as this great world may be, and poor and small as the individual man may be, there [is] none so small, none so destitute, but that he is rich enough to make this great world a debtor to him for something in the way of example, word, or deed more precious than all the gems of the east?—(loud applause).

“THE DAY OF JUBILEE COMES” (1862)

In this short speech, delivered at his church in Rochester, four days before the Emancipation Proclamation was issued, Douglass highlights its significance while also warning that even after chattel slavery has been abolished, whites will endeavor to make [blacks] the slaves “of society at large.”

SOURCE: *Douglass’ Monthly*, January 1863

My Friends:—This is scarcely a day for prose. It is a day for poetry and song, a new song. These cloudless skies, this balmy air, this brilliant sunshine, (making December as pleasant as May,) are in harmony with the glorious morning of liberty about to dawn upon us. Out of a full heart and with sacred emotion, I congratulate you my friends, and fellow citizens, on the high and hopeful condition, of the cause of human freedom and the cause of our common country, for these two causes are now one and inseparable and must stand or fall together. We stand to day in the presence of a glorious prospect. This sacred Sunday in all the likelihoods of the case, is the last which will witness the existence of legal slavery in all the Rebel slaveholding States of America.[1] Henceforth and forever, slavery in those States is to be recognized, by all the departments [of] the American Government, under its appropriate character as an unmitigated robber and pirate, branded as the sum of all villainy,[2] an outlaw having no rights which any man white or colored is bound to respect.[3] It is difficult for us who have toiled so long and hard, to believe that this event, so stupendous, so far reaching and glorious is even now at the door. It surpasses our most enthusiastic hopes that we live at such a time and are likely to witness the downfall, at least the legal downfall of slavery in America. It is a moment for joy, thanksgiving and Praise.

Among the first questions that tried the strength of my childhood mind—was first why are colored people slaves, and the next was will their slavery last forever? From that day onward, the cry that has reached the most silent chambers of my soul, by day and by night has been How long! How long oh! Eternal Power of the Universe, how long shall these things be?

This inquiry is to be answered on the first of January 1863.

That this war is to abolish slavery I have no manner of doubt. The process may be long and tedious but that that result must at last be reached is among the undoubted certainties of the future! Slavery once abolished in the Rebel States, will give the death wound to slavery in the border States. When Arkansas is a free State, Missouri cannot be a slave State.

Nevertheless. This is no time for the friends of freedom to fold their hands and consider their work at an end. The price of Liberty is eternal vigilance.[4] Even after slavery has been legally abolished, and the rebellion substantially suppressed, even when there shall come representatives to Congress from the States now in rebellion, and they shall have repudiated the miserable and disastrous error of disunion, or secession, and the country shall have reached a condition of comparative peace, there will still remain an urgent necessity for the benevolent activity of the men and the women who have from the first opposed slavery from high moral conviction.

Slavery has existed in this country too long and has stamped its character too deeply and indelibly, to be blotted out in a day or a year, or even in a generation. The slave will yet remain in some sense a slave, long after the chains are taken from his limbs, and the master will retain much of the pride, the arrogance, imperiousness and conscious superiority, and love of power, acquired by his former relation of master. Time, necessity, education, will be required to bring all classes into harmonious and natural relations.

But the South will not be the only part of the country demanding vigilance and exertion on the part of the true friends of the colored people. Our chief difficulty will [be] hereafter, as it has been heretofore with proslavery doughfaces, at the North. A dog will continue to scratch his neck even after the collar is removed. The sailor a night or two after reaching land feels his bed swimming from side to side, as if tossed by the sea. Daniel Webster received a large vote in Massachusetts after he was dead.[5] It will not be strange if many Northern men whose politics, habits of thought, and accustomed submission to the slave power, leads them to continue to go through the forms of their ancient servility long after their old master slavery is in his grave.

Law and the sword can and will, in the end abolish slavery. But law and the sword cannot abolish the malignant slaveholding sentiment which has kept the slave system alive in this country during two centuries. Pride of race, prejudice against color, will raise their hateful clamor for oppression of the negro as heretofore. The slave having ceased to be the abject slave of a single master, his enemies will endeavor to make him the slave of society at large.

For a time at least, we may expect that this malign purpose and principle of wrong will get itself more or less expressed in party presses and platforms. Pro-Slavery political writers and speakers, will not fail to inflame the ancient prejudice against the negro, by exaggerating his faults and concealing or disparaging his virtues. A crime committed by one of the hated race, [words missing] while any excellence found in one black man will grudgingly be set to his individual credit. Hence we say that the friends of freedom, the men and women of the land who regard slavery as a crime and the slave as a man will still be needed even after slavery is abolished.

“THE PROCLAMATION AND A NEGRO ARMY” (1863)

In this address at Cooper Institute, New York, Douglass describes the revolutionary effects of the Emancipation Proclamation and the arming of blacks as soldiers.

SOURCE: *Douglass’ Monthly*, March 1863

I congratulate you, upon what may be called the greatest event of our nation’s history, if not the greatest event of the century. In the eye of the Constitution, the supreme law of the land, there is not now, and there has not been, since the first day of January, a single slave lawfully deprived of Liberty in any of the States now recognized as in Rebellion against the National Government. In all those States Slavery is now in law, as in fact, a system of lawless violence, against which the slave may lawfully defend himself. (Cheers.)

In the hurry and excitement of the moment, it is difficult to grasp the full and complete significance of President Lincoln’s proclamation. The change in the attitude of the Government is vast and startling. For more than sixty years the Federal Government has been little better than a stupendous engine of Slavery and oppression, through which Slavery has ruled us, as with a rod of iron. The boast that Cotton is King was no empty boast. Assuming that our Government and people will sustain the President and his Proclamation, we can scarcely conceive of a more complete revolution in the position of a nation. England, no longer ruled by a king, the Pope turned Protestant, Austria—a Republic, would not present a greater revolution.

I hail it as the doom of Slavery in all the States. I hail it as the end of all that miserable statesmanship, which has for sixty years juggled and deceived the people, by professing to reconcile what is irreconcileable. No politician need now hope to rise to power, by crooking the pregnant hinges of the knee to Slavery. We part company forever with that amphibious animal called a Northern man with Southern principles. Color is no longer a crime or a badge of bondage. At last the out-spread wings of the American Eagle afford shelter and protection to men of all colors, all countries, and all climes, and the long oppressed black man may honorably fall or gloriously flourish under the star-spangled banner. (Applause.)

I stand here to-night not only as a colored man and an American, but, by the express decision of the Attorney-General of the United States, as a colored citizen, having, in common with all other citizens, a stake in the safety, prosperity, honor, and glory of a common country.[1] (Cheering.) We are all liberated by this proclamation. Everybody is liberated. The white man is liberated, the black man is liberated, the brave men now fighting the battles of their country against rebels and traitors are now liberated, and may strike with all their might, even if they do by thus manfully striking hurt the Rebels, at their most sensitive point. (Applause.)

I congratulate you upon this amazing change—this amazing approximation toward the sacred truth of human liberty. All the space between man's mind and God's mind, says Parker,[2] is crowded with truths that wait to be discovered and organized into law for the better government of society. Mr. Lincoln has not exactly discovered a new truth, but he has dared, in this dark hour of national peril, to apply an old truth, long ago acknowledged in theory by the nation—a truth which carried the American people safely through the war for independence, and one which will carry us, as I believe, safely through the present terrible and sanguinary conflict for national life, if we shall but faithfully live up to that great truth. (Cheers.)

Born and reared as a slave, as I was, and wearing on my back the marks of the slavedriver's lash, as I do, it is natural that I should value the Emancipation Proclamation for what it is destined to do for the slaves. I do value it for that. It is a mighty event for the bondman, but it is a still mightier event for the nation at large, and mighty as it is for both, the slave and the nation, it is still mightier when viewed in its relation to the cause of truth and justice throughout the world. It is in this last character that I prefer to consider it. There are certain great national acts, which by their relation to universal principles, properly belong to the whole human family, and Abraham Lincoln's Proclamation of the 1st of January, 1863, is one of these acts. Henceforth that day shall take rank with the Fourth of July. (Applause.) Henceforth it becomes the date of a new and glorious era in the history of American liberty. Henceforth it shall stand associated in the minds of men, with all those stately steps of mankind, from the regions of error and oppression, which have lifted them from the trial by poison and fire to the trial by Jury—from the arbitrary will of a despot to the sacred writ of habeas corpus—from abject serfdom to absolute citizenship. It will stand in the history of civilization with Catholic Emancipation, with the British Reform Bill,[3] with the repeal of Corn Laws and with that noble act of Russian liberty, by which twenty millions of serfs, against the clamors of haughty tyrants, have been released from servitude. (Loud cheering.) Aye! It will stand with every distinguished event which marks any advance made by mankind from the thraldom and darkness of error to the glorious liberty of truth.

I believe in the millenium—the final perfection of the race, and hail this Proclamation, though wrung out under the goading lash of a stern military necessity, as one reason of the hope that is in me. Men may see in it only a military necessity. To me it has a higher significance. It is a grand moral necessity.

> "Thrice is he armed who hath his quarrel just,
> And he but naked, though wrapped up in steel,
> Whose conscience with injustice is corrupted."[4]

The conscience of the North has been troubled during all this war. It has seen the inconsistency of fighting for Slavery. It has seen the absurdity of killing the Rebel, while asserting the Rebel's right to his slave. It has seen the folly of fighting the Rebels with our soft white hands, and keeping back our iron black hands. (Cheers.)

This whole subject of the war and the President's proclamation naturally brings us to the consideration of first principles, the nature of truth and error, and their respective powers and prospects, in the Government of mankind. I attempt no scientific definition either of truth or of error. The occasion does not require it. Truth is that view or theory of things which describes them as they really are. It describes a man as a man, a horse as a horse, and never confounds the distinction between men and horses. Error is any and every contradiction of truth, in much or in little. The one is in its nature a unit. The other is in its nature multitudinous. The devil gave his name correctly when he called himself legion[5]—for there are a thousand wrong ways to but one right way.

Nevertheless, truth as one, shall be more than a match for error as a thousand—and all nations shall yet be brought into harmony with its absolute requirements. Either in the truth, or man himself, there is a compensating force, which renders him, in a high sense superior to the numerical advantages of error. By some means or other, whatever may be said of innate depravity, men do and will in the end prefer truth to error, and the right way to the wrong one.

When we meet with facts in our experience of the world, which seem to contradict this, the explanation can always be found in considerations entirely apart from the qualities of truth on the one hand, and of error on the other. Men never prefer the crooked to the straight road, because the one is crooked and the other is straight. It is always done because of some fancied advantage gained, or some disadvantage avoided—and done in the name of expediency, as choosing the least between two evils.

But little hope would there be for this world covered with error as with a cloud of thick darkness, and studded with all abounding injustice, wrong, oppression, intemperance, and monopolies, bigotry, superstition, King-craft, priest-craft, pride of race, prejudice of color, chattel-slavery—the grand sum of all human woes, and villanies[—]if there were not in man, deep down, and it may be very deep down, in his soul or in the truth itself, an elective power, or an attractive force, call it by what name you will, which makes truth in her simple beauty and excellence, ever preferred to the grim and ghastly powers of error.

Hence, though this life voyage of ours offers a thousand opportunities to drown, to only one of being saved; hence, though the sea is broad, and the ship is narrow; hence, though the billows are mighty, and the bark frail, there is a power on board, a captain at the helm whose presence forbids despair even in the darkest hours.

The hope of the world—the progress of nations—the triumph of the truth and the reign of reason and righteousness among men are conditioned on free discussion. Good old John Brown (loud applause) was a madman at Harper's Ferry. Two years pass away, and the nation is as mad as he. (Great cheering.) Every General and every soldier that now goes in good faith to Old Virginia, goes there for the very purpose that sent honest John Brown to Harper's Ferry. (Renewed cheers.)

After discussing the momentous power of Free Speech, he continued: One of the peculiarities of our times compels notice here. Parties have to some extent changed sides on the subject of free speech. The men who would a few years ago mob and hang Abolitionists for exercising the sacred right of free thought and speech, have all at once become the most urgent for the largest liberty of speech. And I must say, detestable as are the motives that have brought them to the defense of free speech, I think they have the right in the controversy. I do not know where I would limit the right of simple utterance of opinion. If any one is base enough to spit upon the grave of his mother, or to shout for Jefferson Davis, let him, and do not lock him up for it. (Cheering.) After that almost inspired announcement of equal rights contained in the Declaration of Independence, Jefferson has left us nothing more worthy of his profound mind than his saying that error may be safely tolerated where truth is left free to combat it. Equally true, though not always equally manifest, is it that error can never be safely tolerated when truth is not left free to combat it. Whence came the terrible conflict which now rocks our land with the thundering tramp of hostile armies? Why does the cold and greedy earth now drink up the warm red blood of our patriot sons, brothers, husbands, and fathers—carrying sorrow and agony into every household? Many answers have been returned to these questions. This, however, is the true one. A stupendous error, long tolerated, and protected even from discussion, held too sacred to be called in question, has at last become belligerent and snatched the sword of treason for permanent dominion.

Nothing strange has happened unto us; the result has been reached naturally. Our trouble is a logical part of the conflict of ages, past, present, and future. It will go on. It cannot be stopped. Here, as elsewhere, the fire will go out only when the fuel is exhausted. The moral chemistry of the universe makes peace between Liberty and Slavery impossible. Moral necessity is upon the slaveholders to stand up for Slavery. The dream and delusion of the hour is the thought of restoring the country to the condition it occupied previous to the war. What good would come of such restoration? What is the tremendous war but the ripened fruit of that past condition? Our present, horrible as it is, is the legitimate child of our previous; and to go back to what we were is simply to ask us to come back again to what we are. The conflict has changed its form from words to blows, and it may change again from blows to words; but the conflict itself, in one form or the other, will go on till truth is slain or error is driven from the field. (Cheers.)

Much as I hate Slavery, and glad as I should be to see it instantly abolished, I would consent gladly to any peace if but the right of speech, and the liberty of peaceably assembling could be secured in every part of the Union. (Applause.) When error consents to reason, truth may also consent to reason. But when error takes the sword, truth must also take the sword. Not to do this, and to cry out "peace at any price," is to desert the truth, and give up the world to the powers of darkness. The man who now preaches peace, preaches treason to his country and to the paramount claims of truth and justice.

The slaveholders are fighting for Slavery. The boldness with which they avow this object would astonish the world, but that the world knows that cunning, not courage, is the cause of their making it. They know that all attempt at concealment would be absurd and fruitless. They are fighting for Slavery[—]and the slave system being against nature—they are fighting against the eternal laws of nature, and though they should for a time succeed—dissolve the Union, capture a part of our territory, compel the North to sue for peace, and obtain peace upon the usual terms of compromise by which the South gets all and the North nothing, (Laughter and cheers) Nature with the aid of free discussion would set herself right in the end. Great is truth, great is humanity, and they must prevail. (Cheering.) A great man once said it was useless to re-enact the laws of God, meaning thereby the laws of Nature. But a greater man than he will yet teach the world that it is useless to re-enact any other laws with any hope of their permanence.

There are said to be some towns in this country which are finished, nothing more will or can be done for them, and that they might be fenced in without detriment. There are individuals of the same description whose greatest alarm seems to be that things may change after they are dead. (Cheers.) As the nerves of one of your dwellers in a finished town would be shocked by the sound of a hammer, those of our respectable Hunkers are shocked by the sound of a newly discovered truth. (Laughter and applause.) They recognize it as a disturber of the world's peace. But the world, like the fish preached to in the stream, moves on in obedience to the laws of its being, bearing away all excresences and imperfections in its progress. It has its periods of illumination as well as of darkness, and often bounds forward a greater distance in a single year than in an age before. The rosy morning light of a great truth breaks upon the vision of some early riser—and straightway he wakes up the drowsy world with the announcement of the day and the work. Sleepy people don't like to be disturbed. They hate the troubler, call him names, draw their curtains, close their blinds, turn their backs to the light—but the sun rises nevertheless, and the most conservative Hunker of them all is compelled in time to acknowledge it. (Cheers.)

Less than one hundred years ago it is said that the people of the West Coast of Ireland thought that the proper way to attach a horse to a plow was by the tail. (Laughter.) It seemed to them that that was what the tail was made for. (Laughter.) Only two hundred years ago, we are told by the pious Godwin, that the Christian people of the British West Indies thought it a sin to baptize persons of color who were slaves. The argument against such baptism was quite logical. They said that negroes are property, and it is not right to baptize property; and a learned divine thought it necessary to write a book to prove that it was not a sin to baptize a negro. (Laughter.)

At a time less remote than that, even in New England, now so remarkable for its enlightenment and its liberality, if any aged woman were in any wise distinguished for talent, and a little eccentric withal, as most gifted women are supposed to be, she stood a smart chance of being hanged as a witch. New England has outgrown this folly, and is condemned by some who reproach her, for refusing now to fall in with the barbarism of Slavery. At one time to hate and despise a Jew, simply for being a Jew, was almost a Christian virtue. The Jews were treated with every species of indignity, and not allowed to learn trades, nor to live in the same part of the city with other people. Now kings cannot go to war without the consent of a Jew. The Jew has come up, and the negro will come up by and by.

The world is not much older than it was when to torture and burn men for a difference of speculative religious belief was deemed simple fidelity to the Christian faith. All the wisdom of Boston could devise no better way a hundred years ago to cure a woman of Quakerism than by the cart-whip.[6] Roger Williams found more toleration among the Indians of Rhode Island than among the Puritans of Massachusetts.[7] It is only thirty years ago when gentlemen of property and standing in the very Athens of America felt it a patriotic duty to mob Wm. L. Garrison and break up a woman's Anti-Slavery prayer-meeting. Only two years ago there remained enough of this brutality and barbarism in Boston to block the streets of that city with a mob of 10,000 men clamoring for the blood of an eminent Boston citizen, for simply daring to speak against Slavery.

These facts are notorious and oft repeated. I mention them here not to cast reproach but as a part of the struggle between truth and error, and as a proof of progress. Fortunately for mankind, error is a bad reasoner. It can fight better than it can reason. It can make mouths, call names, and fling brickbats, but cannot reason except to damage itself. All the powers of the universe fight steadily against it. Brooks could knock down the Senator, but the whole South in arms could not knock down the Senator's argument. Such is my confidence in the potency of truth, in the power of reason, I hold that had the right of free discussion been preserved during the last thirty years, had the Northern parties and politicians been half so diligent in protecting this high constitutional right, from the first ruthlessly struck down all over the South, as they have been in framing laws for the recapture of poor, toil-worn and foot-sore slaves, we should now have no Slavery to breed Rebellion, nor war, black with dismal terror, to drench our land with blood, and fill our dwellings with sorrow and mourning. Slavery would have fallen as it fell in the West Indies, as it has fallen in the Free States, as it has fallen in Russia, and elsewhere, and as it will fall everywhere, when men can assail it with the weapons of reason and the facts of experience. (Applause.)

No men better understand the moral weakness of Slavery than the slaveholders themselves. The simple ones among them may think the system strong in reason; but the leading minds at the South know and confess the contrary. The Columbia (S.C.) *Telegraph* only echoed the sentiment of the whole South when it said thirty years ago:

"Let us declare through the public journals of the country that the question of Slavery is not and shall not be open to discussion, that the moment any private individual shall attempt to lecture upon its evils and immorality, and the necessity of putting means in operation to secure us from them, in that same moment, his tongue shall be cut out and cast upon a dung hill."

The Augusta (Ga.) *Chronicle*, of the same period, speaking of one who had attempted thus to lecture, says:

"He should have been hanged up as high as Haman, to rot till the wind whistled through his bones. The cry of the whole South should be death to the Abolitionists, wherever found."

The Lords of the Lash have often boasted of late that discussion has convinced them that Slavery is right. That in this respect they are wiser than Washington, who desired to see Slavery abolished, and would gladly give his vote for such abolition; wiser than Jefferson, who said he trembled for his country when he reflected that God was just, and that his justice would not sleep forever; wiser than Franklin, who was President of the first Abolition Society in America; wiser than Madison, who did not wish to have it seen in the Constitution that there could be any such thing as property in man; wiser than the Congress of 1807, which abolished the Slave Trade, and wiser than the men of 1787, who abolished Slavery in all the Territory then belonging to the United States.

They tell us that discussion has made them thus wise. Discussion indeed! Discussion which only permits one side to be heard, and compels the other to remain silent, would be likely to produce just such a result. The slaveholder has spoken but the slave has remained dumb. On the side of the oppressor is power, on the side of the slave weakness. The whole array of Southern lawyers, priests, and politicians—the whole power of the Southern press, pulpit, and platform have for 30 years stifled the very groans of the millions in bondage. Valuing itself at twenty hundred millions of dollars—a mountain of gold—it has bribed and bought up all the subtle machinery of religion, science, and law, in favor of Slavery. While denouncing rails, tar and feathers, faggots and fire against any who should dare call in question the accursed system of Slavery, and this they call discussion. Thus the moral eyes of Southern society were put out. They banished from among them every moral antidote for the dreadful evil of Slavery and have chosen to walk blindfold[ed] in to the very jaws of death.

I confess that when I consider the common people of the South, especially helpless women and children, who are often startled at midnight, and made to leave their beds and homes, half clad, to find their way to the woods through darkness, rain, mud, and snow, I feel something like pity for these people, while I feel a burning indignation, for those who have blinded and deceived them. Under the whole heavens there never was a people more completely given over to believe a lie that they might be destroyed. They are suffering all the horrors of war at this moment because [they were] deluded by their moral teachers, both at the North and at the South. Look at it! If they went to the church where men profess to speak by the authority of God, what did they hear on the subject of Slavery? Why, this: That Jesus Christ and his Apostles, though they walked in the presence of Roman Slavery—which was far more severe than ours—nowhere condemned the system; that the New Testament prescribed and enjoined obedience from slaves to their masters; that even to catch and return runaway slaves was in accordance with apostolic example, and that the main feature of the Fugitive Slave bill was in harmony with Paul's Epistle to Philemon. (Laughter.) They learned from their moral teachers that they might whip, hold, buy, and sell men and women, innocently, for Slavery was of Divine appointment, established by the law of Christ. Slaveholders are the modern Abrahams, Isaacs and Jacobs in the Church of God. (Renewed laughter.)

Such was the teaching at the South. Was the case much better at the North? You know and I know that even here, the black mantle of Slavery was everywhere flaunted in our faces from Northern pulpits. If at any time during the last thirty years preceding the firing upon Fort Sumter any slaveholder had consulted the leading divines of the North as to the sinfulness of Slavery, he would have found that the teachings of the Northern pulpit differed very little from that of the South. A few heterodox, and still fewer orthodox ministers, filling humble pulpits and living upon small salaries, have espoused the cause of the slave; but the ministers of high standing—the $5,000 divines—were almost to a man on the side of Slavery, and did their best to defend the system from the assaults of the Abolitionists. They steadily denied the inherent sinfulness of Slavery and so far from being rebuked as an offender, the slaveholder was received and welcomed as a saint.

Every influential pulpit of Rochester, where I live, was open to slaveholders so lately as two or three years ago. The old school General Assembly met there—the city survived it—at that time. (Laughter and applause.) The late Dr. Thornwall, a champion, alike of Secession and of Slavery, was there. He was courted and welcomed by every prominent pulpit of the city, while that faithful champion of the rights of human nature, Dr. George B. Cheever, was coldly repulsed from all such pulpits. What was true of Rochester three years ago, and true of the whole North, would become true again if this war were settled on the basis of compromise. Nay, I should expect that the Press would be fettered at the North nearly as heavily as it is at the South. Slavery would be welcomed and honored in Northern pulpits, with a servility more disgusting and shocking than ever before.

Why do I make these remarks? I will tell you. Much as I value the present apparent hostility to Slavery at the North, I plainly see that it is less the outgrowth of high and intelligent moral conviction against Slavery, as such, than because of the trouble its friends have brought upon the country. I would have Slavery hated for that and more. A man that hates Slavery only for what it does to the white man, stands ready to embrace it the moment its injuries are confined to the black man, and he ceases to feel those injuries in his own person. (Cheers.) I confess, if I could possibly doubt the salvation of this nation, it would not be because the traitors and Rebels are strong, but because we are weak at this vital point. There is yet among us a cowardly shrinking from a full and frank acknowledgment of the manhood of the negro, and a whole-souled recognition of his power to help in the great struggle through which we are passing. (Cheers.)

But to proceed: The saying that the children of this world are in their day and generation wiser than the children of light, is verified in the history of the conflict between Slavery and Freedom. History will accord to the Abolitionists a large measure of wisdom, and heroic courage and fortitude in assailing Slavery in its strongholds of Church and State; but it cannot award to them that prophetic vision that sees the end from the beginning. It is fortunate, I think, that they did not see it—fortunate that they walked by faith and not by sight.[8] Could they have foreseen their country torn and rent by the giant footsteps of this terrible rebellion—could they have seen a million of men, confronting each other, discussing the question of Slavery with cannon—could they have seen the rivers red with blood, and the fields whitened with human bones, they might have shrunk back from the moral contest, and thus only have postponed this physical contest to a future day, and upon a more dreadful scale than the one now going on.

From the very first the enemies of Abolitionism comprehended one feature in the nature of the contest between Freedom and Slavery. They saw at least the evils attendant on that conflict. Merchants saw their trade with the South embarrassed and ruined. Churches saw their denominations divided. The old political parties saw their organizations broken up. Statesmen saw the Union dissolved and terrible border wars inaugurated. Worshiping at mammon's altar themselves they knew the mighty hold which mammon held upon its Southern worshipers. They said that the slaveholders would strike down the Government before they would give up Slavery. They predicted that the South would secede if we did not stop talking and voting against Slavery. By their very predictions, they helped on the fulfillment. The South was flattered and encouraged by what was thus expected of her by leading men at the North. She doubtless expected that those who said she would dissolve her connection with the Union without once denouncing her doing so as a crime, recognized her right to do so, and would rather think her wanting in spirit if she did not do so. Foreseeing the evils thus predicted, these men cried with one accord: "Give us the Union; give us Slavery and prosperity; give us Slavery and peace; give us error, if Slavery be an error; and as for what you call truth and human liberty, crucify them."

The world has seen no greater example of patience and perseverance than that exhibited by the Abolitionists in meeting the objections of their opponents. Weapons of war they had cast from the battle. No Abolitionist ever drew sword against Slavery until Slavery drew its exterminating sword against Liberty on the soil of Kansas. It was only after he saw his brave sons hunted like felons and shot down like wolves, that noble old John Brown went to Harper's Ferry. (Cheers.) Until this, Anti-Slavery men, of all shades of opinion were eminently peaceful. The grand mistake of the Abolitionists was in supposing the American people better than they were. They did not see that an evil so gigantic as Slavery, so interwoven with the social arrangements, manners, and morals of the country, could not be removed without something like the social earthquake now upon us. They ought to have known that the huge Leviathan would cause the deep to boil—aye, to howl, and hiss, and foam in sevenfold agony. Great however, as was our mistake, incomparably greater and vastly more harmful was the mistake of those who flattered themselves and the nation that all was peace and prosperity, and that the nation had nothing to fear from anything but Abolitionists. They thought that this nation could go on year after year and century after century, outraging and trampling upon the sacred rights of human nature, and that it could still enjoy peace, and prosperity. To them the world was without a moral Government and might was right. The war now on our hands is sometimes described as a school for the moral education of the nation. I like the designation. It certainly is a school, and a very severe and costly one. But who will say that it will not be worth all it costs if it shall correct our errors concerning Slavery and free us from that barbarism. (Applause.)

Slavery from the first has not only been our great national crime, but our great national scandal and mistake. The first grand error of which this war is likely to cure us is: That a nation can outlaw one part of its people without endangering the rights and liberties of all the people. They will learn that they cannot put a chain on the ankle of the bondmen without finding the other end of it about their own necks. Hitherto the white laborer has been deluded into the belief that to degrade the black laborer is to elevate the white. We shall learn by-and-by that labor will always be degraded where idleness is the badge of respectability. Whence came the degrading phrases, fast growing popular before the war, "hireling labor," "greasy mechanics," "mudsills of society." The laborer should be "owned by the capitalists."—Poor "white trash"—and a dozen others of the same class: They come from Slavery. I think I never saw anywhere such contempt for poor white people as in the South. (Loud cheers.) Gen. Butler has only made a discovery which any man having two eyes could not fail to make in the South, that the war of the Rebels—is a war of the rich against the poor. Let Slavery go down with the war, and let labor cease to be fettered, chained, flogged, and branded. Let it be paid honest wages for honest work, and then we shall see as never before, the laborers in all sections of this country rising to respectability and power. (Cheers.)

That this war is to abolish Slavery I have no manner of doubt. The process may be long and tedious, but the event will come at last. It is among the undoubted certainties of the future. (Cheering.) It is objected to the Proclamation of Freedom, that it only abolishes Slavery in the Rebel States. To me it seems a blunder that Slavery was not declared abolished everywhere in the Republic. Slavery anywhere endangers the National cause, and should perish everywhere. (Loud applause.) But even in this omission of the Proclamation the evil is more seeming than real. When Virginia is a free State, Maryland cannot be a slave State. When Missouri is a free State, Kentucky cannot be a slave State. (Cheers.) Slavery must stand or fall together. Strike it at either extreme—either on the head or at the heel, and it dies. A brick knocked down at either end of the row brings every brick in it to the ground. (Applause.) You have heard the story of the Irishman who paid the price of two spurs—but refused to carry away but one; on the ground, as he said, that if he could make one side of his horse go, he would risk the other. (Laughter and cheering.) So I say, if we can strike down Slavery in the Rebel States, I will risk the downfall of Slavery in the Border States. (Cheering.)

It is again objected to this Proclamation that it is only an ink and paper proclamation. I admit it. The objector might go a step further, and assert that there was a time when this Proclamation was only a thought, a sentiment, an idea—a hope of some radical Abolitionist—for such it truly was. But what of it? The world has never advanced a single inch in the right direction, when the movement could not be traced to some such small beginning. The bill abolishing Slavery, and giving freedom to eight hundred thousand people in the West Indies, was a paper bill. The Reform bill, that broke up the rotten borough system in England, was a paper bill. The act of Catholic Emancipation was a paper act; and so was the bill repealing the Corn Laws. Greater than all, our own Declaration of Independence was at one time but ink and paper. (Cheering.) The freedom of the American colonies dates from no particular battle during the war. No man can tell upon what particular day we won our national independence. But the birth of our freedom is fixed on the day of the going forth of the Declaration of Independence. In like manner aftercoming generations will celebrate the first of January as the day which brought liberty and manhood to the American slaves. (Loud cheers.) How shall this be done? I answer: That the paper Proclamation must now be made iron, lead and fire, by the prompt employment of the negro's arm in this contest. (Great applause.) I hold that the Proclamation, good as it is, will be worthless—a miserable mockery—unless the nation shall so far conquer its prejudice as to welcome into the army full-grown black men to help fight the battles of the Republic. (Renewed applause.)

I know it is said that the negroes won't fight. But I distrust the accuser. In one breath the Copperheads tell you that the slaves won't fight, and in the next they tell you that the only effect of the

Proclamation is to make the slaves cut their masters' throats (laughter) and stir up insurrections all over the South. The same men tell you that the negroes are lazy and good for nothing, and in the next breath they tell you that they will all come North and take the labor away from the laboring white men here. (Laughter and cheers.) In one breath they tell you that the negro can never learn the military art, and in the next they tell you that there is danger that white men may be outranked by colored men. (Continued laughter.) I may be pardoned if I leave these objections to their own contradictions and absurdities. They are like the Kilkenny cats, and there is a fair probability of their reaching the same result. (Great laughter.)

But we are asked why have the negroes remained silent spectators of the dreadful struggle now going on? I am not annoyed by this question. The course pursued by them is creditable to their wisdom. The negro has proved that he is much like the white man. He will fight, but he must have a reasonable prospect of whipping somebody. Up to the first day of last month there was no earthly chance of success in a rising among the slaves. Both the Union and the Confederate armies were in the field against the negro. Madness itself could not counsel the slaves to rise in such circumstances. Their not doing so should be charged not to their cowardice, but to their good sense.

But who are those who are now opposing the measure of putting arms in the hands of colored men? Who are those who are opposed to raising colored troops? They are the men who would gladly disarm every white soldier now fighting for their country, and hand the country over, bound hand and foot, into the hands of Jefferson Davis. You know the men, and ought to know how much weight should be given to the counsels of such men. Would these men rather drown than be saved by a black man? Would they prefer to see their dwellings burnt to ashes than to have the flames extinguished by colored men? If they would not, then are they traitors in disguise and very thin disguise at that, when they refuse to the country, now in its peril, what they would gladly claim for themselves. They exhibit their unmitigated hollowness by opposing the enrollment of colored troops. (Cheers.)

Do you ask me whether black men will freely enlist in the service of the country? I tell you that that depends upon the white men of the country. The Government must assure them of protection as soldiers, and give them a fair chance of winning distinction and glory in common with other soldiers. (Cheers.) They must not be made the mere hewers of wood and drawers of water for the army. When a man leaves home, family, and security, to risk his limbs and life in the field of battle, for God's sake let him have all the honor which he may achieve, let his color be what it may. If, by the fortunes of war he is flung into the hands of the Rebels, let him be assured that the loyal Government will not desert him, but will hold the Confederate Government strictly responsible, as much for a black as for a white soldier. (Applause.) Give us fair play, and open here your recruiting offices, and their doors shall be crowded with black recruits to fight the battles of the country. (Loud cheers.) Do your part, my white fellow-countrymen, and we will do ours.

Oh! where's the slave so lowly,
Condemned to chains unholy,
Who, could he burst his chains at fight,
Would pine beneath them
slowly?[9]

The colored man only waits for honorable admission into the service of the country. They know that who would be free, themselves must strike the blow, and they long for the opportunity to strike that blow. Thus far, however, the colored men of the Free States, and for the most part, of the Slave States, have had their military ardor chilled by the contempt with which their offer to serve their country has been refused. We asked the Governor of New York if he would accept colored troops, and he said it would be impossible for him to receive them. We asked Gov. Curtin of Pennsylvania, and he would not receive colored soldiers at any rate. So that our ardor was chilled. But I know, colored men now in the army passing for white not much whiter than I, but by shaving their heads very closely they manage to get in. I know one from my own town who has been promoted recently. (Laughter and cheers.) If I could speak loud enough to be heard by the Government at Washington I should say, have a care, lest you let slip the last moment when your call for help can be answered. You have wronged us long and wronged us greatly, but it is not yet too late to retrieve the past. We still stand ready to serve you, and will do it with a will, at the first sound of your war-trumpet. (Cheers.)

I know the colored men of the North; I know the colored men of the South. They are ready to rally under the stars and stripes at the first tap of the drum. Give them a chance; stop calling them "niggers," and call them soldiers. (Applause.) Give them a chance to seek the bauble [bubble] reputation at the cannon's mouth. Stop telling them they can't fight, and tell them they can fight and shall fight, and they will fight, and fight with vengeance. Give them a chance. The most delicate lady in the city of New York can ride by the side of a black man, if he is there as a servant. Even the most fastidious of our Generals can be waited on by colored men. Why should they object to our fighting? We were with you on the banks of the Mobile, good enough to fight with you under Gen. Jackson. Why not let us fight by your side under Gen. Hooker? (Loud cheering.) We shall have a chance yet, and I tell you to whom I am looking for this. I have great faith, as I told you more than a year ago, in the virtue of the people of the North; I have more in the persistent villainy of the South. (Laughter and applause.) I tell you that under their tent we shall yet be able to accept the aid of the colored man. Away with prejudice, away with folly, and in this death struggle for liberty, country, and permanent security, let the black, iron hand of the colored man fall heavily on the head of the slaveholding traitors and rebels and lay them low. Give them a chance! Give them a chance. I don't say they are great fighters. I don't say they will fight better than other men. All I say is, give them a chance. I feel that we are living in a glorious time. I felt so on the first of January, and have been feeling so ever since. I felt whiter, and I have combed my hair with less difficulty. (Cheers and laughter.) You had a grand time here, and we had a grand time at Boston, on the first of January.

We had two machines running—at Music Hall and Tremont Temple—more than three thousand at each. You want to know what the colored people think. I will tell you how joyfully they received the Proclamation of Abraham Lincoln. We were not all colored either; but we all seemed to be about of one color that day. We met in good spirits at 10 o'clock expecting before the adjournment to have the Proclamation. We had waited on each speaker keeping our eye on the door. No Proclamation. The President said we would meet again at two when he had no doubt we should have the Proclamation. We met again but no Proclamation. We did not know whether to shout or hold our peace but we adjourned again with the understanding that it was on the wires and we should certainly see it in the evening. But no Proclamation came. We went on until 11 o'clock and I said, we won't go home till morning. By and by Judge Russell went to one of the newspaper offices and obtained a slip containing the Proclamation. I never saw enthusiasm before. I never saw joy before. Men, women, young and old, were up; hats and bonnets were in the air, and we gave three cheers for Abraham Lincoln and three cheers for almost everybody else. Some prayed and some sang, and finally we adjourned from that place to meet in the Rev. Mr. Grimes' Church; that good old soul (laughter) and we continued greeting them till three o'clock. There was shouting and singing, "Glory, Hallelujah," "Old John Brown," "Marching On," and "Blow Ye, the Trumpet Blow!"—till we got up such a state of enthusiasm that almost anything seemed to be witty—and entirely appropriate to the glorious occasion.

There was one black man who stood in a corner, and I thought I never saw a blacker man and I think I never saw whiter teeth. Occasionally he would bound up like a fish out of water, and as he was standing in a dark place, you could see nothing going up but a little white streak. (Loud laughter.) About the last he said he must speak, and I will make you his speech. It was all in place. We were up to the point when everything was in order. "Brethren," said he, "I was born in North Carolina, where my brother Douglass was born, thank God!" I didn't happen to be born there, but I could not for the life of me interrupt him. Said he, "I was born there, and was born and held a slave there, thank God! (Laughter.) I grew up from childhood to manhood there, thank God!" And the audience shouted. And said he: "When I got to be grown up to man's estate I wanted to marry a wife, thank God!" (Laughter.) And said he: "I courted no less than sixteen women, thank God!" (Great laughter.) And said he: "The woman I married is here to-night, thank God!" We all rose up to see this little woman, and she was told to get up, and we looked at her, and she was nothing extraordinary (laughter); but still it was all in place. The feeling of the whole of this black Congregation—for it was mainly black—was that they were ready to offer their services at any moment this Government should call for them. And I want to assure you, and the Government, and everybody, that we are ready, and we only ask to be called into this service. What a glorious day when Slavery shall be no more in this country, when we have blotted out this system of wrong, and made this United States in fact and in truth what it is in theory—The land of the Free and the Home of the Brave. (Loud applause.)

"THE MISSION OF THE WAR" (1864)

Douglass delivered this influential address at several venues during the winter of 1863–64, including Cooper Institute, New York. It provides the fullest account of what the war meant to him: an "abolition war" and an "abolition peace" that would end racial discrimination.

SOURCE: *New York Daily Tribune*, January 14, 1864

Ladies and Gentlemen: By the mission of the war I mean nothing occult, arbitrary or difficult to be understood, but simply those great moral changes in the fundamental condition of the people, demanded by the situation of the country, plainly involved in the nature of the war, and which if the war is conducted in accordance with its true character, it is naturally and logically fitted to accomplish.

Speaking in the name of Providence, some men tell us that Slavery is already dead, that it expired with the first shot at Sumter. This may be so, but I do not share the confidence with which it is asserted. In a grand Crisis like this, we should all prefer to look facts sternly in the face, and to accept their verdict whether it bless or blast us. I look for no miraculous destruction of Slavery. The war looms before me simply as a great national opportunity, which may be improved to national salvation, or neglected to national ruin. I hope much from the bravery of our soldiers, but in vain is the might of armies if our rulers fail to profit by experience, and refuse to listen to the suggestions of wisdom and justice. The most hopeful fact of the hour is that we are now in a salutary school—the school of affliction. If sharp and signal retribution, long protracted, wide-sweeping and overwhelming, can teach a great nation respect for the long-despised claims of justice, surely we shall be taught now and for all time to come. But if, on the other hand, this potent teacher, whose lessons are written in characters of blood, and thundered to us from a hundred battle-fields shall fail, we shall go down, as we shall deserve to go down, as a warning to all other nations which shall come after us. It is not pleasant to contemplate the hour as one of doubt and danger. We naturally prefer the bright side, but when there is a dark side it is folly to shut our eyes to it or deny its existence.

I know that the acorn involves the oak, but I know also that the commonest accident may destroy its potential character and defeat its natural destiny. One wave brings its treasure from the briny deep, but another often sweeps it back to its primal depths. The saying that revolutions never go backward must be taken with limitations.[1] The revolution of 1848 was one of the grandest that ever dazzled a gazing world. It overturned the French throne, sent Louis Philippe into exile, shook every throne in Europe, and inaugurated a glorious Republic. Looking on from a distance, the friends of democratic liberty saw in the convulsion the death of kingcraft in Europe and throughout the world. Great was their disappointment. Almost in the twinkling of an eye, the latent forces of despotism rallied. The Republic disappeared. Her noblest defenders were sent into exile, and the hopes of democratic liberty were blasted in the moment of their bloom. Politics and perfidy proved too strong for the principles of liberty and justice in that contest. I wish I could say that no such liabilities darken the horizon around us. But the same elements are plainly involved here as there. Though the portents are that we shall flourish, it is too much to say that we cannot fail and fall. Our destiny is not to be taken out of our own hands. It is cowardly to shuffle our responsibilities upon the shoulders of Providence. I do not intend to argue but to state facts.

We are now wading deep into the third year of conflict with a fierce and sanguinary rebellion, one which, at the beginning of it, we were hopefully assured by one of our most sagacious and trusted political prophets, would be ended in less than ninety days: a rebellion which, in its worst features, stands alone among rebellions a solitary and ghastly horror, without a parallel in the history of any nation, ancient or modern: a rebellion inspired by no love of liberty and by no hatred of oppression, as most other rebellions have been, and therefore utterly indefensible upon any moral or social grounds: a rebellion which openly and shamelessly sets at defiance the world's judgment of right and wrong, appeals from light to darkness, from intelligence to ignorance, from the ever-increasing prospects and blessings of a high and glorious civilization to the cold and withering blasts of a naked barbarism: a rebellion which even at this unfinished stage of it, counts the number of its slain not by thousands nor tens of thousands, but by hundreds of thousands. A rebellion which in the destruction of human life and property has rivalled the earthquake, the whirlwind and the pestilence that walketh in darkness, and wasteth at noonday. It has planted agony at a million hearthstones, thronged our streets with the weeds of mourning, filled our land with mere stumps of men, ridged our soil with 200,000 rudely-formed graves, and mantled it all over with the shadow of death. A rebellion which, while it has arrested the wheels of peaceful industry and checked the flow of commerce, has piled up a debt, heavier than a mountain of gold to weigh down the necks of our children's children. There is no end to the mischiefs wrought. It has brought ruin at home, contempt abroad, cooled our friends, heated our enemies, and endangered our existence as a nation.

Now, for what is all this desolation, ruin, shame, suffering, and sorrow? Can anybody want the answer? Can anybody be ignorant of the answer? It has been given a thousand times from this and other platforms. We all know it is Slavery. Less than a half a million of Southern slave-holders—holding in bondage four million slaves—finding themselves outvoted in the effort to get possession of the United States Government, in order to serve the interests of Slavery, have madly resorted to the sword—have undertaken to accomplish by bullets what they failed to accomplish by ballots. That is the answer.

It is worthy of remark that Secession was an afterthought with the Rebels. Their aim was higher; Secession was only their second choice. Wise was going to fight for Slavery in the Union. It was not separation, but subversion. It was not Richmond, but Washington. It was not the Confederate rag, but the glorious Star-Spangled Banner.

Whence came the guilty ambition equal to this atrocious crime? A peculiar education was necessary to this bold wickedness. Here all is plain again. Slavery—the peculiar institution—is aptly fitted to produce just such patriots, who first plunder and then seek to destroy their country. A system which rewards labor with stripes and chains!—which robs the slave of his manhood, and the master of all just consideration for the rights of his fellow-man—has prepared the characters—male and female—that figure in this Rebellion—and for all its cold-blooded and hellish atrocities. In all the most horrid details of torture, starvation and murder, in the treatment of our prisoners, I beheld the features of the monster in whose presence I was born, and that is Slavery. From no source less foul and wicked could such a Rebellion come. I need not dwell here. The country knows the story by heart. But I am one of those who think this Rebellion—inaugurated and carried on for a cause so unspeakably guilty and distinguished by barbarities which would extort a cry of shame from the painted savage—is quite enough for the whole lifetime of any one nation—though that lifetime should cover the space of a thousand years. We ought not to want a repetition of it—nor can we wisely risk a possible repetition of it. Looking at the matter from no higher ground than patriotism—setting aside the high considerations of justice, liberty, progress, and civilization—the American people should resolve that this shall be the last slaveholding Rebellion that shall ever curse this continent. Let the War cost much or cost little—let it be long or short—the work now begun should suffer no pause, no abatement, until it is done and done forever.

I know that many are appalled and disappointed by the apparently interminable character of this war. I am neither appalled nor disappointed. Without pretending to any higher wisdom than other men, I know well enough and often said it—Once let the North and South confront each other on the battle-field, and Slavery and Freedom be the inspiring motives of the respective sections, the contest will be fierce, long and sanguinary. Gov. Seymour charges us with prolonging the war,[2] and I say the longer the better if it must be so—in order to put an end to the hell black cause out of which the Rebellion has risen.

Say not that I am indifferent to the horrors and hardships of the war. I am not indifferent. In common with the American people generally, I feel the prolongation of the war a heavy calamity—private as well [as] public. There are vacant spaces at my hearthstone which I shall rejoice to see filled again by the boys who once occupied them—but which cannot be thus filled while the war lasts—for they have enlisted—"during the war."[3]

But even from the length of this struggle, we who mourn over it may well enough draw some consolation when we reflect upon the vastness and grandeur of its mission. The world has witnessed many wars—and history records and perpetuates their memory, but the world has not seen a nobler and grander war than that which the loyal people of this country are now waging against the slaveholding Rebels. The blow we strike is not merely to free a country or continent—but the whole world from Slavery—for when Slavery falls here—it will fall everywhere. We have no business to mourn over our mission. We are writing the statutes of eternal justice and liberty in the blood of the worst of tyrants as a warning to all after-comers. We should rejoice that there was moral life and health enough in us to stand in our appointed place, and do this great service for mankind.

It is true that the war seems long. But this very slow progress is an essential element of its effectiveness. Like the slow convalescence of some patients the fault is less chargeable to the medicine than to the deep-seated character of the disease. We were in a very low condition before the remedy was applied. The whole head was sick and the whole heart faint. Dr. Buchanan and his Democratic friends had given us up, and were preparing to celebrate the nation's funeral. We had been drugged nearly to death by Pro-Slavery compromises. A radical change was needed in our whole system. Nothing is better calculated to effect the desired change than the slow, steady and certain progress of the war.

I know that this view of the case is not very consoling to the peace Democracy. I was not sent and am not come to console this branch of our political church. They regard this grand moral revolution in the mind and heart of the nation as the most distressing attribute of the war, and howl over it like certain characters of whom we read—who thought themselves tormented before their time.

Upon the whole, I like their mode of characterizing the war. They charge that it is no longer conducted upon constitutional principles. The same was said by Breckinridge and Vallandigham. They charge that it is not waged to establish the Union as it was. The same idea has occurred to Jefferson Davis. They charge that this is a war for the subjugation of the South. In a word, that it is an Abolition war.

For one, I am not careful to deny this charge. But it is instructive to observe how this charge is brought and how it is met. Both warn us of danger. Why is this war fiercely denounced as an Abolition war? I answer, because the nation has long and bitterly hated Abolition, and the enemies of the war confidently rely upon this hatred to serve the ends of treason. Why do the loyal people deny the charge? I answer, because they know that Abolition, though now a vast power, is still odious. Both the charge and the denial tell how the people hate and despise the only measure that can save the country.

An Abolition war! Well, let us thank the Democracy for teaching us this word. The charge in a comprehensive sense is most true, and it is not a pity that it is true, but it would be a vast pity if it were not true. Would that it were more true than it is. When our Government and people shall bravely avow this to be an Abolition war, then the country will be safe. Then our work will be fairly mapped out. Then the uplifted arm of the nation will swing unfettered to its work, and the spirit and power of the Rebellion will be broken. Had Slavery been abolished in the Border States at the very beginning of this war, as it ought to have been—had it been abolished in Missouri, as it would have been but for Presidential interference—there would now be no Rebellion in the Southern States—for instead of having to watch these Border States, as they have done, our armies would have marched in overpowering numbers directly upon the Rebels and overwhelmed them. I now hold that a sacred regard for truth, as well as sound policy, makes it our duty to own and avow before Heaven and earth that this war is, and of right ought to be, an Abolition war.

The abolition of Slavery is the comprehensive and logical object of the war, for it includes everything else which the struggle involves. It is a war for the union, a war for the Constitution, I admit; but it is logically such a war only in the sense that the greater includes the lesser. Slavery has proved itself the strong man of our national house. In every Rebel State it proved itself stronger than the Union, stronger than the Constitution, and stronger than Republican Institutions. It overrode majorities, made no account of the ballot-box, and had everything its own way. It is plain that this strong man must be bound and cast out of our house before Union, Constitution and Republican institutions can become possible. An Abolition war, therefore, includes Union, Constitution, Republican Institutions, and all else that goes to make up the greatness and glory of our common country. On the other hand, exclude Abolition, and you exclude all else for which you are fighting.

The position of the Democratic party in relation to the war ought to surprise nobody. It is consistent with the history of the party for thirty years past. Slavery, and only Slavery, has been its recognized master during all that time. It early won for itself the title of being the natural ally of the South and of Slavery. It has always been for peace or against peace, for war and against war, precisely as dictated by Slavery. Ask why it was for the Florida War,[4] and it answers, Slavery. Ask why it was for the Mexican War, and it answers, Slavery. Ask why it was for the annexation of Texas, and it answers, Slavery. Ask why it was opposed to the habeas corpus when a negro was the applicant, and it answers, Slavery. Ask why it is now in favor of the habeas corpus, when Rebels and traitors are the applicants for its benefits, and it answers, Slavery. Ask why it was for mobbing down freedom of speech a few years ago, when that freedom was claimed by the Abolitionists, and it answers, Slavery. Ask why it now asserts freedom of speech, when sympathizers with traitors claim that freedom, and again Slavery is the answer. Ask why it denied the right of a State to protect itself against possible abuses of the Fugitive-Slave bill, and you have the same old answer. Ask why it now asserts the sovereignty of the States separately, as against the States united, and again Slavery is the answer. Ask why it was opposed to giving persons claimed as fugitive slaves a jury trial before returning them to slavery; ask why it is now in favor of giving jury trial to traitors before sending them to the forts for safe keeping; ask why it was for war at the beginning of the Rebellion; ask why it has attempted to embarrass and hinder the loyal Government at every step of its progress, and you have but one answer, Slavery.

The fact is, the party in question, I say nothing of individual men who were once members of it, has had but one vital and animating principle for thirty years, and that has been the same old horrible and hell-born principle of negro Slavery.

It has now assumed a saintly character. Its members would receive the benediction due to peace-makers. At one time they would stop bloodshed at the South by inaugurating bloody revolution at the North. The livery of peace is a beautiful livery, but in this case it is a stolen livery and sits badly on the wearer. These new apostles of peace call themselves Peace Democrats, and boast that they belong to the only party which can restore the country to peace. I neither dispute their title nor the pretensions founded upon it. The best that can be said of the peace-making ability of this class of men is their bitterest condemnation. It consists in their known treachery to the loyal Government. They have but to cross the Rebel lines to be hailed by the traitors as countrymen, clansmen, kinsmen, and brothers beloved in a common conspiracy. But, fellow-citizens, I have far less solicitude about the position and the influence of this party than I have about that of the great loyal party of the country. We have much less to fear from the bold and shameless wickedness of the one than from the timid and short-sighted policy of the other.

I know we have recently gained a great political victory; but it remains to be seen whether we shall wisely avail ourselves of its manifest advantages. There is danger that, like some of our Generals in the field, who, after soundly whipping the foe, generously allow him time to retreat in order, reorganize his forces, and intrench himself in a new and stronger position, where it will require more power and skill to dislodge him than was required to vanquish him in the first instance. The game is now in our hands. We can put an end to this disloyal party by putting an end to Slavery. While the Democratic party is in existence as an organization, we are in danger of a slaveholding peace, and of Rebel rule. There is but one way to avert this calamity, and that is, destroy Slavery and enfranchise the black man while we have the power. While there is a vestige of Slavery remaining, it will unite the South with itself, and carry with it the Democracy of the North. The South united and the North divided, we shall be hereafter as heretofore, firmly held under the heels of Slavery.

Here is a part of the platform of principles upon which it seems to me every loyal man should take his stand at this hour:

First: That this war, which we are compelled to wage against slaveholding Rebels and traitors, at untold cost of blood and treasure, shall be, and of right ought to be, an Abolition War.

Secondly: That we, the loyal people of the North and of the whole country, while determined to make this a short and final war, will offer no peace, accept no peace, consent to no peace, which shall not be to all intents and purposes an Abolition peace.

Thirdly: That we regard the whole colored population of the country, in the loyal as well as in the disloyal States, as our *countrymen*—valuable in peace as laborers, valuable in war as soldiers—entitled to all the rights, protection, and opportunities for achieving distinction enjoyed by any other class of our countrymen.

Fourthly: Believing that the white race has nothing to fear from fair competition with the black race, and that the freedom and elevation of one race are not to be purchased or in any manner rightfully subserved by the disfranchisement of another, we shall favor immediate and unconditional emancipation in all the States, invest the black man everywhere with the right to vote and to be voted for, and remove all discriminations against his rights on account of his color, whether as a citizen or as a soldier.

Ladies and gentlemen, there was a time when I hoped that events unaided by discussions would couple this Rebellion and Slavery in a common grave. But as I have before intimated, the facts do still fall short of our hopes. The question as to what shall be done with Slavery—and more especially what shall be done with the negro—threaten to remain open questions for some time yet.

It is true we have the Proclamation of January, 1863. It was a vast and glorious step in the right direction. But unhappily, excellent as that paper is—and much as it has accomplished temporarily—it settles nothing. It is still open to decision by courts, canons and Congresses. I have applauded that paper and do now applaud it, as a wise measure—while I detest the motive and principle upon which it is based. By it the holding and flogging of negroes is the exclusive luxury of loyal men.

Our chief danger lies in the absence of all moral feeling in the utterances of our rulers. In his letter to Mr. Greeley the President told the country virtually that the abolition or non-abolition of Slavery was a matter of indifference to him.[5] He would save the Union with Slavery or without Slavery. In his last Message he shows the same moral indifference, by saying as he does say that he had hoped that the Rebellion could be put down without the abolition of Slavery.

When the late Stephen A. Douglas uttered the sentiment that he did not care whether Slavery were voted up or voted down in the Territories, we thought him lost to all genuine feeling on the subject, and no man more than Mr. Lincoln denounced that sentiment as unworthy of the lips of any American statesman. But to-day, after nearly three years of a Slaveholding Rebellion, we find Mr. Lincoln uttering substantially the same heartless sentiments. Douglas wanted Popular Sovereignty; Mr. Lincoln wants the Union. Now did a warm heart and a high moral feeling control the utterances of the President, he would welcome, with joy unspeakable and full of glory, the opportunity afforded by the Rebellion to free the country from the matchless crime and infamy. But policy, policy, everlasting policy, has robbed our statesmanship of all soul-moving utterances.

The great misfortune is and has been during all the progress of this war, that the Government and loyal people have not understood and accepted its true mission. Hence we have been floundering in the depths of dead issues. Endeavoring to impose old and worn-out conditions upon new relations—putting new wine into old bottles, new cloth into old garments, and thus making the rent worse than before.

Had we been wise, we should have recognized the war at the outset as at once the signal and the necessity for a new order of social and political relations among the whole people. We could, like the ancients, discern the face of the sky, but not the signs of the times. Hence we have been talking of the importance of carrying on the war within the limits of a Constitution broken down by the very people in whose behalf the Constitution is pleaded! Hence we have from the first been deluding ourselves with the miserable dream, that the old Union can be revived in the States where it has been abolished.

Now, we of the North have seen many strange things, and may see many more; but that old Union, whose canonized bones we saw hearsed in death and inurned under the frowning battlements of Sumter, we shall never see again while the world standeth. The issue before us is a living issue. We are not fighting for the dead past, but for the living present and the glorious future. We are not fighting for the old Union, nor for anything like it, but for that which is ten thousand times more important; and that thing, crisply rendered, is *National unity.* Both sections have tried Union. It has failed.

The lesson for the statesman at this hour is to discover and apply some principle of Government which shall produce unity of sentiment, unity of idea, unity of object. Union without unity is, as we have seen, body without soul, marriage without love, a barrel without hoops, which falls at the first touch.

The statesmen of the South understood this matter earlier and better than the statesmen of the North. The dissolution of the Union on the old bases of compromise, was plainly foreseen and predicted 30 years ago. Mr. Calhoun and not Mr. Seward, is the original author of the doctrine of the irrepressible conflict. The South is logical and consistent. Under the teachings of their great leader they admit into their form of Government no disturbing force. They have based their Confederacy squarely on their corner-stone. Their two great, and all commanding ideas are first, that Slavery is right, and second, that the slaveholders are a superior order or class. Around these two ideas their manners, morals, politics, religion, and laws revolve. Slavery being right, all that is inconsistent with its entire security is necessarily wrong, and of course ought to be put down. There is no flaw in their logic.

They first endeavored to make the Federal Government stand upon their accursed corner-stone; and we but barely escaped, as you well know, that calamity. Fugitive Slave laws, Slavery Extension laws, and Dred Scott decisions were among the steps to get the nation squarely upon the corner-stone now chosen by the Confederate States. The loyal North is less logical, less consistent, and less definite in regard to the necessity of principles of National Unity. Yet, unconsciously to ourselves, and against our own protestations, we are in reality, like the South, fighting for national unity—a unity of which the great principles of liberty and equality, and not Slavery and class superiority, are the corner-stone.

Long before this rude and terrible war came to tell us of a broken Constitution and a dead Union, the better portion of the loyal people had outlived and outgrown what they had been taught to believe were the requirements of the old Union. We had come to detest the principle by which Slavery had a strong representation in Congress. We had come to abhor the idea of being called upon to suppress slave insurrections. We had come to be ashamed of slave-hunting, and being made the watch-dogs of slaveholders, who were too proud to scent out and hunt down their slaves for themselves. We had so far outlived the old Union four years ago that we thought the little finger of the hero of Harper's Ferry of more value to the world struggling for liberty than all the first families of old Virginia put together.

What business, then, have we to be pouring out our treasure and shedding our best blood like water for that old worn-out, dead and buried Union, which had already become a calamity and a curse? The fact is, we are not fighting for any such thing, and we ought to come out under our own true colors, and let the South and the whole world know that we don't want and will not have anything analogous to the old Union.

What we now want is a country—a free country—a country nowhere saddened by the footprints of a single slave—and nowhere cursed by the presence of a slaveholder. We want a country, and we are fighting for a country, which shall not brand the Declaration of Independence as a lie. We want a country whose fundamental institutions we can proudly defend before the highest intelligence and civilization of the age. Hitherto we have opposed European scorn of our Slavery with a blush of shame as our best defense. We now want a country in which the obligations of patriotism shall not conflict with fidelity to justice and

Liberty. We want a country, and are fighting for a country, which shall be free from sectional political parties—free from sectional religious denominations—free from sectional benevolent associations—free from every kind and description of sect, party, and combination of a sectional character. We want a country where men may assemble from any part of it, without prejudice to their interests or peril to their persons. We are in fact, and from absolute necessity, transplanting the whole South with the higher civilization of the North. The New-England schoolhouse is bound to take the place of the Southern whipping-post. Not because we love the negro, but the nation; not because we prefer to do this, because we must or give up the contest, and give up the country. We want a country, and are fighting for a country, where social intercourse and commercial relations shall neither be embarrassed nor embittered by the imperious exactions of an insolent slaveholding Oligarchy, which required Northern merchants to sell their souls as a condition precedent to selling their goods. We want a country, and are fighting for a country, through the length and breadth of which the literature and learning of any section of it may float to its extremities unimpaired, and thus become the common property of all the people—a country in which no man shall be fined for reading a book, or imprisoned for selling a book—a country where no man can be imprisoned or flogged or sold for learning to read, or teaching a fellow mortal how to read. We want a country, and are fighting for a country, in any part of which to be called an American citizen, shall mean as much as it did to be called a Roman citizen in the palmiest days of the Roman Empire.

We have heard much in other days of manifest destiny. I don't go all the lengths to which such theories are pressed, but I do believe that it is the manifest destiny of this war to unify and reorganize the institutions of this country—and that herein is the secret of the strength, the fortitude, the persistent energy, in a word the sacred significance of this war. Strike out the high ends and aims thus indicated, and the war would appear to the impartial eye of an on-looking world little better than a gigantic enterprise for shedding human blood.

A most interesting and gratifying confirmation of this theory of its mission is furnished in the varying fortunes of the struggle itself. Just in proportion to the progress made in taking upon itself the character I have ascribed to it, has the war prospered and the Rebellion lost ground.

Justice and humanity are often overpowered—but they are persistent and eternal forces—and fearful to contend against. Let but our rulers place the Government fully within these trade winds of Omnipotence, and the hand of death is upon the Confederate Rebels. A war waged as ours seemed to be at first, merely for power and empire, repels sympathy though supported by legitimacy. If Ireland should strike for independence to-morrow, the sympathy of this country would be with her, and I doubt if American statesmen would be more discreet in the expression of their opinions of the merits of the contest, than British statesmen have been concerning the merits of ours. When we were merely fighting for the old Union the world looked coldly upon our Government. But now the world begins to see something more than legitimacy—something more than national pride. It sees national wisdom aiming at national unity; and national justice breaking the chains of a long enslaved people. It is this new complexion of our cause which warms our hearts and strengthens our hands at home, disarms our enemies and increases our friends abroad. It is this more than all else which has carried consternation into the blood-stained halls of the South. It has sealed the fiery and scornful lips of the Roebucks and Lindsays of England, and caused even the eloquent Mr. Gladstone to restrain the expression of his admiration for Jeff. Davis and his Rebel nation. It has placed the broad arrow of British suspicion on the prows of the Rebel rams in the Mersey, and performed a like service for those in France. It has driven Mason, the shameless man-hunter, from London, where he never should have been allowed to stay for an hour, except as a bloodhound is tolerated in Regent Park for exhibition.

We have had from the first warm friends in England. We owe a debt of respect and gratitude to William Edward Forster, John Bright, Richard Cobden, and other British statesmen, in that they outran us in comprehending the high character of our struggle. They saw that this must be a war for human nature, and walked by faith to its defense while all was darkness about us—while we were yet conducting it in profound reverence for Slavery.

I know we are not to be praised for this changed character of the war. We did our very best to prevent it. We had but one object at the beginning, and that was, as I have said, the restoration of the old Union; and for the first two years the war was kept to that object strictly, and you know full well and bitterly with what results. I will not stop here to blame and denounce the past; but I will say that most of the blunders and disasters of the earlier part of the war might have been avoided had our armies and Generals not repelled the only true friends the Union cause had in the Rebel States. The Army of the Potomac took up an anti-negro position from the first, and has not entirely renounced it yet. The colored people told me a few days ago in Washington that they were the victims of the most brutal treatment by these Northern soldiers when they first came there. But let that pass. Few men, however great their wisdom, are permitted to see the end from the beginning. Events are mightier than our rulers, and these Divine forces, with overpowering logic, have fixed upon this war, against the wishes of our Government, the comprehensive character and mission I have ascribed to it. The collecting of revenue in the Rebel ports, the repossession of a few forts and arsenals and other public property stolen by the Rebels, have almost disappeared from the recollection of the people. The war has been a growing war in every sense of the word. It began weak, and has risen strong. It began low, and has risen high. It began narrow, and has become broad. It began with few, and now, behold, the country is full of armed men, ready, with courage and fortitude, to make the wisest and best idea of American statesmanship the law of the land.

Let, then, the war proceed in its strong, high, and broad course till the Rebellion is put down and our country is saved beyond the necessity of being saved again!

I have already hinted at our danger. Let me be a little more direct and pronounced.

The Democratic party, though defeated in the elections last Fall, is still a power. It is the ready organized nucleus of a powerful Pro-Slavery and Pro-Rebel reaction. Though it has lost in numbers, it retains all the elements of its former power and malevolence.

That party has five very strong points in its favor, and its public men and journals know well how to take advantage of them.

First: There is the absence of any deep moral feeling among the loyal people against Slavery itself—their feeling against it being on account of its rebellion against the Government, and not because it is a stupendous crime against human nature.

Secondly: The vast expense of the war and the heavy taxes in money as well as men which the war requires for its prosecution. Loyalty has a strong back, but taxation has often broken it.

Thirdly: The earnest desire for peace which is shared by all classes except Government contractors who are making money out of the war; a feeling which may be kindled to a flame by any serious reverses to our arms. It is silent in victory but vehement and dangerous in defeat.

Fourthly: And superior to all others, is the national prejudice and hatred toward the colored people of the country, a feeling which has done more to encourage the hopes of the Rebels than all other powers beside.

Fifthly: An Abolitionist is an object of popular dislike. The guilty Rebel who with broad blades and bloody hands seeks the life of the nation, is at this hour more acceptable to the northern Democracy than an Abolitionist guilty of no crime. Whatever may be a man's abilities, virtue, or service, the fact that he is an Abolitionist makes him an object of popular hate.

Upon these five strings the Democracy still have hopes of playing themselves into power, and not without reason. While our Government has the meanness to ask Northern colored men to give up the comfort of home, good wages, and personal security, to join the army, endure untold hardships, peril health, limbs and life itself, in its defense, and then degrades them in the eyes of other soldiers, by offering them the paltry sum of $7 per month, and refuses to reward their valor with even the hope of promotion—the Democratic party may well enough presume upon the strength of popular prejudice for support.

While our Republican Government at Washington makes color and not character the criterion of promotion in the army, and degrades colored commissioned officers at New Orleans below the rank to which even the Rebel Government had elevated them, I think we are in danger of a compromise with Slavery.

Our hopeful Republican friends tell me this is impossible—that the day of compromise with Slavery is past. This may do for some men, but it will not do for me.

The Northern people have always been remarkably confident of their own virtue. They are hopeful to the last. Twenty years ago we hoped that Texas could not be annexed; but if that could not be prevented we hoped that she would come in as a Free State. Thirteen years ago we were quite sure that no such abomination as the Fugitive Slave Bill could get itself on our National statute book; but when it got there we were equally sure that it never could be enforced. Four years ago we were sure that the Slave States would not rebel, but if they did we were sure it would be a very short rebellion. I know that times have changed very rapidly, and that we have changed with them. Nevertheless, I know also that we are the same old American people, and that what we have done once we may possibly do again. The leaven of compromise is among us—I repeat, while we have a Democratic party at the North trimming its sails to catch the Southern breeze in the next Presidential election, we are in danger of compromise. Tell me not of amnesties and oaths of allegiance. They are valueless in the presence of twenty hundred millions invested in human flesh. Let but the little finger of Slavery get back into this Union, and in one year you shall see its whole body again upon our backs.

While a respectable colored man or woman can be kicked out of the commonest street car in New York—where any white ruffian may ride unquestioned—we are in danger of a compromise with Slavery. While the North is full of such papers as *The New York World, Express,* and *Herald,* firing the nation's heart with hatred to negroes and Abolitionists, we are in danger of a slaveholding peace. While the major part of all Anti-Slavery profession is based upon devotion to the Union rather than hostility to Slavery, there is danger of a slaveholding peace. Until we shall see the election of November next, and know that it has resulted in the election of a sound Anti-Slavery man as President, we shall be in danger of a slaveholding compromise. Indeed, so long as Slavery has any life left in it, anywhere in the country, we are in danger of such a compromise.

Then there is the danger arising from the impatience of the people on account of the prolongation of the war. I know the American people. They are an impulsive people, impatient of delay, clamorous for change—and often look for results out of all proportion to the means employed in attaining them.

You and I know that the mission of this war is National regeneration. We know and consider that a nation is not born in a day. We know that large bodies move slowly—and often seem to move thus—when, could we perceive their actual velocity, we should be astonished at its greatness. A great battle lost or won is easily described, understood and appreciated, but the moral growth of a great nation requires reflection, as well as observation, to appreciate it. There are vast numbers of voters, who make no account of the moral growth of the nation, and who only look at the war as a calamity to be endured only so long as they have no power to arrest it. Now, this is just the sort of people whose vote may turn the scale against us in the last event.

Thoughts of this kind tell me that there never was a time when Anti-Slavery work was more needed than now. The day that shall see the Rebels at our feet, their weapons flung away, will be the day of trial. We have need to prepare for that trial. We have long been saved a Pro-Slavery peace by the stubborn, unbending persistence of the Rebels. Let them bend as they will bend—there will come the test of our sternest virtues.

I have now given, very briefly, some of the grounds of danger. A word as to the grounds of hope. The best that can be offered is, that we have made progress—vast and striking progress—within the last two years.

President Lincoln introduced his administration to the country as one which would faithfully catch, hold, and return runaway slaves to their masters. He avowed his determination to protect and defend the slaveholder's right to plunder the black laborer of his hard earnings. Europe was assured by Mr. Seward that no slave should gain his freedom by this war. Both the President and the Secretary of State have made progress since then.

Our Generals, at the beginning of the war, were horribly Pro-Slavery. They took to slave-catching and slave-killing like ducks to water. They are now very generally and very earnestly in favor of putting an end to Slavery. Some of them, like Hunter and Butler, because they hate Slavery on its own account, and others, because Slavery is in arms against the Government.

The Rebellion has been a rapid educator. Congress was the first to respond to the instinctive judgment of the people, and fixed the broad brand of its reprobation upon slave-hunting in shoulder-straps. Then came very temperate talk about confiscation, which soon came to be pretty radical talk. Then came propositions for Border-State, gradual, compensated, colonized Emancipation. Then came the threat of a proclamation, and then came the proclamation. Meanwhile the negro had passed along from a loyal spade and pickax to a Springfield rifle.

Hayti and Liberia are recognized, Slavery is humbled in Maryland, threatened in Tennessee, stunned nearly to death in Western Virginia, doomed in Missouri, trembling in Kentucky, and gradually melting away before our arms in the rebellious States.

The hour is one of hope as well as danger. But whatever may come to pass, one thing is clear: The principles involved in the contest, the necessities of both sections of the country, the obvious requirements of the age, and every suggestion of enlightened policy demand the utter extirpation of Slavery from every foot of American soil, and the enfranchisement of the entire colored population of the country. Elsewhere we may find peace, but it will be a hollow and deceitful peace. Elsewhere we may find prosperity, but it will be a transient prosperity. Elsewhere we may find greatness and renown, but if these are based upon anything less substantial than justice they will vanish, for righteousness alone can permanently exalt a nation.

I end where I began—no war but an Abolition war; no peace but an Abolition peace; liberty for all, chains for none; the black man a soldier in war, a laborer in peace; a voter at the South as well as at the North; America his permanent home, and all Americans his fellow-countrymen. Such, fellow-citizens, is my idea of the mission of the war. If accomplished, our glory as a nation will be complete, our peace will flow like a river, and our foundations will be the everlasting rocks.

"PICTURES AND PROGRESS" (1864–65)

During the war Douglass delivered at least four lectures on photography. "Pictures and Progress" is his fullest encapsulation of the links between art and reform, and the importance of photography in ending slavery and uprooting racism.

SOURCE: Frederick Douglass Papers, Library of Congress

In view of the stupendous contest of which this country is now the theatre, this fierce and sanguinary debate between freedom and slavery, between republican institutions and a remorseless oligarchy, upon the decision of which depends for weal or for woe the destiny of this great nation, it may seem almost an impertinence to ask your attention to a lecture on pictures; and yet in this very fact of the all-engrossing character of the war may be found the needed apology for this seeming transgression.

The American people are not remarkable for moderation. They despise halfness. They will go with him who goes farthest and stay with him who stays longest. What the country thinks of half men and half measures is seen by the last election. We repudiate all such men and all such measures. The people said to the Chickahominy hero,[1] "We do abhor and spurn you, and all whose sympathies are like yours"; and to Abraham Lincoln, they say, "Go forward, don't stop where you are, but onward."

This wholeness of American character may be seen in our attention to the war. Intent upon suppressing the rebellion, we have refused to be diverted from that one great object for any cause whatever.

Does Napoleon plant a prince of a detestable family in Mexico?[2] We have but one answer, and that is down with the Rebellion! Does England take advantage of our misfortunes?[3] Our answer is down with the rebellion. Does Brazil assume an unbecoming haughtiness?[4] Our answer is, down with the slaveholding rebellion. Does the tempter at home plead for compromise?[5] Our answer is, sternly, down with the accursed rebellion.

The fact is that the whole thought of the nation during the last four years has been closely and strongly riveted to this one object. Every fact and every phase of this mighty struggle has been made the subject of exhausting discussion. The pulpit, the press, and the platform—political and literary—the street and the fireside, have thought of little else and spoken of little else during all these four long years of battle and blood.

It were easy to commend this almost universal and unceasing thought for the safety of the nation. It is in this deep and heartfelt *solicitude* that the safety of the country is assured.

It may be laid down as an axiom that no man was ever yet lost who seriously thought himself worth saving—and what is true of an individual man the same is true, equally true, of a great nation.

It is said that Nero fiddled when Rome was on fire,[6] and some amongst us have manifested a levity quite as disgraceful and shocking; but the heart of the nation is sound. Those who thought the country not worth saving have found the country entertaining a similar opinion respecting themselves. They are not worth saving, yet we mean to save them by saving the country they would ruin.

It may be assumed, moreover, that this war is now rapidly drawing to its close. The combustible material which caused the explosion is nearly exhausted. It is now seen, even at the South, that cotton is not king, because it has not raised the blockade and given the Confederacy foreign recognition. It is seen too, that slavery, hitherto paramount and priceless, may be less valuable than an army—that the Negro can be more useful as a soldier than as a slave. In all this we see that the rebellion is perishing, not only for the want of men and for the materials and munitions of war, but from a more radical exhaustion—one which touches the vital sources out of which the rebellion sprang.

The people can afford, therefore, to listen for a moment to some other topic. There is no danger of being injuriously diverted from the one grand fact of the hour.

The bow must be unbent occasionally in order to retain its elastic spring and effective power, and the same is true of the mind: A brief excursion in the woods, a change of scene, however trifling, a transient communion with the silent and recuperative forces of nature—the secret sources of pure thought and feeling—constitute an elementary worship, impart tone and vigor to the mind and heart, and enable men to grapple more effectively with the sterner duties and dangers of practical life.

Thoughts that rise from the horrors of the battlefield, like the gloomy exhalations from the dampness and death of the grave, are depressing to the spirit and impair the health. One hour's relief from this intense, oppressive, and heart-aching attention to the issues involved in the war may be of service to all.

The title of my lecture is a very convenient one. It leaves me perfectly free to travel where I list in the realms of thought and experience and to avail myself of any facts and features—any groups or combinations of sentiments, thoughts and ideas from which may be derived either instruction, gratification, or amusement.

The narrowest and shallowest stream from the mountainside may conduct us to the open sea; we have but to go forward to go round the world. No one truth stands alone. Any one truth leads to the boundless realms of all truth: So under the somewhat indefinite title of pictures[7] and by means of pictures, we may be led to the contemplation of great truths—interesting to man in every stage of the journey of life.

Besides, it matters very little what may be the text in these days—man is sure to be the sermon. He is the incarnate wonder of all the ages: and the contemplation of Him is boundless in range and endless in fascination. He is before all books a study—for he is the maker of all books—the essence of all books—the [text] of all books.[8] On earth there is nothing higher than the Human Soul.

Again the books that we write and the speeches that we make—what are they but the extensions, amplifications and shadows of ourselves, the peculiar elements of our individual manhood? Though we read and listen during forty years—it is the same old book and the same old speech, native to the writer's or speaker's heart, and co-extensive with his life—a little shaded by time and events, perhaps, but it is the same old book and speech over again—the pear tree is always a pear tree—and never apple.

Now the speech I was sent into the world to make was an abolition speech. Gough[9] says, whatever may be the subject announced for him the lecture itself is sure to be upon temperance. Sojourner Truth says that she does not speak to tell people what they don't know—but to tell them what she herself knows.

I am somewhat in the condition of Gough—and perhaps also in that of Sojourner Truth.[10] When I come upon the platform the Negro is very apt to come with me. I cannot forget him: and you would not if I did.

Men have an inconvenient habit of reminding each other of the very things they would have them forget.

Wishing to convince me of his entire freedom from the low and vulgar prejudice of color which prevails in this country, a friend of mine once took my arm in New York, saying as he did so—"Frederick, I am not ashamed to walk with you down Broadway." It never once occurred to him that I might for any reason be ashamed to walk with him down Broadway. He managed to remind me that mine was a despised and hated color—and his the orthodox and constitutional one—at the same time he seemed endeavoring to make me forget both. Pardon me if I shall be betrayed into a similar blunder tonight—and shall be found discoursing of Negroes when I should be speaking of pictures.

The saying that happiness depends upon little, not less than upon large things has often encouraged me to speak when otherwise I might have remained silent. And such is the case now. As I cannot bring before you the fruits of deep and thorough culture—which the more favored lecturers are able to do—I am encouraged to present such small things—large to me, small to you, as I have in store such facts, such fancies, such flowers, per chance such reveries—such dreams, images, ideas, and pictures—such earnest outlook into the ever-tempting invisible, unfathomable, and unknown—as have touched my spirit in passing along the mysterious journey of life—may occasionally show themselves in what I have here to say of pictures.

In doing this, hold me to no logical arrangement. I shall probably leave my picture base of supplies about as far in the rear as Sherman left his when he turned his back upon Atlanta for the Atlantic.[11] The most I can promise is that you shall in case of need subsist upon the country through which we pass.

Movement is sometimes the chief end of movement. A trip down the Hudson pays better than a sight of New York. A view from the mountain is more than the mountain. It is not the apex upon which we stand, but the vast and glorious expanse that awes and thrills us.

Our age gets very little credit for poetry or music or indeed for art in any of its branches. It is commonly and often scornfully denominated the age of money, merchandise, and politics, a metallic, utilitarian, dollar-worshipping age; insensible to the song of birds and perfume of flowers: An age which can see nothing in the grand old woods, but timber for ships and cities—nothing in the waterfall but mill power, nothing in the landscape but cotton, corn and cattle; dead alike to the poetic charms both of nature and of art.

That there is much in the tendency of the times to justify this sweeping condemnation, it is needless to deny, and yet, for nothing is this age more remarkable than for the multitude, variety, perfection, and cheapness of its pictures. Indeed the passion for art was never more active and never more productive. The art of today differs from that of other ages, however, only as the education of today differs from that of other ages; only as the printing press of modern times, turning off ten thousand sheets an hour, differs from the tedious and laborious processes by which the earlier thoughts of men were saved from oblivion.

The great discoverer of modern times, to whom coming generations will award special homage, will be Daguerre. Morse has brought the ends of the earth together and Daguerre has made it a picture gallery.[12] We have pictures, true pictures, of every object which can interest us. The aspiration of Burns is now realized.

Men of all conditions and classes can now see themselves as others see them, and as they will be seen by those [who] shall come after them.[13] What was once the special and exclusive luxury of the rich and great is now the privilege of all. The humblest servant girl may now possess a picture of herself such as the wealth of kings could not purchase fifty years ago.[14]

The progress of science has not been more logical than that of art. Both have grown with the increasing wants of men. Franklin brought down the lightning, Morse made it a bearer of dispatches, and in answer to the increasing human demands of progressive human nature, Daguerre has taught the god of day to deck the world with pictures far beyond the art of ancient masters.

As knowledge has left the cloister, pouring itself through the iron gates of the printing press, so art has left the studio for new instruments of expression and multiplication.

Steam has shortened the distance across the ocean, but a voyage is unnecessary to look at Europe. We can see Paris without the steamship, and St. Peters without visiting Rome. You have but to cross the parlor to see both, and with them all the wonders of European architecture, which by the way is about all that the traveler sees abroad that he could not see at home.

That Daguerre has supplied a deep-seated want of human nature is seen less in the eulogies bestowed upon his name than in the universal appropriation of his discovery. The smallest town now has its picture gallery, and even where the roads cross, where stands but a solitary blacksmith shop and a deserted country tavern, there also stands the inevitable gallery—painted yellow, perched upon gutta percha springs, ready to move in any direction, wherever men have the face to have their pictures taken. The farmer boy can get a picture for himself and a shoe for his horse at the same time, and for the same price. The facilities for travelling has sent the world abroad, and the ease with which we get our pictures has brought us all within range of the daguerreian apparatus.

Among the good things growing out of this pictorial abundance, modest distrust of our personal appearance is not greatly distinguished. No one hesitates on account of this sentiment to commit himself to posterity: for a man's picture, however homely, will, like himself, find somebody to admire it. No man contemplates his face in a glass without seeing something to admire. But for this natural self-complacency, the stern severity of the photographic art would repel rather than attract.

A man is ashamed of seeming to be vain of his personal appearance, and yet who ever stood before a glass preparing to sit or stand for a picture without a consciousness of some such vanity?

A man who peddles a patent medicine, writes a book, or does anything out of the common way, may, if he does not give his picture to the public, lay claim to singular modesty. But it so happens that nobody thinks of such an omission.

It is not, however, of such pictures as already intimated that I am here to speak. A wider and grander field of thought lies open before us.

The nature of my discourse is already indicated. What I have said in respect to the character of lectures generally will apply to my own: namely, whatever may be the text, man is sure to be the sermon.

Man, however, is a many-sided being, and the subject I have chosen treats of his best and most interesting side; it is his dreamy, clairvoyant, poetic, intellectual, and shadowy side; the side of religion, music, mystery and passion, wherein illusions take the form of solid reality and shadows get themselves recognized as substance: the side which is better pleased with feeling than reason, with fancies than with facts, with things as they seem, than things as they are, with contemplation rather than action, with thought rather than work.

I have no learned theory of art to present, no rules of wise criticism to explain or enforce, no great pictures to admire, no distinguished artists, ancient or modern, to commend. I bring to the work before me only the eye and thought of a lay man.

It is objected that the crowd, of which I am one, knows nothing of art. The objection is well taken. It however should have only the same weight and application to pictures, where applied, as to poetry and music, for to the eye and spirit, pictures are just what poetry and music are to the ear and heart. One may enjoy all the pleasant sensations arising from the concord of sweet sounds without understanding the subtle principles of music, and the skillful arrangement by which those delightful sensations are produced.

But my discourse has more to do with the philosophy of art than with art itself, with its source, range and influence than with its facts and perfections—with the soul, rather than the body, with the silence of music, rather than sound, and with the ideal forms of excellence floating before the eye of the spirit, rather than with those displayed upon dull canvass.

Man is the only picture-making animal in the world. He alone of all the inhabitants of earth has the capacity and passion for pictures.

Reason is exalted and called Godlike, and sometimes accorded the highest place among human faculties; but grand and wonderful as is this attribute of our species, still more grand and wonderful are the resources and achievements of that power out of which come our pictures and other creations of art.

Reason is said to be not the exclusive possession of men. Dogs and elephants are said to possess it. Ingenious arguments have been framed in support of this claim for the brutes. But no such claim, I believe, has been set up for imagination: This sublime, prophetic, and all-creative power of the human soul—proving its kinship with the eternal sources of life and creation—is the peculiar possession and glory of man.

For man, and for man alone, all nature is richly studded with the material of art. Not only the outside world, but the inside soul may be described as a picture gallery, a magnificent panorama in which things of time and things of eternity are silently portrayed. Within as without there are beautiful thought valleys, varied and far-reaching landscapes, abounding in all the interesting and striking forms and features of external nature. Mountains, plains, rivers, lakes, oceans, woods, waterfalls, outstanding headlands and precipitous rocks have their delightful shadows painted in the soul.

This full identity of man with nature, this affinity for, and this relation to all forms, colors, sounds and movements of external nature that finds music in the slightest whisper of the zephyr-stirred leaf, and in the roaring torrent deep and wild; this all embracing and all sympathizing quality, which everywhere matches the real with the artificial—which endears substances because of its shadow—is our chief distinction from all other beings on earth and the source of our greatest achievements.

A certain class of ethnologists and archeologists, more numerous in our country a few years ago than now and more numerous now than they ought to be and will be when slavery shall have no further need of them, profess some difficulty in finding a fixed, unvarying, and definite line separating what they are pleased to call the lowest variety of our species, always meaning the Negro, from the highest animal.[15]

To all such scientific cavilers, I commend the fact that man is everywhere a picture-making animal, and the only picture-making animal in the world.[16] The rudest and remotest tribes of men manifest this great human power—and thus vindicate the brotherhood of man. All have some idea of tracing definite lines and imitating the forms and colors of things as they appear about them.

Hand in hand, this picture-making power accompanies religion, supplying man with his God, peopling the silent continents of eternity with saints, angels, and fallen spirits, the blest and the blasted, making manifest the invisible, and giving form and body to all that the soul can hope and fear in life and in death.

Humboldt tells of savage tribes of men, remote from commerce and civilization, who nevertheless had coats and other garments, after European patterns, painted on their skin.[17] They no doubt thought themselves very comfortably and very elegantly dressed. The painted coat was a real coat to the savage, and will be 'til latitude and temperature, or some other source of knowledge, shall make him wiser. Until then, let him enjoy his delightful illusion, even as more enlightened men enjoy theirs.

The savage is not the only man nor is savage society the only society dressed out in a painted coat and other habiliments. Examples are all around us. Church and state, religion and patriotism, refinement and learning, manners and morals, all have their counterfeit presentments in paint. You often meet coarse and vulgar persons dressed in the painted appearance of ladies and gentlemen—a slight touch removes the paint and discloses their true character and the class to which they belong. But this is [a] digression.

The unalloyed creations of imagination, conscious of no contradiction, no deception, are solid and flinty realities to the soul. Granite and iron are not more real supports to things material than are those to the subtle architecture of the mind.

"Among eminent persons," says *Emerson*, "those who are most dear to men are not of the class which the economist calls producers: they have nothing in their hands; they have not cultivated corn, nor made bread; they have not led out a colony nor invented a loom. A higher class, in the estimation of this city-building, market-going race of mankind, are the poets, who, from the intellectual kingdom, feed the thought and imagination with ideas and pictures."[18]

This statement of the Concord philosopher is but the repetition or amplification of that of Scripture: "Men do not live by bread alone."[19] It affirms that to be happy is more than to be rich—and that happiness results less from external conditions than from internal exercises. Leaning upon this inner staff of the soul, John Brown went to the gallows as serenely as other men go to church on Sunday morning. He [endured by] seeing the angel with his crown of glory—saying come up higher.[20] With the same support too, the martyr John Huss could shout amid the blazing faggots.[21]

In youth this unreal, apparent, unlimited and shadowy side of our nature, full of faith and poetry—so insubstantial and yet so strong—gilds all our earthly future with bright and glorious visions, and in age and in sickness and in death paves the streets of our paradise with gold and sets all its opening gates with pearls.[22]

It is from this side of his nature that man derives his chief and most lasting happiness. There is no measure for the depth and purity of the happiness that childhood feels in [the] presence of pictures, symbol and song! Among all the soul-awakening powers to which our nature is susceptible, there are none greater than these. A little child in rapt contemplation of a work of art is itself a delightful picture—full of promise both to the child and to the world.

What is the secret of this childhood pleasure in pictures? What power is it that rivets attention to the speechless paint? The great poet explains for us. In certain conditions of the mind, men may

find tongues in trees, books in the running brooks,
Sermons in stones, and good in everything.[23]

This truth childhood realizes in all its fullness and beauty. Could the joy imparted by the contemplation of pictures be analyzed, it would be found to consist mainly in [the] self tenfold much, a gratification of the innate desire for self-knowledge with which every human soul is more or less largely endowed. Art is a special revelation of the higher powers of the human soul. There is in the contemplation of it an unconscious comparison constantly going on in the mind, of the pure forms of beauty and excellence, which are without to those which are within, and native to the human heart.[24]

It is a process of soul-awakening self-revelation, a species of new birth, for a new life springs up in the soul with every newly discovered agency, by which the soul is brought into a more intimate knowledge of its own Divine powers and perfections, and is lifted to a higher level of wisdom, goodness, and joy.

The savage, accustomed only to the wild and discordant war whoop of his tribe, whose only music comes to him from winds, waterfalls, and the weird sounds of the pathless forest, discovers a new place in his heart, a purer and deeper depth in his soul, the first time his ear is saluted by the divine harmonies of scientific music.

To know man civilized we must study him as a savage.

We are all savages in childhood. And men, we are told, are only children of a larger growth. The life of society is analogous to the life of individual men. It passes through the same gradations of progress. California was not Massachusetts at the first and is not now. She was savage even in the manifestation of her justice. Not that which is spiritual is first, but that which is natural. After that, that which is spiritual.

The sound of a common hand organ in the new streets of San Francisco caused tears to roll down the cheeks of the sun-burnt miners. As are songs to the savage, so are pictures to the boy. They are his earliest and most effective teachers. All the pictures in the book are known before a single lesson is learned. The great teacher of Galilee only uttered a truth deep down in nature, when he opened the Kingdom of heaven only to those who came as little children.

To the flinty-hearted materialists, insensible to ought but dull facts, to the miser, whose every thought is gold, to the [weak], whose every impulse is sensual, pictures like flowers have no voice and impart no joy. Theirs is the ministry of youth and self-forgetfulness. They come oftenest and stay longest when the morning sun is just disclosing the mountain peaks leaning against the distant sky.

In the valley, on the hillside, in distant groves, where cloud-flung shadows sweep the green fields in noiseless majesty, far away from the hum and din of town and city, the boy of ten, yet unconscious of spot or blemish, forgetful of time and place, indifferent alike to books and sport, looks up with silence and awe to the blue overhanging sky, and views with dreamy wonder its ever-drifting drapery, tracing in the clouds themselves and in their ever-changing forms and colors colossal figures, mighty men of war, great cities dotted about with vast temples of justice and religion, adorned with domes and steeples, towers and turrets, and sees mighty ships sailing in grandeur around the hollow firmament: break in if you must upon the prayers of monks or nuns, or upon any of the pomp and show of fashionable worship—but here is a devotion which it were sacrilege to disturb.

At this altar man unfolds to himself the divinest of human faculties—for such is the picture-conceiving and the picture-producing faculty or power of the human soul. This devotion is the prelude to the vision and transfiguration, qualifying men and women for the sacred ministry of life. He who has not borne some such fruits—[has not] had some such experiences in child[hood], gives us only barrenness in age.

I have said that man is a picture-making and a picture-appreciating animal, and have cited that fact as the most important line of distinction between him and all others. The point will bear additional emphasis.

The process by which man is able to posit his own subjective nature outside of himself, giving it form, color, space, and all the attributes of distinct personality, so that it becomes the subject of distinct observation and contemplation, is at [the] bottom of all effort and the germinating principles of all reform and all progress. But for this, the history of the beast of the field would be the history of man. It is the picture of life contrasted with the fact of life, the ideal contrasted with the real, which makes criticism possible. Where there is no criticism there is no progress, for the want of progress is not felt where such want is not made visible by criticism. It is by looking upon this picture and upon that which enables us to point out the defects of the one and the perfections of the other.

Poets, prophets, and reformers are all picture-makers—and this ability is the secret of their power and of their achievements. They see what ought to be by the reflection of what is, and endeavor to remove the contradiction.[25]

We can criticize the characters and actions of men about us because we can see them outside of ourselves, and [can] compare them one with another. But self-criticism, out of which comes the highest attainments of human excellence, arises out of the power we possess of making ourselves objective to ourselves—[we] can see our interior selves as distinct personalities, as though looking in a glass.

Men drunk have been heard addressing themselves—as if speaking to a second person—exposing their faults and exhorting themselves to a higher and better life.

It is said that the best gifts are most abused and this among the rest. Be it so. Conscience itself is often misdirected—shocked at delightful sounds, beautiful colors, and graceful movements, yet smiles at persecution, sleeps amid the agonies of war and slavery, hangs a witch, burns an heretic, and drenches a continent in blood!

This picture-making faculty is flung out into the world like all others, capable of being harnessed to the car of truth or error: It is a vast power to whatever cause it is coupled. For the habit we adopt, the master we obey, in making our subjective nature objective, giving it form, color, space, action and utterance, is the one important thing to ourselves and our surroundings. It will either lift us to the highest heaven or sink us to the lowest depths, for good and evil know no limits.

Once fully started in the direction of evil, man runs with ever-increasing speed, a child in the darkness, frightened onward by the distant echoes of his own footfalls.

The work of the revivalist is more than half done when he has once got a man to stand up in the congregation as evidence of his need of religion. The strength of an iron halter was needed for this first act, but now like Rarey's horse he may be led by a straw.[26]

All wishes, all aspirations, all hopes, all fears, all doubts, all determinations grow stronger by action and utterance, by being rendered objective.

Of all our religious denominations, the Roman Catholic understand this picture passion of man's nature best. It addresses the religious consciousness in its own language: the child language of the soul.

Pictures, images, and other symbolical representations speak the language of religion. The mighty fortress of the human heart silently withstands the rifled cannon of reason, but its walls tremble when brought under the magic power of mystery.

Remove from the church of Rome her cunning illusions, her sacred altars, her glowing pictures, her speaking images, her tapers, miters, incense, her solemn pomp and gorgeous ceremonies, the mere outward shows and signs of things fancied or real, and her magical and entrancing power over men would disappear. Take the cross from before the name of the archbishop, and he will stand before the world as James or John like the rest of us.

Protestantism pays less deference to this natural language of religion. It relies more upon words and actions than upon paints and chisels to give form and body to its sentiments and ideas. Nevertheless, her most successful teachers and preachers are painters, and succeed because they are such. Dry logic and elaborate arguments, though knitted as a coat of mail, linked and interlinked, perfect in all their appointments, lay down the law as empty benches.

But he who speaks to the feelings, who enters the soul's deepest meditations, holding the mirror up to nature, revealing the profoundest mysteries of the heart by the magic power of action and utterance to the eye and ear, will be sure of an audience.

The few think, the many feel. The few comprehend a principle, the many require illustration. The few lead, the many follow. The dignified few are shocked by Mr. Lincoln's homely comparisons and quaint stories, but the many like them and elect him president.

There is our national flag: a grand national picture: the glorious red white and blue: nothing of itself but everything for what it represents. We search the woods and bring out the tallest spar: raise our banner, give it ample folds to the breeze, its glorious stars to the sky, and hail with a shout that general who orders to be shot the first man who pulls down that flag. When the hands of Joshua were held up Israel prevailed, when the horns were blown the walls of Jericho fell, and when the flag of the union is borne aloft the country is safe from its foes. The ancient and modern emblems serve the same purpose: nothing in themselves, but everything in what they signify. They speak to the feeling by every mystic fascination.

But feeling and mystery are not the only elements of successful painting, whether of the voice, pen, or brush. Truth is the soul of art, as of all things else. No man can have [a] permanent hold upon his fellows by means of falsehood. "Paint me as I am," said Cromwell,[27] and such is the voice of nature everywhere, when nature is allowed to be natural. Better remain dumb than letter a falsehood—better repeat the old truth forever, than to spin out a pure fiction.

Nevertheless, with the clear perception of things as they are, must stand the faithful rendering of things as they seem. The dead fact is nothing without the living expression. Niagara is not fitly described when said to be a river of this or that volume falling two hundred feet over a ledge of rocks; nor is thunder when simply called a loud noise or a jarring sound. This is truth but truth disrobed of its sublimity and glory: a kind of frozen truth, destitute of motion itself and incapable of exciting emotion in others.

But on the other hand, to give us the glory without some glimpse of the glorified object is a still greater transgression, and makes those who do it as him who beateth the air. The looker and the listener are alike repelled by any straining after effect.

We have learned nothing higher in the art of speech since Shakspeare wrote, "Suit the action to the word, and overstep not the modesty of nature."[28]

Whether we read Shakspeare or look at Hogarth's pictures,

we commune alike with nature and have human beings for society.[29] They are of the earth and speak to us in a known tongue. They are neither angels nor demons, but in their possibilities both. We see in them not only men and women, but ourselves.

The great philosophical truth now to be learned and applied is that man is limited by manhood. He cannot get higher than human nature, even in his conceptions. Laws, religion, morals, manners, and art are but the expressions of manhood, and begin and end in man. As he is enlightened or ignorant, as he is rude or refined, as he is exalted or degraded, so are his laws, religion, morals, manners—and everything else pertaining to him.

"OUR MARTYRED PRESIDENT" (1865)

In this impromptu address at city hall in Rochester on the day Lincoln died, Douglass describes how the assassination would unite black and white Northerners, "making us kin" by creating an interracial national family.

SOURCE: *Rochester Democrat and American*, April 17, 1865

Mayor Moore[1] *and Fellow Citizens:* This call to address you on this occasion was quite unexpected to me, and one to which I find it almost impossible to respond. If you have deep grief in the death of Abraham Lincoln,[2] and feel in it a severe stab at Republican institutions, I feel it on all these accounts and more. I feel it as a personal as well as national calamity; on account of the race to which I belong and the deep interest which that good man ever took in its elevation. This is not an occasion for speech making, but for silence. I have scarcely been able to say a word to any of those friends who have taken my hand and looked sadly in my eyes to-day. A dreadful disaster has befallen the nation. It is a day for silence and meditation; for grief and tears. Yet I feel that though Abraham Lincoln dies, the Republic lives; (cheers;) though that great and good man, one of the noblest men [to] trod God's earth, (applause,) is struck down by the hand of the assassin, yet I know that the nation is saved and liberty established forever. (Loud applause.) The human mind naturally turns from a calamity like this, and endeavors, through its tears and anguish, to catch some gleam of hope—some good that may be born of the tremendous evil. And I think it is not inconsistent with this tearful occasion to discover through the blinding mists that rise from this yawning gulf, the beautiful bow of promise spanning the gloom and giving hope to all. (Applause.)

Only the other day, it seemed as if this nation were in danger of losing a just appreciation of the awful crimes of this rebellion. We were manifesting almost as much gratitude to Gen. Lee for surrendering as to Gen. Grant for compelling him to surrender! (Cheers.) It seemed to me that Gen. Lee was about the most popular man in America. (Applause and laughter.) The crimes of treason and slavery were [line obliterated] amnesty and oblivion in behalf of men whose hands are red with the best blood of the land. (Loud cheers.) Republics have proverbially short memories. I was afraid the American people were growing weak. It may be in the inscrutable wisdom of Him who controls the destinies of Nations, that this drawing of the Nation's most precious heart's blood was necessary to bring us back to that equilibrium which we must maintain if the Republic was to be permanently redeemed. (Applause.)

How I have to-day mourned for our noble President, I dare not attempt to tell. It was only a few weeks ago that I shook his brave, honest hand,[3] and looked into his gentle eye and heard his kindly voice uttering those memorable words—words which will live immortal in history, and be read with increasing admiration from age to age:

Fondly do we hope, fervently do we pray that this mighty scourge of war may speedily pass away. Yet if God will that it continue until all the wealth piled by the bondman's two hundred and fifty years of unrequited toil shall be sunk, and until every drop of blood drawn by the lash shall be paid by another, drawn with the sword, as was said three thousand years ago, so still must it be said, that the judgments of the Lord are righteous altogether. (Long continued applause.)

Brave good words are those; and I think, with Dr. Robinson, that if treason expects to gain anything by this hell-black assassination, it will be awfully disappointed.[4] To-day, to-day as never before this North is a unit! (Great applause.) To-day, to-day as never before, the American people, although they know they cannot have indemnity for the past—for the countless treasure and the precious blood—yet they resolve to-day that they will exact ample security for the future! (Cheers.) And if it teaches us this lesson, it may be that the blood of our beloved martyred President will be the salvation of our country. Good man we call him; good man he was. If "an honest man is the noblest work of God,"[5] we need have no fear for the soul of Abraham Lincoln. (Applause.)

This new demonstration of the guilt of slavery, teaches another lesson. Hereafter we must not despise any hand or any arm that has been uplifted in defence of the Nation's life. Let us not be in too much haste in the work of restoration. Let us not be in a hurry to clasp to our bosom that spirit which gave birth to Booth. When we take to our arms again, as brethren, our Southern foes, let us see to it that we take also our Southern friends. (Cheers.) Let us not forget that justice to the negro is safety to the Nation. When the tall heads[?] of this Rebellion are swept off (as they will be) (applause), in their tracks will spring up another race, their luckless sons, to whom the wretched traitors will bequeath some infernal passions like that which has caused our great bereavement. By their hand other officers of the government will be stricken down. Where is our remedy? It is here: know no man hereafter in all these States[?] by his complexion, but know every man by his loyalty (cheers), and wherever there is a patriot in the North or South, white or black, helping on the good cause, hail him as a citizen, a kinsman, a clansman, a brother beloved! (Great applause.) Let us not remember our enemies and disenfranchise our friends. The black man will not only run everywhere to bring us information and to warn us of dangerous plots, through marsh and fen and forest, will not only bear exposure and privation, and lead and feed our fugitive prisoners, and bind up their wounded feet, sheltering them by day and piloting them in the darkness, will not only build for you ramparts of earth and solid stone, but they offer you ramparts of flesh, and fight the battles of the nation amid contumely and persecution. (Cheers.) For the safety of all, let justice be done to each. I thank you, gentlemen, for the privilege of mingling my sorrows and hopes with yours on this memorable occasion.

"THE FREEDMEN'S MONUMENT TO ABRAHAM LINCOLN" (1876)

In this speech, delivered at the unveiling of the Freedmen's Monument at Lincoln Park in Washington, D.C., before the nation's leading statesmen, Douglass provides the most eloquent and nuanced assessment of Lincoln's legacy in the nineteenth century.

SOURCE: *Washington National Republican*, April 15, 1876

FRIENDS AND FELLOW CITIZENS: I warmly congratulate you upon the highly interesting object which has caused you to assemble in such numbers and spirit as you have to-day. This occasion is in some respects remarkable. Wise and thoughtful men of our race, who shall come after us, and study the lessons of our history in the United States, who shall survey the long and dreary space over which we have traveled, who shall count the links in the great chain of events by which we have reached our present position, will make a note of this occasion—they will think of it, and with a sense of manly pride and complacency. I congratulate you also upon the very favorable circumstances in which we meet to-day. They are high, inspiring and uncommon. They lend grace, glory and significance to the object for which we have met. Nowhere else in this great country, with its uncounted towns and cities, uncounted wealth, and immeasurable territory extending from sea to sea, could conditions be found more favorable to the success of this occasion than here. We stand to-day at the national centre to perform something like a national act, an act which is to go into history, and we are here where every pulsation of the national heart can be heard, felt and reciprocated.

A THOUSAND WIRES,

fed with thought and winged with lightning, put us in instantaneous communication with the loyal and true men all over this country. Few facts could better illustrate the vast and wonderful change which has taken place in our condition as a people, than the fact of our assembling here for the purpose we have to-day. Harmless, beautiful, proper and praiseworthy as this demonstration is, I cannot forget that no such demonstration would have been tolerated here twenty years ago. The spirit of slavery and barbarism, which still lingers to blight and destroy in some dark and distant parts of our country, would have made our assembling here to-day the signal and excuse for opening upon us all the floodgates of wrath and violence. That we are here in peace to-day is a compliment and credit to American civilization, and a prophecy of still greater national enlightenment and progress in the future. I refer to the past not in malice, for this is no day for malice, but simply to place more distinctly in front the gratifying and glorious change which has come both to our white fellow-citizens and ourselves, and to congratulate all upon the contrast between now and then, the new dispensation of freedom with its thousand blessings to both races, and the old dispensation of slavery with its ten thousand evils to both races—white and black. In view then, of the past, the present and the future, with

THE LONG AND DARK HISTORY

of our bondage behind us, and with liberty, progress and enlightenment before us, I again congratulate you upon this auspicious day and hour.

Friends and fellow-citizens: The story of our presence here is soon and easily told. We are here in the District of Columbia;

here in the city of Washington, the most luminous point of American territory—a city recently transformed and made beautiful in its body and in its spirit; we are here, in the place where the ablest and best men of the country are sent to devise the policy, enact the laws and shape the destiny of the Republic; we are here, with the stately pillars and majestic dome of the Capitol of the nation looking down upon us; we are here, with the broad earth freshly adorned with the foliage and flowers of spring for our church, and all races, colors and conditions of men for our congregation; in a word, we are here to express, as best we may, by appropriate forms and ceremonies, our grateful sense of the vast, high and pre-eminent services rendered to ourselves, to our race, to our country and to the whole world

BY ABRAHAM LINCOLN.

The sentiment that brings us here to-day is one of the noblest that can stir and thrill the human heart. It has crowned and made glorious the high places of all civilized nations, with the grandest and most enduring works of art, designed to illustrate characters and perpetuate the memories of great public men. It is the sentiment which from year to year adorns with fragrant and beautiful flowers the graves of our loyal, brave, and patriotic soldiers who fell in defense of the Union and liberty. It is the sentiment of gratitude and appreciation, which often, in the presence of many who hear me, has filled yonder heights of Arlington with the eloquence of eulogy and the sublime enthusiasm of poetry and song; a sentiment which can never die while the Republic lives. For the first time in the history of our people, and in the history of the whole American people, we join in this high worship and march conspicuously in the line of this time-honored custom. First things are always interesting, and this is one of our first things. It is the first time that, in this form and manner, we have sought to do honor to any American great man, however deserving and illustrious. I commend the fact to notice. Let it be told in every part of the Republic; let men of all parties and opinions hear it; let those who despise us, not less than those who respect us, know that now and here, in the spirit of

LIBERTY, LOYALTY, AND GRATITUDE,

let it be known everywhere and by everybody who takes an interest in human progress and in the amelioration of the condition of mankind, that in the presence and with the approval of the members of the American House of Representatives, reflecting the general sentiment of the country; that in the presence of that august body, the American Senate, representing the highest intelligence and the calmest judgment of the country; in presence of the Supreme Court and Chief Justice of the United States, to whose decisions we all patriotically bow; in the presence and under the steady eye of the honored and trusted President of the United States, we, the colored people, newly emancipated and rejoicing in our blood-bought freedom, near the close of the first century in the life of this Republic, have now and here unveiled, set apart, and dedicated a monument of enduring granite and bronze, in every line, feature, and figure of which the men of this generation may read—and those of after-coming generations may read—something of the exalted character and great works of Abraham Lincoln, the first martyr President of the United States.

Fellow citizens: In what we have said and done to-day, and in what we may say and do hereafter, we disclaim everything like

ARROGANCE AND ASSUMPTION.

We claim for ourselves no superior devotion to the character, history and memory of the illustrious name whose monument we have here dedicated to-day. We fully comprehend the relation of Abraham Lincoln, both to ourselves and the white people of the United States. Truth is proper and beautiful at all times and in all places, and it is never more proper and beautiful in any case than when speaking of a great public man whose example is likely to be commended for honor and imitation long after his departure to the solemn shades, the silent continents of eternity. It must be admitted, truth compels me to admit even here in the presence of the monument we have erected to his memory, Abraham Lincoln was not, in the fullest sense of the word, either our man or our model. In his interests, in his associations, in his habits of thought, and in his prejudices, he was a white man. He was preeminently the white man's President, entirely devoted to the welfare of white men. He was ready and willing at any time during the last years of his administration to deny, postpone and sacrifice the rights of humanity in the colored people, to promote the welfare of the white people of his country. In all his education and feelings he was an

AMERICAN OF THE AMERICANS.

He came into the Presidential chair upon one principle alone, namely, opposition to the extension of slavery. His arguments in furtherance of this policy had their motive and mainspring in his patriotic devotion to the interest of his own race. To protect, defend and perpetuate slavery in the States where it existed, Abraham Lincoln was not less ready than any other President to draw the sword of the nation. He was ready to execute all the supposed constitutional guarantees of the Constitution in favor of the slave system anywhere inside the Slave States. He was willing to pursue, recapture, and send back the fugitive slave to his master, and to suppress a slave rising for liberty, though his guilty masters were already in arms against the Government. The race to which we belong were not the special objects of his consideration. Knowing this, I concede to you, my white fellow-citizens, a pre-eminence in this worship at once full and supreme. First, midst and last you and yours were the object of his deepest affection and his most earnest solicitude.

YOU ARE THE CHILDREN

of Abraham Lincoln. We are at best only his step-children, children by adoption, children by force of circumstances and necessity. To you it especially belongs to sound his praises, to preserve and perpetuate his memory, to multiply his statues, to hang his pictures on your walls, and commend his example, for to you he was a great and glorious friend and benefactor. Instead of supplanting you at this altar we would exhort you to build high his monuments; let them be of the most costly material, of the most costly workmanship; let their forms be symmetrical, beautiful and perfect; let their bases be upon solid rocks, and their summits lean against the unchanging blue overhanging sky, and let them endure forever! But while in the abundance of your wealth and in the fullness of your just and patriotic devotion you do all this, we entreat you to despise not the humble offering we this day unveil to view: for while Abraham Lincoln saved for you a country, he delivered us from a bondage, according to Jefferson, one hour of which was worse than ages of the oppression your fathers rose in rebellion to oppose.

Fellow-citizens: Ours is a new-born zeal and devotion, a thing of the hour. The name of Abraham Lincoln was

NEAR AND DEAR TO OUR HEARTS

in the darkest and most perilous hours of the Republic. We were no more ashamed of him when shrouded in clouds of darkness, of doubt and defeat than when crowned with victory, honor and glory. Our faith in him was often taxed and strained to the uttermost, but it never failed. When he tarried long in the mountain; when he strangely told us that we were the cause of the war;[1] when he still more strangely told us to leave the land in which we were born; when he refused to employ our arms in defense of the Union; when, after accepting our services as colored soldiers, he refused to retaliate when we were murdered as colored prisoners; when he told us he would save the Union if he could with slavery; when he revoked the proclamation of emancipation of General Frémont; when he refused to remove the commander of the Army of the Potomac, who was more zealous in his efforts to protect slavery than suppress rebellion; when we saw this, and more, we were at times stunned, grieved and greatly bewildered; but our hearts believed while

THEY ACHED AND BLED.

Nor was this, even at that time, a blind and unreasoning superstition. Despite the mist and haze that surrounded him; despite the tumult, the hurry and confusion of the hour, we were able to take a comprehensive view of Abraham Lincoln, and to make reasonable allowance for the circumstances of his position. We saw him, measured him, and estimated him; not by stray utterances to injudicious and tedious delegations, who often tried his patience; not by isolated facts torn from their connection; not by any partial and imperfect glimpses, caught at inopportune moments; but by a broad survey, in the light of the stern logic of great events—and in view of that divinity which shapes our ends, rough hew them as we will, we came to the conclusion that the hour and the man of our redemption had met in the person of Abraham Lincoln. It mattered little to us what language he might employ upon special occasions; it mattered little to us, when we fully knew him, whether he was swift or slow in his movements; it was enough for us that Abraham Lincoln was at the head of a great movement, and was in living and earnest sympathy with that movement; which, in the nature of things, must go on

TILL SLAVERY SHOULD BE UTTERLY

and forever abolished in the United States. When, therefore, it shall be asked what we have to do with the memory of Abraham Lincoln, or what Abraham Lincoln had to do with us, the answer is ready, full and complete. Though he loved Caesar less than Rome,[2] though the Union was more to him than our freedom or our future, under his wise and beneficent rule we saw ourselves gradually lifted from the depths of slavery to the heights of liberty and manhood; under his wise and beneficent rule, and by measures approved and vigorously pressed by him, we saw that the handwriting of ages, in the form of prejudice and proscription, was rapidly fading away from the face of our whole country; under his rule, and in due time, about as soon after all as the country could tolerate the strange spectacle, we saw our brave sons and brothers laying off the rags of bondage, and being clothed all over in the blue uniforms of the soldiers of the United States; under his rule we saw two hundred thousand of our dark and dusky people responding to the call of Abraham Lincoln, and, with muskets on their shoulders and eagles on their buttons, timing their high footsteps to liberty and union under the national flag; under his rule we saw the independence of the black Republic of Hayti, the special object of slaveholding aversion and horror fully recognized, and her minister, a colored gentleman, duly received here in the city of Washington; under his rule we saw

THE INTERNAL SLAVE TRADE

which so long disgraced the nation abolished, and slavery abolished in the District of Columbia;[3] under his rule we saw for the first time the law enforced against the foreign slave trade and the first slave-trader hanged,[4] like any other pirate or murderer; under his rule and his inspiration we saw the Confederate States, based upon the idea that our race must be slaves, and slaves forever, battered to pieces and scattered to the four winds; under his rule, and in the fullness of time, we saw Abraham Lincoln, after giving the slaveholders three months of grace in which to save their hateful slave system, penning the immortal paper which, though special in its language, was general in its principles and effect, making slavery forever impossible in the United States. Though we waited long, we saw all this and more.

Can any colored man, or any white man friendly to the freedom of all men, ever forget the night which followed the first day of January, 1863? When the world was to see if Abraham Lincoln would prove to be as good as his word? I shall never forget that memorable night, when in a distant city I waited and watched at a public meeting, with three thousand others not less anxious than myself, for the word of deliverance which we have heard read to-day. Nor shall I ever forget the outburst of joy and thanksgiving that rent the air when the lightning brought to us the emancipation. In that happy hour we forgot all delay, and forgot all tardiness, forgot that the President had bribed the rebels to lay down their arms by a promise to withhold the bolt which would smite the slave system with destruction; and we were thenceforward willing to allow the President all the latitude of time, phraseology, and every honorable device that statesmanship might require for the achievement of a great and beneficent measure of liberty and progress.

Fellow-citizens, there is little necessity on this occasion to speak at length and critically of this great and good man, and of his high mission in the world. That ground has been fully occupied and completely covered both here and elsewhere. The whole field of fact and fancy has been gleaned and garnered. Any man can say things that are true of Abraham Lincoln, but no man can say anything new of Abraham Lincoln. His personal traits and public acts are better known to the American people than are those of any other man of his age. He was a mystery to no man who saw him and heard him. Though high in position, the humblest could approach him and feel at home in his presence. Though deep, he was transparent; though strong, he was gentle; though decided and pronounced in his convictions, he was tolerant towards those who differed from him, and patient under reproaches.

Even those who only knew him through his public utterances obtained a tolerably clear idea of his character and his personality. The image of the man went out with his words, and those who read him knew him. I have said that President Lincoln was a white man, and shared the prejudices common to his countrymen towards the colored race. Looking back to his times and to the condition of the country, this unfriendly feeling on his part may safely be set down as one element of his wonderful success in organizing the loyal American people for the tremendous conflict before them, and bringing them safely through that conflict. His great mission was to accomplish two things; first, to save his country from dismemberment and ruin, and second, to free his country from the great crime of slavery. To do one or the other, or both, he must have the earnest sympathy and the powerful cooperation of his loyal fellow-countrymen. Without this primary and essential condition to success, his efforts must have been vain and utterly fruitless. Had he put the abolition of slavery before the salvation of the Union, he would have inevitably driven from him a powerful class of the American people, and rendered resistance to rebellion impossible. Viewed from the genuine abolition ground, Mr. Lincoln seemed tardy, cold, dull, and indifferent: but measuring him by the sentiment of his country, a sentiment he was bound as a statesman to consult, he was swift, zealous, radical, and determined. Though Mr. Lincoln shared the prejudices of his white fellow-countrymen against the negro, it is hardly necessary to say that in his heart of hearts

HE LOATHED AND HATED SLAVERY.

He was willing while the South was loyal that it should have its pound of flesh, because he thought it was so nominated in the bond, but further than this no earthly power could make him go.

Fellow-citizens, whatever else in this world may be partial, unjust and uncertain, *time! time!* is impartial, just and certain in its actions. In the realm of mind, as well as in the realm of matter, it is a great worker, and often works wonders. The honest and comprehensive statesman, clearly discerning the needs of his country, and earnestly endeavoring to do his whole duty, though covered and blistered with reproaches, may safely leave his course to the silent judgment of time. Few great public men have ever been the victims of fiercer denunciation than Abraham Lincoln was during his administration. He was often wounded in the house of his friends. Reproaches came thick and fast upon him from within and from without, and from opposite quarters. He was assailed by abolitionists; he was assailed by slaveholders; he was assailed by men who were for peace at any price; he was assailed by those who were for a more vigorous prosecution of the war; he was assailed for not making the war an abolition war; and he was most bitterly assailed for making the war an abolition war.

BUT NOW BEHOLD THE CHANGE;

the judgment of the present hour is, that taking him for all in all, measuring the tremendous magnitude of the work before him, considering the necessary means to ends, and surveying the end from the beginning, infinite wisdom has seldom sent any man into the world better fitted for his mission than was Abraham Lincoln. His birth, his training, and his natural endowments, both mental and physical, were strongly in his favor. Born and reared among the lowly, a stranger to wealth and luxury, compelled to grapple single-handed with the flintiest hardships from tender youth to sturdy manhood, he grew strong in the manly and heroic qualities demanded by the great mission to which he was called by the votes of his countrymen. The hard condition of his early life, which would have depressed and broken down weaker men, only gave greater life, vigor and buoyancy to the heroic spirit of Abraham Lincoln. He was ready for any kind and any quality of work. What other young men dreaded in the shape of toil, he took hold of with the utmost cheerfulness.

A spade, a rake, a hoe,
A pick-axe or a bill;
A hook to reap, a scythe to mow,
A flail, or what you will.[5]

ALL DAY LONG HE COULD SPLIT HEAVY RAILS

in the woods, and half the night long he could study his English grammar by the uncertain flare and glare of the light made by a pine knot. He was at home on the land with his axe, with his maul, with gluts and his wedges; and he was equally at home on water, with his oars, with his poles, with his planks and with his boathooks. And whether in his flatboat on the Mississippi river, or at the fireside of his frontier cabin, he was a man of work. A son of toil himself he was linked in brotherly sympathy with the sons of toil in every loyal part of the Republic. This very fact gave him tremendous power with the American people, and materially contributed not only to selecting him to the Presidency, but in sustaining his administration of the Government.

Upon his inauguration as President of the United States, an office even where assumed under the most favorable conditions, it is fitted to tax and strain the largest abilities, Abraham Lincoln was met by a tremendous pressure. He was called upon not merely to administer the Government, but to decide, in the face of terrible odds, the fate of the Republic. A formidable rebellion rose in his path before him; the Union was already practically dissolved. His country was torn and rent asunder at the centre. Hostile enemies were already organized against the Republic, armed with the munitions of war which the Republic had provided for its own defense.

THE TREMENDOUS QUESTION

for him to decide was whether his country should survive the crisis and flourish, or be dismembered and perish. His predecessor in office had already decided the question in favor of national dismemberment by denying it the right of self-defense and self-preservation.

Happily for the country, happily for you and for me, the judgment of James Buchanan, the patrician, was not the judgment of Abraham Lincoln, the plebeian. He brought his strong common sense, sharpened in the school of adversity, to bear upon the question. He did not hesitate, he did not doubt, he did not falter, but at once resolved at whatever peril, at whatever cost, the union of the States should be preserved. A patriot himself, his faith was firm and unwavering in the patriotism of his countrymen. Timid men said before Mr. Lincoln's inauguration that we had seen the last President of the United States. A voice in influential quarters said let the Union slide. Some said that a Union maintained by the sword was worthless. Others said a rebellion of 8,000,000 cannot be suppressed. But in the midst of all this tumult and timidity, and against all this Abraham Lincoln was clear in his duty, and had an oath in heaven. He calmly and bravely heard the voice of doubt and fear all around him, but he had an oath in heaven, and there was not power enough on the earth to make this honest boatman, backwoodsman, and broad-handed splitter of rails evade or violate that sacred oath. He had not been schooled in the ethics of slavery; his plain life favored his love of truth. He had not been taught that treason and perjury were the proofs of honor and honesty. His moral training was against his saying one thing when he meant another. The trust which Abraham Lincoln had of himself and in the people was surprising and grand, but it was also enlightened and well founded. He knew the American people better than they knew themselves, and his truth was based upon his knowledge.

Had Abraham Lincoln died from any of the numerous ills to which flesh is heir; had he reached that good old age of which his vigorous constitution and his temperate habits gave promise; had he been permitted to see the end of his great work; had the solemn curtain of death come down but gradually, we should still have been smitten with a heavy grief and treasured his name lovingly. But dying as he did die, by the red hand of violence; killed, assassinated, taken off without warning, not because of personal hate, for no man who knew Abraham Lincoln could hate him, but because of his fidelity to Union and liberty, he is doubly dear to us, and will be precious forever.

Fellow-citizens, I end as I began, with congratulations. We have done a good work for our race to-day. In doing honor to the memory of our friend and liberator we have been doing highest honor to ourselves and those who come after us. We have been fastening ourselves to a name and fame imperishable and immortal. We have also been defending ourselves from a blighting slander. When now it shall be said that the colored man is soulless; that he has no appreciation of benefits or benefactors; when the foul reproach of ingratitude is hurled at us, and it is attempted to scourge us beyond the range of human brotherhood, we may calmly point to the monument we have this day erected to the memory of Abraham Lincoln.

"LESSONS OF THE HOUR" (1894)

In this antilynching address at Washington's Metropolitan A.M.E. church, Douglass describes the success of the South's counterrevolution that created a new order of black unfreedom, and he spells out the ways to combat it.

SOURCE: *Lessons of the Hour, by Hon. Frederick Douglass* (Baltimore: Press of Thomas & Evans, 1894)

FRIENDS AND FELLOW CITIZENS:—No man should come before an audience like the one by whose presence I am now honored, without a noble object and a fixed and earnest purpose. I think that, in whatever else I may be deficient, I have the qualifications indicated, to speak to you this evening. I am here to speak for, and to defend, so far as I can do so within the bounds of truth, a long-suffering people, and one just now subject to much misrepresentation and persecution. Charges are at this time preferred against them, more damaging and distressing than any which they have been called upon to meet since their emancipation.

I propose to give you a colored man's view of the unhappy relations at present existing between the white and colored people of the Southern States of our union. We have had the Southern white man's view of the subject. It has been presented with abundant repetition and with startling emphasis, colored by his peculiar environments. We have also had the Northern white man's view tempered by time, distance from the scene, and his higher civilization.

This kind of evidence may be considered by some as all-sufficient upon which to found an intelligent judgment of the whole matter in controversy, and that therefore my testimony is not needed. But experience has taught us that it is sometimes wise and necessary to have more than the testimony of two witnesses to bring out the whole truth, especially in this the case where one of the witnesses has a powerful motive for concealing or distorting the facts in any given case. You must not, therefore, be surprised if my version of the Southern question shall widely differ from both the North and the South, and yet I shall fearlessly submit my testimony to the candid judgment of all who hear me. I shall do so in the firm belief that my testimony is true.

There is one thing, however, in which I think we shall all agree at the start. It is that the so-called, but mis-called, negro problem is one of the most important and urgent subjects that can now engage public attention. It is worthy of the most earnest consideration of every patriotic American citizen. Its solution involves the honor or dishonor, glory or shame, happiness or misery of the whole American people. It involves more. It touches deeply not only the good name and fame of the Republic, but its highest moral welfare and its permanent safety. Plainly enough the peril it involves is great, obvious and increasing, and should be removed without delay.

The presence of eight millions of people in any section of this country constituting an aggrieved class, smarting under terrible wrongs, denied the exercise of the commonest rights of humanity, and regarded by the ruling class in that section as outside of the government, outside of the law, and outside of society; having nothing in common with the people with whom they live, the sport of mob violence and murder is not only a disgrace and scandal to that particular section but a menace to the peace and security of the people of the whole country.

I have waited patiently but anxiously to see the end of the epidemic of mob law and persecution now prevailing at the South. But the indications are not hopeful, great and terrible as have been its ravages in the past, it now seems to be increasing not only in the number of its victims, but in its frantic rage and savage extravagance. Lawless vengeance is beginning to be visted upon white men as well as black. Our newspapers are daily disfigured by its ghastly horrors. It is no longer local, but national; no longer confined to the South, but has invaded the North. The contagion is spreading, extending and over-leaping geographical lines and state boundaries, and if permitted to go on it threatens to destroy all respect for law and order not only in the South, but in all parts of our country—North as well as South. For certain it is, that crime allowed to go on unresisted and unarrested will breed crime. When the poison of anarchy is once in the air, like the pestilence that walketh in the darkness,[1] the winds of heaven will take it up and favor its diffusion. Though it may strike down the weak to-day, it will strike down the strong to-morrow.

Not a breeze comes to us now from the late rebellious States that is not tainted and freighted with negro blood. In its thirst for blood and its rage for vengeance, the mob has blindly, boldly and defiantly supplanted sheriffs, constables and police. It has assumed all the functions of civil authority. It laughs at legal processes, courts and juries, and its red-handed murderers range abroad unchecked and unchallenged by law or by public opinion. Prison walls and iron bars are no protection to the innocent or guilty, if the mob is in pursuit of negroes accused of crime. Jail doors are battered down in the presence of unresisting jailors, and the accused, awaiting trial in the courts of law are dragged out and hanged, shot, stabbed or burned to death as the blind and irresponsible mob may elect.

We claim to be a Christian country and a highly civilized nation, yet, I fearlessly affirm that there is nothing in the history of savages to surpass the blood chilling horrors and fiendish excesses perpetrated against the colored people by the so-called enlightened and Christian people of the South. It is commonly thought that only the lowest and most disgusting birds and beasts, such as buzzards, vultures and hyenas, will gloat over and prey upon dead bodies, but the Southern mob in its rage feeds its vengeance by shooting, stabbing and burning when their victims are dead.

Now the special charge against the negro by which this ferocity is justified, and by which mob law is defended by good men North and South, is alleged to be assaults by negroes upon white women. This charge once fairly started, no matter by whom or in what manner, whether well or ill-founded, whether true or false, is certain to subject the accused to immediate death. It is nothing, that in the case there may be a mistake as to identity. It is nothing that the victim pleads "not guilty." It is nothing that he only asks for time to establish his innocence. It is nothing that the accused is of fair reputation and his accuser is of an abandoned character. It is nothing that the majesty of the law is defied and insulted; no time is allowed for defence or explanation; he is bound with cords, hurried off amid the frantic yells and cursing of the mob to the scaffold and under its shadow he is tortured till by pain or promises, he is made to think he can possibly gain time or save his life by confession, and then whether innocent or guilty, he is shot, hanged, stabbed or burned to death amid the wild shouts of the mob. When the will of the mob has been accomplished, when its thirst for blood has been quenched, when its victim is speechless, silent and dead, his mobocratic accusers and murderers of course have the ear of the world all to themselves, and the world generally approves their verdict.

Such then is the state of Southern civilization in its relation to the colored citizens of that section and though the picture is dark and terrible I venture to affirm that no man North or South can deny the essential truth of the picture.

Now it is important to know how this state of affairs is viewed by the better classes of the Southern States. I will tell you, and I venture to say if our hearts were not already hardened by familiarity with such crimes against the negro, we should be shocked and astonished by the attitude of these so-called better classes of the Southern people and their lawmakers. With a few noble exceptions the upper classes of the South are in full sympathy with the mob and its deeds. There are few earnest words uttered against the mob or its deeds. Press, platform and pulpit are either generally silent or they openly apologize for the mob. The mobocratic murderers are not only permitted to go free, untried and unpunished, but are lauded and applauded as honorable men and good citizens, the guardians of Southern women. If lynch law is in any case condemned, it is only condemned in one breath, and excused in another.

The great trouble with the negro in the South is that all presumptions are against him. A white man has but to blacken his face and commit a crime to have some negro lynched in his stead. An abandoned woman has only to start the cry that she has been insulted by a black man to have him arrested and summarily murdered by the mob. Frightened and tortured by his captors, confused into telling crooked stories about his whereabouts at the time when the alleged crime was committed and the death penalty is at once inflicted, though his story may be but the incoherency of ignorance or distraction caused by terror.

Now in confirmation of what I have said of the better classes of the South, I have before me the utterances of some of the best people of that section, and also the testimony of one from the North, a lady, from whom, considering her antecedents, we should have expected a more considerate, just and humane utterance.

In a late number of the "Forum" Bishop Haygood, author of the "Brother in Black," says that "The most alarming fact is, that execution by lynching has ceased to surprise us. The burning of a human being for any crime, it is thought, is a horror that does not occur outside of the Southern States of the American Union, yet unless assaults by negroes come to an end, there will most probably be still further display of vengeance that will shock the world, and men who are just will consider the provocation."[2]

In an open letter addressed to me by ex-Governor Chamberlain,[3] of South Carolina, and published in the "Charleston News and Courier," a letter which I have but lately seen, in reply to an article of mine on the subject published in the "North American Review," the ex-Governor says: "Your denunciation of the South on this point is directed exclusively, or nearly so, against the application of lynch law for the punishment of one crime, or one sort of crime, the existence, I suppose, I might say the prevalence of this crime at the South is undeniable. But I read your (my) article in vain for any special denunciation of the crime itself. As you say your people are lynched, tortured and burned for assault on white women. As you value your own good fame and safety as a race, stamp out the infamous crime." He further says, the way to stop lynching is to stamp out the crime.

And now comes the sweet voice of a Northern woman, of Southern principles, in the same tone and the same accusation, the good Miss Frances Willard, of the W. C. T. U. She says in a letter now before me, "I pity the Southerner. The problem on their hands is immeasurable. The colored race," she says, "multiplies like the locusts of Egypt. The safety of woman, of childhood, of the home, is menaced in a thousand localities at this moment, so that men dare not go beyond the sight of their own roof tree." Such then is the crushing indictment drawn up against the Southern negroes, drawn up, too, by persons who are perhaps the fairest and most humane of the negro's accusers. But even they paint him as a moral monster ferociously invading the sacred rights of women and endangering the homes of the whites.

The crime they allege against the negro is the most revolting which men can commit. It is a crime that awakens the intensest abhorrence and invites mankind to kill the criminal on sight. This charge thus brought against the negro, and as constantly reiterated by his enemies, is not merely against the individual culprit, as would be in the case with an individual culprit of any other race, but it is in a large measure a charge against the colored race as such. It throws over every colored man a mantle of odium and sets upon him a mark for popular hate, more distressing than the mark set upon the first murderer. It points him out as an object of suspicion and avoidance. Now it is in this form that you and I, and all of us, are required to meet it and refute it, if that can be done. In the opinion of some of us, it is thought that it were well to say nothing about it, that the least said about it the better. In this opinion I do not concur. Taking this charge in its broad and comprehensive sense in which it is presented, and as now stated, I feel that it ought to be met, and as a colored man, I am grateful for the opportunity now afforded me to meet it. For I believe it can be met and successfully met. I am of opinion that a people too spiritless to defend themselves are not worth defending.

Without boasting, on this broad issue as now presented, I am ready to confront ex-Governor Chamberlain, Bishop Fitzgerald, Bishop Haygood, and Miss Frances Willard[4] and all others, singly or altogether, without any doubt of the result.

But I want to be understood at the outset. I do not pretend that negroes are saints or angels. I do not deny that they are capable of committing the crime imputed to them, but I utterly deny that they are any more addicted to the commission of that crime than is true of any other variety of the human family. In entering upon my argument, I may be allowed to say, that I appear here this evening not as the defender of any man guilty of this atrocious crime, but as the defender of the colored people as a class.

In answer to the terrible indictment, thus read, and speaking for the colored people as a class, I, in their stead, here and now plead not guilty and shall submit my case with confidence of acquittal by good men and women North and South.

It is the misfortune of the colored people in this country that the sins of the few are visited upon the many, and I am here to speak for the many whose reputation is put in peril by the sweeping charge in question. With General Grant and every other honest man, my motto is, "Let no guilty man escape." But while I am here to say this, I am here also to say, let no innocent man be condemned and killed by the mob, or crushed under the weight of a charge of which he is not guilty.

You will readily see that the cause I have undertaken to support is not to be maintained by any mere confident assertions or general denials. If I had no better ground to stand upon than this, I would leave the field of controversy and give up the colored man's cause at once to his able accusers. I am aware, however, that I am here to do in some measure what the masters of logic say cannot be done—prove a negative.

Of course, I shall not be able to succeed in doing the impossible, but this one thing I can and will do. I can and will show that there are sound reasons for doubting and denying this horrible and hell-black charge of rape as the peculiar crime of the colored people of the South. My doubt and denial are based upon two fundamental and invincible grounds.

The first is the well established and well tested character of the negro on the very point upon which he is now violently and persistently accused. The second ground for my doubt and denial is based upon what I know of the character and antecedents of the men and women who bring this charge against him. I undertake to say that the strength of this position will become more manifest as I proceed with my argument.

At the outset I deny that a fierce and frenzied mob is or ought to be deemed a competent witness against any man accused of any crime whatever. The ease with which a mob can be collected and the slight causes by which it may be set in motion, and the elements of which it is composed, deprives its testimony of the qualities that should inspire confidence and command belief. It is moved by impulses utterly unfavorable to an impartial statement of the truth. At the outset, therefore, I challenge the credibility of the mob, and as the mob is the main witness in the case against the negro, I appeal to the common sense of mankind in support of my challenge. It is the mob that brings this charge, and it is the mob that arraigns, condemns and executes, and it is the mob that the country has accepted as its witness.

Again, I impeach and discredit the veracity of southern men generally, whether mobocrats or otherwise, who now openly and deliberately nullify and violate the provisions of the constitution of their country, a constitution, which they have solemnly sworn to support and execute. I apply to them the legal maxim, "False in one, false in all."

Again I arraign the negro's accuser on another ground, I have no confidence in the truthfulness of men who justify themselves in cheating the negro out of his constitutional right to vote. The men, who either by false returns, or by taking advantage of his illiteracy or surrounding the ballot-box with obstacles and sinuosities intended to bewilder him and defeat his rightful exercise of the elective franchise, are men who are not to be believed on oath. That this is done in the Southern States is not only admitted, but openly defended and justified by so-called honorable men inside and outside of Congress.

Just this kind of fraud in the South is notorious. I have met it face to face. It was boldly defended and advocated a few weeks ago in a solemn paper by Prof. Weeks,[5] a learned North Carolinian, in my hearing. His paper was one of the able papers read before one of the World's Auxiliary Congresses at Chicago.

Now men who openly defraud the negro by all manner of artifice and boast of it in the face of the world's civilization, as was done at Chicago, I affirm that they are not to be depended upon for truth in any case whatever, where the rights of the negro are involved. Their testimony in the case of any other people than the negro, against whom they should thus commit fraud would be instantly and utterly discredited, and why not the same in this case? Every honest man will see that this point is well taken, and I defy any argument that would drive me from this just contention. It has for its support common sense, common justice, common honesty, and the best sentiment of mankind, and has nothing to oppose it but a vulgar popular prejudice against the colored people of our country, which prejudice strikes men with moral blindness and renders them incapable of seeing any distinction between right and wrong.

But I come to a stronger position. I rest my conclusion not merely upon general principles, but upon well known facts. I reject the charge brought against the negro as a class, because all through the late war, while the slave masters of the South were absent from their homes in the field of rebellion, with bullets in their pockets, treason in their hearts, broad blades in their blood stained hands, seeking the life of the nation, with the vile purpose of perpetuating the enslavement of the negro, their wives, their daughters, their sisters and their mothers were left in the absolute custody of these same negroes, and during all those long four years of terrible conflict, when the negro had every opportunity to commit the abominable crime now alleged against him, there was never a single instance of such crime reported or charged against him. He was never accused of assault, insult, or an attempt to commit an assault upon any white woman in the whole South. A fact like this, although negative, speaks volumes and ought to have some weight with the American people.

Then, again on general principles, I do not believe the charge because it implies an improbable, if not impossible, change in the mental and moral character and composition of the negro. It implies a change wholly inconsistent with well known facts of human nature. It is a contradiction to well known human experience. History does not present an example of such a transformation in the character of any class of men so extreme, so unnatural and so complete as is implied in this charge. The change is too great and the period too brief. Instances may be cited where men fall like stars from heaven, but such is not the usual experience. Decline in the moral character of a people is not sudden, but gradual. The downward steps are marked at first by degrees and by increasing momentum from bad to worse. Time is an element in such changes, and I contend that the negroes of the South have not had time to experience this great change and reach this lower depth of infamy. On the contrary, in point of fact, they have been and still are, improving and ascending to higher levels of moral and social worth.

Again, I do not believe it and utterly deny it, because those who bring the charge do not, and dare not, give the negro a chance to be heard in his own defence. He is not allowed to explain any part of his alleged offense. He is not allowed to vindicate his own character or to criminate the character and motives of his accusers. Even the mobocrats themselves admit that it would be fatal to their purpose to have the character of his accusers brought into court. They pretend to a delicate regard for the feelings of the parties assaulted, and therefore object to giving a fair trial to the accused. The excuse in this case is contemptible. It is not only mock modesty but mob modesty. Men who can collect hundreds and thousands, if we may believe them, and can spread before them in the tempest and whirlwind of vulgar passion, the most disgusting details of crime with the names of women, with the alleged offense, should not be allowed to shelter themselves under any pretense of modesty. Such a pretense is absurd and shameless. Who does not know that the modesty of womanhood is always an object for protection in a court of law? Who does not know that a lawless mob composed in part of the basest of men can have no such respect for the modesty of women as a court of law. No woman need be ashamed to confront one who has insulted or assaulted her in a court of law. Besides innocence does not hesitate to come to the rescue of justice.

Again, I do not believe it, and deny it because if the evidence were deemed sufficient to bring the accused to the scaffold, through the action of an impartial jury, there could be, and would be, no objection to having the alleged offender tried in conformity to due process of law.

Any pretence that a guilty negro, especially one guilty of the crime now charged, would in any case be permitted to escape condign punishment, is an insult to common sense. Nobody believes or can believe such a thing as escape possible, in a country like the South, where public opinion, the laws, the courts, the juries, and the advocates are all known to be against him, he could hardly escape if innocent. I repeat, therefore, I do not believe it, because I know, and you know, that a passionate and violent mob bent upon taking life, from the nature of the case, is not a more competent and trustworthy body to determine the guilt or innocence of a negro accused in such a case, than is a court of law. I would not, and you would not, convict a dog on such testimony.

But I come to another fact, and an all-important fact, bearing upon this case. You will remember that during all the first years of re-construction and long after the war when the Southern press and people found it necessary to invent, adopt, and propagate almost every species of falsehood to create sympathy for themselves and to formulate an excuse for gratifying their brutal instincts, there was never a charge then made against a negro involving an assault upon any white woman or upon any little white child. During all this time the white women and children were absolutely safe. During all this time there was no call for Miss Willard's pity, or Bishop Haygood's defense of burning negroes to death.

You will remember also that during this time the justification for the murder of negroes was said to be negro conspiracies, insurrections, schemes to murder all the white people, to burn the town, and commit violence generally. These were the excuses then depended upon, but never a word was then said or whispered about negro outrages upon white women and children. So far as the history of that time is concerned, white women and children were absolutely safe, and husbands and fathers could leave home without the slightest anxiety on account of their families.

But when events proved that no such conspiracies; no such insurrections as were then pretended to exist and were paraded before the world in glaring head-lines, had ever existed or were even meditated; when these excuses had run their course and served their wicked purpose; when the huts of negroes had been searched, and searched in vain, for guns and ammunition to prove these charges, and no evidence was found, when there was no way open thereafter to prove these charges against the negro and no way to make the North believe in these excuses for murder, they did not even then bring forward the present allegation against the negro. They, however, went on harassing and killing just the same. But this time they based the right thus to kill on the ground that it was necessary to check the domination and supremacy of the negro and to secure the absolute rule of the Anglo-Saxon race.

It is important to notice that there has been three distinct periods of persecution of negroes in the South, and three distinct sets of excuses for persecution. They have come along precisely in the order in which they were most needed. First you remember it was insurrection. When that was worn out, negro supremacy became the excuse. When that is worn out, now it is assault upon defenseless women. I undertake to say that this order and periodicity is significant and means something and should not be overlooked. And now that negro supremacy and negro domination are no longer defensible as an excuse for negro persecutions, there has come in due course, this heart-rending cry about the white women and little white children of the South.

Now, my friends, I ask what is the rational explanation of this singular omission of this charge in the two periods preceding the present? Why was not the charge made at that time as now? The negro was the same then as today. White women and children were the same then as to-day. Temptations to wrong doing were the same then as to-day. Why then was not this dreadful charge brought forward against the negro in war times and why was it not brought forward in reconstruction times?

I will tell you; or you, yourselves, have already answered the question. The only rational answer is that there was no foundation for such a charge or that the charge itself was either not thought of or was not deemed necessary to excuse the lawless violence with which the negro was then pursued and killed. The old charges already enumerated were deemed all sufficient. This new charge has now swallowed up all the old ones and the reason is obvious.

Things have changed since then, old excuses were not available and the negro's accusers have found it necessary to change with them. The old charges are no longer valid. Upon them the good opinion of the North and of mankind cannot be secured. Honest men no longer believe in the worn-out stories of insurrection. They no longer believe that there is just ground to apprehend negro supremacy. Time and events have swept away these old refuges of lies. They did their work in their day, and did it with terrible energy and effect, but they are now cast aside as useless. The altered times and circumstances have made necessary a sterner, stronger, and more effective justification of Southern barbarism, and hence, according to my theory, we now have to look into the face of a more shocking and blasting charge than either negro supremacy or insurrection or that of murder itself.

This new charge has come at the call of new conditions, and nothing could have been hit upon better calculated to accomplish its purpose. It clouds the character of the negro with a crime the most revolting, and is fitted to drive from him all sympathy and all fair play and all mercy. It is a crime that places him outside of the pale of the law, and settles upon his shoulders a mantle of wrath and fire that blisters and burns into his very soul.

It is for this purpose, as I believe, that this new charge unthought of in the times to which I have referred, has been largely invited, if not entirely trumped up. It is for this purpose that it has been constantly reiterated and adopted. It was to blast and ruin the negro's character as a man and a citizen.

I need not tell you how thoroughly it has already done its wonted work. You may feel its malign influence in the very air. You may read it in the faces of men. It has cooled our friends. It has heated our enemies, and arrested in some measure the efforts that good men were wont to make for the colored man's improvement and elevation. It has deceived our friends at the North and many good friends at the South, for nearly all have in some measure accepted the charge as true. Its perpetual reiteration in our newspapers and magazines has led men and women to regard us with averted eyes, increasing hate and dark suspicion.

Some of the Southern papers have denounced me for my unbelief in their new departure, but I repeat I do not believe it and firmly deny it. I reject it because I see in it evidence of an invention, called into being by a well defined motive, a motive sufficient to stamp it as a gross expedient to justify murderous assault upon a long enslaved and hence a hated people.

I do not believe it because it bears on its face the marks of being a makeshift for a malignant purpose. I reject it not only because it was sprung upon the country simultaneously with well-known efforts now being industriously made to degrade the negro by legislative enactments, and by repealing all laws for the protection of the ballot, and by drawing the color line in all railroad cars and stations and in all other public places in the South;

but because I see in it a means of paving the way for our entire disfranchisement.

Again, I do not believe it, and deny it, because the charge is not so much against the crime itself, as against the color of the man alleged to be guilty of it. Slavery itself, you will remember, was a system of legalized outrage upon the black women of the South, and no white man was ever shot, burned, or hanged for availing himself of all the power that slavery gave him at this point.

Upon these grounds then—grounds which I believe to be solid and immovable—I dare here and now in the capital of the nation and in the presence of Congress to reject it, and ask you and all just men to reject this horrible charge so frequently made and construed against the negro as a class.

To sum up my argument on this lynching business. It remains to be said that I have shown that the negro's accusers in this case have violated their oaths and have cheated the negro out of his vote; that they have robbed and defrauded the negro systematically and persistently, and have boasted of it. I have shown that when the negro had every opportunity to commit the crime now charged against him he was never accused of it by his bitterest enemies. I have shown that during all the years of reconstruction, when he was being murdered at Hamburg, Yazoo, New Orleans, Copiah and elsewhere, he was never accused of the crime now charged against him. I have shown that in the nature of things, no such change in the character and composition of a people as this charge implies could have taken place in the limited period allowed for it. I have shown that those who accuse him dare not confront him in a court of law and have their witnesses subjected to proper legal inquiry. And in showing all this, and more, I have shown that they who charge him with this foul crime may be justly doubted and deemed unworthy of belief.

But I shall be told by many of my Northern friends that my argument, though plausible, is not conclusive. It will be said that the charges against the negro are specific and positive, and that there must be some foundation for them, because as they allege men in their normal condition do not shoot and hang their fellowmen who are guiltless of crime. Well! This assumption is very just, very charitable. I only ask something like the same justice and charity could be shown to the negro as well as to the mob. It is creditable to the justice and humanity of the good people of the North by whom it is entertained. They rightly assume that men do not shoot and hang their fellowmen without just cause. But the vice of their argument is in their assumption that the lynchers are like other men. The answer to that argument is what may be truly predicated of human nature under one condition is not what may be true of human nature under another. Uncorrupted human nature may shudder at the commission of such crimes as those of which the Southern mob is guilty.

But human nature uncorrupted is one thing and human nature corrupted and perverted by long abuse of irresponsible power, is quite another and different thing. No man can reason correctly on this question who reasons on the assumption that the lynchers are like ordinary men.

We are not, in this case, dealing with men in their natural condition, but with men brought up in the exercise of arbitrary power. We are dealing with men whose ideas, habits and customs are entirely different from those of ordinary men. It is, therefore, quite gratuitous to assume that the principles that apply to other men apply to the Southern murderers of the negro, and just here is the mistake of the Northern people. They do not see that the rules resting upon the justice and benevolence of human nature do not apply to the mobocrats, or to those who were educated in the habits and customs of a slave-holding community. What these habits are I have a right to know, both in theory and in practice.

I repeat: The mistake made by those who on this ground object to my theory of the charge against the negro is that they overlook the natural effect and influence of the life, education, and habits of the lynchers. We must remember that these people have not now and have never had any such respect for human life as is common to other men. They have had among them for centuries a peculiar institution, and that peculiar institution has stamped them as a peculiar people. They were not before the war, they were not during the war, and have not been since the war in their spirit or in their civilization, a people in common with the people of the North. I will not here harrow up your feelings by detailing their treatment of Northern prisoners during the war. Their institutions have taught them no respect for human life and especially the life of the negro. It has in fact taught them absolute contempt for his life. The sacredness of life which ordinary men feel does not touch them anywhere. A dead negro is with them a common jest.

They care no more for a negro's right to live than they care for his rights to liberty, or his rights to the ballot. Chief Justice Taney told the exact truth about these people when he said: "They did not consider that the black man had any rights which the white men were bound to respect." No man of the South ever called in question that statement and they never will. They could always shoot, stab, and burn the negro without any such remorse or shame as other men would feel after committing such a crime. Any Southern man who is honest and is frank enough to talk on the subject, will tell you that he has no such idea as we have of the sacredness of human life and especially, as I have said, of the life of the negro. Hence it is absurd to meet my arguments with the facts predicated on our common human nature.

I know I shall be charged with apologizing for criminals. Ex-Governor Chamberlain has already virtually done as much. But there is no foundation for any such charge. I affirm that neither I nor any other colored man of like standing with myself has ever raised a finger or uttered a word in defense of any one really guilty of the dreadful crime now in question.

But, what I contend for, and what every honest man, black or white should contend for, is that when any man is accused of this or any other crime, of whatever name, nature, or extent, he shall have the benefit of a legal investigation; that he shall be confronted by his accusers; and that he shall through proper counsel, be able to question his accusers in open court and in open day-light so that his guilt or his innocence may be duly proved and established.

If this is to make me liable to the charge of apologizing for crime, I am not ashamed to be so charged. I dare to contend for the colored people of the United States that they are a law-abiding people, and I dare to insist upon it that they or any man, black or white, accused of crime, shall have a fair trial before he is punished.

Again, I cannot dwell too much upon the fact that colored people are much damaged by this charge. As an injured class we have a right to appeal from the judgment of the mob to the judgment of the law and the American people. Our enemies have known well where to strike and how to stab us most fatally. Owing to popular prejudice it has become the misfortune of the colored people of the South and of the North as well, to have as I have said, the sins of the few visited upon the many. When a white man steals, robs or murders, his crime is visited upon his own head alone. But not so with the black man. When he commits a crime the whole race is made to suffer. The cause before us is an example. This unfairness confronts us not only here, but it confronts us everywhere else.

Even when American art undertakes to picture the types of the two races it invariably places in comparison not the best of both races as common fairness would dictate, but it puts side by side in glaring contrast the lowest type of the negro with the highest type of the white man and calls upon you to "look upon this picture then upon that."

When a black man's language is quoted, in order to belittle and degrade him, his ideas are put into the most grotesque and unreadable English, while the utterances of negro scholars and authors are ignored. A hundred white men will attend a concert of white negro minstrels with faces blackened with burnt cork, to one who will attend a lecture by an intelligent negro.

On this ground I have a criticism to make, even of the late World's Columbian Exposition. While I join with all other men in pronouncing the Exposition itself one of the grandest demonstrations of civilization that the world has ever seen, yet great and glorious as it was, it was made to show just this kind of unfairness and discrimination against the negro.

As nowhere else in the world it was hoped that here the idea of human brotherhood would have been fully recognized and most gloriously illustrated. It should have been, and would have been, had it been what it professed to be, a World's Exposition. It was, however, in a marked degree an American Exposition. The spirit of American caste made itself conspicuously felt against the educated American negro, and to this extent, the Exposition was made simply an American Exposition and that in one of America's most illiberal features.

Since the day of Pentecost, there has never assembled in any one place or on any one occasion, a larger variety of peoples of all forms, features and colors, and all degrees of civilization, than was assembled at this World's Exposition. It was a grand ethnological lesson, a chance to study all likenesses and differences. Here were Japanese, Soudanese, Chinese, Cingalese, Syrians, Persians, Tunisians, Algerians, Egyptians, East Indians, Laplanders, Esquimaux, and as if to shame the educated negro of America, the Dahomeyans were there to exhibit their barbarism, and increase American contempt for the negro intellect. All classes and conditions were there save the educated American negro. He ought to have been there if only to show what American slavery and freedom have done for him. The fact that all other nations were there and there at their best, made his exclusion the more marked, and the more significant. People from abroad noticed the fact that while we have eight millions of colored people in the United States, many of them gentlemen and scholars, not one of them was deemed worthy to be appointed a Commissioner, or a member of an important committee, or a guide, or a guard on the Exposition grounds. What a commentary is this upon our boasted American liberty and American equality! It is a silence to be sure, but it is a silence that speaks louder than words. It says to the world that the colored people of America are deemed by Americans not within the compass of American law and of American civilization. It says to the lynchers and mobocrats of the South, go on in your hellish work of negro persecution. What you do to their bodies, we do to their souls.

I come now to the question of negro suffrage. It has come to be fashionable of late to ascribe much of the trouble at the South to ignorant negro suffrage. The great measure according suffrage to the negro recommended by General Grant and adopted by the loyal nation is now denounced as a blunder and a failure. They would, therefore, in some way abridge and limit this right by imposing upon it an educational or some other qualification. Among those who take this view are Mr. John J. Ingalls, and Mr. John M. Langston. They are both eloquent, both able, and both wrong. Though they are both Johns neither of them is to my mind a "St. John" and not even a "John the Baptist." They have taken up an idea which they seem to think quite new, but which in reality is as old as despotism and about as narrow and selfish. It has been heard and answered a thousand times over. It is the argument of the crowned heads and privileged classes of the world. It is as good against our Republican form of government as it [is] against the negro. The wonder is that its votaries do not see its consequences. It does away with that noble and just idea of Abraham Lincoln, that our government should be a government of the people, by the people, and for the people, and for *all* the people.

These gentlemen are very learned, very eloquent and very able, but I cannot follow them. Much learning has made them mad. Education is great, but manhood is greater. The one is the principle, the other is the accident. Man was not made as an attribute to education, but education is an attribute to man. I say to these gentlemen, first protect the man and you will thereby protect education. I would not make illiteracy a bar to the ballot, but would make the ballot a bar to illiteracy. Take the ballot from the negro and you take from him the means and motives that make for education. Those who are already educated and are vested with political power and have thereby an advantage, will have a strong motive for refusing to divide that advantage with others, and least of all will they divide it with the negro to whom they would deny all right to participate in the government.

I, therefore, cannot follow these gentlemen in their proposition to limit suffrage to the educated alone. I would not make suffrage more exclusive, but more inclusive. I would not have it embrace merely the elite, but would include the lowly. I would not only include the men, I would gladly include the women, and make our government in reality as in name a government of the people and of the whole people.

But manifestly suffrage to the colored people is not the cause of the failure of good government, or the cause of trouble in the Southern States, but it is the lawless limitations of suffrage that makes the trouble.

Much thoughtless speech is heard about the ignorance of the negro in the South. But plainly enough it is not the ignorance of the negro, but the malevolence of his accusers, which is the real cause of Southern disorder. The illiteracy of the negro has no part or lot in the disturbances there. They who contend for disfranchisement on this ground know, and know very well, that there is no truth whatever in their contention. To make out their case they must show that some oppressive and hurtful measure has been imposed upon the country by negro voters. But they cannot show any such thing.

The negro has never set up a separate party, never adopted a negro platform, never proclaimed or adopted a separate policy for himself or for the country. His assailants know that he has never acted apart from the whole American people. They know that he has never sought to lead, but has always been content to follow. They know that he has not made his ignorance the rule of his political conduct, but the intelligence of white people has always been his guide. They know that he has simply kept pace with the average intelligence of his age and country. They know that he has gone steadily along in the line of his politics with the most enlightened citizens of the country. They know that he has always voted with one or the other of the two great political parties. They know that if the votes of these parties have been guided by intelligence and patriotism, the same may be said for the vote of the negro. They ought to know, therefore, that it is a shame and an outrage upon common sense and common fairness to make the negro responsible, or his ignorance responsible, for any disorder and confusion that may reign in the Southern States. Yet, while any lie may be safely told against the negro and be credited, this lie will find eloquent mouths bold enough to tell it, and pride themselves upon their superior wisdom in denouncing the ignorant negro voter.

It is true that the negro once voted solidly for the candidates of the Republican party, but what if he did? He then only voted with John Mercer Langston, John J. Ingalls, John Sherman, General Harrison, Senator Hoar, Henry Cabot Lodge, and Governor McKinley, and many of the most intelligent statesmen and patriots of whom this country can boast. The charge against him at this point is, therefore, utterly groundless. It is a mere pretense, a sham, an excuse for fraud and violence, for persecution and a cloak for popular prejudice.

The proposition to disfranchise the colored voter of the South in order to solve the race problem I hereby denounce as a mean and cowardly proposition, utterly unworthy of an honest, truthful and grateful nation. It is a proposition to sacrifice friends in order to conciliate enemies; to surrender the constitution to the late rebels for the lack of moral courage to execute its provisions. It says to the negro citizens, "The Southern nullifiers have robbed you of a part of your rights, and as we are powerless and cannot help you, and wish to live on good terms with our Southern brethren, we propose to join your oppressors so that our practice shall be consistent with their theories. Your suffrage has been practically rendered a failure by violence, we now propose to make it a failure by law. Instead of conforming our practice to the theory of our government and the genius of our institutions, we now propose, as means of conciliation, to conform our practice to the theory of your oppressors."

Than this, was there ever a surrender more complete, more cowardly or more base? Upon the statesmen, black or white, who could dare to hint such a scheme of national debasement as a means of settling the race problem, I should inflict no punishment more severe than to keep him at home, and deprived of all legislative trusts forever.

Do not ask me what will be the final result of the so-called negro problem. I cannot tell you. I have sometimes thought that the American people are too great to be small, too just and magnanimous to oppress the weak, too brave to yield up the right to the strong, and too grateful for public services ever to forget them or fail to reward them. I have fondly hoped that this estimate of American character would soon cease to be contradicted or put in doubt. But the favor with which this cowardly proposition of disfranchisement has been received by public men, white and black, by Republicans as well as Democrats, has shaken my faith in the nobility of the nation. I hope and trust all will come out right in the end, but the immediate future looks dark and troubled. I cannot shut my eyes to the ugly facts before me.

Strange things have happened of late and are still happening. Some of these tend to dim the lustre of the American name and chill the hopes once entertained for the cause of American liberty. He is a wiser man than I am who can tell how low the moral sentiment of this republic may yet fall. When the moral sense of a nation begins to decline and the wheel of progress to roll backward, there is no telling how low the one will fall or where the other may stop. The downward tendency already manifest has swept away some of the most important safeguards.

The Supreme Court has surrendered. State sovereignty is restored. It has destroyed the civil rights bill, and converted the Republican party into a party of money rather than a party of morals, a party of things rather than a party of humanity and justice. We may well ask what next?

The pit of hell is said to be bottomless. Principles which we all thought to have been firmly and permanently settled by the late war have been boldly assaulted and overthrown by the defeated party. Rebel rule is now nearly complete in many States, and it is gradually capturing the nation's Congress. The cause lost in the war is the cause regained in peace, and the cause gained in war is the cause lost in peace.

There was a threat made long ago by an American statesman, that the whole body of legislation enacted for the protection of American liberty and to secure the results of the war for the Union, should be blotted from the national statute book. That threat is now being sternly pursued, and may yet be fully realized. The repeal of the laws intended to protect the elective franchise has heightened the suspicion that Southern rule may yet become complete, though I trust, not permanent. There is no denying that the trend is in the wrong way at present. The late election, however, gives us hope that the loyal Republican party may return to its first born.

But I come now to another proposition held up just now as a solution of the race problem, and this I consider equally unworthy with the one just disposed of. The two belong to the same low-bred family of ideas.

This proposition is to colonize the colored people of America in Africa or somewhere else. Happily this scheme will be defeated, both by its impolicy and its impracticability. It is all nonsense to talk about the removal of eight millions of the American people from their homes in America to Africa. The expense and hardships, to say nothing of the cruelty of such a measure, would make success to such a measure impossible. The American people are wicked, but they are not fools, they will hardly be disposed to incur the expense, to say nothing of the injustice which this measure demands. Nevertheless, this colonizing scheme, unworthy as it is, of American statesmanship and American honor, and though full of mischief to the colored people, seems to have a strong hold on the public mind and at times has shown much life and vigor.

The bad thing about it is that it has now begun to be advocated by colored men of acknowledged ability and learning, and every little while some white statesman becomes its advocate. Those gentlemen will doubtless have their opinion of me; I certainly have mine of them. My opinion of them is that if they are sensible, they are insincere, and if they are sincere they are not sensible. They know, or they ought to know, that it would take more money than the cost of the late war, to transport even one-half of the colored people of the United States to Africa. Whether intentionally or not they are, as I think, simply trifling with an afflicted people. They urge them to look for relief, where they ought to know that relief is impossible. The only excuse they can make is that there is no hope for the negro here and that the colored people in America owe something to Africa.

This last sentimental idea makes colonization very fascinating to dreamers of both colors. But there is really for it no foundation.

They tell us that we owe something to our native land. But when the fact is brought to view, which should never be forgotten, that a man can only have one native land, and that is the land in which he was born, the bottom falls entirely out of this sentimental argument.

Africa, according to her advocates, is by no means modest in her demand upon us. She calls upon us to send her only our best men. She does not want our riff raff, but our best men. But these are just the men we want at home. It is true we have a few preachers and laymen with a missionary turn of mind who might be easily spared. Some who would possibly do as much good by going there as by staying here. But this is not the only colonization idea. Its advocates want not only the best, but millions of the best. They want the money to be voted by the United States Government to send them there.

Now I hold that the American negro owes no more to the negroes in Africa than he owes to the negroes in America. There are millions of needy people over there, but there are also millions of needy people over here as well, and the millions here need intelligent men of their numbers to help them, as much as intelligent men are needed in Africa. We have a fight on our hands right here, a fight for the whole race, and a blow struck for the negro in America is a blow struck for the negro in Africa. For until the negro is respected in America, he need not expect consideration elsewhere. All this native land talk is nonsense. The native land of the American negro is America. His bones, his muscles, his sinews, are all American. His ancestors for two hundred and seventy years have lived, and labored, and died on American soil, and millions of his posterity have inherited Caucasian blood.

It is competent, therefore, to ask, in view of this admixture, as well as in view of other facts, where the people of this mixed race are to go, for their ancestors are white and black, and it will be difficult to find their native land anywhere outside of the United States.

But the worse thing, perhaps, about this colonization nonsense is, that it tends to throw over the negro a mantle of despair. It leads him to doubt the possibility of his progress as an American citizen. It also encourages popular prejudice with the hope that by persecution or persuasion the negro can finally be driven from his natural home, while in the nature of the case, he must stay here, and will stay here and cannot well get away.

It tends to weaken his hold on one country while it can give him no rational hope of another. Its tendency is to make him dispondent and doubtful, where he should be made to feel assured and confident. It forces upon him the idea that he is forever doomed to be a stranger and sojourner in the land of his birth, and that he has no permanent abiding place here.

All this is hurtful, with such ideas constantly flaunted before him he cannot easily set himself to work to better his condition in such ways as are open to him here. It sets him to groping everlastingly after the impossible.

Every man who thinks at all must know that home is the fountain head, the inspiration, the foundation and main support not only of all social virtue, but of all motives to human progress and that no people can prosper or amount to much without a home. To have a home, the negro must have a country, and he is an enemy to the moral progress of the negro, whether he knows it or not, who calls upon him to break up his home in this country for an uncertain home in Africa.

But the agitation of this subject has a darker side still. It has already been given out that we may be forced to go at the point of the bayonet. I cannot say we shall not, but badly as I think of the tendency of our times, I do not think that American sentiment will ever reach a condition which will make the expulsion of the negro from the United States by such means possible.

Colonization is no solution of the race problem. It is an evasion. It is not repenting of wrong but putting out of sight the people upon whom wrong has been inflicted. Its reiteration and agitation only serve to fan the flame of popular prejudice and encourage the hope that in some way or other, in time or in eternity, those who hate the negro will get rid of him.

If the American people could endure the negro's presence while a slave, they certainly can and ought to endure his presence as a freeman. If they could tolerate him when he was a heathen, they might bear with him when he is a Christian, a gentleman and a scholar.

But woe to the South when it no longer has the strong arm of the negro to till its soil! And woe to the nation if it shall ever employ the sword to drive the negro from his native land!

Such a crime against justice, such a crime against gratitude, should it ever be attempted, would certainly bring a national punishment which would cause the earth to shudder. It would bring a stain upon the nation's honor, like the blood on Lady Macbeth's hand.[6] The waters of all the oceans would not suffice to wash out the infamy that such an act of ingratitude and cruelty would leave on the character of the American people.

Another mode of impeaching the wisdom of emancipation, and one that seems to give pleasure to our enemies, is, as they say, that the condition of the colored people of the South has been made worse; that freedom has made their condition worse.

The champions of this idea are the men who glory in the good old times when the slaves were under the lash and were bought and sold in the market with horses, sheep and swine. It is another way of saying that slavery is better than freedom; that darkness is better than light and that wrong is better than right. It is the American method of reasoning in all matters concerning the negro. It inverts everything; turns truth upside down and puts the case of the unfortunate negro wrong end foremost every time. There is, however, always some truth on their side.

When these false reasoners assert that the condition of the emancipated is wretched and deplorable, they tell in part the truth, and I agree with them. I even concur with them that the negro is in some respects, and in some localities, in a worse condition to-day than in the time of slavery, but I part with these gentlemen when they ascribe this condition to emancipation.

To my mind, the blame for this condition does not rest upon emancipation, but upon slavery. It is not the result of emancipation, but the defeat of emancipation. It is not the work of the spirit of liberty, but the work of the spirit of bondage, and of the determination of slavery to perpetuate itself, if not under one form, then under another. It is due to the folly of endeavoring to retain the new wine of liberty in the old bottles of slavery. I concede the evil but deny the alleged cause.

The land owners of the South want the labor of the negro on the hardest possible terms. They once had it for nothing. They now want it for next to nothing and they have contrived three ways of thus obtaining it. The first is to rent their land to the negro at an exorbitant price per annum, and compel him to mortgage his crop in advance. The laws under which this is done are entirely in the interest of the landlord. He has a first claim upon everything produced on the land. The negro can have nothing, can keep nothing, can sell nothing, without the consent of the landlord. As the negro is at the start poor and empty handed, he has to draw on the landlord for meat and bread to feed himself and family while his crop is growing. The landlord keeps books; the negro does not; hence, no matter how hard he may work or how saving he may be, he is, in most cases, brought in debt at the end of the year, and once in debt, he is fastened to the land as by hooks of steel. If he attempts to leave he may be arrested under the law.

Another way, which is still more effective, is the payment of the labor with orders on stores instead of in lawful money. By this means money is kept entirely out of the hands of the negro. He cannot save money because he has no money to save. He cannot seek a better market for his labor because he has no money with which to pay his fare and because he is, by that vicious order system, already in debt, and therefore already in bondage. Thus he is riveted to one place and is, in some sense, a slave; for a man to whom it can be said, "You shall work for me for what

I shall choose to pay you and how I shall choose to pay you," is in fact a slave though he may be called a free man.

We denounce the landlord and tenant system of England, but it can be said of England as cannot be said of our free country, that by law no laborer can be paid for labor in any other than lawful money. England holds any other payment to be a penal offense and punishment by fine and imprisonments. The same should be the case in every State in the Union.

Under the mortgage system, no matter how industrious or economical the negro may be, he finds himself at the end of the year in debt to the landlord, and from year to year he toils on and is tempted to try again and again, seldom with any better result.

With this power over the negro, this possession of his labor, you may easily see why the South sometimes brags that it does not want slavery back. It had the negro's labor heretofore for nothing, and now it has it for next to nothing, and at the same time is freed from the obligation to take care of the young and the aged, the sick and the decrepit.

I now come to the so-called, but mis-called "Negro Problem," as a characterization of the relations existing in the Southern States.

I say at once, I do not like or admit the justice or propriety of this formula. Words are things. They certainly are such in this case, and I may say they are a very bad thing in this case, since they give us a misnomer and one that is misleading. It is a formula of Southern origin, and has a strong bias against the negro. It handicaps his cause with all the prejudice known to exist against him. It has been accepted by the good people of the North, as I think, without investigation. It is a crafty invention and is in every way, worthy of its inventors.

The natural effect and purpose on its face of this formula is to divert attention from the true issue now before the American people. It does this by holding up and preoccupying the public mind with an issue entirely different from the real one in question. That which really is a great national problem and which ought to be so considered, dwarfs into a "negro problem."

The device is not new. It is an old trick. It has been oft repeated, and with a similar purpose and effect. For truth, it gives us falsehood. For innocence, it gives us guilt. It removes the burden of proof from the old master class, and imposes it upon the negro. It puts upon a race a work which belongs to the nation. It belongs to that craftiness often displayed by disputants, who aim to make the worse appear the better reason. It gives bad names to good things, and good names to bad things.

The negro has often been the victim of this kind of low cunning. You may remember that during the late war, when the South fought for the perpetuity of slavery, it called the slaves "domestic servants," and slavery "a domestic institution." Harmless names, indeed, but the things they stood for were far from harmless.

The South has always known how to have a dog hanged by giving him a bad name. When it prefixed "negro" to the national problem, it knew that the device would awaken and increase a deep-seated prejudice at once, and that it would repel fair and candid investigation. As it stands, it implies that the negro is the cause of whatever trouble there is in the South. In old slave times, when a little white child lost his temper, he was given a little whip and told to go and whip "Jim" or "Sal" and thus regained his temper. The same is true, to-day on a larger scale.

I repeat, and my contention is, that this negro problem formula lays the fault at the door of the negro, and removes it from the door of the white man, shields the guilty, and blames the innocent. Makes the negro responsible and not the nation.

Now the real problem is, and ought to be regarded by the American people, a great national problem. It involves the question, whether, after all, with our Declaration of Independence, with our glorious free constitution, whether with our sublime Christianity, there is enough of national virtue in this great nation to solve this problem, in accordance with wisdom and justice.

The marvel is that this old trick of misnaming things, so often played by Southern politicians, should have worked so well for the bad cause in which it is now employed—for the Northern people have fallen in with it. It is still more surprising that the colored press of the country, and some of the colored orators of the country, insist upon calling it a "negro problem," or a Race problem, for by it they mean the negro Race. Now—there is nothing the matter with the negro. He is all right. Learned or ignorant, he is all right. He is neither a Lyncher, a Mobocrat, or an Anarchist. He is now, what he has ever been, a loyal, law-abiding, hard working, and peaceable man; so much so, that men have thought him cowardly and spiritless. They say that any other people would have found some violent way in which to resent their wrongs. If this problem depended upon *his* character and conduct, there would be no problem to solve; there would be no menace to the peace and good order of Southern society. He makes no unlawful fight between labor and capital. That problem which often makes the American people thoughtful, is not of his bringing—though he may some day be compelled to talk, and on this tremendous problem.

He has as little to do with the cause of Southern trouble as he has with its cure. There is no reason, therefore, in the world, why he should give a name to this problem, and this lie, like all other lies, must eventually come to naught. A lie is worth nothing when it has lost its ability to deceive, and if it is at all in my power, this lie shall lose its power to deceive.

I well remember that this same old falsehood was employed and used against the negro, during the late war. He was then charged and stigmatized with being the cause of the war, on the principle that there would be no highway robbers if there were nobody on the road to be robbed. But as absurd as this pretense was, the color prejudice of the country was stimulated by it and joined in the accusation, and the negro has to bear the brunt of it.

Even at the North, he was hated and hunted on account of it. In the great city of New York, his houses were burned, his children were hunted down like wild beasts, and his people were murdered in the streets,[7] because "they were the cause of the war." Even the noble and good Mr. Lincoln, one of the best men that ever lived, told a committee of negroes who waited upon him at Washington, that "they were the cause of the war." Many were the men who accepted this theory, and wished the negro in Africa, or in a hotter climate, as some do now.

There is nothing to which prejudice is not equal in the way of perverting the truth and inflaming the passions of men.

But call this problem what you may, or will, the all important question is: How can it be solved? How can the peace and tranquility of the South, and of the country, be secured and established?

There is nothing occult or mysterious about the answer to this question. Some things are to be kept in mind when dealing with this subject and never be forgotten. It should be remembered that in the order of Divine Providence the man who puts one end of a chain around the ankle of his fellow man will find the other end around his own neck. And it is the same with a nation. Confirmation of this truth is as strong as thunder. "As we sow, we shall reap,"[8] is a lesson to be learned here as elsewhere. We tolerated slavery, and it cost us a million graves, and it may be that lawless murder, if permitted to go on, may yet bring vengeance, not only on the reverend head of age and upon the heads of helpless women, but upon the innocent babe in the cradle.

But how can this problem be solved? I will tell you how it can *not* be solved. It cannot be solved by keeping the negro poor, degraded, ignorant, and half-starved, as I have shown is now being done in the Southern States.

It cannot be solved by keeping the wages of the laborer back by fraud, as is now being done by the landlords of the South.

It cannot be done by ballot-box stuffing, by falsifying election returns, or by confusing the negro voter by cunning devices.

It cannot be done by repealing all federal laws enacted to secure honest elections.

It can, however, be done, and very easily done, for where there's a will, there's a way!

Let the white people of the North and South conquer their prejudices.

Let the great Northern press and pulpit proclaim the gospel of truth and justice against war now being made upon the negro.

Let the American people cultivate kindness and humanity.

Let the South abandon the system of "mortgage" labor, and cease to make the negro a pauper, by paying him scrip for his labor.

Let them give up the idea that they can be free, while making the negro a slave. Let them give up the idea that to degrade the colored man, is to elevate the white man.

Let them cease putting new wine into old bottles, and mending old garments with new cloth.

They are not required to do much. They are only required to undo the evil that they have done, in order to solve this problem.

In old times when it was asked, "How can we abolish slavery?" the answer was "Quit stealing."

The same is the solution of the Race problem to-day. The whole thing can be done by simply no longer violating the amendments of the Constitution of the United States, and no longer evading the claims of justice. If this were done, there would be no negro problem to vex the South, or to vex the nation.

Let the organic law of the land be honestly sustained and obeyed.

Let the political parties cease to palter in a double sense and live up to the noble declarations we find in their platforms.

Let the statesmen of the country live up to their convictions.

In the language of Senator Ingalls:[9] "Let the nation try justice and the problem will be solved."

Two hundred and twenty years ago, the negro was made the subject of a religious problem, one which gave our white forefathers much perplexity and annoyance. At that time the problem was in respect of what relation a negro would sustain to the Christian Church, whether he was a fit subject for baptism, and Dr. Godwin, a celebrated divine of his time, and one far in advance of his brethren, was at the pains of writing a book of two hundred pages, or more, containing an elaborate argument to prove that it was not a sin in the sight of God to baptize a negro.

His argument was very able, very learned, very long. Plain as the truth may now seem, there were at that time very strong arguments against the position of the learned divine.

As usual, it was not merely the baptism of the negro that gave trouble, but it was what might follow his baptism. The sprinkling him with water was a very simple thing, but the slave holders of that day saw in the innovation something more dangerous than water. They said that to baptize the negro and make him a member of the Church of Christ, was to make him an important person—in fact, to make him an heir of God and a joint heir of Jesus Christ. It was to give him a place at the Lord's supper. It was to take him out the category of heathenism, and make it inconsistent to hold him as a slave; for the Bible made only the heathen a proper subject for slavery.

These were formidable consequences, certainly, and it is not strange that the Christian slave holders of that day viewed these consequences with immeasurable horror. It was something more terrible and dangerous than the fourteenth and fifteenth amendments to our Constitution. It was a difficult thing, therefore, at that day to get the negro in the water.

Nevertheless, our learned Doctor of Divinity, like many of the same class in our day, was quite equal to the emergency. He was able to satisfy all the important parties to the problem, except the negro, and him it did not seem necessary to satisfy.

The Doctor was [a] skilled dialectician. He did not only divide the word with skill, but he could divide the negro in two parts. He argued that the negro had a soul as well as a body, and insisted that while his body rightfully belonged to his master on earth, his soul belonged to his Master in heaven. By this convenient arrangement, somewhat metaphysical, to be sure, but entirely evangelical and logical, the problem of negro baptism was solved.

But with the negro in the case, as I have said, the argument was not entirely satisfactory. The operation was much like that by which the white man got the turkey and the Indian got the crow. When the negro looked around for his body, that belonged to his earthly master. When he looked around for his soul, that had been appropriated by his Heavenly Master. And when he looked around for something that really belonged to himself, he found nothing but his shadow, and that vanished in the shade.

One thing, however, is to be noticed with satisfaction, it is this: Something was gained to the cause of righteousness by this argument. It was a contribution to the cause of liberty. It was largely in favor of the negro. It was recognition of his manhood, and was calculated to set men to thinking that the negro might have some other important rights, no less than the religious right to baptism.

Thus with all its faults, we are compelled to give the pulpit the credit of furnishing the first important argument in favor of the religious character and manhood rights of the negro. Dr. Godwin was undoubtedly a good man. He wrote at a time of much moral darkness, and property in man was nearly everywhere recognized as a rightful institution. He saw only a part of the truth. He saw that the negro had a right to be baptized, but he could not all at once see that he had a paramount right to himself.

But this was not the only problem slavery had in store for the negro. Time and events brought another and it was this very important one:

Can the negro sustain the legal relation of a husband to a wife? Can he make a valid marriage contract in this Christian country.

This problem was solved by the same slave holding authority, entirely against the negro. Such a contract, it was argued, could only be binding upon men providentially enjoying the right to life, liberty, and the pursuit of happiness, and, since the negro is a slave, and slavery a divine institution, legal marriage was wholly inconsistent with the institution of slavery.

When some of us at the North questioned the ethics of this conclusion, we were told to mind our business, and our Southern brethren asserted, as they assert now, that they alone are competent to manage this, and all other questions relating to the negro.

In fact, there has been no end to the problems of some sort or other, involving the negro in difficulty.

Can the negro be a citizen? was the question of the Dred Scott decision.

Can the negro be educated? Can the negro be induced to work for himself, without a master? Can the negro be a soldier? Time and events have answered these and all other like questions. We have amongst us, those who have taken the first prizes as scholars; those who have won distinction for courage and skill on the battlefield; those who have taken rank as lawyers, doctors and ministers of the gospel; those who shine among men in every useful calling; and yet we are called "a problem;" "a tremendous problem;" a mountain of difficulty; a constant source of apprehension; a disturbing force, threatening destruction to the holiest and best interests of society. I declare this statement concerning the negro, whether by Miss Willard, Bishop Haygood, Bishop Fitzgerald, Ex-Governor Chamberlain or by any and all others as false and deeply injurious to the colored citizen of the United States.

But, my friends, I must stop. Time and strength are not equal to the task before me. But could I be heard by this great nation, I would call to mind the sublime and glorious truths with which, at its birth, it saluted a listening world. Its voice then, was as the trump of an archangel, summoning hoary forms of oppression and time honored tyranny, to judgement. Crowned heads heard it and shrieked. Toiling millions heard it and clapped their hands for joy. It announced the advent of a nation, based upon human brotherhood and the self-evident truths of liberty and equality. Its mission was the redemption of the world from the bondage of ages. Apply these sublime and glorious truths to the situation now before you. Put away your race prejudice. Banish the idea that one class must rule over another. Recognize the fact that the rights of the humblest citizen are as worthy of protection as are those of the highest, and your problem will be solved; and, whatever may be in store for it in the future, whether prosperity, or adversity; whether it shall have foes without, or foes within, whether there shall be peace, or war; based upon the eternal principles of truth, justice and humanity, and with no class having any cause of complaint or grievance, your Republic will stand and flourish forever.

JOURNALISM

“TO MY OLD MASTER” (1848)

On the tenth anniversary of his escape to freedom, Douglass wrote a scathing public letter to his former master, Thomas Auld. He describes his ascent “from degradation to respectability,” emphasizes his common humanity with Auld, and denounces him for keeping his siblings in bondage and treating his grandmother “like an old horse.”

SOURCE: *The North Star*, September 8, 1848

THOMAS AULD:

SIR—The long and intimate, though by no means friendly relation which unhappily subsisted between you and myself, leads me to hope that you will easily account for the great liberty which I now take in addressing you in this open and public manner. The same fact may possibly remove any disagreeable surprise which you may experience on again finding your name coupled with mine, in any other way than in an advertisement, accurately describing my person, and offering a large sum for my arrest. In thus dragging you again before the public, I am aware that I shall subject myself to no inconsiderable amount of censure. I shall probably be charged with an unwarrantable, if not a wanton and reckless disregard of the rights and proprieties of private life. There are those North as well as South who entertain a much higher respect for rights which are merely conventional, than they do for rights which are personal and essential. Not a few there are in our country, who, while they have no scruples against robbing the laborer of the hard earned results of his patient industry, will be shocked by the extremely indelicate manner of bringing your name before the public. Believing this to be the case, and wishing to meet every reasonable or plausible objection to my conduct, I will frankly state the ground upon which I justify myself in this instance, as well as on former occasions when I have thought proper to mention your name in public. All will agree that a man guilty of theft, robbery, or murder, has forfeited the right to concealment and private life; that the community have a right to subject such persons to the most complete exposure. However much they may desire retirement, and aim to conceal themselves and their movements from the popular gaze, the public have a right to ferret them out, and bring their conduct before the proper tribunals of the country for investigation. Sir, you will undoubtedly make the proper application of these generally admitted principles, and will easily see the light in which you are regarded by me, I will not therefore manifest ill temper, by calling you hard names. I know you to be a man of some intelligence, and can readily determine the precise estimate which I entertain of your character. I may therefore indulge in language which may seem to others indirect and ambiguous, and yet be quite well understood by yourself.

I have selected this day on which to address you, because it is the anniversary of my emancipation; and knowing of no better way, I am led to this as the best mode of celebrating that truly important event. Just ten years ago this beautiful September morning, yon bright sun beheld me a slave—a poor, degraded chattel—trembling at the sound of your voice, lamenting that I was a man, and wishing myself a brute. The hopes which I had treasured up for weeks of a safe and successful escape from your grasp, were powerfully confronted at this last hour by dark clouds of doubt and fear, making my person shake and my bosom to heave with the heavy contest between hope and fear. I have no words to describe to you the deep agony of soul which I experienced on that never to be forgotten morning—(for I left by daylight). I was making a leap in the dark. The probabilities, so far as I could by reason determine them, were stoutly against the undertaking. The preliminaries and precautions I had adopted previously, all worked badly. I was like one going to war without weapons—ten chances of defeat to one of victory. One in whom I had confided, and one who had promised me assistance, appalled by fear at the trial hour, deserted me, thus leaving the responsibility of success or failure solely with myself. You, sir, can never know my feelings. As I look back to them, I can scarcely realize that I have passed through a scene so trying. Trying however as they were, and gloomy as was the prospect, thanks be to the Most High, who is ever the God of the oppressed, at the moment which was to determine my whole earthly career. His grace was sufficient, my mind was made up. I embraced the golden opportunity, took the morning tide at the flood, and a free man, young, active, and strong, is the result.

I have often thought I should like to explain to you the grounds upon which I have justified myself in running away from you. I am almost ashamed to do so now, for by this time you may have discovered them yourself. I will, however, glance at them. When yet but a child about six years old, I imbibed the determination to run away. The very first mental effort that I now remember on my part, was an attempt to solve the mystery, Why am I a slave? and with this question my youthful mind was troubled for many days, pressing upon me more heavily at times than others. When I saw the slave-driver whip a slave woman, cut the blood out of her neck, and heard her piteous cries, I went away into the corner of the fence, wept, and pondered over the mystery. I had, through some medium, I know not what, got some idea of God, the Creator of all mankind, the black and the white, and that he had made the blacks to serve the whites as slaves. How he could do this and be *good*, I could not tell. I was not satisfied with this theory, which made God responsible for slavery, for it pained me greatly, and I have wept over it long and often. At one time, your first wife, Mrs. Lucretia, heard me singing and saw me shedding tears, and asked of me the matter, but I was afraid to tell her. I was puzzled with this question, till one night, while sitting in the kitchen, I heard some of the old slaves talking of their parents having been stolen from Africa by white men, and were sold here as slaves. The whole mystery was solved at once. Very soon after this my aunt Jinny and uncle Noah ran away, and the great noise made about it by your father-in-law, made me for the first time acquainted with the fact, that there were free States as well as slave States. From that time, I resolved that I would some day run away. The morality of the act, I dispose as follows: I am myself; you are yourself; we are two distinct persons, equal persons. What you are, I am. You are a man, and so am I. God created both, and made us separate beings. I am not by nature bound to you, or you to me. Nature does not make your existence depend upon me, or mine to depend upon yours. I cannot walk upon your legs, or you upon mine. I cannot breathe for you, or you for me; I must breathe for myself, and you for yourself. We are distinct persons, and are each equally provided with faculties necessary to our individual existence. In leaving you, I took nothing but what belonged to me, and in no way lessened your means for obtaining an *honest* living. Your faculties remained yours, and mine became useful to their rightful owner. I therefore see no wrong in any part of the transaction. It is true, I went off secretly, but that was more your fault than mine. Had I let you into the secret, you would have defeated the enterprise entirely; but for this, I should have been really glad to have made you acquainted with my intentions to leave.

You may perhaps want to know how I like my present condition. I am free to say, I greatly prefer it to that which I occupied in Maryland. I am, however, by no means prejudiced against the State as such. Its geography, climate, fertility and products, are such as to make it a very desirable abode for any man; and but for the existence of slavery there, it is not impossible that I might again take up my abode in that State. It is not that I love Maryland less, but freedom more. You will be surprised to learn that people at the North labor under the strange delusion that if the slaves were emancipated at the South, they would flock to the North. So far from this being the case, in that event, you would see many old and familiar faces back again to the South. The fact is, there are few here who would not return to the South in the event of emancipation. We want to live in the land of our birth, and to lay our bones by the side of our fathers'; and nothing short of an intense love of personal freedom keeps us from the South. For the sake of this, most of us would live on a crust of bread and a cup of cold water.

Since I left you, I have had a rich experience. I have occupied stations which I never dreamed of when a slave. Three out of the ten years since I left you, I spent as a common laborer on the wharves of New Bedford, Massachusetts. It was there I earned my first free dollar. It was mine. I could spend it as I pleased. I could buy hams or herring with it, without asking any odds of any body. That was a precious dollar to me. You remember when I used to make seven or eight, or even nine dollars a week in Baltimore, you would take every cent of it from me every Saturday night, saying that I belonged to you, and my earnings also. I never liked this conduct on your part—to say the best, I thought it a little mean. I would not have served you so. But let that pass. I was a little awkward about counting money in New England fashion when I first landed in New Bedford. I like to have betrayed myself several times. I caught myself saying phip, for fourpence; and at one time a man actually charged me with being a runaway, whereupon I was silly enough to become one by running away from him, for I was greatly afraid he might adopt measures to get me again into slavery, a condition I then dreaded more than death.

I soon, however, learned to count money, as well as to make it, and got on swimmingly. I married soon after leaving you: in fact, I was engaged to be married before I left you; and instead of finding my companion a burden, she was truly a helpmeet. She went to live at service, and I to work on the wharf, and though we toiled hard the first winter, we never lived more happily. After remaining in New Bedford for three years, I met with Wm. Lloyd Garrison, a person of whom you have *possibly* heard, as he is pretty generally known among slaveholders. He put it into my head that I might make myself serviceable to the cause of the slave by devoting a portion of my time to telling my own sorrows, and those of other slaves which had come under my observation. This was the commencement of a higher state of existence than any to which I had ever aspired. I was thrown into society the most pure, enlightened, and benevolent that the country affords. Among these I have never forgotten you, but have invariably made you the topic of conversation—thus giving you all the notoriety I could do. I need not tell you that the opinion formed of you in these circles, is far from being favorable. They have little respect for your honesty, and less for your religion.

But I was going on to relate to you something of my interesting experience. I had not long enjoyed the excellent society to which I have referred, before the light of its excellence exerted a beneficial influence on my mind and heart. Much of my early dislike of white persons was removed, and their manners, habits and customs, so entirely unlike what I had been used to in the kitchen-quarters on the plantations of the South, fairly charmed me, and gave me a strong disrelish for the coarse and degrading customs of my former condition. I therefore made an effort so to improve my mind and deportment, as to be somewhat fitted to the station to which I seemed almost providentially called. The transition from degradation to respectability was indeed great, and to get from one to the other without carrying some marks of one's former condition, is truly a difficult matter. I would not have you think that I am now entirely clear of all plantation peculiarities, but my friends here, while they entertain the strongest dislike to them, regard me with that charity to which my past life somewhat entitles me, so that my condition in this respect is exceedingly pleasant. So far as my domestic affairs are concerned, I can boast of as comfortable a dwelling as your own. I have an industrious and neat companion, and four dear children—the oldest a girl of nine years, and three fine boys, the oldest eight, the next six, and the youngest four years old. The three oldest are now going regularly to school—two can read and write, and the other can spell with tolerable correctness words of two syllables: Dear fellows! they are all in comfortable beds, and are sound asleep, perfectly secure under my own roof. There are no slaveholders here to rend my heart by snatching them from my arms, or blast a mother's dearest hopes by tearing them from her bosom. These dear children are ours—not to work up into rice, sugar and tobacco, but to watch over, regard, and protect, and to rear them up in the nurture and admonition of the gospel—to train them up in the paths of wisdom and virtue, and, as far as we can to make them useful to the world and to themselves. Oh! sir, a slaveholder never appears to me so completely an agent of hell, as when I think of and look upon my dear children. It is then that my feelings rise above my control. I meant to have said more with respect to my own prosperity and happiness, but thoughts and feelings which this recital has quickened unfits me to proceed further in that direction. The grim horrors of slavery rise in all their ghastly terror before me, the wails of millions pierce my heart, and chill my blood. I remember the chain, the gag, the bloody whip, the death-like gloom overshadowing the broken spirit of the fettered bondman, the appalling liability of his being torn away from wife and children, and sold like a beast in the market. Say not that this is a picture of fancy. You well know that I wear stripes on my back inflicted by your direction; and that you, while we were brothers in the same church, caused this right hand, with which I am now penning this letter, to be closely tied to my left, and my person dragged at the pistol's mouth, fifteen miles, from the Bay side to Easton, to be sold like a beast in the market, for the alleged crime of intending to escape from your possession. All this and more you remember, and know to be perfectly true, not only of yourself, but of nearly all the slaveholders around you.

At this moment, you are probably the guilty holder of at least three of my own dear sisters, and my only brother in bondage. These you regard as your property. They are recorded on your ledger, or perhaps have been sold to human flesh mongers, with a view to filling your own ever-hungry purse. Sir, I desire to know how and where these dear sisters are. Have you sold them? or are they still in your possession? What has become of them? are they living or dead? And my dear old grand-mother, whom you turned out like an old horse, to die in the woods—is she still alive? Write and let me know all about them. If my grandmother be still alive, she is of no service to you, for by this time she must be nearly eighty years old—too old to be cared for by one to whom she has ceased to be of service, send her to me at Rochester, or bring her to Philadelphia, and it shall be the crowning happiness of my life to take care of her in her old age. Oh! she was to me a mother, and a father, so far as hard toil for my comfort could make her such. Send me my grandmother! that I may watch over and take care of her in her old age. And my sisters, let me know all about them. I would write to them, and learn all I want to know of them, without disturbing you in any way, but that, through your unrighteous conduct, they have been entirely deprived of the power to read and write. You have kept them in utter ignorance, and have therefore robbed them of the sweet enjoyments of writing or receiving letters from absent friends and relatives. Your wickedness and cruelty committed in this respect on your fellow-creatures, are greater than all the stripes you have laid upon my back, or theirs. It is an outrage upon the soul—a war upon the immortal spirit, and one for which you must give account at the bar of our common Father and Creator.

The responsibility which you have assumed in this regard is truly awful—and how you could stagger under it these many years is marvellous. Your mind must have become darkened, your heart hardened, your conscience seared and petrified, or you would have long since thrown off the accursed load and sought relief at the hands of a sin-forgiving God. How, let me ask, would you look upon me, were I some dark night in company with a band of hardened villains, to enter the precincts of your elegant dwelling and seize the person of your own lovely daughter Amanda, and carry her off from your family, friends, and all the loved ones of her youth—make her my slave—compel her to work, and I take her wages—place her name on my ledger as property—disregard her personal rights—fetter the powers of her immortal soul by denying her the right and privilege of learning to read and write—feed her coarsely—clothe her scantily, and whip her on the naked back occasionally; more and still more horrible, leave her unprotected—a degraded victim to the brutal lust of fiendish overseers, who would pollute, blight, and blast her fair soul—rob her of all dignity—destroy her virtue, and annihilate all in her person the graces that adorn the character of virtuous womanhood? I ask how would you regard me, if such were my conduct? Oh! the vocabulary of the damned would not afford a word sufficiently infernal, to express your idea of my God-provoking wickedness. Yet sir, your treatment of my beloved sisters is in all essential points, precisely like the case I have now supposed. Damning as would be such a deed on my part, it would be no more so than that which you have committed against me and my sisters.

I will now bring this letter to a close, you shall hear from me again unless you let me hear from you. I intend to make use of you as a weapon with which to assail the system of slavery—as a means of concentrating public attention on the system, and deepening their horror of trafficking in the souls and bodies of men. I shall make use of you as a means of exposing the character of the American church and clergy—and as a means of bringing this guilty nation with yourself to repentance. In doing this I entertain no malice towards you personally. There is no roof under which you would be more safe than mine, and there is nothing in my house which you might need for your comfort, which I would not readily grant. Indeed, I should esteem it a privilege, to set you an example as to how mankind ought to treat each other.

I am your fellow man, but not your slave,
FREDERICK DOUGLASS.

P. S.—I send a copy of the paper containing this letter, to save postage.—F. D.

"PREJUDICE AGAINST COLOR" (1850)

While walking down Broadway in New York City with two white female friends, Douglass was attacked and punched in the face. In the wake of the assault, he assails Northern racism, exposing its sources and contradictions.

SOURCE: *The North Star*, June 13, 1850

Let no one imagine that we are about to give undue prominence to this subject. Regarding, as we do, the feeling named above to be the greatest of all obstacles in the way of the anti-slavery cause, we think there is little danger of making the subject of it too prominent. The heartless apathy which prevails in this community on the subject of slavery—the cold-blooded indifference with which the wrongs of the perishing and heart-broken slave are regarded—the contemptuous, slanderous, and malicious manner in which the names and characters of Abolitionists are handled by the American pulpit and press generally, may be traced mainly to the *malign* feeling which passes under the name of prejudice against color. Every step in our experience in this country since we commenced our anti-slavery labors, has been marked by facts demonstrative of what we have just said. The day that we started on our first anti-slavery journey to Nantucket, now nine years ago, the steamer was detained at the wharf in New Bedford two hours later than the usual time of starting, in an attempt on the part of the captain to compel the colored passengers to separate from the white passengers, and to go on the forward deck of that steamer; and during this time, the most savage feelings were evinced towards every colored man who asserted his right to enjoy equal privileges with other passengers. Aside from the twenty months which we spent in England (where color is no crime, and where a man's fitness for respectable society is measured by his moral and intellectual worth), we do not remember to have made a single anti-slavery tour in any direction in this country, when we have not been assailed by this mean spirit of caste. A feeling so universal and so powerful for evil, cannot well be too much commented upon. We have used the term prejudice against color to designate the feeling to which we allude, not because it expresses correctly what that feeling is, but simply because that *innocent* term is usually employed for that purpose.

Properly speaking, *prejudice against color* does not exist in this country. The feeling (or whatever it is) which we call *prejudice*, is no less than a *murderous, hell-born hatred* of every virtue which may adorn the character of *a black man*. It is not the black man's color which makes him the object of brutal treatment. When he is drunken, idle, ignorant and vicious, *"Black Bill"* is a source of amusement: he is called a good-natured fellow: he is the first to touch his hat to the stranger approaching the hotel, and offer his service in holding his horse, or blacking his boots. The white gentleman tells the landlord to give "Bill" *"something to drink,"* and actually drinks with "Bill" himself!—while poor black "Bill" will minister to the pride, vanity and laziness of white American gentlemen. While he consents to play the buffoon for their sport, he will share their regard. But let him cease to be what we have described him to be—let him shake off the filthy rags that cover him—let him abandon drunkenness for sobriety, industry for indolence, ignorance for intelligence, and give up his menial occupation for respectable employment—let him quit the hotel and go to the church, and assume there the rights and privileges of one for whom the Son of God died, and he will be pursued with the fiercest hatred. His name will be cast out as evil; and his life will be embittered with all the venom which hate and malice can generate. Thousands of colored men can bear witness to the truth of this representation. While we are servants, we are never offensive to the whites, or marks of popular displeasure. We have been often dragged or driven from the tables of hotels where colored men were officiating acceptably as waiters; and from steamboat cabins where twenty or thirty colored men in light jackets and white aprons were frisking about as servants among the whites in every direction. On the very day we were brutally assaulted in New York for riding down Broadway in company with ladies, we saw several white ladies riding with *black servants*. These servants were well-dressed, proud looking men, evidently living on the fat of the land—yet they were servants. They rode not for their own, but for the pleasure and convenience of white persons. They were not in those carriages as friends or equals. They were there as appendages; they constituted a part of the magnificent equipages. They were there as the fine black horses which they drove were there—to minister to the pride and splendor of their employers. As they passed down Broadway, they were observed with admiration by the multitude; and even the *poor* wretches who assaulted us might have said in their hearts, as they looked upon such splendor, "We would do so too if we could." We repeat, then, that color is not the cause of our persecution; that is, it *is not our color* which makes our proximity to white men disagreeable. The evil lies deeper than prejudice against color. It is, as we have said, an intense hatred of the colored man when he is distinguished for any ennobling qualities of head or heart. If the feeling which persecutes us were prejudice against color, the colored servant would be as obnoxious as the colored gentleman, for the color is the same in both cases; and being the *same* in both cases, it would produce the *same* result in both cases.

We are then a persecuted people; not because we are *colored*, but simply because that color has for a series of years been coupled in the public mind with the degradation of slavery and servitude. In these conditions, we are thought to be in our place; and to aspire to anything above them, is to contradict the established views of the community—to get out of our sphere, and commit the provoking sin of *impudence*. Just here is our sin: we have been a slave; we have passed through all the grades of servitude, and have, under God, secured our freedom; and if we have become the special object of attack, it is because we speak and act among our fellow-men without the slightest regard to their or our own complexion; and further, because we claim and exercise the right to associate with just such persons as are willing to associate with us, and who are agreeable to our tastes, and suited to our moral and intellectual tendencies, without reference to the color of their skin, and without giving ourselves the slightest trouble to inquire whether the world are pleased or displeased by our conduct. We believe in human equality; that character, not color, should be the criterion by which to choose associates; and we pity the pride of the poor pale dust and ashes which would erect any other standard of social fellowship.

This doctrine of human equality is the bitterest yet taught by the abolitionists. It is swallowed with more difficulty than all the other points of the anti-slavery creed put together. "What makes a negro equal to a *white* man?" "No, we will never consent to that! No, that won't do!" But stop a moment; don't [be in] a passion, keep cool. What *is* a white man that you do so revolt at the idea of making a negro equal with him? Who made him? Is he an angel or a man? "A man." Very well, he is a man, and nothing but a man—possessing the same weaknesses, liable to the same diseases, and under the same necessities to which a black man is subject. Wherein does the white man differ from the black? Why, one is white and the other is black. Well, what of that? Does the sun shine more brilliantly upon the one than it does upon the other? Is nature more lavish with her gifts toward the one than toward the other? Do earth, sea and air yield their united treasures to the one more readily than to the other? In a word, "have we not all one Father?" Why then do you revolt at that equality which God and nature instituted?

The very apprehension which the American people betray on this point, is proof of the fitness of treating all men equally. The fact that they fear an acknowledgment of our equality, shows that they see a fitness in such an acknowledgment. Why are they not apprehensive lest the horse should be placed on an equality with man? Simply because the horse is not a man; and no amount of reasoning can convince the world, against its common sense, that the horse is anything else than a horse. So here all can repose without fear. But not so with the negro. He stands erect. Upon his brow he bears the seal of manhood, from the hand of the living God. Adopt any mode of reasoning you please with respect to him, he is a man, possessing an immortal soul, illuminated by intellect, capable of heavenly aspirations, and in all things pertaining to manhood, he is at once self-evidently a man, and therefore entitled to all the rights and privileges which belong to human nature.—F.D.

"F.D." (1851)

In 1851 Douglass joined the National Liberty Party and made his paper an organ of it. In doing so he changed its name from *The North Star* to *Frederick Douglass' Paper* and removed his initials from his editorials. In this short piece, he explains why he had previously used initials, revealing his influence as an editor and public leader.

SOURCE: *Frederick Douglass' Paper*, June 26, 1851

We have during the last three years signed our editorials with the above initials. The custom originated in a desire to remove certain doubts which were most liberally entertained by the pro-slavery public as to who wrote the leading editorials of the *North Star.* It had been repeatedly denied that an uneducated fugitive slave could write the English language with such propriety and correctness as those early editorials evinced. Well, we pocketed the compliments to our skill, although at the expense of our veracity; and having won the former, we set about to establish the latter by affixing our initials. We have followed the custom now more than three years, and hope we have removed all doubts which our signature can possibly remove in this line. We shall now, therefore, dispense with them, and assume fully the right and dignity of *an Editor*—a Mr. Editor if you please!

"THE WORD 'WHITE'" (1854)

During the debates over the Homestead Bill (which finally passed in 1862), Congress barred blacks from settling on public land in the west. Here Douglass condemns the bill while exposing the fiction of race: the bill benefited only "that part of God's children, who happen to live in a skin which passes for white."

SOURCE: *Frederick Douglass' Paper*, March 17, 1854

The *Homestead Bill,* which has just passed the House of Representatives, and is now likely to pass the Senate, contains a provision limiting the advantages which it is designed to secure, solely to that part of God's children, who happen to live in a skin which passes for white. Blacks, browns, mulattoes, and quadroons, &c., are to have no part or lot in the rights it secures to the settlers on the wild lands of the Republic. In the political eyes of our legislators, these latter have no right to live. The great Legislator above, according to our magnanimous republicans, legislated unwisely, and in a manner which independent Americans can never sanction, in giving life to blacks, browns, mulattoes, and quadroons, equally with his dear white children! and this, Congress is determined to make evident before Heaven and Earth and Hell! Alas! poor, robbed and murdered people! For what were we born? Why was life given us? We may not live in the old states; we may not emigrate to the new, and are told not to settle with any security on the wild lands! Were we made to sport?—given life to have it starved out of us?—provided with blood simply that it may gush forth at the call of the scourge? and thus to gratify the white man's love of torture. Some deeds there are, so wantonly cruel, so entirely infernal, as to stun the feeling, and confound all the powers of reason.—And such an one is this. What kind of men are those who voted for the Homestead Bill with such an amendment! Do they eat bread afforded by our common mother earth? and do they ever pray that God, the common father of mankind, will preserve them from famine? Men that act as they have now acted, do not appear to believe either in the existence of, or in the justice of God. It is impossible for us to argue against such mean, cowardly and wanton cruelty. Americans by birth—attached to the country by every association that can give a right to share in the benefits of its institutions, the first successful tillers of the soil—and yet foreigners, aliens, Irish, Dutch, English and French, are to be made welcome to a quarter section of American land, while we are to be kept off from it by the flaming sword of the Republic. Shame on the outrage!

"IS IT RIGHT AND WISE TO KILL A KIDNAPPER?" (1854)

When the fugitive Anthony Burns was captured in Boston, abolitionists tried to rescue him. In the process a guard was killed. The case became a cause célèbre, and Douglass uses it to justify killing slave catchers and slave owners.

SOURCE: *Frederick Douglass' Paper*, May 26, 1854

A kidnapper has been shot dead while attempting to execute the fugitive slave bill in Boston.[1] The streets of Boston in sight of Bunker Hill Monument have been stained with the warm blood of a man in the act of perpetrating the most atrocious robbery which one man can possibly commit upon another—even the wresting from him his very person and natural powers. The deed of blood, as of course must have been expected, is making a tremendous sensation in all parts of the country, and calling forth all sorts of comments. Many are branding the deed as "murder," and would visit upon the perpetrator the terrible penalty attached to that dreadful crime. The occurrence naturally brings up the question of the reasonableness, and the rightfulness of killing a man who is in the act of forcibly reducing a brother man who is guilty of no crime, to the horrible condition of a slave. The question bids fair to be one of important and solemn interest, since it is evident that the practice of slave-hunting and slave-catching, with all their attendant enormities, will either be pursued indefinitely, or abandoned immediately according to the decision arrived at by the community.

Cherishing a very high respect for the opinions of such of our readers and friends as hold to the inviolability of the human life, and differing from them on this vital question, we avail ourselves of the present excitement in the public mind, calmly to state our views and opinions, in reference to the case in hand, asking for them an attentive and candid perusal.

Our moral philosophy on this point is our own—never having read what others may have said in favor of the views which we entertain.

The shedding of human blood at first sight, and without explanation is, and must ever be, regarded with horror; and he who takes pleasure in human slaughter is very properly looked upon as a moral monster. Even the killing of animals produces a shudder in sensitive minds, uncalloused by crime; and men are only reconciled to it by being shown, not only its reasonableness, but its necessity. These tender feelings so susceptible to pain, are most wisely designed by the Creator, for the preservation of life. They are, especially, the affirmation of God, speaking through nature, and asserting man's right to live. Contemplated in the light of warmth of these feelings, it is in all cases, a crime to deprive a human being of life: but God has not left us solely to the guidance of our feelings, having endowed us with reason, as well as with feeling, and it is in the light of reason that this question ought to be decided.

All will agree that human life is valuable or worthless, as to the innocent or criminal use that is made of it. Most evidently, also, the possession of life was permitted and ordained for beneficent ends, and not to defeat those ends, or to render their attainment impossible. Comprehensively stated, the end of man's creation is his own good, and the honor of his Creator. Life, therefore, is but a means to an end, and must be held in reason to be not superior to the purposes for which it was designed by the All-wise Creator. In this view there is no such thing as an absolute right to live; that is to say, the right to live, like any other human right, may be forfeited, and if forfeited, may be taken away. If the right to *life* stands on the same ground as the right to *liberty,* it is subject to all the exceptions that apply to the right to liberty. All admit that the right to enjoy *liberty* largely depends upon the use made of that liberty; hence Society has erected jails and prisons, with a view to deprive men of their liberty when they are so wicked as to abuse it by invading the liberties of their fellows. We have a right to arrest the locomotion of a man who insists upon walking and trampling on his brother man, instead of upon the highway. This right of society is essential to its preservations; without it a single individual would have it in his power to destroy the peace and the happiness of ten thousand otherwise right minded people. Precisely on the same ground, we hold that a man may properly, wisely, and even mercifully be deprived of life. Of course life being the most precious is the most sacred of all rights, and cannot be taken away, but under the direst necessity; and not until all reasonable modes had been adopted to prevent this necessity, and to spare the aggressor.

It is no answer to this view to say that society is selfish in sacrificing the life of an individual, or of many individuals, to save the mass of mankind, or society at large. It is in accordance with nature, and the examples of the Almighty, in the execution of his will and beneficent laws. When a man flings himself from the top of some lofty monument, against a granite pavement, in that act he forfeits his *right* to live. He dies according to law, and however shocking may be the spectacle he presents, it is no argument against the beneficence of the law of gravitation, the suspension of whose operation must work ruin to the well-being of mankind. The observance of this law was necessary to his preservation; and his wickedness or folly, in violating it, could not be excused without imperilling those who are living in obedience to it. The atheist sees no benevolence in the law referred to; but to such minds we address not this article. It is enough for us that the All-Wise has established the law, and determined its character, and the penalty of its violation; and however we may deplore the mangled forms of the foolish and the wicked who transgress it, the beneficence of the law itself is fully vindicated by the security it gives to all who obey it.

We hold, then, in view of this great principle, or rule, in the physical world, we may properly infer that other law or principle of justice is the moral and social world, and vindicate its practical application to the preservation of the rights and liberties of the race, as against such exceptions furnished in the monsters who deliberately violate it by taking pleasure in enslaving, imbruting and murdering their fellow-men. As human life is not superior to the laws for the preservation of the physical universe, so, too, it is not superior to the eternal law of justice, which is essential to the preservation of the rights, and the security, and happiness of the race.

The argument thus far is to the point that society has the right to preserve itself even at the expense of the life of the aggressor; and it may be said that, while what we allege may be right enough, as regards society, it is false as vested in an individual, such as the poor, powerless, and almost friendless wretch, now in the clutches of this proud and powerful republican government. But we take it to be a sound principle, that when government fails to protect the just rights of any individual man, either he or his friends may be held in the sight of God and man, innocent, in exercising any right for his preservation which society may exercise for its preservation. Such an individual is flung, by his untoward circumstances, upon his original right of self defence. We hold, therefore, that when James Batchelder, the truckman of Boston, abandoned his useful employment, as a common laborer, and took upon himself the revolting business of a kidnapper, and undertook to play the bloodhound on the track of his crimeless brother Burns, he labelled himself the common enemy of mankind, and his slaughter was as innocent, in the sight of God, as would be the slaughter of a ravenous wolf in the act of throttling an infant. We hold that he had forfeited his right to live, and that his death was necessary, as a warning to others liable to pursue a like course.

It may be said, that though the right to kill in defence of one's liberty be admitted, it is still unwise for the fugitive slave or his friends to avail themselves of this right; and that submission, in the circumstances, is far wiser than resistance. To this it is a sufficient answer to show that submission is valuable only so long as it has some chance of being recognized as a virtue. While it has this chance, it is well enough to practice it, as it may then have some moral effect in restraining crime and shaming aggression, but no longer. That submission on the part of the slave has ceased to be a virtue is very evident. While fugitives quietly cross their hands to be tied, adjust their ankles to be chained, and march off unresistingly to the hell of slavery, there will ever be fiends enough to hunt them and carry them back. Nor is this all nor the worst. Such submission, instead of being set to the credit of the poor sable ones, only creates contempt for them in the public mind, and becomes an argument in the mouths of the community, that Negroes are, by nature, only fit for slavery; that slavery is their normal condition. Their patient and unresisting disposition, their unwillingness to peril their own lives, by shooting down their pursuers, is already quoted against them, as marking them as an inferior race. This reproach must be wiped out, and nothing short of resistance on the part of colored men, can wipe it out. Every slave-hunter who meets a bloody death in his infernal business, is an argument in favor of the manhood of our race. Resistance is, therefore, wise as well as just.

At this point of our writing, we meet with the following plea, set up for the atrocious wretch, "gone to his own place," by the Rochester *Daily American*, a Silver Grey paper.

> "An important inquiry arises,—Who are the murderers of Batchelder? There are several. First, and most guilty, are Wendell Phillips, Theodore Parker, and their Fanueil Hall coadjutors. All just minds will regard their conduct as more atrocious than even that of the ruffians who shot and mangled the unfortunate officer. Cold, remorseless, and bloody as the cruel axe, they deliberately worked up the crowd to a murderous frenzy, and pointed out the path which led to murder. The guilt which rests upon the infuriated assassins is light compared with that which blackens the cowardly orators of Fanueil Hall.
>
> "What had Batchelder done, that Phillips, Parker and their minions should steep their souls in his blood? Why did these men make his wife a widow,—his children fatherless, and send his unwarned spirit to the presence of God?"

This is very pathetic. The *widow* and the *fatherless* of this brutal truckman—a truckman who, it seems, was one of the swell-head bullies of Boston, selected for the office of Marshal or Deputy Marshal, solely because of his brutal nature and ferocious disposition.

We would ask Mr. Mann[2] whether if such a wretch should lay his horney paws upon his own dignified shoulders, with a view to reduce him to bondage, he would hold, as a murderer, any friend of his, who, to save him from such a fate, shot down the brute?—There is not a citizen of Rochester worthy of the name, who would not shoot down any man in defence of his own liberty—or who, if set upon, by a number of robbers, would not thank any friend who interposed, even to the shedding of blood, for his release.—*The widow and orphans* are far better off with such a wretch in the grave, than on the earth. Then again, the law which he undertook to execute, has *no tears* for the *widows and orphans* of poor innocent fugitives, who make their homes at the North. With a hand as relentless as that of death, it snatches the husband from the wife, and the father from his children, and this for no crime.—Oh! that man's ideas of justice and of right depended *less* upon the circumstance of color, and *more* upon the indestructible nature of things. For a *white* man to defend his friend unto blood is praiseworthy, but for a *black* man to do precisely the same thing is crime. It was glorious for Patrick Henry to say, "*Give me liberty or give me death!*" It was glorious for Americans to drench the soil, and crimson the sea with blood, *to escape the payment of three-penny tax upon tea;* but it is crime to shoot down a monster in defence of the liberty of a black man and to save him from a bondage "one hour of which (in the language of Jefferson) is worse than ages of that which our fathers rose in rebellion to oppose." Until Mr. Mann is willing to be a slave—until he is ready to admit that human legislation can rightfully reduce him to slavery, by a simple vote—until he abandons the right of self defence—until he ceases to glory in the deeds of Hancock, Adams, and Warren—and ceases to look with pride and patriotic admiration upon the sombre pile at Bunker Hill, where the blood of the oppressor was poured out in torrents making thousands of *widows and orphans,* it does not look graceful in him to brand as *murderers* those that killed the atrocious *Truckman* who attempted to play the blood-hound on the track of the poor, defenceless BURNS.

"OUR PLAN FOR MAKING KANSAS A FREE STATE" (1854)

The Kansas-Nebraska Act, passed in May 1854, repealed the Missouri Compromise and opened Northern territories to slavery. Almost immediately Kansas became a battleground over slavery, as thousands of white Northerners and Southerners emigrated there. Douglass advocated *black* emigration to Kansas, which he argued would protect freedom and prevent violence there.

SOURCE: *Frederick Douglass' Paper*, September 15, 1854

The momentous question, Shall Kansas be a Free State? continues to engage the thoughts, and to exercise the minds of the best friends of Freedom throughout the Republic. But we do not observe, among all the plans now submitted, having for their object the prevention of Slavery in that Eden-like country, one which we deem half so likely to accomplish that most desirable, and solemnly important object, as would be the one which we are now about to submit, were it but promptly put into execution.—This plan is, simply, the settlement, in the Kansas Territory, at the earliest possible period, a large and well-disciplined body of Free Colored People from the Northern States. There is nothing, confessedly, which slaveholders more dread than the presence of a numerous population of industrious, enlightened, and orderly Colored men—and just such a population as that, we believe, could be most easily flung into that much-coveted Territory.

Certain it is, that the Laws of the United States oppose no insurmountable barrier to settlements of that description. Even the infamous Nebraska Bill, mischievous in all its parts and particulars, has not closed this door against Colored Americans. The Homestead Bill, to be sure, denies them the rights of pre-emption. But this injustice is so utterly base and scandalous, that we believe the common sense, honor and magnanimity of most of the white population of Kansas would render it inoperative and void. The Law permits a meanness which the honest people will not perpetrate. There is something so mean and so shocking about the crime of denying to a man the benefit of his own hard-earned improvements, that we doubt whether there is one in ten in the Territory who would possess the hardihood to commit the deed.

We say again, the coast is clear. Colored men, Colored Citizens—for such they really are—native born Citizens to boot, can emigrate to Kansas, and can safely occupy lands located therein. And the question is *Ought they not to do so?* We believe they ought to do so. Whether regarded from the point of duty to the Slave—its effect being to weaken the slave power—or from the point of duty to themselves—its effect being to increase their welfare, and to elevate their condition—*they ought to go* into that Territory as *permanent* settlers.

There is now no question, that Kansas is one of the finest countries in the world. The testimony on this point, from those who have resided there, and those who have traversed its fertile prairies, is uniform and conclusive. The climate, soil, and productions are precisely such as are adapted to develop the energies of Colored laborers, reared in the Middle and Northern States of the Union. To emigrate thither is *far* better than to emigrate to Liberia, to the West Indies, or to Central America, and especially on account of its tendency to make Kansas a Free State. Let it be known throughout the country that one thousand Colored families, provided with all the needful implements of pioneers, and backed up by the moral influence of the Northern people, have taken up their abode in Kansas, and slaveholders, who are now bent upon blasting that fair land with Slavery, would shun it, as if it were infested by famine, pestilence, and earthquakes. They would stand as a wall of living fire to guard it. The true antidote, in that Territory, for *black slaves,* is an enlightened body of black freemen—and to that Territory should such freemen go.

To the question, Can this thing be accomplished? we answer—

Yes! Three cities can, at once, be named, in which, if proper means be adopted, *nine hundred* of the *one thousand* families can be obtained in three months, who would take up their abode as permanent settlers in Kansas the coming spring. New York City and its vicinity could send three hundred families. Philadelphia and its vicinity would gladly spare three hundred families more. Cincinnati and vicinity could afford three hundred families for such a purpose; and Boston, with the aid of New England, could easily send the additional one hundred—making an army of One Thousand families. When once in Kansas, armed with spades, rakes and hoes, and other useful implements, they need not be driven out, without *"their own consent"*; and we doubt very much if any attempt would be made to dislodge them from their adopted homes. But, for fear of the worst, let one hundred families settle upon lands near the center of the Territory, and let the remaining nine hundred spread themselves out in a circle of twenty-five or fifty miles from the center; and let all go manfully and soberly to work, minding their own business, respecting the just rights of each other, and those of all settlers in the Territory, with whom they are brought in contact; and thus, we believe, Kansas may be secured for Liberty, without conflict, without bloodshed, and without Government interference. That the announcement of this plan, and the attempt to put it into execution, would call forth loud threats from the Lords of the lash may be expected. They have already threatened and resolved. They have talked of Bowie-knives and Revolvers; but to no purpose. Emigration is going on, and *will* go on. A principal recommendation of our plan is that it exactly meets the slaveholder on his own ground. The line of argument which establishes the right of the South to settle their black slaves in Kansas is equally good for the North in establishing the right to settle black freemen in Kansas. The theory is that the Territory acquired by the treasure of all the States, belongs alike and equally to all the States;—that the Missouri restriction was an odious, unjust, and unconstitutional discrimination against the South—not allowing such *Patriarchs* as Senator Badger to settle his black *Mammy* on Territory belonging as much to the *South,* as to the *North.*

Well! the South has repealed the restriction; and now, as they think, they occupy an equal footing with the Northern States, they can drive their scarred and fettered Negroes upon those fertile Prairies. The Law allows it, and the Court awards it.—What is done, is done. Repeal is out of the question. A platform on that single stick would not admit of foot-room for half a dozen. Since this is the case, if the North is wise, it will profit by the Southern argument. The Free States have as clear a right, certainly, to send into that Territory *black Freemen,* and to protect them there, as the Southern States have to send in black Slaves, and to hold them there. We should say to the South, Freedom is not less a Northern Institution, than Slavery is a Southern one; and since you have flung down the wall which separated the two, and have invited the conflict, Let it come, and God protect the Right!

We are not to listen to the argument that the settlement of Colored Freemen, virtually excludes the white slaveholder from the Territory of Kansas. Such an argument was addressed to the South, in behalf of the free, white working-man. They scouted it; and told the free, white working-man, if the presence of slaves offended him, he might keep *out* of the Territory. Very well; we avail ourselves again of a Southern argument; and we say, that, if the presence of *free* Negroes in Kansas is offensive to slaveholders, *let them keep out of it!*—that's all! "What is fair for the *Goose,* is fair for the *Gander!*" It is the boast of Douglas,[1] that his Bill leaves Liberty and Slavery on terms of equality.

Again; when the day of election comes, and these people, with the other settlers of the territory, shall meet to determine what shall be the character of their institutions, we should like to see the argument based on the principle or doctrine of popular sovereignty[2] against their voting, and voting for whom they please. But even if debarred from voting, they would not be without influence, and there is no question on which side that influence would be wielded. The Nebraska bill says "every free white male inhabitant of the age of twenty-one years, who shall be an actual resident of said territory, and shall possess the qualifications hereinafter prescribed, shall be entitled to vote at the first election." This, of course, is entirely unconstitutional. For the Constitution of the United States makes no such discrimination on account of color in the exercise of any rights under it; and, deeming it so, the people might prefer to conform to the Constitution, at a point so important to popular sovereignty. We repeat that the

Constitution of the United States makes no distinction among citizens on account of color, but says, "that the citizens of each State shall be entitled to all the privileges and immunities of citizens of the several States."

But again; while this otherwise wicked Nebraska bill mentions the kind of persons who may vote, it does not mention the sort who may not vote; at least it does not mention the color of the parties who shall not vote, but simply restricts the right *"of suffrage, and holding office, to citizens of the United States."* Now, under this, the public opinion of the neighborhood, agreeing thereto, the colored man might exercise the elective franchise at the very first election.—But whether voting or non-voting, their presence in the territory would, of itself, form a powerful barrier to the inflowing of a large slave and slaveholding population, and secure the territory to freedom and to free institutions.

But how shall we begin, (the South has already begun). Let an association of wealthy men be at once formed, having for its object the emigration of respectable free colored people to Kansas. Let them appoint two agents for each of the large cities named—men capable of inspiring confidence—and let the latter lay the subject of emigration to Kansas before the colored people, assuring such as are disposed to improve their fortunes by emigration, that they will be aided and protected in their rights in the territory. Let a fund be raised—say forty thousand dollars—(it will be a grand, benevolent investment)—to all such as are too poor to undertake the journey upon their own means. The first hundred families could soon be raised and put on their way; and the second and third would soon follow, and so on to the end of the chapter. Let the press of the North take hold of this idea and press it upon the public mind, and Kansas need not be a slave State, and your cities need not have an unequal share of the free colored people of the North. Meanwhile, let white free working men flock into the territory by thousands. There is room and work for all. Will the people of the North aid such a movement as is here contemplated? We believe they will, and will do so joyfully.—Those who are themselves going to Kansas may not have time or attention to bestow upon the plan for colonizing colored men in Kansas, but there are hundreds of thousands who, while they cannot go themselves, still look with the deepest interest upon that territory, and feel an abiding concern for the possible results of the struggle now going on with regard to its future character and destiny. Among these thousands are men of mind, and men of money, and men of heart. These men will give time, money, talents, influence, and dignity to the enterprise. The work to be done is to launch it; set it in motion. Get it once before the people, once on the waves of public opinion, and it will float itself. We broach the idea, and so much (very little we know) is done. We leave others to do the rest, promising, however, to lend a hand, a pen, a voice, or anything else we possess, to make the plan successful.

If it be said that there are all-sufficient means in operation to keep slavery out of Kansas, the answer is, slavery is already there—and there is reason to believe that while many good and true men are going to that territory who can neither be frightened nor bought into supporting slavery, there are others quite of a different stamp. Congress is not the only place to find doughfaces.—They are among the peoples as well as among the peoples' representatives; and some may seek to better their fortunes by availing themselves of the emigration societies now scattered over the country. Besides, the Southern slaveholders are generally hard to beat. When they set about an enterprise for slavery, they are *"dreadfully"* apt to succeed. It is, therefore, unwise in a conflict like this, where so much is at stake, and where the right is so clearly on our side, to omit any effort or neglect any plan to secure a victory for freedom—a victory which may decide the whole controversy with slavery forever.

We call now for judgment upon this plan. It is imperfectly presented, we know. The wise heads of the press may improve upon it; we ask that it be considered and tried.—We make no apology for the heading we have seen fit to put to this article. Stephen A. Douglas has given his plan for getting slavery into Kansas; and we see not why Frederick Douglass should not submit his plan for keeping slavery out of Kansas.

Friends of Freedom! what say you to meeting the enemy on this vantage ground? You can meet them and beat them in the way here indicated; and if you do not do it, the responsibility is yours.

"THE DOOM OF THE BLACK POWER" (1855)

In the 1850s most Northerners believed that a cabal of powerful slaveholders, known as the "Slave Power," sought to nationalize slavery by extending it into the territories and free states. Here Douglass refers to the Slave Power as the Black Power and predicts its demise.

SOURCE: *Frederick Douglass' Paper*, July 27, 1855

The days of the Black Power are numbered. Its course, indeed, is onward, but with the swiftness of an arrow, it rushes to the tomb. While crushing its millions, it is also crushing itself.—The sword of Retribution, suspended by a single hair, hangs over it. That sword must fall. Liberty must triumph. It possesses an inherent vitality, a recuperative energy, to which its opposite is a stranger. It may to human appearances be dead, the enemy may rejoice at its grave, and sing its funeral requiem, but in the midst of the triumphal shout, it leaps from its well guarded sepulchre, asserts the divinity of its origin, flashes its indigant eye upon the affrighted enemy, and bids him prepare *for the last battle, and the grave*.

We were never more hopeful, than at the present time, of the final triumph of the great Principles which underlie the Abolition movement. We rest our hopes upon a consciousness of their inherent Righteousness. Truth is mighty, and will prevail. This is a maxim, which we do not regard as a mere rhetorical flourish. We are conscious that there is a black side to our picture. The developments of the Slave Power, are anything but pleasant to contemplate. The Present, with its inflexible realities, seems to be but an echo of the terribleness of the Past. We have lived through the one, we are now grappling with the other. We should not, as an oppressed People, grow despondent. Fear and despondency prevent us from working for the overthrow of our common enemy, with that hopeful spirit which causes us to keep our head above the waters, despite the raging of the elements. If we can at the present crisis, catch but one soft, low whisper of peace to our troubled souls, let us cling to it. Let us rejoice in Hope. The arm of the enemy will yet be paralyzed, and *with our withered arm made whole,* we'll rise in all the majesty and might of *Freemen,* and crush the crushers of the dangerous element of Abolitionism.

Whoever will contemplate the diversified phases of the Abolition Movement, from its inception to the present, will readily discern, that at no period of its history, has it presented so favorable an aspect as at the present. Truth is progressive. It ever has been; it always will be. Retrogression cannot be written on its brow. To the gaze of the world, error may appear, robed in the habiliments of gladness, and riding upon the wings of the wind. Truth may seemingly lag behind, and stop to rest upon the weeping willow. But the progress of the latter is sure and steady. The race is not to the swift; Error will soon lie down and die, but Truth will live forever. Let these reflections continually inspire us while battling with the oppressor.

Again: we should rejoice that the People are beginning to read, mark, and inwardly digest the truth. The attention of the masses is being directed to the enormity, the crushing cruelty, the ever-grasping cupidity of Slavery.—They begin to feel and know that Slavery is as relentless as the greedy grave, that its thirst for human blood can only be satiated for the time being; even a gift of nearly a half a million square miles only cools, *pro tempore,* the ardor of its ferocity. They have found out to their hearts' content, the utter inutility of attempting to compromise, or enter into any kind of contract with it, that so soon as compromises and contracts cease to conduce to its own aggrandizement, it spurns the compromise, and those who were gulled by it, and tramples on the contract. They have also found out that the Slavery question is one in which white men, as well as black men, are immediately interested, that Slavery invades the rights of man, irrespective of color and condition. They now begin to realize as Truth, that which a short time ago, they were wont to regard as the freak of disordered imaginations. Hence, the wolfish cry of "*fanaticism,*" has lost its potency; indeed the "*fanatics*" are looked upon as a pretty respectable body of People. Some consolation can be deduced from this reflection.

Another thought: we regard the present developments of the Slave Power as precipitating the era of its disastrous doom. It has overreached itself, in its efforts to abolish Freedom in the United States, and erect its black standard upon every hill-top and valley in the land. It never wore an aspect so repulsive, as it does to-day. It has made such a frightful noise of late, that the attention of the world is directed toward it. The passage of the Fugitive Slave Act, and the Nebraska Bill; the recent marauding movements of the oligarchy in Kansas, all the ebullitions of its pent-up wrath, are fatal stabs in the monster side. The Anti-Slavery sentiment of the North, has been strengthened and increased by these developments; indeed, the Abolitionists have now a most potent ally in the Slave Power. Slaveholders are unconsciously performing good service in the cause of Liberty, by demonstrating in their conduct, the truthfulness of the sentiments advanced and advocated by Abolitionists. The Anti-Slavery men of the land have faithfully admonished the whole country, and held up the Slave Power, as an Oligarchy determined on swaying the sceptre of universal dominion. But they have been regarded fanatics, and enthusiasts, crying wolf, when there was no wolf, inciting peaceful citizens to Rebellion, turning the country upside down, striving to destroy the Union. These and a host of similar allegations have been brought against them.

But now the great masses of the People find out by experience, that the wolf is indeed among them. They see his red, glaring eyes, and they cry out, "*kill the wolf;* he must not be permitted to go any farther in his depredations; our eyes have been opened." Thanks to the Fugitive Slave and Nebraska Bills. They have sealed the doom of the Black Power.

Lastly, we behold that doom written in unmistakable characters, by the great Republican Movement, which is sweeping like a whirlwind over the Free States. We rejoice in this demonstration. It evinces the fact of a growing determination on the part of the North, to redeem *itself* from bondage, to bury party affinities, and predilections, and also the political leaders who have hitherto controlled them; to unite in one grand phalanx, and go forth, and whip the enemy. *We* cannot join this party, because we think it lacks vitality; it does not go far enough in the right direction; it gives aid and comfort to the Slaveholder, by its concessions, and its willingness to "let Slavery alone where it is"—This is the very place where it should be attacked. We cannot attack it very well where it is not. But we have in former articles commented at length on the inconsistency and absurdity of that phase of Anti-Slavery sentiment and action, denominated Free-Soilism. We are, however, hopeful that this Republican Party as it grows in numbers, will also grow *"in the knowledge of the Truth."* A few more pro-Slavery demonstrations, a few more presses thrown into the river, a few more northern ministers driven from the South and West, a few more recaptures of Fugitives, near Bunker Hill, and Plymouth Rock, causing the People to see the system in all its native ugliness, and hate it with indescribable intenseness, and all will be well. We have no fears of ultimate success. Let each man do his duty. Let him continue to *agitate* in the circle in which he moves. Let him not lose sight of his individual responsibility, for this gives tone and vigor to associated action. The Slave's complaint must be heard at the fireside, in the street, in the counting house, in the prayer meeting, in the conference room, from the pulpit, in synods, and associations, and conferences, and especially *at the Polls.* We must follow the oppressor whithersoever he goeth, irrespective of the form in which he may develop himself, or the habiliments he may assume. Use the proper means, fight with the right weapons, let there be no cessation of the warfare, no diversion from the *real cause of the battle,* and we shall yet witness the *end of the Black Power in America.*

"CAPT. JOHN BROWN NOT INSANE" (1859)

Douglass was a close friend of John Brown and supported his militancy. But when Brown asked Douglass to join him on the Harpers Ferry raid, part of a scheme to free the slaves, Douglass declined because he predicted (accurately) that it would fail. Most of the raiders were captured or killed, and many Northerners called Brown insane. In this piece Douglass defends his friend, likening him to the biblical Samson and the heroes of Bunker Hill.

SOURCE: *Douglass' Monthly*, November 1859

One of the most painful incidents connected with the name of this old hero, is the attempt to prove him insane. Many journals have contributed to this effort from a friendly desire to shield the prisoner from Virginia's cowardly vengeance. This is a mistaken friendship, which seeks to rob him of his true character and dim the glory of his deeds, in order to save his life. Was there the faintest hope of securing his release by this means, we would choke down our indignation and be silent. But a Virginia court would hang a crazy man without a moment's hesitation, if his insanity took the form of hatred of oppression; and this plea only blasts the reputation of this glorious martyr of liberty, without the faintest hope of improving his chance of escape.

It is an appalling fact in the history of the American people, that they have so far forgotten their own heroic age, as readily to accept the charge of insanity against a man who has imitated the heroes of Lexington, Concord, and Bunker Hill.

It is an effeminate and cowardly age, which calls a man a lunatic because he rises to such self-forgetful heroism, as to count his own life as worth nothing in comparison with the freedom of millions of his fellows. Such an age would have sent Gideon to a madhouse, and put Leonidas in a strait-jacket. Such a people would have treated the defenders of Thermopylae as demented, and shut up Caius Marcus in bedlam. Such a marrowless population as ours has become under the debaucheries of Slavery, would have struck the patriot's crown from the brow of Wallace, and recommended blisters and bleeding to the heroic Tell. Wallace was often and again as desperately forgetful of his own life in defense of Scotland's freedom, as was Brown in striking for the American slave; and Tell's defiance of the Austrian tyrant, was as far above the appreciation of cowardly selfishness as was Brown's defiance of the Virginia pirates. Was Arnold Winkelried insane when he rushed to his death upon an army of spears, crying "make way for Liberty!" Are heroism and insanity synonyms in our American dictionary? Heaven help us! when our loftiest types of patriotism, our sublimest historic ideals of philanthropy, come to be treated as evidence of moon-struck madness. Posterity will owe everlasting thanks to John Brown for lifting up once more to the gaze of a nation grown fat and flabby on the garbage of lust and oppression, a true standard of heroic philanthropy, and each coming generation will pay its installment of the debt. No wonder that the aiders and abettors of the huge, overshadowing and many-armed tyranny, which he grappled with in its own infernal den, should call him a mad man; but for those who profess a regard for him, and for human freedom, to join in the cruel slander, "is the unkindest cut of all."

Nor is it necessary to attribute Brown's deeds to the spirit of vengeance, invoked by the murder of his brave boys. That the barbarous cruelty from which he has suffered had its effect in intensifying his hatred of slavery, is doubtless true. But his own statement, that he had been contemplating a bold strike for the freedom of the slaves for ten years, proves that he had resolved upon his present course long before he, or his sons, ever set foot in Kansas. His entire procedure in this matter disproves the charge that he was prompted by an impulse of mad revenge, and shows that he was moved by the highest principles of philanthropy. His carefulness of the lives of unarmed persons—his humane and courteous treatment of his prisoners—his cool self-possession all through his trial—and especially his calm, dignified speech on receiving his sentence, all conspire to show that he was neither insane or actuated by vengeful passion; and we hope that the country has heard the last of John Brown's madness. The explanation of his conduct is perfectly natural and simple on its face. He believes the Declaration of Independence to be true, and the Bible to be a guide to human conduct, and acting upon the doctrines of both, he threw himself against the serried ranks of American oppression, and translated into heroic deeds the love of liberty and hatred of tyrants, with which he was inspired from both these forces acting upon his philanthropic and heroic soul. This age is too gross and sensual to appreciate his deeds, and so calls him mad; but the future will write his epitaph upon the hearts of a people freed from slavery, because he struck the first effectual blow.

Not only is it true that Brown's whole movement proves him perfectly sane and free from merely revengeful passion, but he has struck the bottom line of the philosophy which underlies the abolition movement. He has attacked slavery with the weapons precisely adapted to bring it to the death. Moral considerations have long since been exhausted upon slaveholders. It is in vain to reason with them. One might as well hunt bears with ethics and political economy for weapons, as to seek to "pluck the spoiled out of the hand of the oppressor" by the mere force of moral law. Slavery is a system of brute force. It shields itself behind *might,* rather than right. It must be met with its own weapons. Capt. Brown has initiated a new mode of carrying on the crusade of freedom, and his blow has sent dread and terror throughout the entire ranks of the piratical army of slavery. His daring deeds may cost him his life, but priceless as is the value of that life, the blow he has struck, will, in the end, prove to be worth its mighty cost. Like Samson, he has laid his hands upon the pillars of this great national temple of cruelty and blood, and when he falls, that temple will speedily crumble to its final doom, burying its denizens in its ruins.

“TO THE *ROCHESTER DEMOCRAT AND AMERICAN*” (1859)

Douglass was wanted as a conspirator in the Harpers Ferry raid and fled to Canada to avoid arrest. After one of the raiders accused him of cowardice for not participating in it, Douglass responded with this editorial. He denies that he promised to participate, but emphasizes that he would make war on the proslavery government if there was “a reasonable hope for success.”

SOURCE: *New York Herald* (reprinted from the *Rochester Democrat and American*), November 4, 1859

Canada West, Oct. 31, 1859.

Mr. Editor:

I notice that the telegraph makes Mr. Cook (one of the unfortunate insurgents at Harper’s Ferry, and now in the hands of the thing calling itself the Government of Virginia, but which in fact is but an organized conspiracy by one party of the people against the other and weaker,) denounce me as a coward—and to assert that I promised to be present at the Harper’s Ferry insurrection. This is certainly a very grave impeachment, whether viewed in its bearing upon friends or upon foes, and you will not think it strange that I should take a somewhat serious notice of it. Having no acquaintance whatever with Mr. Cook, and never having exchanged a word with him about the Harper’s Ferry insurrection, I am induced to doubt that he could have used the language concerning me which the wires attribute to him. The lightning, when speaking for itself, is among the most direct, reliable, and truthful of things; but when speaking for the terror-stricken slaveholders at Harper's Ferry, it has been made the swiftest of liars. Under their nimble and trembling fingers, it magnified seventeen men into seven hundred—and has since filled the columns of the New York *Herald* for days with interminable contradictions. But, assuming that it has told only the simple truth, as to the sayings of Mr. Cook in this instance, I have this answer to make to my accuser: Mr. Cook may be perfectly right in denouncing me as a coward. I have not one word to say in defence or vindication of my character for courage. I have always been more distinguished for running than fighting—and, tried by the Harper' Ferry insurrection test, I am most miserably deficient in courage—even more so than Cook, when he deserted his old brave captain, and fled to the mountains. To this extent Mr. Cook is entirely right, and will meet no contradiction from me or from anybody else. But wholly, grievously, and most unaccountably wrong is Mr. Cook, when he asserts that I promised to be present in person at the Harper's Ferry insurrection. Of whatever other imprudence and indiscretion I may have been guilty, I have never made a promise so rash and wild as this. The taking of Harper's Ferry was a measure never encouraged by my word or by my vote, at any time or place; my wisdom or my cowardice has not only kept me from Harper's Ferry, but has equally kept me from making any promise to go there. I desire to be quite emphatic here—for of all guilty men, he is the guiltiest who lures his fellow-men to an undertaking of this sort, under promise of assistance, which he afterwards fails to render. I therefore declare that there is no man living, and no man dead, who if living, could truthfully say that I ever promised him or anybody else, either conditionally or otherwise, that I would be present in person at the Harper's Ferry insurrection. My field of labor for the abolition of slavery has not extended to an attack upon the United States arsenal. In the teeth of the documents already published, and of those which hereafter may be published, I affirm no man connected with that insurrection, from its noble and heroic leader down, can connect my name with a single broken promise of any sort whatever. So much I deem it proper to say negatively.

The time for a full statement of what I know, and of *all* I know, of this desperate but sublimely disinterested effort to emancipate the slaves of Maryland and Virginia, from their cruel taskmasters, has not yet come, and may never come. In the denial which I have now made, my motive is more a respectful consideration for the opinions of the slave's friends, than from my fear of being made an accomplice in the general *conspiracy* against Slavery. I am ever ready to write, speak, publish, organize, combine, and even to conspire against Slavery, when there is a reasonable hope for success. Men who live by robbing their fellowmen of their labor and liberty, have forfeited their right to know anything of the thoughts, feelings, or purposes of those whom they rob and plunder. They have by the single act of slaveholding voluntarily placed themselves beyond the laws of justice and honor, and have become only fitted for companionship with thieves and pirates—the common enemies of God and of all mankind. While it shall be considered right to protect oneself against thieves, burglars, robbers and assassins, and to slay a wild beast in the act of devouring his human prey, it can never be wrong for the imbruted and whip-scarred slaves, or their friends, to hunt, harass, and even strike down the traffickers in human flesh. If anybody is disposed to think less of me on account of this sentiment, or because I may have had a knowledge of what was about to occur and did not assume the base and detestable character of an informer, he is a man whose good or bad opinion of me may be equally repugnant and despicable. Entertaining this sentiment, I may be asked, why I did not join John Brown—the noble old hero whose one right hand has shaken the foundation of the American Union, and whose ghost will haunt the bed-chambers of all the born and unborn slaveholders of Virginia through all their generations, filling them with alarm and consternation! My answer to this has already been given, at least, impliedly given: "The tools to those that can use them." Let every man work for the abolition of Slavery in his own way. I would help all, and hinder none. My position in regard to the Harper's Ferry insurrection may be easily inferred from these remarks, and I shall be glad if those papers which have spoken of me in connection with it would find room for this brief statement.

I have no apology for keeping out of the way of those gentlemanly United States Marshals, who are said to have paid Rochester a somewhat protracted visit lately, with a view to an interview with me. A government recognizing the validity of the *Dred Scott* decision, at such a time as this, is not likely to have any very charitable feelings towards me; and if I am to meet its representatives, I prefer to do so, at least, upon equal terms. If I have committed any offence against Society, I have done so on the soil of the State of New York, and I should be perfectly willing *there* to be arraigned before an impartial jury; but I have quite insuperable objections to being caught by the hands of Mr. Buchanan, and "*bagged*" by Gov. Wise. For this appears to be the arrangement. Buchanan does the fighting and hunting, and Wise "*bags*" the game.

Some reflections may be made upon my leaving on a tour to England, just at this time. I have only to say that my going to that country has been rather delayed than hastened by the insurrection at Harper's Ferry. All knew that I had intended to leave here in the first week of November.

FREDERICK DOUGLASS

"THE CHICAGO NOMINATIONS" (1860)

Douglass explains why Lincoln, a dark horse, won the Republican nomination. John Brown was partly responsible, he argues, for his raid "frightened" the frontrunner William Seward into conceding to the demands of Southerners, thus calling into question his antislavery credentials.

SOURCE: *Douglass' Monthly*, June 1860

The nomination of Mr. Lincoln has taken the people of this part of the Country by surprise. The popular feeling in favor of Mr. Seward was nowhere stronger, or more earnest, than in this part of the State. The people felt that he had a stronger claim upon his party than any other man, having done more to give that party shape, and to systematise the elements composing it, and to furnish it with ideas, than any other man in the nation.

The Republican party is justly proud of Mr. Seward, proud of his history, proud of his talents, and proud of his attainments as a statesman, and it is not without strong feeling that it sees him shoved aside to make room for a man whose abilities are untried, and whose political history is too meagre to form a basis on which to judge of his future.

Still there does not appear to be the slightest disposition, on the part of Mr. Seward's friends to be factional under their disappointment, but they acquiesce in the decision of the Convention, with a grace which speaks much in praise of the party discipline in the Republican ranks.

There are a few of the more radical men, who regard Mr. Seward's defeat as a sort of political "judgment" upon him for his late speech in the Senate.[1] To them, that speech was so full of concession to the slave power, so clear a bid for the nomination at Chicago, and so nearly sunk the progressive statesman in the political trimmer, that they are well content with his defeat.

The road to the Presidency does not lead through the swamps of compromise and concession any longer, and Mr. Seward ought to have made that discovery, before John Brown frightened him into making his last great speech. In that speech he stooped quite too low for his future fame, and lost the prize that tempted the stoop after all. He had far better have lost it while standing erect.

Mr. Lincoln is a man of unblemished private character; a lawyer, standing near the front rank at the bar of his own State, has a cool, well balanced head; great firmness of will; is perseveringly industrious; and one of the most frank, honest men in political life. He cannot lay claim to any literary culture beyond the circle of his practical duties, or to any of the graces found at courts, or in diplomatic circles, but must rely upon his "good hard sense" and honesty of purpose, as capital for the campaign, and the qualities to give character to his administration. His friends cannot as yet claim for him a place in the front rank of statesmanship, whatever may be their faith in his latent capacities. His political life is thus far to his credit, but it is a political life of fair promise rather than one of rich fruitage.

It was, perhaps, this fact that obtained for him the nomination. Our political history has often illustrated the truth that a man may be too great a statesman to become President. The failure of Webster, Clay and Silas Wright in the Presidential race, is in point here, and the success of Harrison, Polk, Taylor and Pierce, tends to prove the same proposition.

If, therefore, Mr. Lincoln possesses great capacities, and is yet to be proved a great statesman, it is lucky for him that a political exigency moved his party to take him on trust and before his greatness was ripe, or he would have lost the chance. But when once elected it will be no longer dangerous for him to develop great qualities, and we hope that in taking him on a "profession of his faith," rather than on the recommendations of his political life, his party will witness his continual "growth in grace," and his administration will redound to the glory of his country, and his own fame.

As to his principles, there is no reason why the friends of Mr. Seward should not heartily support him. He is a radical Republican, and is fully committed to the doctrine of the "irrepressible conflict." In his debates with Douglas, he came fully up to the highest mark of Republicanism, and he is a man of will and nerve, and will not back down from his own assertions. He is not a compromise candidate by any means. Mr. Bates was to have played that part, with Horace Greeley for prompter. But the Chicago Convention did not fall into the melting mood. Greeley "piped unto them but they would not dance;" he mourned unto them, but they did not "lament," and his "betweenity" candidate fell flat between the two stools of Somewhere and Nowhere. Mr. Greeley has the greatest passion for making political nominations from the ranks of his enemies of any man in America. His candidates are like the frogs bred along the Nile; the head begins to croak and show signs of life while the body is yet plain mud. So Mr. Greeley is forever digging up some man for a candidate, whose head just begins to appear, while his whole body is yet enveloped in proslavery mud, and we are glad he was defeated.

The Presidential contest this fall is likely to be rather sharply defined. If Mr. Douglas is put on the course, the old personal rivalry between him and Mr. Lincoln will render the campaign especially spicy.

Illinois will form a sort of pivot, around which the waves of the political sea will sweep and dash with great force.

The nomination of Bell and Everett will tend to divert strength from the Democracy, and give advantage to Lincoln, but will have no great influence on the general result. Slavery propagandism, whether led by the vigorous and impulsive "little giant," or by the more staid and conservative Bell, will be the great enemy which the Republican party must meet.

For ourselves, we are sorry that the hosts of freedom could not have been led forth upon a higher platform, and have had inscribed upon their banners, "Death to Slavery," instead of "No more Slave States." But the people will not have it so, and we are compelled to work and wait for a brighter day, when the masses shall be educated up to a higher standard of human rights and political morality.

But as between the hosts of Slavery propagandism and the Republican party—incomplete as is its platform of principles—our preferences cannot hesitate.

While we should be glad to co-operate with a party fully committed to the doctrine of "All rights to all men," in the absence of all hope of rearing up the standard of such a party for the coming campaign, we can but desire the success of the Republican candidates.

It will be a great work accomplished when this Government is divorced from the active support of the inhuman slave system. To pluck executive patronage out of the hands of the pliant tools of the whip and the chain; to turn the tide of the National Administration against the man-stealers of this country and in favor of even a partial application of the principles of justice, is a glorious achievement, and we hope for its success.

To save a prospective empire, yet to be planted in the Great West, from the desecrating foot prints of inhuman oppression, and open these mountain slopes and river bottoms, to a hardy, industrious, and enlightened population of freemen, who are sure to follow the "Star of Empire"[2] toward the Pacific, marching to the inspiring songs of "Free labor and free men,"[3] is a consummation devoutly to be wished—a vision of prospective good, inspiring to the patriot.

It is a sad fact that the people of this country are, as yet, on a plane of morality and philanthropy far below what the exigencies of the cause of human progress demands. It is to be regretted that they will not come up to the glorious work of striking the shackles from four million slaves at a single blow—but even though they persist in approaching the blood-cemented Bastille of oppression, by the slow processes of a cautious siege, rather than by the more brave and inspiring march of a storming party, we are compelled to submit for the present, and take with gratitude the little good thus proffered.

"THE INAUGURAL ADDRESS" (1861)

Lincoln's Inaugural Address outraged Douglass. He called it "little better than our worst fears." In his address Lincoln sought to conciliate with the newly formed Confederacy in the hopes of restoring the Union peacefully. In so doing, Douglass argues, the president repudiated his platform of seeking the "ultimate extinction" of slavery.

SOURCE: *Douglass' Monthly*, April 1861

Elsewhere in the columns of our present monthly, our readers will find the Inaugural Address of Mr. Abraham Lincoln, delivered on the occasion of his induction to the office of President of the United States. The circumstances under which the Address was delivered, were the most extraordinary and portentous that ever attended any similar occasion in the history of the country. Threats of riot, rebellion, violence and assassination had been freely, though darkly circulated, as among the probable events to occur on that memorable day. The life of Mr. Lincoln was believed, even by his least timid friends, to be in most imminent danger. No mean courage was required to face the probabilities of the hour. He stood up before the pistol or dagger of the sworn assassin, to meet death from an unknown hand, while upon the very threshold of the office to which the suffrages of the nation had elected him. The outgoing Administration, either by its treachery or weakness, or both, had allowed the Government to float to the very verge of destruction. A fear, amounting to agony in some minds, existed that the great American Republic would expire in the arms of its newly elected guardian upon the very moment of his inauguration. For weeks and months previously to the 4th of March, under the wise direction and management of General Scott,[1] elaborate military preparations were made with a view to prevent the much apprehended outbreak of violence and bloodshed, and secure the peaceful inauguration of the President elect. How much the nation is indebted to General Scott for its present existence, it is impossible to tell. No doubt exists that to him, rather than to any forbearance of the rebels, Washington owes its salvation from bloody streets on the fourth of March. The manner in which Mr. Lincoln entered the Capital was in keeping with the menacing and troubled state of the times. He reached the Capital as the poor, hunted fugitive slave reaches the North, in disguise, seeking concealment, evading pursuers, by the underground railroad, between two days, not during the sunlight, but crawling and dodging under the sable wing of night.[2] He changed his programme, took another route, started at another hour, travelled in other company, and arrived at another time in Washington. We have no censure for the President at this point. He only did what braver men have done. It was, doubtless, galling to his very soul to be compelled to avail himself of the methods of a fugitive slave, with a nation howling on his track. The great party that elected him fairly wilted under it. The act, in some sense, was an indication of the policy of the new Government—more cunning than bold, evading rather than facing danger, outwitting rather than bravely conquering and putting down the enemy. The whole thing looked bad, but it was not adopted without reason. Circumstances gave to an act which, upon its face, was cowardly and mean, the merit of wisdom, forethought and discretion.

Once in Washington, Mr. Lincoln found himself in the thick atmosphere of treason on the one hand, and a cowardly, sentimental and deceitful profession of peace on the other. With such surroundings, he went to work upon his Inaugural Address, and the influence of those surroundings may be traced in the whole character of his performance. Making all allowance for circumstances, we must declare the address to be but little better than our worst fears, and vastly below what we had fondly hoped it might be. It is a double-tongued document, capable of two constructions, and conceals rather than declares a definite policy. No man reading it could say whether Mr. Lincoln was for peace or war, whether he abandons or maintains the principles of the Chicago Convention upon which he was elected. The occasion required the utmost frankness and decision. Overlooking the whole field of disturbing elements, he should have boldly rebuked them. He saw seven States in open rebellion, the Constitution set at naught, the national flag insulted, and his own life murderously sought by slave-holding assassins. Does he expose and rebuke the enemies of his country, the men who are bent upon ruling or ruining the country? Not a bit of it. But at the very start he seeks to court their favor, to explain himself where nobody misunderstands him, and to deny intentions of which nobody had accused him. He turns away from his armed enemy and deals his blows on the head of an innocent bystander. He knew, full well, that the grand objection to him and his party respected the one great question of slavery extension. The South want to extend slavery, and the North want to confine it where it is, "where the public mind shall rest in the belief of its ultimate extinction." This was the question which carried the North and defeated the South in the election which made Mr. Abraham Lincoln President. Mr. Lincoln knew this, and the South has known it all along; and yet this subject only gets the faintest allusion, while others, never seriously in dispute, are dwelt upon at length.

Mr. Lincoln opens his address by announcing his complete loyalty to slavery in the slave States, and quotes from the Chicago platform a resolution affirming the rights of property in slaves, in the slave States. He is not content with declaring that he has no lawful power to interfere with slavery in the States, but he also denies having the least *"inclination"* to interfere with slavery in the States. This denial of all feeling against slavery, at such a time and in such circumstances, is wholly discreditable to the head and heart of Mr. Lincoln. Aside from the inhuman coldness of the sentiment, it was a weak and inappropriate utterance to such an audience, since it could neither appease nor check the wild fury of the rebel Slave Power. Any but a blind man can see that the disunion sentiment of the South does not arise from any misapprehension of the disposition of the party represented by Mr. Lincoln. The very opposite is the fact. The difficulty is, the slaveholders understand the position of the Republican party too well. Whatever may be the honied phrases employed by Mr. Lincoln when confronted by actual disunion; however silvery and beautiful may be the subtle rhetoric of his long-headed Secretary of State when wishing to hold the Government together until its management should fall into other hands; all know that the masses at the North (the power behind the throne) had determined to take and keep this Government out of the hands of the slave-holding oligarchy, and administer it hereafter to the advantage of free labor as against slave labor. The slaveholders knew full well that they were hereafter to change the condition of rulers to that of being ruled; they knew that the mighty North is outstripping the South in numbers, and in all the elements of power, and that from being superior, they were to be doomed to hopeless inferiority. This is what galled them. They are not afraid that Lincoln will send out a proclamation over the slave States declaring all the slaves free, nor that Congress will pass a law to that effect. They are no such fools as to believe any such thing; but they do think, and not without reason, that the power of slavery is broken, and that its prestige is gone whenever the people have made up their minds that Liberty is safer in the hands of freemen than in those of slaveholders. To those sagacious and crafty men, schooled into mastery over bondmen on the plantation, and thus the better able to assume the airs of superiority over Northern doughfaces, Mr. Lincoln's disclaimer of any power, right or inclination to interfere with slavery in the States, does not amount to more than a broken shoe-string! They knew it all before, and while they do not accept it as a satisfaction, they do look upon such declarations as the evidence of cowardly baseness, upon which they may safely presume.

The slaveholders, the parties especially addressed, may well inquire if you, Mr. Lincoln, and the great party that elected you, honestly entertain this very high respect for the rights of slave property in the States, how happens it that you treat the same rights of property with scorn and contempt when they are set up in the Territories of the United States?—If slaves are property, and our rights of property in them are to be so sacredly guarded in the States, by what rule of law, justice or reason does that property part with the attributes of property, upon entering into a Territory owned in part by that same State? The fact is, the slaveholders have the argument all their own way, the moment that the right of property in their slaves is conceded under the Constitution. It was, therefore, weak, uncalled for and useless for Mr. Lincoln to begin his Inaugural Address by thus at the outset prostrating himself before the foul and withering curse of slavery. The time and the occasion called for a very different attitude. Weakness, timidity and conciliation towards the tyrants and traitors had emboldened them to a pitch of insolence which demanded an instant check. Mr. Lincoln was in a position that enabled him to wither at a single blast their high blown pride. The occasion was one for honest rebuke, not for palliations and apologies. The slaveholders should have been told that their barbarous system of robbery is contrary to the spirit of the age, and to the principles of Liberty in which the Federal Government was founded, and that they should be ashamed to be everlastingly pressing that scandalous crime into notice. Some thought we had in Mr. Lincoln the nerve and decision of an Oliver Cromwell; but the result shows that we merely have a continuation of the Pierces and Buchanans, and that the Republican President bends the knee to slavery as readily as any of his infamous predecessors. Not content with the broadest recognition of the right of property in the souls and bodies of men in the slave States, Mr. Lincoln next proceeds, with nerves of steel, to tell the slaveholders what an excellent slave hound he is, and how he regards the right to recapture fugitive slaves a constitutional duty; and lest the poor bondman should escape being returned to the hell of slavery by the application of certain well known rules of legal interpretation, which any and every white man may claim in his own case, Mr. Lincoln proceeds to cut off the poor, trembling Negro who had escaped from bondage from all advantages from such rules. He will have the pound of flesh, blood or no blood, be it more or less, a just pound or not. The Shylocks of the South, had they been after such game, might have exclaimed, in joy, an Abraham come to judgment! But they were not to be caught with such fodder. The hunting down a few slaves, the sending back of a few Lucy Bagleys, young and beautiful though they be, to the lust and brutality of the slave-breeders of the Border States, is to the rapacity of the rebels only as a drop of water upon a house in flames. The value of the thing was wholly in its quality. "Mr. Lincoln, you will catch and return our slaves if they run away from us, and will help us hold them where they are;" what cause, then, since you have descended to this depth of wickedness, withholds you from coming down to us entirely? Indeed, in what respect are you better than ourselves, or our overseers and drivers who hunt and flog our Negroes into obedience?—Again, the slaveholders have a decided advantage over Mr. Lincoln, and over his party. He stands upon the same moral level with them, and is in no respect better than they. If we held the Constitution, as held by Mr. Lincoln, no earthly power could induce us to swear to support it. The fact is, (following the lead of the Dred Scott decision, and all the Southern slaveholding politicians, with all the doughfaces of the North who have been engaged in making a Constitution, for years, outside of the Constitution of 1789,) Mr. Lincoln has taken everything at this point in favor of slavery for granted. He is like the great mass of his countrymen, indebted to the South for both law and gospel.

But the Inaugural does not admit of entire and indiscriminate condemnation. It has at least one or two features which evince the presence of something like a heart as well as a head. Horrible as is Mr. Lincoln's admission of the constitutional duty of surrendering persons claimed as slaves, and heartily as he seems determined that that revolting work shall be performed, he has sent along with his revolting declaration a timid suggestion which, tame and spiritless as it is, must prove as unpalatable as gall to the taste of slaveholders. He says: "In any law on this subject, ought not all the safeguards of liberty known in humane and civilized jurisprudence be introduced, so that a free man be not in any case surrendered as a slave." For so much, little as it is, let the friends of freedom thank Mr. Lincoln. This saves his Address from the gulf of infamy into which the Dred Scott decision sunk the Supreme Court of the United States. Two ideas are embraced in this suggestion: First, a black man's rights should be guarded by all the safeguards known to liberty and to humane jurisprudence; secondly, that slavery is an inhuman condition from which a free man ought by all lawful means to be saved. When we remember the prevailing contempt for the rights of all persons of African descent, who are mostly exposed to the operation of these slave-catching laws, and the strenuous efforts of the American Church and clergy to make slavery a divine relation, and especially blissful to our much hated variety of the human family, we are disposed to magnify and rejoice over even this slight recognition of rights, and this implied acknowledgment of the hatefulness of slavery. One of the safeguards of liberty is trial in open court. Another is the right of bringing evidence in one's own favor, and of confronting and questioning opposing witnesses. Another is the trial by a jury of our peers. Another is that juries are judges both of the law and the evidence in the case. There are other safeguards of liberty which we might specify, any one of which, faithfully applied, would not only make it difficult to surrender a free man as a slave, but would make it almost impossible to surrender any man as such. Thanking Mr. Lincoln for even so much, we yet hold him to be the most dangerous advocate of slave-hunting and slave-catching in the land.

He has laid down a general rule of legal interpretation which, like most, if not all general rules, may be stretched to cover almost every conceivable villainy. "*The intention of the law-giver is the law,*" says Mr. Lincoln. But we say that this depends upon whether the *intention* itself is lawful. If law were merely an arbitrary rule, destitute of all idea of right and wrong, the intention of the lawgiver might indeed be taken as the law, provided that intention were certainly known. But the very idea of law carries with it ideas of right, justice, and humanity. Law, according to Blackstone, commands that which is right and forbids that which is wrong. A law authorizing murder is not law, because it is an outrage upon all the elements out of which laws originate. Any man called to administer and execute such a law is bound to treat such an edict as a nullity, having no binding authority over his action or over his conscience. He would have a right to say, upon the authority of the Supreme Court, that "laws against fundamental morality are void"; that a law for murder is an absurdity, and not only from the purpose of all law and government, but wholly at war with every principle of law. It would be no avail in such a case to say that the "intention of law-makers is the law." To prove such an intention is only to destroy the validity of the law.

But the case is not murder, but simply the surrendering of a person to slavery who has made his or her escape from slavery into a free State. But what better is an act of this kind than murder? Would not Mr. Lincoln himself prefer to see a dagger plunged to the hilt into the heart of his own daughter, than to see that daughter given up to the lust and brutality of the slaveholders of Virginia, as was poor, trembling Lucy Bagley given up a few weeks ago by the Republicans of Cleveland? What is slavery but a slow process of soul murder? What but murder is its chief reliance? How do slaveholders hold their slaves except by asserting their right and power to murder their slaves if they do not submit to slavery? Does not the whole slave system rest upon a basis of murder? Your money or your life, says the pirate; your liberty or your life, says the slaveholder. And where is the difference between the pirate and the slaveholder?

But the "intention of the law is the law." Well, suppose we grant it in the present case, that the intention of the law-maker is the law, and two very important questions arise—first, as to who were the makers, and, secondly, by what means are we required to learn their intentions? Who made the Constitution? The preamble to the Constitution answers that question. "We, the people, do ordain and establish this Constitution." The people, then, made the law. How stood their intention as to the surrender of fugitive slaves? Were they all agreed in this intention to send slaves to bondage who might escape from it? Or were only a part? and if a part, how many? Surely, if a minority only were of the intention, that intention could not be the law, especially as the law itself expresses no such intention. The fact is, there is no evidence whatever that any considerable part of the people who made and adopted the American Constitution intended to make that instrument a slave-hunting or a slave-holding instrument, while there is much evidence to prove the very reverse. Daniel Webster, even in his famous 7th of March speech, was sufficiently true to the letter of the Constitution, and to the history of the times in which the Constitution was framed and adopted, to deny that the Constitution required slaves to be given up, and quoted Mr. James Madison in corroboration of his statement. This is Mr. Webster's language: "It may not be important here to allude to that—I had almost said celebrated—opinion of Mr. Madison. You observe, sir, that the term slavery is not used in the Constitution. The Constitution does not require that fugitive slaves shall be delivered up; it requires that persons bound to service in one State escaping into another, shall be delivered up. Mr. Madison opposed the introduction of the term slave, or slavery, into the Constitution; for he said he did not wish to see it recognized by the Constitution of the United States of America, that there could be property in men."

How sadly have the times changed, not only since the days of Madison—the days of the Constitution—but since the days even of Daniel Webster. Cold and dead as that great bad man was to the claims of humanity, he was not sufficiently removed from the better days of the Republic to claim, as Mr. Lincoln does, that the surrender of fugitive slaves is a plain requirement of the Constitution.

But there comes along a slight gleam of relief. Mr. Lincoln tremblingly ventures to *inquire* (for he is too inoffensive to the slaveholders to assert and declare, except when the rights of the black men are asserted and declared away) if it "might not be well to provide by law for the enforcement of that clause in the Constitution which guarantees that the citizens of each State shall be entitled to all the privileges and immunities of citizens in the several States."

Again we thank Mr. Lincoln. He has, however, ventured upon a hazardous suggestion. The man has not quite learned his lesson. He had not been long enough in Washington to learn that Northern citizens, like persons of African descent, have no rights, privileges or immunities that slaveholders are bound to respect. To break open a man's trunk, to read the letters from his wife and daughters, to tar and feather him, to ride him on a rail and give him the alternative of being hanged or of leaving town the same hour, simply because he resides in a free State, is a privilege and immunity which our Southern brethren will not give up, though the requirement were made in every line of the Constitution. Yet, we say, we are thankful. It is something even to have a sickly intimation that other American citizens, not belonging to the privileged slaveholding class, have rights which it "*might be well*" to secure by law, and that the mere fact of living in a free State ought not to subject the unfortunate traveler either to being whipped, hanged or shot. Yes, this is something to be thankful for and is more than any other American President has ever ventured to say, either in his Inaugural Speech or Annual Message. It is, perhaps, this latter fact that gives Mr. Lincoln's casual remark its chief importance.—Hitherto our Presidents had pictured the South as the innocent lamb, and the greedy North as the hungry wolf, ever ready to tear and devour.

From slave-catching, Mr. Lincoln proceeds to give a very lucid exposition of the nature of the Federal Union, and shows very conclusively that this Government from its own nature and the nature of all Governments, was intended to be perpetual, and that it is revolutionary, insurrectionary and treasonable to break it up. His argument is excellent; but the difficulty is that the argument comes too late. When men deliberately arm themselves with the avowed intention of breaking up the Government; when they openly insult its flag, capture its forts, seize its munitions of war, and organize a hostile Government, and boastfully declare that they will fight before they will submit, it would seem of little use to argue with them. If the argument was merely for the loyal citizen, it was unnecessary. If it was for those already in rebellion, it was casting pearls before swine. No class of men in the country understood better than the rebels themselves the nature of the business on which they are engaged.—They tell us this in the thousands of pounds of powder they have been buying, and the millions of money and arms they have been stealing. They know that unless the Government is a miserable and contemptible failure, destitute of every attribute of a Government except the name, that that Government must meet them on the field and put them down, or be itself put down. To parley with traitors is but to increase their insolence and audacity.

It remains to be seen whether the Federal Government is really able to do more than hand over some John Brown to be hanged, suppress a slave insurrection, or catch a runaway slave—whether it is powerless for liberty, and only powerful for slavery. Mr. Lincoln says, "I shall take care that the laws of the Union shall be faithfully executed in all the States"—that is, he will do so as *"as far as practicable,"* and *unless* the American people, his masters, shall, in some authoritative manner direct the contrary. To us, both these provisions had better have been omitted. They imply a want of confidence in the ability of the Government to execute its own laws, and open its doors to all that border tribe who have nothing but smiles for the rebels and peace lectures for the Government. The American people have placed the Government in the hands of Abraham Lincoln for the next four years, and his instructions are in the Constitution. He had no right to suppose that they will reverse those instructions in a manner to give immunity to traitors; and it was a mistake to admit such a possibility, especially in the presence of the very traitors themselves. But we are dwelling longer upon Mr. Lincoln's speech than we had intended, and longer than we are warranted either by the patience of our readers, or the extent of our space. The perusal of it has left no very hopeful impression upon our mind for the cause of our down-trodden and heart-broken countrymen. Mr. Lincoln has avowed himself ready to catch them if they run away, to shoot them down if they rise against their oppressors, and to prohibit the Federal Government *irrevocably* from interfering for their deliverance. With such declarations before them, coming from our first modern anti-slavery President, the Abolitionists must know what to expect during the next four years, (should Mr. Lincoln not be, as he is likely to be, driven out of Washington by his rival, Mr. Jeff. Davis, who has already given out that should Mr. Lincoln attempt to do, what he has sworn to do—namely, execute the laws, fifty thousand soldiers will march directly upon Washington!) This might be taken as an empty threat on the part of the President of the Confederated States, if we did not see with what steadiness, promptness and certainty the rebels have from the first executed all their designs and fulfilled all their promises. A thousand things are less probable than that Mr. Lincoln and his Cabinet will be driven out of Washington, and made to go out, as they came in, by the Underground Railroad. The game is completely in the hands of Mr. Jefferson Davis, and no doubt he will avail himself of every advantage.

"A TRIP TO HAITI" (1861)

Lincoln's Inaugural Address prompted Douglass to plan a trip to Haiti with an eye toward emigrating there. But the bombing of Fort Sumter created "a tremendous revolution" for ending slavery, and he canceled his trip.

SOURCE: *Douglass' Monthly*, May 1861

A dream, fondly indulged, a desire, long cherished, and a purpose, long meditated, are now quite likely to be realized. At this writing, we are on the eve of starting for a visit of a few weeks to Haiti; and before the announcement can reach all our readers and friends, especially those in Great Britain, we shall probably be well on our ocean-way to the shores of *la Republic de l'Haiti*.

For this piece of good fortune (for such we esteem it, and hope it will prove to be) we are indebted for all, save the disposition to go the voyage, to the considerate kindness of the Haitian Government. That Government has removed an important obstacle out of the way, which might have delayed, though it could not have prevented our long-desired visit. Too late to apprize our readers in our April number of the fact, we were informed that a steamer was being chartered by the Haitian Bureau at Boston to carry emigrants and passengers to Haiti from the United States. The intimation was accompanied with a generous offer of a free passage to ourself and daughter to and from Haiti, by Mr. Redpath, the Haitian Consulate at Philadelphia. We are not more thankful for this generous offer from the quarter whence it comes, than sensible of the kind consideration which it implies.

We gratefully appreciate both, and shall promptly avail ourselves of the double favors.

The steamer secured for the voyage is to sail from New Haven, Connecticut, about the 25th of April, and will, if all be well, reach *Port-au-Prince* by the first of May.

In making this announcement, we do not wish in any wise to conceal the fact that we are much elated by the prospect of standing once upon the soil of San Domingo, the theatre of many stirring events and heroic achievements, the work of a people, bone of our bone, and flesh of our flesh.

We began life too late to accomplish much. More than twenty-one years of it were lost for all proper educational advantage. Slavery stole from us those years when study and travel should do most for a man; but the world is still new and beautiful to us, and we still rejoice in any opportunity to increase our knowledge of its works and ways. We have seen much of it, but mostly its sterner features. Clouds and storms, ice and snow, moral as well as physical, have been our familiar elements. We have felt the keenly cutting, frosty air, from off the desolate coast of Labrador, amid the snows of winter; but we have never felt the beams of a tropical sun, seen the luminous stars of the tropical sky, heard the sweet warblings of tropical birds, inhaled the fragrance of tropical breezes, nor beheld the endless wealth of a tropical soil. We are going to a land where nature is in full dress, and unfolds her charms in all their loveliness. But we go to Haiti not to enjoy its delightful and soothing climate, to rest in the shadow of its stately palms, nor to luxuriate in its delicious fruits, and its glorious flowers. While not insensible to those delightful attractions, we are drawn towards the sunny region at this time by other considerations than those of pleasure—considerations connected with the sacred cause to which we have gladly given twenty years of unremitting toil.

A visit to Haiti at any time would be a high privilege to us. Our whole experience makes such a visit desirable. Born a slave as we were, in this boasted land of liberty, tinged with a hated color, despised by the rulers of the State, accustomed from childhood to hear the colored race disparaged and denounced, their mental and moral qualities held in contempt, treated as an inferior race, incapable of self government, and of maintaining, when left to themselves, a state of civilization, set apart by the laws of our being to a condition of slavery—we, naturally enough, desire to see, as we doubtless shall see, in the free, orderly and Independent Republic of Haiti, a refutation of the slanders and disparagements of our race. We want to experience the feeling of being under a Government which has been administered by a race denounced as mentally and morally incapable of self-government.

While, however, we shall go to Haiti with strong prepossessions in its favor, we hope to go with the eyes of a truthful observer, able to see things as they really are, to consider the circumstances, and report the philosophy as well as the facts of the situation. Truth can hurt nobody, and we have no fear to tell even that which may seem to make against our cause, if truth shall require it. One thing we know in advance, of Haiti, and that is, her people are *"naught but men and women"*; and that men and women under a vertical sun, where nature responds at the merest touch of industry to every physical want, will not tax themselves to make the same exertion as when in a colder climate and upon a sterner soil.—Another thing we know in advance, which is this: that against all disparagements from the United States against the crafty machinations of two continents to crush her, Haiti has during more than sixty years maintained a free and independent system of government and that no hostile power has been able to bend the proud necks of her people to a foreign yoke. She stands forth among the nations of the earth richly deserving respect and admiration.

Both the press and the platform of the United States have long made Haiti the bugbear and scare-crow of the cause of freedom. Ignorant of her real character in some instances; willfully blind to her obvious virtues in others, we have done her people the most marked injustice. The fact is, white Americans find it hard to tell the truth about colored people. They see us with a dollar in their eyes. Twenty hundred millions of dollars invested in the bodies and souls of the Negro race in this Republic—a mountain of gold—constitutes a standing bribe, a perpetual temptation to do injustices to the colored race. Haiti has thus constantly been the victim of something like a downright conspiracy to rob her of the natural sympathy of the civilized world, and to shut her out of the fraternity of nations. No people have been compelled to meet and live down a prejudice so stubborn and so hatefully unjust. For a time it was fashionable to call them even in our Congress a nation of murderers and cut-throats, and for no better reason than that they won their freedom by their arms. It is quite time that this interesting people should be better understood. Though a city set on an hill, she has been hid; and though a light of glorious promise, she has been compelled to shine only under a bushel. A few names of her great men have been known to the world; but her real character as a whole, we are persuaded, has been grossly misunderstood and perversely misrepresented. One object of our mission, therefore, will be to do justice to Haiti, to paint her as she is, and to add the testimony of an honest witness to honest worth.

But besides these general motives, there are special ones growing out of the state of things at present existing in this country.—During the last few years the minds of free colored people in all the States have been deeply exercised in relation to what may be their future in the United States. To many it has seemed that the portents of the moral sky were all against us. At the South they have been taught to believe that they must soon be forced to choose between slavery or expulsion. At the North there are, alas! too many proofs that the margin of life and liberty is becoming more narrow every year. There are many instances where the black man's places are taken by the white man, but few where, in the free States, the places of the white man are taken by the man of sable hue. The apprehension is general, that proscription, persecution and hardships are to wax more and more rigorous and more grievous with every year; and for this reason they are now, as never before, looking out into the world for a place of retreat, an asylum from the apprehended storm which is about to beat pitilessly upon them.

Without attempting to dispel this apprehension by appeals to facts, which have failed to satisfy, and to general principles of development and progress, which most of our people have deemed too abstract and transcendental for practical life, we propose to act in view of the settled fact that many of them are already resolved to look for homes beyond the boundaries of the United States, and that most of their minds are turned towards Haiti. Though never formally solicited by any organized body of our people to acquire information which may be useful to those who are looking to that country for a home, we have been repeatedly urged to do so by individuals of the highest character and respectability. Without at all discrediting the statements of others, we have desired to see for ourselves. For the next six or eight weeks, therefore, we know of no better use to which we can put ourselves, than in a tour of observation in this modern land of Canaan, where so many of our people are journeying from the rigorous bondage and oppression of our modern Egypt.

—Since this article upon Haiti was put in type, we find ourselves in circumstances which induce us to forego our much desired trip to Haiti, for the present. The last ten days have made a tremendous revolution in all things pertaining to the possible future of the colored people of the United States. We shall stay here and watch the current of events, and serve the cause of freedom and humanity in any way that shall be open to us during the struggle now going on between the slave power and the government. When the Northern people have been made to experience a little more of the savage barbarism of slavery, they may be willing to make war upon it, and in that case we stand ready to lend a hand in any way we can be of service. At any rate, this is no time for us to leave the country.

"THE FALL OF SUMTER" (1861)

Douglass was one of the first journalists to recognize that the war created a social revolution in the North. In making war on the slaveholding South, the government also fought for liberty, Douglass notes. As a result, abolitionists enjoyed newfound respect.

SOURCE: *Douglass' Monthly*, May 1861

As a friend of freedom, earnestly laboring for the abolition of slavery, we have no tears to shed, no lamentations to make over the fall of Fort Sumter. By that event, one danger which threatened the cause of the American slave has been greatly diminished. Through many long and weary months, the American people have been on the mountain with the wily tempter, and have been liable at any moment of weakness to grant a new lease of life to slavery. The whole power of the Northern proslavery press, combined with the commercial and manufacturing interests of the country, has been earnestly endeavoring to purchase peace and prosperity for the North by granting the most demoralizing concessions to the insatiate Slave Power. This has been our greatest danger. The attack upon Fort Sumter bids fair to put an end to this cowardly, base and unprincipled truckling. To our thinking, the damage done to Fort Sumter is nothing in comparison with that done to the secession cause. The hail and fire of its terrible batteries has killed its friends and spared its enemies. Anderson lives, but where are the champions of concession at the North? Their traitor lips are pale and silent.

While secession confined its war operation to braggart threats, pompous declarations, exciting telegrams, stealing arms, planting liberty poles, wearing cockades, and displaying palmetto and rattlesnake flags, it exercised a potent influence over the public mind, and held the arm of the Government paralyzed. It commanded the artillery of a thousand cannon. But the secessionists themselves have now "smashed" up these magnificent machines, and have spiked their own most efficient guns. They have completely shot off the legs of all trimmers and compromisers, and compelled everybody to elect between patriotic fidelity and proslavery treason.

For this consummation we have watched and wished with fear and trembling. God be praised! that it has come at last. We should have been glad if the North, of its own proper virtue, had given this *quietus* to doubt and vacillation. She did not do it, and perhaps it is best that she did not. What her negative wisdom withheld has now come to us through the vengeance and rashness of slaveholders. Another instance of the wrath of man working out the purposes and praise of eternal goodness!

Had Mr. Jefferson Davis continued to allow Major Anderson, with his harmless garrison, to receive his daily bread from the markets of Charleston, or even permitted the Government at Washington to feed his men, the arm of the nation might have slept on, and the South might have got the most extravagant concessions to its pet monster, slavery. Every Personal Liberty Bill might have been swept from the statute books of the North, and every trembling fugitive hunted by Northern bloodhounds from his hiding place to save the Union. Already the hateful reaction had begun. Chicago and Cleveland, headquarters of Republicanism, had both betrayed innocent blood, while "down with Abolition" was fast becoming the cry of the mob on the one hand, and clergy on the other. The color of the Negro, always hated, was fast becoming more hated, and the few rights and liberties enjoyed by the free colored citizen were threatened. But now, thanks to the reckless impetuosity of the dealers in the bodies and souls of men, their attack upon Sumter has done much to arrest this retrograde and cowardly movement, and has raised the question as to the wisdom of thus pampering treason. Our rulers were ready enough to sacrifice the Negro to the Union so long as there was any hope of saving the Union by that means. The attack upon Sumter, and other movements on the part of the cotton lords of the lash, have about convinced them that the insatiate slaveholders not only mean peace and safety of slavery, but to make themselves masters of the Republic. It is not merely a war for slavery, but it is a war for slavery dominion. There are points in which different nations excel.—England is mighty on the land, but mightier on the water. The slaveholders have always surpassed the North in the matter of party politics. In the arts of persuasion, the management of men, in tact and address, they have ever been remarkably successful. Accustomed to rule over slaves, and to assume the airs of vaunted superiority, they easily intimidate the timid, overawe the servile, while they artfully cultivate the respect and regard of the brave and fearless.

It remains to be seen whether they have acted wisely in transferring the controversy with the North from the halls of diplomacy, to the field of battle. They were not forced to the measure. The Government at Washington stood waiting to be gracious. It treated treason in its embryo form, merely as an *"eccentricity,"* which a few months would probably cure. They had no purpose to resort to the straight jacket. To some of us there was far too little importance attached to the slaveholding movement by the Government at Washington. But all is changed now. The Government is active, and the people aroused. Again, we say, out of a full heart, and on behalf of our enslaved and bleeding brothers and sisters, thank God!—The slaveholders themselves have saved our cause from ruin! They have exposed the throat of slavery to the keen knife of liberty, and have given a chance to all the righteous forces of the nation to deal a death-blow to the monster evil of the nineteenth century.—*Friends of freedom! be up and doing;—now is your time.* The tyrant's extremity is your opportunity! Let the long crushed bondman arise! and in this auspicious moment, snatch back the liberty of which he has been so long robbed and despoiled. Now is the day, and now is the hour!

Is it said that we exult in rebellion? We repel the allegation as a slander. Every pulsation of our heart is with the legitimate American Government, in its determination to suppress and put down this slave-holding rebellion. The *Stars and Stripes* are now the symbols of liberty. The Eagle that we left last month something like as good as dead, has revived again, and screams terror in the ears of the slaveholding rebels. None but the worst of traitors can now desire victory for any flag but that of the old Confederacy.

He who faithfully works to put down a rebellion undertaken and carried on for the extension and perpetuity of slavery, performs an anti-slavery work. Even disunion Abolitionists, who have believed that the dissolution of the Union would be the dissolution of slavery, will, we have no doubt, rejoice in the success of the Government at Washington, in suppressing and putting down this slaveholding rebellion.

"FRÉMONT AND HIS PROCLAMATION" (1861)

In August 1861, General John C. Frémont issued the first wartime emancipation proclamation, declaring free all slaves of rebel masters in Missouri. Lincoln revoked the proclamation. Douglass describes the significance of Frémont's proclamation and assails Lincoln's rationale for revoking it.

SOURCE: *Douglass' Monthly*, December 1861

We have recently seen some interesting samples of young men, dressed in military costume, and bound for the seat of war. As we looked upon those noble beings, so promptly responding to their country's call, we felt an involuntary sinking within ourselves, and silently inquired, "When shall this fratricidal war have an end?" The question necessarily induced its legitimate train of thought, legitimate to us, and as follows:

Before this war is terminated, the men who comprehend its nature, and realize in some measure its design, (for it is too momentous an affair to be accidental,) will have something to do in directing those measures which are eventually to bring it to a successful issue. The measures hitherto adopted strike one as inadequate to accomplish the object for which they have been inaugurated. The apparent trifling with matters of the last importance to the stability and perpetuity of any Government; the want of firmness in rigidly enforcing fitting penalties against offenders—as the treatment of traitors as belligerents in honorable warfare—all go to undermine the confidence of reflecting men in the strength and true dignity of a Government which they ardently love. We have for a time expected, with almost every returning sun, that some blow would be struck to give relief to a picture whose sombre hues have, up to the present time, saddened many a hopeful heart. But disappointment has succeeded disappointment until we feel compelled to look in another direction, and to other men, to relieve the country from this direful scourge, and place it upon a basis whose *quality* shall be twin brother to its *claims*.

We venture the assertion that a majority among the intelligent and thoughtful of the nation were *never* more hopeful since the commencement of this war, and never gave vent to feelings so jubilant with satisfaction, as when they read the fearless and earnest Proclamation of John C. Frémont, given in the Department of Missouri. Honest men of all parties hailed it as auspicious of a speedy salvation from the evils that at present afflict us. But alas! politicians who have sometimes been mistaken for statesmen, and who affect to see goblins in all shadows which do not directly follow themselves, saw either an extinguishment of their own hopes of preferment, or some other equally important evil to result from this Proclamation; and it and its author were quietly laid aside under pretexts equally frivolous. If the people were as ready to listen to complaints originated in the chafing of some ambitious and restless spirit, many of our leaders would undoubtedly be found to "live in glass houses." But John C. Frémont and his *timely* Proclamation are not forgotten; nor can any amount of well feigned prosecution, or equally bitter persecution, entomb the instrument and its author.—In *three years more* the people will sanction the death of slavery *in the man of their choice*. And, too, this unnatural war will render its death constitutional.

Complaints of mistakes and extravagance might be very common. Where are the mistakes of Bull Run, Ball's Bluff, and many others of like character, though of seemingly less significance? And why, in the midst of the councils of the nation, in the face of the grand army, and where money is lavished without stint, have the enemy been allowed to blockade the Potomac, and been permitted to hurl defiance in the teeth of the Government, under the very eaves of the Capitol? But we will not complain. He whose genius has dealt a well directed blow at the evil which has provoked this war, and whose indomitable energy would have carried out his purpose, must be required by this insatiate monster as a sacrifice; but Nature is remunerative, and, Phoenix-like, he shall arise from the ashes around the altar upon which he has been offered, and with the might of his unswerving purpose, destroy the monster that has, up to the present, performed all its devilish orgies in the very halls of our National Legislature, and made its horrid feasts upon the heart's blood of its best interests. In this we have not spoken with any reference to our prevailing predilections in regard to the hateful institution of slavery, but to facts as they shadow themselves before us in the horoscope of the future.

"THE PRESIDENT AND HIS SPEECHES" (1862)

In August 1862, President Lincoln met with Washington, D.C., black leaders and encouraged them to leave the country. He blamed the war on blacks and said the two races could never live together in harmony. Douglass was outraged and called Lincoln a representative American racist.

SOURCE: *Douglass' Monthly*, September 1862

The President of the United States seems to possess an ever increasing passion for making himself appear silly and ridiculous, if nothing worse. Since the publication of our last number he has been unusually garrulous, characteristically foggy, remarkably illogical and untimely in his utterances, often saying that which nobody wanted to hear, and studiously leaving unsaid about the only things which the country and the times imperatively demand of him. Our garrulous and joking President has favored the country and the world with two speeches, which if delivered by any other than the President of the United States, would attract no more attention than the funny little speeches made in front of the arcade by our friend John Smith, inviting customers to buy his razor strops.—One of the speeches of the President was made at a war meeting in Washington in vindication of Mr. Stanton,[1] and in justification of himself against the charge that he had failed to send reinforcements to Gen. McClellan.[2] Very little need be said of this first speech. In comparison with some speeches made on that occasion, the President's is short, but in comparison to the amount of matter it contains, it is tediously long, full of repetitions, and so remarkably careless in style that it reminds one strongly of the gossiping manner in which a loquacious old woman discusses her neighbors and her own domestic affairs, and explaining herself so lucidly that her audience, after listening with all due patience, are in the end as well informed about the subject in question as before the exposition. In short, the speech does not prove anything except that the Secretary of War is not responsible, but that the President is responsible for the failure to send re-enforcements to General McClellan. We may at once have done with this speech, especially since the information it contains was explicitly given to the country full three weeks before its utterance at the War meeting in Washington.

The other and more important communication of the President it appears was delivered in the White House before a committee of colored men assembled by his invitation. In this address Mr. Lincoln assumes the language and arguments of an itinerant Colonization lecturer, showing all his inconsistencies, his pride of race and blood, his contempt for Negroes, and his canting hypocrisy. How an honest man could creep into such a character as that implied by this address we are not required to show. The argument of Mr. Lincoln is that the difference between the white and black races renders it impossible for them to live together in the same country without detriment to both. Colonization, therefore, he holds to be the duty and the interest of the colored people. Mr. Lincoln takes care in urging his colonization scheme to furnish a weapon to all the ignorant and base, who need only the countenance of men in authority to commit all kinds of violence and outrage upon the colored people of the country. Taking advantage of his position and of the prevailing prejudice against them he affirms that their presence in the country is the real first cause of the war, and logically enough, if the premises were sound, assumes the necessity of their removal.

It does not require any great amount of skill to point out the fallacy and expose the unfairness of the assumption, for by this time every man who has an ounce of brain in his head, no matter to which party he may belong, and even Mr. Lincoln himself, must know quite well that the mere presence of the colored race never could have provoked this horrid and desolating rebellion.

Mr. Lincoln knows that in Mexico, Central America and South America, many distinct races live peaceably together in the enjoyment of equal rights, and that the civil wars which occasionally disturb the peace of those regions never originated in the difference of the races inhabiting them. A horse thief pleading that the existence of the horse is the apology for his theft or a highway man contending that the money in the traveler's pocket is the sole first cause of his robbery are about as much entitled to respect as is the President's reasoning at this point. No, Mr. President, it is not the innocent horse that makes the horse thief, not the traveler's purse that makes the highway robber, and it is not the presence of the Negro that causes this foul and unnatural war, but the cruel and brutal cupidity of those who wish to possess horses, money and Negroes by means of theft, robbery, and rebellion. Mr. Lincoln further knows or ought to know at least that Negro hatred and prejudice of color are neither original nor invincible vices, but merely the offshoots of that root of all crimes and evils—slavery. If the colored people instead of having been stolen and forcibly brought to the United States had come as free immigrants, like the German and the Irish, never thought of as suitable objects of property, they never would have become the objects of aversion and bitter persecution, nor would there ever have been divulged and propagated the arrogant and malignant nonsense about natural repellancy and the incompatibility of races.

Illogical and unfair as Mr. Lincoln's statements are, they are nevertheless quite in keeping with his whole course from the beginning of his administration up to this day, and confirm the painful conviction that though elected as an anti-slavery man by Republican and Abolition voters, Mr. Lincoln is quite a genuine representative of American prejudice and Negro hatred and far more concerned for the preservation of slavery, and the favor of the Border Slave States, than for any sentiment of magnanimity or principle of justice and humanity. This address of his leaves us less ground to hope for anti-slavery action at his hands than any of his previous utterances. Notwithstanding his repeated declarations that he considers slavery an evil, every step of his Presidential career relating to slavery proves him active, decided, and brave for its support, and passive, cowardly, and treacherous to the very cause of liberty to which he owes his election. This speech of the President delivered to a committee of free colored men in the capital explains the animus of his interference with the memorable proclamation of General Fremont. A man who can charge this war to the presence of colored men in this country might be expected to take advantage of any legal technicalities for arresting the cause of Emancipation, and the vigorous prosecution of the war against slaveholding rebels. To these colored people, without power and without influence, the President is direct, undisguised, and unhesitating. He says to the colored people: I don't like you, you must clear out of the country. So too in dealing with anti-slavery Generals, the President is direct and firm. He is always brave and resolute in his interferences in favor of slavery, remarkably unconcerned about the wishes and opinions of the people of the North; apparently wholly indifferent to the moral sentiment of civilized Europe; but bold and self-reliant as he is in the ignominious service of slavery, he is as timid as a sheep when required to live up to a single one of his anti-slavery testimonies. He is scrupulous to the very letter of the law in favor of slavery, and a perfect latitudinarian as to the discharge of his duties under a law favoring freedom. When Congress passed the Confiscation Bill, made the Emancipation of the slaves of rebels the law of the land, authorized the President to arm the slaves which should come within the lines of the Federal army, and thus removed all technical objections, everybody who attached any importance to the President's declarations of scrupulous regard for law, looked at once for a proclamation emancipating the slaves and calling the blacks to arms. But Mr. Lincoln, formerly so strict and zealous in the observance of the most atrocious laws which ever disgraced a country, has not been able yet to muster courage and honesty enough to obey and execute that grand decision of the people. He evaded his obvious duty, and instead of calling the blacks to arms and to liberty he merely authorized the military commanders to use them as laborers, without even promising them their freedom at the end of their term of service to the government, and thus destroyed virtually the very object of the measure. Further when General Halleck issued his odious order No. 3, excluding fugitive slaves from our lines, an order than which none could be more serviceable to the slaveholding rebels, since it was a guarantee against the escape of their slaves, Mr. Lincoln was deaf to the outcry and indignation which resounded through the north and west, and saw no occasion for interference, though that order violated a twice adopted resolution of Congress. When General McClellan employed our men guarding rebel property and even when Gen. Butler committed the outrage paralleled only by the atrocities of the rebels—delivering back into bondage thousands of slaves—Mr. Lincoln again was mute and did not feel induced to interfere in behalf of outraged humanity.

The tone of frankness and benevolence which he assumes in his speech to the colored committee is too thin a mask not to be seen through. The genuine spark of humanity is missing in it, no sincere wish to improve the condition of the oppressed has dictated it. It expresses merely the desire to get rid of them, and reminds one of the politeness with which a man might try to bow out of his house some troublesome creditor or the witness of some old guilt. We might also criticize the style adopted, so exceedingly plain and coarse threaded as to make the impression that Mr. L. had such a low estimate of the intelligence of his audience, as to think any but the simplest phrases and constructions would be above their power of comprehension. As Mr. Lincoln, however, in all his writings has manifested a decided awkwardness in the management of the English language, we do not think there is any intention in this respect, but only the incapacity to do better.

"MEN OF COLOR, TO ARMS!" (1863)

Douglass was a principal recruiter for the 54th Massachusetts Volunteer Infantry Regiment. His two sons were among the first recruits, and this broadside, also published in his newspaper, circulated through the North and helped fill the regiment in less than a month.

SOURCE: Broadside, Philadelphia, 1863

When first the rebel cannon shattered the walls of Sumter and drove away its starving garrison, I predicted that the war then and there inaugurated would not be fought out entirely by white men. Every month's experience during these dreary years has confirmed that opinion. A war undertaken and brazenly carried on for the perpetual enslavement of colored men, calls logically and loudly for colored men to help suppress it. Only a moderate share of sagacity was needed to see that the arm of the slave was the best defense against the arm of the slaveholder. Hence with every reverse to the national arms, with every exulting shout of victory raised by the slaveholding rebels, I have implored the imperiled nation to unchain against her foes, her powerful black hand. Slowly and reluctantly that appeal is beginning to be heeded. Stop not now to complain that it was not heeded sooner. It may or it may not have been best that it should not. This is not the time to discuss that question. Leave it to the future. When the war is over, the country is saved, peace is established, and the black man's rights are secured, as they will be, history with an impartial hand will dispose of that and sundry other questions. Action! Action! not criticism, is the plain duty of this hour. Words are now useful only as they stimulate to blows. The office of speech now is only to point out when, where, and how to strike to the best advantage. There is no time to delay. The tide is at its flood that leads on to fortune. From East to West, from North to South, the sky is written all over, "Now or never." Liberty won by white men would lose half its luster. "Who would be free themselves must strike the blow." "Better even die free, than to live slaves." This is the sentiment of every brave colored man amongst us. There are weak and cowardly men in all nations. We have them amongst us. They tell you this is the "white man's war"; that you will be "no better off after than before the war"; that the getting of you into the army is to "sacrifice you on the first opportunity." Believe them not; cowards themselves, they do not wish to have their cowardice shamed by your brave example. Leave them to their timidity, or to whatever motive may hold them back. I have not thought lightly of the words I am now addressing you. The counsel I give comes of close observation of the great struggle now in progress, and of the deep conviction that this is your hour and mine. In good earnest then, and after the best deliberation, I now for the first time during this war feel at liberty to call and counsel you to arms. By every consideration which binds you to your enslaved fellow-countrymen, and the peace and welfare of your country; by every aspiration which you cherish for the freedom and equality of yourselves and your children; by all the ties of blood and identity which make us one with the brave black men now fighting our battles in Louisiana and in South Carolina, I urge you to fly to arms, and smite with death the power that would bury the government and your liberty in the same hopeless grave. I wish I could tell you that the State of New York calls you to this high honor. For the moment her constituted authorities are silent on the subject. They will speak by and by, and doubtless on the right side; but we are not compelled to wait for her. We can get at the throat of treason and slavery through the State of Massachusetts. She was first in the War of Independence; first to break the chains of her slaves; first to make the black man equal before the law; first to admit colored children to her common schools, and she was first to answer with her blood the alarm cry of the nation, when its capital was menaced by rebels. You know her patriotic governor, and you know Charles Sumner. I need not add more.

Massachusetts now welcomes you to arms as soldiers. She has but a small colored population from which to recruit. She has full leave of the general government to send one regiment to the war, and she has undertaken to do it. Go quickly and help fill up the first colored regiment from the North. I am authorized to assure you that you will receive the same wages, the same rations, the same equipments, the same protection, the same treatment, and the same bounty, secured to the white soldiers. You will be led by able and skillful officers, men who will take especial pride in your efficiency and success. They will be quick to accord to you all the honor you shall merit by your valor, and see that your rights and feelings are respected by other soldiers. I have assured myself on these points, and can speak with authority. More than twenty years of unswerving devotion to our common cause may give me some humble claim to be trusted at this momentous crisis. I will not argue. To do so implies hesitation and doubt, and you do not hesitate. You do not doubt. The day dawns; the morning star is bright upon the horizon! The iron gate of our prison stands half open. One gallant rush from the North will fling it wide open, while four millions of our brothers and sisters shall march out into liberty. The chance is now given you to end in a day the bondage of centuries, and to rise in one bound from social degradation to the plane of common equality with all other varieties of men. Remember Denmark Vesey of Charleston; remember Nathaniel Turner of Southampton; remember Shields Green and Copeland, who followed noble John Brown, and fell as glorious martyrs for the cause of the slave. Remember that in a contest with oppression, the Almighty has no attribute which can take sides with oppressors. The case is before you. This is our golden opportunity. Let us accept it, and forever wipe out the dark reproaches unsparingly hurled against us by our enemies. Let us win for ourselves the gratitude of our country, and the best blessings of our posterity through all time. The nucleus of this first regiment is now in camp at Readville, a short distance from Boston. I will undertake to forward to Boston all persons adjudged fit to be mustered into the regiment, who shall apply to me at any time within the next two weeks.

"VALEDICTORY" (1863)

Douglass became outraged over the treatment of black soldiers and went to Washington to complain. He met with President Lincoln and Secretary of War Edwin Stanton, who promised him a commission to raise troops in the South. As a result, he ended his paper and published this "Valedictory." The commission never went through, and so he ended his paper on a false promise.

SOURCE: *Douglass' Monthly*, August 1863

Rochester, N. Y., Aug 16th, 1863

My Respected Readers:

I beg to state that my relation to you as the Editor and publisher of a Journal devoted to the cause of Emancipation is, for the present, ended. That journal which has continued, under one form and designation or another, during nearly sixteen years, covering a period remarkable for the intensity and fierceness of the moral struggle between slavery and freedom, will be discontinued from the date of this publication.

In making this simple announcement emotions are excited for which I shall not attempt to find words to give suitable expression.—Although the result has been reached naturally, logically and necessarily, it is nevertheless accepted reluctantly and sadly. My relation to my readers has been in a high degree friendly, and in taking this formal leave of those readers, at home and abroad, I feel that I am taking leave of my true and tried friends. Great principles of justice and the most enduring sympathies known to the heart of man have united us in the cause of the American slave and swept us along the tide of these eventful sixteen years together. I know well enough, and knew from the first that my hold upon you, was not the result of shining talents or hight mental attainments. I came to you fresh from the house of American bondage, with only such learning as I had stolen or picked up in the darkness of twenty-two years of slavery, and in a few years of liberty and toil. Yet you were pleased to receive me, and were not ashamed to cheer me on in my mission of deliverance to my enslaved people. Out of a full heart, my dear respected friends, I thank you at this parting, for your long continued and ever faithful cooperation. I shall never cease to regard these years of editorial toil on my part and of sympathy and support on your part, as among the most cheerful and happy of my life.

But you will ask me, Why do you cease the publication of your paper? "Why not continue to speak and write as formerly—Slavery is not yet abolished." The inquiry is pertinent and I will give it my answer: and to answer it more perfectly I will first answer it negatively. First then, I wish it distinctly understood, that I do not discontinue the publication of my paper because it can no longer be supported. In this respect my paper has been highly favored from the first. The kind friends, who in England, seventeen years ago gave me the means of purchasing a printing press, have stood by me through all the years of my journal and generously helped me in every time of need. The same friends would doubtless help me hereafter as heretofore, if the journal were continued, and needed their help for its continuance.

Again, I cannot allow that my course is dictated by a love of change or adventure. My stability is quite equal to that of most men. My paper ends its existence in the same room on the same street where it began. It has been during these sixteen years, immovable in its principles as it has been permanent in its local habitation. Often called elsewhere as more desirable localities for being heard and felt over the country, I have still remained in Rochester, and shown no taste for experimenting anywhere. Many times I could have sold my establishment, and formed alliances with other papers, but remembering that those who put me in possession of the press desired me to conduct it, I have refused all proposals for either sale or alliance. Neither do I discontinue the paper because I think that speaking and writing against slavery and its twin monster prejudice against the colored race are no longer needful. Such writing and speaking will be necessary so long as slavery and proscription shall remain in this country and in the world. Happily, however, I can write now through channels which were not opened fully to these subjects, when my journal was established. It will be grateful to my friends, especially to those over the sea, to know that the New York *Independent* and the New York *Tribune,* both powerful periodicals, counting their readers by the hundred thousand, welcome to their ample columns the best utterances in behalf of my race of which I am capable. These journals with many others, in my own town and elsewhere, are now quite ready to listen to what the colored man has to say for himself and for his much questioned and doubted people. Besides these, there is now, as there was not, at the beginning, a paper published in the city of New York by colored men entitled *"The Anglo-African,"* to whose columns all colored writers may gain access. I, at least have never been refused a place in its columns.—Indeed, I may say with gratitude and without boasting, that humble as I am in origin and despised as is the race to which I belong, I have lived to see the leading presses of the country, willing and ready to publish any argument or appeal in behalf of my race, I am able to make. So that while speaking and writing are still needful, the necessity for a special organ for my views and opinions on slavery no longer exists. To this extent at least, my paper has accomplished the object of its existence. It has done something towards battering down that dark and frowning wall of partition between the working minds of two races, hitherto thought impregnable. It found me an illiterate fugitive from slavery, and by the mental exercise in reflection and reading its publication imposed, and made indispensable, it has educated myself, and other colored men up to the average power of thought and expression of our times.

Let it also be understood that I do not abandon my paper, because I shall cease to think and write upon vital social questions concerning colored men and women. I shall think, write and speak as I have opportunity, while the slave needs a pen to plead his cause, or a voice to expose his wrongs before the people.

So much dear readers, negatively, and to prevent misapprehension. I will now tell affirmatively and directly why I lay down my pen and paper. The United States are now in the bitterest pangs of civil war. Slavery is the cause of this terrible war, and its abolition is decreed by one of the parties to the war. I am with the abolition party in war as in peace. I discontinue my paper because I can better serve my poor bleeding country-men whose great opportunity has now come, by going South and summoning them to assert their just liberty, than I can do by staying here. I am going South to assist Adjutant General Thomas in the organization of colored troops who shall win for the millions in bondage the inestimable blessings of liberty and country.

Slavery has chosen to submit her claims to the decision of the God of battles. She has deliberately taken the sword and it is meet that she should perish by the sword. Let the oppressor fall by the hand of the oppressed, and the guilty slaveholder, whom the voice of truth and reason could not reach, let him fall by the hand of his slave. It is in accordance with the All-wise orderings of Providence that it should be so. Eternal justice can thunder forth no higher vindication of her majesty nor proclaim a warning more salutary to a world steeped in cruelty and wickedness, than in such a termination of our system of slavery. Reason, argument, appeal,—all moral influences have been applied in vain. The oppressor has hardened his heart, blinded his mind, and deliberately rushed upon merited destruction. Let his blood be upon his own head. That I should take some humble part in the physical as well as the moral struggle against slavery and urge my long enslaved people to vindicate their manhood by bravely striking for their liberty and country is natural and consistent. I have indicated my course. You may not approve it, but I am sure you will appreciate the convictions of duty which impel me to it. With a heart full and warm with gratitude to you for all you have done in furtherance of the cause of these to whom I have devoted my life, I bid you an affectionate farewell.

FREDERICK DOUGLASS

"WOMAN SUFFRAGE MOVEMENT" (1870)

Douglass was among the foremost male feminists of the nineteenth century and frequently spoke out and wrote on their behalf. In this essay, published after the Fifteenth Amendment denied women suffrage, he explains the foundations of equal rights and accuses the government of treating women like animals.

SOURCE: *New National Era*, October 20, 1870

The simplest truths often meet the sternest resistance, and are slowest in getting general acceptance. There are none so blind as those who will not see, is an old proverb. Usage and prejudice, like forts built of sand, often defy the power of shot and shell, and play havoc with their besiegers. No simpler proposition, no truth more self-evident or more native to the human soul, was ever presented to human reason or consciousness than was that which formed our late anti-slavery movement. It only affirmed that every man is, and of right ought to be, the owner of his own body; and that no man can rightfully claim another man as his property. And yet what a tempest and whirlwind of human wrath, what clouds of ethical and theological dust, this simple proposition created. Families, churches, societies, parties, and States were riven by it, and at last the sword was called in to decide the questions which it raised. What was true of this simple truth was also true as to the people's right to a voice in their own Government, and the right of each man to form for himself his own religious opinions. All Europe ran blood before humanity and reason won this sacred right from priestcraft, bigotry, and superstition. What to-day seems simple, obvious, and undeniable, men looking through old customs, usages, and prejudices in other days denied altogether. Our friends of the woman's suffrage movement should bear this fact in mind, and share the patience of truth while they advocate the truth. It is painful to encounter stupidity as well as malice; but such is the fate of all who attempt to reform an abuse, to urge on humanity to nobler heights, and illumine the world with a new truth.

Now we know of no truth more easily made appreciable to human thought than the right of woman to vote, or, in other words, to have a voice in the Government under which she lives and to which she owes allegiance. The very admission that woman owes allegiance, implies her right to vote. No man or woman who is not consulted can contract an obligation, or have an obligation created for him or her as the case may be. We can owe nothing by the mere act of another. Woman is not a consenting party to this Government. She has never been consulted. Ours is a Government of men, by men, each agreeing with all and all agreeing with each in respect to certain fundamental propositions, and women are wholly excluded. So far as respects its relation to woman, our Government is in its essence a simple usurpation, a Government of force, and not of reason. We legislate for woman, and protect her, precisely as we legislate for and protect animals, asking the consent of neither.

It is nothing against this conclusion that our legislation has for the most part been eminently just and humane. A despotism is no less a despotism because the reigning despot may be a wise and good man. The principle is unaffected by the character of the man who for the moment may represent it. He may be kind or cruel, benevolent or selfish, in any case he rules according to his own sovereign will—and precisely such is the theoretical relation of our American Government toward woman. It simply takes her money without asking her consent and spends the same without in any wise consulting her wishes. It tells her that there is a code of laws which men have made, and which she must obey or she must suffer the consequences. She is absolutely in the hands of her political masters: and though these may be kind and tender hearted, (the same was true of individual slave masters, as before stated,) this in nowise mitigates the harshness of the principle—and it is against this principle we understand the woman's suffrage movement to be directed. It is intended to claim for woman a place by the side of man, not to rule over him, not to antagonize him, but to rule with him, as an equal subject to the solemn requirements of reason and law.

To ourselves the great truth underlying this woman's movement is just as simple, obvious, and indisputable as either of the great truths referred to at the beginning of this article. It is a part of the same system of truths. Its sources are individuality, rationality, and sense of accountability.

If woman is admitted to be a moral and intellectual being, possessing a sense of good and evil, and a power of choice between them, her case is already half gained. Our natural powers are the foundation of our natural rights; and it is a consciousness of powers which suggests the exercise of rights. Man can only exercise the powers he possesses, and he can only conceive of rights in presence of powers. The fact that woman has the power to say "I choose *this* rather than *that*" is all-sufficient proof that there is no natural reason against the exercise of that power. The power that makes her a moral and an accountable being gives her a natural right to choose the legislators who are to frame the laws under which she is to live, and the requirements of which she is bound to obey. By every fact and by every argument which man can wield in defence of his natural right to participate in government, the right of woman so to participate is equally defended and rendered unassailable.

Thus far all is clear and entirely consistent. Woman's natural abilities and possibilities, not less than man's, constitute the measure of her rights in all directions and relations, including her right to participate in shaping the policy and controlling the action of the Government under which she lives, and to which she is assumed to owe obedience. Unless it can be shown that woman is morally, physically, and intellectually incapable of performing the act of voting, there can be no natural prohibition of such action on her part. Usage, custom, and deeply rooted prejudices are against woman's freedom. They have been against man's freedom, national freedom, religious freedom, but these will all subside in the case of woman as well as elsewhere. The thought has already been conceived; the word has been spoken; the debate has begun; earnest men and women are choosing sides. Error may be safely tolerated while truth is left free to combat it, and nobody need fear the result. The truth can hurt nothing which ought not to be hurt, and it alone can make men and women free.

"LETTER FROM THE EDITOR" (ON THE BURNING DOWN OF HIS ROCHESTER HOUSE) (1872)

After the war Douglass moved to Washington, D.C., and began editing the *New National Era*. In this editorial, he responds to the burning down of his Rochester home, where family members still resided. The fire was caused by arson, he concludes, and he links it to the rise of the "Ku-Klux spirit" pervading the era.

SOURCE: *New National Era*, June 13, 1872

Dear Readers:

I am here among the ashes of my old home in Rochester, New York. As soon as I learned of the fire I hurried here from Washington, and have been here ever since. A summons home to find one's house in ashes is almost like going home to a funeral, and though only sadness greets one at the end of the journey no speed is too great to bring him there. The house destroyed had been my home during more than twenty years; and twenty years of industry and economy had there brought together many things valuable in themselves, and rendered more valuable by association. Several questions are naturally suggested by every fire; First, How did it happen? How was it extinguished? What was saved? What was lost? What was damaged? I do not mean to answer these questions in detail, nor to indulge in sentimental description. The fire was doubtless the work of an incendiary.[1] It began in a barn well filled with hay on the south side of the house, and was first seen at midnight, when the family of my son-in-law (who occupied the dwelling) had been in bed two hours. No fire or light had been carried into the barn by any of the family for months. What could be the motive? Was it for plunder, or was it for spite, or was it mere wanton wickedness on the part of persons of the baser sort, who wander on the outskirts of cities by starlight at late hours? I do not know and I cannot guess. One thing I do know and that is, while Rochester is among the most liberal of Northern cities, and its people are among the most humane and highly civilized, it nevertheless has its full share of that Ku-Klux spirit which makes anything owned by a colored man a little less respected and secure than when owned by a white citizen. I arrived in Rochester at one o'clock in the night in thick darkness and drenching rain, and not knowing where my family might be, I applied for shelter at two of the nearest hotels and was at first refused by both, with the convenient excuse that "We are full," till it was known that my name was Frederick Douglass, when a room was readily offered me, though the house was full! I did not accept, but made my way to the police headquarters, to learn if possible where I might find the scattered members of my family. Such treatment as this does not tend to make a man secure either in his person or property. The spirit which would deny a man shelter in a public house, needs but little change to deny him shelter, even in his own house. It is the spirit of hate, the spirit of murder, the spirit which would burn a family in their beds. I may be wrong, but I fear that the sentiment which repelled me at Congress Hall burnt my house.

The fire did its work quick and with marked thoroughness and success. Scarcely a trace of the building, except brick walls and stone foundations, is left, and the trees surrounding the building, planted by my own hands and of more than twenty years' growth were not spared, but were scorched and charred beyond recovery. Much was saved in the way of furniture and much was lost, and much was damaged. Eleven thousand dollars worth of government securities (of which I have fortunately the numbers) were destroyed. Sixteen volumes of my old paper the *North Star* and Frederick Douglass' paper, were destroyed; a piano worth five hundred dollars was saved, but much damaged, the same with three sofas, and many mahogany chairs, and other furniture. My loss, not covered with insurance, will reach from four to five thousand dollars. Every effort possible was made by the police and fire department to save property, and the neighbors (all white) did everything in their power to afford relief to the shelterless family. Assured of the sympathy of my readers in this calamity, I have felt at liberty to make this brief statement, as an apology for absence from my post of public duty, which after all will not be long.

FREDERICK DOUGLASS

"GIVE US THE FREEDOM INTENDED FOR US" (1872)

With the rise of racism and antiblack violence during Reconstruction, Douglass urges Congress to honor the enforcement clauses of the Reconstruction amendments, which charged that body to pass legislation upholding equal protection under the law, citizenship rights, and unrestricted male suffrage for all Americans.

SOURCE: *New National Era*, December 5, 1872

We are often cautioned against demanding too much for the colored people of this country. This cautioning is invariably accompanied with a full narration of what has already been done for our people, and we are further exhorted to remember that within the past decade we were slaves without any rights entitled to respect, and that in this short space of time we have been freed and transformed into American citizens, with the right to exercise the elective franchise extended to us by amendment to the National Constitution. Having been the recipients of these very valuable gifts, it is asserted by some who have taken an active part in the giving, that we should be satisfied at least long enough to allow the nation to take breath after its strenuous exertions in the accomplishment of the results so beneficial to us. To such persons the fact that we have been oppressed, outraged, and wronged for more than two centuries seems to be no argument why the nation should hasten to undo the wrong it has sanctioned against us, now that if fully admits the evil perpetrated upon us.

The elective franchise without protection in its exercise amounts to almost nothing in the hands of a minority with a vast majority determined that no exercise of it shall be made by the minority. Freedom from the auction block and from legal claim as property is of no benefit to the colored man without the means of protecting his rights. The black man is not a free American citizen in the sense that a white man is a free American citizen; he cannot protect himself against encroachments upon the rights and privileges already allowed him in a court of justice without an impartial jury. If accused of crime, he is tried by men who have a bias against him by reason of his race, color, or previous condition of servitude. If he attempts to send his children to the nearest public school where a free white American citizen, who pays no more taxes, can have the privilege without question, he is driven away and has no redress at law. If, after purchasing tickets for a ride in a first-class railway carriage, a colored person is hustled out into a smoking car, he or she has no redress at law because a custom prevails which allows injustice in this respect to colored persons.

We claim that the thirteenth, fourteenth, and fifteenth amendments to the Constitution of the United States were intended to give full freedom to every person without regard to race or color in the United States; and, in order that this intention should be carried out and acted upon, power for that purpose was given by conferring upon Congress the right to enforce the amendments by appropriate legislation. It cannot be denied that the violent interference with the black man to prevent him from exercising the elective franchise in accordance with his own views is an abridgement of his freedom as is also the refusal of a trial by a jury of his peers; nor can it be denied that the forcing of colored men to pay for what they do not get by railroad corporations or the refusal to allow the same accommodation to them as to other citizens of the United States, is an invidious discrimination amounting to an abridgement of citizenship rights.

We cannot be asking too much when we ask this Congress to carry out the intention of this Nation as expressed in the thirteenth, fourteenth and fifteenth amendments. We are not free. We cannot be free without the appropriate legislation provided for in the above amendments. We say to those who think we are demanding too much that it is idle to point us to the amendments and ask us to be satisfied with them and wait until the nation is educated up to giving us something more. The amendments are excellent but they need to be enforced. The result intended to be reached by the nation has not been reached. Congress has neglected to do its full duty. The people one month ago reiterated in thunder tones their demand "that complete liberty and *exact equality* in the enjoyment of all civil, political, and public rights should be established and effectually maintained throughout the Union by efficient and appropriate State and Federal legislation."[1] We join in this demand those who think we are asking too much to the contrary notwithstanding.

The people on the 5th of November last ratified the following: "The recent amendments to the national Constitution should be cordially sustained because they are right, not merely tolerated because they are law, and should be carried out *according to their spirit* by appropriate legislation."[2] The Liberal Democratic platform took similar ground as follows, and all the voters in the country voted for similar principles: "We recognize the equality of all men before the law and hold that it is the duty of Government in its dealings with the people to mete out equal and exact justice to all of whatever nativity, race, color or persuasion religious or political. We pledge ourselves to maintain the Union of these States, emancipation and enfranchisement and to oppose any reopening of the questions settled by the thirteenth, fourteenth, and fifteenth amendments to the Constitution."[3] In view of this can a Republican Congress longer refuse to enact into law such a bill as Senator Sumner brought forward[4] in the last session of Congress and which is by far the best measure yet proposed for establishing "complete liberty and exact equality in the enjoyment of all civil, political, and public rights"?

"THE COLOR LINE" (1881)

Douglass explores the history and philosophy of racism, and argues that it is not a natural or instinctive phenomenon but a social construction, which can be abolished through protest and legislation.

SOURCE: *North American Review*, June 1881

Few evils are less accessible to the force of reason, or more tenacious of life and power, than a long-standing prejudice. It is a moral disorder, which creates the conditions necessary to its own existence, and fortifies itself by refusing all contradiction. It paints a hateful picture according to its own diseased imagination, and distorts the features of the fancied original to suit the portrait. As those who believe in the visibility of ghosts can easily see them, so it is always easy to see repulsive qualities in those we despise and hate.

Prejudice of race has at some time in their history afflicted all nations. "I am more holy than thou" is the boast of races, as well as that of the Pharisee. Long after the Norman invasion and the decline of Norman power, long after the sturdy Saxon had shaken off the dust of his humiliation and was grandly asserting his great qualities in all directions, the descendants of the invaders continued to regard their Saxon brothers as made of coarser clay than themselves, and were not well pleased when one of the former subject race came between the sun and their nobility. Having seen the Saxon a menial, a hostler, and a common drudge, oppressed and dejected for centuries, it was easy to invest him with all sorts of odious peculiarities, and to deny him all manly predicates. Though eight hundred years have passed away since

Norman power entered England, and the Saxon has for centuries been giving his learning, his literature, his language, and his laws to the world more successfully than any other people on the globe, men in that country still boast their Norman origin and Norman perfections. This superstition of former greatness serves to fill out the shriveled sides of a meaningless race-pride which holds over after its power has vanished. With a very different lesson from the one this paper is designed to impress, the great Daniel Webster once told the people of Massachusetts (whose prejudices in the particular instance referred to were right) that they "had conquered the sea, and had conquered the land," but that "it remained for them to conquer their prejudices."[1] At one time we are told that the people in some of the towns of Yorkshire cherished a prejudice so strong and violent against strangers and foreigners that one who ventured to pass through their streets would be pelted with stones.

Of all the races and varieties of men which have suffered from this feeling, the colored people of this country have endured most. They can resort to no disguises which will enable them to escape its deadly aim. They carry in front the evidence which marks them for persecution. They stand at the extreme point of difference from the Caucasian race, and their African origin can be instantly recognized, though they may be several removes from the typical African race. They may remonstrate like Shylock—"Hath not a Jew eyes? hath not a Jew hands, organs, dimensions, senses, affections, passions? fed with the same food, hurt with the same weapons, subject to the same diseases, healed by the same means, warmed and cooled by the same summer and winter, as a Christian is?"—but such eloquence is unavailing. They are Negroes—and that is enough, in the eye of this unreasoning prejudice, to justify indignity and violence. In nearly every department of American life they are confronted by this insidious influence. It fills the air. It meets them at the workshop and factory, when they apply for work. It meets them at the church, at the hotel, at the ballot-box, and worst of all, it meets them in the jury-box. Without crime or offense against law or gospel, the colored man is the Jean Valjean of American society. He has escaped from the galleys, and hence all presumptions are against him. The workshop denies him work, and the inn denies him shelter; the ballot-box a fair vote, and the jury-box a fair trial. He has ceased to be the slave of an individual, but has in some sense become the slave of society. He may not now be bought and sold like a beast in the market, but he is the trammeled victim of a prejudice, well calculated to repress his manly ambition, paralyze his energies, and make him a dejected and spiritless man, if not a sullen enemy to society, fit to prey upon life and property and to make trouble generally.

When this evil spirit is judge, jury, and prosecutor, nothing less than overwhelming evidence is sufficient to overcome the force of unfavorable presumptions.

Everything against the person with the hated color is promptly taken for granted; while everything in his favor is received with suspicion and doubt.

A boy of this color is found in his bed tied, mutilated, and bleeding, when forthwith all ordinary experience is set aside, and he is presumed to have been guilty of the outrage upon himself; weeks and months he is kept on trial for the offense, and every effort is made to entangle the poor fellow in the confused meshes of expert testimony (the least trustworthy of all evidence). This same spirit, which promptly assumes everything against us, just as readily denies or explains away everything in our favor. We are not, as a race, even permitted to appropriate the virtues and achievements of our individual representatives. Manliness, capacity, learning, laudable ambition, heroic service, by any of our number, are easily placed to the credit of the superior race. One drop of Teutonic blood is enough to account for all good and great qualities occasionally coupled with a colored skin; and on the other hand, one drop of negro blood, though in the veins of a man of Teutonic whiteness, is enough on which to predicate all offensive and ignoble qualities. In presence of this spirit, if a crime is committed, and the criminal is not positively known, a suspicious-looking colored man is sure to have been seen in the neighborhood. If an unarmed colored man is shot down and dies in his tracks, a jury, under the influence of this spirit, does not hesitate to find the murdered man the real criminal, and the murderer innocent.

Now let us examine this subject a little more closely. It is claimed that this wonder-working prejudice—this moral magic that can change virtue into vice, and innocence to crime; which makes the dead man the murderer, and holds the living homicide harmless—is a natural, instinctive, and invincible attribute of the white race, and one that cannot be eradicated; that even evolution itself cannot carry us beyond or above it. Alas for this poor suffering world (for four-fifths of mankind are colored), if this claim be true! In that case men are forever doomed to injustice, oppression, hate, and strife; and the religious sentiment of the world, with its grand idea of human brotherhood, its "peace on earth and good-will to men," and its golden rule, must be voted a dream, a delusion, and a snare.

But is this color prejudice the natural and inevitable thing it claims to be? If it is so, then it is utterly idle to write against it, preach, pray, or legislate against it, or pass constitutional amendments against it. Nature will have her course, and one might as well preach and pray to a horse against running, to a fish against swimming, or to a bird against flying. Fortunately, however, there is good ground for calling in question this high pretension of a vulgar and wicked prepossession.

If I could talk with all my white fellow-countrymen on this subject, I would say to them, in the language of Scripture: "Come and let us reason together." Now, without being too elementary and formal, it may be stated here that there are at least seven points which candid men will be likely to admit, but which, if admitted, will prove fatal to the popular thought and practice of the times.

First. If what we call prejudice against color be natural, *i.e.*, a part of human nature itself, it follows that it must be co-extensive with human nature, and will and must manifest itself whenever and wherever the two races are brought into contact. It would not vary with either latitude, longitude, or altitude; but like fire and gunpowder, whenever brought together, there would be an explosion of contempt, aversion, and hatred.

Second. If it can be shown that there is anywhere on the globe any considerable country where the contact of the African and the Caucasian is not distinguished by this explosion of race-wrath, there is reason to doubt that the prejudice is an ineradicable part of human nature.

Thirdly. If this so-called natural, instinctive prejudice can be satisfactorily accounted for by facts and considerations wholly apart from the color features of the respective races, thus placing it among the things subject to human volition and control, we may venture to deny the claim set up for it in the name of human nature.

Fourthly. If any considerable number of white people have overcome this prejudice in themselves, have cast it out as an unworthy sentiment, and have survived the operation, the fact shows that this prejudice is not at any rate a vital part of human nature, and may be eliminated from the race without harm.

Fifthly. If this prejudice shall, after all, prove to be, in its essence and in its natural manifestation, simply a prejudice against condition, and not against race or color, and that it disappears when this or that condition is absent, then the argument drawn from the nature of the Caucasian race falls to the ground.

Sixthly. If prejudice of race and color is only natural in the sense that ignorance, superstition, bigotry, and vice are natural, then it has no better defense than they, and should be despised and put away from human relations as an enemy to the peace, good order, and happiness of human society.

Seventhly. If, still further, this aversion to the Negro arises out of the fact that he is as we see him, poor, spiritless, ignorant, and degraded, then whatever is humane, noble, and superior, in the mind of the superior and more fortunate race, will desire that all arbitrary barriers against his manhood, intelligence, and elevation shall be removed, and a fair chance in the race of life be given him.

The first of these propositions does not require discussion. It commends itself to the understanding at once. Natural qualities are common and universal, and do not change essentially on the mountain or in the valley. I come therefore to the second point—the existence of countries where this malignant prejudice, as we know it in America, does not prevail; where character, not color, is the passport to consideration; where the right of the black man to be a man, and a man among men, is not questioned; where he may, without offense, even presume to be a gentleman. That there are such countries in the world there is ample evidence. Intelligent and observing travelers, having no theory to support, men whose testimony would be received without question in respect of any other matter, and should not be questioned in this, tell us that they find no color prejudice in Europe, except among Americans who reside there. In England and on the Continent, the colored man is no more an object of hate than any other person. He mingles with the multitude unquestioned, without offense given or received. During the two years which the writer spent abroad, though he was much in society, and was sometimes in the company of lords and ladies, he does not remember one word, look, or gesture that indicated the slightest aversion to him on account of color. His experience was not in this respect exceptional or singular. Messrs. Remond, Ward, Garnet, Brown, Pennington, Crummell, and Bruce, all of them colored, and some of them black, bear the same testimony. If what these gentlemen say (and it can be corroborated by a thousand witnesses) is true, there is no prejudice against color in England, save as it is carried there by Americans—carried there as a moral disease from an infected country. It is American, not European; local, not general; limited, not universal, and must be ascribed to artificial conditions, and not to any fixed and universal law of nature.

The third point is: Can this prejudice against color, as it is called, be accounted for by circumstances outside and independent of race or color? If it can be thus explained, an incubus may be removed from the breasts of both the white and the black people of this country, as well as from that large intermediate population which has sprung up between these alleged irreconcilable extremes. It will help us to see that it is not necessary that the Ethiopian shall change his skin, nor needful that the white man shall change the essential elements of his nature, in order that mutual respect and consideration may exist between the two races.

Now it is easy to explain the conditions outside of race or color from which may spring feelings akin to those which we call prejudice. A man without the ability or the disposition to pay a just debt does not feel at ease in the presence of his creditor. He does not want to meet him on the street, or in the market-place. Such meeting makes him uncomfortable. He would rather find fault with the bill than pay the debt, and the creditor himself will soon develop in the eyes of the debtor qualities not altogether to his taste.

Some one has well said, we may easily forgive those who injure us, but it is hard to forgive those whom we injure. The greatest injury this side of death, which one human being can inflict on another, is to enslave him, to blot out his personality, degrade his manhood, and sink him to the condition of a beast of burden; and just this has been done here during more than two centuries. No other people under heaven, of whatever type or endowments, could have been so enslaved without falling into contempt and scorn on the part of those enslaving them. Their slavery would itself stamp them with odious features, and give their oppressors arguments in favor of oppression. Besides the long years of wrong and injury inflicted upon the colored race in this country, and the effect of these wrongs upon that race, morally, intellectually, and physically, corrupting their morals, darkening their minds, and twisting their bodies and limbs out of all approach to symmetry, there has been a mountain of gold—uncounted millions of dollars—resting upon them with crushing weight. During all the years of their bondage, the slave master had a direct interest in discrediting the personality of those he held as property. Every man who had a thousand dollars so invested had a thousand reasons for painting the black man as fit only for slavery. Having made him the companion of horses and mules, he naturally sought to justify himself by assuming that the Negro was not much better than a mule. The holders of twenty hundred million dollars' worth of property in human chattels procured the means of influencing press, pulpit, and politician, and through these instrumentalities they belittled our virtues and magnified our vices, and have made us odious in the eyes of the world. Slavery had the power at one time to make and unmake Presidents, to construe the law, dictate the policy, set the fashion in national manners and customs, interpret the Bible, and control the church; and, naturally enough, the old masters set themselves up as much too high as they set the manhood of the Negro too low. Out of the depths of slavery has come this prejudice and this color line. It is broad enough and black enough to explain all the malign influences which assail the newly emancipated millions to-day. In reply to this argument it will perhaps be said that the Negro has no slavery now to contend with, and that having been free during the last sixteen years, he ought by this time to have contradicted the degrading qualities which slavery formerly ascribed to him. All very true as to the letter, but utterly false as to the spirit. Slavery is indeed gone, but its shadow still lingers over the country and poisons more or less the moral atmosphere of all sections of the republic. The money motive for assailing the negro which slavery represented is indeed absent, but love of power and dominion, strengthened by two centuries of irresponsible power, still remains.

Having now shown how slavery created and sustained this prejudice against race and color, and the powerful motive for its creation, the other four points made against it need not be discussed in detail and at length, but may only be referred to in a general way.

If what is called the instinctive aversion of the white race for the colored, when analyzed, is seen to be the same as that which men feel or have felt toward other objects wholly apart from color; if it should be the same as that sometimes exhibited by the haughty and rich to the humble and poor, the same as the Brahmin feels toward the lower caste, the same as the Norman felt toward the Saxon, the same as that cherished by the Turk against Christians, the same as Christians have felt toward the Jews, the same as that which murders a Christian in Wallachia, calls him a "dog" in Constantinople, oppresses and persecutes a Jew in Berlin, hunts down a socialist in St. Petersburg, drives a Hebrew from an hotel at Saratoga, that scorns the Irishman in London, the same as Catholics once felt for Protestants, the same as that which insults, abuses, and kills the Chinaman on the Pacific slope—then may we well enough affirm that this prejudice really has nothing whatever to do with race or color, and that it has its motive and mainspring in some other source with which the mere facts of color and race have nothing to do.

After all, some very well informed and very well meaning people will read what I have now said, and what seems to me so just and reasonable, and will still insist that the color of the Negro has something to do with the feeling entertained toward him; that the white man naturally shudders at the thought of contact with one who is black—that the impulse is one which he can neither resist nor control. Let us see if this conclusion is a sound one. An argument is unsound when it proves too little or too much, or when it proves nothing. If color is an offense, it is so, entirely apart from the manhood it envelops. There must be something in color of itself to kindle rage and inflame hate, and render the white man generally uncomfortable. If the white man were really so constituted that color were, in itself, a torment to him, this grand old earth of ours would be no place for him. Colored objects confront him here at every point of the compass. If he should shrink and shudder every time he sees anything dark, he would have little time for anything else. He would require a colorless world to live in—a world where flowers, fields, and floods should all be of snowy whiteness; where rivers, lakes, and oceans should all be white; where islands, capes, and continents should all be white; where all the men, and women, and children should be white; where all the fish of the sea, all the birds of the air, all the "cattle upon a thousand hills," should be white; where the heavens above and the earth beneath should be white, and where day and night should not be divided by light and darkness, but the world should be one eternal scene of light. In such a white world, the entrance of a black man would be hailed with joy by the inhabitants. Anybody or anything would be welcome that would break the oppressive and tormenting monotony of the all-prevailing white.

In the abstract, there is no prejudice against color. No man shrinks from another because he is clothed in a suit of black, nor offended with his boots because they are black. We are told by those who have resided there that a white man in Africa comes to think that ebony is about the proper color for man. Good old Thomas Whitson—a noble old Quaker—a man of rather odd appearance—used to say that even he would be handsome if he could change public opinion.

Aside from the curious contrast to himself, the white child feels nothing on the first sight of a colored man. Curiosity is the only feeling. The office of color in the color line is a very plain and subordinate one. It simply advertises the objects of oppression, insult, and persecution. It is not the maddening liquor, but the black letters on the sign telling the world where it may be had. It is not the hated Quaker, but the broad brim and the plain coat. It is not the hateful Cain, but the mark by which he is known. The color is innocent enough, but things with which it is coupled make it hated. Slavery, ignorance, stupidity, servility, poverty, dependence, are undesirable conditions. When these shall cease to be coupled with color, there will be no color line drawn. It may help in this direction to observe a few of the inconsistencies of the color-line feeling, for it is neither uniform in its operations nor consistent in its principles. Its contradictions in the latter respect would be amusing if the feeling itself were not so deserving of unqualified abhorrence. Our Californian brothers, of Hibernian descent, hate the Chinaman, and kill him, and when asked why they do so, their answer is that a Chinaman is so industrious he will do all the work, and can live by wages upon which other people would starve. When the same people and others are asked why they hate the colored people, the answer is that they are indolent and wasteful, and cannot take care of themselves. Statesmen of the South will tell you that the Negro is too ignorant and stupid properly to exercise the elective franchise, and yet his greatest offense is that he acts with the only party intelligent enough in the eyes of the nation to legislate for the country. In one breath they tell us that the Negro is so weak in intellect, and so destitute of manhood, that he is but the echo of designing white men, and yet in another they will virtually tell you that the Negro is so clear in his moral perceptions, so firm in purpose, so steadfast in his convictions, that he cannot be persuaded by arguments or intimidated by threats, and that nothing but the shot-gun can restrain him from voting for the men and measures he approves. They shrink back in horror from contact with the Negro as a man and a gentleman, but like him very well as a barber, waiter, coachman, or cook. As a slave, he could ride anywhere, side by side with his white master, but as a freeman, he must be thrust into the smoking-car. As a slave, he could go into the first cabin; as a freeman, he was not allowed abaft the wheel. Formerly it was said he was incapable of learning, and at the same time it was a crime against the State for any man to teach him to read. To-day he is said to be originally and permanently inferior to the white race, and yet wild apprehensions are expressed lest six millions of this inferior race will somehow or other manage to rule over thirty-five millions of the superior race. If inconsistency can prove the hollowness of anything, certainly the emptiness of this pretense that color has any terrors is easily shown. The trouble is that most men, and especially mean men, want to have something under them. The rich man would have the poor man, the white would have the black, the Irish would have the Negro, and the Negro must have a dog, if he can get nothing higher in the scale of intelligence to dominate. This feeling is one of the vanities which enlightenment will dispel. A good but simple-minded Abolitionist said to me that he was not ashamed to walk with me down Broadway arm-in-arm, in open daylight, and evidently thought he was saying something that must be very pleasing to my self-importance, but it occurred to me, at the moment, this man does not dream of any reason why I might be ashamed to walk arm-in-arm with him through Broadway in open daylight. Riding in a stage-coach from Concord, New Hampshire, to Vergennes, Vermont, many years ago, I found myself on very pleasant terms with all the passengers through the night, but the morning light came to me as it comes to the stars; I was as Dr. Beecher says he was at the first fire he witnessed, when a bucket of cold water was poured down his back—"the fire was not put out, but he was." The fact is, the higher the colored man rises in the scale of society, the less prejudice does he meet.

The writer has met and mingled freely with the leading great men of his time,—at home and abroad, in public halls and private houses, on the platform and at the fireside,—and can remember no instance when among such men has he been made to feel himself an object of aversion. Men who are really great are too great to be small. This was gloriously true of the late Abraham Lincoln, William H. Seward, Salmon P. Chase, Henry Wilson, John P. Hale, Lewis Tappan, Edmund Quincy, Joshua R. Giddings, Gerrit Smith, and Charles Sumner, and many others among the dead. Good taste will not permit me now to speak of the living, except to say that the number of those who rise superior to prejudice is great and increasing. Let those who wish to see what is to be the future of America, as relates to races and race relations, attend, as I have attended, during the administration of President Hayes, the grand diplomatic reception at the executive mansion, and see there, as I have seen, in its splendid east room the wealth, culture, refinement, and beauty of the nation assembled, and with it the eminent representatives of other nations,—the swarthy Turk with his "fez," the Englishman shining with gold, the German, the Frenchman, the Spaniard, the Japanese, the Chinaman, the Caucasian, the Mongolian, the Sandwich Islander and the Negro,—all moving about freely, each respecting the rights and dignity of the other, and neither receiving nor giving offense.

"Then let us pray that come it may,
As come it will for a' that,
That sense and worth, o'er a' the earth,
May bear the gree, and a' that;

"That man to man, the world o'er,
Shall brothers be, for a' that."

FREDERICK DOUGLASS.

“THE FUTURE OF THE COLORED RACE” (1886)

In this hopeful essay, Douglass predicts that African Americans will be integrated and absorbed into the white race and notes that a new race has already arisen, “which is neither white nor black” but both.

SOURCE: *North American Review*, May 1886

It is quite impossible, at this early date, to say with any decided emphasis what the future of the colored people will be. Speculations of that kind, thus far, have only reflected the mental bias and education of the many who have essayed to solve the problem.

We all know what the negro has been as a slave. In this relation we have his experience of two hundred and fifty years before us, and can easily know the character and qualities he has developed and exhibited during this long and severe ordeal. In his new relation to his environments, we see him only in the twilight of twenty years of semi-freedom; for he has scarcely been free long enough to outgrow the marks of the lash on his back and the fetters on his limbs. He stands before us, to-day, physically, a maimed and mutilated man. His mother was lashed to agony before the birth of her babe, and the bitter anguish of the mother is seen in the countenance of her offspring. Slavery has twisted his limbs, shattered his feet, deformed his body and distorted his features. He remains black, but no longer comely. Sleeping on the dirt floor of the slave cabin in infancy, cold on one side and warm on the other, a forced circulation of blood on the one side and chilled and retarded circulation on the other, it has come to pass that he has not the vertical bearing of a perfect man. His lack of symmetry, caused by no fault of his own, creates a resistance to his progress which cannot well be overestimated, and should be taken into account, when measuring his speed in the new race of life upon which he has now entered. As I have often said before, we should not measure the negro from the heights which the white race has attained, but from the depths from which he has come. You will not find Burke, Grattan, Curran and O'Connell among the oppressed and famished poor of the famine-stricken districts of Ireland. Such men come of comfortable antecedents and sound parents.

Laying aside all prejudice in favor of or against race, looking at the negro as politically and socially related to the American people generally, and measuring the forces arrayed against him, I do not see how he can survive and flourish in this country as a distinct and separate race, nor do I see how he can be removed from the country either by annihilation or expatriation.

Sometimes I have feared that, in some wild paroxysm of rage, the white race, forgetful of the claims of humanity and the precepts of the Christian religion, will proceed to slaughter the negro in wholesale, as some of that race have attempted to slaughter Chinamen, and as it has been done in detail in some districts of the Southern States. The grounds of this fear, however, have in some measure decreased, since the negro has largely disappeared from the arena of Southern politics, and has betaken himself to industrial pursuits and the acquisition of wealth and education, though even here, if over-prosperous, he is likely to excite a dangerous antagonism; for the white people do not easily tolerate the presence among them of a race more prosperous than themselves. The negro as a poor ignorant creature does not contradict the race pride of the white race. He is more a source of amusement to that race than an object of resentment. Malignant resistance is augmented as he approaches the plane occupied by the white race, and yet I think that that resistance will gradually yield to the pressure of wealth, education, and high character.

My strongest conviction as to the future of the negro therefore is, that he will not be expatriated nor annihilated, nor will he forever remain a separate and distinct race from the people around him, but that he will be absorbed, assimilated, and will only appear finally, as the Phœnicians now appear on the shores of the Shannon, in the features of a blended race. I cannot give at length my reasons for this conclusion, and perhaps the reader may think that the wish is father to the thought, and may in his wrath denounce my conclusion as utterly impossible. To such I would say, tarry a little, and look at the facts. Two hundred years ago there were two distinct and separate streams of human life running through this country. They stood at opposite extremes of ethnological classification: all black on the one side, all white on the other. Now, between these two extremes, an intermediate race has arisen, which is neither white nor black, neither Caucasian nor Ethiopian, and this intermediate race is constantly increasing. I know it is said that marital alliance between these races is unnatural, abhorrent and impossible; but exclamations of this kind only shake the air. They prove nothing against a stubborn fact like that which confronts us daily and which is open to the observation of all. If this blending of the two races were impossible we should not have at least one-fourth of our colored population composed of persons of mixed blood, ranging all the way from a dark-brown color to the point where there is no visible admixture. Besides, it is obvious to common sense that there is no need of the passage of laws, or the adoption of other devices, to prevent what is in itself impossible.

Of course this result will not be reached by any hurried or forced processes. It will not arise out of any theory of the wisdom of such blending of the two races. If it comes at all, it will come without shock or noise or violence of any kind, and only in the fullness of time, and it will be so adjusted to surrounding conditions as hardly to be observed. I would not be understood as advocating intermarriage between the two races. I am not a propagandist, but a prophet. I do not say that what I say *should* come to pass, but what I think is likely to come to pass, and what is inevitable.[1] While I would not be understood as advocating the desirability of such a result, I would not be understood as deprecating it. Races and varieties of the human family appear and disappear, but humanity remains and will remain forever. The American people will one day be truer to this idea than now, and will say with Scotia's inspired son:

"A man's a man for a' that."

When that day shall come, they will not pervert and sin against the verity of language as they now do by calling a man of mixed blood, a negro; they will tell the truth. It is only prejudice against the negro which calls every one, however nearly connected with the white race, and however remotely connected with the negro race, a negro. The motive is not a desire to elevate the negro, but to humiliate and degrade those of mixed blood; not a desire to bring the negro up, but to cast the mulatto and the quadroon down by forcing him below an arbitrary and hated color line. Men of mixed blood in this country apply the name "*negro*" to themselves, not because it is a correct ethnological description, but to seem especially devoted to the black side of their parentage. Hence in some cases they are more noisily opposed to the conclusion to which I have come, than either the white or the honestly black race. The opposition to amalgamation, of which we hear so much on the part of colored people, is for most part the merest affectation, and, will never form an impassable barrier to the union of the two varieties.

FREDERICK DOUGLASS.

"INTRODUCTION TO *THE REASON WHY THE COLORED AMERICAN IS NOT IN THE WORLD'S COLUMBIAN EXPOSITION*" (1892)

In this satirical piece, Douglass emphasizes that slavery has persisted even after emancipation and is the reason why blacks have been excluded from the Columbian Exposition. Douglass contributed a chapter to the pamphlet "The Convict Lease System." Other contributors included Ida B. Wells, the famous antilynching activist, and her future husband Ferdinand Barnett.

SOURCE: Pamphlet, Chicago, 1892

The colored people of America are not indifferent to the good opinion of the world, and we have made every effort to improve our first years of freedom and citizenship. We earnestly desired to show some results of our first thirty years of acknowledged manhood and womanhood. Wherein we have failed, it has been not our fault but our misfortune, and it is sincerely hoped that this brief story, not only of our successes, but of trials and failures, our hopes and disappointments will relieve us of the charge of indifference and indolence. We have deemed it only a duty to ourselves, to make plain what might otherwise be misunderstood and misconstrued concerning us. To do this we must begin with slavery. The duty undertaken is far from a welcome one.

It involves the necessity of plain speaking of wrongs and outrages endured, and of rights withheld, and withheld in flagrant contradiction to boasted American Republican liberty and civilization. It is always more agreeable to speak well of one's country and its institutions than to speak otherwise; to tell of their good qualities rather than of their evil ones.

There are many good things concerning our country and countrymen of which we would be glad to tell in this pamphlet, if we could do so, and at the same time tell the truth. We would like for instance to tell our visitors that the moral progress of the American people has kept even pace with their enterprise and their material civilization; that practice by the ruling class has gone on hand in hand with American professions; that two hundred and sixty years of progress and enlightenment have banished barbarism and race hate from the United States; that the old things of slavery have entirely passed away, and that all things pertaining to the colored people have become new; that American liberty is now the undisputed possession of all the American people; that American law is now the shield alike of black and white; that the spirit of slavery and class domination has no longer any lurking place in any part of this country; that the statement of human rights contained in its glorious Declaration of Independence, including the right to life, liberty and the pursuit of happiness is not an empty boast nor a mere rhetorical flourish, but a soberly and honestly accepted truth, to be carried out in good faith; that the American Church and clergy, as a whole, stand for the sentiment of universal human brotherhood and that its Christianity is without partiality and without hypocrisy; that the souls of Negroes are held to be as precious in the sight of God, as are the souls of white men; that duty to the heathen at home is as fully recognized and as sacredly discharged as is duty to the heathen abroad; that no man on account of his color, race or condition, is deprived of life, liberty or property without due process of law; that mobs are not allowed to supersede courts of law or usurp the place of government; that here Negroes are not tortured, shot, hanged or burned to death, merely on suspicion of crime and without ever seeing a judge, a jury or advocate; that the American Government is in reality a Government of the people, by the people and for the people, and for all the people; that the National Government is not a rope of sand, but has both the power and the disposition to protect the lives and liberties of American citizens of whatever color, at home, not less than abroad; that it will send its men-of-war to chastise the murder of its citizens in New Orleans or in any other part of the south, as readily as for the same purpose it will send them to Chile, Haiti or San Domingo; that our national sovereignty, in its rights to protect the lives of American citizens is ample and superior to any right or power possessed by the individual states; that the people of the United States are a nation in fact as well as in name; that in time of peace as in time of war, allegiance to the nation is held to be superior to any fancied allegiance to individual states; that allegiance and protection are here held to be reciprocal; that there is on the statute books of the nation no law for the protection of personal or political rights, which the nation may not or can not enforce, with or without the consent of individual states; that this World's Columbian Exposition, with its splendid display of wealth and power, its triumphs of art and its multitudinous architectural and other attractions, is a fair indication of the elevated and liberal sentiment of the American people, and that to the colored people of America, morally speaking, the World's Fair now in progress, is not a whited sepulcher.

All this, and more, we would gladly say of American laws, manners, customs and Christianity. But unhappily, nothing of all this can be said, without qualification and with flagrant disregard of the truth. The explanation is this: We have long had in this country, a system of iniquity which possessed the power of blinding the moral perception, stifling the voice of conscience, blunting all human sensibilities, and perverting the plainest teaching of the religion we have here professed, a system which John Wesley truly characterized as the sum of all villainies, and one in view of which Thomas Jefferson, himself a slaveholder, said he "trembled for his country" when he reflected "that God is just and that His justice cannot sleep forever." That system was American slavery. Though it is now gone, its asserted spirit remains.

The writer of the initial chapter of this pamphlet, having himself been a slave, knows the slave system both on the inside and outside. Having studied its effects not only upon the slave and upon the master, but also upon the people and institutions by which it has been surrounded, he may therefore, without presumption, assume to bear witness to its baneful influence upon all concerned, and especially to its malign agency in explaining the present condition of the colored people of the United States, who were its victims; and to the sentiment held toward them both by the people who held them in slavery, and the people of the country who tolerated and permitted their enslavement, and the bearing it has upon the relation which we the colored people sustain to the World's Fair. What the legal and actual condition of the colored people was previous to emancipation is easily told.

It should be remembered by all who would entertain just views and arrive at a fair estimate of our character, our attainments and our worth in the scale of civilization, that prior to the slaveholder's rebellion thirty years ago, our legal condition was simply that of dumb brutes. We were classed as goods and chattels, and numbered on our master's ledgers with horses, sheep and swine. We were subject to barter and sale, and could be bequeathed and inherited by will, like real estate or any other property. In the language of the law: A slave was one in the power of his master to whom he belonged. He could acquire nothing, have nothing, own nothing that did not belong to his master. His time and talents, his mind and muscle, his body and soul, were the property of the master. He, with all that could be predicated of him as a human being, was simply the property of his master. He was a marketable commodity. His money value was regulated like any other article; it was increased or diminished according to his perfections or imperfections as a beast of burden.

Chief Justice Taney truly described the condition of our people when he said in the infamous Dred Scott decision, that they were supposed to have no rights which white men were bound to respect. White men could shoot, hang, burn, whip and starve them to death with impunity. They were made to feel themselves as outside the pale of all civil and political institutions. The master's power over them was complete and absolute. They could decide no question of pursuit or condition for themselves. Their children had no parents, their mothers had no husband and there was no marriage in a legal sense.

But I need not elaborate the legal and practical definition of slavery. What I have aimed to do, has not only been to show the moral depths, darkness and destitution from which we are still emerging, but to explain the grounds of the prejudice, hate and contempt in which we are still held by the people, who for more than two hundred years doomed us to this cruel and degrading condition. So when it is asked why we are excluded from the World's Columbian Exposition, the answer is Slavery.[1]

Outrages upon the Negro in this country will be narrated in these pages. They will seem too shocking for belief. This doubt is creditable to human nature, and yet in view of the education and training of those who inflict the wrongs complained of, and the past condition of those upon whom they are inflicted as already described, such outrages are not only credible but entirely consistent and logical. Why should not these be inflicted?

The life of a Negro slave was never held sacred in the estimation of the people of that section of the country in the time of slavery, and the abolition of slavery against the will of the enslavers did not render a slave's life more sacred. Such a one could be branded with hot irons, loaded with chains, and whipped to death with impunity when a slave. It only needed be said that he or she was impudent or insolent to a white man, to excuse or justify the killing of him or her. The people of the south are with few exceptions but slightly improved in their sentiments towards those they once held as slaves. The mass of them are the same to-day that they were in the time of slavery, except perhaps that now they think they can murder with a decided advantage in point of economy. In the time of slavery if a Negro was killed, the owner sustained a loss of property. Now he is not restrained by any fear of such loss.

The crime of insolence for which the Negro was formerly killed and for which his killing was justified, is as easily pleaded in excuse now, as it was in the old time and what is worse, it is sufficient to make the charge of insolence to provoke the knife or bullet. This done, it is only necessary to say in the newspapers that this dead Negro was impudent and about to raise an insurrection and kill all the white people, or that a white woman was insulted by a Negro, to lull the conscience of the north into indifference and reconcile its people to such murder. No proof of guilt is required. It is enough to accuse, to condemn and punish the accused with death. When he is dead and silent, and the murderer is alive and at large, he has it all his own way. He can tell any story he may please and will be believed. The popular ear is open to him, and his justification is sure. At the bar of public opinion in this country all presumptions are against the Negro accused of crime.

The crime to which the Negro is now said to be so generally and specially addicted, is one of which he has been heretofore, seldom accused or supposed to be guilty. The importance of this fact cannot be overestimated. He was formerly accused of petty thefts, called a chicken thief and the like, but seldom or never was he accused of the atrocious crime of feloniously assaulting white women. If we may believe his accusers this is a new development. In slaveholding times no one heard of any such crime by a Negro. During all the war, when there was the fullest and safest opportunity for such assaults, nobody ever heard of such being made by him. Thousands of white women were left for years in charge of Negroes, while their fathers, brothers and husbands were absent fighting the battles of the rebellion; yet there was no assault upon such women by Negroes, and no accusation of such assault. It is only since the Negro has become a citizen and a voter that this charge has been made. It has come along with the pretended and baseless fear of Negro supremacy. It is an effort to divest the Negro of his friends by giving him a revolting and hateful reputation. Those who do this would make the world believe that freedom has changed the whole character of the Negro, and made of him a moral monster.

This is a conclusion revolting alike to common sense and common experience. Besides there is good reason to suspect a political motive for the charge. A motive other than the one they would have the world believe. It comes in close connection with the effort now being made to disfranchise the colored man. It comes from men who regard it innocent to lie, and who are unworthy of belief where the Negro is concerned. It comes from men who count it no crime to falsify the returns of the ballot box and cheat the Negro of his lawful vote. It comes from those who would smooth the way for the Negro's disfranchisement in clear defiance of the constitution they have sworn to support—men who are perjured before God and man.

We do not deny that there are bad Negroes in this country capable of committing this, or any other crime that other men can or do commit. There are bad black men as there are bad white men, south, north and everywhere else, but when such criminals, or alleged criminals are found, we demand that their guilt shall be established by due course of law. When this will be done, the voice of the colored people everywhere will then be "Let no guilty man escape." The man in the South who says he is for Lynch Law because he honestly believes that the courts of that section are likely to be too merciful to the Negro charged with this crime, either does not know the South, or is fit for prison or an insane asylum.

Not less absurd is the pretense of these law breakers that the resort to Lynch Law is made because they do not wish the shocking details of the crime made known. Instead of a jury of twelve men to decently try the case, they assemble a mob of five hundred men and boys, and circulate the story of the alleged outrage with all its concomitant, disgusting detail. If they desire to give such crimes the widest publicity, they could adopt no course better calculated to secure that end than by a resort to Lynch Law. But this pretended delicacy is manifestly all a sham, and the members of the blood-thirsty mob bent upon murder know it to be such. It may deceive people outside of the sunny South, but not those who know as we do the bold and open defiance of every sentiment of modesty and chastity practiced for centuries on the slave plantations by this same old master class.

We know we shall be censured for the publication of this volume. The time for its publication will be thought to be ill chosen. America is just now, as never before, posing before the world as a highly liberal and civilized nation, and in many important respects she has a right to this reputation. She has brought to her shores and given welcome to a greater variety of mankind than were ever assembled in one place since the day of Pentecost. Japanese, Javanese, Soudanese, Chinese, Senegalese, Syrians, Persians, Tunisians, Algerians, Egyptians, East Indians, Laplanders, Esquimaux, and as if to shame the Negro, the Dahomians are also here to exhibit the Negro as a repulsive savage.

It must be admitted that to outward seeming, the colored people of the United States have lost ground and have met with increased and galling resistance since the war of the rebellion. It is well to understand this phase of the situation. Considering the important services rendered by them in suppressing the late rebellion and the saving of the Union, they were for a time generally regarded with a sentiment of gratitude by their loyal white fellow citizens. This sentiment, however, very naturally became weaker as, in the course of events, those services were retired from view and the memory of them became dimmed by time and also by the restoration of friendship between the North and the South. Thus, what the colored people gained by the war they have partly lost by peace.

Military necessity had much to do with requiring their services during the war, and their ready and favorable response to that requirement was so simple, generous and patriotic, that the loyal states readily adopted important amendments to the constitution in their favor. They accorded them freedom and endowed them with citizenship and the right to vote and the right to be voted for. These rights are now a part of the organic law of the land and as such, stand today on the national statute book. But the spirit and purpose of these have been in a measure defeated by state legislation and by judicial decisions. It has nevertheless been found impossible to defeat them entirely and to relegate colored citizens to their former condition. They are still free.

The ground held by them to-day is vastly in advance of that they occupied before the war, and it may be safely predicted that they will not only hold this ground, but that they will regain in the end much of that which they seem to have lost in the reaction. As to the increased resistance met with by them of late, let us use a little philosophy. It is easy to account in a hopeful way for this reaction and even to regard it as a favorable symptom. It is a proof that the Negro is not standing still. He is not dead, but alive and active. He is not drifting with the current, but manfully resisting it and fighting his way to better conditions than those of the past, and better than those which popular opinion prescribes for him. He is not contented with his surroundings, but nobly dares to break away from them and hew out a way of safety and happiness for himself in defiance of all opposing forces.

A ship rotting at anchor meets with no resistance, but when she sets sail on the sea, she has to buffet opposing billows. The enemies of the Negro see that he is making progress, and they naturally wish to stop him and keep him in just what they consider his proper place.

They have said to him "you are a poor Negro, be poor still," and "you are an ignorant Negro, be ignorant still and we will not antagonize you or hurt you." But the Negro has said a decided no to all this, and is now by industry, economy, and education wisely raising himself to conditions of civilization and comparative well being beyond anything formerly thought possible for him. Hence, a new determination is born to keep him down. There is nothing strange or alarming about this. Such aspirations as his when cherished by the lowly are always resented by those who have already reached the top. They who aspire to higher grades than those fixed for them by society are scouted and scorned as upstarts for their presumptions.

In their passage from an humble to a higher position, the white man in some measure goes through the same ordeal. This is in accordance with the nature of things. It is simply an incident of a transitional condition. It is not the fault of the Negro, but the weakness, we might say the depravity, of human nature. Society resents the pretentions of those it considers upstarts. The newcomers always have to go through with this sort of resistance. The old and established are ever adverse to the new and aspiring. But the upstarts of to-day are the elite of tomorrow. There is no stopping any people from earnestly endeavoring to rise. Resistance ceases when the prosperity of the rising class becomes pronounced and permanent.

The Negro is just now under the operation of this law of society. If he were white as the driven snow, and had been enslaved as we had been, he would have to submit to this same law in his progress upward. What the Negro has to do then, is to cultivate a courageous and cheerful spirit, use philosophy and exercise patience. He must embrace every avenue open to him for the acquisition of wealth. He must educate his children and build up a character for industry, economy, intelligence and virtue. Next to victory is the glory and happiness of manfully contending for it. Therefore, contend! contend!

That we should have to contend and strive for what is freely conceded to other citizens without effort or demand may indeed be a hardship, but there is compensation here as elsewhere. Contest is itself ennobling. A life devoid of purpose and earnest effort is a worthless life. Conflict is better than stagnation. It is bad to be a slave, but worse to be a willing and contented slave. We are men, and our aim is perfect manhood, to be men among men. Our situation demands faith in ourselves, faith in the power of truth, faith in work, and faith in the influence of manly character. Let the truth be told, let the light be turned on ignorance and prejudice, let lawless violence and murder be exposed.

The Americans are a great and magnanimous people, and this great exposition adds greatly to their honor and renown, but in the pride of their success, they have cause for repentance as well as complaisance, and for shame as well as for glory, and hence we send forth this volume to be read of all men.

"TOUSSAINT L'OUVERTURE" (CA. 1891)

Douglass penned this essay as an introduction to the American edition of *Vie de Toussaint-Louverture* (1889) by the French abolitionist and statesman Victor Schoelcher. The planned edition fell through, however, and the essay is published here for the first time. It is Douglass's only extended assessment of Toussaint.

SOURCE: Frederick Douglass Papers, Library of Congress

To give the world a full and fair estimate of the character, qualities and works of a great black man of the period in which Toussaint L'Ouverture lived and worked, is a task not easily performed. Whether this task is undertaken by a white man or a black man, a Frenchman or an American, there is danger of an inability to reach a satisfactory conclusion. There may be in the author the best intention and the most conscientious endeavor to hold the scales steady and perfectly level, yet the force of the moral atmosphere and the inequality of its pressure in which he must work will be apt to cause some deviation from the right line and ensure defeat to his honest purpose to tell the whole truth in respect to him.

It is the misfortune of men of the African race that they rest under a heavy cloud which time and events have yet to dispel. Every man in whose veins there is found a trace of African blood is on first sight prejudged and falls under the depressing weight of an unfavourable popular opinion. In respect of him the verdict is usually made up and ready for presentation in advance of all vindicating evidence and argument.

Few things are more blinding than prejudice, and few things more persistently and inflexibly defy the assaults of reason and common sense. It may be well hoped that the contents of this volume of the life and times of a great black man will prove a valuable auxiliary in the work of combatting this prejudice, especially as here it is most prevalent and exerts a more powerful influence than in any other part of the civilized world.

But the difficulty of writing a correct life of Toussaint L'Ouverture is not wholly one-sided. Possible prejudices for, as well as those against, though less likely to intervene, may prove a hindrance in attaining a just estimate of the character and deeds of this remarkable black man. He may be unduly exalted by reason of the very influences that have caused him to be disparaged and depressed. Though the danger in one direction is much less than in the other, neither can be wisely ignored where truth and impartiality are sought.

A man of tender and humane impulses, deeply penetrated with a sense of the wrongs inflicted upon the Negro for ages, and aware of the unjust judgment by which he has been oppressed, despised, and depressed may be easily led in a spirit of magnanimity to magnify his virtue or conceal or apologize for his faults, not only by way of atonement for such wrongs but by a spirit of combativeness. He may also be carried away by an enthusiasm perfectly natural, arising out of surprise and gratification at the discovery in his hero of so many qualities which are in point blank contradiction to the prevalent opinion of the race and which transcend in excellence his own expectations. Extremes beget extremes, and the pendulum swung too far in one direction inevitably swings too far in the other.

Besides, there is much in the career of this hero of Santo Domingo to touch and warm the heart of our common humanity, as well as to the poetic side of human nature. The generally accepted theory of the inferiority of the Negro, combined with the common disposition to be in accord with surroundings and to conform individual opinions to that which is held by the multitude on the one hand, and humane and poetic feeling on the other, are the two obvious dangers to be guarded against in this and similar cases. They constitute the Scylla and Charybdis between which an author, like a mariner, must steer.

Another element in the history of the man before us, calculated to mislead and confuse the mental and moral vision, is the practical existence of a dual standard of measurement of the character and deeds of men. One is the ethnological standard which determines excellence according to race, and the other is the standard which arises out of common human nature, and applies to all men alike. Unhappily for the Negro, he is made to stand outside of this broad and comprehensive standard of measurement. The world looked upon the example of George Washington, battling with England during seven years for the freedom and independence of his people and country, from a point entirely different from that of Toussaint L'Ouverture battling against France for the freedom and independence of his people and country. To the one was extended the warmest sympathy and was regarded with admiration as a model of manhood, a paragon of patriotism; while the other was detested as a savage insurgent and a villainous cut-throat. One was fighting against political abuses, and the other against personal slavery, one hour of which, according to Jefferson, himself a slave-holder, was worse than ages of that which Washington rose in rebellion to oppose. Yet one was lauded to the skies as an example for mankind, and the other is branded as a moral monster for whom the prison and the halter are too good. This standard of measurement, which was in full force in the days of these two great men, obtains in some degree today. As it worked injustice then, so it works injustice now. Nathaniel Turner, the Negro who in 1831 struck for the freedom of himself and brothers at Southampton, Virginia, was, in the estimation of his times, a blood-thirsty murderer fit only for the gallows. A white man who should do the same thing today would be hailed as a saint or a hero.

But again there is another difficulty in the way of a just view of the black hero of Santo Domingo. It is that greatness is relative and not easily arrived at when standing alone. It is discoverable better by analogy, than by being viewed separately. For the most part, men appear either great or small by comparison. A ship sailing alone on a smooth sea, with its broad canvass filled with a favourable breeze, will seem to those who stand upon her deck to be making much better speed than when another of equal size and canvass is alongside, sailing the same way and with equal rate of speed.

Just here is the difficulty of the case of Toussaint L'Ouverture. There is no fit example with which to compare him. His circumstances were as peculiar as his character was unique. He stands alone as a liberator, warrior and statesman, separate and apart from all other heroes and leaders of men. Others may have risen higher but none have started from a point lower. Greater things have been done by other men, but none have done greater things than he with conditions so unfavourable and means so small as his.

Circumstances sometimes make men great, but greater men than those who were made by circumstances were those that made their own. Toussaint L'Ouverture was one of this latter class of great men. He created the sea upon which he floated. He imparted to others strength, and infused the valour which gave himself and them the victory.

Other redeemers and liberators of men come from heaven; this one came to us from the hell of slavery. From such a quarter no such man as Toussaint L'Ouverture could have been expected. It is your free-born, educated, and sensitive man whose neck has never been bowed or calloused by the yoke, whose soul is capable of being stung to madness by oppression, and whose spirit, ambition and eloquence are able to rouse the oppressed to rise in revolt against powerful slaveholders and tyrants. It is the hand of little employment that hath the daintier touch. The condition of a slave is not favourable to this sensitiveness. The natural effect of slavery is to blunt all the finer feelings of the human soul, destroy self-respect and reduce a man simply to a beast of burden, and to divest him of all manly ambition. In fact, it may be said that to treat a slave well, to deal tenderly with him, to give him a good bed to sleep upon, to provide him good food to eat, ample time for sleep, rest and recreation, is the best preparation that can be devised to make him discontented and to equip him as a leader of revolt against slavery.

The case of Toussaint L'Ouverture is an illustration of this theory only in part. He was a slave, but a favoured slave. His position as his master's coachman was one of comparative ease. He had time to think, and his contact with his master and his master's family was in some degree a school. The more light it brought to him, the more clearly he could see the false and unjust position he occupied. He was a slave, but had in him a spirit too strong for slavery to crush. He knew the value of liberty by being denied its possession. To outward seeming, he was no doubt a contented slave, when the desire to be free was burning in every throb of his manly heart. His comparatively easy condition on the one hand, and his low estate as a bondsman alike, rendered it improbable that in him could be the great qualities displayed by him as a leader of a fierce and sanguinary rebellion against slavery.

He was, in fact, a gigantic surprise. He came upon the world like a bolt from a clear sky, or rather like one forced to the surface by a sudden and violent disturbance underground, an upheaval from impenetrable depths and darkness, a furious outburst of valour, smoke, and volcanic fire, destined to fill all the air of his country with odours, pestilence and death. He is seen as [if] by the lurid glare of a furnace, infernal in the midst of horrors where men came to glut over warm, smoking, human blood, to laugh at human agony, and mock at human despair and death. In this conflict between the white and the black, the slave and the master, men seemed transformed into devils and earth into a hell, till the very name of Santo Domingo sent a shudder around the world. Since the horrors of the inquisition, when bigotry and priest-craft in the name of religion taxed human ingenuity to the extent of all its powers in the invention of engines of cruelty, there has been nothing with which to compare the scenes enacted in Santo Domingo. Indian savages on our western borders, with their gleaming tomahawks and scalping knives, with their war-whoops and death dances, sparing in their fury neither age nor sex, have given examples of cruelty not more shocking than that perpetrated in the interest of slavery in Santo Domingo. Every outrage by the French brought retaliation by the Negroes. Each brought with it some added element of horrors.

It is remarkable that the man who might have been expected to be the most cruel and blood-thirsty, in view of that for which he struggled and the terrible power against which he had to contend, was distinguished above all for the quality of mercy, and this man was Toussaint L'Ouverture.

Toussaint L'Ouverture was an unmixed Negro. The busts and portraits I have seen of him in Hayti do him full justice in this respect. Happily no part of his greatness can be ascribed to blood relationship to the white race. His colour, his features, his hair proclaim him at once a Negro. True, he had a high broad forehead, and a dignified and thoughtful expression of face, but he was in all respects a typical Negro. He therefore demonstrates beyond cavil or doubt the possibilities of the Negro race. We may take him as an unanswerable argument against all detractors of his race on account of colour and features. It enables the Negro to say to the world that what the Negro has done once, he can do again; what he has done in the past he may do in the future. If there has been one Toussaint, there may be yet another. The material is not exhausted or decreased. It is said that he is an exception. So he is. All Englishmen are not Peels, Gladstones, Brights, or Broughams; and all Americans are not Clays, Conklings, Websters or Sumners; but the races that produced them can produce more like them. The black race may well enough contemplate Toussaint with the complacency with which other races contemplate their great men. In the light of this reasoning they may well gain courage to resist the forces operating against them here and elsewhere.

But the beneficent example of Toussaint is not confined to the Negro race, or to the Negro's relations—as all are calling Negroes who have any Negro blood in their veins. To the white people of this country, he has a mission scarcely less important than that of the Negro. His example is fitted [for] oppressors of whatever land or colour, that there is a danger of goading too far the energy that may "slumber in the black man's arm"; that out of the depth of misery and oppression there may come another black man, not inferior to Toussaint in talent, zeal, and organizing ability, who may convert the Gulf States into another Santo Domingo. In such a contest it should be remembered, in the language of Thomas Jefferson, that the Almighty has no attribute that will take the side of the oppressor. Besides, conditions are more favourable to the Negro than was the case when Toussaint rose against slavery in Santo Domingo. Then, almost the whole Christian world was against him, and thought him only fit for slavery. All the greatest states were slave-holding. England,

France, Spain, Holland, Portugal, Central and South America as well as the United States were slave-holding nations. Now, the reverse is true. The whole Christian and civilized world has pronounced against it, and now there is a generous feeling in favour of giving the Negro a fair chance in the race of life. In no part of the world now is the lesson taught by Toussaint more needed than in the United States. For though the system of slavery is here abolished, the spirit of slavery is still visibly alive, active and baneful. A large debt is due not only to the author, but to Mr. Stanton for translating and publishing this in this country.

In this volume the reader will observe that there is nothing sensational beyond the measure of the simple truth. There is no straining after effect. The author is not a searcher after fame and evidently has no desire to attract attention to himself. He has passed beyond the time of such ambition. His work is the work of a venerable statesman, a member of the French Senate, a position of honour to which mere authorship can add nothing. He is not only aged and venerable, but he is one who can look back over a long line of public service and has had the good fortune and satisfaction to see some of his most radical and cherished ideas accepted by his countrymen and organized into law. His life of Toussaint comes to us from under the solid weight of four score years, and was probably meant by him to be, as it well might be so meant, as the crowning work of a long and useful life. He could have done few things more appropriate and serviceable to mankind. His work has given us in a calm, clear light a true view of a great man, a figure of which we have heretofore only had glimpses, and one, too, that was rapidly vanishing from the vision of the world, and one that the world could poorly afford to lose sight of.

No one is perhaps so well qualified as Victor Schoelcher to perform this work. His years extend back to the time when the character and deeds of Toussaint were much talked of. All that we know of Victor Schoelcher proves that he would be likely to take a deep interest in the misfortunes of a man like Toussaint and endeavour to know all that could be known about him. Not less fitted by fullness of knowledge (as his work shows) than by sympathy with the fallen chief to do justice to his merits. Aside from this, his own history, his name and station are a guarantee of the quality of his work and proof of its value. No temptation of fame or wealth has induced him to write this book. It comes from his pen as [a] labour of love and a contribution to the truth of history. If he has departed a hair's breadth from the strict line of truth in his estimate of Toussaint, no man who knows him will think for a moment it is due to anything but his intense love of liberty and his equally intense and outspoken hatred of oppression. The Negro, to Mr. Schoelcher, is a man and a man among men, with all the attributes and dignity of manhood. Hence if in this book he has leaned to either side, it is to the side of a deeply wronged people. While, however, he has spoken well of Toussaint and of the race of which he is a conspicuous example, he has been too just and impartial to flatter the variety of the race by imputing to Toussaint qualities which he did not possess. While he has allowed nothing to escape him which could serve to illustrate the greatness of his hero, he has not withheld his faults. Nor has he refrained from exposing in fitting language the terrible crimes of those against whom Toussaint fought.

Nothing other, or less, than this could have been expected from a man like Victor Schoelcher. A man without bigotry or prejudices, and fearless of criticism, a born philanthropist, a friend of progress, a patron of education, a champion of liberty, could do no other than expose and denounce the shocking outrages perpetrated against the Negroes of Santo Domingo.

Schoelcher is to France what Wilberforce was to England, and Sumner was to the United States. The proud position now held by France on the slavery question is largely due to his statesmanship. He had the sagacity to see the golden opportunity for freeing his country from the crime of slavery, and what is better still, he had the moral firmness to improve the opportunity, the courage to strike the blow required at the moment when it could be most effective. This opportunity might have been as plain to other men as to himself, and yet have been lost on various grounds of fancied expediency. No better eulogy could be pronounced upon our author than the way in which he accomplished emancipation in the French colonies.

His agency in that measure stamps him as one of the noblest among the patriots and wisest of the statesmen who took part in the Revolution of 1848. He was at that time a secretary under the provisional government which succeeded the downfall of Louis Philip. It was a time when men in his position did not lack for employment. They were in the midst of pressing affairs. Though Victor Schoelcher was as busy as the busiest of them, he did not forget the slaves of the French Colonies. There was much in the occupation furnished [to] him at home which to another mind than his might have excused forgetfulness of those abroad, but Schoelcher was not of the sort to forget a manifest duty where liberty was concerned, whether at home or abroad; and he pressed upon the colonial minister the duty of freeing the slaves with such eloquence and urgency as at last to bring that scientist and statesman to support and carry out the measure. When told that emancipation would bring on a war of races, Schoelcher said, on the contrary, a failure to emancipate would bring on such a war, and boldly declared that he would advise the slaves to rise if they were not emancipated. It was this bold and lofty spirit of the true statesman of the hour that brought Arago to his support, and it was the hand of this man who wrote the memorable *decree*, signed by M. Arago, that freed France from all participation in the shame and guilt of slavery, and now the same hand that wrote that decree, has written this voluminous history of the life and times of Toussaint L'Ouverture.

It was my good fortune while in Paris four years ago to have several interviews with the author of this life of Toussaint. I was first introduced to him in the chamber of the French Senate, and afterwards met him on two occasions with Mr. Theodore Stanton at his house. To say I was very much impressed by M. Schoelcher's conversation, bearing, and surroundings is to say almost nothing. I look back to my calls upon him as among the most interesting and memorable of the many I have had the privilege of making upon distinguished public men in America and in Europe. M. Schoelcher was at that time nearly 80 years old, and though his form implied as much, I found him still about as warmly alive to all that was going on in the world, as if in the midst of his years. He was still in the busy world and taking his full part in it abreast with the men whose locks were unhinged by time and toil. He seemed to have no idea of quitting work on account of declining health or weight of years. It was here I learned of his purpose to write the life of Toussaint L'Ouverture. I confess, in view of his years, his many duties and his engagements as a senator, I felt some amazement at his announcement; but remembering the long lives attained by European statesmen, I could not but hope that his intention would be carried out. So I told him, then and there, if an American edition were published of his work, I would write an introduction to it. In fulfillment of this promise I have written what, I hope, may pass as not an entirely unsuitable introduction of his work to my countrymen.

I learned much of the life and good works of the author while in Paris, and could say much about him and them, but willingly leave this material to the pen of Mr. Theodore Stanton, whom I learn is to write a sketch of the author's life. I must, however, be allowed to say I was considerably surprised to find in Paris any house having such emblems of barbarism as I found in his. The room in which M. Schoelcher received me was itself eloquent. It proclaimed the character and history of the man more forcibly than any words of mine can do. The walls were decorated with slave-whips, broken chains, fetters, hand-cuffs, and iron collars which had been used on the backs, necks and limbs of slaves. They were sent to him from the colonies by emancipated Negroes, in grateful recognition of the noble liberator's services in bringing their bondage to an end. There were, too, in the room other evidences of the gratitude of the emancipated people of the colonies to their friend and benefactor. These memorials came from Martinique and Guadeloupe. It was evident that the venerable philanthropist valued highly these grateful testimonials. Several coloured members of the Corps Legislatif called upon him while I was there, and were received by the grand old statesman with dignified cordiality. They came mostly to obtain the benefit of his experience and counsel, and I think showed their wisdom in applying to that source.

At the time of my visit to M. Schoelcher I had no idea that I should be appointed Minister-resident to Hayti, the land of Toussaint L'Ouverture. I am sorry to say, one of the painful impressions made upon me here was the small appreciation in which the memory of Hayti's greatest man is held in Hayti. His case is another illustration of the scripture saying that a prophet is without honour in his country and among his own kinsmen. In my search for the cause of this lack of grateful remembrance, I found that it was not pretended that Toussaint was not a great man and a friend to the liberty of his people, but it was said that he was a Frenchman and was for keeping his country as a colony of France. It is also alleged that his government was hard in that it insisted upon keeping the productions of the island up to the point at which slavery left them. Small faults these, if faults they were, in comparison with the eminent services performed and the lustre shed on the Negro race by this illustrious personage. This man, like many another Moses, finds his fiercest critics among those he has served best, and on the other hand, the highest appreciation among impartial observers under no special obligations to him.

To his countrymen, his skillful generalship, his enlightened statesmanship, and heroic courage while contending for the liberty of his people, and his splendid vindication of Negro ability, seem to count for nothing in Hayti because of a political difference of opinion, entirely sincere on his part, and which was quite natural to a loyal soul like his. Besides, his allegiance to France was conditional. He was for France with liberty, but against the whole world for the freedom of his people and country.

Appendix: On Genealogical Self-Fashioning

These excerpts from Douglass's three autobiographies show how he changed the identities of his mother and father, revealing the evolution of his own identity.

SOURCES: *Narrative of the Life of Frederick Douglass, an American Slave* (Boston: Anti-Slavery Office, 1845); *My Bondage and My Freedom* (New York and Auburn, New York: Miller, Orton & Mulligan, 1855); *Life and Times of Frederick Douglass* (Hartford, CT: Park Publishing Co., 1881)

FROM *NARRATIVE OF THE LIFE OF FREDERICK DOUGLASS, AN AMERICAN SLAVE*

My mother was named Harriet Bailey. She was the daughter of Isaac and Betsey Bailey, both colored, and quite dark. My mother was of a darker complexion than either my grandmother or grandfather.

My father was a white man. He was admitted to be such by all I ever heard speak of my parentage. The opinion was also whispered that my master was my father; but of the correctness of this opinion, I know nothing; the means of knowing was withheld from me. My mother and I were separated when I was but an infant—before I knew her as my mother. It is a common custom, in the part of Maryland from which I ran away, to part children from their mothers at a very early age. Frequently, before the child has reached its twelfth month, its mother is taken from it, and hired out on some farm a considerable distance off, and the child is placed under the care of an old woman, too old for field labor. For what this separation is done, I do not know, unless it be to hinder the development of the child's affection toward its mother, and to blunt and destroy the natural affection of the mother for the child. This is the inevitable result.

I never saw my mother, to know her as such, more than four or five times in my life; and each of these times was very short in duration, and at night. She was hired by a Mr. Stewart, who lived about twelve miles from my home. She made her journeys to see me in the night, travelling the whole distance on foot, after the performance of her day's work. She was a field hand, and a whipping is the penalty of not being in the field at sunrise, unless a slave has special permission from his or her master to the contrary—a permission which they seldom get, and one that gives to him that gives it the proud name of being a kind master. I do not recollect of ever seeing my mother by the light of day. She was with me in the night. She would lie down with me, and get me to sleep, but long before I waked she was gone. Very little communication ever took place between us. Death soon ended what little we could have while she lived, and with it her hardships and suffering. She died when I was about seven years old, on one of my master's farms, near Lee's Mill. I was not allowed to be present during her illness, at her death, or burial. She was gone long before I knew any thing about it. Never having enjoyed, to any considerable extent, her soothing presence, her tender and watchful care, I received the tidings of her death with much the same emotions I should have probably felt at the death of a stranger.

Called thus suddenly away, she left me without the slightest intimation of who my father was. The whisper that my master was my father, may or may not be true; and, true or false, it is of but little consequence to my purpose whilst the fact remains, in all its glaring odiousness, that slaveholders have ordained, and by law established, that the children of slave women shall in all cases follow the condition of their mothers; and this is done too obviously to administer to their own lusts, and make a gratification of their wicked desires profitable as well as pleasurable; for by this cunning arrangement, the slaveholder, in cases not a few, sustains to his slaves the double relation of master and father.

* * *

I have had two masters. My first master's name was Anthony. I do not remember his first name. He was generally called Captain Anthony—a title which, I presume, he acquired by sailing a craft on the Chesapeake Bay. He was not considered a rich slaveholder. He owned two or three farms, and about thirty slaves. His farms and slaves were under the care of an overseer. The overseer's name was Plummer. Mr. Plummer was a miserable drunkard, a profane swearer, and a savage monster. He always went armed with a cowskin and a heavy cudgel. I have known him to cut and slash the women's heads so horribly, that even master would be enraged at his cruelty, and would threaten to whip him if he did not mind himself. Master, however, was not a humane slaveholder. It required extraordinary barbarity on the part of an overseer to affect him. He was a cruel man, hardened by a long life of slaveholding. He would at times seem to take great pleasure in whipping a slave. I have often been awakened at the dawn of day by the most heart-rending shrieks of an own aunt of mine, whom he used to tie up to a joist, and whip upon her naked back till she was literally covered with blood. No words, no tears, no prayers, from his gory victim, seemed to move his iron heart from its bloody purpose. The louder she screamed, the harder he whipped; and where the blood ran fastest, there he whipped longest. He would whip her to make her scream, and whip her to make her hush; and not until overcome by fatigue, would he cease to swing the blood-clotted cowskin. I remember the first time I ever witnessed this horrible exhibition. I was quite a child, but I well remember it. I never shall forget it whilst I remember any thing. It was the first of a long series of such outrages, of which I was doomed to be a witness and a participant. It struck me with awful force. It was the blood-stained gate, the entrance to the hell of slavery, through which I was about to pass. It was a most terrible spectacle. I wish I could commit to paper the feelings with which I beheld it.

* * *

My master's family consisted of two sons, Andrew and Richard; one daughter, Lucretia, and her husband, Captain Thomas Auld. They lived in one house, upon the home plantation of Colonel Edward Lloyd. My master was Colonel Lloyd's clerk and superintendent. He was what might be called the overseer of the overseers. I spent two years of childhood on this plantation in my old master's family. It was here that I witnessed the bloody transaction recorded in the first chapter; and as I received my first impressions of slavery on this plantation, I will give some description of it, and of slavery as it there existed. The plantation is about twelve miles north of Easton, in Talbot county, and is situated on the border of Miles River. The principal products raised upon it were tobacco, corn, and wheat. These were raised in great abundance; so that, with the products of this and the other farms belonging to him, he was able to keep in almost constant employment a large sloop, in carrying them to market at Baltimore. This sloop was named Sally Lloyd, in honor of one of the colonel's daughters. My master's son-in-law, Captain Auld, was master of the vessel; she was otherwise manned by the colonel's own slaves. Their names were Peter, Isaac, Rich, and Jake. These were esteemed very highly by the other slaves, and looked upon as the privileged ones of the plantation; for it was no small affair, in the eyes of the slaves, to be allowed to see Baltimore.

FROM *MY BONDAGE AND MY FREEDOM*

If the reader will now be kind enough to allow me time to grow bigger, and afford me an opportunity for my experience to become greater, I will tell him something, by-and-by, of slave life, as I saw, felt, and heard it, on Col. Edward Lloyd's plantation, and at the house of old master, where I had now, despite of myself, most suddenly, but not unexpectedly, been dropped. Meanwhile, I will redeem my promise to say something more of my dear mother.

I say nothing of *father*, for he is shrouded in a mystery I have never been able to penetrate. Slavery does away with fathers, as it does away with families. Slavery has no use for either fathers or families, and its laws do not recognize their existence in the social arrangements of the plantation. When they *do* exist, they are not the outgrowths of slavery, but are antagonistic to that system. The order of civilization is reversed here. The name of the child is not expected to be that of its father, and his condition does not necessarily affect that of the child. He may be the slave of Mr. Tilgman; and his child, when born, may be the slave of Mr. Gross. He may be a *freeman*; and yet his child may be a *chattel*. He may be white, glorying in the purity of his Anglo-Saxon blood; and his child may be ranked with the blackest slaves. Indeed, he *may* be, and often *is*, master and father to the same child. He can be father without being a husband, and may sell his child without incurring reproach, if the child be by a woman in whose veins courses one thirty-second part of African blood. My father was a white man, or nearly white. It was sometimes whispered that my master was my father.

But to return, or rather, to begin. My knowledge of my mother is very scanty, but very distinct. Her personal appearance and bearing are ineffaceably stamped upon my memory. She was tall, and finely proportioned; of deep black, glossy complexion; had regular features, and, among the other slaves, was remarkably sedate in her manners. There is in *"Prichard's Natural History of Man,"* the head of a figure—on page 157—the features of which so resemble those of my mother, that I often recur to it with something of the feeling which I suppose others experience when looking upon the pictures of dear departed ones.

Yet I cannot say that I was very deeply attached to my mother; certainly not so deeply as I should have been had our relations in childhood been different. We were separated, according to the common custom, when I was but an infant, and, of course, before I knew my mother from any one else.

The germs of affection with which the Almighty, in his wisdom and mercy, arms the helpless infant against the ills and vicissitudes of his lot, had been directed in their growth toward that loving old grandmother, whose gentle hand and kind deportment it was the first effort of my infantile understanding to comprehend and appreciate. Accordingly, the tenderest affection which a beneficent Father allows, as a partial compensation to the mother for the pains and lacerations of her heart, incident to the maternal relation, was, in my case, diverted from its true and natural object, by the envious, greedy, and treacherous hand of slavery. The slave-mother can be spared long enough from the field to endure all the bitterness of a mother's anguish, when it adds another name to a master's ledger, but *not* long enough to receive the joyous reward afforded by the intelligent smiles of her child. I never think of this terrible interference of slavery with my infantile affections, and its diverting them from their natural course, without feelings to which I can give no adequate expression.

I do not remember to have seen my mother at my grandmother's at any time. I remember her only in her visits to me at Col. Lloyd's plantation, and in the kitchen of my old master. Her visits to me there were few in number, brief in duration, and mostly made in the night. The pains she took, and the toil she endured, to see me, tells me that a true mother's heart was hers, and that slavery had difficulty in paralyzing it with unmotherly indifference.

My mother was hired out to a Mr. Stewart, who lived about twelve miles from old master's, and, being a field hand, she seldom had leisure, by day, for the performance of the journey. The nights and the distance were both obstacles to her visits. She was obliged to walk, unless chance flung into her way an opportunity to ride; and the latter was sometimes her good luck. But she always had to walk one way or the other. It was a greater luxury than slavery could afford, to allow a black slave-mother a horse or a mule, upon which to travel twenty-four miles, when she could walk the distance. Besides, it is deemed a foolish whim for a slave-mother to manifest concern to see her children, and, in one point of view, the case is made out—she can do nothing for them. She has no control over them; the master is even more than the mother, in all matters touching the fate of her child. Why, then, should she give herself any concern? She has no responsibility. Such is the reasoning, and such the practice. The iron rule of the plantation, always passionately and violently enforced in that neighborhood, makes flogging the penalty of failing to be in the field before sunrise in the morning, unless special permission be given to the absenting slave. "I went to see my child," is no excuse to the ear or heart of the overseer.

* * *

I learned, after my mother's death, that she could read, and that she was the *only* one of all the slaves and colored people in Tuckahoe who enjoyed that advantage. How she acquired this knowledge, I know not, for Tuckahoe is the last place in the world where she would be apt to find facilities for learning. I can, therefore, fondly and proudly ascribe to her an earnest love of knowledge. That a "field hand" should learn to read, in any slave state, is remarkable; but the achievement of my mother, considering the place, was very extraordinary; and, in view of that fact, I am quite willing, and even happy, to attribute any love of letters I possess, and for which I have got—despite of prejudices—only too much credit, *not* to my admitted Anglo-Saxon paternity, but to the native genius of my sable, unprotected, and uncultivated *mother*—a woman, who belonged to a race whose mental endowments it is, at present, fashionable to hold in disparagement and contempt.

Summoned away to her account, with the impassable gulf of slavery between us during her entire illness, my mother died without leaving me a single intimation of *who* my father was. There was a whisper, that my master was my father; yet it was only a whisper, and I cannot say that I ever gave it credence. Indeed, I now have reason to think he was not; nevertheless, the fact remains, in all its glaring odiousness, that, by the laws of slavery, children, in all cases, are reduced to the condition of their mothers. This arrangement admits of the greatest license to brutal slaveholders, and their profligate sons, brothers, relations and friends, and gives to the pleasure of sin, the additional attraction of profit. A whole volume might be written on this single feature of slavery, as I have observed it.

One might imagine, that the children of such connections, would fare better, in the hands of their masters, than other slaves. The rule is quite the other way; and a very little reflection will satisfy the reader that such is the case. A man who will enslave his own blood, may not be safely relied on for magnanimity. Men do not love those who remind them of their sins—unless they have a mind to repent—and the mulatto child's face is a standing accusation against him who is master and father to the child. What is still worse, perhaps, such a child is a constant offense to the wife. She hates its very presence, and when a slaveholding woman hates, she wants not means to give that hate telling effect. Women—white women, I mean—are IDOLS at the south, not WIVES, for the slave women are preferred in many instances; and if these *idols* but nod, or lift a finger, woe to the poor victim: kicks, cuffs, and stripes are sure to follow. Masters are frequently compelled to sell this class of their slaves, out of deference to the feelings of their white wives; and shocking and scandalous as it may seem for a man to sell his own blood to the traffickers in human flesh, it is often an act of humanity toward the slave-child to be thus removed from his merciless tormentors.

It is not within the scope of the design of my simple story, to comment upon every phase of slavery not within my experience as a slave.

But, I may remark that, if the lineal descendants of Ham are only to be enslaved, according to the scriptures, slavery in this country will soon become an unscriptural institution; for thousands are ushered into the world, annually, who—like myself—owe their existence to white fathers, and, most frequently, to their masters, and master's sons. The slave-woman is at the mercy of the fathers, sons or brothers of her master. The thoughtful know the rest.

After what I have now said of the circumstances of my mother, and my relations to her, the reader will not be surprised, nor be disposed to censure me, when I tell but the simple truth, viz: that I received the tidings of her death with no strong emotions of sorrow for her, and with very little regret for myself on account of her loss. I had to learn the value of my mother long after her death, and by witnessing the devotion of other mothers to their children.

There is not, beneath the sky, an enemy to filial affection so destructive as slavery. It had made my brothers and sisters strangers to me; it converted the mother that bore me, into a myth; it shrouded my father in mystery, and left me without an intelligible beginning in the world.

My mother died when I could not have been more than eight or nine years old, on one of old master's farms in Tuckahoe, in the neighborhood of Hillsborough. Her grave is, as the grave of the dead at sea, unmarked, and without stone or stake.

* * *

Although my old master—Capt. Anthony—gave me at first, (as the reader will have already seen,) very little attention, and although that little was of a remarkably mild and gentle description, a few months only were sufficient to convince me that mildness and gentleness were not the prevailing or governing traits of his character. These excellent qualities were displayed only occasionally. He could, when it suited him, appear to be literally insensible to the claims of humanity, when appealed to by the helpless against an aggressor, and he could himself commit outrages, deep, dark and nameless. Yet he was not by nature worse than other men. Had he been brought up in a free state, surrounded by the just restraints of free society—restraints which are necessary to the freedom of all its members, alike and equally—Capt. Anthony might have been as humane a man, and every way as respectable, as many who now oppose the slave system; certainly as humane and respectable as are members of society generally. The slaveholder, as well as the slave, is the victim of the slave system. A man's character greatly takes its hue and shape from the form and color of things about him. Under the whole heavens there is no relation more unfavorable to the development of honorable character than that sustained by the slaveholder to the slave. Reason is imprisoned here, and passions run wild. Like the fires of the prairie, once lighted, they are at the mercy of every wind, and must burn till they have consumed all that is combustible within their remorseless grasp. Capt. Anthony could be kind, and, at times, he even showed an affectionate disposition. Could the reader have seen him gently leading me by the hand—as he sometimes did—patting me on the head, speaking to me in soft, caressing tones and calling me his "little

Indian boy," he would have deemed him a kind old man, and, really, almost fatherly. But the pleasant moods of a slaveholder are remarkably brittle; they are easily snapped; they neither come often, nor remain long. His temper is subjected to perpetual trials; but, since these trials are never borne patiently, they add nothing to his natural stock of patience.

Old master very early impressed me with the idea that he was an unhappy man. Even to my child's eye, he wore a troubled, and at times, a haggard aspect. His strange movements excited my curiosity, and awakened my compassion. He seldom walked alone without muttering to himself; and he occasionally stormed about, as if defying an army of invisible foes. "He would do this, that, and the other; he'd be d—d if he did not,"—was the usual form of his threats. Most of his leisure was spent in walking, cursing and gesticulating, like one possessed by a demon. Most evidently, he was a wretched man, at war with his own soul, and with all the world around him. To be overheard by the children, disturbed him very little. He made no more of *our* presence, than of that of the ducks and geese which he met on the green. He little thought that the little black urchins around him could see, through those vocal crevices, the very secrets of his heart. Slaveholders ever underrate the intelligence with which they have to grapple. I really understood the old man's mutterings, attitudes and gestures, about as well as he did himself. But slaveholders never encourage that kind of communication with the slaves, by which they might learn to measure the depths of his knowledge. Ignorance is a high virtue in a human chattel; and as the master studies to keep the slave ignorant, the slave is cunning enough to make the master think he succeeds. The slave fully appreciates the saying, "where ignorance is bliss, 'tis folly to be wise." When old master's gestures were violent, ending with a threatening shake of the head, and a sharp snap of his middle finger and thumb, I deemed it wise to keep at a respectable distance from him; for, at such times, trifling faults stood, in his eyes, as momentous offenses; and, having both the power and the disposition, the victim had only to be near him to catch the punishment, deserved or undeserved.

FROM *LIFE AND TIMES OF FREDERICK DOUGLASS*

My first experience of life, as I now remember it, and I remember it but hazily, began in the family of my grandmother and grandfather, Betsey and Isaac Bailey. They were considered old settlers in the neighborhood, and from certain circumstances I infer that my grandmother, especially, was held in high esteem, far higher than was the lot of most colored persons in that region. She was a good nurse, and a capital hand at making nets used for catching shad and herring, and was, withal, somewhat famous as a fisherwoman. I have known her to be in the water waist deep, for hours, seine-hauling. She was a gardener as well as a fisherwoman, and remarkable for her success in keeping her seedling sweet potatoes through the months of winter, and easily got the reputation of being born to "good luck." In planting-time Grandmother Betsey was sent for in all directions, simply to place the seedling potatoes in the hills or drills; for superstition had it that her touch was needed to make them grow. This reputation was full of advantage to her and her grandchildren, for a good crop, after her planting for the neighbors, brought her a share of the harvest.

Whether because she was too old for field service, or because she had so faithfully discharged the duties of her station in early life, I know not, but she enjoyed the high privilege of living in a cabin separate from the quarters, having imposed upon her only the charge of the young children and the burden of her own support. She esteemed it great good fortune to live so, and took much comfort in having the children. The practice of separating mothers from their children and hiring them out at distances too great to admit of their meeting, save at long intervals, was a marked feature of the cruelty and barbarity of the slave system; but it was in harmony with the grand aim of that system, which always and everywhere sought to reduce man to a level with the brute. It had no interest in recognizing or preserving any of the ties that bind families together or to their homes.

My grandmother's five daughters were hired out in this way, and my only recollections of my own mother are of a few hasty visits made in the night on foot, after the daily tasks were over, and when she was under the necessity of returning in time to respond to the driver's call to the field in the early morning. These little glimpses of my mother, obtained under such circumstances and against such odds, meager as they were, are ineffaceably stamped upon my memory. She was tall and finely proportioned, of dark, glossy complexion, with regular features, and amongst the slaves was remarkably sedate and dignified. There is, in "Prichard's Natural History of Man," the head of a figure, on page 157, the features of which so resemble my mother that I often recur to it with something of the feelings which I suppose others experience when looking upon the likenesses of their own dear departed ones.

Of my father I know nothing. Slavery had no recognition of fathers, as none of families. That the mother was a slave was enough for its deadly purpose. By its law the child followed the condition of its mother. The father might be a freeman and the child a slave. The father might be a white man, glorying in the purity of his Anglo-Saxon blood, and the child ranked with the blackest slaves. Father he might be, and not be husband, and could sell his own child without incurring reproach, if in its veins coursed one drop of African blood.

* * *

Once established on the home plantation of Col. Lloyd—I was with the children there, left to the tender mercies of Aunt Katy, a slave woman, who was to my master what he was to Col. Lloyd. Disposing of us in classes or sizes, he left to Aunt Katy all the minor details concerning our management. She was a woman who never allowed herself to act greatly within the limits of delegated power, no matter how broad that authority might be. Ambitious of old master's favor, ill-tempered and cruel by nature, she found in her present position an ample field for the exercise of her ill-omened qualities. She had a strong hold upon old master, for she was a first-rate cook, and very industrious. She was therefore greatly favored by him—and as one mark of his favor she was the only mother who was permitted to retain her children around her, and even to these, her own children, she was often fiendish in her brutality. Cruel, however, as she sometimes was to her own children, she was not destitute of maternal feeling, and in her instinct to satisfy their demands for food she was often guilty of starving me and the other children. Want of food was my chief trouble during my first summer here. Captain Anthony, instead of allowing a given quantity of food to each slave, committed the allowance for all to Aunt Katy, to be divided by her, after cooking, amongst us. The allowance consisted of coarse corn-meal, not very abundant, and which, by passing through Aunt Katy's hands, became more slender still for some of us. I have often been so pinched with hunger as to dispute with old "Nep," the dog, for the crumbs which fell from the kitchen table. Many times have I followed, with eager step, the waiting girl when she shook the table-cloth, to get the crumbs and small bones flung out for the dogs and cats. It was a great thing to have the privilege of dipping a piece of bread into the water in which meat had been boiled, and the skin taken from the rusty bacon was a positive luxury. With this description of the domestic arrangements of my new home, I may here recount a circumstance which is deeply impressed on my memory, as affording a bright gleam of a slave-mother's love, and the earnestness of a mother's care. I had offended Aunt Katy. I do not remember in what way, for my offences were numerous in that quarter, greatly depending upon her moods as to their heinousness, and she had adopted her usual mode of punishing me: namely, making me go all day without food. For the first hour or two after dinner time, I succeeded pretty well in keeping up my spirits; but as the day wore away, I found it quite impossible to do so any longer. Sundown came, but no bread; and in its stead came the threat from Aunt Katy, with a scowl well-suited to its terrible import, that she would starve the life out of me. Brandishing her knife, she chopped off the heavy slices of bread for the other children, and put the loaf away, muttering all the while her savage designs upon myself. Against this disappointment, for I was expecting that her heart would relent at last, I made an extra effort to maintain my dignity, but when I saw the other children around me with satisfied faces, I could stand it no longer. I went out behind the kitchen wall and cried like a fine fellow. When wearied with this, I returned to the kitchen, sat by the fire and brooded over my hard lot. I was too hungry to sleep.

While I sat in the corner, I caught sight of an ear of Indian corn upon an upper shelf. I watched my chance and got it; and shelling off a few grains, I put it back again. These grains I quickly put into the hot ashes to roast. I did this at the risk of getting a brutal thumping, for Aunt Katy could beat as well as starve me. My corn was not long in roasting, and I eagerly pulled it from the ashes, and placed it upon a stool in a clever little pile. I began to help myself, when who but my own dear mother should come in. The scene which followed is beyond my power to describe. The friendless and hungry boy, in his extremest need, found himself in the strong, protecting arms of his mother. I have before spoken of my mother's dignified and impressive manner. I shall never forget the indescribable expression of her countenance when I told her that Aunt Katy had said she would starve the life out of me. There was deep and tender pity in her glance at me, and, at the same moment, a fiery indignation at Aunt Katy, and while she took the corn from me, and gave in its stead a large ginger-cake, she read Aunt Katy a lecture which was never forgotten. That night I learned as I had never learned before, that I was not only a child, but somebody's child. I was grander upon my mother's knee than a king upon his throne. But my triumph was short. I dropped off to sleep, and waked in the morning to find my mother gone and myself at the mercy again of the virago in my master's kitchen, whose fiery wrath was my constant dread.

My mother had walked twelve miles to see me, and had the same distance to travel over again before the morning sunrise. I do not remember ever seeing her again. Her death soon ended the little communication that had existed between us, and with it, I believe, a life full of weariness and heartfelt sorrow. To me it has ever been a grief that I knew my mother so little, and have so few of her words treasured in my remembrance. I have since learned that she was the only one of all the colored people of Tuckahoe who could read. How she acquired this knowledge I know not, for Tuckahoe was the last place in the world where she would have been likely to find facilities for learning. I can therefore fondly and proudly ascribe to her an earnest love of knowledge. That in any slave State a field-hand should learn to read is remarkable, but the achievement of my mother, considering the place and circumstances, was very extraordinary. In view of this fact, I am happy to attribute any love of letters I may have, not to my presumed Anglo-Saxon paternity, but to the native genius of my sable, unprotected, and uncultivated mother—a woman who belonged to a race whose mental endowments are still disparaged and despised.

* * *

Fifty years have passed since I entered upon that work,[1] and now that it is ended, I find myself summoned again by the popular voice and by what is called the negro problem, to come a second time upon the witness stand and give evidence upon disputed points concerning myself and my emancipated brothers and sisters who, though free, are yet oppressed and are in as much need of an advocate as before they were set free. Though this is not altogether as agreeable to me as was my first mission, it is one that comes with such commanding authority as to compel me to accept it as a present duty. In it I am pelted with all sorts of knotty questions, some of which might be difficult even for Humboldt, Cuvier or Darwin, were they alive, to answer. They are questions which range over the whole field of science, learning and philosophy, and some descend to the depths of impertinent, unmannerly and vulgar curiosity. To be able to answer the higher range of these questions I should be profoundly versed in psychology, anthropology, ethnology, sociology, theology, biology, and all the other ologies, philosophies and sciences. There is no disguising the fact that the American people are much interested and mystified about the mere matter of color as connected with manhood. It seems to them that color has some moral or immoral qualities and especially the latter. They do not feel quite reconciled to the idea that a man of different color from themselves should have all the human rights claimed by themselves. When an unknown man is spoken of in their presence, the first question that arises in the average American mind concerning him and which must be answered is, Of what color is he? and he rises or falls in estimation by the answer given. It is not whether he is a good man or a bad man. That does not seem of primary importance. Hence I have often been bluntly and sometimes very rudely asked, of what color my mother was, and of what color was my father? In what proportion does the blood of the various races mingle in my veins, especially how much white blood and how much black blood entered into my composition? Whether I was not part Indian as well as African and Caucasian? Whether I considered myself more African than Caucasian, or the reverse? Whether I derived my intelligence from my father, or from my mother, from my white, or from my black blood? Whether persons of mixed blood are as strong and healthy as persons of either of the races whose blood they inherit? Whether persons of mixed blood do permanently remain of the mixed complexion or finally take on the complexion of one or the other of the two or more races of which they may be composed? Whether they live as long and raise as large families as other people? Whether they inherit only evil from both parents and good from neither? Whether evil dispositions are more transmissible than good? Why did I marry a person of my father's complexion instead of marrying one of my mother's complexion? How is the race problem to be solved in this country? Will the negro go back to Africa or remain here? Under this shower of purely American questions, more or less personal, I have endeavored to possess my soul in patience and get as much good out of life as was possible with so much to occupy my time; and, though often perplexed, seldom losing my temper, or abating heart or hope for the future of my people. Though I cannot say I have satisfied the curiosity of my countrymen on all the questions raised by them, I have, like all honest men on the witness stand, answered to the best of my knowledge and belief, and I hope I have never answered in such wise as to increase the hardships of any human being of whatever race or color.

Notes

INTRODUCTION

1. Prior to his *Narrative*, Douglass had published only a few letters in newspapers. See, for example, "Frederick Douglass in Behalf of Geo. Latimer," *The Liberator*, November 18, 1842; Douglass, "Explanation," *The Liberator*, August 30, 1844; Douglass, "Milton Clarke—Liberty Party—George Bradburn," *The Liberator*, November 1, 1844.
2. John Stauffer, Zoe Trodd, and Celeste-Marie Bernier, *Picturing Frederick Douglass: The Most Photographed American in the Nineteenth Century* (New York: W. W. Norton, 2015).
3. James McCune Smith, "Introduction," to Frederick Douglass, *My Bondage and My Freedom*, ed. John Stauffer (1855; reprint, New York: Modern Library, 2003), xli, xlix; John Eaton, quoted from *In Memoriam: Frederick Douglass*, ed. Helen Douglass (1897; reprint, Freeport, NY: Books for Libraries Press, 1971), p. 71; Philip S. Foner, ed., *The Life and Writings of Frederick Douglass*, vol. 3, *The Civil War, 1861–1865* (New York: International Publishers, 1952), p. 45.
4. Douglass, "Pictures," n.d. (ca. Nov. 1864–March 1865), Frederick Douglass Papers, Library of Congress (quoted); Aristotle, *Poetics*, tr. Malcolm Heath (New York: Penguin Books, 1996), pp. 6–7 (3.1: "The Anthropology and History of Poetry, Origins"); W. J. T. Mitchell, "Representation," in *Critical Terms for Literary Study*, 2nd ed., Frank Lentricchia and Thomas McLaughlin, eds. (Chicago: University of Chicago Press, 1995), pp. 11–17.
5. John Stauffer, *The Black Hearts of Men: Radical Abolitionists and the Transformation of Race* (Cambridge, MA: Harvard University Press, 2002), pp. 50–51; Stauffer, "Frederick Douglass and the Aesthetics of Freedom," *Raritan* 25:1 (Summer 2005): 114–36.
6. John W. Blassingame, "Introduction to Series One," *The Frederick Douglass Papers, Series One: Speeches, Debates, and Interviews*, vol. 1, *1841–46* (New Haven, CT: Yale University Press, 1979),

pp. xxi–lxix; Elizabeth Cady Stanton, quoted from *Majestic in His Wrath: A Pictorial Life of Frederick Douglass*, ed. Frederick S. Voss (Washington, D.C.: Smithsonian Institution Press, 1995), p. v (quoted); Douglass, *Life and Times of Frederick Douglass* (1892; reprint, New York: Collier Books, 1962), p. 511 (quoted).

7. "Biographies," *Putnam's Monthly Magazine* 6:35 (November 1855): 547; "From the 'Pen' of a Slave," *The National Era*, August 9, 1855; "My Bondage and My Freedom," *The National Era*, October 11, 1855; John W. Blassingame, "Introduction to Series Two," in *The Frederick Douglass Papers, Series Two: Autobiographical Writings*, vol. 2, *My Bondage and My Freedom* (New Haven, CT: Yale University Press, 2003), p. xxxi.
8. Douglass to Gerrit Smith, May 23, 1856, Gerrit Smith Papers, Syracuse University; Blassingame, "Introduction to Series Two," p. xxxi.
9. The only comparable book is the one-volume selection from Philip Foner's five-volume *Life and Writings of Frederick Douglass*; Philip S. Foner, ed., *Frederick Douglass: Selected Speeches and Writings* (Chicago: Lawrence Hill Books, 1999). But Foner's book focuses chiefly on Douglass's journalism.
10. Douglass, *Narrative*, in this volume, pp. 36–38.
11. Douglass, *Narrative*, in this volume, p. 59; Caleb Bingham, *The Columbian Orator*, ed. David W. Blight (New York: New York University Press, 1998); Henry Louis Gates, Jr., "Frederick Douglass's Camera Obscura: Representing the Antislave 'Clothed and in Their Own Form,'" *Picturing Frederick Douglass*, p. 200; Gates, *Figures in Black: Words, Signs, and the "Racial" Self* (New York: Oxford University Press, 1989), chaps. 3–4; Kenneth Cmiel, *Democratic Eloquence: The Fight over Popular Speech in Nineteenth-Century America* (New York: W. Morrow, 1990), chaps. 2–3; Jeanne Fahnestock, *Rhetorical Style: The Uses of Language in Persuasion* (New York: Oxford University Press, 2011), pp. 410, 417.
12. Blight, "Introduction," in *Columbian Orator*, pp. xiii–xxvii, xxviii.n.9.
13. In this volume, p. 42.
14. Douglass, *My Bondage*, pp. 73, 88.
15. Cmiel, *Democratic Eloquence*, pp. 96–98, quotation from p. 96; Robert Alter, *Pen of Iron: American Prose and the King James Bible* (Princeton, NJ: Princeton University Press, 2010), p. 1. Douglass quotes from the King James Bible, and Cmiel notes that it was the standard Bible in the United States from the seventeenth century until the 1850s.
16. Douglass, *Narrative*, in this volume, p. 35.
17. Ibid., in this volume, p. 58.
18. Ibid., in this volume, p. 64.

19. Dickson J. Preston, *Young Frederick Douglass: The Maryland Years* (Baltimore: Johns Hopkins University Press, 1980), pp. 148–49; Christopher Phillips, *Freedom's Port: The African American Community of Baltimore, 1790–1860* (Urbana: University of Illinois Press, 1997), p. 58; Barbara Jeanne Fields, *Slavery and Freedom on the Middle Ground: Maryland during the Nineteenth Century* (New Haven, CT: Yale University Press, 1985), p. 62.
20. *Frederick Douglass Papers, Series One*, vol. 1, p. 3.
21. Douglass, *Narrative*, in this volume, p. 15; Douglass, "Farewell to the British People: An Address Delivered in London, England, on 30 March 1847," *Frederick Douglass Papers, Series One*, vol. 2, ed. John W. Blassingame (New Haven, CT: Yale University Press, 1982), p. 42.
22. Douglass, *My Bondage*, in this volume, pp. 543, 547–48. See also James McCune Smith's assessment of Douglass's genealogical self-fashioning in "Introduction to the 1855 Edition," *My Bondage and My Freedom*, ed. John Stauffer (New York: Modern Library, 2003), pp. liii–liv.
23. Douglass, "Life and Times," *Autobiographies*, ed. Henry Louis Gates, Jr. (New York: Library of America, 1994), p. 961; Douglass, "The Future of the Colored Race," in this volume, pp. 515; Werner Sollors, *Neither Black Nor White Yet Both: Thematic Explorations of Interracial Literature* (New York: Oxford University Press, 1997).
24. Abraham Lincoln, "Address before the Wisconsin State Agricultural Society," September 30, 1859, in *The Collected Works of Abraham Lincoln*, vol. 3, ed. Roy P. Basler (New Brunswick, NJ: Rutgers University Press, 1953), p. 478.
25. Douglass, "The Claims of the Negro Ethnologically Considered," in this volume, p. 235.
26. Peter F. Walker, *Moral Choices: Memory, Desire, and Imagination in Nineteenth-Century American Abolition* (Baton Rouge: Louisiana State University Press, 1978). See also Henry Louis Gates, Jr., "Frederick Douglass and the Language of the Self," *Yale Review*, 70:4 (July 1981): 592–611.
27. Douglass, "Pictures and Progress," in this volume, pp. 357.
28. For good historical overviews of the *Creole* rebellion, see Howard Jones, "The Peculiar Institution and National Honor: The Case of the *Creole* Slave Revolt," *Civil War History* 21:1 (1975), 28–50; George Hendrick and Willene Hendrick, *The* Creole *Mutiny: A Tale of Revolt aboard a Slave Ship* (Chicago: Ivan R. Dee, 2003); Walter Johnson, "White Lies: Human Property and Domestic Slavery aboard the Slave Ship *Creole*," *Atlantic Studies* 5:2 (2008): 237–63; and Robert S. Levine, John Stauffer, and John R. McKivigan, "Introduction," in *The Heroic Slave: A Cultural and Critical Edition* (New Haven, CT: Yale University Press, 2015), pp. xi–xxxi.

29. "Letter from Wm. C. Nell," *Frederick Douglass' Paper*, March 18, 1852; "Brooklyn Items," *New York Daily Tribune*, February 25, 1852; Levine, Stauffer, and McKivigan, "Introduction," pp. xxvi–xxxiii; Stauffer, *The Black Hearts of Men: Radical Abolitionists and the Transformation of Race,* chaps. 1, 5.
30. Douglass, *Heroic Slave*, in this volume, p. 172; *Frederick Douglass Papers, Series One*, vol. 2, p. 60; Levine, Stauffer, and McKivigan, "Introduction," pp. xxxi–xxxiii.
31. On Douglass's speeches, the best overview is John W. Blassingame, "Introduction to Series One," in *Frederick Douglass Papers, Series One*, vol. 1, pp. xxi–lxix. On Douglass's journalism, see Shelley Fisher Fishkin and Carla L. Peterson, "'We Hold These Truths to Be Self-Evident': The Rhetoric of Frederick Douglass's Journalism," in *Frederick Douglass: New Literary and Historical Essays*, ed. Eric J. Sundquist (Cambridge: Cambridge University Press, 1990), pp. 189–204.
32. Douglass, *Narrative*, in this volume, p. 93; Garrison, quoted from Henry Mayer, *All On Fire: William Lloyd Garrison and the Abolition of Slavery* (New York: St. Martin's Press, 1998), p. 120.
33. Douglass, "The Day of Jubilee Comes," in this volume, p. 305; Douglass, "Toussaint L'Ouverture," in this volume, p. 532.
34. Gates, *Figures in Black*; William L. Andrews, *To Tell a Free Story: The First Century of Afro-American Autobiography, 1760–1820* (Urbana: University of Illinois Press, 1986); Eric J. Sundquist, *To Wake the Nations: Race in the Making of American Literature* (Cambridge, MA: Harvard University Press, 1998), part 1; Ezra Greenspan, ed., *William Wells Brown: A Reader* (Athens: University of Georgia Press, 2008), pp. 321–22; Greenspan, *William Wells Brown: An American Life* (New York: W. W. Norton, 2014); Robert K. Wallace, *Douglass and Melville, Anchored Together in Neighborly Style* (New Bedford, MA: Spinner Publications, 2005); Wallace, "Douglass, Shaw, Melville," in *Frederick Douglass and Herman Melville: Essays in Relation*, eds. Robert S. Levine and Samuel Otter (Chapel Hill: University of North Carolina Press, 2008), pp. 39–68; Robert S. Levine and Samuel Otter, "Introduction," in *Frederick Douglass and Herman Melville*, pp. 1–18; Levine, *Martin Delany, Frederick Douglass, and the Politics of Representative Identity* (Chapel Hill: University of North Carolina Press, 1997), pp. 58–98; David S. Reynolds, *Mightier than the Sword:* Uncle Tom's Cabin *and the Battle for America* (New York: W. W. Norton, 2011), pp. 111–14; Julia Sun-Joo Lee, *The American Slave Narrative and the Victorian Novel* (New York: Oxford University Press, 2010), pp. 3–24, 113–30; Jean Fagan Yellin, *Harriet*

Jacobs: A Life (New York: Basic/Civitas, 2004), pp. 145–48; Jennifer Fleischner, *Mrs. Lincoln and Mrs. Keckly: The Remarkable Story of the Friendship between a First Lady and a Former Slave* (New York: Broadway Books, 2003), pp. 145–46, 173–89, 262–64, 311–12; Fleischner, *Mastering Slavery: Memory, Family, and Identity in Women's Slave Narratives* (New York: New York University Press, 1996), pp. 93–132; Carl F. Wieck, *Refiguring Huckleberry Finn* (Athens: University of Georgia Press, 2000), pp. 20–39; Booker T. Washington, *Frederick Douglass* (Philadelphia: George W. Jacobs & Co., 1906), pp. 5–7; Gates, *Loose Cannons: Notes on the Culture Wars* (New York: Oxford University Press, 1992), pp. 30, 59; Gates, *The Signifying Monkey: A Theory of African-American Literary Criticism* (New York: Oxford University Press, 1988), pp. 170–73; Robert B. Stepto, *A Home Elsewhere: Reading African American Classics in the Age of Obama* (Cambridge, MA: Harvard University Press, 2010), pp. 3–50, 100–120; Stepto, *From Behind the Veil: A Study of Afro-American Narrative* (Urbana: University of Illinois Press, 1979); Gregory Stephens, *On Racial Frontiers: The New Culture of Frederick Douglass, Ralph Ellison, and Bob Marley* (Cambridge: Cambridge University Press, 1999), pp. 54–147; James Smethurst, *The African American Roots of Modernism, from Reconstruction to the Harlem Renaissance* (Chapel Hill: University of North Carolina Press, 2011), pp. 44–51, 100–104, 212; Charles Chesnutt, *Frederick Douglass* (Boston: Small, Maynard & Co., 1899); Mel Watkins, "The Fire Next Time This Time," in *James Baldwin*, updated ed., ed. Harold Bloom, Bloom's Modern Critical Views (New York: Infobase Publishing, 2007), pp. 178–79.

35. Blight, "Introduction," in *Columbian Orator*, p. xviii; Gates, *Figures in Black*, p. 108. See also William L. Andrews, *To Tell a Free Story*.

AUTOBIOGRAPHICAL WRITINGS

Narrative of the Life of Frederick Douglass, an American Slave

1. **"gave the world assurance of a MAN":** Quoted from Shakespeare's *Hamlet*, III.iv.62.
2. **"created but . . . the angels":** Quoted from Psalm 8:5; Hebrews 2:7.
3. **JOHN A. COLLINS:** Collins (1810–79) toured with Douglass as an orator for the American Anti-Slavery Society in the early 1840s. In 1843 he resigned his position as general agent of the society to focus on Fourierism, a utopian land reform movement.

4. **"grow in grace . . . of God":** Quoted from 2 Peter 3:18.
5. **Charles Lenox Remond:** Remond (1810–73) was a black abolitionist leader from Massachusetts, after whom Douglass named his third son, Charles Remond Douglass.
6. **"He that knoweth his master's will . . . many stripes":** Masters often quoted this line from Luke 12:47 to their slaves.
7. **"rather bear those ills . . . knew not of":** Quoted from *Hamlet*, III.i.80–81.
8. **David Ruggles:** Ruggles (1810–49) was a leading New York City black abolitionist who devoted his energies to helping fugitives. Virtually blind by 1841, he joined an interracial utopian commune in western Massachusetts called the Northampton Association of Education and Industry.
9. ***Darg* case:** An 1838 fugitive slave case that received national attention. Ruggles was arrested for harboring the fugitive Thomas Hughes, whose owner, John P. Darg, accused him of stealing nine thousand dollars. The case was never prosecuted.
10. **J. W. C. Pennington:** James William Charles Pennington (1807–70) was a well-known black abolitionist, minister, and orator who was then living in Brooklyn, New York. Having escaped slavery in the Eastern Shore of Maryland in 1828, he became the first African American to attend classes at Yale. In 1841 he published *A Text Book of the Origin and History . . . of the Colored People*, often considered the first history of African Americans; and in 1849 he published his autobiography, *The Fugitive Blacksmith*.
11. **"Lady of the Lake" . . . "Douglass":** Lord James of Douglas, a Scottish chieftain revered for his bravery and unjustly outlawed, is a main character in Sir Walter Scott's poem *The Lady of the Lake* (1810).
12. **"I was hungry . . . he took me in":** Quoted from Matthew 25:35.
13. **"Shall I not visit . . . nation as this?":** Quoted from Jeremiah 5:9.
14. **A PARODY:** Douglass parodies the popular Southern hymn "Heavenly Union."

From *My Bondage and My Freedom*

1. **"William Dixon," in New York:** Dixon, or Jake, was a slave of Dr. William T. Allender from Baltimore. In 1837 he was arrested as a fugitive, but the black leader David Ruggles raised money for an attorney and argued successfully for Dixon's right to a jury trial. There was not enough evidence to extradite him. Soon after he was released, he met Douglass.

2. **"I am among the Quakers . . . am safe":** The religious Society of Friends, known as Quakers, was the first organized group of white abolitionists. Members embraced an ethic of simplicity, pacifism, and humility.
3. **Hood's laborer . . . "give me work":** Quoted from Thomas Hood, "The Lay of the Labourer," stanza 6.
4. **known as the Zion Methodists:** African Methodist Episcopal (A.M.E.) Zion Church, officially founded in New York City in 1821.
5. **ISAAC KNAPP:** Knapp (1804–43) was the printer and copublisher of William Lloyd Garrison's *Liberator*. He stepped down as copublisher in 1838 owing to ill health and deteriorating finances.
6. **"father the devil":** Quoted from John 8:44.
7. **"You are the man . . . from bondage":** A paraphrase of 2 Samuel 12:7.
8. **"Who or what . . . at the sound":** A paraphrase of Psalm 124.
9. **James N. Buffum:** Buffum (1807–87) was a wealthy white abolitionist who helped desegregate public transportation in Massachusetts in the early 1840s.
10. **The Hutchinson Family:** An internationally renowned singing group committed to abolitionism, consisting of Judson (1817–59), John (1821–1908), Asa (1823–84), and Abby Hutchinson (1829–92).
11. **"I am a stranger . . . all my fathers were":** Quoted from Psalm 39:12.
12. **Louis Kossuth and Mazzini:** Kossuth (1802–94) led the 1848 revolution for Hungarian independence and was known in the United States as the "father of Hungarian democracy." Giuseppe Mazzini (1805–72) was an Italian republican revolutionary who collaborated with several British and American abolitionists.
13. **Joseph Sturge:** An internationally renowned British abolitionist, Sturge (1793–1859) founded the British and Foreign Anti-Slavery Society and in 1841 came to the United States to campaign against slavery.
14. **Dr. Campbell:** John Campbell (1795–1867) was a Scottish Congregational minister who abandoned the pulpit in 1848 to edit the *British Banner*, a reform paper. He urged Douglass to remain in England until American slavery had been abolished, and he offered to raise money to bring Douglass's family to England.
15. **tenderness of Melancthon . . . boldness of Luther:** Philipp Melancthon (1497–1560), the German reformer and intellectual, spearheaded with Martin Luther (1483–1546) the Protestant Reformation.
16. **George Thompson:** A member of Parliament, Thompson (1804–78) was a renowned abolitionist orator who spent several years in the United States beginning in 1835. He helped unite the British and American abolition movements.

17. **Free Church of Scotland:** The Free Church of Scotland broke from the Church of Scotland in 1843 to obtain greater independence from the state. Free Church members accused the Church of Scotland of a patronage system that allowed wealthy gentry to select local ministers. Douglass accused the Free Church of its own patronage system, which solicited and received money from slave owners for evangelizing purposes.
18. **the great Evangelical Alliance:** The International Evangelical Alliance, organized during Douglass's speaking tour, proposed a world union of Protestant denominations.
19. **Dr. Cox:** The Reverend Dr. Samuel Hanson Cox (1793–1880) was born into a Quaker family, became a Presbyterian minister, and in 1840 helped suppress antislavery petitions sent to the General Assembly of the American Presbyterian Church.
20. **Doctors Chalmers, Cunningham, and Candlish:** Thomas Chalmers (1780–1847), William Cunningham (1805–61), and Robert Smith Candlish (1806–73) organized the Free Church of Scotland.
21. **Henry C. Wright:** A well-known abolitionist and pacifist, Wright (1797–1870) spent four years in the British Isles, from 1842 to 1846, protesting against slavery, war, and militarism.
22. **"have greatness forced upon them":** A slight revision of Shakespeare's *Twelfth Night*, II.v.158.

FICTION

The Heroic Slave

1. **"Oh! child of grief . . . sorrow lingers there?":** Quoted from the popular folk hymn "God Is Love."
2. **"black, but comely":** Quoted from Song of Solomon 1:5.
3. ***Shakspeare*:** Quoted from *Henry VI, Part II*, IV.i.1-7. Douglass uses a popular nineteenth-century spelling of Shakespeare.
4. **"that hearest the raven's cry":** A paraphrase of Psalm 147:9.
5. **"With thee . . . all things are possible":** A paraphrase of Matthew 19:26.
6. **"I have seen the affliction . . . deliver them":** A paraphrase of Acts 7:34.
7. **Zacheus:** Zacchaeus, a rich tax collector, climbed a tree to see Jesus, who saw him in the tree and converted him (Luke 19:1–10). [Note that in Bible it's spelled "Zacchaeus"; Douglass spells it "Zacheus."]
8. **"to deliver the spoiled . . . the spoiler":** A paraphrase of Jeremiah 21:12.
9. **bread to the hungry . . . the naked:** A paraphrase of Ezekiel 18:7 and Matthew 25:36.

10. ***Childe Harold*:** Quoted from Lord Byron, *Childe Harold's Pilgrimage* (1812–18), canto 4, stanza 141.
11. **Dryburgh Abbey:** A Scottish monastery and the burial place of Sir Walter Scott.
12. **"a sweet morsel":** Quoted from Job 20:12.
13. **"without compromise and without concealment":** Quoted from the motto of the abolitionist paper *National Anti-Slavery Standard.*
14. ***"villainously low"*:** A paraphrase from Shakespeare's *Tempest*, IV.i.248.
15. ***Moore*:** Quoted from the Irish poet Thomas Moore's "Where Is the Slave" (1848).
16. ***Childe Harold*:** Quoted from Byron's *Childe Harold's Pilgrimage*, canto 2, stanza 76.

SPEECHES

"What to the Slave Is the Fourth of July?"

1. **Three score years . . . individual men:** An allusion to Psalm 90:10.
2. **"Trust no future . . . and God overhead":** Quoted from Henry Wadsworth Longfellow's "A Psalm of Life."
3. **Sydney Smith:** A British minister, Smith (1771–1845) was famous for his satirical essays and speeches.
4. **"Abraham to our father":** Quoted from Luke 3:8.
5. **"The evil that men do, . . . with their bones":** Quoted from Shakespeare's *Julius Caesar*, III.ii.76.
6. **"lame man leap as an hart":** Quoted from Isaiah 35:6.
7. **"By the rivers of Babylon . . . my mouth":** Quoted from Psalm 137:1–6.
8. **"I will not equivocate; I will not excuse":** Douglass quotes from William Lloyd Garrison's famous editorial in the first issue of *The Liberator*, January 1, 1831.
9. **Ex-Senator Benton:** Thomas Hart Benton (1782–1858) was U.S. senator from Missouri from 1821 to 1851, having lost his bid for reelection in 1850.
10. **Austin Woolfolk:** Austin Woolfolk, one of the largest slave traders in antebellum America, owned slave markets in Baltimore and New Orleans.
11. **"Is this the land . . . slumber in?":** A close paraphrase of John Greenleaf Whittier's "Stanzas for the Times" (1835).
12. **"*mint, anise* and *cummin*":** Quoted from Matthew 23:23.
13. **Fillmore:** Millard Fillmore, president from 1850 to 1853, signed into law the notorious Fugitive Slave Act of 1850.

14. **Thomas Paine, Voltaire, and Bolingbroke:** Paine (1737–1809), Voltaire (1694–1778), and Henry St. John, Viscount Bolingbroke (1678–1751), all deists, were attacked by orthodox Christians.
15. **"*pure and undefiled*" . . . "*without hypocrisy*":** Quoted from James 1:27.
16. **"Bring no more . . . plead for the widow":** Quoted from Isaiah 1:13–17.
17. **"There is no power . . . not sustained in it":** Quoted from the Reverend Albert Barnes's (1798–1870) antislavery tract, *An Inquiry into the Scriptural Views of Slavery* (1846).
18. **"that, of one blood, . . . all the earth":** A paraphrase of Acts 17:26, frequently quoted by abolitionists.
19. **"*is worse than ages . . . oppose*":** Douglass quotes from Thomas Jefferson's well-known letter of June 26, 1786.
20. **"To palter with us . . . to the heart":** A paraphrase of Shakespeare's *Macbeth*, V.viii.20–22.
21. **Ex-Vice-President Dallas:** George Mifflin Dallas (1792–1864) was vice president under James K. Polk.
22. **"*The arm of the Lord is not shortened*":** A paraphrase of Isaiah 59:1.
23. **"*Let there be Light*":** Quoted from Genesis 1:3.
24. **"*Ethiopia shall stretch . . . unto God*":** A reference to Psalm 68:31.
25. **"God speed the year of jubilee . . . driven":** Douglass quotes Garrison's poem "The Triumph of Freedom" (1845).

"The Claims of the Negro Ethnologically Considered"

1. **Clay in eloquence. . . and directness:** Henry Clay (1777–1852), John C. Calhoun (1782–1850), and Daniel Webster (1782–1852) were leading statesmen, known as the "great triumvirate" in the U.S. Senate for their influence and eloquence. They were also apologists for slavery.
2. **"man is distinguished . . . his circumstances":** Douglass most likely refers to the ethnologist Samuel Stanhope Smith's book *An Essay on the Causes of the Variety of Complexion and Figure in the Human Species* (1810).
3. **the Notts, the Gliddens, . . . and Mortons:** Josiah Nott (1804–73), George Gliddon (1809–57), Louis Agassiz (1807–73), and Samuel Morton (1799–1851) were among the nation's leading scientists—specifically ethnologists, the precursors to anthropologists—whose racist doctrines formed what became known as the American school of ethnology.
4. **Rev. Dr. Anderson:** Martin Brewer Anderson (1815–90) was president of the University of Rochester from 1853 to 1889 and published numerous essays on history, religion, and ethnology.

5. **the learned and pious Godwin . . . negroes and Indians:** Douglass refers to the Anglican clergyman Morgan Godwyn's book *Negro's and Indian's Advocate* (1680).
6. ***"the wish is father to the thought"*:** A paraphrase of Shakespeare's *Henry IV, Part II*, IV.v.91.
7. ***Crania Americana*:** In the following paragraphs, Douglass quotes and paraphrases from Morton's *Crania Americana: or, A Comparative View of the Skulls of Various Aboriginal Nations of North and South America* (1839).
8. **Dr. Prichard . . . Combs' *Constitution of Man*:** Douglass refers to James Cowles Prichard's *Researches into the Physical History of Mankind*, 5 vols. (1813); and George Combe's *Constitution of Man Considered in Relation to External Objects*, 3rd ed. (1834).
9. **The heads of . . . others I could mention:** Douglass lists some of the leading black writers and intellectuals of his day.
10. **"delicate and voluptuous . . . representation":** Douglass quotes and paraphrases Dominique Vivant Denon's *Travels in Upper and Lower Egypt, during the Campaigns of General Bonaparte in That Country*, 2 vols. (1802), which went through several editions and translations.
11. **Eschylus:** Aeschylus (525–456 BCE), the ancient Greek playwright.
12. **"I suspect . . . like the mulattoes":** Douglass quotes Constantin de Volney, Baron Larrey, and John Ledyard in Prichard's *Researches into the Physical History of Mankind*, vol. 2.
13. **"A short . . . and Arabia":** Quoted from Robert Gordon Latham, *Man and His Migrations* (1852).
14. **"The typical woolly haired races . . . or art":** Quoted from Charles Hamilton Smith, *The Natural History of the Human Species: Its Typical Forms, Primeval Distribution, Filiations, and Migrations* (1854).
15. ***Types of Mankind*, by Nott and Glidden:** Douglass refers to the best-selling and widely influential work by the ethnologists Josiah Nott and George Glidden, who argued that blacks were subhuman.
16. **GRATTAN, of CURRAN, of O'CONNELL . . . SHERIDAN:** Douglass refers to leading Irish politicians, writers, and intellectuals: Henry Grattan, John Philpot Curran, Daniel O'Connell, and Richard B. Sheridan.
17. **Dr. JAMES MCCUNE SMITH . . . its composite character:** A close friend of Douglass, Smith (1813–65) was the foremost black intellectual before W. E. B. Du Bois and the first professionally trained black physician in the United States. In his essay "Civilization: Its Dependence on Physical Circumstances," first published in 1844, he undermined ethnological racism by emphasizing the composite nature of Americans and a similar comingling of races and ethnicities in other nations.

18. **The most terrible nation . . . of the world:** A reference to Russia and the Crimean War that lasted from 1853 until 1856.
19. ***"A man's a man for a' that"*****:** Quoted from Robert Burns's famous poem "For A' That and A' That."
20. **the eloquent CURRAN, "No matter . . . him":** Douglass quotes from Thomas Davis, ed., *The Speeches of the Right Honorable John Philpot Curran* (1845).
21. **"Whatsoever things are true, . . . these things":** Quoted from Philippians 4:8.

"The Dred Scott Decision"

1. **"David, you know, . . . had slain his foe":** A reference to the famous fight between David and Goliath in 1 Samuel 17:4–51.
2. **It has risen from a grain . . . crowd its branches:** A paraphrase of Matthew 13:31–32.
3. **Politicians go . . . by night:** A reference to Exodus 13:21.
4. **In 1850 it was again settled . . . the former settlements:** A reference to the Compromise of 1850 and the Kansas-Nebraska Act of 1854, which inflamed the sectional crisis over slavery.
5. **"There is a law," says Brougham, "above all . . . in man":** A paraphrase of Lord Brougham's speech in Parliament in July 1830.
6. **Jefferson said . . . sleep forever:** A paraphrase of Thomas Jefferson's famous statement in *Notes on the State of Virginia* (1787): "Indeed I tremble for my country when I reflect that God is just: that his justice cannot sleep forever."
7. **the Hoffers and Tells, the noblest heroes of history:** A reference to Andreas Hofer and William Tell, famous folk heroes.
8. **Dred Scott . . . declares for freedom:** Shortly before the Dred Scott decision, John M. Wimer, an antislavery advocate, was elected mayor of St. Louis.
9. **"Do justice, though the heavens fall":** Douglass paraphrases the famous statement by Lord Mansfield in the Somerset decision of 1772, which effectively outlawed slavery in England and became an important legal foundation for antislavery politicians in the United States: "let justice be done, though the heavens may fall."
10. **Burns and Simms:** A reference to the famous fugitive slave cases of Anthony Burns in 1854 and Thomas Sims in 1851. Burns and Sims were both arrested in Boston and sent back into slavery, though after Burns was remanded, Bostonians raised money, purchased his freedom, and sent him to Oberlin College, where he trained for the ministry.
11. **It has told us . . . from its words:** Douglass refers to Chief Justice John Marshall's statement from *Sturges v. Crowninshield* (1819),

that "the spirit" of the Constitution "is to be collected chiefly from its words." Douglass then quotes the Constitution's emphasis on liberty and tranquility and notes that there is no mention of slavery, slaveholder, slave, or Negro in it.

12. **"It is difficult, . . . the Constitution":** Douglass quotes and paraphrases Chief Justice Roger Taney's summary opinion in Dred Scott.
13. **In 1780, that denomination . . . "proper means":** Douglass quotes or paraphrases from the Annual Conference of the Methodist Episcopal Church in 1780, 1784, and 1785.
14. **"1st Timothy, . . . of the earth":** Douglass quotes from the Larger Catechism of the Presbyterian Church in 1794.
15. **Washington and Jefferson . . . Fathers of the Republic:** Douglass refers to the antislavery convictions of the Founding Fathers.
16. **"There is not a man living, . . . be wanting":** Douglass quotes and paraphrases Washington's well-known letter to Robert Morris of April 12, 1786.
17. **Our Savior . . . their traditions:** Douglass refers to Jesus' denunciation of the Pharisees in Mark 7:9 and 7:13.

"The Significance of Emancipation in the West Indies"

1. **Chas. Van Loon . . . the poor of this land:** The Baptist minister Charles Van Loon (1819–47) was viciously attacked for championing abolitionism and total abstinence from alcohol. Most black and white abolitionists, including Douglass, abstained from alcohol.
2. **Millard Fillmore, . . . Doctor Lord in the other:** Douglass refers to President Fillmore's and the Reverend John Chase Lord's support for the fugitive slave law.
3. **The great poet has told us . . . world akin:** A reference to Shakespeare's *Troilus and Cressida*, III.iii.175.
4. **They are as a city set upon a hill:** A reference to Matthew 5:14, widely cited by Americans to distinguish themselves from Europeans. Douglass reverses the metaphor, calling Britain a city on a hill for ending slavery.
5. **Even the doctrine . . . abolitionists in England:** Elizabeth Heyrick's pamphlet *Immediate, Not Gradual Abolition; or, An Inquiry into the Shortest, Safest, and Most Effectual Means of Getting Rid of West Indian Slavery* (1824) was widely seen as helping launch the movement to abolish slavery immediately rather than gradually.
6. **"that he who makes . . . grew before":** Quoted from Jonathan Swift's *Gulliver's Travels* (1726).
7. **Arkwright, Watt, Fulton, Franklin, Morse, and Daguerre:** A list of famous inventors. Richard Arkwright patented the cotton spinning

machine; James Watt developed the steam engine; Robert Fulton developed the steamboat; Benjamin Franklin pioneered research in electricity; Samuel Morse invented the telegraph; and Louis Daguerre created the daguerreotype, the first popular form of photography.

8. **"What shall it profit . . . his own soul":** A paraphrase of Mark 8:36.
9. **"Men do not live by bread alone," said the great Redeemer:** A paraphrase of Matthew 4:4.
10. **We have bowed down . . . ashes under us:** A reference to Isaiah 58:5.
11. **It has been said that corporations have no souls:** A reference to the English judge Sir Edward Coke's famous statement from 1605 that corporations "cannot commit treason, nor be outlawed nor excommunicated, for they have no souls."
12. **with nations might is the standard of right:** The phrase "might makes right" was often attributed to Plato's *Republic*, Book 1.
13. **self-interest governs the world:** A reference to Adam Smith's *Wealth of Nations* (1776).
14. **"Glory to God . . . be glad":** A paraphrase of Luke 2:14.
15. **"The Lord God omnipotent reigneth":** Quoted from Revelation 19:6.
16. **"And I saw another angel . . . and people":** Quoted from Revelation 14:6.
17. **Senator Sumners . . . stunned and bleeding:** Douglass refers to the caning of Massachusetts senator and abolitionist Charles Sumner (1811–74), who was almost killed on the Senate floor in 1856 by South Carolinian Preston Brooks for his "Crime against Kansas" speech.
18. **We are brothers and friends of . . . slavery:** Douglass lists famous British philanthropists and champions of freedom.
19. **Senator Toombs . . . ever existed:** Douglass refers to Georgia senator Robert Toombs's speech in Boston in January 1856.
20. **Christianity itself . . . for his own house:** A reference to 1 Timothy 5:8.
21. **We may fight, . . . under white officers:** Douglass refers to the Sepoy Rebellion of 1857 in India, in which native soldiers rose up against their British commanders.
22. **Margaret Garner:** A Kentucky slave, Garner escaped with her family to Ohio in 1856, but was pursued and surrounded by slave catchers and marshals. Rather than see her two-year-old daughter be sent back into slavery, she killed her with a butcher knife. The case was national news and became the inspiration for Toni Morrison's *Beloved* (1987).

23. **William Thomas:** In 1853 Thomas, a fugitive working as a waiter in Wilkes-Barre, Pennsylvania, jumped into the Susquehanna River to avoid being apprehended by marshals and told them that he would rather drown than be taken alive. During the standoff, Wilkes-Barre residents drove away the marshals and enabled his escape.
24. **The fugitive Horace, . . . service to our cause:** In 1857 marshals and slave catchers tried to arrest the fugitive Addison White, also known as Horace, in Mechanicsburg, Ohio. White shot one marshal and escaped, drawing national attention.
25. **Parker and his noble band of fifteen at Christiana:** In 1851 the Maryland planter Edward Gorsuch, along with his son and neighbors, tried to recover four fugitives who had taken refuge in the home of William Parker, himself a fugitive, in Christiana, Pennsylvania. A battle ensued, and the fugitives killed Gorsuch, wounded his son, and escaped to Canada. Douglass helped Parker in his flight through Rochester to Canada.
26. **the rescue of Jerry, and Shadrack:** Douglass refers to two of the most famous slave cases. In 1851 the fugitive William Henry, known as Jerry, was arrested and jailed in Syracuse. Several hundred black and white abolitionists freed him and helped him reach safety in Canada. That same year, Shadrach Minkins was arrested and jailed in Boston. A group of mostly black abolitionists broke into the jail and carried him away before officers could respond, enabling him to flee to Canada.

"The Trials and Triumphs of Self-Made Men"

1. **"The proper study of mankind is man":** Quoted from Alexander Pope, *An Essay on Man*, Epistle II, lines 1–2.
2. **Franklin:** John Franklin (1786–1847), one of Britain's most famous nineteenth-century explorers.
3. **Hugh Miller:** Miller (1802–56), a poor quarryman, became an internationally famous geologist and writer.
4. **Elihu Burritt:** Burritt (1810–79), a Connecticut blacksmith, became a leading humanitarian and peace advocate.
5. **Benjamin Bannecker:** Banneker (1731–1806), born free in Maryland, became the foremost African American scientist of the eighteenth century.
6. **William Dietz:** Dietz, a black servant from Albany, New York, became a wealthy businessman and architect.
7. **A king can mak' a belted knight, . . . and a' that:** A paraphrase of Robert Burns's poem "For A' That and A' That."

"The Day of Jubilee Comes"

1. **This sacred Sunday . . . slaveholding States of America:** Douglass delivered this speech at his A.M.E. Zion church in Rochester four days before President Lincoln signed the final Emancipation Proclamation into law.
2. **the sum of all villainy:** A paraphrase of slave trading by Methodism's founder John Wesley.
3. **an outlaw having no rights . . . bound to respect:** An allusion to Chief Justice Roger Taney's opinion of the legal status of blacks in the 1857 Dred Scott decision.
4. **The price of Liberty is eternal vigilance:** Douglass paraphrases the Irish politician and judge John Philpot Curran (1750–1817).
5. **Daniel Webster . . . was dead:** Although Massachusetts senator Daniel Webster died in October 1852, a month later, over 1,500 Massachusetts Whigs voted for him for president rather than support the Whig candidate Winfield Scott.

"The Proclamation and a Negro Army"

1. **I stand here to-night . . . a common country:** Douglass refers to the November 1862 ruling by Attorney-General Edward Bates (1793–1869), who declared that free blacks were citizens of the United States. In doing so, Bates gave legal support to Congress's Second Confiscation Act of July 1862 and Lincoln's Final Emancipation Proclamation, which went into effect on January 1, 1863. Both documents authorized the arming of blacks as U.S. soldiers, and there was a precedent, going back to the Revolutionary War, of soldiers being recognized as citizens.
2. **Parker:** Douglass paraphrases Theodore Parker (1810–60), the radical abolitionist and transcendentalist from Boston.
3. **British Reform Bill:** Britain's 1832 Reform Act gave more representation in the House of Commons to workingmen in industrial towns.
4. **"Thrice is he armed . . . corrupted":** Quoted from Shakespeare's *Henry VI, Part II*, III.ii.233–35.
5. **The devil gave his name . . . legion:** A paraphrase of Luke 8:30.
6. **All the wisdom of Boston . . . cart-whip:** From the 1650s to 1677 Boston's Puritan leaders forbade Quakers from entering Massachusetts and punished offenders with whipping and expulsion. It became known as the "Cart and Whip Act."
7. **Roger Williams found . . . Massachusetts:** Williams (1603–83), an English theologian and early champion of religious freedom, settled

in the Massachusetts Bay Colony. After running afoul of Puritan authorities, he took refuge with the Pokanoket tribe.

8. **walked by faith and not by sight:** A paraphrase of 2 Corinthians 5:7.
9. **Oh! where's the slave . . . slowly:** Quoted from Thomas Moore, "Where Is the Slave."

"The Mission of the War"

1. **The saying that . . . with limitations:** A reference to William Seward's famous "Irrepressible Conflict" speech.
2. **Gov. Seymour charges us with prolonging the war:** Douglass refers to New York's antiabolition Democratic governor Horatio Seymour (1810–86), who argued that Republicans' emancipationist war aims were prolonging the war and bankrupting the Union.
3. **There are vacant spaces . . . "during the war":** Two of Douglass's sons, Lewis and Charles, were among the first recruits in the 54th Massachusetts Volunteer Infantry Regiment. Lewis was badly wounded during the storming of Fort Wagner in July 1863.
4. **Ask why it was for the Florida War:** A reference to the Second Seminole War (1835–42).
5. **In his letter to Mr. Greeley . . . to him:** Douglass refers to Lincoln's famous letter to Horace Greeley, editor of the *New-York Tribune*, in August 1862, in which he declared that his chief aim was to preserve the Union rather than end slavery.

"Pictures and Progress"

1. **Chickahominy hero:** Douglass refers to the 1864 Democratic presidential candidate George McClellan (1826–85), known satirically as the "Chickahominy hero."
2. **Does Napoleon . . . in Mexico:** Maximilian I of Austria schemed with Napoleon III to rule Mexico after Napoleon invaded it in 1861 and then three years later declared himself Emperor of Mexico. In referring to Maximilian's family as "detestable," Douglass alludes to widespread but unfounded rumors that Maximilian was the offspring of an illicit affair between his mother, Sophie, and his first cousin Napoleon II.
3. **Does England take advantage of our misfortunes:** During the Civil War, England sold over $100 million worth of supplies, including arms, to the Confederacy. Its sympathies with the Confederacy were economic; over 80 percent of its cotton came from the United States.

4. **Does Brazil assume an unbecoming haughtiness:** By 1861 slavery had been abolished everywhere in South America except Brazil. It was the only country on the continent to declare neutrality in the Civil War and the only one to extend rights to Confederate vessels.
5. **Does the tempter . . . compromise:** Douglass refers to Copperhead "Peace" Democrats, who opposed emancipation and sought a negotiated settlement with the Confederacy.
6. **It is said . . . Rome was on fire:** Douglass refers to the legend of Nero, Rome's unpopular emperor who allegedly "fiddled while Rome burned" during a great fire in 64 CE.
7. **under the somewhat indefinite title of pictures:** Douglass frequently changed the titles of his lectures. He titled this talk "Pictures and Progress" on the first page of the holograph, but here he refers to it as simply "Pictures." We have not found contemporaneous reviews of this speech or any reference to it in the press.
8. **the [text] of all books:** Douglass's phrase may be "the test of all books" rather than "the text of all books." It is unclear in the manuscript.
9. **Gough:** John B. Gough (1817–86), a reformed drunkard, was the nation's most popular temperance lecturer and the author of three autobiographies (1846, 1870, 1880), the first two bestsellers.
10. **Sojourner Truth:** Truth (1797–1883), born Isabella Baumfree, was an eloquent orator and one of the best-known African American women in the Civil War era.
11. **I shall probably . . . for the Atlantic:** In September 1864, General William T. Sherman's army took Atlanta, thus salvaging Lincoln's reelection. In early November Sherman began marching through Georgia to Savannah, and by early 1865 he had reached the Carolinas. He and his troops lived off the land while destroying property in a "scorched earth" campaign to break Confederates' will to fight.
12. **Morse has brought . . . picture gallery:** Like most Americans, Douglass credited Louis Daguerre (1787–1851) with having invented photography in 1839, even though the Englishman Henry Fox Talbot (1800–77) simultaneously developed the calotype, a negative-to-positive form of photography. Talbot's invention was not popular in America, however. Samuel Morse (1791–1872) patented the telegraph in 1847.
13. **The aspiration of Burns . . . after them:** From Robert Burns's poem "To a Louse, On Seeing One on a Lady's Bonnet at Church" (1786).
14. **The humblest servant . . . fifty years ago:** With Louis Daguerre's invention of the daguerreotype in 1839, photography became the most democratic form of portraiture, cheaper than sitting for a painted portrait or miniature. Daguerreotypes, along with subse-

quent formats, from tintypes and ambrotypes to cartes-de-visite, cost as little as one dollar.

15. **A certain class . . . from the highest animal:** Douglass refers to scientists of race, particularly Louis Agassiz, Josiah Nott, and George R. Gliddon, who argued that blacks were subhuman or a separate species. He attacked them in his 1854 speech "The Claims of the Negro Ethnologically Considered."
16. **I commend the fact . . . animal in the world:** Douglass borrows from Aristotle's *Poetics* to refute the proslavery ideal articulated in Aristotle's *Politics*, along with contemporary racist and "protoracist" justifications for slavery. See Aristotle, *Poetics*, tr. Malcolm Heath (New York: Penguin Books, 1996), pp. 6–7 (3.1: "The Anthropology and History of Poetry, Origins."); Aristotle, *The Politics*, tr. T. A. Sinclair (New York: Penguin Books, 1981), pp. 67, 58.
17. **Humboldt tells . . . painted on their skin:** Douglass refers to Alexander von Humboldt (1769–1859), whose *Personal Narrative of Travels to the Equinoctial Regions of the New Continent, during the Years 1799–1804*, translated into English and first published in the United States in 1815, reached a wide audience. In it Humboldt describes how some natives imitated European clothes by painting their skin. He also argued that all humans form one "great family," a "single organic type, modified by circumstances."
18. **"Among eminent persons, . . . ideas and pictures":** Douglass quotes from Emerson's "Swedenborg; or, the Mystic," in *Representative Men* (1850).
19. **"Men do not live by bread alone":** Douglass paraphrases Luke 4:4 and Matthew 4:4.
20. **John Brown went . . . come up higher:** Douglass refers to his friend John Brown, who was executed in December 1859 after raiding the federal arsenal at Harpers Ferry with an interracial army. The raid helped split the national Democratic Party, opening the way for Lincoln's election, and was an important cause of secession. Most of the states' Declarations of Secession refer to the Harpers Ferry raid. In launching his raid, Brown believed that he was heeding God's will. While in prison and facing execution, he acted with great nobility.
21. **the martyr John Huss . . . blazing faggots:** Jan Hus (often referred to as John Huss in English) was a fourteenth-century Czech priest and reformer, whose writings influenced the rise of Protestantism a century later. Hus was convicted of heresy against Catholic doctrines and burned at the stake. As more wood was thrown upon the fire, Hus purportedly shouted out, "Sancta simplicitas" (holy simplicity).

22. **paves the streets . . . gates with pearls:** Douglass borrows from Revelation 21, in which John sees "the holy city," a "new Jerusalem," "a new heaven and a new earth," with twelve gates of pearl, "and the street of the city was pure gold." Revelation 21:1–2 and 21:21.
23. **find tongues . . . in everything:** Quoted from Shakespeare's *As You Like It*, II.i.16–17.
24. **This truth childhood realizes . . . the human heart:** In this paragraph, Douglass builds upon Aristotle's *Poetics* and Catholics' emphasis on icons, both of which highlight the role of art as an engine of individual and social reform.
25. **Poets, prophets, and reformers . . . remove the contradiction:** In this original conceptualization of the relationship between art and reform, Douglass revised Carlyle's analysis of heroes in *On Heroes, Hero-Worship, and the Heroic in History* (1841). Carlyle refers to poets, prophets, and seers as reformers; but he emphasizes that ideals can never be realized and that great men should not strive to realize them, in order to prevent disorder, anarchy, and revolution. Douglass seeks to "remove the contradiction" between ideals and reality, between "what is" and "what ought to be."
26. **like Rarey's horse he may be led by a straw:** John Solomon Rarey (1827–66) was a world-renowned horse trainer from Ohio. He wrote and lectured widely on the subject, and in 1861 he toured the States demonstrating his training techniques. During the Civil War the Union Army invited him to train its cavalry.
27. **"Paint me as I am," said Cromwell:** Douglass invokes a popular legend about Oliver Cromwell (1599–1658), Lord Protector of England, Scotland, and Ireland. The source of the legend is Horace Walpole, who quoted Cromwell's purported instructions to the portraitist Peter Lely: "I desire you would use all your skill to paint my picture truly like me, and not flatter me at all; but remark all these roughnesses, pimples, warts, and every thing as you see me, otherwise I never will pay a farthing for it." Walpole's quote was shortened to "Paint me as I am" and became a popular aphorism.
28. **"Suit the action . . . modesty of nature":** Quoted from *Hamlet*, III.ii.17–19.
29. **Whether we read . . . beings for society:** William Hogarth (1697–1764), a British painter, printmaker, and political satirist, was one of the most popular Anglo-American artists of the eighteenth century.

"Our Martyred President"

1. ***Mayor Moore*:** Daniel David Tompkins Moore (1820–92), the mayor of Rochester.
2. **the death of Abraham Lincoln:** Lincoln died at 7:22 a.m. on April 15, 1865, the morning of Douglass's address.
3. **It was only a few weeks ago . . . brave, honest hand:** Douglass attended Lincoln's Second Inaugural and the reception at the White House. It was the third time he had met with the president.
4. **Dr. Robinson . . . awfully disappointed:** Ezekiel Gilman Robinson (1815–94), a professor at Rochester Theological Seminary, had recently declared that traitors would be "disappointed."
5. **"an honest man . . . God":** Quoted from Alexander Pope, *An Essay on Man*, Epistle IV, line 248.

"The Freedmen's Monument to Abraham Lincoln"

1. **when he strangely told us . . . cause of the war:** A reference to Lincoln's August 1862 address to Washington, D.C., black leaders, in which he championed black colonization and blamed the war on blacks: "But for your race among us there could not be war."
2. **Though he loved Caesar less than Rome:** A paraphrase of Shakespeare's *Julius Caesar*, III.ii.21–22.
3. **slavery abolished in the District of Columbia:** In April 1862 Lincoln signed into law a bill abolishing slavery and compensating masters in Washington, D.C.
4. **the first slave-trader hanged:** Captain Nathaniel Gordon was the first and only American executed for violating the ban on international slave trading after it was outlawed in 1808. Gordon appealed to Lincoln for a commutation of his sentence to life in prison, but Lincoln refused.
5. **A spade, a rake . . . what you will:** A paraphrase of Thomas Hood's poem "The Lay of the Laborer."

"Lessons of the Hour"

1. **like the pestilence that walketh in the darkness:** A paraphrase of Psalm 91:6.
2. **Bishop Haygood, . . . "the provocation":** Atticus Green Haygood (1839–96), a Methodist minister, editor, and president of Emory University, was considered a Southern progressive on race. Douglass adapts sentences from Haygood's article "The Black Shadow in the South," *The Forum* 14 (October 1893): 167–75.

3. **ex-Governor Chamberlain:** Raised in Massachusetts, Daniel Henry Chamberlain (1835–1907) settled in South Carolina after the war and was elected the state's first Republican governor in 1872. He returned north to New York City following his failed reelection bid in 1876, amid widespread violence against blacks and Republicans.
4. **Bishop Fitzgerald, . . . and Miss Frances Willard:** Oscar Penn Fitzgerald (1829–1911), a well-known Nashville divine, and Frances Willard (1839–98), a suffragette and president of the Woman's Christian Temperance Union, along with Bishop Haygood, condoned the lynchings that plagued the South.
5. **Prof. Weeks:** Stephen Beauregard Weeks (1865–1918), a professor of history and political science, cofounded the Southern History Association and in 1894 became a researcher at the U.S. Bureau of Education.
6. **like the blood on Lady Macbeth's hand:** A reference to the sleepwalking scene in Shakespeare's *Macbeth*, V.i.
7. **Even at the North, . . . murdered in the streets:** Douglass refers to the 1863 draft riots in New York City, in which antiwar and anti-abolition Democrats lynched several blacks and looted the city in their protest against conscription.
8. **"As we sow, we shall reap":** Quoted from Galatians 6:7.
9. **Senator Ingalls:** Douglass quotes from the 1890 Senate speech of John J. Ingalls (1833–1900) of Kansas.

JOURNALISM

"Is It Right and Wise to Kill a Kidnapper?"

1. **A kidnapper . . . in Boston:** Douglass refers to James Batchelder, a guard who was killed as abolitionists stormed the Boston courthouse in their effort to free Anthony Burns.
2. **Mr. Mann:** Alexander Mann (1811–1860) was the editor of the *Rochester Daily American.*

"Our Plan for Making Kansas a Free State"

1. **the boast of Douglas:** Stephen Douglas (1813–1861), U.S. senator from Illinois.
2. **popular sovereignty:** Illinois senator Stephen Douglas popularized the doctrine, which called for allowing settlers in a territory to regulate slavery themselves and vote it up or down.

"The Chicago Nominations"

1. **his late speech in the Senate:** John Brown's raid on Harpers Ferry galvanized secessionists in the South, prompting Senator William Seward (1801–72), the front-runner for the 1860 Republican nomination, to try to appease conservatives. He avoided references to his previous endorsements of "higher law" and his assertion that slave owners had created an "irrepressible conflict" between slave labor and free labor. Instead he declared that he had "never loved the representatives of other sections more than now."
2. **"Star of Empire":** A phrase reflecting the widespread belief that westward expansion in the United States had been ordained by God.
3. **"Free labor and free men":** A motto of the Republican Party.

"The Inaugural Address"

1. **General Scott:** Winfield Scott (1786–1866), the nation's commanding general, oversaw the peaceful transition to Lincoln's Republican administration. Amid fears that Southerners would try to prevent Lincoln from taking office, Scott deployed troops throughout Washington and helped prevent a plot to assassinate the president as he traveled through Baltimore to the capital.
2. **He reached the Capital . . . under the sable wing of night:** Lincoln left Baltimore for Washington in disguise and at night, owing to evidence of a plot to assassinate him.

"The President and His Speeches"

1. **Mr. Stanton:** Edwin Stanton (1814–69), Secretary of War, had an excellent working relationship with Lincoln. See Doris Kearns Goodwin, *Team of Rivals: The Political Genius of Abraham Lincoln* (New York: Simon and Schuster, 2005).
2. **reinforcements to Gen. McClellan:** Douglass refers to Lincoln's address on August 6, 1862, which attempted to silence criticisms against General George McClellan and Stanton in the wake of the failure of the Peninsular Campaign.

"Letter from the Editor" (On the Burning Down of His Rochester House)

1. **The fire . . . incendiary:** No one was charged for arson, and Douglass never found out how the fire started.

"Give Us the Freedom Intended for Us"

1. **"that complete liberty . . . legislation":** Douglass quotes from the platform of the Republican National Convention in Philadelphia in June 1872, which reelected Ulysses S. Grant.
2. **"The recent amendments . . . legislation":** Douglass quotes from the platform of the Republican National Convention, ratified in November.
3. **The Liberal Democratic platform . . . "Constitution":** Douglass quotes from the platform nominating Horace Greeley for president that sought to unite progressive Democrats with Republicans who opposed Grant, called the Liberal Republican Party.
4. **bill as Senator Sumner brought forward:** Douglass refers to Charles Sumner's civil rights bill to desegregate all public establishments in the nation, from graveyards to restaurants and schools. Passed in a watered-down form in 1875, it was overturned by the Supreme Court eight years later for violating states' rights. Sumner's bill served as the blueprint for President Johnson's 1964 Civil Rights Act.

"The Color Line"

1. **Daniel Webster . . . "conquer their prejudices":** Douglass refers to Webster's support of the Fugitive Slave Law speeches. In an 1850 speech in Boston to his Massachusetts constituents, he urged them to conquer their prejudices against catching slaves. His most famous speech urging Northerners to "conquer their prejudices" against slave catching was his three-hour Senate speech on March 7, 1850, which outraged New Englanders and destroyed his political career.

"The Future of the Colored Race"

1. **I would not be understood . . . inevitable:** In 1884, following the death of his first wife, Anna, Douglass had married Helen Pitts, a white woman. The marriage was criticized by both whites and blacks.

"Introduction to *The Reason Why the Colored American Is Not in the World's Columbian Exposition*"

1. **So when it is asked . . . the answer is Slavery:** This pamphlet, to which Douglass wrote the introduction, was a protest against the failure to appoint any African American as commissioner, committee member, guide, or guard at the Columbian Exposition in Chicago. Douglass

also wrote chapter 3, "The Convict Lease System." The other authors were Ida B. Wells, who wrote "Class Legislation" and "Lynch Law," Irving Garland Penn, who wrote "The Progress of the Afro-American since Emancipation," and Ferdinand Barnett, Ida B. Wells's future husband, who detailed the reasons why blacks had no role in the Columbian Exposition.

APPENDIX

1. Douglass refers to his work as an abolitionist, fighting "the slave system."